Jihad in Central Asia

Foreign Fighters, the Islamic State of
Khorasan, the Chechens and Uyghur
Islamic Front in China

Jihad in Central Asia

Foreign Fighters, the Islamic State of
Khorasan, the Chechens and Uyghur
Islamic Front in China

Musa Khan Jalalzai

Vij Books India Pvt Ltd
New Delhi (India)

Published by

Vij Books India Pvt Ltd
(Publishers, Distributors & Importers)
2/19, Ansari Road
Delhi – 110 002
Phones: 91-11-43596460, 91-11-47340674
Mobile: 98110 94883
e-mail: contact@vijpublishing.com
www.vijbooks.com

Contents

Introduction

The Washington Post revelations about the failure of American army in Afghanistan demonstrate that no state can be vanquished, stooped and genuflected by nuclear missiles, extrajudicial killings, war crimes and Mother of Bombs. The Paper warned that senior US officials were lurking the truth of their failure in Afghanistan. "Every data-point was altered to present the best picture possible," Bob Crowley, an Army colonel who served as a senior counterinsurgency adviser to US military commanders in 2013 and 2014, told government interviewers. "Surveys, for instance, were totally unreliable but reinforced that everything we were doing was right and we became a self-licking ice cream cone," Bob said. Pentagon and CIA in the Bush, Obama and Trump administrations were painting different pictures of their failure in Afghanistan.

The CIA and Pentagon spent more than $1 trillion in Afghanistan, but couldn't succeed to bring Gallus-Gallus chicken to the White House. According to the Washington Post, that the 2,000 pages interviews with more than 400 generals, diplomats, and other officials directly involved in the war exposed incompetence of so-called superpower that killed innocent Afghans with impunity. Many officials described a sustained effort by the US government to hide the truth from the American public. The Post also released hundreds of pages of previously classified memos about the Afghan war dictated by former US Defence Secretary Donald Rumsfeld.

Unsurprisingly, the war dragged on; making it the longest the United States has ever fought. Negotiations were taking place between the Trump administration and the terrorist Taliban leadership as the US debated whether to withdraw 13,000 troops from Afghanistan with or without a deal with the Terrorists. But

1

U.S. military officials consistently warned against a "premature" withdrawal from the country, assuring that progress was being made. "At least American participation in the war in Afghanistan comes to an end when our interests are met, and I think that'll be met through a negotiated settlement with the Taliban, and I think we're seeing some progress," Chairman of the Joint Chiefs of Staff Gen. Mark Milley said.

After a complete failure in Afghanistan, now CIA and Pentagon want to turn Central Asia into a new battlefield. Nationals of the five Central Asian states who joined ISIS in Syria and Afghanistan may possibly serve the interests of the United States when they return to the region. They might inflict huge fatalities on civilian population by taking part in combat on the side of jihadist groups like the Islamic State, and by carrying out terrorist attacks inside and outside their home regions. Most Central Asian states face their greatest risk of domestic instability and violent extremism as a reaction to political repression and counterterrorism policies of their governments. In Central Asia, the focus of Jihadists groups has been the Tajikistan, Turkmenistan and Russian Federation. But it is unclear how many Central Asian fighters will ultimately seek to return to their countries of origin, and if they do, whether any of them will remain committed to ISIS.

Before the rise of ISIS, the Islamic Movement of Uzbekistan (IMU) was the main Central Asian extremist organization in the field. Its base of operations is in Afghanistan and Pakistan. Central Asian fighters linked to ISIS headquarters in Syria also participated in acts of terrorism in other countries. The ISIS has previously restrained from getting involved in attacks in Central Asia as the group's leadership emphasised that attacking this region was not the highest priority. In July 2018, five Tajik men killed four foreign cyclists in a car-ramming attack, accompanied by an on-foot gun and knife assault in the Khatlon province of Tajikistan. The presence of Daesh in Iraq and Afghanistan, and participation of Central Asian jihadists in it prompted consternation in the region. In Syria, the radical Islamic militants from Central Asia established terrorist organisations of their own. These terrorists have Salafi-Wahhabi inclinations and are among the backers of al-

Qaeda, al-Nusra Front, and Daesh group. In his Diplomat analysis (20 September 2016), Uran Botobekov, documented videos and extrajudicial killing in Iraq and Syria:

"Recently, Central Asians saw on YouTube a terrible video of a teenager, Babur Israilov from Jalal-Abad in southern Kyrgyzstan, on his way to becoming a suicide bomber. In the video, Babur cries before being sent to his death in an armoured car laden with explosives in Fua, Syria. One of the fighters gathered around encourages him, saying in Uzbek that Satan intervenes at crucial moments to confuse a Muslim's mind, so he should think only of Allah. Further in the video sentimental Arabic music plays, the armoured personnel carrier moves, and, at the fatal moment, the bomb explodes. According to Radio Free Europe/Radio Liberty, Babur Israilov was a member of an extremist group of Uzbeks–Imam Bukhari Jamaat–which fights alongside Jabhat al-Nusra in Syria. Just like the father of the British boy JoJo, resident of Suzak district in the Jalal-Abad region of Kyrgyzstan Tahir Rahitov saw his son Babur via video. According to Tahir, his wife died in 1995 and the boy was raised by his grandmother. In November 2013 Babur left for Russia in search of work. In March 2014 he arrived in Syria via Turkey, joined Imam Bukhari Jamaat, and fought alongside Jabhat al-Nusra against the government of Bashar al-Assad".

The four Central Asian States (Kyrgyzstan, Tajikistan, Kazakhstan, and Uzbekistan) security agencies and government have adopted several law and order measures to effectively fight against radicalization, but some states failed to intercept the infiltration of the ISIS militants from Afghanistan into the region. The power structures, social institutions and local authorities of the Central Asian states are unable to work with radical Islamic groups. Analyst Uran Botobekov has also warned that presence of Central Asian minors in Daesh ranks might possibly cause huge fatalities when they translate their ideologies into violent actions:

"According to the special services of Kyrgyzstan, about 140 minors have been taken from Kyrgyzstan to training camps in Iraq and Syria. The vast majority of children are under the age of 14, with an estimated 85 children under the age of 10. Authorities have not reported how many children have come to the Islamic State from Kazakhstan, Tajikistan, Turkmenistan, and Uzbekistan. According to human rights organizations more than 600 children from Central Asia are in ISIS-controlled areas of Iraq and Syria. Most children were brought into the conflict zone by their parents. According to various estimates, there are 4,000 Central Asians fighting with various groups in Iraq and Syria. Estimates of the number of children from the former republics of the Soviet Union vary, and no one can pinpoint the exact number".

Aside from an Islamic State-linked attack on foreign cyclists, Tajikistan had largely been spared from significant attacks by both international terrorist organizations and radicalized individuals. The ISIS recruitment of Tajikistanis relies heavily on the glorification of celebrity jihadist commanders. Despite this, ISIS recruitment in Tajikistan is perhaps the least organized of all the Central Asian states as Tajikistanis fighting for ISIS maintain no dedicated official media outlet or spokesman. The Tajikistani government restricted religious freedom to an exceptional degree. All but 500 to 1,000 ethnic Uzbekistanis were also fighting in Syria during 2015, with a majority of them believed to be from southern Kyrgyzstan. However, more than 400 to 500 Islamist fighters with ties to Uzbekistan participated in the battlefields of Syria and Iraq.

After March 2015, Uzbekistan changed its tactics and started to actively downplay the threat ISIS internally poses to the country and to show that ISIS was subverting true Islam. Tajikistanis fighting for ISIL repeatedly threatened to return and wage jihad in Tajikistan, but they failed. In January 2015, members of an IMU cell planned to attack a police station were arrested in Tajikistan. Monitoring of the Central Asian Salafi-jihadi groups activities showed that since 2018, al Qaeda-linked Katibat Imam al Bukhari (KIB) stepped up its participation in the terror attacks against the Afghan Armed Forces. This Uzbek terrorist group has a high level of trust among the leaders al Qaeda and Taliban and has become a link in their strategic ties. Analyst, Mr. Uran Botobekov has noted the group has established two important branches to maintain its army:

> "It is known that KIB has two branches. The group's main fighting force of more than 500 militants, led by leader Abu Yusuf Muhojir today is based in the Syrian province Idlib. Despite the fact that KIB positions itself as an "independent" faction it is closely connected with Ahrar al Sham who has had al Qaeda operatives embedded in its own ranks. The KIB's second branch is concentrated in Afghanistan, which positions itself as an integral part of the Taliban. Even the emblem and the name of the KIB branch are closely associated with the Taliban. It is known that the Taliban refers to itself as "the Islamic Emirate of Afghanistan" and has the website under the same name. With the Taliban's consent KIB leaders gave their branch the name "Katibat Imam al Bukhari of the Islamic Emirate of Afghanistan". After pledging an oath of allegiance to Taliban leader Mullah Omar, KIB became a reinforcing factor of the strategic ties of the Taliban and al Qaeda. It should be noted that the US State Department designated KIB to the list of global terrorist organizations on March 22, 2018".

The establishment of the ISIS networks in Tajikistan and Uzbekistan raised several question including the failure of Tajik law enforcement agencies to intercept infiltration of ISIS fighter into the country. The Islamic State is now recruiting young people into its ranks, and supports them financially. In view of this development, Tajikistan introduced new legislation in 2015 allowing authorities to pardon citizens who voluntarily return home and express regret that they joined militant groups abroad, but, notwithstanding this legislation, people of all walks of life are joining Daesh consecutively. On 06 November 2019, BBC reported terror attack of the ISIS fighters on Checkpost of Tajik border with Uzbekistan, and killed 17 people. Analyst Damon Mehl in his paper (Damon Mehl, CTC Sentinel, November 2018, Volume-11, Issue-10) noted some aspects of the development of ISIS networks in Tajikistan:

"Jamaat Ansarullah, an Afghanistan-based Tajikistani terrorist group, was formed in 2010 with likely fewer than 100 members and has since received support from the IMU, the Taliban, and al-Qaeda. The group's stated mission is to bring an 'Islamic' government to Tajikistan. Beginning with its foundation, Jamaat Ansarullah sporadically published videos and disseminated messages through its website, which has been inactive since 2016. The group's leader Amriddin Tabarov was killed in Afghanistan in December 2015 and Tabarov's son-in-law Mavlavif Salmon was appointed as the new leader by the end of 2016. In 2014, Jamaat Ansarullah sent some of its members to fight in Syria with Jabhat al-Nusra, an al-Qaeda-aligned group now known as Hayat Tahrir al-Sham. At a point in 2014 or 2015, some Jamaat Ansarullah members ended up fighting alongside the Islamic State. The Islamic State subsequently began financially supporting Ansarullah according to Afghanistan expert Antonio Giustozzi, citing a Jamaat Ansarullah commander. This support reportedly caused fissures between Jamaat Ansarullah and al-Qaeda, and by 2015, Ansarullah received 50 percent of its financial backing from the Islamic State. In October 2014, a Jamaat Ansarullah member going by the name Mansur stated on the group's website that Jamaat Ansarullah considered the Islamic State a jihadi organization, but had paused its decision on whether to accept the Islamic State's claim of being the caliphate".

In 2010, Jamaat Ansarullah extremist group was formed in Afghanistan, with possibly 100 members and trained by the Islamic Movement of Uzbekistan to fight the Tajik forces effectively. The group's leader Amriddin Tabarov was killed in Afghanistan in December 2015 and Tabarov's son-in-law Mavlavif Salmon was appointed as the new leader by the end of 2016. Analyst Damon Mehl in his paper (Damon Mehl, CTC Sentinel, November 2018, Volume-11, Issue-10) has documented the activities of Daesh in Tajikistan, and a Tajik language audio, in which the Islamic State member Abu Usama Noraki threatened Tajikistan President Emomali Rahmon:

"In early August 2018, a week following the attack on the cyclists, a nine-minute, Tajik-language audio message from Islamic State member Abu Usama Noraki threatened Tajikistan president Emomali Rahmon. Abu Usama Noraki is very probably synonymous with a Syria-based Islamic State member whom Tajik authorities identified as 31-year-old Tojiddin Nazarov in March 2018. Tajik authorities stated Abu Usama was from Norak, located in Khatlon province southeast of Dushanbe, and called him the "Islamic State's most dangerous recruiter among Tajiks." According to the same Tajik authorities, Abu Usama Noraki joined the Islamic State in Syria and Iraq in 2014, previously worked with the IMU, and was radicalized when he was a migrant laborer working in Russia. Noraki is a prominent Islamic State spokesperson to a Tajik-language audience and since at least 2015 has frequently disseminated audio speeches through an Islamic State-affiliated, Tajik-language Zelloi channel that now has approximately 15,000 subscribers. Noraki's early August 2018 message regarding the Tajikistan President was likewise disseminated via Zello and social media sites. Noraki stated Rahmon was acting against Islam and that Islamic State Mujahideen would soon move to Tajikistan and overthrow the government. Noraki claimed the killing of foreigners, an obvious reference to the July 29, 2018, attack, was the "first bell" for future jihad and attacks in Tajikistan. Noraki also called on Tajik government officials to join Islamic State ranks and praised a certain Shaykh Abu Malik for providing the Islamic State with Tajik military insight. Shaykh Abu Malik is the nom de guerre of the former commander of Tajikistan's OMON (Special Purpose Police Unit) Colonel Gulmurod Khalimov who defected to the Islamic State in 2015, was appointed Islamic State War Minister in 2016, and may have been killed in 2017".

Chechen fighters have also established networks across Russian Federation and want to retrieve sophisticated weapons. The group in Afghanistan receive military training to strengthen its army for the future war against Russia. Pakistan have also trained Chechen commanders years ago, while during their jihad against Russia, some reports confirmed the participation of over 1000 Pakistani jihadists and retired military officers in fighting alongside their fighters. Analyst and researcher, Mr. Christian Bleuer noted the presence of Chechen leadership in Afghanistan:

> "Extremist members of Chechnya's rebel movement adhere to ideas tied to jihad and the creation of an Islamist state. Afghan and foreign officials say as many as 7,000 Chechens and other foreign fighters could be operating in the country, loosely allied with the Taliban and other militant groups. Local reporting by Pajhwok News, sourced to the Logar governor's spokesman, was slightly different, naming the targets as "Taliban Commanders Mullah Saber, Mullah Sabawon and Mullah Bashir," but also noting the presence of Chechens–in this case, three Chechen women who were allegedly killed. Khaama Press also reported the incident, noting that "[f]oreign insurgents fighting the Afghan forces is not new as scores of militants from Chechnya and other countries are routinely reported killed during the fight with the Afghan forces," with the caveat that "[t]he anti-government armed militant groups have not commented regarding the report so far."

With the presence of Jihadist Groups and the ISIS in Central Asia, the use of chemical, biological and nuclear weapons cannot be ruled out, the fact is that the ISIS found these weapons in Syria and Iraq. If they used these weapons, reaction of Central Asia States and Russian would be violent, and they might attack the US and NATO installations inside Afghanistan. Researchers and analysts Keir A. Lieber and Daryl G. Press in their paper have warned that if state transferred nuclear or biological weapons to jihadist groups and ISIS in Central Asia, this will change the whole picture of war in Afghanistan:

"The concern that a state might transfer nuclear weapons to terrorists, however, is among the greatest of these worries, and to many analysts it is the most compelling justification for costly actions—including the use of military force—aimed at preventing proliferation. Despite the issue's importance, the danger of deliberate nuclear weapons transfer to terrorist's remains understudied. Scholars have scrutinized many other proliferation concerns more extensively. Analysts have investigated the deductive and empirical bases for claims that new nuclear states would be deterrable; the likelihood that Iran, in particular, would behave rationally and avoid using nuclear weapons recklessly; and the risks of proliferation cascades, "loose nukes," and nuclear-armed states using their weapons as a shield for aggression or blackmail. To the extent that analysts have debated the possibility of covert state sponsorship of nuclear terrorism, however, the arguments have consisted mostly of competing deductive logics—with little empirical analysis. This article assesses the risk that states would give nuclear weapons to terrorists".

Moreover, Mr. Truls Hallberg Tonnessen has noted arguments of some experts and security analysts about the use of CBRN and nuclear weapons by ISIS in the region. The ISIS group found these weapons in Syria, and Iraq that caused huge consternation:

"There has been no shortage of politicians and security analysts warning that Islamic State (or other terrorist organisations) may use various forms of CBRN weapons, even nuclear weapons, for an attack. And there is no doubt that the motivation to use CBRN weapons indeed is present – in 2014 it was estimated that there have been 50 registered incidents where al-Qaida or its affiliates have attempted to acquire, produce or deploy CBRN weapons during the last two decades. There have also been a handful of incidents in Europe where CBRN materials have been considered in the planning phase of a terrorist attack. However, the low number of actual incidents including CBRN indicates that ambition fortunately has so far exceeded capabilities. Jihadists' lack of competence and lack of development within the field of CBRN has been confirmed by a 2015 study based on the discussions of CBRN weapons and various CBRN "recipes" posted on online jihadist forums. Symptomatically, terrorist groups have so far primarily used the least advanced form of CBRN – chemical weapons. The University of Maryland's Global Terrorism Database (GTD) has registered 303 incidents of terrorist attacks including chemical weapons worldwide. In comparison, GTD has registered

32 incidents of biological terrorism worldwide, resulting in 9 fatalities, no incidents of nuclear terrorism, and 13 incidents of (attempted) radiological terrorism, resulting in no fatalities. Of the al-Qaida affiliates, it is the Islamic State and its predecessors that have been regarded as the most successful in the development and use of chemical weapons".

The prospect of nuclear terrorism in Central Asia and might possibly in Russia, is crystal clear as the ISIS groups, and US army are making thing worse. There are possibilities that terrorists can acquire nuclear material or a complete warhead to use it in Central Asia, or possibly in Russia. The risk of a complete nuclear device falling into the hands of terrorists will cause consternation in the region. Over the past several years, the prospect of a terrorist group armed with a nuclear weapon has frequently been cited as a genuine and overriding threat to the security of Central Asia and Russia.

If terrorist groups such as ISIS or Lashkar-e-Taiba determine to go nuclear, what will be the security preparations in Central Asia to intercept these groups? These and other Pakistan based groups can attempt to manufacture the fissile material needed to fuel a nuclear weapon—either highly enriched uranium or plutonium, and then use it. Moreover, there are possibilities that Pakistan, Afghanistan and Central Asia based extremist and jihadist groups can purchase fissile material in black market or steal it from a military or civilian facility and then use that material to construct an improvised nuclear device. The US tensions with Russia receded and nuclear strategy came to seem like a relic of a bygone era. Yet today, with Russia rising again as a military power, the grim logic of nuclear statecraft is returning. In his nuclear risk analysis, Simon Saradzhyan (Russia Matters, Simon Saradzhyan, (August 06, 2019) argued that there are possibility of nuclear war between Russia and the United States:

"Is the risk of a nuclear war between the U.S. and Russia now higher than at the height of the Cold War? Yes, it is, according to an article former U.S. Energy Secretary Ernie Moniz and former U.S. Sen. Sam Nunn have penned for Foreign Affairs. "Not since the 1962 Cuban Missile Crisis has the risk of a U.S.-Russian confrontation involving the use of nuclear weapons been as high as it is today," the co-chairs of the Nuclear Threat Initiative warn in their commentary published on Aug. 6, 2019. To back their claim, the two American statesmen describe an imaginary scenario in which Russian air defense systems shoot down a NATO aircraft that has accidentally veered into Russian airspace during a wargame in Russia's Kaliningrad exclave in 2020".

All but, 15 years ago, Graham Allison (September/October 2004) noted the possiblity of nuclear terrorism in Russia by Chechen terrorists. Chechen have had a long-standing interest in acquiring nuclear weapons and material to use in their campaign against Russia. He is of the opinion that Chechen had access to nuclear materials, and their experts were able to make nuclear explosive devices:

"To date, the only confirmed case of attempted nuclear terrorism occurred in Russia on November 23, 1995, when Chechen separatists put a crude bomb containing 70 pounds of a mixture of cesium-137 and dynamite in Moscow's Ismailovsky Park. The rebels decided not to detonate this "dirty bomb," but instead informed a national television station to its location. This demonstration of the Chechen insurgents' capability to commit ruthless terror underscored their long-standing interest in all things nuclear. As early as 1992, Chechnya's first rebel president, Dzhokhar Dudayev, began planning for nuclear terrorism, including a specific initiative to hijack a Russian nuclear submarine from the Pacific Fleet in the Far East. The plan called for seven Slavic-looking Chechens to seize a submarine from the naval base near Vladivostok, attach explosive devices to the nuclear reactor section and to one of the nuclear-tipped missiles on board, and then demand withdrawal of Russian troops from Chechnya. After the plot was discovered, Russian authorities disparaged it, and yet it is ominous to note that the former chief of staff of the Chechen rebel army, Islam Khasukhanov, had once served as second-in-command of a Pacific Fleet nuclear submarine".

The ISIS found dangerous weapons in Syria and Iraq and killed thousands innocent women and children. In Central Asia and Russian Federation, there are several extremist and terrorist groups that seek nuclear weapons to use it against local security forces. Chechen extremist groups have also consistently expressed the desire to obtain, build, and utilize unconventional devices against selected targets, and have innovated by incorporating hazardous materials into their ordnance. The war in Syria and Iraq has significantly altered modern terrorism, with radical Islamic militants from Central Asia being no exception. The terrorists' method for recruiting forces is almost the same in most of the countries in the Central Asia.

While the majority of ISIS recruits originate in the Middle East, the Maghreb, and Western Europe. Central Asia is the third largest source of foreign fighters in Syria. More than 4,000 Central Asian fighters are believed to have joined armed groups fighting in Syria, with an estimated 2,500 arriving there in 2014 and early 2015 alone. Russian President Vladimir Putin once stated that as many as 7,000 fighters from Russia and Central Asia have joined the ranks of the Islamic State.

The Takfiri groups of al-Nusra Front and the so-called Islamic Jihad Union are also employing nationals from Central Asia. In some countries, the process of employment is done through indigenous people. Efforts of terrorists to get access to nuclear materials and technologies appear to be increasing at the same time as there is a race for developing nuclear power projects in the Middle East, Africa and Asia. This might create fertile soil for the rise of nuclear terrorism on a global scale. There is evidence that terrorist groups have tried to acquire the material needed to construct a crude nuclear explosive device, or a dirty bomb. Terrorists use biological agents because they are often difficult to detect. In 2016, after the two ISIS brothers involved in the Brussels bombings, Khalid and Ibrahim el-Bakraoui, were killed and captured, authorities discovered they had been secretly watching a Belgian nuclear scientist who worked at the Tihange Nuclear Power Station.

Nuclear terrorism remains a constant threat to global peace. Access of terrorist organizations to nuclear material is a bigger threat to civilian population. Terrorist groups can gain access to highly enriched uranium or plutonium, because they have the potential to create and detonate an improvised nuclear device. Since the ISIS has already retrieved nuclear materials from Mosul city of Iraq, we can assert that terrorist groups like ISIS and Katibat Imam Bukhari, and Chechen extremist groups can make access to biological and nuclear weapons with the help of local experts. Nuclear facilities also often store large amounts of radioactive material, spent fuel, and other nuclear waste products that terrorists could use in a dirty bomb. Without access to such fissile materials, extremist and radicalized groups can turn their attention toward building a simple radiological device. The most difficult part of making a nuclear bomb is acquiring the nuclear material, but some Muslim and non-Muslim state might facilitate the ISIS, Lashkar-e-Taiba, Chechen extremist groups and Afghanistan and Pakistan based groups to attack nuclear installations in Russia and Central Asia.

Information on how to manipulate nuclear material to produce an explosive device—an improvised nuclear device, which would produce a nuclear explosion and a mushroom cloud, or a radiation-dispersal device, which would spread dangerous radioactive material over a substantial area—is now available widely. Daesh (ISIS) seized control of the Iraqi city of Mosul in 2014. Pakistan has also been heavily dependent on outside supply for many key direct- and dual-use goods for its nuclear programs. It maintains smuggling networks and entities willing to break supplier country laws to obtain these goods. Many of these illegal imports have been detected and stopped. These illegal procurements have led to investigations and prosecutions in the supplier states, leading to revelations of important details about Pakistan's complex to make nuclear explosive materials and nuclear weapons. According to some reports that weapons-grade and weapons-usable nuclear materials have been stolen by terrorist groups from some states. Once a crude weapon is in a country, terrorists would transport it in a vehicle to city and then detonate it in a crowded area.

The ISIS magazine (Dabiq-May 2015) published article of British journalist John Cantlie, in which he warned that the ISIS terrorist group had gained capabilities to launch major terrorist attack: "Let me throw a hypothetical operation onto the table. The Islamic State has billions of dollars in the bank, so they call on their wilayah in Pakistan to purchase a nuclear device through weapons dealers with links to corrupt officials in the region. The weapon is then transported overland until it makes it to Libya, where the mujāhidīn move it south to Nigeria. Drug shipments from Columbia bound for Europe pass through West Africa, so moving other types of contraband from East to West is just as possible. The nuke and accompanying mujāhidīn arrive on the shorelines of South America and are transported through the porous borders of Central America before arriving in Mexico and up to the border with the United States. From there it's just a quick hop through a smuggling tunnel and hey presto, they're mingling with another 12 million "illegal" aliens in America with a nuclear bomb in the trunk of their car".

On 25 March 2016, Daily Telegraph reported militants plan to attack the Brussels nuclear plant: "In the wake of claims the Brussels attackers had planned to set off a radioactive 'dirty bomb', Yukiya Amano, the Director General of the International Atomic Energy Agency said: "Terrorism is spreading and the possibility of using nuclear material cannot be excluded. The material can be found in small quantities in universities, hospitals and other facilities. "Dirty bombs will be enough to (drive) any big city in the world into panic. And the psychological, economic and political implications would be enormous," said Mr Amano. One security expert suggested that the terrorists could have been plotting to kidnap the nuclear researcher they had been filming with a view to coercing the scientist into helping them make a 'dirty bomb'. The Newspaper reported. State sponsorship of nuclear terrorism in Central Asia is matter of great concern as some states support terrorist groups such as the ISIS, Taliban, Katibat Imam al Bukhari, Chechen groups, and Lashkar-e-Taiba, and provide dangerous weapons. These states can sponsor terrorist groups to launch nuclear attack inside Russia or Central Asia.

Musa Khan Jalalzai

February-2020 London

14

Chapter 1

The Region that isn't: China, Russia and the Failure of Regional Integration in Central Asia

Sebastian Krapohl and Alexandra Vasileva-Dienes

Abstract

The failure of regionalism in Central Asia is a puzzle. Whereas almost all world regions have seen a rise of regional organisations since the end of the Cold War attempts to establish durable regional cooperation among Kazakhstan, Kyrgyzstan, Tajikistan, Turkmenistan and Uzbekistan proofed unsuccessful. Although some of the Central Asian countries participate in wider regional organisations like the Eurasian Economic Union (EAEU) and the Shanghai Cooperation Organisation (SCO), the genuine Central Asian Cooperation Organisation (CACO) was dissolved in 2005. Given the cultural, economic and political similarities between the five Central Asian countries, this lack of a regional organisation is surprising.

In contrast to previous work, this paper argues that the failure of regionalism in Central Asia is not so much due to domestic political factors, but more to the extra-regional economic dependence of the regional economies and the impact of external powers within Central Asia. Challenged by the rise of China, Russia uses the

15

EAEU in order to preserve its hegemonic influence over the former Soviet Republics. By joining the Russian dominated EAEU, Central Asia's regional power Kazakhstan enjoys economic benefits which outweigh the potential gains of Central Asian cooperation within CACO by far. Consequently, Kazakhstan follows its extra-regional interests in closer cooperation with Russia at the cost of regional cooperation with its Central Asian neighbours. As a result, the Central Asian countries are unable to build up a unified regional block in relation to extra-regional powers like China or Russia.

Introduction

The five 'Stans' of Central Asia—Kazakhstan, Kyrgyzstan, Tajikistan, Turkmenistan and Uzbekistan—are clearly recognisable as a region, whose member states have more in common with each other than with external neighbours. The five countries share a moderate Islam as majority religion, they all look back on a common history as former Soviet republics under Russian dominance, and they are currently all governed by (semi-)authoritarian presidents. Nevertheless, whereas the spread of the new regionalism since the 1990s has led to the emergence of regional organisations in almost all world regions (Mansfield and Milner 1999), a genuine Central Asian integration project does not exist. The Central Asian Cooperation Organisation (CACO) was dissolved in 2005, and Kazakhstan and Kyrgyzstan joined the Russian-dominated Eurasian Economic Community (EurAsEC) and later the Eurasian Economic Union (EAEU) (Bohr 2004; Pomfret 2009). Thus, two of the five Central Asian countries participate in some form of regionalism today, but Central Asia as such is nevertheless one of the very few world regions which have not managed to establish a regional organisation on its own.

The comparative regionalism literature deals extensively with the emergence of regional organisations all around the world since the 1990s (Mansfield and Milner 1999), but it has not yet explored under which circumstances regions fail to establish regional organisations. Scholars usually analyse prominent regional organisations like the Association of Southeast Asian Nations (ASEAN), the Common Market of South America (MERCOSUR) or the Southern African

Development Community (SADC) (Krapohl 2017a), which exist since several decades and are relatively stable. Thus, we know that the new regionalism has been a reaction to globalisation (Schirm 2002), and that successful integration of one world region triggers integration in other world regions (Mattli 1999), but we do not know under which circumstances these forces reach their limits and regionalism collapses.

Different schools of international relations theory stress different structural factors to explain the success of regionalism. Realists argue that it needs a regional hegemon or leader, which provides a regional order on behalf of all other regional countries (Lake 2009; Mattli 1999). This poses a problem for Central Asia, where Kazakhstan and Uzbekistan rival for regional leadership. Whereas Kazakhstan is economically much stronger than Uzbekistan, the latter has a larger population and more military power. Constructivists stress the importance of a regional identity (Acharya 2005), which they deem to be necessary for regional integration.

Such a common regional identity seems to be weak in Central Asia, and consequently the prospects for regionalism are poor. Finally, liberals concentrate on domestic interests within regional states in order to explain the success or failure of regional cooperation (Moravcsik 1998). In this respect, the authoritarian political structures in Kazakhstan, Kyrgyzstan, Tajikistan, Turkmenistan and Uzbekistan are problematic for regionalism, because political elites and especially the presidents avoid regional cooperation to avoid opening up their countries and losing political control (Bohr 2004; Collins 2009; Spechler 2002).

The problem is that none of these variables—neither hegemony, nor regional identity, nor authoritarian political systems— is able to explain the complex pattern of success or failure of regionalism in different world regions. MERCOSUR in South America and SADC in Southern Africa are both dominated by regional hegemons, but Brazil and South Africa have not always provided the necessary leadership and damaged regionalism with unilateral actions (Krapohl et al. 2014). A regional identity is slowly emerging in ASEAN (Acharya 2005), but it is unclear why this happens in a culturally diverse region as Southeast Asia and not in a culturally more homogeneous region like Central Asia. Finally, authoritarian-ruled countries like Myanmar or Zimbabwe participate in regional organisations like ASEAN or SADC, and Kazakhstan and Kyrgyzstan themselves are members of the EAEU (Roberts and Moshes 2016). Thus, authoritarianism alone does not necessarily prevent regionalism (Allison 2008).

We argue that the failure of regionalism in Central Asia is due to two interrelated factors: First, like in other developing regions of the global south, intra-regional economic interdependence is low in Central Asia. This does not mean that there exists no demand for regional integration in Central Asia, but the demand is different to that in economically well-developed regional organisations like the Europe Union (EU). The main economic demand for European integration results from the utilisation of comparative cost advantages, and economies of scale in the single market (Mattli 1999), where, the trade of EU member states is more than 60% of their exports and imports. In contrast, the share of intraregional trade within Central Asia is only about 10% (see 'Economic dependency of Central Asia' section below). The Central Asian economies are dependent on the export of agricultural products and a few commodities like gas and oil to extra-regional markets.

Thereby, they all share the fundamental infrastructure problems of landlocked countries at the periphery of the global market (Bobokulov 2006; Gleason 2001; Myant and Drahokoupil 2008). The Central Asian countries could improve their trade infrastructure and their standing on the global market considerably, if they cooperated with each other. Here, the gains of regional integration would not so much derive from an intraregional economic exchange, but from an improved interaction with extra-regional actors and markets (Krapohl 2017a). Other regional organisations of the global south (for example ASEAN; Krapohl 2017b) have managed to utilise such extra-regional economic by cooperating successfully at the regional level gains (for example within the Chiang-Mai-Initiative of the ASEAN+3). However, the five Central Asian countries do not address their problems in common, but a regional organisation does not exist, and the region is distinguished by high internal trade barriers.

Second, at the same time when the success of regionalism depends very much on taking a united stance in relation to extra-regional actors, Central Asia is subject of the 'Second Great Game', wherein extra-regional powers—most notably China and Russia—compete for access to Central Asia's fossil resources (Cooley 2012). Within this 'Second Great Game', Russia uses Eurasian regionalism— namely EurAsEC and later the EAEU—to restore its influence in Central Asia. For Kazakhstan, membership in EurAsEC and the EAEU guarantees safe access to the Russian market and pipeline network.

This constitutes an important extra-regional economic privilege, which weights much more for Central Asia's largest economy than economic integration with its regional neighbours Kyrgyzstan, Tajikistan, Turkmenistan and Uzbekistan ever could (Collins and Bekenova 2017). Thus, Kazakhstan becomes a regional 'Rambo' (Krapohl 2017a) and prioritised its relations with Russia over regional integration in Central Asia. Because the Russian-led EAEU forms a customs union, Kazakhstan is locked into Eurasian regionalism and Central Asian regionalism becomes impossible. Thus, the 'Second Great Game' between China and Russia has torn Central Asia apart, and a genuine Central Asian regionalism could not survive.

The paper proceeds by developing the theoretical argument in 'Regionalism in the shadow of dependency' section. Here, it demonstrates how economic dependency on extra-regional markets influences the demand for and supply of regional cooperation in developing regions of the global south. 'The failure of regionalism in Central Asia' section analyses the emergence of Eurasian at the cost of Central Asian regionalism. It becomes visible that the Central Asian economies are highly dependent on economic exchange with China and Russia, and that the Russian strategy of Eurasian regionalism stopped the preliminary attempts of Central Asian regionalism. The conclusion summarises the findings of the empirical analysis and discusses the lessons of the Central Asian case for the academic field of comparative regionalism.

Regionalism in the shadow of dependency

The academic literature on regionalism still suffers from a divide between studies of the European Union (EU) and the field of comparative regionalism (Söderbaum and Sbragia 2011; Warleigh-Lack and Rosamond 2010). On the one hand, EU studies have developed a well-equipped theoretical toolbox in order to analyse the processes of European integration and policymaking within the EU. On the other hand, theories like liberal intergovernmentalism (Moravcsik 1998), neofunctionalism (Haas 1961) or various institutionalist approaches (Pollack 2003) are hardly applicable to cases of regionalism outside of Europe. Europe is an economically advanced region, and the regional economies profit a lot from mutual exchange on a liberalised single market.

Intraregional trade makes up for 60–65% of member states' international trade (Krapohl and Fink 2013). In contrast, most other regional organisations (with the exception of the North American Free Trade Agreement, NAFTA) are composed of developing countries and emerging markets, which have much less potential to trade with each other. Thus, the share of intraregional trade in regional organisations of the global south rarely exceeds 20%, and developing regions are dependent on economic exchange with other world regions. European integration theories do not account for these different economic structures, which, however, have a huge impact on regional integration.

The demand for regional integration

In order that regionalism succeeds, there needs to be demand for regional cooperation. In well-developed regions like Europe, the economic gains of regionalism result from the utilisation of comparative cost advantages and economies of scale by trading on the regional market (Mattli 1999). However, developing countries are distinguished by less diversified economies, which are dependent on the export of few commodities. The regional neighbours usually do not constitute important export markets for these goods because the regional economies are rarely compatible. Thus, the utilisation of comparative cost advantages and economies of scale generates less demand for cooperation in developing than in economically diversified regions.

Regionalism in developing world regions takes place in the shadow of extra-regional dependency. Developing countries are usually dependent on investment from and trade with more developed economies outside of their own region. Only developed economies possess the necessary capital and technology for productive investments and are able to grant significant amounts of development aid. Besides, developed economies constitute the main export market for primary goods, and they are the destination of labour migration which then leads to high remittance flows. Given this economic dependency, it seems that developing countries would be better off by cooperating with well-developed extra-regional partners than by setting up regional organisations together with their equally poor neighbours. Thus, the question arises, why regionalism actually exists within developing regions of the global south.

Regionalism in the global south is an instrument for developing countries to escape marginalisation on the global market (Schirm 2002). Many developing countries—maybe with the exception of Brazil, Russia, India and China (the so-called BRICs)—face the problem of being small and insignificant players on the global market and in international politics. As such, they do not constitute attractive partners for private businesses or intergovernmental cooperation. As a result, the terms of exchange will be unfavourable for them. Regionalism improves the standing of these developing countries because it bears positive size and stability effects. A regional market is necessarily bigger than each of its member states' markets on its own. Besides, regionalism improves the political stability of a region and reduces the risk of violent conflicts, because the member states of regional organisations have more peaceful means to settle their disputes (Haftel 2007). Both the size and stability effects make regions more attractive as locations for investments or as partners for international cooperation. Thus,

21

successful regionalism constitutes a competitive advantage for the regional member states.

To sum up, the gains of regionalism in developing regions of the global south are fundamentally different from the gains of regionalism in economically advanced regions of the global north. Whereas the gains of European integration are created inside of the region, the gains of regionalism in developing regions are created by improving the regions' standing in relation to extra-regional actors. We can thus speak of the intraregional and the extra-regional logics of regionalism (Krapohl 2017a). Both rationales for regionalism exist in well-developed and developing regions, but their relative weight depends on the degrees of intraregional economic interdependence and extra-regional economic dependence.

The supply of regional integration

The fact that there exists some demand for regional cooperation in developing regions does not necessarily imply that regionalism is supplied quasi automatically (Krapohl et al. 2014; Mattli 1999). Global competition for economic gains or political influence does not stop at the regional borders, and regional member states also compete with each other. Regional cooperation may improve the standing of developing regions in international politics and on the global market, but this does not mean that all regional member states profit from it to the same degree. There need to be net benefits for all the regional countries, because single member states do not cooperate for regional gains if their individual losses exceed their share of these gains.

In a first scenario, extra-regional actors reward regional cooperation of a particular developing region systematically, and the extra-regional logic of regional cooperation is successful (Krapohl 2017a). Thus, the extra-regional relations of all regional member states improve as long as they cooperate with each other and implement regional agreements. Regional cooperation can be achieved relatively easily because every member state enjoys a net benefit. The regional member states may still disagree about the concrete form of regional agreements, and they may bargain about the distributive consequences of these agreements, but they all prefer cooperation over defection. In sum, the preference constellation resembles battle-of-the-sexes, wherein coordination is not trivial, but possible (Stein 1982).

In a second scenario, extra-regional actors do not reward regional cooperation systematically but rather grant privileges to single member states of a particular developing region (Krapohl et al. 2014). These privileges may—for example—be bilateral trade agreements, access to important infrastructure or an opening up of the labour market for one particular regional member state. Such extra-regional privileges constitute an important competitive advantage for the respective developing country, but they may be at odds with regionalism. For example, bilateral trade agreements with extra-regional partners are incompatible with regional customs unions. Because of the dependency on extra-regional relations, a privileged member state of a developing region is likely to put its extra-regional interests first. The respective member state becomes a regional 'Rambo' (Holzinger 2003; Zürn 1993), which defects from regional cooperation in order to follow its extra-regional interests.

Often, it is one of the larger regional economies or even the regional power that is able to benefit from privileged extra-regional relations and that gains the least from regional integration. Regional powers are the most attractive partners within the region. This allows them to interact with extra-regional actors on more favourable terms. Besides, large regional member states profit the least from the size and stability effect of regionalism since they need to provide these goods on behalf of their smaller neighbours. In contrast to the argument of realists (Lake 2009; Mattli 1999), the dominance of one particular state usually does not have positive effects on regionalism in the global south, as regional powers put their own extra-regional interests before the common interests of the region (Krapohl et al. 2014; Krapohl 2017a). Due to their extra-regional economic dependence, they opt for privileged relations with important extra-regional actors, even if these privileges are in conflict with the goals of regional integration.

As a result of economic dependency, extra-regional actors have a huge impact on the prospects of regionalism in the global south. If extra-regional actors support regional cooperation, invest in the regional market and negotiate interregional trade and security agreements, regionalism in the global south can succeed. An example for this is ASEAN, which gained a new integration dynamic in the 2000s, because it profited a lot from extra-regional cooperation with China and Japan within the ASEAN+3 framework (Krapohl 2017b). However, if extra-regional actors grant privileges such as bilateral agreements to single member states, the chances for regional cooperation among developing countries decline.

An example for this is SADC, where the bilateral Trade, Development and Cooperation Agreement (TDCA) between the EU and South Africa became a stumbling stone for deeper regional integration (Muntschick 2017). This can go to such lengths that extra-regional governments may employ a divide-and-conquer strategy in order to prevent successful regionalism. By offering significant extra-regional privileges to important regional countries, they can prevent these privileged countries from successful cooperation with their regional neighbours and hinder the development of a stronger regional organisation.

The failure of regionalism in Central Asia

Although Central Asia was at the centre of a Eurasian trade network—the Silk Roads—in medieval times (Frankopan 2016), today it is a peripheral region in the global economy (Allison 2004). All five Central Asian countries look back on a history as Soviet republics during the Cold War. This implies that their economies enjoyed some rudimentary form of industrialisation, but also that infrastructure and trade relations were heavily oriented towards Russia (Pomfret 2009). Despite the end of the Cold War and the political independence of the five countries, the economic reliance on Russia can still be seen in current trade relations (Jenish 2015, see 'Economic dependency of Central Asia' section below for details).

However, the Russian dominance is increasingly challenged by a rising China, which invests heavily in Central Asia in order to access the region's fossil fuels and other mineral reserves (Sheives 2006). Today, Central Asia and its natural resources are at the centre of a 'Second Great Game',[1] in which China and Russia (and to a lesser extent also the EU and the USA) compete for influence (Cooley 2012; Samokhvalov 2016; von Hauff 2018). Within this 'Second Great Game', regional organisations dominated by China (i.e. the Shanghai Cooperation Organisation, SCO) and Russia (i.e. EurAsEC and later the EAEU) have become strategic instruments of power projection, and they have prevented the successful development of a genuine Central Asian regionalism (Stronski and Ng 2018; International Crisis Group 2017).

Economic dependency of Central Asia

Like in other developing regions, intraregional trade among the Central Asian countries is low, and it has been even declining since the dissolution of the Soviet Union at the beginning of the 1990s.[2] In Kyrgyzstan and Tajikistan, it halved over the past 20 years, falling from 30 to 40% of total international trade in the mid-1990s to 20% in 2017. Uzbekistan does not exhibit strong regional trade links either, with the respective trade share falling from 15% in the 1990s to 10% today. Kazakhstan stands out as the least regionally integrated country, because its intraregional trade share declines from a modest 6.5% in the 1990s to only 5% nowadays.

Kyrgyzstan's International Trade. UN Comtrade database (comtrade.un.org). No data was available for Kyrgyz trade in 1997–1999 and in 2014. The average between figures for 1996 and 2000, as well as between figures for 2013 and 2015, were taken instead. Tajikistan's International Trade. Tajikistan does not report trade data to the UN. Therefore, data were obtained from the official website of the Statistical Agency of Tajikistan (www.stat.tj/ru). Missing data for trade with China, Kazakhstan and Kyrgyzstan from 1995 to 2003 were mirrored from the UN Comtrade database. No trade data were available for 2017.

Uzbekistan's International Trade

Total trade figures were obtained from UN Uzbekistan (data. mdg-stat.uz/ru/data_finder/3332 and data.mdg-stat.uz/ru/data_finder/3332). Data for trade with China, Russia, Kazakhstan, Kyrgyzstan and Tajikistan in 2006–2017 were obtained from the official website of the Statistical Agency of Uzbekistan (https://stat.uz/ru). Data for Uzbekistan's trade in 1995–2005 and its trade with the EU were mirrored from UN Comtrade data of the respective trade partners

Due to low levels of regional economic interdependence, the intraregional gains of market integration are insufficient to promote regional cooperation in Central Asia. The Central Asian countries have relatively similar commodity-dependent economies that are competing rather than complementing each other (Wang 2014). As a result, rather than developing a regional market, the Central Asian countries have repeatedly deployed protectionist measures against each other. Trade barriers such as cumbersome controls on borders persist despite the proclaimed goal of regional cooperation. This makes Central Asian states among the most difficult places in the world for cross-border trade. For example, exporters to Kazakhstan need an average of 5 days to prepare documentation and four for custom clearance, at a total cost of around 700 USD (Russel 2019, p. 8; Doing Business 2019). Even 'informal regionalism' in the form of local trade and businesses in transboundary areas has hardly gained foothold in the region (Bohr 2004). All this has exacerbated the dependence on the extra-regional export of commodities like gas and oil.

While intraregional trade is low in Central Asia, trade dependence on external actors, foremost Russia but also increasingly China, is high. Russia has been the most important trading partner for Central Asia since the early 1990s and at least up until the financial crisis of 2008/9 (Jenish 2015). During that period Russia's trade share has increased in Kyrgyzstan (from around 20 to 35%), Tajikistan (from 15 to 25%) and Uzbekistan (figures fluctuate between 15 and 20%). Cooperation with Russia is crucial for the Central Asian economies. The country has not only been a traditional market for many Central Asian goods, but it is also the economic gateway to Europe, as 70% of Central Asian exports reach Europe through Russia. As a legacy from Soviet times, Central Asia's infrastructure is still heavily oriented north rather than connecting the five regional countries with each other (Kubicek 1997). Moreover, the countries are interested in access to Russian finances, discounted energy prices and free movement of labour, which leads to high remittances flows from emigrants (Bobokulov 2006; Spechler 2002).

China has been steadily expanding its influence in Central Asia since the 1990s (Peyrose and Raballand 2015). Until the mid-2000s, the share of trade with China was below 10% for all Central Asian countries, but it has been constantly rising since then. This has been due to the acceleration of Chinese growth and to its increasing interest in Central Asian resources (Jenish 2015). Noteworthy, and in stark contrast with the Russian trade, the Chinese trade share did not decline in the 2008/9 crisis. Even though Russia still remains the most important trading partner for Kazakhstan (after the EU) and Tajikistan, China has already caught up in the case of Kyrgyzstan and Uzbekistan. The rising role of China in Central Asia leads to a growing competition for influence—or, in other words, a new 'Great Game' between China and Russia (Cooley 2012; Stronski and Ng 2018).

Up to here, the economic structure of Central Asia is surprisingly similar to that of Southeast Asia, where ASEAN constitutes one of the most advanced regional organisations in the developing world (Krapohl and Fink 2013; Krapohl 2017b). Intraregional trade within ASEAN is also relatively low (around 25% of member states international trade), and it was even lower in the past (ASEAN exists since 1967). Besides, the ASEAN member states also trade heavily with two extra-regional partners in the wider neighbourhood, namely with China and Japan. However, in contrast to the Central Asian countries, the ASEAN member states managed to keep their unity and were not torn apart by the power struggle between China and Japan.

On the contrary, they were able to take advantage of the situation and ASEAN profits a lot from cooperation with China and Japan within the ASEAN+3 frameworks (e.g. the Chiang-Mai-Initiative; Krapohl 2015, 2017b). One reason for this is that there exists no regional power with extra-regional economic privileges within ASEAN. The four biggest economies—Indonesia, Malaysia, Singapore and Thailand—balance each other to some degree and none of them could achieve a unilateral advantage by cooperating on its own with either China or Japan. This marks an important difference to Central Asia, where Kazakhstan dominates the region in economic terms and is able to gain huge economic advantages by cooperating with Russia on its own.

Kazakhstan is Central Asia's regional power in economic terms, although its population (18.5 mln) is less than that of Uzbekistan (30 mln). Kazakhstan's economy is based on vast hydrocarbon and mineral reserves (foremost coal and uranium), but also developed a more advanced manufacturing sector, for instance in chemical industry (Guliev and Mekhdiev 2017; Sultanov 2014, p. 106). As a result of rising energy prices during the 2000s, Kazakhstan's GDP surged from a mere $ 9 bln in the 1990s to $ 160 bln today[3] and is triple the size of the Uzbek economy ($ 48 bln) and more than 20 times larger than the Tajik or Kyrgyz economies (about $ 7 bln each).[4]

As a result, the Russian-Chinese rivalry has been particularly pronounced in the case of Kazakhstan. Russia was the destination of up to 50% of Kazakh exports back in the 1990s. However, the relative importance of Kazakhstan's trade with Russia has been in constant decline since the 1990s and fell down to 21% nowadays. At the high of the financial crisis in 2008/9, when oil prices collapsed, trade with Russia even fell to a historical low of 10%. At the same time, China caught up and raised its trade share from below 5% during the 1990s to 13% today.

Oil forms the backbone of Kazakhstan's economy and most of the Kazakh oil exports go to Europe. Thus, the share of Kazakhstan's trade with the EU is quite high (almost 40%). However, the intense economic exchange with Europe does not reduce but rather contributes to Kazakhstan's dependency on Russia. Being a landlocked country and sharing a 7000 km border with Russia, Kazakhstan relies on Russian pipelines in order to export its oil to Europe (Jenish 2015). Among the most important pipelines are the Uzen-Atyrau-Samara pipeline, a northbound link to Russia's distribution system, and the Caspian Consortium pipeline, which brings Kazakh oil to the Russian Black Sea port of Novorossiysk (Eurasian Review 2012).

About 85% of Kazakh oil is exported to or via Russia. One of the few pipelines bypassing Russia is the Baku-Tbilisi-Ceyhan pipeline, which is however hard to reach (Kazakh oil is brought by tanker across the Caspian Sea) and transports only a very small share of Kazakh oil. The only connection to China is the Kazakhstan-China pipeline, running 2230 km from Kazakhstan's Caspian shore to Xinjiang in China, which was completed in 2005 and is currently being expanded. Oil exports to China are rapidly growing and make up 15% of the total volume. This share is likely to grow in the future, indicating an increasing Chinese influence in Central Asia (Kembayev 2018; Guliev and Mekhdiev 2017).

The 'Second Great Game' and Russian interests in Central Asia

Russia has been historically the pre-eminent power in Central Asia, having colonised the region during Tsarism in the nineteenth century and incorporated it into the Soviet Union after the Bolshevik revolution. In the twenty-first century, Russia's traditional dominance became increasingly challenged by China, so that Russia has been seeking to counterbalance a growing Chinese influence in the region. Moscow is keen on the region's natural resources and strives to control the routes of their transport and export (Melnykovska et al. 2012). To keep up with the supply obligations to Europe, Russian energy companies grew increasingly reliant on imports of Central Asian gas and oil (Cooley 2012, p. 65; Kuzmina 2010).

Among the five Central Asian countries, Kazakhstan is Russia's most important economic partner in the region. Apart from being a major supplier of oil, Kazakhstan is also an important crossroad territory for the transit of Turkmen and Uzbek gas, which goes to Russia and China (about 99 bln m3 per year). The export of Kazakhstan's own gas is negligible (13 bln m3 in 2017), but is rapidly growing, and before the end of 2017 it was entirely sold to Russia (BP 2018; Mazorenko 2014; Guliev and Mekhdiev 2017).[5] Hydroenergy from Kyrgyzstan and Tajikistan also reaches Russia through the territory of Kazakhstan (Kuzmina 2010). Access to Kazakhstan's rich uranium reserves is also of primary interest to Russia as a major uranium manufacturer. Moreover, Russian companies, especially state monopolists, have substantial stakes in Kazakh oil fields, refineries, hydroelectric stations, pipelines and uranium enrichment plants (ibid).

Central Asia is furthermore a crucial region for Russia's national security interests (Jonson 2001). Among the main concerns are terrorism, drug trafficking, the fight against Islamic fundamentalism[6] and regional separatism. Moscow has been trying to consolidate its military presence in the region by deploying military bases in Kazakhstan, Kyrgyzstan and Tajikistan, and by binding these three countries into the Collective Security Treaty Organisation (CSTO) (Mesheryakov 2012; Bobokulov 2006).[7] For Russia's security interests, Kazakhstan is again the most important country of Central Asia, and the two countries cooperate closely in military-industrial complexes, in atomic industry and in space. As a legacy from Soviet times, most Russian satellites are launched from the Kazakh space station Baikonur (Kuzmina 2010).

Since the collapse of the Soviet Union, Russia has always used regionalism as an instrument to keep or gain influence in the former Soviet republics. This began already with the establishment of the Commonwealth of Independent States (CIS) in 1991. However, the CIS proved to be rather dysfunctional, and economic integration could not prevail against the eagerness for independence in the former Soviet republics (Kubicek 1997). A new approach of economic integration was started in 2000 with the establishment of the Eurasian Economic Community (EurAsEC) by Belarus, Kazakhstan, Kyrgyzstan, Russia and Tajikistan. Uzbekistan joined EurAsEC in 2005 but left it again in 2008.[8] After the financial crisis of 2008, the three bigger EurAsEC member states—Belarus, Kazakhstan and Russia—formed a customs union, which was further institutionalised and renamed to Eurasian Economic Union (EAEU) in 2015 (Vinokurov 2018; Roberts and Moshes 2016).

Armenia and Kyrgyzstan joined the EAEU within the same year, whereas Tajikistan's accession is still pending today. Unlike the CIS, the EAEU is underpinned by serious financial commitments and has nascent supranational institutions modelled upon the EU. Though an alliance with former Soviet republics has been always important to Russia, the strategic shift towards Eurasian integration became particularly pertinent since the deterioration of relations with the West in the wake of the annexation of Crimea (Trenin 2017; Krickovic and Bratersky 2016). Moreover, through the promotion of the EAEU, Russia has been seeking to counterbalance the rising Chinese influence in Central Asia (Kembayev 2018).

China's economy is growing rapidly and increasingly needs access to Central Asia's natural resources, in particular oil and gas but also metals and rare earths. China is also keen on getting access to Eurasian markets for its exports of cheap consumer goods, and views Central Asia as an important transit corridor for its exports to Europe (Peyrose and Raballand 2015; Melnykovska et al. 2012). Like Russia, China also has security interests in Central Asia, which neighbours its politically unstable province of Xinjiang (Rolland 2017; Bobokulov 2006). In order to fight political extremism and the simmering threat of Uyghur separatism in Xinjiang, China puts emphasis on the economic development of the province through intensified trade links with Central Asia (Raballand and Andresy 2007).

Despite being a potential competitor, China shares a common interest with Russia in preserving the political status quo in the region (rather than promoting democratisation), as well as keeping Western influence in Central Asia to the minimum (Stronski and Ng 2018). Therefore, China tried not to alienate Russia and pursue joint economic cooperation with Central Asia through the Shanghai

Cooperation Organisation (SCO)—a regional organisation originating in the 1990s and comprising Russia, China and all Central Asian republics (except Turkmenistan) (Naarajärvi 2012; Yuan 2010). However, fearing the expansion of Chinese influence in Central Asia,[9] Russia vehemently opposed Chinese proposals such as a joint SCO free trade area and a development bank. China answered on this by launching the Asian Infrastructure Investment Bank without Russian involvement (Kembayev 2018; Gabuev 2017).

More recently, China has been spearheading a gigantic infrastructure and development project titled 'Belt and Road' initiative (initially called 'One Belt, One Road'). It aims at reviving the ancient Silk Road by erecting a Eurasian transport-linked corridor for bringing Chinese exports to Europe via land roads in Central Asia (Dave and Kobayashi 2018; Rolland 2017). Among the 29 heads of state who attended the Belt and Road summit were the presidents of Kazakhstan, Kyrgyzstan and Uzbekistan (The Diplomat 2017). The presence of Vladimir Putin was perhaps symbolic for the ambivalent relationship between China and Russia as partners and competitors in Central Asia. Also indicative in this respect was the signing of a general agreement on 'trade and economic cooperation' between the Eurasian Economic Union and China in autumn 2017 (Eurasian Economic Commission 2017).

The increasing strength and influence of China threatens Russia's dominance and interests in the region. Remaining an important security provider, Russia loses its economic clout in Central Asia, with China increasingly becoming the economic driver of the region (Stronski and Ng 2018). In the framework of the Belt and Road initiative, China has pledged and started investing billions of dollars in Central Asian infrastructure, primarily roads and railways, in this way expanding overland routes to Europe for the export of Chinese goods. Chinese investment entails increasing indebtedness. For example, Kyrgyzstan owes 40% of its foreign debt to China. In Tajikistan, debt to China, the country's single largest creditor, accounts for 80% increase in Tajikistan's external debt over the past 10 years (Hurley et al. 2018).

In the context of the rising economic role of China, Russia wants to remain the gatekeeper for Central Asian trade with Europe and in particular to preserve its monopoly on the export of Central Asian hydrocarbons (Xin and Daleng 2015; Guangcheng 2015). Increased Central Asian exports of oil and gas to China could deprive Russia of transit fees and drive down the global oil price. At the same time, the economic downturn in Russia since 2014, exacerbated by Western sanctions and the continuously relatively low oil price, makes Russia less attractive as a market for Central Asian exports and as an origin of remittances, which went down considerably given the crisis and the depreciation of the rouble (IMF 2016).[10] Additionally, the lack of pressure from China on political-military orientation, unlike from Russia, makes China an attractive partner for many Central Asian states. Chinese soft power influence is also on the rise, illustrated by the increasing numbers of Central Asian—primarily Kazakh—students obtaining their degrees in China. Still, most Central Asian students studying abroad go to Russia (Stronski and Ng 2018).

In the context of the 'Second Great Game', the Central Asian countries basically have two options. On the one hand, they can attempt to develop a unified regional stance in relation to extra-regional actors and to profit from the rivalry between China and Russia. This strategy has been successfully applied by the Southeast Asian countries, which use the regional organisation ASEAN in order to cooperate with the extra-regional powers China and Japan (Krapohl 2017b). On the other hand, the Central Asian countries can opt for closer bilateral relations with extra-regional actors at the expense of the genuine Central Asian integration. This happened for example in Southern Africa, where the regional power South Africa enjoyed privileged economic relations with the EU (Krapohl et al. 2014). Which of the two strategies prevails depends very much on Kazakhstan, which is a crucial player for regional integration in Central Asia, but which is also highly dependent on its economic relations with Russia.

From the CAU to the EAEU

There have been repeated efforts to establish a genuine Central Asian regional organisation in the last 25 years, but all of them have remained unsuccessful so far (Kubicek 1997; Pomfret 2009). We argue that the most important reason for the failure of Central Asian regionalism is the pull of extra-regional actors, foremost Russia, which has torn the region apart. As part of Russia's strategy within the 'Second Great Game', Eurasian integration provided economic and political gains for Kazakhstan that exceeded the possible gains of Central Asian regionalism by far. Thus, the regional power Kazakhstan opted for closer cooperation with Russia rather than cooperating with its regional neighbours. As a result, the Central Asian countries gave up their own attempts to create a regional organisation and some of them joined the Russian-led Eurasian integration project.

In the wake of the demise of the Soviet Union, the leaders of the five Central Asian countries met in 1992 to discuss options for regional cooperation. Turkmenistan's President Saparmurat Niyazov suggested to create a 'Confederation of Central Asian States' as an alternative to joining the Russian-lead CIS, but the other leader disagreed with Niyazov's proposal and opted for joining the CIS. A year later, it became clear that the CIS did not offer an effective framework to address the economic challenges of post-communist transformation in Central Asia. Following an initiative of the Uzbek president Islam Karimov, the Central Asian states decided to form their own regional organisation (Kubicek 1997). Turkmenistan refused to join, since president Niyazov remained suspicious of his colleagues after they refused his idea of the Confederation (Mesheryakov 2012). Being a neutral country according to the constitution and possessing abundant natural resource reserves, Turkmenistan did not participate in any regional integration initiatives since then (Yapıcı 2018).

The integration process of the remaining four Central Asian states was driven by Kazakhstan and Uzbekistan, who had been traditionally competing for leadership in Central Asia. Integration was institutionalised in 1994, when Kazakhstan, Uzbekistan and

Kyrgyzstan established the Central Asian Union (CAU). The Union was modelled upon the example of west-European integration and envisaged the creation of a single economic space with the goal of free movement of goods, capital, services and labour (Bobokulov 2006). Contrary to the CIS, the CAU had an economic rather than an ideological rationale and moved beyond joint declarations by establishing regional institutions such as the Intergovernmental Council, the Executive Committee and a bank designated to finance common projects.

A further commitment to regional integration was signalled in 1995, when Uzbekistan worked out a regional development strategy until 2000 (Kubicek 1997). Tajikistan joined the regional organisation following the end of the civil war in 1998, and CAU was renamed as the Central Asian Economic Community (CAEC). Another 4 years later, the regional organisation once again changed its name to become the Central Asian Cooperation Organisation (CACO). The goals of CACO were broader than its predecessor organisations. Next to regional economic integration, the organisation addressed the new threats of terrorism and aimed to promote regional security (Mesheryakov 2012).

Despite ambitious goals, regionalism in Central Asian has not yielded desired results. CACO and its predecessor organisations have failed to develop an effective coordination of regional economic and trade policy. Instead, disagreements and protectionism persisted. For example, Kyrgyzstan's accession to the WTO in 1998 and the related liberalisation of its trade regime led to differences in trade policies and custom legislation among the members of CACO. When Kyrgyzstan became a major trading hub for the re-export of Chinese consumer goods, Kazakhstan and Uzbekistan took protectionist measures to shield their industries.

Uzbekistan, which borders all other Central Asian states, has repeatedly closed its border with Kyrgyzstan and Tajikistan, which partly rely on transit through Uzbekistan in order to export their goods to Russia and Europe (Bohr 2004). Additionally, CACO suffered from disagreements between Kazakhstan and Uzbekistan, which were competing for regional leadership, and had different policy interests. Whereas Kazakhstan was concerned about economic instability and separatism, Uzbekistan focused more on fighting religious extremism (Mesheryakov 2012). By 2003, CACO had become largely ineffective, and regional integration in Central Asia stalled.

Central Asian regionalism was captured by Russia and its Eurasian integration project. Russia always strove to become involved in Central Asian regionalism and became an observer to CAU and CAEC in the 1990s. When CACO was established in 2002, Russia made a decisive move and applied for membership in the organisation. The accession of Russia in 2004 meant de facto a fusion of CACO with the Russia-centred EurAsEC (Ministry of Foreign Affairs of the Russian Federation 2005), which had existed since 2000 and included the four Central Asian countries Kazakhstan, Kyrgyzstan, Tajikistan and Uzbekistan (Bobokulov 2006).

The formal decision to abolish CACO in 2005 meant the end of genuinely Central Asian attempts at integration (Mesheryakov 2012). Today's EAEU, the successor organisation of EurAsEC, includes only Kazakhstan and Kyrgyzstan, but not the other Central Asian countries. Uzbekistan had already left EurAsEC in 2008, and Tajikistan has not yet been able to meet the preconditions of the EAEU's customs union. Thus, the external border of the EAEU's customs union runs through Central Asia and divides it into two parts.

In the context of a strong Russian pull, the economic priority of Central Asia's largest economy was a crucial factor in the failure of Central Asian regionalism. Sharing a border with Russia and being home to a large Russian minority, Kazakhstan has always seen Russia as part of any region that it belongs to and viewed Eurasian integration with Russia as a political priority (Kassenova 2012). Aside of oil exports to Europe, Russia is Kazakhstan's major trading partner so that economic gains of integrating with Russia by far outweigh gains from cooperation with Central Asian neighbours (trade figures discussed in 'Economic dependency of Central Asia' section corroborate that). The structural dependencies on the

Russian pipeline system for the export of oil to Europe are another reason for seeking closer economic integration with Russia. Thus, Kazakhstan supported Eurasian integration together with Russia from the start. In fact, it was Kazakh president Nursultan Nazarbayev who aired his grand vision of a 'Eurasian Union' as early as 1994 (Konopelko 2018; Spechler 2002).

When choosing between Central Asian regionalism and extra-regional (i.e. Eurasian) economic privileges, Kazakhstan became a regional Rambo, which put its extra-regional interests first. Russia did not reward regional cooperation in Central Asia systematically, but instead aimed to include Kazakhstan in the Eurasian integration project. Membership in the EAEU includes significant economic benefits for Central Asia's regional power. Kazakhstan gets access to the Russian market, gets disproportionally high investments and has access to the Russian pipeline network. Regional cooperation in Central Asia had not produced any of these benefits.

Thus, when choosing between deepening the ties with its Central Asian neighbours and joining the EAEU, Kazakhstan opted for the latter, even when most of the Central Asian countries did not join the Russian-led organisation. Since the EAEU is a customs union, Kazakhstan's membership is not compatible with bilateral trade agreements and other forms of economic integration in the region, which effectively prevents Central Asian regionalism. As a result, the region has not been successful in establishing a common stance in relation to Russia and China. Instead of taking advantage of the rivalry between the two external powers, Central Asia is torn apart in the 'Second Great Game'.

Conclusion

The empirical analysis has demonstrated that the extra-regional interests of Kazakhstan and the external influence of Russia have led to the abandonment of regionalism in Central Asia. The failure of various regional organisations in Central Asia cannot conclusively be explained by blaming the lack of a regional hegemon, the weak regional identity or the authoritarian political systems of Kazakhstan, Kyrgyzstan, Tajikistan, Turkmenistan and

Uzbekistan. The example of ASEAN demonstrates that regions can cooperate successfully and develop a regional identity despite lacking a regional hegemon and including authoritarian states. The Central Asian countries have not managed to cooperate regionally and to integrate their economies because they are torn apart in the 'Second Great Game'.

Russia needs to balance a rapidly growing Chinese influence in Central Asia, and it used Eurasian integration as a strategic instrument to project power in the region. Thereby, EurAsEC and the EAEU have provided important economic (and political) gains for Kazakhstan, and regional cooperation with its Central Asian neighbours could never have been a substitute for that. As a result, Central Asia's largest economy put its extra-regional interests first, and Central Asian regionalism was doomed to fail. Instead of establishing a unified stance in the 'Second Great Game', Central Asia is fragmented and suffers from trade barriers, closed borders and political conflicts. The crucial question for the academic field of comparative regionalism is, under which circumstances regional organisations constitute themselves successfully and when they are likely to fail. A comparison of Southeast Asia and Central Asia may be fruitful in this respect. Both regions consist of relatively small countries and constitute playing fields for the rivalry of larger external powers. However, whereas Central Asia has not been able to build up a unified position in relation to China and Russia, the ASEAN member states have established a stable regional organisation, which has become an important player in the wider neighbourhood and balances the influences of China and Japan (Stubbs 2014).

This striking difference between the two regions can be due to several factors. The timing may have been much more favourable for ASEAN, which existed long before the rise of China and the resulting competition for regional hegemony with Japan. Besides, the Russian influence may be much more dominant in Central Asia than the Chinese or Japanese influence in Southeast Asia, because the Central Asian countries were de facto governed by Russia since Tsarist times. But all these are simple ad hoc explanations, and more research is necessary to get convincing answers.

European integration theories like or liberal intergovernmentalism (Moravcsik 1998), neofunctionalism (Haas 1961) or institutionalist approaches (Pollack 2003) cannot contribute much to the comparison of different developing regions, since they do not conceptualise the extra-regional dimension of regional integration. The European theories were developed on the example of an economically well-developed region, and they take intraregional economic interdependence for granted. However, intraregional economic exchange is much less important in developing regions, which are economically and politically much more dependent on extra-regional countries. This dependency leads to a huge influence of external actors on regionalism in developing regions— as the example of Russia's influence in Central Asia has shown. In order to bridge the gap between the two academic fields of comparative regionalism and EU studies (Söderbaum and Sbragia 2011; Warleigh-Lack and Rosamond 2010), we need to develop integration theories which systematically conceptualise the intraregional as well as the extra-regional effects of regionalism.

The region that isn't: China, Russia and the failure of regional integration in Central Asia Sebastian Krapohl1 & Alexandra Vasileva-Dienes1,2 *Received: 21 January 2019 / Revised: 30 April 2019 / Accepted: 1 May 2019. Krapohl, S. &Vasileva-Dienes, A. Asia Eur J (2019). https://doi.org/10.1007/s10308-019-00548-0.* *Sebastian Krapohl s.krapohl@uva.nl Alexandra Vasileva-Dienes alexandra.dienes@fes-vienna.org.*

Chapter 2

Jihadists from Ex-Soviet Central Asia: Where Are They? Why Did They Radicalize? What Next?

Edward Lemon Vera Mironova William Tobey

Foreword by Simon Saradzhyan

In the fall of 2016 Fletcher School professor Monica Duffy Toft and I were completing work on an issue brief[1] in which we argued that the Islamic State should be further rolled back and dismantled rather than allowed to remain in the hopes that it would somehow become a normal state. IS was already in retreat at the time, having lost much of the territories it had once controlled in Syria and Iraq. Watching this made me, like many other analysts of political violence, wonder what surviving foreign fighters—which, at the time, included an estimated 5,000-10,000 individuals from post-Soviet Eurasia—would do next if IS and other jihadist Salafi groups in the Levant disintegrated.

To ascertain their next moves, one had to begin by discerning what made them leave their home countries and eventually go to IS in the first place, and whether/how their motivation may have evolved in the course of their stay with the group. As someone focusing on Eurasia, I was particularly worried about what nationals of the Central Asian states would decide to do next and what impact their decisions and actions would have as some of the regimes in these countries were considerably more fragile and, therefore, more vulnerable than, say, Vladimir Putin's government. Another reason behind my interest in the subject is that the threat by violent extremists hailing from Central Asia had not been, in my view, as thoroughly examined as that posed by jihadists in and from Russia's North Caucasus.

Specifically, I had three sets of questions in mind:

(1) What causes nationals of Central Asia to take up arms and participate in political violence and what might those of them who have gone to fight in Iraq/Syria decide to do next?;

(2) if they decide to return to post-Soviet Central Asia en masse, can this region become a major source of violent extremism that transcends borders, and possibly continents, in the wake of IS's demise?; and

(3) is there a threat that chemical, biological, radiological or nuclear materials stored anywhere in Central Asia will be used by the returning nationals of Central Asia or others for purposes of WMD terrorism (considering that al-Qaeda has sought nuclear weapons and IS has used chemical weapons) and, if so, how serious is this threat? We asked three scholars to answer these questions.

Vera Mironova is best known for her research on individual level behavior in conflict environments and her fieldwork involving extensive interviews with former and active fighters. Edward Lemon is known for his research examining the intersection of authoritarian governance, religion, security and migration in Eurasia, along with his fieldwork in the region. Finally, William Tobey offers unparalleled expertise and years of experience in the U.S. government's nuclear security and non-proliferation initiatives. Fortunately, they all agreed to delve into the issues, refining my initial questions in ways that made their answers even more illuminating than I had hoped for. The results of their tremendous efforts are presented here, skillfully fused into one narrative by Russia Matters editor Natasha Yefimova-Trilling with assistance from our project's editorial assistant and student associates, in what I think is an insightful paper on the threat of violent extremism within and emanating from Central Asia.

Executive Summary

In the summer of 2018, the scenic, impoverished Central Asian nation of Tajikistan appeared in international headlines when Islamic State terrorists claimed credit[2] for the killing of four Western cyclists who were run over by a car, then shot and stabbed to death. This was the first known terrorist attack on foreigners in Central Asia since a suicide bombing[3] of the Chinese Embassy in Kyrgyzstan in 2016, and it appears to have been inspired by IS propaganda, though we do not know how much the group was involved in planning the attack, if at all.

The violence serves as a jarring reminder that Islamist radicals from the five Central Asian nations once under Moscow's control—Kazakhstan, Kyrgyzstan, Tajikistan, Turkmenistan and Uzbekistan—have become noteworthy players on the field of international terrorism. Thousands of radicals from formerly Soviet Central Asia have travelled to fight alongside IS in Syria and Iraq; hundreds more are in Afghanistan. Not counting the fighting in those three war-torn countries, nationals of Central Asia have been responsible for nearly 100 deaths in terrorist attacks outside their home region in the past five years. But many important aspects of the phenomenon need more in-depth study.

This research paper attempts to answer four basic sets of questions adapted from the ones mentioned in the foreword:

(1) Is Central Asia becoming a new source of violent extremism that transcends borders, and possibly continents? (2) If so, why? What causes nationals of Central Asia to take up arms and participate in political violence? (3) As IS has been all but defeated in Iraq and Syria, what will Central Asian extremists who have thrown in their lot with the terrorist group do next? And (4) Do jihadists from Central Asia aspire to acquire and use weapons of mass destruction? If so, how significant a threat do they pose and who would be its likeliest targets? None of the answers is as straightforward as we would like, and far more attention should

be paid to the differences and similarities among the five Central Asian states. But key findings generated by our research include the following:

- The civil war in Syria and the rise of IS in the Middle East have spurred an increase in the number of Central Asians participating in extremist violence beyond their home region; however, comparatively speaking, the international threat should not be exaggerated: Although Central Asians make up about 1 percent of the world's population, they were responsible for 0.14 percent of the world's terrorist attacks in the past decade, based on data from the Global Terrorism Database.[4]

- While the causes of radicalization vary widely, field research by two of the authors, as well as other scholars, suggests that two significant factors are (a) real and/or perceived injustices or failures that lead to an extreme rejection of society and (b) affinity for "a culture of violence." These factors can overlap with a search for adventure and/or a sense of belonging and meaning. Contrary to popular belief, relative poverty, religiosity and lack of education do not seem to be strong predictors of radicalization.

- These authors' research also suggests that a significant number of Central Asian extremists who went to fight in the Middle East became radicalized abroad, primarily while working in Russia or Turkey.

- Other scholars' research suggests that recent terrorist attacks and plots with a jihadist agenda in peaceful countries have more often been the work of local residents without combat experience than by former combatants.

- The next steps of Central Asian jihadists in foreign combat zones are exceedingly difficult to predict. Those who manage to escape from Iraq and Syria will have three basic options: to continue their fight in a different conflict zone, Afghanistan being the most likely; to go back to Central Asia, which does not seem like an option many find appealing; and to settle in a third country, whether to live peacefully or to keep fighting.

- The evidence indicates that Afghanistan-based militant groups, most notably the Islamic State Khorasan Province (ISKP), are targeting Central Asian recruits. But the inflow of foreign fighters is less intense than to Syria and Iraq in 2014-2015.

- While lone attackers attempting to commit acts of violence— whether inspired by radical propaganda or other factors—will continue to be difficult to identify before they do damage, policymakers and law-enforcement authorities would be wise to cooperate across borders in tracking those Central Asian extremists who plug into networks of like-minded radicals and/or criminal groups.

- Much work needs to be done to provide better security for the radiological sources in use in Central Asia; however, the threat vectors for chemical, biological, radiological and nuclear weapons involving Central Asia appear not to pose an imminent danger either within the region or outside it.

Central Asia and International Terrorism Today

Nationals of the five Central Asian states once under Moscow's rule have been prominent in the global landscape of violent extremism in two ways in recent years: by taking part in combat on the side of jihadist groups like the Islamic State and by plotting and/or carrying out terrorist attacks in non-war zones inside and outside their home region. Quantitatively, relative to the region's population, the available data suggest that Central Asia as a whole accounts for a disproportionately high percentage of foreign fighters in Syria and Iraq, but a disproportionately low number of terrorist attacks worldwide. This is a much generalized summary, to be sure, accounting neither for individual variation among the five countries nor for the non-quantifiable aspects of violent extremism, but it a starting point. It is also a basis to say with confidence that Central Asia has become a source of violent extremism that transcends borders and continents.

As far as foreign fighters are concerned, prior to the start of Syria's civil war in 2011 the former Soviet republics of Central Asia had periodically seen trickles of citizens leaving to fight for radical causes abroad, mostly in Afghanistan/Pakistan. But the expanding war in Syria and the rise of IS there and in Iraq in 2013, opened the doors for Central Asians to engage with extremist violence on a much larger scale than before. While coming up with accurate figures is next to impossible, a tally of the most recent estimates of how many fighters have gone to Syria and Iraq from ex-Soviet Central Asia ranges approximately from 2,000 to upwards of 4,000, totaling perhaps one-third to nearly one-half of the contingent from the former Soviet Union and 5-10 percent of "foreign terrorist fighters" worldwide, to borrow the European Commission's terminology.[5] Considering that the ex-Soviet Central Asian states account for less than one percent of the world's population,[6] this figure suggests a disproportionately high representation among the foreign-fighter contingent in the Middle East.

Country of Origin (2017 est. pop.)[7]	High Estimate (Year)	Low Estimate (Year)	Fighters per 100K of population
Kazakhstan (18 mln)	600[8] (2017)	150[9] (2015)	0.8-3.3
Kyrgyzstan (6.2 mln)	595[10] (2016)	295[11] (2016)	4.8-9.6
Tajikistan[12] (8.9 mln)	1, 699[13] (2018)	941[14] (2017)	10.6-12.3
Turkmenistan (5.6 mln)	400[15] (2015)	360[16] (2015)	6.3 – 7.1
Uzbekistan (32.4 mln)	1, 500[17] (2016)	200[18] (2015)	0.6-4.6
TOTALS	4,195	1,946 2.	7-5.8

Table 1: Estimated Number of Central Asian Fighters Who Have Gone to Iraq and Syria.

An equally confounding problem for counterterrorism analysts is the potential for violence among individuals from Central Asia residing outside their home region that have not fought in combat zones or undergone intensive military training. Between 2014 and 2017, according to our tally, men from Uzbekistan and Kyrgyzstan carried out five high-profile terrorist attacks in New York, Stockholm, Istanbul, St. Petersburg and Karachi, four of them just last year. While two of those cases (Pakistan and Turkey) involved assailants with significant military training, two of the other attacks (Sweden and Russia) were perpetrated by men who may have tried but failed to join IS, though evidence in the Russia case isspotty; and the fifth attacker, in the U.S., clearly had no combat experience or military training with extremist groups. Three of the attacks took place in countries with significant Central Asian Diasporas: Russia (3-7 million), the U.S. (about 250,000), Turkey (100,000-200,000) and Europe (under 100,000). Overall, in the past five years terrorist attacks carried out by perpetrators from Central Asia have killed more people outside the region than inside it over the past decade—96 versus 91, not counting attackers. (See tables below.)

That said, as noted above, citizens of Central Asia have been involved in relatively few of the world's recent terror attacks. Based on data from the EU Terrorism Situation and Trend reports[19] for 2014-2017, Central Asians perpetrated just one of the 65 attacks in the European Union,[20] one of the 77 attacks in Turkey, one of the 27 attacks in the United States and one of the 153 alleged attacks in Russia.[21] The more comprehensive Global Terrorism Database,[22] or GTD, based at the University of Maryland, includes at least two other fatal attacks in Russia reportedly committed by Central Asians, though available details on these are spotty. They include an attack on police in the city of Astrakhan (some perpetrators reportedly[23] born in Kazakhstan or were Russian-born ethnic Kazakhs), as well as the widely reported[24] beheading of a four-year-old by an Uzbek nanny whom investigators said could have been mentally ill. Worldwide, between 2008 and 2017, Central Asians were involved in 68 of the 48,546 terrorist attacks recorded in the GTD, excluding those that took place in Syria, Iraq and Afghanistan—or just 0.14 percent.

Aside from actual attacks, Central Asian nationals have been detained in numerous incidents on suspicion of plotting attacks or aiding those who might carry them out. As noted below, some of these cases may involve political manipulation or shoddy investigative work. In the U.S., which has a relatively robust legal system, as well as a practice of counterterrorism stings,[25]several terror-related cases have centered on suspects from Central Asia. For example, three Brooklyn men—one citizen of Kazakhstan and two of Uzbekistan—were arrested[26] in 2015 on charges of conspiring to give material support to IS; according to the State Department, [27] in 2015 an Uzbek refugee was sentenced to 25 years in prison by a U.S. court after planning bomb attacks for which he sought advice from the Islamic Movement of Uzbekistan, or IMU, ii and in late 2016 a Dutch-Turkish citizen was convicted in the U.S. for serving as an IMU fundraiser and facilitator; this June a refugee from Uzbekistan residing in Colorado was found guilty[28] of trying to aid the Islamic Jihad Union, a splinter group of the IMU.

Year	Location	Affiliated Group	Fatalities	Origin of Perpetrator(s)
2014	Karachi	IMU[2]	39[29](inc. 10 attackers)	Uzbekistan[3]
2016 (March)	Moscow	-	1	Uzbekistan
2017 (Jan.)	Istanbul	ISIS	39	Uzbekistan
2017 (April)	St. Petersburg	-	14 (inc. 1 attacker)	Kyrgyzstan[4]
2017 (April)	Astrakhan	ISIS	2	Kazakhstan
2017 (April)	Stockholm	ISIS	4	Uzbekistan
2017 (Oct.)	New York	ISIS	8	Uzbekistan
TOTAL	-	-	107 (inc. 11 attackers)	-

Table 2: Attacks by Central Asians outside the Region (with Fatalities), 2008-2017.

These disturbing numbers have led some scholars to contend that the international terrorist threat emanating from Central Asia is "a reality that cannot be ignored,"[30] while media headlines have declared the region to be a "growing source of terrorism"[31] and "fertile ground" [32] for recruitment. While radicalization clearly does occur in Central Asia, some research suggests that the primary recruiting ground for Central Asian fighters among jihadist groups may be in Russia among the millions of Central Asian migrants' therein; this, however, is not a consensus view. In Central Asia itself, recruitment has been particularly active in the agricultural south of Tajikistan (Khatlon province),[33] isolated mining and oil-drilling cities in the western Kazakh desert (Zhezkazgan, Aktobe, Atyrau) and in predominantly ethnic Uzbek communities in Kyrgyzstan's Ferghana Valley.[34]

The destructive potential of violent extremists from Central Asia may be amplified by their ability to cooperate with other groups, particularly from elsewhere in the former Soviet Union, though not only. Some Central Asians have risen to positions of authority within IS and other international terrorist organizations, expanding their networks and clout: Most notably, Col. GulmurodHalimov, the U.S.-trained head of Tajikistan's paramilitary police, or OMON, rose to become the Islamic State's "minister of war" after spectacularly defecting to the group in May 2015.

Also, in 2015, the IMU—which has long worked with al-Qaeda and the Taliban in Afghanistan and Pakistan, and claimed joint responsibility[35] withTehrik-i-Taliban Pakistan for the 2014 airport attack in Karachi—declared its allegiance to the Islamic State. The extremist groupImam Bukhari Jamaat, labelled by the U.S. State Department as "the largest Uzbek fighting force in Syria," and possibly a second, much smaller Uzbek group, cooperated with al-Nusra FrontandAhrar al-Sham to overrun Idlib in July 2015. [36] These examples notwithstanding, it is also worth noting that wartime alliances are often unstable, as illustrated by the acrimonious split in 2013 within JaishMuhajireenwal Ansar between fighters from the Caucasus and from Central Asia.[37]

As noted above, the number of fatalities resulting from terror attacks by Central Asian jihadists outside the region has exceeded the number within it, but that does not mean acts of domestic terrorism have been insignificant. It is interesting to note that, unlike the instances of extremist violence abroad, most of the 18 deadly attacks within Central Asia in 2009-2018 targeted government officials, including police, rather than civilians. This is clearly reflected in the fatality counts: 80 representatives of the state, 11 civilians and 50 attackers. Moreover, four of the five Central Asian countries have been shaken by other forms of political violence, claiming well over 1,500 lives between 2005 and 2012. (Insular Turkmenistan has had neither political violence nor terror attacks that we know of.)

Attacks by Central Asians Within the Region (with Fatalities), 2009-2018

Year	Location	Group(s) Claiming Responsibility	Group(s) Blamed by Government	Fatalities	Breakdown: State/ Civilian/ Attacker
2009	Uzbekistan (Khanabad / Andijan)	Islamic Jihad Union	Islamic Jihad Union	2	1/0/1
2009	Tajikistan (Isfara)	IMU	IMU	1	1/0/0
2010	Tajikistan (Khujand)	Jamaat Ansurallah	Jamaat Ansurallah	4	3/0/1
2010	Tajikistan (Kamarob)	IMU	IMU	25	25/0/0
2012	Tajikistan (Khorog)	--	--	1	1/0/0
2014	Tajikistan (Khorog)	--	--	1	0/0/1
2015	Tajikistan (Dushanbe / Vahdat)	--	IRPT[22]	39	14/0/25

Year	Location	Group(s) Claiming Responsibility	Group(s) Blamed by Government	Fatalities	Breakdown: State/ Civilian/ Attacker
2018	Tajikistan (Danghara)	IS	IRPT[23]	8	0/4/4
2015	Kyrgyzstan (Bishkek)	--	Jaysh al-Mahdi[24]	1	1/0/0
2016	Kyrgyzstan (Bishkek)	--	Turkestan Islamic Party / al-Nusra Front[25]	1	0/0/1
2011	Kazakhstan (Aktobe)	--	Organized Crime	1	0/0/1
2011	Kazakhstan (Aktobe)	--	Organized Crime	3	3/0/0
2011	Kazakhstan (Atyrau)	Jund al-Khalifa[26]	--	1	0/0/1
2011	Kazakhstan (Taraz)	Jund al-Khalifa	--	7	4/2/1
2012	Kazakhstan (Almaty)	--	Jihadist Salafis	14	14/0/0
2012	Kazakhstan (Almaty)	--	--	1	1/0/0
2016	Kazakhstan (Aktobe)	--	IS	21	4/3/14
2016	Kazakhstan (Almaty)	--	Jihadist Salafis	10	8/2/0
	TOTALS			141	80/11/50

Despite the abundance of media reports and other research available, many questions about Central Asians' developing role in international terrorism remain unanswered, and any quest for those answers will be complicated by several factors. One is the extent to which various actors—including authorities in all the countries concerned—have manipulated or exaggerated the terrorist threat and can continue to do so.[40] Indeed, Tajikistan's official position[41] on this summer's fatal attack on the cyclists has been that it was perpetrated by the country's main political opposition group,[42] banned in 2015, the Islamic Renaissance Party of Tajikistan; this claim persisted despite a video posted by the IS media outlet Amaq showing four of the attackers pledging allegiance to the Islamic State. In another example of muddied waters, after Kazakhstan's deadliest attack thus far, in Aktobe in June 2016, the authorities could not agree on a narrative, vaguely stating[43] that the attack had been "ordered from abroad" without providing evidence or details. Uzbekistan, according to the U.S. State Department,[44] "routinely uses security concerns related to terrorism as a pretext for detention of suspects, including of religious activists and political dissidents."

Another global problem with access to reliable information is that violent extremists who work alone or in small groups often undergo radicalization out of public view, making them particularly difficult to identify before they do damage. The United States has experienced this repeatedly, including the cases of the 2013 Boston Marathon bombers—ethnic Chechens who had spent part of their childhood in Kyrgyzstanvi—and the Uzbek immigrant who killed eight people[45] in New York with a rented truck in 2017. In light of these constraints, it is important to recognize the limits of what we can actually know about the transnational threat coming from Central Asia.[46]

Drivers of Radicalization

Each individual's exact pathway to terrorism is different and catchall explanations of recruitment fail to reflect the complex dynamics at play. It is possible, however, to make some general observations about why Central Asians join terrorist groups. Perhaps surprisingly, research has indicated that poverty, lack of education and high levels of religiosity do not necessarily correlate with susceptibility to recruitment; conversely, the evidence suggests that many recruits are better off financially and better educated than the average person in Central Asia,[47] and also not particularly religious prior to radicalization. Instead, leitmotifs in fighters' biographies include a culture of violence—whether through previous combat experience, petty crime or combat sports—and disillusionment or de-socialization stemming from unfulfilled aspirations, a sense of injustice, disengagement from social support networks, a diminished sense of selfworth or some combination of these factors.

Many of the cases of Central Asian fighters for whom we have sufficient evidence to draw conclusions about their radicalization mirror a phenomenon observed by French political scientist Olivier Roy in Europe among first-generation migrants and their descendants—namely, that a diminished sense of status, accomplishment, fulfillment and/or social connectedness leads individuals to reject society, and radical ideologies provide justification for an extreme but empowering form of that rejection. Thus, Roy argues that we are seeing "not the radicalization of Islam, but the Islamization of radicalism."[48] For Roy, "the typical radical is a young, second-generation immigrant or convert, very often involved in episodes of petty crime, with practically no religious education, but having a rapid and recent trajectory of conversion/reconversion."[49]

Studies among Kyrgyz, Uzbek and Tajik communities—including field research conducted by two of this paper's authors—indicate that, often, recruits to extremist militant causes have experienced real and/ or perceived personal injustices or failure as migrants, whether through discrimination, failed romantic relationships, thwarted career aspirations or other experiences of powerlessness.[50] Here, it is important to note that migration in and of itself does not cause radicalization: Central Asians have been migrating to Russia for more than 20 years, while joining terrorist organizations is a more recent phenomenon affecting a small fraction of migrants.

Among that minority, however, their experience as migrants can be a significant catalyst for their radical rejection of society and embrace of political violence. An example from Edward Lemon's fieldwork in Moscow in 2015 is illustrative of this. In April of that year, young Tajik construction workers were living in converted shipping containers as they built a new overpass near Moscow's Spartak stadium for the 2018 soccer World Cup. They recounted how recruiters whom they believed to be from Chechnya had come around their encampment calling people to Islam. One young man, whom they called Nasim, was drawn to the group:

He arrived in Moscow back in 2013. He was a smart guy, spoke good Russian and wanted to find a good job. But he couldn't. So he ended up in construction. In 2014, he went home and married a girl from his village. But soon after he came back the marriage was not good. He became more angry and bitter. When the recruiters came, he found their promises attractive. He never prayed before or talked about religion, but now he talked about jihad. One day he disappeared. The next thing we heard he was in Syria.

One Uzbek former fighter who joined Islamic State on his own initiative told a similar story of disillusionment in a long interview with another of this report's authors, Vera Mironova. In describing his journey from Moscow to Syria, Mohammed (not his real name) became visibly frustrated recalling the discrimination he experienced in Russia, where he came when he was 16. "People considered us second-rate," he said, noting as an example that he could not approach local girls because they would never consider him, or any other poor, uneducated migrant from Central Asia, as a possible partner. (In Syria Mohammed married a 16-year-old Kazakh girl who came there with her family.)

Like Nasim and Mohammed, many young Central Asians who have experienced personal failures and marginalization start to feel alienated and disillusioned with their lives—whether abroad, at home or in an adopted country where they have settled as immigrants. Terrorist groups, including IS, have capitalized on this potential for resentment in their messaging, specifically targeting vulnerable individuals and offering them the promise of a different life. Such groups offer recruits meaning, a collective identity and individual fulfilment. Islamic State, in its propaganda, also claimed the absence of any discrimination in its fledgling caliphate, pointing to the equality of all Muslims. The heroic image of jihadis projected by such organizations, the promise of a wage and welfare, the adventure and brotherhood of membership in a violent extremist group can be appealing to a small minority of disillusioned individuals.

As noted above, a sense of injustice or disillusionment strong enough to lead to radicalization can arise among non-migrant Central Asians as well, often nudged along by the region's repressive and corrupt governments. For example, a key recruiting ground in Kyrgyzstan, as mentioned before, has been the Uzbek community in the Ferghana Valley. This ethnic minority bore the brunt of interethnic violence in 2010, sometimes facilitated[51] by local officials and followed[52] by little government effort to investigate or hold perpetrators accountable. More broadly, the former Soviet republics of Central Asia have some of the worst corruption[53] and least reliable[54] systems of justice in the world. They have also tended to regulate religious practices with a heavy hand.

All the Central Asian ex-fighters interviewed by Vera Mironova mentioned the severe restrictions on religious freedoms in their home countries and for some this was a factor in their decision to leave. Both Tajikistan and Uzbekistan, for example, have either explicit or de facto limitations on men's right to wear beards and women's right to wear hijabs. Some of the Uzbek interviewees also pointed out that they had been under surveillance by local law enforcement for their religious activities, so they felt like they had no option but to leave.

For most recruits from Central Asia, however, religion seems to play a limited role in their lives until they begin to be exposed (and receptive) to extremist content. They often discover or rediscover Islam with a neophyte's zeal, rapidly embracing a simplistic, good-versus-evil takfiri narrative that pits believers against non-believers. Evidence from the Tajik case reflects this. Most of them leave behind close-knit communities and an authoritarian system where the government has closely monitored and restricted religious practices for the past hundred years. They find themselves in migrant communities where religion in its different guises is discussed more openly. While most maintain close links to their relatives and communities at home, some become alienated in their new environment[55] and seek new sources of connection or meaning. Contrary to Islamophobic stereotypes, those with high levels of religious knowledge have often proved integral to counter-radicalization efforts.[56]

Our field research also indicates that there seems to be a link, in some cases, between recruitment to wage jihad in the Middle East and a prior connection to what the Russian scholar Vitaly Naumkin calls a "culture of violence," whether through crime, combat, violent sports or some combination of these. In one example, a Tajik named Anvar had served a short prison sentence for theft as a young man and then migrated in 2013 to Russia to work on a construction site in Moscow. He spent much of his free time at a gym, training in mixed martial arts. An IS recruiter operating out of the gym began grooming him, making him believe it was his duty as a Muslim to go to Syria; Anvar left to join IS in early 2014. Some of the most prominent fighters hailing from Central Asia were battle-hardened veterans, as described in more detail below. Many recruits had been petty criminals in their youth.[57] Tajik militant leader Nusrat Nazarov, for example, had been a drug dealer in Kulob.[58] Others have been active in combat sports. [59] Alan Chekranov, a Tajik fighter prominent on social media, was a three-time national champion in mixed martial arts.[60] Naumkin contends that terrorism offered these men an opportunity to express their masculinity and live out violent fantasies.[61]

It is also worth pointing out that many Central Asians are pulled into violent extremist groups through their social networks, recruited by people who know them.[62] Such networks work through both offline and online contact. After Nasim left for Syria in 2014, for example, he was joined by two other individuals from his village in southern Tajikistan. In some villages in Kazakhstan, Kyrgyzstan and Tajikistan entire extended families, numbering up to 40, have left for Syria and Iraq. Finally, it is worth noting that those who choose violent forms of radicalism may confront very different logistical challenges: Carrying out an unsophisticated terrorist attack—for example, mowing down people with a vehicle—takes less planning and involves fewer chances both to be interdicted and to have a change of heart than does joining a terrorist group in a foreign country, which requires obtaining travel documents, crossing multiple borders and paying for the journey.

What Might They Do Next?

In examining the question of Central Asian militants' next steps, most analysts of international security have focused on the extremists affected by the decline of ISIS and Jabhat Fateh al-Sham—formerly known as the al-Nusra Front, an al-Qaeda affiliate—in Syria and Iraq. We will do the same. What will happen to these men and their families if their host groups lose all their territory in the region? Surviving ex-fighters have three basic options other than detention by local authorities: join a violent group in another conflict zone, migrate to a peaceful country or return home, with the latter two options possible both for those who want to demilitarize and for those who want to keep the fight going.

All of these scenarios require money and connections to leave the region, doing which has become increasingly difficult[63] over the past few years. After the IS stronghold of Raqqa fell in 2017, prices for smuggling non-Arab foreigners out of Syria rose to around $10,000 per adult, and about one-third that for a child, so not many people could afford it, especially those with families. Moreover, people from Central Asia often look different than other jihadists in the region, so it was harder for them—even compared to fighters from other parts of the former Soviet Union, like Russia—to pass unnoticed though government or Kurdish checkpoints.

Existing evidence suggests that a mass return to Central Asia remains unlikely, largely due to local authorities' heavy-handed policies[64] Our tally from earlier this year, based on open sources, showed only about 300 returnees to all five countries combined, not including non-combatant family members.[65] Some analysts have even speculated that sending radicalized citizens to fight in Syria and Iraq may benefit the regimes in the region, helping them transfer the threat of Islamic terrorism out of their own countries.[66] In all of the Central Asian states, an influx of former fighters would certainly pose a huge challenge in terms of demobilization and reintegration. Jailing ex-combatants en masse could create new problems: In November 2018, IS reportedly claimed responsibility[67] for a prison riot in Tajikistan that left at least 23 dead.[68] While that claim has not been verified, Tajikistan's foreign minister said the unrest was provoked by members of extremist organizations.[69]

This leaves the other two options: new war zone or third country. As noted at the beginning of this report, the most likely conflict zone for migration would seem to be Afghanistan, while the peaceful countries that could serve as sanctuaries for ex-fighters include Ukraine, Turkey and potentially some European Union states.[70] According to various reports,[71] over 800 Central Asians have been killed in the Middle East. If the numbers of dead and returnees, given above, are accurate, this would leave between 850 and over 3,000 survivors, including an undisclosed number in prison.[72]

In order to better predict where certain individuals could go next, it may be useful to consider why they went to the Middle East in the first place. In general, the migration of Central Asians to join IS and other radical violent groups in Syria and Iraq can be divided into three "waves" as described below. Readers should note, however, that this is very much a generalization. For example, at the time of the first wave, made up largely of veteran militants, there were also some early recruits who had been working or studying in Syria at the time that protests broke out in early 2011.

• The first wave, primarily in 2011-2012, mostly included people with combat experience in Tajikistan's civil war (1992-1997) and Afghanistan/Pakistan (Waziristan), with the Taliban and Taliban affiliated groups. These men went with the explicit goal of fighting. At that point, in the very beginning of the armed conflict, there were no major armed coalitions, only many separate groups, or jamaats, of foreign fighters largely segregated by language. With time, some of those groups merged with IS, while others continued fighting against Bashar al-Assad's forces as semi-independent formations, sometimes in an alliance with the al-Nusra Front. According to former IS fighters interviewed by Vera Mironova, these people were among the most professional and experienced foreign combatants in Syria. Many of them started, as did other Russian-speaking fighters, in the Jaish Muhajireenwa Ansar under the command of Omar (or Umar) al-Shishani, an ethnic Chechen from Georgia, and followed him to IS after he became a military commander for the jihadist group. Because of their experience, many assumed positions as trainers. For example, according to one interviewed ex-fighter, his military base had a Kazakh sniper instructor who had cut his teeth in Waziristan and several Uzbek experts in explosives and topography, which also had come via Waziristan.

• The second wave, roughly in 2012-2014, was made up largely of fighting-age males with no combat experience, coming mostly from Russia and Turkey where they had been working. While some were actively recruited, others travelled on their own initiative and sometimes had a hard time getting to the Syrian battlefield. For instance, Mohammed, the Uzbek who recalled feeling like a second-class citizen in Russia, said in an interview that he had been working and studying in Moscow when events in Syria caught his attention and, although he was not religious, he felt the need to go fight against Assad. It was easier said than done. First, he asked around at mosques, but was kicked out because people assumed he was a mole or provocateur working for the Russian security service. Then he searched on Russian-language social media and eventually found people already fighting in Syria. At first, they also did not believe him, but ultimately agreed to take him in if he flew to Turkey. He bought a ticket and soon joined Jaish Muhajireenwa Ansar, later moving to al-Nusra and then to IS. It's worth noting that not everyone wanted to fight for IS, which some fighters accused of excessive violence or misguided religious ideology. As of August 2018, within the anti-Assad rebel bloc, Central Asians were fighting with the Turkistan Islamic Party, Katibat al-Tawhid wal Jihad and Liwa Mujahedeen wal Ansar, among other groups. Although they are considered semi-independent, they often coordinate their military activities with al-Nusra, which publicly cut its ties to al-Qaeda in 2016 and changed its name to Jabhat Fateh al-Sham.

• The third wave of people, which trickled in with the first two but intensified significantly after the declaration of a caliphate in 2014,[73] included whole families, together with women and children, eager to start a new life in what they saw as a newly established country, a Promised Land for Muslims. Central Asia has long experienced widescale out-migration, so the idea of moving to a different country was not new. Many of these people sold their apartments and cars back home and bought houses in IS-controlled territory. They took along schoolbooks to continue their children's education in their native language. They even took their diplomas and other educational certificates—further suggesting that their goal was a new life, not a suicide mission. Some of the men did not go through boot camp or own a weapon. In the Middle East they managed to live relatively normal lives, working as engineers or social workers, caring, for example, for the families of killed IS fighters. In short, for many this was a "one-way journey," whether seeking adventure, martyrdom or a new life.[74]

Based on Vera Mironova's research, Central Asian fighters who have managed to leave IS can be divided into two basic subgroups: those who had given up on the idea of a caliphate, or had grown disillusioned with the ideology of IS, and those from the IS leadership and intelligence service (Amnivii) who left with money and are considering regrouping in another geographic area. The former include a small, elusive group sometimes called the "excessive" takfirists, who consider IS insufficiently stringent in its pursuit of sharia-based rule. Many of these are currently living peacefully and working in civilian occupations in their countries of hiding; some are even actively working to discourage potential IS supporters. The second subgroup is a dangerous one. These ex-fighters are looking for countries with weak security where they could take control of territory, such as Afghanistan.

Among the world's existing conflict zones, it is indeed Afghanistan—with its geographical proximity and linguistic affinities with Central Asia—that appears to be a logical destination for ex-fighters and new recruits alike.[75] Three radical groups operating there have roots in post-Soviet Central Asia: the Tajik group Jamaat Ansurallah, which pledged allegiance to IS in 2017 after having once been affiliated with al-Qaeda, which, in turn, had been strong in Afghanistan prior to 9/11; Uzbekistan's IMU, often referred to by Afghan officials as Jundallah; and its splinter group, the Islamic Jihad Union, or IJU, which has a base[76] in Sar-e Pul, less than 100 miles from the border with Turkmenistan, albeit with an estimated 25 fighters. All these organizations, however, have been weakened by years of war, and it has been the Islamic State - Khorasan Province (ISKP) that has been most active in trying to recruit fighters from Central Asia.[77]

The group declared its existence as an affiliate of IS in January 2015. Like IS, it has developed a sophisticated media presence outmatching the Taliban's[78] and it has targeted Central Asian recruits directly: In March 2018, for example, the group released a video in which Uzbek fighters called on militants in Syria and Iraq to join it.[79] ISKP's messaging, like IS's, stresses the purity of its Salafi ideology and the obligation of believers to engage in jihad and romanticizes life as a fighter. ISKP propaganda also projects a transnational cause centered on apocalyptic narratives from the Prophet Muhammed about jihadis from Khorasan winning a decisive victory near the end of times.[80] ("Khorasan" is a Persian word referring to the territory of modern-day Afghanistan and parts of Central Asia.) For recruits from Central Asia, the ISKP's promises of expansion into the region may be more appealing than the Taliban's nationalist vision, which focuses strictly on Afghanistan and has ruled out northern expansion.

The ISKP's actual strength, in numbers and influence, remains contentious and hard to ascertain.[81] Over its nearly four years, the ISKP extended its presence beyond its initial base in Nangarhar province to establish control of two districts in Jowzjan in northern Afghanistan, only to be routed there by the Taliban in July 2018. Russian officials have consistently emphasized the group's might, with a top Russian military commander estimating in April 2018 that the ISKP has 10,000 fighters.[82] A U.S. military spokeswoman said[83] around the same time that the group was believed to have only about 2,000 fighters, and the general in charge of U.S. Central Command, Joseph Votel, said earlier that year that "Moscow has exaggerated the presence of the ISIS-K threat."[84] According to U.N.

estimates, 3,500 to 4,000 militants are fighting with ISKP, with 750 of them originating in Central Asia.[85]

Afghan officials, meanwhile, have estimated that the ISKP has 3,000 foreign fighters alone.[86] (In August 2017 a senior Afghan security official put the number[87] of foreigners fighting for both IS and the Taliban in his country at roughly 7,000, most of them from Pakistan, Uzbekistan and Tajikistan; this is much less than the estimates of foreign fighters in Syria and Iraq, which have run as 40,000.[88]) The ISKP has faced all matter of challenges: With its coercive approach to governance and unpopular policies, such as publicly banning poppy cultivation while benefitting[89] from the trade, the group has struggled to gain a foothold in Afghanistan. Three of its emirs have been killed[90] and, in November 2017, NATO claimed that U.S. forces had killed 1,600 of its militants.[91] Fighting with Taliban factions has also weakened the organization, despite occasional attempts at détente.[92] Veteran Afghanistan researcher Antonio Giustozzi concluded[93] in late 2017 that the ISKP, damaged by infighting, dependency on external funding and setbacks in the Middle East, "is past its peak in Afghanistan, if not in terms of military capabilities, certainly in terms of jihadist image."[94]

For now, the flow of foreign fighters to Afghanistan seems insignificant when compared with the peak of IS recruiting from Central Asia in 201415. Moreover, if IS's proto-caliphate in Syria and Iraq became attractive to some foreigners when it controlled significant territory and really had come to resemble a state, Afghanistan's radical groups do not seem to offer that: While the Taliban remains extremely powerful, it has full control of only 4 percent of the country's provinces, according to a BBC estimate[95] from January; around the same time, Afghan officials reportedly said[96] that rebels control 14.5 percent of the country's territory, while another 29 percent is contested by both sides.

The ISKP controls far less territory[97] than that, mostly in eastern Afghanistan on the border with Pakistan, and the group has not managed to create the same state functions as IS did in its heyday in Syria/Iraq. That said, the damage it inflicts locally is substantial: According to an October 2018 U.N. report[98] on Afghanistan, the

ISKP accounted for more than half the year-on-year increase in civilian casualties caused by "anti-government elements" in the first nine months of the year (and 25 percent of the absolute total of such casualties), while Nangarhar province, its home base, recorded the most civilian casualties for that time period, with 554 deaths and 940 injured.

There is no question that Central Asians are among the foreigners fighting in Afghanistan. In addition to the Uzbeks and Tajiks in the Taliban, many of the non-Afghans in today's ISKPx are militants from Pakistan and Uzbekistan who have fought in the region since the 1990s According to Giustozzi,[99] in the summer of 2017, the ISKP split into two factions, one of them led by an ethnic Uzbek former IMU commander known as Moawiya,[100] or sometimes referred to in press reports as Mawlavi Habib ul-Rahman; his men were mainly Central Asians—including members "of the Omar Ghazi Group (an offshoot of the IMU which fully joined IS) and Shamali Khilafat, a group made up of Afghan Tajiks and Uzbeks"—and his group claimed to have 3,800 members. There is also evidence that fighters from other Central Asian republics have joined the group, particularly from Tajikistan, which shares with Afghanistan both a border and closely related languages (Tajik and Dari).

In the summer of 2018, for instance, over 100 IS fighters from Moawiya's group[101] including[102] children, surrendered[103] to Afghan authorities after combat with the Taliban. The local governor said[104] there had been numerous foreign fighters in the group, Uzbeks and Tajiks among them, who had not surrendered and may have wound up with the Taliban. (A video[105] that reportedly circulated days later on pro-Taliban social media seemed to show 25 captured Central Asian fighters not only from Tajikistan and Uzbekistan, but a few from Kazakhstan and Kyrgyzstan as well.) Indeed, Tajik President Emomali Rahmon claimed in May 2018 that dozens of his citizens had joined the ISKP.[106] That same month Kabul extradited to Tajikistan three alleged IS sympathizers, who had crossed into Afghanistan from Iran, a route of major concern to Afghan authorities.[107] (Linguistically, Tajik and Dari are closely related to Farsi.)

About 10 cases of Tajiks entering the country via Iran have been reported in the media since mid-2017—for example, that of 18-year-old Shodidjon Boyev, who had worked as a labor migrant in Russia before trying to travel to Syria via Turkey. Having failed to reach Syria, he reportedly[108] traveled to Iran before crossing into Afghanistan in December 2017 and ending up in an IS training camp. Ex-fighters could also settle in a stable third country. After leaving IS, many fighters end up in Turkey, which shares a border with Syria, but in 2016 Ankara started a crackdown on ex-IS fighters on its territory. (Egypt, Georgia and Malaysia have likewise gotten stricter than before.) In Turkey, some fleeing militants get detained for extradition to their homeland; others are offered the option of buying a ticket to a third country where a visa is not required.[109] Given that Ukraine has a visa-free regime with most post-Soviet states, and was once a place where fake identification papers were relatively cheap and easy to buy, it has become a transit zone for many Russian-speaking ex-fighters, but is unlikely to be their final destination.

Many of the ex-fighters interviewed by Vera Mironova said they aimed to travel to former Soviet republics where they could find work and blend in more easily in their ethnic communities, but most hoped to settle ultimately in Western Europe, and some have already entered Europe illegally. It is difficult to predict where exactly these fighters will go because many of their decisions hinge on changes in government policies and illegal networks to buy documents, which they monitor closely. As noted above, these people could try to embark on a peaceful life, disillusioned with jihad, or they could plot attacks, whether of their own volition or following someone's orders.

Thus far, IS-related attacks and plots outside of Syria, Iraq and Afghanistan have more often been the work of local residents sympathizing with the group than of former foreign fighters.[110] Militants from Central Asia seem to follow this pattern to some extent—the stark exceptions being the 2014 Karachi attack, carried out by IMU militants, and the Istanbul attack of 2017: Abdulkadir Masharipov, who killed 39 revelers in a nightclub on Jan. 1, 2017, had trained in an al-Qaeda camp in Afghanistan in 2011 and confessed to carrying out the attack on orders from Islam Atabiyev, a Russian, Raqqa-based IS leader also known as Abu Jihad.[111] The Stockholm attack in April 2017 was something of a "hybrid": It was carried out by RakhmatAkilov who had been deported back to Sweden from Turkey in 2015 after he was caught attempting to join IS.[112]

The charges against Akilov stated that he had been in contact with more than 30 Islamic State fighters in Iraq, Syria and Afghanistan prior to the attack; according to Akilov's testimony, he had been "prepared" by Abu Dovud, the nom de guerre of Tajikistan native Parviz Saidrakhmonov.[113] Claims to a connection with foreign fighters in the St. Petersburg case are more tenuous: The accused suicide bomber, AkbarzhonJalilov, had migrated with his family to the city and lived there from 2011 to 2015. In November of that year he reportedly[114] moved to Turkey, where he lived until December 2016 when he was deported for overstaying his visa and moved back to St. Petersburg. Russia's state-owned-TASS news agency reported:[115]within days of the attack that law-enforcement officials suspected that he may have left Turkey for Syria and trained with IS.

One early, unverified claim[116] of responsibility came from a little known group claiming links to al-Qaeda; other media reports,[117] citing unnamed Russian and Kyrgyz security sources, said the suspected mastermind of the attack was, like Jalilov, an ethnic Uzbek from Kyrgyzstan, who commanded a group of Central Asian fighters in Syria and was suspected by Kyrgyz authorities of organizing the 2016 attack against the Chinese Embassy. Russian investigators have reportedly[118] accused Jalilov's alleged accomplices of receiving and then passing on money for the attack from "an active member of an international terrorist organization" in Turkey.

Most Central Asian ex-fighters hoping to return to a peaceful life seem wary of heading back to their home countries. As noted above, our tally showed only about 300 returnees. The region's governments, like Russia's, [119] have often been heavy-handed with returning ex-fighters and have not been keen to develop re-integration policies for those who engaged in combat. The governments of Tajikistan and Kazakhstan, for example, have amended legislation to revoke the citizenship of those convicted of being members of terrorist organizations, giving the state the right to bar or deport them.

Tajikistan has introduced an amnesty program, but its success seems to be limited: While dozens of ex-fighters have been pardoned,[120] a provincial police chief said earlier this[121] year that, of 72 amnestied fighters, 34 had returned to IS. According to several former IS members now in hiding, comrades who were extradited to Russia, Turkmenistan and Uzbekistan have never been heard from again. The ex-fighters are particularly afraid of torture at the hands of authorities back home, which made many of their brothers-in-arms opt to stay in Syria and die there. So real was the fear of torture or "being disappeared" that one ex-fighter awaiting extradition from Turkey to Tajikistan slit his wrists before he could be returned, according to his cellmate in a deportation prison in Istanbul.

Central Asian Nuclear, Chemical and Biological Terrorism Threat Vectors

Central Asia could be relevant to the threat of chemical, biological, radiological or nuclear (CBRN) terrorism in several ways. First, because the region was the home of significant Soviet-era production and testing activities, it could be a source of material. Second, because many of the Islamic State's foreign fighters came from the region those who survive the conflicts in Syria and Iraq and return to it could potentially bring with them CBRN expertise and nihilist motivations gained from IS efforts. Third, because large and sensitive Russian facilities are located close to the region, and the borders are relatively porous, Central Asian countries could be used as a haven or trans-shipment point to exploit any thefts from Russian facilities; for example, the closed city of Ozersk, which contains one of Russia's largest nuclear weapons-related facilities with thousands of weapons' worth of fissile material, lies less than 175 miles from Russia's frontier with Kazakhstan—the world's longest contiguous land border.[122]

Central Asia as a Potential Source of CBRN Material

Kazakhstan, Kyrgyzstan, Tajikistan, Turkmenistan and Uzbekistan are all "states parties" to the Biological and Chemical Weapons Conventions and the Non-proliferation Treaty, which prohibit them from holding stocks of nuclear, chemical or biological weapons. There are, moreover, no current, public and credible claims that any of these countries are violating that treaty obligations.[123] Thus, the regional threat of diversion or theft of nuclear, chemical or biological weapons or materials from existing state programs is negligible.

Central Asia was, however, the home of significant Soviet-era nuclear weapons activities. The Soviets mined and milled 10,000 tonnes of uranium in Tajikistan.[124] They set off over 450 nuclear detonations at Semipalatinsk, Kazakhstan.[125] About a tenth of those tests were of such low yields that the fissile material was left "readily recoverable" should terrorists have been sufficiently knowledgeable and motivated to take it.[126] The Soviet authorities also left behind in Kazakhstan 600 kilograms of 90-percent-enriched uranium, mostly in the form of metal chunks and oxide pellets—enough for about two dozen nuclear weapons—at the unsecured Ulba Metallurgy Plant,[127] and spent fuel containing 10 tonnes of highly enriched uranium and 3 tonnes of weapons-grade plutonium in a relatively unsecure facility at Aktau on the shores of the Caspian Sea.[128]

Central Asia was also beset by Soviet biological weapons activities. Vozrozhdeniye Island, a biological-weapons test site straddling present day Uzbekistan and Kazakhstan, is the world's largest dumping ground for anthrax agent. Soviet scientists and technicians moved hundreds of tonnes of the deadly brew there in 1988 to cover up the illicit Soviet biological-weapons program, from their production facility at Sverdlovsk.[129] Moreover, another one of at least six Soviet biological-weapons production plants operated at Stepnogorsk, Kazakhstan—the only one outside of Russia—and was capable of churning out about 300 tons of agent in 220 days.[130]

When the Soviet Union dissolved, this lethal mess fell to the fledgling Central Asian republics. Fortunately, their governments welcomed U.S. cooperative threat-reduction assistance[131] and signal nonproliferation successes followed—sometimes in cooperation with Russia, including in the return of fresh and spent highly enriched reactor fuel from Central Asian research reactors. Only a short distance ahead of metal scavengers active in the area, the U.S. and Kazakh governments completed work in 2012 to secure the highly enriched uranium and plutonium left from Soviet nuclear tests, under a project that spanned the Bush and Obama administrations.[132] Earlier, Project Sapphire removed 600 kilograms of highly enriched uranium from Ulba in 1994.[133] The U.S. National Nuclear Security Administration funded a massive effort to repackage and transport spent fuel from the BN-350 reactor at Aktau to a secure storage site in northeastern Kazakhstan completed in 2010.

The United States also facilitated the dismantlement of the biological facilities at Stepnogorsk, remediation of the dumping ground on Vozrozhdeniye Island and deployment of physical protection and accounting measures in Kazakhstan and Uzbekistan.[134] This has largely negated the threat posed by biological facilities and materials abandoned by the Soviet Union. Thus, the legacy of nuclear and biological materials left by the Soviet Union and the implicit threat that they could fall into terrorist hands were effectively addressed by international cooperative efforts to consolidate, secure and dispose of the material.

Radiological sources remain in Central Asia and, if stolen, could be used in unconventional attacks by terrorists. They have been less well addressed by cooperative threat-reduction efforts because they serve ongoing and important industrial and medical purposes. Approximately 1,000 Category 1-3 radiological sources are currently in use in Central Asia, with the overwhelming majority in Kazakhstan.[135] Generally located in hospitals, universities and industrial sites, these sources are often less well-protected than nuclear facilities.[136]

Returning Fighters as a Source of CBRN Threat

The fate of defeated Central Asian fighters from the Islamic State and other violent extremist groups will obviously play a critical role in their ability to spread an IS-related CBRN threat. From 2014 to 2017, the Islamic State produced and used chemical weapons in 37 separate attacks,[137] but there is only one recorded incident of an IS chemical-weapons capability being transferred outside of Iraq or Syria, and it was to Australia,[138] with no public evidence of participation by Central Asians.

IS also surveilled the home of a Belgian nuclear official, although the purpose of that action remains obscure. In 2015, the IS publication Dabiq alluded to an interest in nuclear terrorism. The article with murky intent and provenance warned: "Let me throw a hypothetical operation onto the table. The Islamic State has billions of dollars in the bank, so they call on their wilāyah in Pakistan to purchase a nuclear device through weapons dealers with links to corrupt officials in the region. The weapon is then transported overland until it makes it to Libya, where the mujāhidīn move it south to Nigeria."[139]

No concrete plots or preparations by ISIS to obtain nuclear weapons or material, however, have been discovered and publicly disclosed. Moreover, even in 2015 when IS controlled far more people, resources and territory than they do today, David Albright and Sarah Burkhard concluded that "Daesh's public boasts and fantasies about its easy pathways to nuclear weapons should be dismissed."[140] In Mosul, Iraq, IS controlled facilities that housed two large Cobalt-60 radiological sources, but, possibly unaware of what they had, the militants left them unmolested.[141] Thus, there is no publicly available evidence that any fleeing Central Asian Islamic State fighters are linked to any IS CBRN efforts in Syria or Iraq, or that they have undertaken such activities after their departure from IS-held territory. While mindful of the need to avoid argumentum ad ignorantiam, it does not appear that the out-migration of Central Asian IS fighters from the Middle East poses a current CBRN terrorism threat vector.

Proximity of Sensitive Russian Facilities to Central Asia

Much of Russia's nuclear archipelago is strewn across the Urals, originally chosen by Stalin's secret police for the region's isolation and therefore security. These vast facilities house sufficient fissile material for thousands of nuclear weapons in hundreds of buildings.[142] The closed cities are no longer embedded in a totalitarian police state. They now face changing demographics and the emergence of ideologies that might undermine the security of the facilities. The Carnegie Moscow Center's researchers Alexey Malashenko and Alexey Staroshin noted: "There have been significant changes in the composition and distribution of Russia's Muslim community during the era of President Vladimir Putin. In particular, as Islam expands in the Ural Federal District, religious and political life there is evolving. Much of this expansion is due to the arrival of Muslim migrants from Central Asia and the Caucasus, and some migrants bring with them religious radicalism—a challenge that requires a more effective official response."[143]

While the threat that stolen Russian materials could be transferred to Central Asia—or used elsewhere—for terrorist purposes are a plausible concern, no publicly available evidence reveals such a plot. Russia attracts millions of Central Asians as seasonal workers and manual laborers, many of them in Russia illegally. Because of their status, these workers are often exploited and abused by their employers, contributing to the possibility that their migrant experience fosters extremism.[144] While such workers are unlikely to have direct access to weapons-usable materials, they could form a network to be employed by insiders to smuggle pilfered material out of Russia for fabrication into a viable weapon or transshipment to another region. As noted above, the closed city of Ozersk lies within 170 miles of the Kazakh border. Theft from these facilities, albeit mostly non-nuclear, is a common occurrence.[145] Moreover; smuggling of arms and narcotics in the region is so prevalent that it threatens, according to one researcher, to "curtail Central Asia's development."[146] Authorities have interdicted trafficking of radiological sources from Russia into Kazakhstan, although the purpose of the smuggling is unclear.[147]

Net Assessment

When the Soviet Union dissolved, Central Asia was left with a large inventory of CBRN materials and facilities. Cooperative threat reduction efforts by the U.S. government and those of Central Asian states eliminated or greatly reduced the vulnerability of that material. Moreover, it is likely that any terrorist group that succeeded in obtaining CBRN weapons or materials would seek a target more lucrative than a Central Asian state. It is plausible that CBRN material stolen in Russia could be taken to Central Asia for transshipment or fabrication into a usable weapon. Much work needs to be done to provide alternatives to or better security for the radiological sources in use in Central Asia. The international spread of perhaps thousands of Central Asian IS fighters could pose a severe security threat. Their activities bear close scrutiny, particularly to ensure that they do not attempt to use knowledge that might have been gained in Iraq or Syria regarding CBRN attacks. Moreover, ongoing vigilance in securing sensitive facilities is critical, as complacency leads to vulnerability. Nonetheless, so far, from publicly available information, the CBRN threat vectors involving Central Asia appear not to pose an imminent peril either within the region or externally.

For Further Consideration

As we have noted throughout this paper, the threat of violent extremism emanating from Central Asia has raised many as yet unanswered questions. Research on the topic is complicated by the many overlapping, sometimes tangled lines of inquiry worth pursuing: Some violent actors are radicalized at home, others abroad; some choose to perpetrate violence in low-cost ways as lone actors, while others go to great lengths to travel to distant war zones; getting access to those who have participated in jihadist violence is not easy; official assessments of the threat are often warped by political considerations; the list of complicating factors goes on.

That said, it is worth restating some of our basic conclusions:

- The turmoil in Syria and the rise of IS allowed thousands of Central Asians to take part in extremist violence outside their countries of residence, and perhaps inspired violent actions by a small number of individuals who did not travel to the war zone; however, nationals of Central Asian countries have been behind only 0.14 percent of attacks recorded in the Global Terrorism Database over the past decade, while making up about 1 percent of the world's population.

- Research suggests that two significant causes of radicalization are (a) a rejection of society based on real and/or perceived injustices or failures and (b) experience with or attraction to "a culture of violence," whether through previous combat experience, violent sports or crime.

- A large number of Central Asians fighting in the Middle East seem to have been radicalized outside of Central Asia, while working as labor migrants in Russia or Turkey.

- It is extremely difficult to say what Central Asian jihadists' next moves might be. The three main options seem to be: move on to a different conflict zone, with Afghanistan as the likeliest destination; return to Central Asia, where local governments are not rolling out the welcome mat; move to a third country, which requires money and/or connections, whether to abandon the fight or pursue it further.

- IS's Afghanistan branch is actively recruiting Central Asians but the flow of fighters is much lower than to the Middle East three or four years ago.

- Based on other researchers' work, recent terrorist attacks and plots in the West have more often been the work of local residents than itinerant former IS fighters.

- Tracking networked jihadists will require international cooperation among law-enforcers and other stakeholders.

71

- There does not seem to be an imminent danger of WMD attacks emanating from Central Asia, although better security is needed for radiological sources in use in the region.

The questions that still need to be answered are myriad. A good list of them can be found at the end of the December 2017 report "Russian-Speaking Foreign Fighters in Iraq and Syria:[148] Assessing the Threat from (and to) Russia and Central Asia" by the Center for Strategic and International Studies. A few that interest us in particular include the following:

1. We have a good understanding of how Central Asians have been recruited, but why are certain individuals more susceptible than others?

2. Here we have focused on the 0.005 percent of the region's population who have joined violent extremist groups, and on the relatively small number of attacks they have committed. But what factors have made 99.995 percent of the population not take this route and put up with hardships without resorting to violence?

3. On a practical level, will countries in Central Asia take back their citizens who are currently in prison in the greater Middle East? (Formally they refuse to do so; however, it is possible that some of these people may have been quietly let back into their countries of origin if considered "useful" by the authorities.)

4. Finally, what are the salient distinctions among the five Central Asian countries in the context of radicalization and international terrorism?

Until we know more in answer to these and other questions it seems like a fool's errand to make policy recommendations. Nonetheless, a few obvious suggestions do come to mind for officials and the various international and non-governmental organizations working in the relevant fields:

- Examine the decision-making processes of fighters who joined IS and other extremist groups as closely as possible. If they left their country, why? How did they choose their destination, militant group and/or targets? What made violence attractive? And so on. Interview them directly with the help of trained professionals to learn about the underlying problems that pushed them to jihad.

- Find ways to reduce the perceived injustices that can make individuals vulnerable to recruitment, such as corruption, abuse of power by law enforcement and other officials and discrimination against certain groups, e.g., ethnic Uzbeks in southern Kyrgyzstan. (Further strengthening community policing may be one step in this direction.)

- Provide better security for the radiological sources in use in Central Asia.

- Ensure that information about potential terrorist threats is not skewed by Central Asian governments to get more money for military equipment or counterterrorism measures or to justify heavy-handed practices.

- Since so many Central Asian jihadists are recruited as labor migrants, help develop sustainable modes of improving economic opportunities at home where they will continue to have social support networks while earning a living.

Russia Matters is a project launched in 2016 by Harvard Kennedy School's BelferCenter for Science and International Affairs and made possible with support from Carnegie Corporation of New York. The project's main aim is to improve the understanding of Russia and the U.S.-Russian relationship among America's policymakers and concerned public. It does so by showcasing the best expertise on Russia and its relationships with the rest of the world by providing top-notch analysis, relevant factual data and related digests of news and analysis. Initially, the project's contributors and institutional partners will be primarily U.S.-based and its main platform for pursuing its goals will be this website. The specific aims of Russia Matters are to help: U.S. policymakers and the general public gain a better understanding of why and how Russia matters to the United States now and in the foreseeable future and what drivers propel the two countries' policies in areas of mutual concern; Ensure that U.S. policies toward Russia are conducive to the advancement of long-term U.S. vital national interests, but that they also improve cooperation in areas where interests converge and mitigate friction in areas of divergence; Foster a new generation of Russia experts. Russia Matters likewise endeavors to build bridges between academe and the policymaking community. Russia Matters BelferCenter for Science and International Affairs Harvard Kennedy School 79 John F. Kennedy Street Cambridge, MA 02138. Edward Lemon is the DMGS-Kennan Institute Fellow at the Daniel Morgan Graduate School. Dr. Lemon was previously a Mellon Postdoctoral Teaching Fellow at the Harriman Institute at Columbia University. He gained his PhD in international studies from the University of Exeter in the United Kingdom in 2016. Vera Mironova is a visiting scholar in Harvard University's Economics Department, and is also affiliated with the Davis Center. From 2015 to 2018, she was an International Security Fellow at the BelferCenter for Science and International Affairs. William Tobey is a senior fellow at Harvard's BelferCenter for Science and International Affairs and the director of Belfer's U.S.-Russia Initiative to Prevent Nuclear Terrorism. Russia Matters BelferCenter for Science and International Affairs Harvard Kennedy School 79 John F. Kennedy Street Cambridge, MA 02138. www.russiamatters.org. https://www.russiamatters.org/analysis/ jihadists-ex-soviet-central-asia-where-are-they-why-did-they-radicalize-what-next. *Russia Matters was founded in 2016 with a mission: to advance a deeper understanding of U.S.-Russia relations among America's policymaking community and concerned public. To that end, we invite readers to share our high-caliber content, including RM's exclusive reports and analyses. If you would like to reprint one of these articles, a blog post written by RM staff, one of our infographics or a fact-check, we ask that you follow these guidelines: Include a prominent attribution to Russia Matters as the source and link back to the original at RussiaMatters.org. Retain the hyperlinks used in the original content. Do not change the meaning of the article in any way.*

Chapter 3

The Return of Foreign Fighters to Central Asia: Implications for U.S. Counterterrorism Policy

Thomas F. Lynch III, Michael Bouffard, Kelsey King, and Graham Vickowski

Executive Summary

Central Asia is the third largest point of origin for Salafi jihadist foreign fighters in the conflagration in Syria and Iraq, with more than 4,000 total fighters joining the conflict since 2012 and 2,500 reportedly arriving in the 2014–2015 timeframe alone. As the Islamic State of Iraq and the Levant (ISIL) continues to lose territory under duress from U.S.-led anti-ISIL coalition activities, some predict that many may return home bent on jihad and generating terror and instability across Central Asia. Yet several factors indicate that such an ominous foreign fighter return may not materialize. Among these factors are that a majority of Central Asians fighting for ISIL and the al-Nusra Front in Syria and Iraq are recruited while working abroad in Russia, often from low-wage jobs under poor conditions making the recruits ripe for radicalization. In addition, many of those heading for jihad in Syria and the Levant expect that they are on a "one way journey," some to martyrdom but most for a completely new life, and do not plan a return.

Most Central Asian states face their greatest risk of domestic instability and violent extremism as a reaction to political repression and counterterrorism (CT) policies that counter productively conflict political opposition and the open practice of Islam with a domestic jihadist threat. If improperly calibrated, greater U.S. CT assistance to address foreign fighter returns may strengthen illiberal regime short-term focus on political power consolidation, overplay the limited risks of foreign fighter returns, and increase the risks of domestic unrest and future instability.

The United States has few means to pressure Central Asian regimes into policies that address the main drivers of domestic radicalization, such as political inclusion and religious freedom. Although an imperfect instrument, U.S. security assistance—and the specific subset of CT assistance—is a significant lever. U.S. CT assistance for Central Asia should eschew additional general lethal assistance and instead scope security attention toward border security intelligence and physical capacity enhancements. This CT aid should be paired with important, complementary socioeconomic programs that help with countering violent extremism, including greater religious and political openness along with support for the Central Asian diaspora.

Introduction

The Islamic State of Iraq and the Levant (ISIL) and similar Salafi jihadist organizations, such as the al-Nusra Front and other al Qaeda affiliates, have presented the United States with serious counterterrorism (CT) challenges since ISIL expanded its reach in Syria and Iraq in 2014.[1] Among these serious challenges, stemming the flow of foreign fighters to this conflict area as well as preparing for the eventual return of these fighters to their home countries have become issues of significant concern for U.S. policymakers.[2] The region of Central Asia has played an important, if often overlooked, role in supplying fighters to various violent extremist organizations (VEOs) in Syria and Iraq. The United States, along with Russia and other adjoining countries, could confront serious threats to CT interests in Central Asia as foreign fighters return to this region after having been radicalized and battle-hardened.

This paper assesses the current status and future risk potential for return of the thousands of Central Asian foreign fighters who have joined Salafi jihadist groups in Syria and Iraq since mid-2011. The analysis and policy recommendations draw upon authors' findings from a review of primary source publications from the region, field trips there from 2013 to 2015, and research into English-language and other secondary sources that culminated in June 2016.

Balancing Security, Stability and Socioeconomic Factors

Central Asia is important to overall U.S. CT efforts, having received increasing levels of security assistance since the terrorist attacks of September 11, 2001.[3] With Afghanistan bordering three of the five Central Asian states, U.S. security assistance in the region increased with the intensification of U.S. efforts in Afghanistan and Pakistan over the past decade (see map). After a steady increase, there has been some reduction in overall security assistance after 2010.[4] The United States also has a stated policy interest in seeing that Central Asian governments are accountable to their people for basic human rights and liberties, as well as capable of providing economic opportunities. Although U.S. economic and governance assistance to these states has increased in absolute terms over the past decade, non–security assistance first decreased as a proportion of overall U.S. assistance between 2009 and 2013, and then eclipsed security assistance by 2014.

U.S. non–security assistance to Central Asian states is projected to remain greater than security-related assistance through 2017. With a general trend toward authoritarianism in several of these states in recent years, specifically Tajikistan and Uzbekistan, the United States faces a policy dilemma. Should, on one hand, greater security assistance in the form of CT support again be prioritized with less attention paid to the development of accountable-governance and civil and religious liberties? If, on the other hand, the United States does press Central Asian countries for reform in these areas by denying or conditioning security assistance, will Russia simply fill the gap, damaging and perhaps removing U.S. influence in the region?

These questions are all the more significant because Central Asians have been recruited in great numbers as foreign fighters by Islamic jihadist groups such as ISIL. ISIL recruitment from Central Asian countries has benefited from local government policies that have eroded the space for the open and peaceful practice of Islam while also removing outlets of legitimate political opposition. Central Asians as a group have been disproportionately represented as foreign fighters in Syria and Iraq, with close to 20 percent of all foreign fighters originating from Central Asia while this region accounts for less than 5 percent of global Muslims.[5] According to the International Centre for the Study of Radicalization and Political Violence (ICSR), Central Asia is the third largest source of foreign fighters for ISIL and other VEOs in Iraq and Syria.[6]

Poor economic conditions in most of Central Asia, especially Tajikistan and Kyrgyzstan, contribute to restlessness and wanderlust among many there. An overarching—and in some states increasingly—repressive political climate generates disaffection and can make populations vulnerable to radicalization and recruitment by VEOs. An absence of capable border controls and credible reintegration programs makes most Central Asian governments appear at risk for continuing as a supplier of Salafi jihadist foreign fighters for Syria and Iraq, and at risk from instability and violence upon their return home.[7] As ISIL steadily loses strength and territory in the Levant region, Central Asian governments will need to address the risks of increasing terrorism and instability if thousands of foreign fighters return home. Increasing the amount of U.S. security assistance, including CT assistance, is unlikely to help these governments weather the turbulence of returning jihadis if there is not an accompanying adjustment in the political-religious climate.

The threat of returned fighters moving underground and engaging in terrorist attacks is greater if there is no process to reintegrate and absorb them into a reasonably open society. The United States can foster an increase in religious and political opening through non-kinetic forms of assistance and public diplomacy. But the returns of such soft power assistance are harder to quantify in the short term than security forces training or weapons transfers. The

United States will have to find a balance between military and non-military aid to each of the Central Asian republics, keeping in mind the local context in each state. Mitigating rather than contributing to violence and extremism in Central Asia is the challenge that the United States faces at this important time in the region's history.

ISIL and U.S. Global Counterterrorism Concerns ISIL changed the terrorist landscape in the Middle East, which had ripple effects around the globe. Skillful marketing has given ISIL greater reach than previously established Islamic VEOs such as al Qaeda.[8] Manifestations of ISIL's reach have shown up in places where dramatic jihadist terrorism was not an expected threat, such as Brussels and Paris. ISIL has built its ranks by recruiting fighters from across the globe.[9] The potential for fighters to return to their home states with an objective to practice organized jihad is a major international security concern. It is also a concern for global U.S. CT efforts. The 2011 U.S. CT strategy calls for coordinating, enabling, and improving capabilities of partner nations.[10]

U.S. CT leaders have consistently named places where foreign fighter returns from Syria and Iraq may necessitate additional partnership, and Central Asian states—especially Tajikistan—are on that list.[11] Among the key questions for U.S. security partnerships worldwide is whether Central Asian states merit a $20–$50 million increase in CT security assistance in 2016–2017 to address legitimate risks they face.[12] While the majority of ISIL recruits originate in the Middle East, the Maghreb, and Western Europe, Central Asia is the third largest source of foreign fighters in Syria.[13] Central Asians also are overrepresented among jihadist VEOs in Iraq and Syria, making up over 17 percent of the foreign fighters there, despite constituting just 5 percent of the global ummah.[14] More than 4,000 Central Asian fighters are believed to have joined armed groups fighting in Syria, with an estimated 2,500 arriving there in 2014 and early 2015 alone.[15] Russian President Vladimir Putin has stated that as many as 7,000 fighters from Russia and Central Asia have joined the ranks of the Islamic State.[16] While many of the Central Asians fighting in Syria and Iraq align with ISIL, they also are present in a number of other Salafi jihadist outfits there, some under the al Qaeda–affiliated umbrella group known as the al-Nusra Front.

Among the prominent groups with known Central Asian participation are Jaish al-Muhajireenwal-Ansar, Jamaat Sabri (a mostly Uzbek group), and Imam Bukhari Jamaat (also predominantly Uzbek). Central Asians also make up small percentages of primarily Chechen-led Caucasian VEOs.[17] Many analysts have written about the "blowback potential" from these foreign fighters, speculating about an increase terrorism and instability across Central Asia but with divergent and often uncertain conclusions. An early 2015 International Crisis Group report labeled the risks of instability from the inevitable return of these Central Asian fighters as great, observing that the governments know of the dangers but are not properly preparing, instead using the forecast threat to bolster domestic political agendas and curtail more civil liberties.[18]

Another regional observer noted, "Although a threat from jihadist returnees does exist, it has been exaggerated by the Central Asian governments . . . playing on the population's fear . . . to legitimate . . . repressive measures."[19] His sentiments are shared by other regional experts who view the risks from foreign fighter blowback as less significant than those from violent opposition from within.[20] Still others have argued that Central Asia faces great risks from foreign fighter repatriation and that this mandates significant scope for policy action and outside security assistance.[21]

Among those sounding the more worrisome alarm are those who point to reports that children of Uzbek and Tajikistani origin are being indoctrinated in radicalism and the practice of jihad by ISIL zealots in Syria and in Turkey.[22] Policymakers require a more discerning assessment of the actual risks from foreign fighter blowback in the Central Asian countries. The number of expatriates from there fighting in Iraq and Syria is not the sole indicator or even the best indicator of blowback risk. Many Central Asian foreign fighters do not expect to return home; some are there to culminate their martyrdom and most have gone to start a whole new life in an Islamic caliphate. With ISIL currently on the defensive during 2016, its recruiting strategies for Central Asians and others appear to be more centered on bolstering ranks within Iraq and Syria than spreading instability elsewhere.[23]

U.S. Policy in Central Asia Pre-2016—a Balancing Act

In March of 2015, Deputy Secretary of State Antony Blinken outlined U.S. policy in the Central Asian region as founded on two distinct ideas: "first that our own security is enhanced by a more stable, secure Central Asia that contributes to global efforts to combat terrorism and violent extremism, and second that stability can best be achieved if the nations of Central Asia are sovereign and independent countries . . . benefiting from governments that are accountable to their citizens."[24] Current U.S. policy emphasizes both security assistance and democracy and governance programing equally.[25] In most of the past decade, U.S. aid to Central Asia has been imbalanced toward more security assistance focused on tactical training and equipping than on democracy and governance programming.[26] The most recent example of this policy was the waiver of sanctions on Tajikistan after being designated a country of particular concern regarding religious liberty.[27]

However, the U.S. policy challenge is more than one of disproportional funding between hard and soft power programs. U.S.-sponsored countering violent extremism (CVE) workshops and other governance/democratization programming confront limited effectiveness when constrained by wary Central Asian governments and if not buttressed by firm but flexible pressure from Washington's most senior leaders. The United States walks a challenging path with a dual concentration on CT assistance and fostering human rights and democratic governance in Central Asia. The difficulties for cohesive U.S. policy in Central Asia are many. Chief among them is the wide disparity in key factors found in the individual regional states. Repressive national political and human rights policies contribute to radicalization and recruitment to the Syria-Iraq front. A one-size-fits-all U.S. policy approach to what are distinct and diverse political and economic national conditions across the five Central Asian countries could have counterproductive results.

The United States faces a number of challenges with implementing effective policy in the region. First, America is not the only—or the preferred—guarantor of security in Central Asia. Historic and contemporary security ties between Russia and the Central Asian states remain strong. Additionally, the United States has few levers to pull when trying to influence Central Asian republics.

Table 1. U.S. Aid to Central Asia, 2014

Country	Military and Police Aid	Humanitarian and Development Aid.	Arms Sales (Deliveries)	Trainees
Kazakhstan	$19,452,079	$6,438,000	$1,084,188	275
Kyrgyzstan	$8,902,880	$37,506,150	$307,400	358
Tajikistan	$29,214,516	$26,644,000	$4,263,198	119
Turkmenistan	$1,054,809	$4,078,000	$38,613	35
Uzbekistan	$13,674,055	$9,352,200	$4,004,190	127
Floating Regional Funds	$7,000,000	$31,422,000	N/A	N/A
Total	$79,298,339	115,440,350	$9,697,589	914

The option to cut off security assistance to Central Asia exists. However, an end to security assistance would, by extension, cut off the military-to-military relationships that those assistance programs develop. Additional challenges arise in trying to strike a balance between maintaining ties and assistance while not tying the United States to autocratic regimes. Given its historic ties in the region, Russia remains the primary security partner for the Central Asian republics.[28] Russia provides engagement through bilateral and multilateral cooperation, including tactical-level training and equipping, and military professionalization training at the Frunze Academy in Moscow. Within the region, those trained at the Frunze Academy are regarded as part of an elite network of officers, upon which career and promotions depend.

While the United States does provide some military professionalization training,[29] it is not currently seen as at the same level as Russian training.[30] Despite Russian military attention currently focused on Syria and the recent Russian economic downturn, U.S. influence in the region is unlikely to surpass longstanding Russian ties. At the same time, Russia is trying to retain its relevance in the region, whether through its leadership of the Collective Security Treaty Organization, its membership in the Shanghai Cooperation Organization, or bilateral joint-level security and CT exercises with regional countries. Central Asian governments will participate in ventures such as the North Atlantic Treaty Organization's Partnership for Peace as far as it will benefit them, but there is relatively little buy-in for large institutional reform initiatives emanating from the United States or Western Europe. Conditioning U.S. security assistance on improved governance and political opening is unlikely to work. Rather this will likely drive Central Asia further into Russia's sphere of influence, severely eroding if not ending military-to-military ties between the United States and Central Asia.

In 2014, the most recent year with a full set of security assistance data, the United States spent $194,738,689 on Central Asian security and economic aid—$79,289,339 of which was security oriented aid (≈ 41 percent). The United States trained 914 Central Asian security personnel (see table 1).[31] The volume of U.S. security, governance, and economic aid to the states of Central Asia grew and then declined over the past decade from a relative low point in 2005 to a high in 2010 and then to a smaller amount in 2014.[32] So too did the proportion of general security (military and police aid) in that assistance. In 2005, the United States spent $221,059,971 on Central Asian security and economic aid; $88,729,971 (≈ 40 percent) of that was security-oriented aid. It also trained 993 Central Asian security personnel. In 2010, the United States spent $385,159,747 on Central Asian security and economic aid; $216,707,698 (≈ 56 percent) was security-oriented aid. It also trained 678 Central Asian security personnel.[33]

From 2010 through 2014, the proportion of U.S. regional assistance given as security assistance declined from 56 percent per year back to roughly 41 percent in 2014. Incomplete data for U.S. aid to Central Asia in 2015 indicate that the overall amount of aid dropped by almost 50 percent from 2014, falling to $111,282,000; $25,702,000 of this amount (23 percent) was general military police and security aid. If all U.S. Department of Defense (DOD) Counterterrorism Partnership Funds (CTPF) earmarked for Central Asia—up to $20 million in fiscal year 2016 and up to $30 million in fiscal year 2017—are applied, then 60 percent of the total planned U.S. $51,870,000 security assistance to Central Asia for 2017 will come from CTPF. Projected U.S. economic and development aid for Central Asia in 2017 is almost $140,000,000. Thus the percentage of U.S. security assistance of the overall projected $191,808,000 in total U.S. assistance to Central Asia in 2017 will be 27 percent (see table 2).[34] The forecast remix of overall U.S. aid to Central Asia by 2017 appears calibrated to emphasize economic, development, and governance programs nested around CVE initiatives.[35] The re-scope of U.S. military and police aid to a less significant proportion of overall U.S. aid and a specific focus on CTPF programs seem aimed to provide sustained but targeted assistance to selected CT programs in Central Asian states.

Table 2. Forecast U.S. Aid to Central Asia, 2017

Country	Military and Police Aid	Humanitarian and Development Aid	Arms Sales (Deliveries)	Trainees
Kazakhstan	$ 2,600,000	$6,183,000	N/A	Unknown
Kyrgyzstan	$ 3,060,000	$47,696,000	N/A	Unknown
Tajikistan	$ 6,515,000	$35,055,000	N/A	Unknown
Turkmenistan	$715,000	$4,100,000	N/A	Unknown
Uzbekistan	$1,780,000	$9,828,000	N/A	Unknown

Floating Regional Funds	$37,200,000	$37,076,000	N/A	N/A
Total	$51,870,000	$139,938,000	N/A	Unknown

Foreign Fighter Flows: Why, How, and from Where?

Before the rise of ISIL, the Islamic Movement of Uzbekistan (IMU) was the main Central Asian VEO of notable consequence in the region.[36] Its historic base of operations is in Afghanistan and Pakistan. The case of IMU is informative when assessing the risk of fighters returning to Central Asia from Iraq and Syria. Observers report a conspicuous absence of IMU foreign fighter return to Uzbekistan as of early 2016. Some analysts suggest that this demonstrates IMU members—and other Central Asian jihadists traveling to Syria—view their trip as a one-way ticket, some committed to remaining with the Islamic State forever and others understanding the untenable repercussions they could face if they try to return home.[37] As mentioned earlier, most respected estimates indicate that, as of 2015, Central Asia accounted for the third largest source of Islamist foreign fighters in Syria and Iraq.[38] These estimates indicate a political environment that contributes to the radicalization and subsequent recruitment of a significant number of Central Asian Muslims.

Indeed, the governments of Central Asia display various deficiencies in the areas of political and religious freedom, some to a much more serious degree than others. Although the absolute number of Central Asian fighters in the Syrian civil war is high, the per capita foreign fighter flows from Central Asia are lower than those from the states of the Middle East and North Africa (MENA). Kazakhstan (1 in 72,000), Kyrgyzstan (1 in 56,000), Tajikistan (1 in 40,000), and Uzbekistan (1 in 58,000) have lower per capita foreign fighter flows into Syria than Turkmenistan (1 in 14,000). Turkmenistan alone has reported per capita foreign fighter flows more comparable to MENA states.[39]

MENA state foreign fighter flow rates are those from Jordan (1 in 5,300), Lebanon (1 in 6,500), Tunisia (1 in 7,300), Saudi Arabia (1 in 18,200), and Morocco (1 in 22,000). The proximity of MENA states to ISIL territory is likely a pertinent contributing factor, but the lower per capita flows may indicate other mitigating factors in Central Asia. Some Central Asian fighters originate via recruitment cells actually found in Central Asia. Often these are small, secretive, and sometimes extensions of prayer groups. Not everyone in a prayer group will be aware of the activities of other members or the connection to Syria.[40] A significant number of these radicalized fighters, however, travel directly from Russian territory, which demonstrates a major radicalization factor for Central Asian states—the difficult working conditions and religious and ethnic persecution faced by the Central Asian diaspora within Russian territory.[41]

Separated from their home communities, families, and local imams, and with little or no support from their home governments, it is easy to imagine how Central Asian migrant workers in Russia might become socially alienated and more susceptible to radicalization and VEO recruitment.[42] Many working in Russia turn to in-person and online social media–based Islamic communities to explore their faith, particularly when it previously was not a strong part of their identity. As they interact with online faith communities in their native languages, many are targeted by extremist recruiters. If they are co-opted, migrants then travel directly to Syria or Iraq to fight with violent extremist organizations.[43] In his 2015 Central Asian Involvement in the Conflict in Syria and Iraq: Drivers and Responses, Central Asia expert Noah Tucker demonstrates that economic migration is one of the primary factors that leads to Central Asian recruitment by Islamist extremists, with the majority of Central Asians being recruited outside of the area.[44]

Given often limited economic opportunities, many Central Asians migrate to Russia or Germany for work. As Russian economic stagnation has increased in the past couple years, Moscow has introduced additional laws and restrictions on economic migrants. These laws have further isolated the Central Asian diaspora in Russia.[45] While the majority of Central Asian economic migrants go to Russia; more are looking to Germany as an option. In 2000, 546,823 Central Asians lived in Germany, whereas 4,501,585 lived in Russia. In 2015, these numbers were 4,950,593 in Russia and 1,178,397 in Germany.[46] As Central Asian migrant flows increase, the percent growth from 5 years previously (2010–2015) of those going to Germany (3.45 percent growth) outpaces the growth of total migration from Central Asia (2.65 percent growth), whereas migration to Russia shows less growth (1.91 percent). Russia is the destination for 64.63 percent of Central Asian migrants, whereas Germany is the destination of 15.38 percent. Ukraine is the destination for 6.79 percent, followed by intra–Central Asia migration.

Country	Remittances from Russia (% of GDP)	Total Remittance from Russia (USD)
Tajikistan	41.45	$3,831,000,000
Kyrgyzstan	27.36	$2,026,000,000
Uzbekistan	8.91	$5,581,000,000
Kazakhstan	0.22	$480,000,000
Turkmenistan	0.065	$31,000,000

Table 3. Russian Remittances to Central Asia, 2014 Source: Bank of Russia, "External Sector Statistics," available at www.cbr.ru/eng/statistics/?PrtId=svs

Despite the Russian economic downturn from 2014–2016, much of the Central Asian economy still relies on remittances from migrants living in Russia. Remittances from the Russian central bank comprise a sizeable portion of the Tajik, Kyrgyz, and Uzbek gross domestic products in order of decreasing magnitude (see table 3). Whether radicalized in Central Asia and transiting Russia onto Iraq and Syria or radicalized and recruited from the diaspora in Russia, there are a number of "celebrity cases," demonstrating the leadership role Central Asians play in ISIL's operations. Most notable is GulmurodKhalimov, who formerly commanded the Tajikistani Special Purpose Mobility Unit (Otryad Mobilny Osobogo Naznacheniya or, OMON). Colonel Khalimov participated in five separate U.S.-led training programs between 2003 and 2014, three of which were on U.S. soil.[47] In early September 2016, Khalimov reportedly was elevated to the position of ISIL "Minister of War," succeeding an ethnic Chechen who held the post before being killed in a July 2016 U.S. airstrike.[48] In August of 2014, a Tajikistani was appointed as emir of the Raqqa Province, which is the location of the Islamic State's eponymous capital.[49]

There are a few ethnic Uzbeks, veterans of the Afghan jihad, who are leading brigades in ISIL and the al-Nusra Front.[50] Central Asian foreign fighters linked to ISIL headquarters in Syria also have participated in significant acts of terrorism in other countries. Most notably, a Kyrgyzstani and an ethnic Uzbek from Central Asia were among the three suicide terrorist attackers/bombers at Istanbul airport that killed over 40 and wounded more than 200 others on June 28, 2016.[51] Given the diverse nature of the Central Asian states, we address the key factors and context for Islamist radicalization and recruitment in each. This assessment considers ethnic and political aspects, number of fighters recruited, and influence of social media or Russian information operations in each Central Asian country.

Kazakhstan

ICSR estimates that a moderate number of 250 foreign fighters had traveled from Kazakhstan to the Levant to "do jihad" as of early 2015.[52] Many of these are believed to have been radicalized and recruited while in Russia. ISIL propaganda has tried to exploit the diverse ethnic and demographic nature of Kazakhstan through its al-Hayat media wing. Al-Hayat has also played up the presence of women and children in ISIL to portray ISIL as both a multinational and multigenerational movement. This has provoked harsh backlash against ISIL from many Kazakhstanis, including independent Islamic groups online (both strict reformists and Salafists) who reject what they see as exploitation of Kazakhstani society and who reject any relationship between ISIS and Islam.[53]

The Kazakhstani state enforces some restrictions on free speech and religion, but Kazakhstan is perceived to be relatively free compared to other Central Asian republics. Kazakhstan has participated in U.S. CVE activities by hosting the regional CVE conference in June 2015 in cooperation with the U.S. and other international partners and ensuring ample media coverage for the conference.[54] The Kazakhstani government does not deny the fact that some Kazakhstanis have gone to fight in Iraq and Syria. Kazakhstani leaders and its press report that Russian information operations blame the United States for the creation of ISIL and al Qaeda. Russian information activities focus on increasing the public perception of a meaningful threat from ISIL and other VEOs in Kazakhstan as part of an effort to isolate the United States and pull Kazakhstan further into Russia's sphere of influence.

Kyrgyzstan

After a peaceful electoral transition of government in 2011, Kyrgyzstan touts its credentials as an "Island of Democracy" amid the more repressive authoritarian regimes in Central Asia. Recent fears that Islamic extremism is growing in Kyrgyzstan, particularly among the ethnic Uzbek minority in southern Kyrgyzstan, should be tempered by the fact that Kyrgyzstan does not border other states where ISIL is active and that its populace is targeted less by online recruiters than other Central Asian states.[55] However, the Kyrgyzstani government has been using fear of ISIL terrorism to justify cracking down on political opposition. There is no official number of suspected Kyrgyzstani foreign fighters doing jihad in the Levant. In February 2015, the head of Kyrgyzstan's Interior Ministry reported that 22 of its citizens had been killed in fighting in Syria and some 200 total citizens, 30 of them women, had gone to Syria.

He also reported that investigators had uncovered 83 cases of people attempting to recruit Kyrgyzstani citizens to go to Syria.[56] Details on these radicalization and recruitment patterns were not provided. Among the Kyrgyzstanis who have left to fight in Syria, a common profile emerges: "identifiable Kyrgyzstani participants in the Syrian conflict are primarily politically and economically marginalized ethnic Uzbeks from southern Kyrgyzstan whose messaging, recruiting, and social media activity is primarily in the Uzbek language and largely ignored by the Kyrgyzstani media."[57] Best available independent data on fighter flows also indicate that an estimated 500 to 1,000 ethnic Uzbeks were fighting in Syria during 2015, with a majority of them likely from southern Kyrgyzstan.[58] While many foreign fighters are transiting to Syria and Iraq to fight with ISIL, data on foreign fighter flows suggest most Kyrgyzistani/Uzbek fighters are traveling to Syria to fight with al-Nusra Front.[59]

One of the well-respected voices in the fight against ISIL in Kyrgyzstan has been that of Rashot Kamalov, a prominent imam in the southern town of Kara-Suu near the Uzbek border. Kamalov took over the mosque after his father was killed in a Kyrgyzstani security services operation in 2006. He gained prominence for his willingness to criticize local and state officials, as well as to speak openly against terrorist organizations, including ISIL. In October 2015, a judge in southern Kyrgyzstan sentenced the Kamalov to 5 years in jail for "inciting religious hatred" and "possessing extremist materials."[60] The prosecution used sections from Kamalov's sermons condemning ISIL to demonstrate the state narrative that he was allegedly supporting ISIL. Although the Kyrgyzstani government advertises its actions as necessary for security, the sequential persecution of Kamalov, other religious leaders, and the common ethnic people following them not only risks their good will toward the government but also may be increasing the internal risks to domestic stability.

Tajikistan

Tajikistan is the poorest country of the former Soviet Republics and its economy continues to face major challenges. It has a deep dependence on remittances from Tajikistanis working in Russia, exhibits pervasive government corruption, and struggles with a major narcotrafficking role in the country's informal economy.[61] The Tajikistani government estimates that up to 1,000 citizens have left to fight in Syria and Iraq, while ICSR reports a far more conservative figure of 190 as of early 2015.[62] This reporting discrepancy may indicate a motivated inflation of foreign fighter numbers by the Tajikistani government or it may reflect the fact that the government reports its diaspora in Russia in its accounting, while ICSR data do not.

ISIL recruitment of Tajikistanis relies heavily on the glorification of celebrity jihadist commanders, such as Gulmurod Khalimov, who interact with independent journalists and religious leaders in Tajikistan via correspondence from the frontlines.[63] Despite this, ISIL recruitment in Tajikistan is perhaps the least organized of all the Central Asian states as Tajikistanis fighting for ISIL maintain no dedicated official media outlet or spokesman.[64] The Tajikistani government restricts religious freedom to an exceptional degree. The Islamic Renaissance Party of Tajikistan (IRPT) was Central Asia's only legally registered Islamist political party until it was banned by the government of President Emomali Rahmon in 2015, leaving the political opposition without any venue for peaceful political redress.[65] The government continually tries to tie ISIL to Tajikistan's domestic opposition, specifically the IRPT, and to a "Western" plot to "destabilize" the country, effectively amplifying information operations coming from Moscow.[66]

The government has engaged in acts such as forcible beard shavings and strict regulation of Friday mosque content, prompting the resignation of some of the more influential (and anti-ISIL) clerics in the country, including Kulobi imam Hoji Mirzo.[67] Analysts of Tajikistan point out that while no change appears to be forthcoming on these repressive policies, "the Tajikistani state has attempted to show a changed approach to returnees, granting at least six Tajikistani citizens who had participated in the conflict in Syria amnesty." In two specific cases, two 22-year-old Tajikstanis, RizvonAkhmadov and Farrukh Sharifov, were among at least six currently reported Tajikistani citizens to take advantage of an amnesty offer. Sharifov and Akhmedov were migrant laborers in Russia when they chose to join ISIL.

They have told their story on television and in talks around the country, warning others of the Islamic State brutality that motivated them to leave what they thought would be a paradise when they joined. In the view of many Tajikistanis on social media, allowing returnees to speak for themselves and granting them amnesty may be the only effective response to the ISIL threat adopted by the government so far and one that appears to enjoy broad public support.[68] Much of U.S. policy in Tajikistan is predicated on the worry of militant "overflow" from bordering Afghanistan. Drug-trafficking has been a consistent concern along the Tajikistani Afghan border, and it remains unclear whether the current upswing in border incidents is due to traffickers or militants. This ambiguity is further obfuscated by the murky relations between opium production and the Taliban in Afghanistan.[69]

Turkmenistan

Turkmenistan's opacity makes it difficult to comprehensively analyze the local government policy regarding the threat from ISIL and other VEOs. Citizens are subject to stringent travel restrictions. The government limits independent news media and restricts certain Web sites. State-run (and oriented) news sources persistently deny Russian claims that there is an "active threat" within Turkmenistan.[70] While tight control of travel in and out of the country limits the likelihood of attacks inside Turkmenistan, individual experiences with Draconian restrictions may contribute to radicalization.

ICSR estimates that the number of Turkmen in Syria and Iraq was 360 as of early 2015.[71] What remains to be seen is whether estimates of Turkmen in Syria and Iraq differentiate between ethnic Turkmen native to the Levant area and Turkey with Turkmens coming from Turkmenistan.[72] Current Turkmen ISIL activity does not exceed what would be expected of an estimated 30–60 person population with origins in Central Asia: "Evidence observed from jihadist media by the Digital Islam project over the past two years would not support claims for an estimate larger than perhaps a few dozen Turkmenistan militants. No Turkmen language messaging targeting the public in Turkmenistan has been observed."[73]

Uzbekistan

As noted already, an estimated 500 to 1,000 ethnic Uzbekistanis were fighting in Syria during 2015, with a majority of them believed to be from southern Kyrgyzstan.[74] As many Uzbekistani-national jihadists have been expatriates for many years, we can safely assume that there may be as many as 400 to 500 more Islamist fighters with ties to Uzbekistan who have made it onto the battlefields of Syria and Iraq. This accounts for widespread reporting of many Uzbekspeaking militants fighting in the conflict across the Levant. Much of Uzbek language messaging that extols the virtues of jihad in Syria was disrupted throughout 2013–2014 due in large part to the short lifecycle of Uzbek fighters in the field there. However, ISIL's language messaging strategy continues to target all Uzbek speakers, those in Uzbekistan, throughout Central Asia, and in Russia.[75] Uzbek language media, both domestic and international (such as BBC), portray ISIL as the primary jihadist threat for Uzbekistan, and largely ignores the Uzbekistani-led battalions and groups fighting for al-Nusra Front and the Syrian Islamic Front.

A majority of Uzbekistani fighters are believed to be aligned with Islamic Movement of Uzbekistan (IMU). Although the IMU declared an official affiliation to ISIL in September 2015, some of its splinter groups retain ties to al Qaeda and reportedly fight with al-Nusra Front.[76] In February 2015, Uzbekistan's domestic intelligence agency announced that it had intercepted militant communications claiming that terrorist attacks were planned across the country for that spring. These attacks did not materialize, leading outside analysts to believe that reports of ISIL activities and risks in Uzbekistan, as across Central Asia, are highly politicized and speculative.[77] At the same time, changes to Uzbekistani policy since March 2015 demonstrate that religious openness can be effective in countering radicalization propaganda—even in the repressive Central Asian context and within a highly authoritarian system such as that of Uzbekistan—if the government actually commits to it. Uzbekistan's movement toward greater tolerance for the open expression of Islam's beliefs has come without any direct U.S. policy intervention.

After the March 2015 presidential election that again stamped authoritarian strongman former President Islam Karimov's longstanding lock on power, Uzbekistan has changed its tactics and started to actively downplay the threat ISIL internally poses to the country and to show that ISIL is subverting true Islam.[78] The Uzbekistani government has begun empowering religious leaders to speak out against ISIL.[79] Former President Karimov took the unprecedented step of releasing Hayrulla Hamidov, a highly respected Islamic poet and teacher, from jail to make him the face of the anti-ISIL campaign. Hamidov was jailed on dubious terrorism charges in 2010, but since his release he is still seen as a legitimate and popular religious figure, despite working in concert with the Uzbekistani government. Hamidov's efforts to counter ISIL messaging have become extremely popular among ethnic Uzbekistanis. This tactic achieved immediate resonance, attracted significant attention, and prompted an official response from IMU and other dissenting radical Uzbekistani Islamic figures.

Whither Blowback? What Is Its True Potential in Central Asia?

There is significant anxieties regarding the prospect of jihadists returning from the conflict zone who are intent on overthrowing governments in Central Asia.[80] Regional governments in particular fear such a scenario and have used this fear to justify stricter laws on religious practice and personal liberties. The risks of returning fighters, however, are not uniform across the region and are far from certain as a whole. Central Asian governments do face violent threats, but most of the important threats have originated from domestic rather than foreign sources. As of mid 2016, there is little evidence of Central Asian fighters returning in significant numbers, and even less that those who have returned are organized for jihad. Many are likely to have been killed in Syria. A blanket description of all migrants to ISIL-controlled territory as potential returnees fails to recognize the motivations that prompted them to leave in the first place.

Tajikistanis fighting for ISIL have repeatedly threatened to return and wage jihad in Tajikistan, but they have remained in Syria so far. In January 2015, members of an IMU cell planning to attack a police station were arrested in Tajikistan[81] Yet as of mid-2016, instability and violence due to extremism has yet to materialize. It may be that ISIL's current need for fighters in Syria (in order to bolster ranks depleted by coalition efforts) outweighs the desire of fighters to return home and fight, assuming that desire for return exists in the first place. Ongoing, low level violence along Tajikistan's border with Afghanistan is generally attributed to narcotrafficking despite contrasting government claims that the violence is terrorism related.[82] In Turkmenistan, the threat of instability due to returned fighters is not high. The government is more concerned with issues along its Afghan border than it is with Turkmens leaving to fight for ISIL or returning. Formal and informal restrictions prevent many Turkmen from leaving the country in the first place. The security services in Turkmenistan take an active role in dominating the narrative against ISIL.

The Turkmens fighting in Syria and Iraq are not particularly organized and as such do not present a threat to Turkmenistan.[83] However, Turkmenistan has requested security assistance from the United States in response to issues along its border with Afghanistan.[84] Unlike Russia and its Central Asian neighbours, Kazakhstan has rarely seen attacks by Muslim hardliners. This does not mean that it has no risk of returning fighters because an estimated 250 fighters of Kazakhstani origin have left the country for Syria and Iraq. In early June 2016, 17 people, including 11 "extremists,'" were killed in Aktobe, near the site of attacks in 2011. The government claimed that the attackers followed radical, non-traditional religious movements.[85] However, security services "often imitate counter-terrorism operations by accusing average criminals of siding with religious fighters." It remains unclear if the June 2016 reported attack was a case of violent religious extremism or a case of armed gangs robbing commercial shops and being accused of terrorist activities.[86] Kazakhstan has taken a relatively more constructive approach to addressing ISIL recruitment.

95

In contrast to its post-Soviet neighbours, it has refrained from hyping the threat as a means of justifying internal religious repression, and it is much less reliant on remittances from migrant workers in Russia. This helps to reduce a major recruitment dynamic faced by neighbouring countries such as Tajikistan.[87] Kyrgyzstan has made significant progress in implementing democratic reforms over the past several years. The government, however, has recently begun using a seemingly exaggerated threat of Islamic extremism as justification to crack down on political and religious opposition leaders. Rather than discouraging already marginalized people away from extremist organizations and recruiters, government heavy handedness plays into the narratives that extremist recruiters use. By silencing the moderate voices, the Kyrgyzstani government risks pushing marginalized communities towards more radical action.

Regional Recommendations

Any overarching U.S. policy addressing fighter flows from Central Asia must acknowledge that the region is first and foremost dominated by Russia's security interests and capacity. Russian policy there will be focused on maintaining security and predominant influence. Some Russian interlocutors may acknowledge the long-term importance of addressing drivers of radicalization, but most observe that Russia will prioritize regime stability over human rights in the Central Asian countries.[88] Russia wishes to see jihadist groups in Afghanistan that are isolated there denied access to Central Asia and Russia itself. But this potential point for security cooperation with the United States is presently lost in rhetoric from Moscow accusing Washington of intentionally orchestrating the deterioration of security in Afghanistan and the expansion of the Islamic State there.[89]

Combined with the visceral Russian opposition to U.S. influence in Central Asia, there seems little room for U.S.-Russian cooperation on Central Asian foreign fighter or radicalization issues directly in those countries. Even with a significant downturn in the Russian economy and the subsequent drop in remittances from Russia to Tajikistan and other Central Asian states, historic ties remain strong. At the same time, Central Asian states do want cooperation with and assistance from America, especially in the area of security. Simultaneously, they will remain resistant to U.S. calls for socioeconomic reform when receiving U.S. assistance, routinely criticizing the United States for pushing nefarious "Western influence."

Rather than increasing direct general security assistance, the United States should pursue targeted increases in limited CT-focused security assistance and pair this with an increase funding for soft power activities such as CVE and civil society building, as well as its support for diaspora labor migrants. Because the U.S. Agency for International Development can no longer operate in Russia, the United States should facilitate skills training and information access for Central Asian labor migrants while still in Central Asia. These initiatives would not be as immediately visible as security assistance activities, but their long-term dividends are too important to ignore. Instead of delivering additional general military aid to governments that likely use it for more repressive and counterproductive purposes, selective CT security assistance and enhanced socioeconomic aid could sow the seeds of gradual social and political change—change far more meaningful for dampening the incentives for radicalization.

In parallel with the soft power focus, U.S. security assistance given to Central Asian states should prioritize greater CT border patrol intelligence cooperation that improves national abilities to track and intercept foreign fighters in Iraq and Syria who might return to their home countries, particularly through Afghanistan, Pakistan, Iran, and Turkey. In this context, the current DOD Counterterrorism Partnership Funds proposal for $20–$50 million in fiscal year 2016–2017 for Central Asia security programs (aimed at assisting regional border security forces to improve border security intelligence, facilities, and mobility) seems prudently targeted for best effect—if the proposal remains limited to those specific aims.[90]

Tajikistan

Issues facing Tajikistan are some of the most nuanced in Central Asia. Thus, a nuanced U.S. security and socioeconomic assistance policy is required. Hard policy decisions must be made: Is the main U.S. assistance priority that of stability? Is it maintaining U.S. influence? Or is it facilitating democratization? To some extent, tenets of these priorities may be mutually exclusive. Policymakers should be aware of the possibility that continued security assistance to Tajikistan would be seen as an endorsement of the occasional heavy-handed crackdowns on "radical Islamist threats" emanating from Dushanbe. To the threat perception of radical Islam in Tajikistan, Central Asia experts John Heathershaw and David Montgomery of Exeter University have stated, the Government's response to the conflict may increase the likelihood of outbreaks of Islamic militancy in the longer term."[91] A case in point is the recent forced beard-shaving campaign conducted under the guise of an "anti-radicalisation campaign."[92] If the roots of radicalism were in facial hair, this would indeed be an astute policy approach. Unfortunately, this potential risk factor has been struck from the list of correlates to jihad.

The actions taken by the Tajikistani government to counter extremism quite predictably will, as a consequence of "being detained in the street and forcibly taken to the police department or a barber shop," create legitimate grievances among the 13,000 Muslims, and some may take things further.[93] In counteracting ISIL messaging to Tajikistanis, prominent cleric HojiMirzoIbronov has been moderately successful, and this should be capitalized on. Having taken such drastic measures against the Islamic Renaissance Party of Tajikistan, while allowing HojiMirzo to remain in the public arena takes away from the perception of his independence and as such delegitimizes his message, as effective as it may be. A good start for Tajikistan would be to empower other imams across the country to speak out against ISIL, allowing them independence while removing restrictions such as state approval of sermons or forcible shaving of beards.

It remains to be seen whether the Tajikistani government can reverse course and what amount of political Islam it can tolerate, but even a token political group, independent from governmental Islam, would have a positive effect, as the IRPT has previously. Russian information operations have saturated Central Asian Internet forums and social media. They state that ISIL is the result of U.S. meddling and conspiracy. The United States could be effective in advocacy, however, by pressuring the Tajikistani government to release imprisoned political activists (especially those involved with the IRPT). U.S. support for democracy should result in concrete gains for the Tajikistani public. Given Russian control of the information sphere, this is one of the few places America could improve its image.

The United States reportedly provided $29 million in security and defense assistance aid to Dushanbe in 2014 and about $8 million in 2015, but the amount could jump again because the CTFP proposed in February 2016 to allocate $50 million to Central Asia over the next 2 years to help counter the Taliban, Islamic State, and other militant groups, with a priority focus on assistance for Tajikistan.[94] The CTFP proposal for Tajikistan in fiscal year 2016–2017 must exercise discipline when making the country a "feature state" for its CT approach, limiting the scope of activities to prudent security increases along critical borders with a focus on intelligence, facilities, and mobility there.[95] Simultaneously, the United States should resist initiatives to extend or expand general Tajikistani military and paramilitary capabilities to prevent more capable and repressive activities against ethnic and religious minorities across the country.

Concurrently, the United States should tether additional targeted CT assistance to Tajikistan with the government's willing participation in conferences and other activities aimed to improve national capabilities to counter violent extremism, building on the CVE seminar hosted by the U.S. Embassy in Dushanbe in February 2016.[96] Turkmenistan The threat of instability in Turkmenistan is not particularly high. The Turkmens fighting in Syria and Iraq are not particularly organized and as such do not present a threat to Turkmenistan.[97] The government of Turkmenistan is more concerned with issues along its Afghan border than with Turkmen leaving to fight for ISIL or coming back. Since Turkmenistan has requested security assistance from the United States in response to issues along its border with Afghanistan, that aid might come with U.S. conditionality targeted at greater openness in stability collaboration and in expanding socioeconomic opportunities across the country.[98]

Kazakhstan

Kazakhstan has taken a relatively more constructive approach to addressing ISIL recruitment. That said, degrees of religious persecution are still evident and the government must take significant steps in other areas. President Nursultan Nazarbayev is widely praised for turning Kazakhstan into one of the most prosperous former Soviet states. But his rule has grown increasingly heavy handed with political opponents jailed and marginalized.[99] The United States should continue to solicit Kazakhstan's support in carrying out CVE activities, including by hosting conferences like the one in January 2015.[100] Furthermore, while Kazakhstan has acknowledged the recruitment of some of its own citizens by ISIL, it has often resorted to censorship of online and independent media outlets in order to maintain its control over the narrative and convince its citizens that it there is no significant problem posed by ISIL that it cannot control. Ultimately, the significant degree of government censorship is counterproductive; it inhibits potentially moderating voices from Muslims who are strongly anti-ISIL.

As with all Central Asian states, Russian information operations penetrate the public and private discourse in Kazakhstan. While ISIL is not portrayed as an existential threat to Kazakhstani territory, which necessitates the repression of Kazakhstani Muslims, ISIL is frequently depicted as a bogus threat created by the United States. In response, the United States should seek to demonstrate tangible support for moderate and anti-ISIL voices wherever possible, including bringing pressure to release imprisoned imams and to recognize the efforts of moderating voices.

Kyrgyzstan

Kyrgyzstan has made significant progress in implementing democratic reforms over the past several years. However, the government appears to have begun to use of an exaggerated threat of Islamic extremism as a justification a crackdown on political and religious opposition leaders. By silencing moderate voices, the Kyrgyzstani government risks distancing the marginalized ethnic Uzbek minority even more. This may lead to greater domestic instability and animus toward the Kyrgyzstani government, either from indigenous religious extremism or renewed ethnic violence.The United States should advocate for moderate and anti-ISIL voices wherever possible. Addressed earlier in this paper, RashotKamalov is an imam who gained prominence for his willingness to criticize local and state officials as well as speak openly against terrorist organizations, including ISIL. Kamalov was sentenced to 5 years in jail for "inciting religious hatred" and "possessing extremist materials" in October 2015.101 However, his arrest and sentencing were almost certainly in response to his criticisms of corrupt local and state officials.[102]

Uzbekistan

Although former President Karimov's March 2015 release of Islamic Imam HayrullaHamidov from jail and Karimov's tolerance of greater open discussion of Islam and Islamic beliefs has been noteworthy, the U.S. State Department continues to assess Uzbekistan's human rights conditions as of "serious concern." Despite some press reporting from the state-controlled media, the threat of Islamist-inspired instability in Uzbekistan is not high. State-run security agencies have tight control and reportedly resort to exceptional measures of torture and depredation to maintain it.[103] In the past, the U.S. State Department has issued waivers for direct security assistance to Uzbekistan, and this has led to sharp criticism of America from a wide array of international human rights agencies, including Amnesty International.

Uzbek-language ISIL radicalization and recruiting propaganda is broad-based in its targeting and tends to have most impact upon

Uzbekistani expatriates and migrant workers. Thus, the direct danger to Uzbekistan stability from that propaganda is less within and more outside of the country. Neither the United States nor its allies would generate much advantage in trying to support Uzbekistan's longstanding efforts to tightly control media or social media messaging. As in Kyrgyzstan, the United States should seek to demonstrate support for religious and political openness. To the extent that HayrullaHamidov represents a figure of moderate Islam, the United States should support his and other similar voices in Uzbekistan. President Karimov's successor will certainly be selective and clever in the assistance he or she seeks from Washington. However, the United States should not agree to direct support of Uzbekistan's repressive security apparatus and should instead emphasize support for political and economic openings that will provide all Uzbekistanis with greater opportunities and more reasons not to leave the country and join with jihadist groups.

Conclusions

From 2012–2015, ISIL has attracted a coalition of Central Asian jihadists and sympathizers with a network of links in the region and in the nearby areas of Xinjiang, China, and the Caucasus. Dangerous violent extremist organizations such as the Islamic Movement of Uzbekistan have leveraged affiliations in Syria and Iraq to gain traction lost across Central and South Asia in years prior to 2012. But the clear operational nexus of Central Asian jihadists in the heart of the Middle East does not mean that the repressive governments of Central Asia confront a dire or certain blowback threat from jihadist violence at home. The risks are present, but properly assessed in mid-2016, the problem is not dramatic. Many factors mitigate against a return to Central Asia of a critical mass of Syria-trained jihadists capable of toppling regional governments and establishing an extension of the ISIL-led caliphate. Many Central Asian governments are using—and often overstating—the risks of foreign fighter return to bolster repressive political agendas, curtail civil liberties, and seek additional lethal assistance from outside donors. In this manner, they are exploiting rather than realistically addressing the problems of radicalization and instability.

These governments must be encouraged to create balanced and viable CVE action plans. Such plans must feature programs to reduce the risk factors for radicalization and generate credible rehabilitation programs for those seeking to return from doing jihad in Syria or elsewhere abroad. This kind of balance can only be struck when the leaders of the region move away from repressive-only approaches and expand political, economic and educational opportunities while at the same time ending ruthless security services practices that generate widespread distrust and fear. The United States, as other outside security partners, is best advised to refrain from any hasty favourable response for greater, more lethal general security assistance by these governments as the best means to combat returning foreign fighters. Instead, the U.S. should offer the Central Asian governments additional and targeted border and intelligence CT security assistance, simultaneously extending to them the more robust socio-economic assistance necessary to expand domestic opportunities and establish de-radicalization programs as part of wider CVE initiatives for those seduced by ISIL or other jihadist propaganda.

The Return of Foreign Fighters to Central Asia: Implications for U.S. Counterterrorism Policy by Thomas F. Lynch III, Michael Bouffard, Kelsey King, and Graham Vickowski. Center for Strategic Research Institute for National Strategic Studies National Defense University. The Institute for National Strategic Studies (INSS) is National Defense University's (NDU's) dedicated research arm. INSS includes the Center for Strategic Research, Center for Complex Operations, Center for the Study of Chinese Military Affairs, and Center for Technology and National Security Policy. The military and civilian analysts and staff who comprise INSS and its subcomponents execute their mission by conducting research and analysis, publishing, and participating in conferences, policy support, and outreach. The mission of INSS is to conduct strategic studies for the Secretary of Defense, Chairman of the Joint Chiefs of Staff, and the unified combatant commands in support of the academic programs at NDU and to perform outreach to other U.S. Government agencies and the broader national security community. Institute for National Strategic Studies Strategic Perspectives, No. 21. Series Editor: Laura J. Junor. Dr. Thomas F. Lynch III is the Distinguished Research Fellow for South Asia, the Near East, and Radical Islam in the Center for Strategic Research, Institute for National Strategic Studies, at the National Defense University (NDU). Michael Bouffard is a Master of Arts Candidate in Security Policy Studies in the Elliott School of International Affairs at The George Washington University. Kelsey King and Graham Vickowski are 2016 Graduates of the Master of Arts in International Affairs from the Elliott School of International Affairs at The George Washington University.

Chapter 4

Islamic Movement of Uzbekistan a Strategy of Survival in Afghanistan-Pakistan Region Re-shift of Focus to Central Asia

Sayed Mujtaba Hashimy

Islamic Movement of Uzbekistan (IMU) is one of the few foreign militant groups operating in the Afghanistan-Pakistan region. The group is associated with al-Qaeda, and the Afghan and Pakistani Taliban. IMU is known as a disciplined organization with die-hard and experienced cadre. Its origin goes back to the aftermath of the collapse of the Soviet Union when it grew under the leadership of Tahir Yaldashev, a young Mullah and JumaNamangani, a former Soviet paratrooper out of a religious movement called Adolat (justice). IMU was designed towards the goal to establish an Islamic state in Uzbekistan. However, immediate military measures undertaken by the Uzbek government urged IMU to seek sanctuaries in Afghanistan during the Taliban regime in late 1998. For it to survive and remain relevant, the group had to promote the goals of the local militant factions in the Afghanistan-Pakistan region.

The survival strategy led IMU to be exploited by local militant and transnational terrorist factions. When IMU sought sanctuaries in Afghanistan during the Taliban regime for its 600 members, the Taliban willingly provided it and IMU leadership had to take oath of loyalty to the Taliban leader Mullah Omar as Amirul Momineen and its members to fight alongside the Taliban against Northern Alliance. While in Afghanistan, IMU came in close contact with al-Qaeda and it was gradually influenced to subscribe to al-Qaeda's global jihad movement. Both the groups benefited from each other- al Qaeda from IMU's military capabilities and IMU from al-Qaeda's vast financial network across the Arab World.

Following the collapse of the Taliban regime in 2001, IMU confronted a new wave of challenges. It sustained heavy human losses alongside the Taliban in the US-led invasion and felt compelled to retreat to Pakistan. There the group, to ensure sanctuaries for it, had to fight war on two fronts- joining the Pakistani Taliban against the Pakistani government and the Afghan Taliban against the Afghan government and the US-led coalition forces in Afghanistan. The former helped the group to build a foothold for itself in the Federally Administered Tribal Areas (FATA) of Pakistan despite opposition from the Pakistani government, local population and even certain elements within the Pakistani Taliban in FATA. Under U.S. pressure, Pakistani government directed several military operations to drive out foreign militants including IMU from the FATA region. Operation Al Mizan in June 2002 and operation Kalosha II in March 2004 were conducted for this purpose. But the Mehsud faction of the Pakistani Taliban, IMU and other foreign militants fought on and held their grounds.

Despite the hardship it faced and the dependence it had on the local militant groups, IMU built its image as a die-hard, disciplined and a significant militant group in Afghanistan-Pakistan region. It has been behind some of the remarkable suicide attacks on the US-led coalition forces in Afghanistan and indigenous security forces in the Afghanistan- Pakistan region. On 19 May 2010, IMU executed a suicide attack on Bagram, the largest US airbase in Afghanistan. On 04 April 2012, it executed a suicide attack that killed 12 people, including three ISAF troops in northern Faryab province. On 19 October 2013, another IMU suicide attack targeted the ISAF convoy near Bagram airbase in killing several American and Afghan soldiers.

The group claimed two of three suicide attacks in Panjshir, the most secure province in Afghanistan. It included the suicide attack on Panjshir governor house in which five IMU members were involved. And in Pakistan, IMU on June 11, 2014 executed coordinated suicide attack on Jinnah International Airport in Karachi that killed at least 18 people, including 11 security personnel. Two months later, the group launched similar attacks on two Pakistani airbases in Quetta in conjunction with the Pakistani Taliban, which killed 35 security officials, destroyed one ammunition depot and two fighter aircrafts. Attacks of such magnitude display the military ability of IMU and significance of the group to both Afghan and Pakistani Taliban.

However, IMU did not make a single incursion into Central Asia since 2001. This could be a tactical move by IMU, probably prioritizing to consolidate its foothold in Afghanistan-Pakistan region by engaging with local militant. The current relevance the group achieved and the foothold it created in the Afghanistan-Pakistan region points towards the deliberate shift of focus from Central Asia especially Uzbekistan for short term.

Now that the US-led withdrawal from Afghanistan is underway, there is likelihood that IMU will re-shift focus to Central Asia as a prime area for its operations. During the security transitioning from NATO to the Afghan security forces from July 2011 to June 2013, IMU expanded operations to a number of provinces in north and northwest of Afghanistan. It has been behind increasing violence in Badghis, Faryab, Takhar, Badakhshan and Kunduz provinces- all of which share border with Central Asia. Security in Faryab province, for example, after the security transition in May 2012 got steadily worse and locals in this province attributed it to increase inflow of the IMU fighters. On October 16, 2014, the leader of Jundullah a chapter of IMU was killed following an airstrike in Badakhshan province. All this could be an indication of increasing presence of IMU in the Northern provinces and its gradual pivot to Central Asia in the years to come.

IMU is now an important group in the broader theatre of terrorism. IMU's exit from Uzbekistan in 1998 rendered the group dependent upon other Islamist entities but its strategy since 2001 helped the group not only to survive but also to become a battle-hardened group. It now remains a more serious threat to Central Asia particularly Uzbekistan. It's loss of former leadership and close links with transnational militant groups paved the way for a more radical cadre to be in reins with transnational agenda to pursue. They now not only dream of establishing an Islamic state in Uzbekistan but also subscribe to Caliphate campaign across the Muslim world bringing the whole of Central Asia into the new mandate of IMU.

Courtesy: Centre for Conflict and Peace Studies Main Office Darul Aman Main Road Phase # 06 Karte Sae Street # 09 House No 577 Kabul, Afghanistan. CAPS commentaries provide well-timed and relevant study of current developments in Afghanistan and the broader region. Views of the author are his own and do not necessarily reflect the official policy or position of CAPS. These commentaries may be republished electronically or in print with due recognition to the author. Sayed Mujtaba Hashimy serves as Research Analyst with Centre for Conflict and Peace Studies (CAPS), Kabul. His research area covers security and terrorism in the Afghanistan-Pakistan region.

Central Asian Jihadists under Al Qaeda's & Taliban's Strategic Ties

Uran Botobekov

At the time when the Uzbek authorities held an international conference on Afghanistan on March 26-27, 2018, and the Uzbek Foreign Minister AbdulazizKamilov hosted the Afghan Taliban delegation led by the Movement's political chief Sher Mohammad Abbas Stanikzai on August 6-10, 2018, Taliban-backed Uzbek Salafi-jihadi groups continued their military operations against the Afghan government forces. Uzbekistan's President Shavkat Mirziyoyev's diplomatic efforts to establish a direct dialogue between the Afghan government and the Taliban have not yet produced the desired result. Moreover, these two important events in Tashkent city could not diminish the terrorist activity of jihadist groups from the Ferghana Valley, which are under the dual patronage of al Qaeda and the Taliban.

The dispute between the UN and the US about the al Qaeda's and the Taliban's strategic ties

Monitoring of the Central Asian Salafi-jihadi groups activities showed that since 2018 al Qaeda-linked Katibat Imam al Bukhari (KIB) has stepped up its participation in the terror attacks against the Afghan Armed Forces. This Uzbek terrorist group has a high level of trust among the leaders al Qaeda and Taliban and has become a link in their strategic ties. The ongoing strategic ties between al Qaeda and the Taliban were also noted in the United Nations' twenty-second comprehensive report, which was published on July 27, 2018.The UN Security Council emphasized that "Al-Qaida and its affiliates remain stronger than ISIL, while its alliance with the Taliban and other terrorist groups in Afghanistan remains firm despite rivalry from the local ISIL affiliate" (page 3, section "Summary"). In this regard, it should be noted that the Pentagon and some high-ranking generals maintained that the strategic ties between al Qaeda and the Taliban were terminated. The US Department of Defense in its biannual report "Enhancing Security and Stability in Afghanistan" in June 2018 wrote that "… there is no evidence of strategic ties between the two organizations and the Taliban likely seeks to maintain distance from al-Qa'ida" (page 26, section "Threats from Insurgent and Terrorist Groups").

However, the UN report and the KIB activities show that the strategic ties between al Qaeda and the Taliban continue to function successfully. KIB is not the only group from Central Asia that is affiliated with al Qaeda and conducts terror operations under the Taliban's leadership in Afghanistan. The authors of the UN's report devoted a whole paragraph to jihadist organizations from Central Asia, which play a key role in strategic cooperation between al Qaeda and the Taliban. Citing information provided by its Member States, the UN its report claims: "The Islamic Movement of Uzbekistan still commands about 500 fighters in Afghanistan, concentrated in Faryab, Sari Pul, Jowzjan, Kunduz, Baghlan, Takhar and Badakhshan provinces. Around another 500

Central Asian fighters are distributed between Khatibat Imam Al-Bukhari, Katibat al Tawhid wal Jihad, Islamic Jihad Union... The Eastern Turkistan Islamic Movement commands 400 fighters in Badakhshan" (page 15-16, section "Central and South Asia").

As an expert who is researching an ideological doctrine of the Central Asian Salafi-jihadi groups, I want to note that the above facts in the UN report may require some adjustment. First, of all the above-mentioned terrorist groups, only Katibat Imam al-Bukhari and the Eastern Turkistan Islamic Movement, more commonly known as the Turkistan Islamic Party (TIP) from northwest China, today jointly conduct attacks against the Afghan government forces.

Militant of Katibat Imam al Bukhari in the joint terror operation Khandak with the Taliban

Secondly, the presence of Katibat al Tawhid wal Jihad (KTJ) militants in Afghanistan raises serious questions for experts on Central Asia. This Salafi-jihadi group, which consists of Islamists from Kyrgyzstan and Uzbekistan, is fighting alongside other Al Qaeda-linked groups in Syria and has not yet formed its branch in Afghanistan. Although KTJ, is a strong mouthpiece of al Qaeda in the Central Asian region. The KTJ's leader Abu Saloh became an effective mechanism in spreading the ideology of al Qaeda in the Ferghana Valley and the recruitment of new militants.

Thirdly, after the killing of the Islamic Movement of Uzbekistan's (IMU) leader Usman Ghazi and his more than 100 militants by the Taliban for the betrayal to ISIS at a base in Zabul Province, the group was practically extinct. In June 2016, a new faction of the IMU announced itself, denouncing ISIS and expressing its loyalty to the Taliban and al Qaeda. But after this incident, al Qaeda and the Taliban leaders do not strongly trust the new IMU faction. Therefore, the IMU is unable to become an effective player in strengthening strategic ties between al Qaeda and the Taliban. Among the Central Asian jihadi groups who fight in Afghanistan, only KIB, TIP and Islamic Jihad Union (IJU) have the highest confidence among al Qaeda and the Taliban leaders.

Uzbek jihadists in a double embrace

It is known that KIB has two branches. The group's main fighting force of more than 500 militants, led by leader Abu Yusuf Muhojir today is based in the Syrian province Idlib. Despite the fact that KIB positions itself as an "independent" faction it is closely connected with Ahrar al Sham who has had al Qaeda operatives embedded in its own ranks. The KIB's second branch is concentrated in Afghanistan, which positions itself as an integral part of the Taliban. Even the emblem and the name of the KIB branch are closely associated with the Taliban. It is known that the Taliban refers to itself as "the Islamic Emirate of Afghanistan" and has the website under the same name. With the Taliban's consent KIB leaders gave their branch the name "Katibat Imam al Bukhari of the Islamic Emirate of Afghanistan".After pledging an oath of allegiance to Taliban leader Mullah Omar, KIB became a reinforcing factor of the strategic ties of the Taliban and al Qaeda. It should be noted that the US State Department designated KIB to the list of global terrorist organizations on March 22, 2018.

KIB's Media Centeris located in Idlib, which promotes the activities of both branches in the social media. In his propaganda materials and public speaking during Jumu'ah (congregational prayer on Friday), KIB leader Abu Yusuf Muhojr regularly makes reference to the religious preaching of the founder al Qaeda Osama bin Laden and the group's current amir Ayman al-Zawahiri. Radical Salafism and militant Takfirism are the fundamental basis of the jihadi ideology of the KIB. In accordance with the ideological doctrine of KIB, the group considers its goal the construction of an Islamic state in Central Asia, the overthrow of the regime of Bashar al-Assad, and the protection and spread of Salafi-jihadi ideology around the world by force. Also, Abu Yusuf Muhojir describes with admiration the military successes of the Taliban Mujahideen and calls them "the faithful warriors of Allah."

Since the spring of 2018, Uzbek jihadists, together with the Taliban, have conducted more than ten terror operations called Khandak and Mansuri. After each terrorist attack, the KIB's Media Center published video and photo materials on the captured military equipment, weapons, and cited the data of the killed soldiers of the Afghan Army on the Telegram channel. For example, on July 18, 2018, the Media Center reported that "in the framework of the joint Operation Khandak, the Mujahideen of Kathibat Imam Bukhori neutralized four military personnel who had undergone military training NATO and destroyed one infantry fighting vehicle and 3 Hummer."At the end information, the KIB confirmed its loyalty to the Taliban according to the Bay'ah (oath of allegiance in the world of jihadism). This indicates that the KIB continue its historical fealty to the Taliban and alQaeda.

As the recent battles for the city of Ghazni have shown, the Taliban has been able to significantly increase its combat readiness and expand its presence to the borders of Uzbekistan, Turkmenistan and Tajikistan. This means that Uzbek jihadists are closer and closer to their homes, where they intend to create an Islamic Caliphate. The KIB, IJU and TIP continue to attract followers, gain battlefield experience and make international connections.

The Central Asian countries seriously fear that the Taliban's dominant role in the intra-Afghan war can inspire the jihadists from the Fergana Valley into terrorist attacks in their homeland. But the "Stans" governments do not have military, political and economic levers to pressure the Taliban so that it refuses patronage over Uzbek and Uyghur Salafi-jihadi groups. The Afghan peace conference in Tashkent and the ongoing talks between Uzbekistan and the Taliban do not give much optimism that the terrorist threat KIB, IJU and TIP will decrease in the future.

Since 2001, there have been many attempts to organize a negotiation process with the "moderate" wing of the Taliban in various formats. International conferences were held under the aegis of the UN, like the Tashkent one. Al Qaeda leader Ayman al Zawahiri has sworn allegiance to the Taliban's new amir, Mullah Haibatullah Akhundzada in June 2016. Therefore, it can be expected that the strategic ties between the Taliban and al Qaeda will continue in the future, and their patronage over the Central Asian Salafi-jihadi terror groups will not interfere.

Causes and consequences of jihadism

In conclusion, it should be noted that the UN statistics on the number of Central Asian jihadists is very conditional. Counting al Qaeda backed Sunni radical group's membership in Central Asia and the Middle East is a difficult task. In practice, their number is several times higher. In my opinion, the controversy over the continuation or termination of al Qaeda's and Taliban's strategic ties in Afghanistan, as well as the allegation of a quarrel between al Qaeda and Hayat Tahrir al-Sham in Syria is of secondary importance. Despite internal contradictions and temporary conflicts for leadership in the jihadist world, al Qaeda, the Taliban and ISIS united by the common extremist Salafist-takfiri ideology. The purpose of this ideology is the construction of the Caliphate in the world and the struggle with the crusaders of the West.

The UN in its report was unable to name the exact number of Sunni Muslims who share the Salafi-jihadi ideology. While the ideology of Salafism and Wahhabism is alive, the number of Islamist terrorists in the world can only grow, and jihad cannot be stopped. After analyzing the UN's and the Pentagon's reports it can be concluded that world powers are struggling not with causes, but with the consequences of jihadism. But the fight against the ideology of radical Islamism is primarily a responsibility of the Islamic world.

Modern diplomacy August 23, 2018. Modern Diplomacy is an invaluable platform for assessing and evaluating complex international issues that are often outside the boundaries of mainstream Western media and academia. We provide impartial and unbiased qualitative analysis in the form of political commentary, policy inquiry, in-depth interviews, special reports, and commissioned research. We are a leading European opinion-maker with far-reaching influence across the Middle East, Africa, and Asia. What we are not is a pure news-switchboard: we do not just provide information but expose readers to analysis that goes deeper than standard media exposes. Today's world already has an avalanche of information, real and fake. What it needs more of are knowledge platforms that provide shared experiences, honestly told opinions, and unique takes informed by rigorous analytical logic. Determined to voice will to power, to question but not dictate, to freely engage the intellectual arena and encourage passionate but respectful debate and discussion, MD does not stand behind any specific agenda, narrative, or school of thought. We aim to expose all ideas, thinkers, and arguments to the light and see what remains valid and sound. Contrary to the majority of news platforms, MD welcomes all imaginative and talented writers who are not hesitant to voice an opinion but diligent to support those opinions with firm, fair, and rational argumentation. This is the raison d'etre of Modern Diplomacy.https://moderndiplomacy.eu/

Chapter 5

Central Asian Jihadists in the Front Line

Ely Karmon

Abstract

Since the beginning of 2017, a string of jihadist terrorist attacks involved Central Asian citizens, mainly of Uzbek and Kirgiz origin, notably in Turkey, Russia and Sweden. Another element, which should not be underestimated, is the Uighur jihadists, original from the Xinjiang Region in China. The final demise of the Islamic State, the disappearance of its territorial base and the pressure of the various coalition forces in Iraq and Syria on the surviving foreign fighters, will compel them to flee to ungoverned states, like Yemen and Libya, but for the various Central Asian jihadists, Afghanistan and the Pakistan tribal areas seem the most suitable refuge. From there they can swarm in case of need for attacks into Europe, Central Asia, China, India and beyond.

Keywords: Syria, Iraq, Turkey, Afghanistan, Russia, China, Europe, Central Asian jihadists

Introduction

Since the beginning of 2017, a string of jihadist terrorist attacks involved Central Asian citizens, mainly of Uzbek and Kirgiz origin. The latest noticeable attacks were the April 2017 bombing of St. Petersburg's Metro and the ramming of a stolen truck into a

115

crowd in central Stockholm, Sweden. Interestingly, in three major cases there is a Turkish connection to the terrorists involved.

The St. Petersburg Metro Attack

On 3 April 2017, an explosive device contained in a briefcase detonated in the Saint Petersburg Metro, killing 15 people and injuring at least 45 others. A second explosive device was found and defused. Authorities in Kyrgyzstan informed that the suspected perpetrator, Akbarzhon Jalilov, was an ethnic Uzbek born in the southern city of Osh (Fergana Valley, Kyrgyzstan) but was a citizen of Russian Federation and had lived there since the age of 16.

Chinara Esengul, an expert on radical Islam based in Kyrgyzstan, said that according to official figures, about 850 people from Kyrgyzstan have joined the Islamic State in Syria and Iraq. There are hundreds of thousands of Central Asian emigres living and working in the Russian Federation.[1] A search of the apartment rented by Jalilov uncovered double-sided tape, metallic foil, and "other objects" similar to those comprising the unexploded device, which indicates that Jalilov assembled both explosive devices in the apartment. The Fontanka.ru agency said Jalilov had traveled to Syria in 2014 and trained with Islamic State militants. The report said that Russian investigators had ascertained that the device used in the subway attack bore the hallmarks of "Syrian know-how," specifically traces of burned sugar.[2]

One theory, investigated in conjunction with the Kyrgyz National Security Committee, is that Jalilov might have committed the attack under the influence of the Jama'at al-Tawhid wal-Jihad terror group, which operates in Syria. The group includes hundreds of Uzbeks, including those who used to live in Kyrgyzstan's Osh Region. In 2016 Kyrgyz security services had carried out a large-scale operation in the region against militants who had returned from Syria and were actively recruiting new members and preparing terrorist attacks. The Osh court banned the group as a terrorist organization. The militants then went underground and set up online recruiting operations.

Russia's Federal Security Service (FSB) detained near Moscow AbrorAzimov from former Soviet Central Asia, born in 1990. He was accused as one of the organizers of the attack, and the one who had trained Jalilov.[3] However, Azimov refused to admit his guilt in court during the hearing. By the end of April, the FSB arrested 12 people of Central Asian descent in the Kaliningrad region suspected of involvement with the Jihad-Jamaat Mujahedin extremist group. The alleged leader of the cell was placed by Uzbekistan on a Wanted List for extremist crimes. Two suspected supporters of the ISIS, who were planning a "high-profile" terror attack in Russia's Far East, were arrested on April 26 in Yuzhno-Sakhalinsk, a city on the Pacific island of Sakhalin. One of the two suspects is from a Central Asian state while the other is a citizen of Russia.[4]

Stockholm, Sweden

On April 7, 2017, RakhmatAkilov, a 39-year-old Uzbek man, rammed a stolen truck into a crowd in central Stockholm, killing five people and wounding 15. Bomb disposal experts found an improvised explosive device packed into a suitcase inside the hijacked beer truck. It is not known why the IED failed to detonate. Speaking in a mixture of Russian and Swedish, the suspect confessed to the crime as soon as he was apprehended. Akilov's Swedish residency application had been rejected in 2016 but police said there was nothing to indicate he might be planning an attack. Akilov was known to the police and posted ISIS jihadist propaganda on social media.

An Uzbek man, living at the same address as Akilov, ran a cleaning company that was part of a 2015 police investigation into an Uzbek crime ring in the Stockholm area which was alleged to have generated significant sums of money for ISIS. Five people were charged and three were convicted on grounds of financial impropriety.[5] Swedish Radio News has discovered links on the Russian social media website Odnoklassniki between the suspected Stockholm terrorist and a network around a jihadist leader, Abu Saloh, who was wanted by Interpol for terror financing and a suicide attack in 2016 in Kyrgyzstan. Extremists use Odnoklassniki accounts as go-betweens to connect violent jihadists and possible recruits – especially focusing on Central Asian migrant workers like RakhmatAkilov. According to a source within the Russian police, the suspected organizer of the attack is none other than Abu Saloh.[6]

In November 2015, a group of Uzbek citizens arrested in Uzbekistan's capital, Tashkent, were allegedly planning to go to Syria to join the Jannat Oshiqlari (Loving Paradise) group in Syria. Jannat Oshiqlari is also known as Tawhid wal-Jihad (TWJ), an Uzbek-led group based in Syria's Aleppo province. TWJ had pledged allegiance to Al-Qaeda and runs a propaganda operation that broadcasts its activities in Syria. The group has two websites, a Facebook page, and a YouTube channel on which it posts professionally made videos with footage of battles in which TWJ militants are fighting, as well as speeches by the group's leader, Abu Saloh.[7]

The Turkish Connection

According to a senior Turkish official, AkbarzhonJalilov, the man who blew up the St. Petersburg metro wagon, had entered Turkey in late 2015 and was deported to Russia in December 2016 because of immigration violations. While in Turkey, Jalilov "was deemed suspicious due to some connections he had, but no action was taken as he had not done anything illegal and there was no evidence of wrongdoing."[8] Turkish authorities detained RakhmatAkilov, the Uzbek national suspected of mowing down pedestrians with a truck in Stockholm on April 7, while he tried to join the ranks of ISIS in Syria in 2015. Given his refugee status, he was deported back to Sweden. Uzbek authorities had added Akilov to an international Wanted List in late February, after a criminal case based on "religious extremism" was opened against him. However, the Turkish roots of Central Asian jihadists are deeper and broader than the cases in St. Petersburg and Stockholm attest.

Attack on Istanbul's Main Airport

On June 28, 2016, three assailants, armed with AK-47 rifles, became involved in a firefight with security and police near Istanbul

Atatürk Airport's x-ray security checkpoint, after which at least two of the gunmen detonated suicide bombs, leaving 43 people dead and some 200 injured. A senior Turkish official identified the three suicide attackers as nationals of Russia, Uzbekistan and Kyrgyzstan. Two suicide bombers were identified as Vadim Osmanov and RakhimBulgarov, while the third was never named.

U.S. Rep. Michael McCaul, Chairman of the House Committee on Homeland Security, claimed that AkhmedChatayev, commander of the Chechen battalion in Syria, directed this attack at Istanbul's airport. The CIA and White House declined to comment on McCaul's assertion. Turkish officials were also not able to confirm Chatayev's role. The Sabah newspaper, which is close to the Turkish government, said police, had launched a manhunt for him. The 35-year-old militant had fought in Chechnya against Russian forces in the early 2000s before fleeing to the West. He was placed on the U.S. list of suspected terrorists in 2015. Although no one has claimed responsibility for the airport attack, Turkish President Recep Tayyip Erdogan said that ISIS was "most probably" behind it.[9]

After the airport attack, authorities arrested 42 suspects, with four more still on the run. Those held, including suspects from Russia, Algeria and Turkey are due to go on trial in November 2017. The authorities have said a large number of those linked to the attack are from ex-Soviet Central Asia or from Russia's mainly Muslim northern Caucasus region.[10] The investigation into the Istanbul airport attack has revealed the Islamic State ran a training center in Turkey, which the airport attacker Vadim Osmanov had attended. This center was used for the initial training of foreign fighters coming to Turkey to join the Islamic State and also to arrange their transfers to Syria.[11]

The Istanbul Reina Nightclub Attack

Contrary to the investigation in the Istanbul airport bombings, the attack on the Reina nightclub in Istanbul, on December 31, 2016, has provided important information about the wide network and deep implantation of Central Asian jihadists on Turkish territory.

The attack was carried out eight weeks after Islamic State leader Abu Bakr al-Baghdadi had called for all-out war against Turkey in an audio released on November 2, 2016. On January 16, 2017, after a massive manhunt, the Reina attacker, identified as Uzbek national Abdulkadir Masharipov (alias Muhammed Horasani) from a small town in Kyrgyzstan with a predominantly Uzbek population, was finally captured alive in Istanbul. Investigations revealed that he had been directed to launch the attack by a senior Islamic State operative in Raqqa, Syria, and had been provided logistical and financial support in Istanbul by a large Islamic State network operating clandestinely in the city.[12]

Born in 1983, Masharipov had graduated from Fergana State University in Uzbekistan with a major in physics and a minor in computer science. He has been involved with jihadi terrorist organizations since 2011, according to information provided to Interpol by Uzbekistan, where he was a known terrorist and subject to a national arrest warrant. He speaks Uzbek, Arabic, Chinese, and Russian. Masharipov told investigators that he had received military training at an al-Qaida camp in Afghanistan after traveling there in 2010. At some later point, while he was in Pakistan, Masharipov became a member of the Islamic State, pledging allegiance to Abu-Bakr al-Baghdadi.[13]

About a year before the Reina attack, he had been given orders by an Islamic State emir in Raqqa to travel to Turkey to establish himself, along with his wife and two children, in Konya - a city in the middle of Turkey - and await further orders. It appears that at some point, while he was in Pakistan, he had established remote contact with the group's leadership in Syria. According to his statement to the police, after traveling from Pakistan, Masharipov was arrested inside Iran and detained there for over a month before Iranian authorities deported him in January 2016 across the Iranian-Turkish border, without informing the Turkish police or customs agents.

Masharipov arrived in Konya, central Turkey, with his family at the beginning of 2016, assuming the name Ebu Muhammed Horasani. Police reportedly found Masharipov along with his four-year-old son at the home of a Kyrgyz friend in the city. His friend was also detained, along with three women. In the apartment, police found two aerial drones, two handguns, several cell phone SIM cards, and $197,000 in cash.[14] Masharipov is believed to be part of a sleeper cell to which several Uighurs, Syrians and Daghestanis also belonged.[15] According to Masharipov's testimony, on December 25, 2016, he was directed, via the messaging app Telegram, by Islamic State emir in Raqqa Abu Shuhada, responsible for Islamic State operations in Turkey, to launch an attack on New Year's Eve in Istanbul. Masharipov claimed he was provided before the attack with an AK-47 assault rifle, six loaded magazines and three stun grenades by an Islamic State member, whose name was never made known to him.

Masharipov's wife was detained in an operation that captured 11 suspects on January 12, 2017. Nurullayeva stated that her husband left their Istanbul lodgings three days before the attack and that she and their daughter were then transferred to an Islamic State safe house by Islamic State members. It was later revealed that Russian authorities had arrested Nurullayeva in 2011 on charges of being a member of a terrorist organization.[16] Hurriyet reported that an ISIS cell of Uzbeks, operating in the central region of Konya, provided Masharipov with support. Uzbek fighters have become deeply embedded in ISIS and have fought alongside the Taliban in Afghanistan. They are also said to have secret outposts in some major Russian cities as well as having ties to Muslim extremists in China.[17] In March 2017, Turkish Police detained in Istanbul's Kağıthane district two ISIS suspects who held Uzbekistani citizenship. They were planning a "major attack similar to the Reina nightclub." Police seized in their apartment two Kalashnikov rifles with two full chargers with 500 bullets, and also found numerous digital and written documents containing information about the terrorist group.[18]

The Central Asian Jihadists in Syria and Iraq

Already by the end of 2014, it was estimated that there were between one and three thousand Caucasians fighting alongside armed groups within Syria and Iraq (whether affiliated to IS or the al-Nusra Front). The Caucasians are divided between those who have arrived from Chechnya, Georgia, Daghestan or Azerbaijan, and those who migrated from countries of asylum like Europe and Turkey. Most of the Chechen fighters living in Europe went to the Arab world during 2012 and 2013. Some proceeded from Grozny to Turkey, while others used Bosnia and Kosovo as their transit routes. Chechens have become an important element of ISIS, despite their small numbers in comparison with other ethnic groups. In Syria and Iraq there are four active groups, some under the banner of the ISIS and others belonging to the al-Nusra Front (the al-Qaeda faction in Syria), while still others operate independently.[19]

According to recent reports, 6,000 militants from Central Asia and the Caucasus have already been enlisted in ISIS ranks. The largest radical group in Uzbekistan, Imam Bukhari Jamaat, has joined ISIS in Syria. Experts say there are over one thousand Uzbek and Tajik militants still fighting under the banner of ISIS.[20] The Chechens in Syria represent a domestic security problem in Europe and Turkey, because many originate from the diaspora. Considerable numbers come from Georgia and Turkey, but there are also dozens from Austria and France and fewer from Belgium, Scandinavia and Germany.

In October 2016, police in Germany had conducted raids in five regions as part of a probe into alleged extremism by asylum-seekers from Chechnya. It was part of an investigation which began against a 28-year-old Russian of Chechen origin that was suspected of "preparing an act of violence against the state." The Chechen jihadist scene in Berlin is substantial and high-profile. Chechen groups in Syria trained foreigners, including Germans of different ethnic origins; following a long tradition of sympathy for Chechnya among German jihadists.[21] The fighters coming from Central Asia to Syria, especially the Uzbeks, possess extensive practical expertise of warfare due to their participation in various theatres of war, such as Afghanistan and Pakistan. Many of them have undertaken numerous operations at the local and regional levels in the past. The Islamic Movement of Uzbekistan was the most prominent Central Asian group active in Afghanistan and

Pakistan. It has been decimated after the US coalition occupied Afghanistan. Most of the Uzbek fighters taking part in Syria's jihad have come from their countries of exile, particularly Russia, Kyrgyzstan, Turkey and Saudi Arabia.[22]

Another element, which should not be underestimated, is the Uighur jihadists, originating from the Xinjiang region in China.

Rami Abdurrahman, who heads the Britain-based Syrian Observatory for Human Rights, said there are about 5,000 Chinese fighters in Syria, who, together with their families, add up to 20,000 people. Li Wei, a terrorism expert at China's Institute of Contemporary International Relations, believes the real numbers are much lower, about 300 Chinese fighters who brought with them about 700 family members. Some have joined al-Qaida's branch in the country previously known as al-Nusra Front, others paid allegiance to ISIS and a smaller number joined factions such as the Islamist Ahrar al-Sham. The majority of Chinese jihadis are with the Turkistan Islamic Party (TIP), a very secretive organization. They are organized, battled-hardened and have been instrumental in ground offensives against regime forces. They are active in parts of Idlib and in the strategic town of Jisr al-Shughour, as well as the Kurdish Mountains in the western province of Latakia.[23]

Christina Lin, an expert in China-Mideast relations at SAIS-Johns Hopkins University, sustains that while from the 1990s to the late 2000s, China's terrorist threats were largely localized in Xinjiang and bordering countries, especially Afghanistan and Pakistan, after Uighur militants based in AfPak began to migrate to Syria in 2012, the Middle East became the "forward front for China's War on Terror." There was an increase of terrorist attacks in China (e.g. in Beijing 2013, and in Kunming and Urumqi in 2014) directed from abroad. Lin mentions the August 14, 2016 deal by China to provide humanitarian aid, military training, and intelligence sharing with the Syrian government, as a possible trigger to the August 30 suicide bomb attack on the Chinese embassy in Kyrgyzstan. According to Bishkek authorities, the terrorist attack was ordered by Uighur jihadists in Syria, financed by the rebranded a Jabhat Fatah al-Sham (JFS, former Jabhat al-Nusra), coordinated from Turkey, and carried out by a member of the Turkistan Islamic Party (TIP/ETIM).[24]

Afghanistan as new/old Base

After the demise of ISIS and the destruction of the Caliphate as a territorial entity, many foreign fighters, especially those from Caucasus, Central and Southeast Asia will either return home or more probably will flow to the "liberated" territories in Afghanistan and the Pakistan tribal areas - a revival of the 1990s situation. They will try to build an ISIS territorial basis there but many will probably strengthen the ranks of al-Qaeda in the region as its ally, the Taliban, has successfully weakened the pro-ISIS groups that tried to challenge it in the region.[25]

On January 26, 2015, Abu Muhammed al-Adnani, Islamic State's chief spokesperson, declared the establishment of Wilayat Khorasan, an IS province "encompassing Afghanistan, Pakistan and other nearby lands." Wilayat Khorasan has pursued a campaign of expansion and consolidation in the region, mostly in eastern and southeastern Afghanistan. The group, however, has experienced several setbacks on the battlefield. The most crushing defeat suffered by Wilayat Khorasan was the annihilation of the Islamic Movement of Uzbekistan (IMU), which had pledged allegiance to the Islamic State in August 2015. In October 2015, the Taliban established a special unit, comprised of highly skilled and experienced militants, to combat ISIS and by December 2015 had killed hundreds of IMU fighters in Zabul, including its emir, Uthman Ghazi. Taliban militants, Afghan security forces, and local militias have also chipped away at Wilayat Khorasan-held territory in Nangarhar province along the Pakistani border.[26]

General John Nicholson, the most senior US commander in Afghanistan, has claimed American efforts have killed about one-third of ISIS fighters, including its leader, Hafiz Saeed Khan, in a drone strike in August 2016, and shrunk its territory in Afghanistan by two-thirds.[27] However, ISIS has not given up its attempt to implant itself in Afghanistan and has recently carried out a series of deadly operations. It claimed responsibility for an attack (with over 80 killed) on a peaceful demonstration by Hazara protesters in the Afghan capital Kabul in July 2016, and also on a Shiite mosque in Kabul in June 2016, with the intention to inflame sectarian tensions. In March 2017, ISIS gunmen dressed as medics fought security forces for hours in an assault on a military hospital in the Afghan capital, killing 38. By the end of May 2017, in one of Afghanistan's worst terrorist attacks ever, at least 150 people were killed and 300 others, including women and children, were injured in the huge suicide explosion in the Kabul diplomatic quarter, near the Germany Embassy and the Afghan presidential palace.

The rise of ISIS in Afghanistan poses serious security concerns for Russia, according to a September 2016 statement by Zamir Kabulov, the Russian Foreign Ministry's director of the Second Asian Department in Afghanistan. Kabulov claimed that about 2,500 ISIS combatants are in Afghanistan and the organization is preparing to expand from Afghanistan into other Central Asian countries and Russia, giving Moscow reasons to worry.[28] IS' Khorasan Province consists mainly of disgruntled former Taliban and insurgents from South and Central Asia, who represent a key pillar of support for the ISIS's affiliate.

Among them, the Uzbek militants show growing assertiveness. The son of Tahir Yuldashev, the powerful Uzbek leader of the outlawed Islamic Movement of Uzbekistan, who was killed in a US missile strike in Pakistan in 2009, is leading efforts to help expand ISIS influence in Afghanistan. According to Anatol Lieven, a regional expert at Georgetown University's Qatar campus, the number of Uzbeks, Tajiks, Turkmen and other fighters from the former USSR living in Afghanistan range from 6,000 to 25,000, many of them are intermarried with Afghans of a similar ethnic background.[29]

The Uighurs' Growing Footprint

Since 2010, Uighurs was involved in several international terrorist plots. In July 2010, three men were arrested in Norway for plotting terror attacks in Europe, an Iraqi Kurd named ShawanSadek Saeed Bujak. Bujak, an Uzbek national named David Jakobsen, and a Norwegian citizen of Uighur origins named Mikael Davud, arrived in Norway in 1999. A European intelligence official said the three men were members of TIP.[30] BahrunNaim, a major Indonesian jihadist, plotted several terrorist attacks against the police and other targets in Indonesia since 2015. He created in September 2015 a terrorist cell in Bekasi, in West Java, which included ArifHidayatullah, and Faris Abdullah Cuma (alias Ali), a Uighur. Naim also ran a cell in Batam, dedicated to smuggle Uighur terrorists into Indonesia for training in Poso and bombing operations in Java. It also arranged outbound trips for Indonesians who wanted to join ISIS in Syria.[31]

In Bangkok, on August 17, 2015, 20 people were killed in a pipe-bomb attack at the Erawan Shrine, a popular destination for Chinese tourists, and most of the bombing's victims were ethnically Chinese. However, even after two suspects had been caught - both of them ethnic Uighurs - the Thai authorities initially refused to confirm their Chinese nationality, and insisted they were merely part of a people-smuggling gang frustrated over police operations constricting their business. This official story has remained unchanged to this day, notwithstanding the discovery of large quantities of bomb-making materials in the same apartment where Bilal Mohammed, the first suspect, had been apprehended. Earlier in 2015, Thailand had deported around 100 Uighurs back to China after they had escaped to Thailand with hopes of reaching refuge in Turkey.[32] The attack on the Erawan Shrine is likely to have been in revenge for this deportation.

In December 2016, five people were killed in the remote county of Karakax, in Xinjiang, after attackers drove a vehicle into the Communist Party compound and set off an explosive device. The five fatalities include the four attackers, who were shot in the incident.[33] In mid-February 2017; eight people were killed in Pishan county in southern Xinjiang, including three knife-wielding assailants, in one of the latest outbreak of violence in the region. Local security forces have put Pishan under lockdown. At least two Uighurs have been detained for sharing videos of the scene. The official statement about the incident did not say whether the assailants were linked to ETIM.[34]

Two weeks later, Uighur jihadists posted a video in western Iraq in which they vow to return home and "shed blood like rivers" - the first ISIS threat against Chinese targets. The video showed fighters, including heavily armed children, giving speeches, praying, and killing "informants."[35] Michael Clarke, a specialist on Xinjiang at the Australian National University, asserted that it is the first time Uighur militants have claimed allegiance to ISIS. He suggested that the video could indicate a possible split among Uighur fighters, as it included a warning to those fighting with the al-Qaeda-aligned Turkestan Islamic Party in Syria. In April, a suspected terrorist accused by the authorities of organizing terrorist operations overseas, was arrested in an armed raid in China's Hainan province. The suspect was said to have led a major group in Turkey. "When he was in Turkey, he had a team of more than 100 people under his command," Wu Tengfei, a member of the anti-terror squad which carried out the arrest, told state television. China is concerned that a growing number of Uighurs have gone to Syria and Iraq to receive terrorist training through Southeast Asia and Turkey after leaving the country illegally through its southern borders.[36]

Conclusion

It is possible that the involvement of Central Asian foreign fighters in attacks in Europe and Russia is the result of the great reservoir of these jihadists with fighting experience in Syria, Iraq, Turkey and Afghanistan; the relative ease of receiving asylum refugee status in Europe; and the difficulty of law enforcement agencies to monitor this big mass of jihadists speaking "strange" languages. The final demise of the Islamic State, the disappearance of its territorial base and the pressure of the various coalition forces in Iraq and Syria on the surviving foreign fighters, will compel them to flee to ungoverned states, like Yemen and Libya. However, for the various Central Asian jihadists, Afghanistan and the Pakistan tribal areas would appear to be the most suitable places of refuge.

From there they can swarm (if ordered to attack) into Europe, mainly Scandinavia and Germany, Russia, the Central Asian Muslim republics, China and India, South-East Asia and beyond. Russia will have to pay special attention to this new/old threat. One of the critical challenges faced by Russia and its affected European neighbors, however, is the problem of intelligence sharing and operational cooperation against a common enemy under current circumstances in light of the tensions created between Russia and the West as a result of Russia's interventions in Ukraine and Syria and the sanctions against the Russian Federation.

About the Author: Ely Karmon is Senior Research Scholar at the International Institute for Counter-Terrorism (ICT) and the Institute for Policy and Strategy (IPS) at the Interdisciplinary Center (IDC) in Herzliya, Israel. Dr. Karmon lectures on International Terrorism and CBRN terrorism at the M.A. Counterterrorism Studies at IDC. His fields of research include political violence, international terrorism, CBRN terrorism, and the strategic influence of terrorism and subversion in the Middle East and worldwide. This work is licensed under a Creative Commons Attribution 3.0 License. Vol 11, No 4 (2017) Karmon. Perspectives on Terrorism is a journal of the Terrorism Research Initiative and the Center for Terrorism and Security Studie.

Chapter 6

Talebs in Tajikistan: The 'Terrorist Spill-Over' Hype

Thomas Ruttig

If one listens to ISAF and to Central Asian governments, there are overlapping networks of jihadist terrorists subverting Afghanistan and Tajikistan, if not the whole region. Those networks, it is said, link the Taleban and the Islamic Movement of Uzbekistan (IMU) with al-Qaeda and other Pakistan-based groups. Few of these reports are substantiated by details that can be independently scrutinised. But they are often picked up by media and other outlets, presented as proven facts and amplified by repetition. This creates a data mist that helps Central Asian governments to exaggerate, if not invent, events asserting groups are present and concealing their own repressive policies against all manner of opposition forces. AAN's Thomas Ruttig, continuing his series from Tajikistan, looks at the 'Afghan connection' in such reporting and weighs its substance.

He delivers his in-depth analysis in two parts. Part 1, published today, deals with the perception and presentation of the jihadist threat in Tajikistan, finding that much of the jihadist activity is home-grown, not instigated from abroad. Part 2 will deal specifically with the role of the Islamic Movement of Uzbekistan (IMU) and the Taleban-IMU nexus. Find it online tomorrow. After Moscow signed a 30 year agreement for a military base in

Tajikistan, the leading Russian news agency, RIA-Nowosti, quoted Russian and international analysts in October 2012 as saying that, "the price includes [the] risk of placing Russian servicemen under fire" in an expected "Taleban face-off ... after the US forces pull out of Afghanistan in 2014".

Regional governments and some foreign terrorism analysts are blowing the same alarmist horn. During the current UN General Assembly, the foreign ministers of Uzbekistan and Kazakhstan warned of "serious threats to regional and global security from terrorism, extremism and drug trafficking emanating out of Afghanistan after 2014". In late September 2013, at the summit of the Russian-dominated Collective Security Treaty Organisation (CSTO) in Sochi, Tajik President Emomali Rahmon already had mentioned "growing threats from Afghanistan" because of "its weak military security [situation]" and said that while three or four years ago drug trafficking had been the "main threat", now it was the "movement of centres of insecurity" to the CSTO borders. Already in 2010, Stratfor, a US-based think tank, wrote:

The Afghan question also looms large. With the United States and NATO set to begin withdrawing troops from Afghanistan... Central Asian countries will face a much less restrained Taliban in Afghanistan. The Taliban's relative weakness in northern Afghanistan will mitigate this threat, but the region will nonetheless be in limbo after NATO withdraws. For their part, Central Asia's militants hope the Western withdrawal and the hoped-for Taliban rise to power will restore Afghanistan as a militant safe haven from which to pursue their home-country ambitions. Newsweek's Daily Beast blog provided another version of an overspill, already apparently happening in 2010. They quoted a "Taliban sub-commander in the northern Afghan province of Kunduz":

... jihadist allies from Central Asia have started heading home ... encouraged by relentless American drone attacks against the fighters' back bases in Pakistan's tribal areas ... they're expanding their range across the unguarded northern Afghan border into Tajikistan to create new Taliban sanctuaries there, assist Islamist rebels in the region, and potentially imperil the Americans' northern supply lines ... [beginning] in late winter 2009.... In Kunduz they joined up with fighters from the Islamic Movement of Uzbekistan (IMU).

Even some Afghan politicians, otherwise eager to build up an "everything under control" narrative, have predicted that Taleban "could penetrate into the Central Asian states such as Tajikistan" from Pakistan, as the spokesman of Badakhshan's provincial governor did in late August 2013. On the other side, many call for caution. Scott Radnitz and Marlene Laruelle, for example, two US-based Central Asia analysts, call predictions of a violent overspill from Afghanistan into Central Asia "alarmism ... based on faulty assumptions". In an article for the National Interest, the two authors add that, "it is of course important for government agencies to prepare for any eventuality, including the direst. Yet ... proponents of the 'spillover' are highly selective in the data points they bring to bear [and neglect] details such as culture, history and political practices."[1]

The first question is whether violence is already spilling over from Afghanistan into Tajikistan or other parts of Central Asia and, if so, how big a problem this is. The second question is whether relatively recent unrest in Tajikistan–mainly between 2008 and 2011–has been strongly influenced by external factors and foreign fighters or whether it is largely home-grown. The third question is whether a strong joint jihadist network is covering northern Afghanistan, that is, areas close to the border with Tajikistan and other Central Asian republics, and why the influence and activity of one particular organisation is getting a lot of coverage in this context: the Islamic Movement of Uzbekistan. A fourth question is whether "the Taleban and its associate militant groups have increasingly come to see Tajikistan as a significant arena," as the author of a report funded by the OSCE and published in December 2012 claims, or whether they are even active there.

Another question – whether the Central Asian populations have significantly changed their earlier negative attitude towards Afghan militants – has already been answered with a negative, in the first part of our Tajikistan series (here and earlier reporting here). The

131

Taleban movement does not have much appeal to Tajiks, even those who might harbour less-secular inclinations than prescribed by the Tajik constitution. The cultural-linguistic barrier seems to stand in the way of such a relationship and even the Taleban's relative success in making inroads into northern Afghanistan's Tajik and Uzbek clergy and population (see an AAN study about the 'insurgents of the north' here) has not changed this situation.

Tajikistan's terrorist threat list

If one believes the government of President Imam Ali Rahmon, the potential terrorist threat to Tajikistan is high. Since 2001, the country's prosecutor general has banned at least 14 'extremist' organisations (no official Tajik website has the list; see media reporting here and here). Not all of them are jihadist or even Muslim; the list also includes Jehovah's Witnesses. The OSCE report already quoted divides the 'Islamic' groups into three sub-categories:

- "Jihadi groups that have a well-known history of armed opposition to what they perceive as un-Islamic governments": the Islamic Movement of Uzbekistan (IMU), al-Qaeda, the Islamic Party of Turkestan/Eastern Turkestan Islamic Movement (IPT/ETIM),[2] Lashkar-e Tayba (LeT) and the Taleban; another group that was banned in May 2012 after the report came out, Jamaat Ansarullah would also belong in this category;

- "Political Islamist groups" that "advocate profound societal changes based on their interpretation of Islam": Jamaat-e Tablighi, the Muslim Brotherhood, Hezb ul-Tahrir and the Salafiya;

- "Relatively unknown and obscure local Tajik groups": Dawa and Tojikiston-e Ozod.[3]

The Tajik government's list reveals some oddities. On one hand, some groups that it had cracked down on earlier are missing, such as a local one called Bayat (Oath of Allegiance) that emerged in 1997. About Bayat, the OSCE report says that, "some have speculated that ... it doesn't even exist and was an invention of the security apparatus". Analysts in Dushanbe told AAN something similar about Ansarullah: it might have been infiltrated by the security forces and used to drive a wedge into the underground Islamist forces; they point out that the group's website (www.irshod. com) is still operating and was when the author last checked on 19 September.[4] Another oddity is that although two groups called Jundullah and Mujohedin-e Tajikistan have reportedly either carried out attacks or had members arrested, they apparently are not on the list of banned groups.

On the other hand, at least four of the groups included are not really active in the country's territory: the Muslim Brotherhood, the Pakistani group Lashkar-e Tayba, the Islamic Party of Turkestan/Eastern Turkestan Islamic Movement (IPT/ETIM) and the Taleban. The inclusion of IPT/ETIM–a group mainly active in Xinjiang, a Muslim-inhabited province of China, and cooperating with the Pakistani Taleban (TTP), the Haqqani network and the IMU in Pakistan's tribal areas –can be read as a nod towards Beijing. For the Chinese leadership, 'separatism' is one of the three 'evils' to be jointly fought with the Central Asian republics in the framework of the Shanghai Cooperation Organisation.[5] Al-Qaeda and LeT are banned as terrorist entities by the UN, the US and the EU–in contrast to the Taleban and the Muslim Brotherhood. The list also does not specify whether 'Taleban' means the Afghan Islamic Movement of the Taleban (now mostly calling itself the 'Islamic Emirate of Afghanistan') or the Pakistani Tehrik-e Taleban-e Pakistan (TTP).

Al-Qaeda can only be counted as active in Tajikistan if one accepts the definition that the IMU or IPT/ETIM or both are its 'associates', as many terrorism analysts and governments do.[6] Meanwhile, the only reports about the Muslim Brotherhood and the Afghan Taleban in Tajik territory are for minor activities–and some of the cases are from far in the past, not fully confirmed or only allegations. As Tajik and foreign analysts AAN talked to in Dushanbe in August confirmed, the Muslim Brothers have never been active except that leaflets (or shabname, 'night-letters', here, as in Afghanistan) distributed some ten years ago were signed in the name of the Brotherhood.

As for the Taleban, Reuters cited Tajik authorities on 11 September 2010 as saying that government forces had killed "at least 20 Taleban fighters ... in a clash along the border with Afghanistan" while they were attempting to enter Tajik territory. The clash, according to the report, took place on the banks and islands of the Panj River that forms the border between the two countries in that area. The ownership of some islands in the Panj River and further west in the Amu Darya is disputed due to the rivers often changing course.

The terrorism watch blog The Long War Journal (LWJ) reported that these forces attempting to enter Tajikistan were "Taliban and IMU fighters ... thought to have been fleeing an ISAF and Afghan operation in Kunduz". In the same piece, as background, the Journal added that the US (in 2010) had been hunting IMU commanders in the northern Afghan provinces of Kunduz, Baghlan, and Takhar, where the terror group had, the Journal contended, integrated its operations with the Taleban's. IMU commanders had taken on "senior roles in the Taliban's commander structure", it said, and on 2 September 2010, the US had killed an IMU leader "who also served as Takhar's deputy shadow governor". This is only one example of how ISAF claims about Taleban-IMU links are repeated as fact. In this case, the "killed IMU leader" was a civilian known to AAN. We researched this case of mistaken identity in which he and nine other civilians – all election workers – were killed in an US air strike.[7]

The 11 September 2010 border clash was not the first incident in this area. Analysts based in Dushanbe told AAN about another group of Taleban that seems to have spent a previous winter in Shurobod district (Khatlon province) in Tajik territory, an area more easily accessible from the Afghan than the Tajik side of the river. A Caucasian jihadi website, Kavkaz center, mentioned an insurgent attack on a Tajik border post there in 2008. But the sources for that report were Tajik officials and Kavkaz center definitely had no way to verify such reports. About more recent incidents, in May 2012 and April 2013, independent media reports do not mention insurgents any more but instead 'armed smugglers'.

Another case of alleged Afghan involvement on the Tajik side of Panj River was the July 2012 fighting in Khorog, the capital of Gorno Badakhshan, an autonomous Tajik region. Rather than insurgent activity, this was a conflict between both governments on the one hand and a smuggling network related to former opposition members on the other hand (see earlier AAN reporting here and here, an independent Tajik view here and Jonathan Goodhand's 2000 study of the opium trade in Badakhshan here). Tajik officials and some Russian media, however, gave many reports that 'rebels' in Gorno Badakhshan had links with the Taleban on the Afghan side of the border and that eight mysterious Afghans had been arrested during the fighting (read AAN reporting here). As it turned out, these reports stood on weak evidence: four of the Afghans were working in a local garage and staying in the country on work visas.

Nobody asked why the Taleban would attack Tajik border guards, without any signs of activities deeper in Tajik territory. The answer lies in further Tajik explanations of the 11 September 2010 incident: many weapons as well as extremist literature were found on the islands. This seems to indicate that the Taleban used the island as a depot, rather than a staging ground for intrusions into Tajikistan. Assertions, like in the OSCE report, that there is a "regional dimension of the overall Jihadi struggle" and that "Tajikistan may [author's emphasis] well be considered a legitimate target from the perspective of the Taliban because of the support of the Tajik government to ISAF" are highly exaggerated. The rare clashes along the Afghan-Tajik border are no threat to Tajikistan's overall stability; they are no more than a local threat to Tajikistan's border security.

Home-grown militant action

When talking about a jihadist threat, the Tajik government refers to a string of clashes between its forces and former opposition fighters that happened between 2008 and early 2011 in the Gharm region (see here, here, here) and that was characterised as the "most serious political violence in Tajikistan for ten years". These clashes allegedly had an Afghan connection which, however, remained dodgy for the lack of convincing facts. A central figure in this fighting was MulloAbdullo, a former Tajik opposition commander who had rejected the 1997 Tajik peace agreement and has lived in Afghanistan after that.

In 2010, Abdullo reportedly returned to Tajikistan with 100 fighters – an exaggerated figure – and was joined by local ex-commanders and fighters.[8] The government sent in troops, most of the commanders involved were killed, including Abdullo, and many fighters arrested. At various times, these fighters were described by the Tajik government as IMU members or IMU-affiliated and as including Russian nationals from Dagestan, Chechnya and even St Petersburg. When, on 20 August 2010, 46 of those arrested broke out of the high security prison belonging to the State Committee for National Security (SCNS), located about 150 metres from the president's official residence (already a surprising event), the group was now also said to include "Afghans and two Uzbeks" according to official Tajik sources.

While the escapees dispersed some reportedly to Afghanistan, another local group of fighters ambushed a Tajik army convoy one month later, killing as many as 35 troops. The government claimed the fighters had been assisted by the IMU, saying that an IMU spokesman had phoned a radio station in Dushanbe confirming this. Tajik officials claimed further–but "without providing evidence", according to a report by the International Crisis Group (ICG)–that MulloAbdullo had been appointed al-Qaeda chief for Tajikistan.[9]

Western reporting picked up and repeated these allegations without much apparent hesitation. For Stratfor, the prison escape was "conducted" by the IMU; the Jamestown Foundation, another terrorism watchdog, in contrast, saw a Jamaat-e Ansarullah connection. The Institute for War and Peace Reporting (IWPR) said the IMU connection was "possible if the likes of MulloAbdullo have spent time in Pakistan's frontier provinces" – the 'if' in this sentence remains the last word on the matter. There is only one, relatively obscure report that Abdullo "supported the IMU" in Afghanistan in 1999 and 2000 but none that he really went to Pakistan. The Tajik government also refused to return the corpses of the killed fighters to their families, so checking their real identities became even less possible. According to Jamestown, a group tried as IMU members in a Tajik court, in April 2012, were exclusively ethnic Tajiks from northern Tajikistan. Their IMU membership was likely established by forced confessions. "Torture, beatings and other ill-treatment are routine in places of detention in Tajikistan and thrive in a climate of widespread corruption and impunity," Amnesty International wrote in a report in 2012.

The Tajik fighting was over by January 2011 (here a report about the last incident). Since then, not a single further incident with IMU participation was reported from any Central Asian country by any of the major terrorism watch websites such as LWJ, the Small Wars Journal, Jamestown or the CTC Sentinel of the Combatting Terrorism Center at West Point. But then, in September 2010, Tajikistan's first-ever reported suicide car bomb attack happened and the previously unknown group Jamaat-e Ansarullah emerged. The attack occurred in Khojand in the country's north, though, far from areas known for militant activity either in the 1990s or more recently. According to official Tajik sources, another suicide attack followed in March 2012, close to Dushanbe's central bus terminal. Analysts in Dushanbe told AAN that whether they actually had been suicide attacks was not fully established in either case.[10]

Authorities blamed the IMU again, but responsibility for the Khojand attack was later claimed by Jamaat-e Ansarullah. In 2011, an Ansarullah video surfaced with a "bearded man wearing Afghan-style clothes" uttering threats against "advocates of democracy...that pray and fast but are non-believers" nevertheless. In the most recent case, when Tajik authorities said they had arrested ten members of a terrorist group on 23 September 2013 who had allegedly planned to blow up "four gates to Dushanbe as well as buildings of the Ministry of Interior and the State Committee for National Security and several other government buildings in Dushanbe," again an IMU-connection was alleged.

137

Tajik authorities claimed the group's leader had been trained in IMU camps in Pakistan.

The already quoted 2001 ICG report says what many observers have thought and written: the Tajik fighting that had ended in early 2011 was not initiated by any jihadis but was an attempt "by the president to remove one of the last [Tajik opposition] veterans with any regional influence." Jamestown adds that, "in many of the recent terrorism cases in Tajikistan, prosecutors have alleged a nexus [with] Pakistani-based militant groups... Given the corruption and politicization of Tajikistan's judicial system, such claims are hard to verify." Christian Bleuer, one of the best independent Central Asia observers, summarises that, "much of the violence in Tajikistan is tied to local issues and has few, if any, strong connections to international networks of radical Islamists." Talking up such connections is an attempt to legitimise a domestic top-down power struggle as part of the fight against international jihadism. The role, and even the existence, of Jamaat-e Ansarullah, meanwhile, remains obscure.

Talebs in Tajikistan? Part 2 on the alleged IMU-Taleban nexus

If one listens to ISAF and to Central Asian governments, there are overlapping networks of jihadist terrorists subverting Afghanistan and Tajikistan, if not the whole region. Few of these reports are substantiated by details that can be independently scrutinised. But they are often picked up by media and other outlets, presented as proven facts and amplified by repetition. This creates a data mist that helps Central Asian governments to exaggerate, if not invent, events, asserting groups are present and concealing their own repressive policies against all manner of opposition forces. AAN's Thomas Ruttig, continuing his series from Tajikistan, looks at the 'Afghan connection' in such reporting and weighs its substance.

After Part 1 (read here) dealt with the perception and presentation of the jihadist threat in Tajikistan (finding that much of the jihadist activity is home-grown, not instigated from abroad), part 2 looks at the most prominent case of a jihadist organisation, the Islamic

Movement of Uzbekistan (IMU), allegedly bridging Afghanistan and Central Asia. Although including the IMU in Tajikistan's terror list makes more sense after its past activity, some analysts are careful when estimating the scope of the group's activity in Central Asia. The usually not very dovish Institute for the Study of War states in the Tajikistan and Afghanistan overview on its website that:

It is believed that the IMU is still active in Central Asia (Tajikistan, Uzbekistan, Kyrgyzstan, and Kazakhstan), and in some countries it has allegedly reconstituted itself as the Islamic Movement of Turkestan.

The Jamestown Institute even writes that "the last major attacks in Uzbekistan associated with the Islamic Movement of Uzbekistan (IMU) were carried out in 2004"–obviously expressing doubt about an IMU role in the sporadic 2009-2011 fighting. And Noah Tucker, in a recent article on the Registan blog, adds that the IMU "rarely mentions Uzbekistan, and never mentions the country at all in terms of operational plans and priorities," but rather refers to the Taliban's government as "our Emirate of Afghanistan", projecting itself less as a national, "Uzbekistani" actor than one in a "global jihad". Tucker concludes that "it seems sometimes that in all the chatter about the supposedly imminent threat of an IMU invasion of Central Asia the only people not talking about it are the IMU themselves."

Consequently, IMU activity in Central Asian countries seems to be comparatively minimal. It also seems to originate from within those countries, not from Afghanistan. In May 2009, for example, it was reported that, a small armed group attacked a border post, then a police station in Uzbekistan but that it had "crossed from Kyrgyzstan". In January 2013, when Tajik forces arrested two small groups of alleged IMU fighters, it was again in the north of the country, in the Ferghana Valley with its confusing border lines between Tajikistan, Uzbekistan and Kyrghyzstan (but not Afghanistan).

A Jamestown report confirms that, throughout 2012, Dushanbe has regularly reported about arrests of IMU members in the Tajikistan part of the Ferghana Valley. However, many analysts doubt that they have real connection with the IMU leadership. "There is no IMU branch in Tajikistan now. Maybe there are some remnants of the IMU in Tajikistan, but I am not sure that most of the so-called IMU members have real links with Afghanistan," it quoted Daniil Kislov, director of the analytical-information agency Ferghana.

Still, even the usually reliable ICG became alarmist about cross-border IMU activities into Central Asia. In its 2011 report, it stated that, "limited infiltration of armed guerrillas from Afghanistan has been taking place for several years" and "a small number of fighters from the North Caucasus have also been active in Tajikistan in recent years." But it does not give any proof, merely noting that "Afghan officials believe that Pakistan was directly involved in the IMU's build-up in the north [of Afghanistan]" and that "Afghan officials and politicians and German intelligence analysts ... expected a further deterioration in that part of the country in 2011." Furthermore, the ICG report refers to an April 2011 statement by the head of Kyrgyzstan's state security service that appears to be exaggerated.

He claimed that "400 Kyrgyz citizens, predominantly of Uzbek ethnicity", were receiving terrorist training in Afghanistan and Pakistan. (This was the only report on such a large group that surely would have been noticed by other sources sooner or later.) ICG itself states in the same report, concerning similar allegations about "some 200 young ethnic Uzbeks from [southern Kyrghyzstan]" who had "gone to Afghanistan for military training" in 2010 that even a senior government minister with responsibility for the area had seen "no information to substantiate this claim". The authors of the report also concede that "little is known about the IMU's organisation or aims" in general.

Bleuer, commenting on the ICG report in his blog, talks about an overestimated "external threat" and a "pervasive exaggeration" of the IMU:

In the vast majority of analysis out there, the Islamic Movement of Uzbekistan is the undying bogeyman of the terrorist/insurgency world... The Pakistani and Afghan security forces want to blame foreigners for everything. And many in the US government and military are blindly consuming this. It should also not be forgotten that the IMU "started as a relatively peaceful Islamic movement", in the sense that it did not aim at overthrowing the government, according to Central Asian scholars, KamoludinAbdullaev (here) and Bakhtiyar Babajanov (quoted here). According to the latter, the IMU originated from Adolat, "a voluntary group to provide protection for the local entrepreneurs against racketeers and patrol cities at night" in 1989 in the Ferghana valley. A few years later, it "took religious orientation and was renamed the Islam Lashkarlari". By 1992 or 1993, writes Abdullaev, it had taken "steps to forcibly introduce an Islamic state in Ferghana [and was] persecuted by the Uzbek regime." This it had in common with all other opposition groups, including moderate ones.[11] Most IMU activists left Uzbekistan for Tajikistan where they fought alongside the local Islamists against the secular government from 1992 to 1997.

There, Abdullaev continues, "this Islamist alliance of Tajiks and Uzbeks was ruined in 1996, however, in favour of ethnic nationalism. Being deprived of political participation in Uzbekistan and finding no place in reconciled [post-civil-war] Tajikistan, [it] joined the regional geopolitical terrorist network," moved to Afghanistan and allied itself with the Taleban regime. From there, it was forced to migrate even further away from its country of origin, to distant Waziristan in 2001, following its defeated Afghan allies. In its own propaganda, Tucker notes, the IMU even claims that its then leader, Yuldashev, played a key role in turning the Afghan jihad against its Pakistani funders and in founding the Pakistani Taleban umbrella, the TTP.

Stratfor stated in a 2010 report that the IMU was "largely wiped out after 9/11 and the subsequent US invasion of Afghanistan in the battle of Kunduz … its remaining members relocated … to northwestern Pakistan [and] the group is no longer the coherent movement it was in the late 1990s." By 2009, the IMU had lost its two original leaders in US drone strikes, first JumaNamangani in 2001 in Kunduz and then Tahir Yuldashev in Pakistan in 2009.[12] The OSCE report quoted above, says that, of the "estimated 2000 fighters" belonging to the IMU between 1998 and 2001 when it was based in the Taleban's Islamic Emirate, only 1,000 escaped to Waziristan.[13] From there, the OSCE report continues, "a significant part" had recently relocated to northeastern Afghanistan. But how many out of 1,000 is a "significant part", particularly when the OSCE report, elsewhere in its text, says that only 600 IMU fighters were in the Taleban Emirate's period? It skates on thin ice with its estimates. The 'small groups' the Taleban commander mentioned in the Daily Beast story might be closer to reality, and less of a threat. Stratfor even casts a doubt on whether the IMU as such continues to exist:

... Governments frequently use the IMU as a catchall phrase for Islamists in Central Asia who would like to overthrow the regions' governments. In reality, various factors divide the region's militants, and continuing to use convenient labels like IMU frequently masks real shifts and complexities in Central Asia's militant landscape.... The name IMU to a large degree has become a generic label for Islamic militant activity in a similar fashion to how the devolution of al Qaeda has shifted the original understanding of the group and its name.

The case of the IMU convincingly shows how the persecution of opposition forces by Central Asian regimes has contributed to home-grown radicalisation and how those pushed into 'the mountains' or the underground come back helpfully as bogeymen for the same regimes, who now shop in the West in their fight against terrorism (see here. The latest crackdown against the legal Islamist opposition party in Tajikistan (see the second part of our Tajikistan series) could lead to similar effects.

The Taleban-IMU nexus

Since 2010, many reports say that the Afghan Taleban and the IMU not only conduct joint operations but have somehow merged their structures in a three-way coalition that also includes al-Qaeda. Most of these reports originate from ISAF in northern Afghanistan, like the one referred to earlier concerning the ten election workers who were killed in September 2010 (quoted

142

here; the Long War Journal described the killing of "a dual-hatted Taliban sub-commander and al Qaeda group leader" who was also "a senior leader of the Islamic Movement of Uzbekistan in Kunduz".[14] A March 2011 article in the Small Wars Journal mentions IMU activity in southern Afghanistan: "In places like the DehChopan district of Zabul province, the IMU is a critical piece of the local insurgency."

The author concludes, without including any detail about other districts, that, "though its members and operations are focused in only a handful of districts in Afghanistan, the IMU's disciplined fighters form an elite training cadre acting as a true combat multiplier for the Afghan Taliban, and thus its influence is felt exponentially across much of the country's south." He also writes that the relocation of IMU fighters from Waziristan to Day Chopan was not voluntary but the result of conflicts with Pakistani Taleban factions in Waziristan – and definitely not a sign of strength.

According to ISAF, the IMU regularly appoints chiefs for its operations in Afghanistan and "ISAF and Afghan forces have killed the IMU's top commander in Afghanistan three times since April 2011". Both after suicide attacks on the US PRT in Panjshir and on the Bagram air base in October 2011 (here and here) as well as a the so-called complex attack (using multiple suicide bombers) against Panjshir's provincial administration compound in late May 2013, ISAF reported that "the IMU and the Taleban claimed responsibility for what they said was a joint attack on the provincial governor's compound in Panjshir".

The IMU-Taleban claims reported in connection with the May 2013 Panjshir incident, which included an announcement of "future conquests in the Mawr-an-nahr region" – a historical term for the area between the Amu Darya and Syr Darya rivers north of the Afghan borders – do not contain direct proof that both organisations were really involved in the attack. In fact, the only 'proof' available were "a statement on the Internet claiming the Panjshir attack, and ... two photos of four of the suicide bombers", reported the Long War Journal, referring to the original ISAF report on the incident. Internet communiqués and photos without

143

any 'action' on them can easily be uploaded; usually, jihadi groups use video footage to bolster claims of attacks. Consequently, such statements might be worth as much as the Taleban's almost-daily pronouncements via social media about their attacks and the massive losses of the 'invaders' and 'hirelings' – like here, here or here – that are rarely confirmed by any independent source.

The same goes for an IMU list of 87 'martyrs' killed over the previous year published in November 2011. It included the names of 64 Afghans. Verifying these names is impossible. As AAN's Kate Clark wrote in another context, it is still "highly unusual for … an Afghan to be a member of the IMU." She added that, however, this "appears to be a fairly routine allegation for ISAF to make when Special Forces kill or capture any Afghan who is an ethnic Uzbek whom they suspect of being a Taleb."

How dead terrorists can be connected to any particular ethnic group remains questionable, too. The 2013 Panjshir suicide bombers, for example, all reportedly died in the incident but were, nevertheless, identified as including "two Uzbeks and one Kyrgyz" by ISAF. Bleuer, who has convincingly assessed recurrent reports about Chechens fighting in Afghanistan as a myth, mentioned in a recent paper how such 'identification' is done, quoting communication with a "former ISAF officer with several years' experience in northern Afghanistan":

We see it here [in Mazar-e Sharif] in the provincial hospital, where dead bodies of insurgent KIAs [killed in action] are brought to. When the bodies are not claimed by family members they are automatically labeled Foreign Fighters and depending on their faces: Asiatic = Uzbeks; dark-skinned = Pakistani; and Caucasian = Chechens. This is done by doctors as well as police and everybody takes it at face value.

Sophie Roche and John Heathershaw, two renowned Central Asian analysts, provide another example, this one from Tajikistan in 2010 (here – not-really-about-radical-islam):

The claim that foreign terrorists take part in the fights stems from bodies found after the government's bombing of Ahmadov's [a former opposition commander] house in Gharm. However, local people claim that these were Kyrgyz workers who were building his house. Kyrgyz from Djirgatol have been working on Gharmi construction sites for many years. It is claimed that these Kyrgyz were among the victims of the recent military attacks and falsely identified as international terrorists.

AAN's Kate Clark comments: Labelling dead ethnic Uzbek Afghans as IMU adds to the narrative of an external 'terrorist' threat and makes whoever was killed or captured sound extremely dangerous. From our point of view, it just underlines that international security forces have a blurred picture about whom they are opposing and that not much is known about IMU and its links to the Taleban, al-Qaeda and other militant Islamist organisations.

Conclusion: Exaggerated Alarmism

To realistically assess the dangers of an Afghan conflict overspill into Central Asia, particularly one linked to armed jihadists, filtering out the hard facts from unproven claims in official statements is necessary. Statements by Central Asian governments contain high doses of self-serving alarmism, seem to exaggerate and misrepresent relatively small incidents, and describe scenarios that could only become true if different groups significantly increased the intensity, scope and coordination of their activities. Whether this will ever happen simply cannot be predicted. To speak of an already existing high-level threat is simply unrealistic. Labelling all domestic dissent as 'Islamist' or 'terrorist' is a long-established pattern. This form of alarmism has proven highly successful: some Central Asian leaders mobilised support from Western governments for their alleged fight against jihadist or Islamist terrorism despite their human rights violations and the home-grown causes of much of the internal tensions in their countries.

Increasing official Afghan reporting of the involvement of alleged foreign fighters in the domestic insurgency reflects an interest in projecting that most insurgent activity in the country's north emanates from beyond the borders. The alleged IMU activity is only one case.

Exaggerating the jihadist threat is also part of the re-opened power games in the 'Greater Central Asia' (the term has recently come into use among Russian academics and politicians and includes the Central Asian republics plus Afghanistan) expected after most NATO combat troops have withdrawn by the end of 2014. Transition in and withdrawal from Afghanistan is increasing some neighbouring countries' interest in the Afghan situation. With regard to Russia, this interest is epitomised by its ongoing discussion about possibly returning its troops to the border with Tajikistan where they had been from Tajikistan's independence in 1992 until 2005. After the recent CSTO summit in Sochi on 23 September, the organisation's secretary general said surprisingly, however, that there was "no need" to send Russian border guards to Tajikistan and those Tajik troops will be provided with military and technical assistance instead.

The claimed nexus between the Taleban, IMU and other groups does exist in Waziristan – where the IMU's focus of activity moved in 2001 and partly in northern Afghanistan, but no evidence of it exists beyond Afghan borders. The scope of the alleged overlap between the Taleban, IMU, al-Qaeda and other groups is difficult to confirm given the lack of open and verifiable detail. According to Roche and Heathershaw, there is also "no evidence" that the Islamic Revival Party of Tajikistan (IRPT), the legal Islamist opposition party, consented to the former civil war commanders' actions during the 2008–2011 fighting or that the party is radicalising as a result of the current government crackdown (see the second part of our Tajikistan series, here).

For Afghanistan, it is far from clear whether fear that the Taleban will take over all or most of the country, or show significant gains in its north, are realistic. But even if that happened, the likelihood of an aggressive spill-over, in the form of cross-border attacks, seems low. This is neither indicated by Taleban leader Mulla Muhammad Omar's statements (as in his 6 August 2013 Eid-ul-Fitr address) where he reiterated that the insurgent movement wants good relations with all countries, including the neighbours; he also did not express any Taleban concern about those countries' involvement in the Northern Distribution Network (more AAN analysis here).

But more importantly, the Taleban's practical behaviour indicates a lack of interest in any substantial cross-border activity. Stirring up Central Asia would lead the Taleban into direct confrontation, not only with the region's five governments, but also with Russia and possibly China. Those countries have built up regional security mechanisms like the Shanghai Cooperation Organisation (SCO) and the CSTO. Such a confrontation would ultimately jeopardise any hypothetical Taleban gains, as happened when al-Qaeda's 9/11 attacks led to the fall of its Islamic Emirate. It would make Afghanistan a pariah again in the international community.

Much of the information about jihadi terrorist groups' activities is classified. What comes into the public's view is likely twisted – part of psychological warfare operations (or just propaganda) – or at least blown out of proportion by the proliferating military and intelligence-related analysis industry that does not put its sources on display for public scrutiny. As the reports about alleged joint IMU-Taleban attacks in Panjshir and Bagram and statements about forays into 'Mawr-an-nahr' show, they are exclusively based on insurgent material, such as photos or statements on websites that might as well be complete invention cooked up in propaganda units or internet cafés by jihadists knowing that such material will create media attention and busy the intelligence community. Real incidents in Central Asia that involve Afghan insurgents are very rare and limited to border areas. Insurgents have not targeted deeper into Tajik or any other territory in the region and are driven by the cross-border drug trade in most cases.

Regional analysts, although not immune to threat scenarios, are often much more nuanced about the possible quality of a spill-over from Afghanistan than their government or Western analysts. IWPR quoted from three different countries recently who, more or less unanimously, said the same thing. "Instability in Afghanistan presents a threat to its neighbours only because conditions for radicals will improve," said Almaty-based Kazak political analyst Marat Shibutov. Alexei Malashenko, a specialist on Central Asian politics and political Islam at the Carnegie Centre in Moscow, points to succession debates in both Uzbekistan and, less prominently, in Tajikistan, saying in possible "power struggles to replace Central Asia's ageing leaders… political groups on the losing side might turn to [internal and external] Islamic groups for support". Alexander Zelitchenko, director of the Central Asia Centre for Drug Policy in Bishkek, confirms that the Taleban "have never made any claims to the territory of others". This sounds quite different as a narrative that implies a forthcoming IMU-Taleban offensive towards Buchara and Samarkand. In Tajikistan itself, jihadist terrorism or other forms of Islamist violence seem to be the exception 16 years after the civil war ended.

Talebs in Tajikistan? The 'terrorist spill-over' hype. Author: Thomas Ruttig. Part 1 and 2. Date: 10 and 11 October 2013. The Afghanistan Analysts Network (AAN) is an independent non-profit policy research organisation. It aims to bring together the knowledge, experience and drive of a large number of experts to better inform policy and to increase the understanding of Afghan realities. It is driven by engagement and curiosity and is committed to producing analysis on Afghanistan and its region, which is independent, of high quality and research-based. Our aim is to be bi-taraf but not bi-tafawut – impartial, but not indifferent. Since its establishment in 2009 AAN's publications have informed and influenced the work of policymakers, journalists, academics and development workers working on Afghanistan. AAN's analysts are regularly asked to speak at conferences and briefings around the world, and frequently appear as commentators in the media. AAN's publications include in-depth thematic reports, shorter policy briefings, quick discussion papers and dispatches from the field. AAN's publications are widely read and often quoted. All of AAN's research and analysis is publicly available and can be found on the AAN website. The Afghanistan Analysts Network is registered in Germany as an association (eingetragener Verein, e.V.) with registration number VR28652B, and as a non-profit research organisation at the Ministry of Economy in Kabul under registration number 341, dated 17.6.1388. The institutional structure of AAN consists of the three co-directors and founders, a Kabul-based core team of analysts and researchers, and a network of contributors with long-standing expertise in the fields of Afghan politics, governance, and rule of law, human rights, security, and regional affairs. AAN has a permanent office in Kabul. https://www. afghanistan-analysts.org/about-us/

Chapter 7

Kazakhstan, Kyrgyzstan, Tajikistan, Turkmenistan, Uzbekistan

Nodirbek Soliev

In 2018, terrorism posed a multi-faceted and continued threat to Central Asia. While the dynamics and characteristics of the terrorist threat may differ across Kazakhstan, Kyrgyzstan, Tajikistan, Turkmenistan and Uzbekistan, certain challenges are visible across the board. The major regional risks that Central Asian countries continued to face in 2018 are: (i) transnational terrorism in the form of Central Asian terrorist units fighting in foreign conflict zones; (ii) the growth of clandestine terrorist sleeper cells in the region; (iii) homegrown attacks inspired by online extremist ideologies; (iv), and the radicalisation of Central Asian migrant communities abroad.

Central Asian Militants Split between Islamic State and Al-Qaeda

In the context of Central Asia, Islamic State (IS) and Al-Qaeda (AQ)-linked groups represent an equally significant threat. Most recent official estimations from the region indicate that nearly 5,500 Central Asians, including 2,000 nationals of Uzbekistan, 1,300 to 2,000 of Tajikistan, 850 of Kyrgyzstan and 500 to 600 of Kazakhstan, travelled to Syria and Iraq to join jihadist groups fighting there.[1] Despite media reports regarding 360 Turkmens drawn to the war in Syria, the Turkmen government has denied the involvement of its citizens in this conflict.[2] There are significant variations in the ethnic composition of Central Asian militant units aligned with IS and of those with Hayat Tahrir al-Sham (HTS), the successor of AQ's former Syrian affiliate Al-Nusra Front. The majority of Kazakh and Tajik fighters have merged with IS as militant divisions known as 'Kazakh Jamaat' and 'Tajik Jamaat'. In comparison, Uzbeks have joined Kateebat at Tawhid wal Jihad (KTJ) and Kateebat Imam Al-Bukhari (KIB), which have close battlefield ties to HTS. Each group presents its own challenges that will be discussed below.

Islamic State Seeks to Reinforce its Influence

In 2018, Tajikistan saw two separate attacks that were carried out by individuals inspired by IS. This was a significant development as it was the first IS-claimed attack in Central Asia. IS has previously restrained from getting involved in attacks in Central Asia as the group's leadership emphasised that attacking this region was not the highest priority.[3] In July 2018, five Tajik men killed four foreign cyclists in a car-ramming attack, accompanied by an on-foot gun and knife assault in the Khatlon province of Tajikistan. The victims consisted of two Americans, a Swiss and a Dutch national. In response, the Tajik government blamed elements of the Islamic Renaissance Party of Tajikistan (IRPT), a former opposition party banned as an extremist group in 2015. IS unhesitatingly claimed that it's 'soldiers had carried out the attack in response to calls to target citizens of the coalition countries'.[4]

In November 2018, a group of terrorist inmates staged a riot at a high-security prison in Khujand province in Tajikistan, leading to the deaths of two prison guards and 21 inmates. Through Amaq media agency, IS leadership claimed responsibility by stating that one of its fighters was responsible for the outbreak of the riot.[5] It is worth noting that IS preferred to remain silent when a group of 27 gunmen attacked two commercial gun stores and attempted to storm a military base in Kazakhstan's Aktobe city in June 2016. The Kazakh government believed that the gunmen were inspired by the speeches of IS' spokesperson Abu Mohammad al-Adnani, who was killed in an airstrike in Syria in 2016.

The two recent IS-linked attacks in Tajikistan aligns with the group's grand strategy of global expansion after continued territorial defeats in Syria and Iraq.[6] Similar to other regions, IS is seeking to increase its ideological and operational influence in Central Asia. However, before its territorial defeat, the main purpose of IS' propaganda activities in Central Asia was to recruit and mobilise potential fighters from the region for its contingents in the Middle East. IS needed more fighters to survive the onslaught it was facing in Syria and Iraq.

In 2018, IS has continued to disseminate online propaganda statements and materials in Central Asian languages, notably in Kazakh, Tajik and Russian. IS' associated Central Asian units, including Tajik and Kazakh Jamaat, do not have their own media wings responsible for propaganda operations. IS' extremist messages focusing on Central Asia are often produced and published directly by the group's main media structures such as Al-Hayat Media and Wilayah of Khayr Media. In terms of its content, graphic design and process of online promotion, the materials in Central Asian languages have shown the markings of IS' typical media production.

A case in point was the release of the 13 minute footage, entitled Subul as-Salam (Pathways to Peace), by Wilayah of Khayr Media in January 2018. Featuring a number of Kazakh militants fighting in Syria's Deir alZor Governorate, the video clip is of high quality and is subtitled with Arabic translations of speeches from Kazakh and Russian languages. The video was distributed via multiple online social networking platforms such as Twitter, Facebook and Odnoklassniki and encrypted messaging platforms including, Telegram and Zello. The main themes in this video included delegitimising secular governments in the region and calling on local supporters to conduct low-tech attacks[7], which have become IS' global trademark. In the video, a fighter named Abu Sayf al-Kazakhi, appealed to the people of Kazakhstan and claimed that Muslims have a caliphate now and they are now obliged to travel to the lands of caliphate. He stated that, "if you see any attempt to stop you from migrating to the caliphate…you have to crucify or stab the kuffar (infidels) or destroy their cars".

Kateebat at Tawhid wal Jihad and Kateebat Imam Al-Bukhari Remain Focused on Syria

Although AQ-linked Central Asian groups have not conducted any attacks in Central Asia since 2016, KTJ and KIB are operationally more capable than IS. The attacks claimed by IS in Central Asia involved simple, unsophisticated and low cost tactics that were not necessarily directed by IS. In contrast, KTJ conducted two high profile attacks in Kyrgyzstan and Russia: the suicide car bombing at the Chinese embassy in Bishkek in August 2016 and the metro bombing in Saint Petersburg in April 2017. KTJ's leader, Abu Saloh, ran these operations directly from Turkey and Syria after employing complex and expensive methods with the use of trained fighters.[8]

KTJ and KIB are now among the largest foreign militant groups that have actively taken part in militant offensives against the regime in Syria's Idlib and Hama provinces. Both of these groups have managed to survive and expand their strength largely due to the support and protection offered by HTS. In return, KTJ and KIB have provided HTS with manpower on the ground. Unlike IS' Central Asian fighters, KTJ and KIB have their own media divisions, which are called 'Jannat Oshiqlari' (Lovers of Paradise) and 'Al-Bukhari Media' respectively. These media outlets extensively produce and disseminate extremist content in the online domain. In 2018 alone, KTJ and KIB released more than 100 audio statements and videos on their Uzbeklanguage blogging websites. The groups' supporters have re-distributed these files to other online domains such as YouTube, Facebook, VK, Odnoklassniki and Telegram.

Unlike IS, which has shifted its strategy towards encouraging attacks in Central Asia, KTJ and KIB are still focused in calling their supporters and sympathisers to travel to Syria. In a video statement released in November 2018, KTJ's leader Abu Saloh pointed out that his group remains committed to 'preserve jihad in the land of Sham' until the rafideen (rejectionists)[9] regime is overthrown in Syria. Since August 2018, there has been a noticeable decline in the production of KIB's and KTJ's online extremist materials in comparison to the same period over the last year. This coincides with Turkey and Russia's agreement to create a demilitarised buffer zone in Syria's Idlib province in September 2018. The ceasefire agreement has significant implications for KTJ and KIB in Syria as the core structures and their family members are located in the areas where the demilitarised regime is going to be established. The successful implementation of the Idlib agreement could possibly lead KTJ, KIB and relevant groups, to leave their key positions in the province and look for a new safe haven elsewhere.

Idlib Agreement Impacts the Future of KTJ and KIB

After the Idlib ceasefire agreement, the future of KTJ and KIB in Syria remains largely unclear. According to the agreement, Turkey has taken responsibility to convince both moderate rebels and jihadist fighters, including the HTS coalition that comprises KTJ and KIB, to hand over their heavy weaponry in the de-escalation zone. Disarmed militants would then migrate to Turkish-controlled safe zones in the north of Syria such as Afrin and Al Bab. At this juncture, it is difficult to predict if the core groups in the HTS coalition will comply with Turkey. Given their close battlefield relationship, it can be expected that the greater contingent of KTJ and KIB fighters would merely follow the existing dynamics within the HTS core. In October 2018, HTS released an online statement that outlined its vision regarding the future of the Syrian war. However, the organisation has avoided revealing its formal position regarding the ceasefire.

Despite this, it remains likely that HTS would endorse Turkey's appeal. Rejecting Turkey's demands could undermine the long-standing support that HTS is believed to have tacitly received from Turkey.[10] It is possible that some members of KTJ and KIB do not want to leave the buffer zone and continue to fight against the Syrian regime, while others may defect to different terrorist factions or relocate to Turkey. Afghanistan could be another possible destination for potential Central Asian jihadists fleeing Syria. Afghanistan already hosts at least five Central Asian militant groups – the Islamic Movement of Uzbekistan (IMU), the Islamic Jihad Union (IJU), Jund al-Khilafah, Jamaat Ansarullah and KIB's Afghan wing. As all of these groups in Afghanistan maintain close ties with AQ and the Taliban, KIB and KTJ fighters fleeing Syria could end up joining anyone of them. Likewise, pro-IS Central Asian fragments may move to Afghanistan to merge with the Islamic State of Khurasan (ISK), which is believed to have up to 6,000 active fighters.[11]

In September 2018, Andrey Novikov, the head of the Anti-Terrorism Center of the Commonwealth of Independent States (CIS), stated that IS has been seeking to build its stronghold in Central Asia and create new sleeper cells and activate existing ones. According to Kyrgyz Deputy Prime Minister ZhenishRazakov, militants attempted to cross into the region from northern Afghanistan with the purpose of targeting Central Asia.[12] However, in the online extremist domain, there have been no indications of Central Asian terrorist groups relocating to Afghanistan. Furthermore, existing Central Asian groups in Afghanistan have been largely quiet and almost inactive as they struggle to survive after being expelled from Pakistan's tribal areas between 2014 and 2015.

On 22 March 2018, the United States (US) Department of State included KIB to its list of specially designated global terrorist organisations. A statement released on the State Department website noted that the objective of the move is to deny KIB the resources it needs to plan and carry out attacks.[13] Although both KTJ and KIB are outlawed as terrorist organisations by Central Asian countries, KTJ has not been designated as a terrorist organisation by the United Nations (UN), US or EU. Given the close operational ties of KTJ with HTS and its growing ideological affiliation to AQ, these global actors should consider blacklisting the group.

Such criminalisation measures have proven to be very effective in curbing the threat of transnational terrorism. For instance, the US' decision to designate KIB as a terrorist organisation had a visible demoralising effect on the group due to the fear of possible US air strikes after the ban. This has been evident from the content of the statement released by KIB on its Telegram channel not long after the ban. KIB stated that it 'was surprised' by the US decision and tried to deny its connections to AQ by claiming that 'it does not have ideological or intellectual ties with any faction internationally enlisted'.

Radicalisation of Central Asian Diaspora Communities

In the past, there were limited cases of radicalisation within the Central Asian diaspora mostly concentrated in Russia, Turkey and the US. Yet an unprecedented surge in attacks by Central Asians across Bishkek, Istanbul, Stockholm, Saint Petersburg and New York were reported between 2016 and 2017. This indicated that the migrant and diaspora radicalisation remains a key challenge. Although members of the Central Asian diaspora and migrant communities did not carry out any attacks in other countries in 2018, dozens of Central Asians were arrested in Russia during antiterrorism investigations.

In March 2018, for instance, Russian counterterrorism agencies cracked down on the activities of a large network of IS recruitment cells and document forgery syndicates in Moscow. The clandestine network that was made up of 60 foreigners, including individuals from Central Asia, had recruited foreign and local nationals in Russia for IS and facilitated their illegal journey to the Middle East. The authorities uncovered three fake documentation-producing labs in 17 locations that they raided.[14]

It is pertinent that recent terrorist attacks by Central Asians living abroad were part of a larger trend in a number of Western countries with minority Muslim populations. The advent of digital media and communications, combined with the heightened interest and propaganda capabilities in terrorist groups to exploit migrant vulnerabilities, cases of radicalisation and recruitment have become more frequent among Central Asians living abroad. The vulnerability of immigrants is directly related to their geographical distance from home.

The limited knowledge of language, culture and socio-economic conditions in the destination country often leads to a sense of alienation and injustice within migrant communities, making them more susceptible to extremist indoctrination. The extensive use of the internet and encrypted networking tools by terrorists has also allowed their ideology to gain traction. Studies suggest that between 80 to 90% of the Kyrgyz, Tajik and Uzbek nationals who went to the Middle East to fight were radicalised and recruited while working as foreign labourers in Russia.[15] It is estimated that nearly 5 million Central Asians now live in Russia–2.6 million Kazakhs, 1.1 million Uzbeks, 590,000 Kyrgyzs, 470,000 Tajiks and 190,000 Turkmens.[16]

Outlook

The future trajectory of the Central Asian terrorist threat will be determined by two main factors: the ongoing armed conflicts in the Middle East and Afghanistan and the future of IS and AQ. With many Central Asian jihadists committed to die as 'martyrs' in the 'holy war', most of them may not return home. According to official reports, 470 Tajik and 150 Kyrgyz nationals were killed in Syria and Iraq since the conflict started.[17]

Meanwhile, there were a number of video clips that showed militants burning their passports in a symbolic renunciation of their former national identities. The recent attacks in Tajikistan have shown that IS' influence is spreading through the virtual domain despite its territorial losses. IS will attempt to inspire and sustain low-tech attacks through decentralised local cells or lone actors using its persistent propaganda efforts. KTJ and KIB will likely survive and maintain their combat capacity in Syria. The Bishkek and Saint Petersburg attacks indicate that suicide bombing will remain a favourite tactic for KTJ's future operations in Central Asia. In an audio statement released on YouTube in August 2018, Abu Saloh claimed that more than 25 trained militants in his group were 'waiting their turn for a fidayeen (suicide) operation'.[18]

The decrease in the production of online extremist materials is a positive development as it is expected to impede radicalisation and calls for violence. Central Asian governments have identified and blocked nearly 600 websites that promote extremist ideas.[19] However, these efforts are not overwhelmingly effective as the terrorist groups have been quite resilient in creating new websites and social media accounts to spread propaganda. The shift by terrorist groups from open-end to encrypted messaging platforms has made their detection and prevention of attacks more challenging.

Given the fact that the Central Asian international diaspora is expanding, radicalisation involving individuals who had come from the region remains a security concern for both Central Asian republics and host countries in the long term. VK and Odnoklassniki are Russia-based online social networking services that are popular in Russia, Central Asia, Trans-Caucasus (Armenia, Azerbaijan and Georgia) and some parts of Eastern Europe. Although these social networking sites were initially launched in Russian, they are now available in several languages. Russian national legislation criminalises posting and re-sharing of extremist content in the online domain and obliges local internet providers and tech companies to block and remove such content.

In compliance with this regulation, both VK and Odnoklassniki have shown their determination and ability to disrupt the extremist exploitation of their services. Despite this, online extremist resources remain largely available for Central Asians who study, live and work overseas. For example, dozens of video and audio lectures of pro-Al Qaeda Central Asian ideologues like TakhirYuldash (now deceased), Abu Saloh, Salakhuddin Haji Yusuf (now deceased) and Abu Yusuf Muhojir still remain on YouTube and Odnoklassnik. This is partly due to the lack of manpower with knowledge of Central Asian languages who could help detect and block terrorist content in these languages. As such, it remains essential to remove these online extremist materials to curb radicalisation among Central Asians both at home and abroad.

Nodirbek Soliev is a Senior Analyst at the International Centre for Political Violence and Terrorism Research, a specialist unit within the S. Rajaratnam School of International Studies, Singapore. He can be contacted at isnsoliev@ntu.edu.sg.

The S. Rajaratnam School of International Studies (RSIS) is a professional graduate school of international affairs at the Nanyang Technological University (NTU), Singapore. RSIS' mission is to develop a community of scholars and policy analysts at the forefront of security studies and international affairs. Its core functions are research, graduate education and networking. It produces cutting-edge research on Asia Pacific Security, Multilateralism and Regionalism, Conflict Studies, Non-Traditional Security, International Political Economy, and Country and Region Studies. RSIS' activities are aimed at assisting policymakers to develop comprehensive approaches to strategic thinking on issues related to security and stability in the Asia Pacific. For more information about RSIS, please visit www.rsis.edu.sg. XW The International Centre for Political Violence and Terrorism Research (ICPVTR) is a specialist research centre within the S. Rajaratnam School of International Studies (RSIS) at Nanyang Technological University, Singapore. ICPVTR conducts research and analysis, training and outreach programmes aimed at reducing the threat of politically motivated violence and mitigating its effects on the international system. The Centre seeks to integrate academic theory with field research, which is essential for a complete and comprehensive understanding of threats from politically-motivated groups. The Centre is staffed by academic specialists, counter-terrorism analysts and other research staff. The Centre is culturally and linguistically diverse, comprising of functional and regional analysts from Asia, the Middle East, Africa, Europe and North America as well as Islamic religious scholars. Journal Article is Open Access, Kazakhstan, Kyrgyzstan, Tajikistan, Turkmenistan, and Uzbekistan. NodirbekSolie.www.rsis.edu.sg/ research/icpvtr/

Chapter 8

Understanding the Factors Contributing to Radicalisation among Central Asian Labour Migrants in Russia

Mohammed S Elshimi with Raffaello Pantucci, Sarah Lain and Nadine L Salman

Preface

This project took seven months to complete. The first phase involved the formulation of the research design in a three-day workshop in Moscow at the end of May 2017 that was led by the Royal United Services Institute (RUSI) and hosted by the Institute of Oriental Studies at the Russian Academy of Science (RAS), which also provided key substantive input into the initial project development and implementation process. The research team comprised researchers from various countries and the three project stakeholders: Search for Common Ground (SFCG), RAS and RUSI. The team met to standardise key terms, concepts and the methodology, including training in research ethics.

The second phase of the project included fieldwork and data collection in Russia. This was undertaken by Central Asian researchers identified by SFCG (from the three target Central Asian communities, on the assumption that common linguistic and cultural background would facilitate access) and RAS researchers, who had ensured appropriate permissions from

Russian authorities and played a critical role in facilitating the interviews. Fieldwork took place between 1 and 28 June 2017 across thirteen cities in Russia, in seven geographical regions. The following sites were included in the research design because they are the key locations for the migration and settlement of Central Asian migrant workers:

- Far East: Khabarovsk.

- Siberia: Krasnoyarsk, Irkutsk, Novosibirsk.

- Ural: Yekaterinburg.

- Volga: Samara, Saratov.

- South: Astrakhan, Krasnodar, Sochi.

- Central: Moscow and Moscow region.

- North-West: St Petersburg.

The third phase of the project involved transcription of interviews and their translation into English. The fourth phase saw the research teams analyse the data. Given the volume of data, these two stages overlapped. Mid-way through the analysis cycle, RAS, SFCG and RUSI convened a three-day workshop in Almaty, Kazakhstan, to discuss preliminary findings, conceptual issues and drafting. The final stage was drafting the reports. There are five reports, each for a different audience: first, a report in English principally drafted by RUSI analysts; a report in Russian principally authored by RAS; and one report each on Kyrgyzstan, Uzbekistan and Tajikistan. Each offers policy recommendations for the Russian Federation and Central Asian governments. They are all analysing the same data, but, given the different audiences and lead authors, offer slightly different recommendations and conclusions.

Executive Summary

This Occasional Paper examines the factors contributing to radicalisation and violent extremism among labour migrants from Kyrgyzstan, Tajikistan and Uzbekistan in Russia. The researchers conducted 218 interviews (67 Uzbeks, 83 Kyrgyz and 68 Tajiks) with migrant labour workers, experts and local officials in thirteen cities across seven areas in Russia. This investigation looks through the lens of radicalisation and violent extremism rather than the economics of migration or the sociological experience of being a labour migrant. The aim of this research is to understand the broader political, economic, social, institutional and cultural conditions that might under certain circumstances generate violent extremism or leave individuals vulnerable to extremist messaging.

This report frames the research findings in terms of perceptions of the factors contributing to violent extremism rather than the causal factors leading to violent extremism. From a methodological perspective, an ideal research project would have had access to violent extremists themselves, but for various practical and ethical reasons this was not possible. Consequently, the research is about the milieu in which radicalisation takes place. Many respondents spoken to in this study had never encountered anyone who had been radicalised or recruited to violent extremism. However, some interviewees did know someone directly who had been radicalised or recruited to violent extremism. Data derived from the interviews with individuals who knew somebody closely who was radicalised is more reliable than others in the sample. This report draws more heavily on their accounts.

The baseline for violent extremism and terrorism among Central Asians working in Russia is low

There is a low incidence of violent extremism in terms of terrorist attacks, plots and supply of foreign fighters among Central Asian labour migrants in Russia. Even considering the upper estimates for numbers of Central Asian individuals who have gone to fight in Syria and Iraq, these are at most a few thousand. Of these, only some are identifiable as having worked in Russia, out of a community of labour migrants in Russia that numbers 2 million (in low estimates – some unofficially place the number as more than double that). It is ultimately only a tiny minority of migrants that become involved in violent extremist activity.

Perceptions of structural motivations

There is no clear evidence of a direct link between the marginalisation of labour migrants and the 'push' factors that might drive individuals towards violent extremism. However, notwithstanding the different migration experience among individuals from different Central Asian countries, there is some evidence of structural factors within the process of labour migration leading to marginalisation, exclusion and alienation across all three groups (Kyrgyz, Tajik and Uzbek) that are the focus of this study. These findings corroborate the wider discourse and limited literature that exists about life as a labour migrant in Russia.

The data shows three potential structural motivations. First, the challenges migrants experience with the administrative, legal and financial process of registering forces some migrants to avoid registering legally and instead work in Russia on an illegal basis. Illegal migrants are then exposed to wider vulnerabilities. Second, the economic exploitation by some actors of migrants, concomitant with the financial hardship and poverty migrants must endure, compels a minority to pursue other means of surviving. Last, the stigmatisation and securitisation of labour migrants in general can lead to their social marginalisation, as well as foster grievances. All of these factors can impact the process of radicalisation, but at the same time, are not necessarily determinants of it taking place.

Perceptions of enabling factors in violent extremism: there is some fragmented but limited evidence that violent extremists are deliberately recruiting Central Asian labour migrants in Russia. While the data conveyed who the recruiters were believed to be and what techniques they use to lure recruits in, overall there remains a lacuna in our understanding of these groups/ organisations/ networks in Russia and the broader region. A considerable number of interviewees spoke about the role of social media in the radicalisation and recruitment process. It was seen as important in providing access to watch violent extremism videos, as well as receiving content through communications applications. This greater exposure to violent-extremist content was also seen to be

163

more prevalent in Russia than in Central Asian countries because smartphones are more affordable and access to the internet is better.

There was also a perception that Russia is a more conducive environment for the adoption of violent extremist ideas than Central Asian countries. Interviewees perceived Russia as having a more tolerant recent record of accommodating religion than governments in Central Asia. Finally, some culturally displaced migrants living in Russia who find themselves unable to adapt to their environment in some cases adopt a more categorical form of identity, such as a global Islamic identity, which potentially makes them more susceptible to mobilising for international causes. Violent extremists have exploited this enabling environment.

Perceptions of individual incentives for engaging in violent extremism

There is no conclusive evidence for why labour migrants from Central Asia working in Russia would go to fight in a third country. However, most interviewees believed that a monetary incentive ('greed') was the primary motive for joining violent-extremist groups. The second-most-cited incentive for migrants engaged in violent extremism was religion. This finding is striking because in most literature on radicalisation, the 'greed' (money) narrative is less salient than the 'creed' (religion/ideology) narrative.

While some respondents did mention that a few individuals were motivated by more emotional reasons, such as a duty to defend Muslims in Syria against perceived oppression, or by idealistic motives of contributing to the building of a new utopian society, many interviewees were in fact cynical about the role of religion in violent extremism. Many interviewees viewed religion to be a ruse used by recruiters to fulfil their objectives. There was also a notable lack of knowledge on ideology among interviewees, both in terms of its doctrinal features and the role it plays in violent extremism.

However, dominant perception among participants must be contrasted with respondents who actually knew someone who had been recruited and radicalised to violent extremism, who stressed that money was not the motivation. Instead, they stressed spiritual, religious and ideological motivations.

Perceptions of who is most at-risk and vulnerable to violent extremism

There is no typical profile of a violent extremist or a pre-existing vulnerability to radicalisation of labour migrants. There is also little or no clear and conclusive evidence about what makes Central Asian Labour migrants in Russia vulnerable to violent extremism. This fact is complicated further by the cultural, ethnic and historical differences between the three different groups of labour migrants examined (those from Kyrgyzstan, Tajikistan and Uzbekistan). However, the data identifies four types of people that participants believed to be more vulnerable and at-risk to violent extremism: (1) youth; (2) illegal migrants; (3) uneducated migrants; and (4) lonely individuals.

Perceptions of existing sources of resilience

Radicalisation and recruitment to violent extremism remains a marginal issue among labour migrants in Russia. Explanations for this low rate of violent extremism offered by interviewees focus on contextual rather than personal factors, which include: the sometimes-positive role of the Russian authorities at a local level; the role of community leaders, such as diaspora leaders, leaders of civil society organisations, consular and diplomatic officials, entrepreneurs, foremen and union leaders in the workplace, and religious leaders; community and social support; employment; the role of the family, including the guidance of family elders or foremen in the workplace; the positive influence of religion; and a level of education. Each explanation is plausible but not sufficient to comprehensively explain resilience. It is likely that these factors acting in concert have restrained violent extremism among labour migrants.

Recommendations

Greater regional cooperation to address violent extremism

The governments of Russia and Uzbekistan, Tajikistan and Kyrgyzstan need to strengthen existing regional counterterrorism and countering violent extremism initiatives. There are already several regional institutions that look at these problems and seek to address issues through the lens of violent extremism. For example, the Collective Security Treaty Organisation's (CSTO) Anti-Terrorist Centre is engaged with this issue directly and it has a southern branch in Bishkek. The Shanghai Cooperation Organisation focuses on it as well. There is a safety on the internet initiative between Russia and the CSTO under cyber security which deals with violent extremism. The effectiveness of these initiatives, however, is currently unclear.

Continue engagement by Russian authorities with diaspora communities

Law enforcement and security agencies in some cases already have a productive relationship with Central Asian communities on security issues, and a positive engagement based on trust should continue. Additionally, greater support for leaders of the Central Asian diaspora communities should be encouraged, as they are already doing great unpublicised work in protecting their communities against violent extremism.

Develop a strategy to address the return of foreign terrorist fighters (FTFs) to Russia and Central Asian countries

The report does not examine what is to be done about the return of violent extremists (or FTFs) to Russia or their home country in Central Asia because the question fell outside the scope of the investigation. During the research, this reverse flow became increasingly prominent in the discussion around the topic of radicalisation. Stories have already emerged of people returning from the battlefield. Identifying how to manage this flow back to Russia and Central Asia requires a careful effort. Some countries, like Kyrgyzstan, have already adopted legislation to prevent such individuals from returning, and have arrested a number of reported returnees.

Further research to fill identified knowledge gaps

Priorities for further research should be: (1) in-depth investigation into the role of extremist organisations and international networks operating in Russia (and their potential links to the North Caucasus – a detail repeatedly referenced by interview subjects); (2) understanding the vulnerability of illegal labour migrants in Russia and their relationship, if any, to violent extremism. The data shows that immigration is a tough experience – this is the case everywhere else and not only in Russia, but how exactly it affects the propensity to become radicalised requires more research, including interviews with different types of respondents; and (3) better understanding of how to address the return of FTFs to the Russian Federation and the broader Russian-speaking world from conflict zones in the Middle East.

Introduction

RaffaelloPantucci and Mohammed S Elshimi

Radicalization in Central Asia (defined as the five countries of Kazakhstan, Kyrgyzstan, Tajikistan, Turkmenistan and Uzbekistan) has been a longstanding concern both in the region and internationally.[1] Yet violence emanating from the region and these communities has historically been rare. The civil war in Tajikistan in the 1990s and the conflict in Afghanistan (both before and after the Soviet withdrawal) drew in some Central Asians and helped foster networks of Central Asian jihadists, but attacks in the region or further afield involving Central Asians during this period were rare. More recently, however, there have been several incidents across the globe involving individuals of Central Asian origin conducting terrorist attacks to further Daesh (also known as the Islamic State of Iraq and Syria, ISIS) goals. Most recently, in 2017, attacks in New York, Stockholm, St Petersburg and Istanbul were all linked to Central Asians. And in August 2016, an attack against the Chinese Embassy in Bishkek, possibly linked to the conflict in Syria, highlighted how the threat could materialise back home.[2]

In addition, Central Asians have also been identified as having gone to fight in Syria and Iraq – though whether they have all come from Russia, Central Asia or elsewhere and where they were radicalised is not always clear.[3] In nearby Afghanistan and Pakistan, Central Asians have appeared in the conflicts for some time, though numbers are disputed.[4] It is clear that it is a minority of Central Asians who become involved in terrorist activity or go to jihadist battlefields, but understanding exactly what drives those that do is an important gap that needs to be filled in the current research around radicalisation to violence.

Migration, and in particular economic migration, has recently been measured as a factor associated with an increased susceptibility of Central Asian individuals to radicalisation and recruitment into extremist groups.[5] While there has yet to be detailed data collection on how and why Central Asians are recruited, sources including martyrdom statements and arrest reports show that a high number of individuals who end up fighting in Syria and Iraq started their journeys to Syria and Iraq from outside Central Asia, with many coming from Russia.[6] Whilst it is unlikely that this provides an explanation for all Central Asians who have joined extremist groups (there is evidence of Central Asians going to Syria and Iraq directly from their home countries[7]), several of those who have ended up on the battlefield in Iraq and Syria have shared economic migration as a background factor.

Experts in countering violent extremism (CVE) and the region have stated that isolation, discrimination, stigmatisation and resentment may play a greater role in radicalisation among labour migrants in Russia than extreme religious beliefs.[8] Central Asian labour migrants face xenophobia and discrimination after moving to Russia. Many seek protection and belonging among fellow nationals or other minority groups by joining local mosques and prayer rooms, even though they may not have actively practised Islam in their home countries. Research has shown that Tajiks in

Russia in particular have been exposed to recruitment in gyms, suggesting that it is more about community than religion.[9]

The existing literature on this topic is limited. Noah Tucker focuses on the alleged motivations of Central Asians who have gone to fight in Syria and Iraq. He identifies economic motives among those outside Central Asia as the major identifiable driver of radicalisation, and shows that a great deal of recruitment and messaging takes place online. He points to three principal motivations to fight in Syria and Iraq: the perception of a 'just war' in Syria to protect Muslims who are suffering there; Daesh's manipulation of the feeling of marginalisation by offering an attractive 'Muslim utopia' in their caliphate; and a narrative that suggests that there is a Muslim 'state' that needs to develop to counter the West.[10]

Edward Lemon instead focuses on Tajiks, exploring the degree to which radicalisation happens at home and within Russia, and the Tajik government's response.[11] The International Crisis Group focuses on the phenomenon of fighters going to Syria from the region, highlighting the important role of online communications in their mobilisation, and the role of local drivers.[12] Others, like John Heathershaw and David Montgomery, focus on the 'myth' of radicalisation in the region.[13] Writing about this topic in 2013, Eric McGlinchey considers labour migration as a potential preventive factor for radicalisation among Central Asians.[14] There are other reports that have been written on these topics, but few appear based on primary data.

The most substantial empirical work looking at questions complementary to this Occasional Paper was undertaken by the International Organization for Migration (IOM) with the support of the Kazakh government and USAID, focusing on migrants who had been deported from or returned from working abroad, principally in Russia. It focused on migrant vulnerabilities and on the fact that:

[W]hile it has not been shown that migration is in itself sufficient to account for cases of radicalisation of migrants, the study points to the impact of the economic downturn, the presence of radical

messages in religious communities in both the country of destination and origin and the sense of social injustice and desperation, felt by certain migrants when faced with the loss of legal status and an uncertain economic future.[15]

Migrants in this situation may 'become more receptive to ideological messages that are actively disseminated by extremist organizations and preachers when they display a combination of economic and social vulnerabilities'[16] While the IOM report does not make a direct causal link given the difficulty to ascribe general reasons to an individual's radicalisation, it highlights how negative aspects of the migration experience, exclusion and an inability to make money as a labour migrant can leave people prone to becoming involved in extremist activity. Remittances sent back by labour migrants working in Russia continue to be a major source of income for Central Asian economies – something that leaves them dependent on the Russian government's attitude towards Central Asian migrant workers.

This brief literature review does not include Russian-language publications, though Russian partners in this project did not identify any major reports on the subject. Nevertheless, the review did bring to light two issues that have been reported as playing a significant role in the recruitment of labour migrants in Russia. First, as Russia has made its migration laws increasingly strict, many Central Asian migrant labourers face pressure to legalise their status after arriving; failure to do so can leave them vulnerable to radicalisation. Second, online influence is playing a role in the recruitment of labour migrants. This online influence can take many forms, both impersonal, with online propaganda, and personal, with social media communications.

It is important to reiterate that only a small fraction of Central Asian labour migrants have become drawn to extremist ideas. Exact numbers are impossible to know. But even if one takes the upper estimates of how many Central Asians are believed to have gone to Syria and Iraq (for example, a report from the International Crisis Group in January 2015 identified between 2,000 and 4,000, while a report from the Soufan Group in December 2015 identified just over 2,000 foreign fighters from Central Asia[17]), this is a fraction of the overall numbers of Central Asian labour migrants that are reported to be in Russia (which Russian sources place at between 2.7 million and 4.2 million[18]), and of course it is not clear that all of the Central Asians in Syria and Iraq started as labour migrants. Nevertheless, given the frequency of stories and narratives of Central Asians in Syria coming from Russia, it is clearly a topic that requires greater research.

This Occasional Paper approaches the topic using an innovative research methodology focused on the milieu in which radicalisation takes place, and draws on interview data with labour migrants and those living in the communities around them in Russia. It offers recommendations for the government of the Russian Federation, the governments of Central Asia, and outside powers to help address this specific aspect of radicalisation to violent extremism.

Methodology

This report seeks to answer the question: what are the factors contributing to radicalisation and violent extremism among labour migrants from Kyrgyzstan, Tajikistan and Uzbekistan in Russia? The aim of this research project is to enhance the understanding of radicalisation and violent extremism among labour migrants in Russia from the three countries investigated. It develops the evidence base on factors that contribute to radicalisation and violent extremism among labour migrants in Russia to improve policy on preventing violent extremism. This study has two objectives:

1. To establish the context in which radicalisation takes place.

2. To understand, as far as possible, the possible range of contributing motivational factors (structural, enabling and micro) to radicalisation and violent extremism among labour migrants from Kyrgyzstan, Tajikistan and Uzbekistan in Russia.

Qualitative interviews were used to gather the data. Interviews followed a semi-structured format, in which a set of fixed and open-ended questions were put to subjects, which the research teams, RUSI and RAS developed together in Moscow. The benefit of using semi-structured interviews was that it enabled consistent themes to be generated among the respondents, while also providing the researchers the flexibility to probe beyond the standard questions to elicit greater variations in the response of interviewees.

The sampling of respondents was determined by the interviewers on the ground, who either would go to areas where labour migrants were known to gather or reach out through networks to identify labour migrants. In addition to these direct interviews with labour migrants, several interviews with elites – including local officials, experts and others–were conducted. Thus, the sample for each of three ethnic-national groups includes participants from other ethnic-national backgrounds, who are considered as 'elites' in this report. While efforts were made to ensure a balance of subjects by gender, age, experience and so on, given the topicality and sometimes difficult nature of the locations in which interviews took place, this was difficult to maintain. In the end, a total of 218 people were interviewed.

To ensure that the data was analysed systematically and rigorously, three approaches were adopted. First, an integrated approach to coding was applied; using a system developed by RUSI which drew on terms and subjects that consistently emerged from the data, alongside a few key terms linked to the subject matter at the heart of the research. Second, a conceptual framework was developed to help shape the formulation of the questions, but also to organise the large data-set in a coherent and accessible way (details are given in the next section, Analytical Framework). Third, various sources of knowledge were triangulated as much as possible from across the data and other sources of information.

Researchers were neither able nor expected to interview actual violent extremists. This created a clear difficulty in trying to reach the goal of understanding violent extremism. A way around this problem was to apply an innovative milieu-based qualitative methodology. The approach uses a pyramid model of radicalisation, which posits that violent extremists emerge from broader communities of support known as the 'radical milieu'.[19] Together, these communities comprise the physical or social setting in which radicalisation occurs.

Although no interviews were ultimately conducted with those who have been recruited or radicalised, some interviewees had information based on actual (primarily second-hand but also anecdotal) knowledge of radicalisation processes. The research is therefore based on the understanding that the information received was not simply assumptions among migrant workers about potential grievances or incentives driving radicalisation, but in some cases, was based on knowledge of radicalisation – on their lived experiences of friends, colleagues and family members. The responses of participants are divided into the following four classifications, which form a hierarchy of evidence:

1. Direct experience (that is to say, have been approached) of radicalisation/recruitment.

2. Know someone who has been radicalised/recruited.

3. Heard of someone (second-hand source or informed opinion, for instance, expert opinion) being radicalised/ recruited.

4. No personal knowledge (that is to say, knowledge obtained from the media, word of mouth or hearsay) of radicalisation/recruitment.

Most respondents interviewed in the fieldwork fall under classification 4. This explains why this report frames the research findings as 'perceptions' of radicalisation to violent extremism, instead of causal factors. However, there are a number of interviewees who either had a direct connection to recruitment to violent extremism or had an informed knowledge of radicalisation and recruitment. This project therefore prioritised classifications 2 and 3 in the data (classification 1 is beyond the scope of this study), focusing on the case studies of individuals who knew someone who was radicalised and recruited. This allows the report to build a profile of the violent extremists who went to fight in Syria or Iraq, as well as those who committed acts of terrorism.

Analytical Framework

The analytical framework used in this research was developed by RUSI in response to one of the biggest challenges of conducting research on radicalisation to violent extremism – how to interview radical individuals without easy access to a community radicalised to violence. It addresses the pertinent methodological question: in the absence of a radicalised cohort, how does one research radicalisation? In response, RUSI researchers have formulated an analytical framework that aims to analyse the drivers of radicalisation that takes into consideration the importance of context, and encompasses the widest possible range of interconnected factors. The framework is also used to systematise analysis and reduce bias. The framework is captured in Box 1.[20]

Radicalisation is a complex, multidimensional phenomenon, emerging from the interaction of micro-individual, enabling environment (socio-cultural) and macro-structural factors: it cannot be predicted by one variable alone. This report examines the findings gleaned from the data in relation to the inter-connected relationship between these dimensions. For violent extremist movements to develop, and for individuals to join them, requires an alignment of situational, social/cultural and individual factors. Using this framework, the research teams were able to use an analytical structure which helped understand the interaction between enabling factors, individual incentives and structural causes among the community of Central Asian labour migrants, as well as explore what effective resilience factors might already exist to help shape recommendations.

Box 1: A

Typology of Factors of Radicalisation Structural motivators: Commonly known as 'push factors', these include factors such as: repression; corruption; unemployment; inequality; discrimination;

a history of hostility between identity groups; and intervention by other states.

Individual incentives

Commonly understood in terms of 'pull factors', including: a sense of purpose (generated through acting in accordance with perceived ideological tenets); adventure; belonging; acceptance; identity; status; material enticements; coercion; and expected rewards in the afterlife.

Enabling factors

Not associated with individual motivations but with the presence of people, ideas, resources and spaces that encourage the development of radicalisation to occur, including: the presence of 'radical' mentors (including religious leaders, individuals from social networks, and so on); access to 'radical' online communities; social networks with violent-extremist associations; access to weaponry or other relevant items; a comparative lack of state influence; the presence of narratives; identity politics; an absence of familial support; the presence of vulnerable people (such as youth or criminals).

Resilience

Refers to the capability of individuals and communities to overcome adversity. At an individual level these include: personal experience, beliefs and values; family and friends; access to resources; personal attributes such as confidence and self-esteem; job; religion; and education. At a community (social level) these include: bonds between families and friends; and 'trust'. At a political level (structural), these can include: the rule of law; state welfare provisions; and just law enforcement agencies.

Definitions and Concepts

Research on radicalisation to violent extremism is beset by definitional and conceptual challenges. Other than the term 'migrant', this report adopts the definitions and concepts from

175

RUSI's Preventing and Countering Violent Extremism Training Curriculum for the European Commission,[21] to address key terms:

Migrant

IOM defines a migrant as 'any person who is moving or has moved across an international border or within a State away from his/her habitual place of residence, regardless of (1) the person's legal status; (2) whether the movement is voluntary or involuntary; (3) what the causes for the movement are; or (4) what the length of the stay is'.[22]

Violent extremism is the use of and support for violence in pursuit of ideological, religious or political goals.[23] Extremist violence is differentiated from other forms of violence by its motivation, it seeks to achieve ideological, religious or political goals. Violent extremism therefore includes terrorism, other forms of politically motivated violence, and some forms of communal violence.[24]

Violent extremism is not, however, a simple or uncontroversial concept. Of course, 'extreme' is a relative concept that can only be understood in relation to the 'norm', and as such it is unavoidably subjective. A difficulty arises from the relationship between violent manifestations of extremism and non-violent ones. The UN secretary-general has acknowledged this difficulty in the Plan of Action to Prevent Violent Extremism. This expressly avoids defining violent extremism, and acknowledges at the outset that 'violent extremism is a diverse phenomenon, without clear definition'.[25]

Radicalisation is commonly understood as the social and psychological process of incrementally experienced commitment to extremist ideologies.[26] Radicalisation describes a process where an individual's beliefs move from being relatively mainstream to seeking a drastic change in society. Radicalisation does not necessarily mean that those who experience it will become violent. However, once an individual decides that terror and violence are justified to achieve ideological, political or social change, that individual has become a violent extremist. Since radicalisation is a process, the term reflects a certain complexity as to how persons come to accept and support the use of terrorist means to achieve political objectives.

Radicalisation is a complex and potentially problematic concept and there are three issues that need to be understood:

a. Some authorities take the concept to imply that the end point of radicalisation is violence, whereas others take it to mean that the end point may be merely 'extreme' views (that is to say, without necessarily advocating/being involved in violence);

b. Radicalisation tends to imply unwarranted degrees of consistency and linearity in the trajectory from 'non-radical' to 'radical' (downplaying the extent to which everyone has their own path);

c. Radicalisation implies that a change in behaviour is the result of a change in belief. Mainstream psychology however shows that the relationship between beliefs and behaviours is surprisingly weak, and research into terrorism has shown that it is possible to hold extreme beliefs and to be non-violent, while some very violent extremists have not been influenced strongly by ideology.[27]

When trying to analyse the process of radicalisation to violence, extremism or somewhere in between, it is never a direct causal chain. Reflecting the complicated nature of human behaviour, it tends to be highly personal and individualised. There is no single clear path to radicalisation.

Recruitment is often used in conjunction with 'radicalisation'. However, the terms are not interchangeable. Recruitment implies that there is some external agent or influence that draws persons into engaging in terrorism, which is essentially a top-down process. Involvement in violent extremism, however, is not merely the result of recruiters looking out for potential recruits. In reality individuals are often proactive about becoming involved and as such the process are commonly more bottom-up than is implied by the term 'recruitment'.

Resilience refers to the capability of individuals and communities to overcome adversity. The EU defines resilience to violent

177

extremism as the capability of people, groups and communities to rebut and reject proponents of terrorism and the ideology they promote.[28] Despite the lack of agreed definitions of resilience in CVE policy and practice, it could nevertheless be regarded as a broad concept that captures a wide range of factors – ideas, institutions, issues, trends or values – that enable individuals and communities to resist or prevent violence, as well as recover or 'bounce back' from violent extremism. In this respect, resilience can be helpfully separated into protective factors (considered as a more passive type of logic, such as being able to 'absorb' an attack or threat) and responsive factors (a more proactive logic, for instance moving forward with life in a new and enhanced direction).

Vulnerability is defined as the condition of being capable of being injured; difficult to defend; open to moral or ideological attack. Within CVE, the word describes factors and characteristics associated with being susceptible to radicalisation.[29]

'At-Risk' refers to the criteria used to distinguish potential beneficiaries of targeted interventions at key 'at-risk' demographics. 'At-risk' individuals and communities have been identified through a needs assessment to be vulnerable to radicalisation and recruitment by violent extremists. Both ideas implicitly refer to individuals and groups of people who could potentially and are in fact exposed to the possibility of being radicalised or recruited. But a second dimension to the concept of both 'vulnerability' and 'at-risk' is the idea that a person is in need of special care, support, or protection because of the threat of violent extremism.

Limitations of the Research

This research captures the potential range of factors that contribute to the broader context within which cases of violent extremism emerge among Central Asian labour migrants in Russia. But the evidence base necessary for a detailed, comprehensive and methodologically rigorous assessment of violent extremism among Central Asian labour migrants in Russia is limited. The low volume of incidents and the relatively small number of individuals implicated in violent extremism mean that an empirical and causal explanation for the radicalisation of a minority of Central Asian migrants in Russia cannot be asserted. In addition, the psychological and sociological diversity of violent-extremist militants, coupled with the individualised, contextspecific nature of pathways towards violence, makes it difficult to definitively answer the questions of how and why a minority of Central Asian labour migrants went to fight in a third country. This challenge is made particularly acute without a sample of violent extremists to interview, and without longitudinal studies and ethnographic fieldwork.

The research design reflects some limitations. First, there is the issue of access to violent extremists – though this is mitigated through the milieu approach. Second, it is possible that the sample size does not necessarily reflect the community of radicalised individuals or labour migrants more broadly. Third, it is impossible to guarantee that interview subjects will honestly respond to questions on a sensitive topic such as extremism to someone they do not know. In addition, there is a huge diversity among Uzbek, Tajik and Kyrgyz communities and the cities and contexts in which the subjects live. All these factors make sweeping comparisons or comprehensive policy recommendations a challenge. A final point to highlight is that a number of the interviews were incomplete or included subjects not relevant to the research. This was a result of the difficult circumstances under which the interview teams operated.

Labour Migrants from Uzbekistan

Mohammed S Elshimi

This section is divided into five sub-sections that follow the analytical framework used to analyse the data. This includes: perceptions of structural motivation; perceptions of enabling factors; perceptions of individual incentives; perceptions of vulnerable and at-risk populations; and perceptions of resilience. This framework aims to analyse the drivers of radicalisation that takes into consideration the importance of context, as well as encompass the widest possible range of interconnected factors.

Perceptions of Structural Motivation

Migration Experience

According to eleven respondents (21%), there was a correlation between the adverse effects of migration to Russia in some instances – working illegally and ending up in severe financial debt – and being at more risk and vulnerable to violent extremism. Indeed, nine interviewees (17%) held the perception that the administrative and legal complexity of working in Russia discouraged labour migrants from seeking legal status, forcing many to live outside the law. In fact, 20 participants (38%), as well as all three in the focus group, highlighted the complexity and difficulties of the current administrative and legal procedure for registration as a major issue. According to interviewees, the process of registering legally for work in Russia entails registering for a visa and work patents (documents naturalising the status of migrants); the cost of completing the necessary paperwork; Russian language and history exams for migrants; and the short time-frame by which to do all of this.

One recurring complaint among respondents was about the complexity and difficulties of the registration process. A construction worker from Novosibirsk claimed, 'If we didn't have these problems with work and papers, then we would be able to solve our problems' (Novo 15).1 The leader of the Uzbek diaspora and now-Russian citizen in Astrakhan said of the difficulty of the language and history tests: 'Also, Russian literature and history exams for migrants are unrealistic, even Russian state officials can't pass them' (Astr 12). Four respondents also emphasised that the long and demanding process was not helped by the short window provided to complete all the paperwork and tests: the entire process has to be completed within one month or applicants are fined.

As a medium-sized business owner in Ekaterinburg remarked,7 days for a permit and 30 days to process documents is not enough' (Ekat 9). Moreover, interviewees shared the view that the process had become much more expensive. By the estimates of a business owner from Novosibirsk (Novo 16), it costs 40,000 roubles for a migrant to get all the necessary paperwork. A Russian professor in St Petersburg explained the consequences of an expensive administrative process: 'this [the expense] leads to the fact that many migrants from Tajikistan and Uzbekistan do not get patents because of their cost. I think it's almost half' (StPb 4).

Exploitation and Financial Hardship

Fifteen interviewees made a link between the precarious financial situation in which many labour migrants find themselves (especially illegal migrants) and an increased vulnerability to being targeted by violent extremist recruiters. A prevalent perception among 20 respondents (38%) was that economic vulnerability could be attributed to exploitation by various organisations and actors. For example, both legal and illegal migrants were being said to be exploited by intermediary organisations, employers, landlords, insurance companies, criminal networks and violent extremists, among others. A manager of a transportation company in Khabarovsk described this as 'Migrants are the "milking cow" for everyone: both countries, the different agencies, and now with terrorism as well ... corruption is booming on the backs of migrants' (Krsk 11). Indeed, a major consequence of the complex and costly administrative process for registration has been the emergence of companies and organisations that act as intermediaries who offer to help migrants with the registration process – for a fee. This is explained below by an Uzbek who created a cultural and adaptation centre in Samara:

The first problem is that the FMS [Federal Migration Service] does not cope with such a flow of migrants, especially during the season of work. Therefore, there are huge queues, so there are all sorts of intermediaries, including black [market] mediators. And that's why many migrants simply do not register and do not get patents, trying to stay here as long as possible, to earn as much as possible and go home knowing that at the border he will get a stamp with refusal of entry for a year. In a year, everything repeats itself again. But they are the first to be at risk, especially if they meet a recruiter. (Sama 10)

181

The problem with intermediaries is that they exploit migrants and either charge a lot of money for their services or end up defrauding their clients. For example, a Tatar assistant at a mosque in Samara highlighted the fact that 'Some come to the mosque, it turns out that they do not have any money, sometimes they were deceived by the mediators' (Sama 22). An employee at a centre that helps migrant workers in Krasnodar spoke about a case of embezzlement involving fifteen Uzbeks and an intermediary organisation: 'At the moment 15 people from Uzbekistan were scammed out of almost 3.5m [roubles] and these cases often happen' (Kdar 7).

Another reason some of the migrants are exploited is due to their legal status. Many interviewees argued that illegal migrants were particularly at risk due to their precarious position and poor working conditions. As the businessman from Novosibirsk put it, 'they don't have to pay an illegal much and they can be fired whenever' (Novo 16). The fact that illegal migrants do not enjoy any protection legally means that they are exploited by some employers, who are believed to offer work to illegal migrants through verbal agreement instead of work contracts, and who then subsequently benefit from their free labour before reneging on their verbal agreements. Illegal labour migrants are unlikely to complain about unpaid wages for fear that their employers would report them to the authorities. In addition, nine interviewees (17%) revealed that other actors also exploit the migration situation, like public officials and the insurance industry. The word used by one anonymous interviewee in Samara was 'corruption':

[It is] difficult for them to legalise, that is, to obtain documents permitting work, there is almost no social support, difficulties with residence and housing, and so on. Migrants are surrounded by corruption, starting with the employees of the Federal Migration Service and ending with medical personnel … it turns out that they do not have any money, sometimes they were deceived by the mediators. (Sama 22)

A sense for the cumulative effects of these costs was highlighted by a female Uzbek factory cleaner in Samara:

The patent is expensive; to get it is a whole story, a lot of expenses, including various black [market] intermediaries. The apartment also takes a lot of money, about 10 thousand roubles. Registration is also a difficult matter. In order to have at least something to send home you need to work for 16–17 hours. It's hard. (Sama 7)

One Uzbek male respondent working in construction in Novosibirsk highlighted the significance of these payments for an ordinary migrant: 'We only work 7 or 8 months of [the] year but we must spend almost 2 months' salary getting these (work) papers' (Novo 15). In effect, whether the migrant is legal or illegal, they begin life in Russia in considerable debt and having to endure considerable hardships.

Stigma and Securitisation

Almost half of the respondents complained about labour migrants facing discrimination from the authorities, the media and wider society. For some interviewees, there was growing stigma attached to being a labour migrant in Russia. Whilst only two (Mosc 3 and Kdar 7) linked this directly with radicalisation and recruitment, other participants highlighted the alienation and marginalisation resulting from the stigmatisation of labour migrants. One interviewee, a male in Krasnodar who works in a centre assisting migrant workers, said that 'People treat them [migrants] badly; even if they are Russians who were born in Uzbekistan and then came to Russia. It is very hard to earn money' (Kdar 7). According to the leader of a diaspora organisation in Astrakhan: 'In the media, they're artificially making the migrants the scapegoats, blaming them for all problems. People don't get to hear what benefits they are bringing for Russia, for the economy here, for development' (Astr 12).

There is a wider contextual reality of growing xenophobia being expressed in the press. This was explained by a Russian university professor in St Petersburg:

Understanding the Factors Contributing to Radicalisation among Central Asian Labour Migrants in Russia

Moscow has traditionally been wary of those who arrived. Previously, the word 'overrun' was attached to the temporary resident workers, to the Caucasians ... In just 2012–14, there has been an increase in labour migration ... Previously, and the context of the discussion was different. For example, 'compatriots abroad' help them and so on. And 'compatriots' was sometimes understood in the sense of fellow citizens of the former USSR. As for labour migration, they started talking actively about it in the media since the 2000s, more and more. (StPb 4)

Moreover, in Russia there is an increasingly securitised migration rhetoric that frames migrants as a threat. Several interviewees stated that police attention had increased since the St Petersburg bombing of April 2017. A male Uzbek from Ekaterinburg said 'because of these explosions, the attitude of the population and even the police has become worse' (Ekat 6). Others worried about police raids and, according to one Uzbek respondent from Ekaterinburg, 'people don't like to gather in flats, especially of late', also complaining that migrants were being treated 'as if we are all guilty' (Ekat 8). The mistreatment of labour migrants, where they are 'treated like cattle' and in which some policeman might abuse their powers by extracting payment ('a bottle'), was described by a market trader in Samara:

Then, under round-ups, people are treated like cattle, as enemies. But we are not enemies; we respect their President, Putin ... Then after the round-up everything ends with additional fees, [if] you cannot pay them, they will kick you back to your homeland. Because of high fees, many simply do not get patents and work illegally, but leave far away to the fields. There everything is decided with the policeman for a bottle. (Sama 6)

One of the interviewees, a teacher living in Ekaterinburg, described police arresting migrants 'to fill their quota of criminal arrests' (Ekat 7). A foreman from Moscow explained how the police sometimes raid mosques and temporarily detain them.

Because of such raids, 'young people stop coming to the mosque and create their own jamaats [groups]' (Mosc 3). He also said that migrants should 'not be humiliated by raids or put like prisoners into concentration camps' because this only prevents assimilation and creates hatred (Mosc 3). On migrants, he says, 'Their tolerance is strong but should not be tested all the time' (Mosc 3). Similarly, a worker at a migration adaptation centre in Krasnodar describes how an otherwise normal migrant might become adversely impacted: 'the raids on migrants begin. And if at such a moment, a good and unspoiled person let's say, doesn't have any documents, he starts hiding somewhere and gradually changes and begins to become different' (Kdar 7).

When asked about whom in the community can prevent radicalisation, a foreman in Astrakhan was sceptical: *and who said that we are reading to become Wahhabis, or how you say, radicals? Why do we have to 'work' with us? I often hear these words on the television, 'radical-shmadikal', 'extremists-pextremists' ... I even asked them 'there' [points up indicating law enforcement] what is this 'radicalism-padicalism'. Even they 'there' do not know. Everyone simply says that everyone in a mosque – is almost a radical. (Astr 11)*

His comments challenged the idea that there was a problem of migrant radicalisation to begin with. This wider discursive framing of migration in conjunction with the everyday experience of stigma makes some migrants conscious of their ethnic difference and low social status in Russian society.

Perceptions of the Enabling Factors

Recruitment to Violent Extremism

Of the 52 interviewees, two respondents (4%) had direct knowledge of recruitment and radicalisation – in other words, they knew someone who has been radicalised – while another three (6%) had an informed knowledge of radicalisation, in that they have either have conducted research on the issue or have seen court transcripts. More than a quarter of respondents mentioned that Caucasians (Dagestanis, Chechens, Azerbaijanis and Avars) were primarily responsible for recruitment, especially Chechens.

The comment in Box 2 is from an Uzbek female respondent who sheds light on the recruitment process in more detail.

Box 2: Informed Knowledge of Recruitment

In this case, the interviewee explains instances of recruitment based on court transcripts they have claimed to have seen (emphasis added):

Recruitment is primarily done by those from the Caucasus, everyone knows that. They do it through other recruits from Uzbek, Tajik and Kyrgyz communities. As our guys will be more open to speak and can only listen to their own. This is particularly important for Uzbeks – to have contact with their own. Then they transfer to the hands of the Caucasians and other people in a big circle. Begin to visit their lessons, read their literature. From court material I know, this is done in places far away, for example, in a forest in an abandoned children's camp. I know of a case where an Uzbek from the Bukinsky district [located in Uzbekistan] was involved in a jamaat …. He was involved in repairing the school. The Foreman was Tajik, who went to the Historical Mosque of Samara. He said find a couple of other guys. During his work he played films. For example, 'we shot down a plane', which was taken, as you know, after ISIS shot down a plane. He played it loud, not hiding from anyone. Then every evening this Tajik guy conducted conversations and working these guys. Then they were caught, likely reported by people from other brigades. [He] was later acquitted, as he cooperated with the investigation. They arrested the others … That were around February 2016 … there are more such examples (Sama 8).

Whilst the main recruiters at the top of the network are Caucasians, direct recruitment at the point of contact is done through the same ethnic group as those being recruited. The reliability of these comments regarding knowledge of recruitment can be questioned if taken on its own. However, the interviewee, who leads an organisation addressing migrant issues, bases her comments on 'court material'. In addition, a similar assertion was made by two other respondents, who suggested that Uzbek recruiters take their orders and are paid by Caucasian recruiters. There is also another possibility in the data that extremism is being transmitted into Russia from Central Asian countries.

This would posit that governments in Central Asian countries expel religious extremists, who then make their way to Russia where they find a more hospitable environment within which to operate and recruit. For example, an Uzbek diaspora leader in Novosibirsk believed extremists were largely from certain areas and cities in Uzbekistan, 'those from Fergana valley – Jalalabat and Osh Uzbeks' and those from 'the Namangan, JalalAbad and Andijan regions' (Novo 17). The businessman from Novosibirsk reiterated this view, saying that some Central Asians in Russia were 'already infected with extremism and they mix with Caucasians, Azeris and Tajiks who are Wahhabis like them, especially Uzbeks from Kyrgyzstan' (Novo 16).

Surprisingly, fifteen respondents (28%) spoke at length about methods of recruitment. According to these interviewees, recruiters use a variety of methods to recruit people. By far the most common method of recruitment is a monetary incentive. A female Uzbek court translator from Samara said that 'People were helped financially, giving small bonuses. And then, in their spare time, they were taught how to read the Qur'an, then they explained what "right Islam" is, what jihad is and so on' (Sama 8).

This use of deception as a tactic – dangling monetary incentives to lure recruits – was also highlighted by an Uzbek diaspora leader in Astrakhan. He reports that he has heard from 'a reliable person' that young recruits are given money and told they will work in construction. But when they get there 'they put a machine gun in their hands ... by then it is too late' (Astr 8). While the veracity of these comments is unreliable, his account nevertheless echoes comments made by another interviewee whose nephew was at the receiving end of violent extremist recruitment (see Box 3). As an Uzbek businessman living in Moscow said: 'They snare them with beautiful words, money and lies' (Mosc 1). Another tactic deployed by recruiters was forging friendships with their target. An Uzbek labourer in Novosibirsk (see Box 3) described first-

187

hand how his nephew was almost recruited in Kazan. Moreover, the same interviewee thought that recruiters seek those with military training (like his nephew), an assertion repeated by the businessman from Novosibirsk, who knew of attempts at recruitment in Uzbekistan. According to him, 'They choose guys who have served in the army or are physically strong ... They are also psychologists, they study whether someone could be used a suicide bomber' (Novo 16).

Box 3: Direct Knowledge of Recruitment In this case, a construction worker in Novosibirsk explained how his nephew was almost recruited in Kazan (emphasis added)

Those who are deceived are mostly young people who don't have money or believe the lies of the recruiters. That's how they tried to lure in my nephew. It's good that I was with him in Kazan. What would have happened otherwise? He'd be toast. He's only 23 years old. But he served in the army. He wanted to stay in the army but they wouldn't let him. People say that at first an Uzbek guy started hanging around him and then a Tajik and some Tatars. But a guy from my hometown warned me that my nephew was in contact with bad people. I immediately started to question him about it. I even beat him several times. But he wouldn't say anything. Then I took him here to Novosibirsk. But he wouldn't even do his work properly. But the boss understood and let him go. Now my nephew doesn't come to Russia any more, they found him work back home.

They promised him a good job in Turkey and said that sometimes he would have to travel to other countries. These recruiters know already that even though they are inexperienced, young people have heard about Syria and Iraq and would be afraid, refusing to go there. And everyone thinks that Turkey is paradise. Although I haven't heard how my nephew is getting on and what's happened to him. They also lure people in with promises of work in other Arabic countries.

But when these ... tried to fill his head with nonsense in Kazan, he changed a lot. It was like he was on drugs. (Novo 15)

Box 4: Direct Knowledge of Recruitment

In this case, a former Islamist explains how his employee's brother was recruited (emphasis added):

My employee ... younger brother was swindled by them. He understood when he stopped answering calls. When ... asked me to visit his brother, I sensed something was wrong with him and we went together to his place of work in Domodedovo. There we found his foreman. This guy was a fool and an alcoholic. We have a saying, the bad shepherd the sheep will die.

In one word, we began to ask the guys in the brigade what and how. It turned out that he often went on his phone, downloaded all sorts of videos. Then he changed completely and did not go to work. Then a Tajik came with him, redeemed his documents and they disappeared. Unfortunately, we did not find a guy... And before that, he began to stare at his phone which ... himself gave him as a present. That's what you need to take away from such young fool.

The young guy got caught by their tricks. I feel sorry for his family: the woman was left alone. Well, he died, probably. They do not live there for long.

They reach youth either through da'wat [to proselytise], or via the Internet ... I think there are many reasons and they all work together. For example, if we say that it's only about money, then we can say that, yes, the guys really are short on money. But in this case, too, he was brainwashed. And then, for sure, he is still being told that he will go to protect the Muslim brothers. There are a lot of reasons, I think, and that's how you should investigate this.

I think that the ways are different and da'watchi usually studies their victims ... But I would, of course, start by processing the possible victim. I would ask any usual, but very uncomfortable questions. For example, he would ask: 'Do you love your Koran? Do you love your belief/religion? Do you love your Prophet?'... Then he would ask ... 'Why then do not you defend your religion,

189

your Qu'ran, or you're Prophet?' These are the questions they ask, these servant of Satan. (Mosc 1)

In addition, this method of using entrapment was echoed by a market trader in Samara (Sama 6) who shared the story of how the son of a person he knew from his village in Uzbekistan was lured to Turkey by recruiters with the promise of a better job than the one he had in Russia. Another tactic is to appeal to people's emotions and generate emotional guilt. This is done through a narrative that espouses the notion that Muslims are being attacked and are suffering in different places, and the solution to this tragedy is to leave one's country and travel to Syria to defend Muslims against tyranny and injustice. A foreman in Astrakhan shed more light on this approach to recruitment: *'They approached a few of the guys on the sly - started to ask about their life, family. Then they tried to teach how to pray properly and spoke about Syria. They say, Muslims are killed there, but we are sitting quietly here, as if nothing is happening' (Astr 11).*

In terms of places of recruitment, most participants mentioned the mosque as the main site of recruitment, especially non-mainstream mosques, which were referred to as 'Wahhabi' by several respondents. A foreman from Astrakhan mentioned the 'red mosque':

Elshimi with Pantucci, Lain and Salman 21

Here there is a mosque - 'Red mosque'. When the Imam was Tatar, everything was fine. Then there was someone from Dagestan and they say the mosque became Wahhabi. I told the guys not to go there. We heard that they recruited 2-3 people there. It was shown on local TV. (Astr 11)

With respect to getting to Syria, eleven respondents (21%) said Russia to Turkey was the main route of travel. An interviewee from Krasnodar (Kadr 7) claimed that two ferries from Russia sailed to Turkey when relations were good between the two countries. Many travelled, he claimed, through the Caucasus too.

Box 5: Informed Knowledge of Recruitment

In this case, a Russian professor in Astrakhan reflects on whether there have been instances of recruitment of migrants in Astrakhan, including women (emphasis added):

[Going] there it's mostly Caucasians ... including long-time residents of Astrakhan. There have been cases amongst Tajiks and Uzbeks. True, I cannot speak of statistics. But there have been cases in the last 2–3 years, including those that were not announced in the media widely, but in private seminars or meetings. In the press, it sometimes slips out. Including the cases among migrants. Of course, most of these attempts were stopped by the law-enforcement agencies before they were sent on literally their 'last journey'. But, as for migrants, I would say that this is not a mass issue. According to my calculations, at first about one hundred people left the Astrakhan region for ISIS ... in 2013–14 and part of 2015. Although the numbers were defined in different ways – from 70 to 90–100. This group comprised of Avars, local Kazakhs [from Astrakhan], those of Kazakh and Avar mixed heritage, but there were Uzbeks with Tajiks. The bulk of them were local citizens. I did not hear about women. Now, as I heard in these forums, it has really subsided. Many were killed there and many people here know about it ... I do not know whether this is due to enlightenment or resources have dried up, generally a clear decline (Astr 10).

Box 6: Informed Knowledge of Recruitment

In response to the statement, 'Uzbeks are getting "wahhabisised" or are inclined to gather in jamaats', a professor of sociology responded (emphasis added):

56 people were detained in the prayer house ... In one of our new neighbourhoods almost beyond the city, on the outskirts beyond the city, on the outskirts. At first I thought it was an exaggeration. But then they say weapons were found. Here you cannot escape. (Sama 11).

The Internet

In Russia, the internet can be regarded as more of an enabling factor in processes of violent extremism than in Central Asian countries. This is primarily because Uzbeks in Russia have more and cheaper access to the internet than in Uzbekistan. Three interviewees (6%) specifically mentioned smartphones and seven (13%) spoke about the internet as a major information source. More importantly, nearly half of interviewees mentioned online recruitment and the availability of extremist material online. Eleven respondents (21%) mentioned videos with extremist content. An Uzbek in Moscow stated that 'the internet is and will remain a method of recruitment for these jamaats' (Mosc 3) and a business owner in Ekaterinburg said he guarded against this because 'It's true that the young guys watch other stuff on the internet. Us older guys warn them about this all the time. We understand that is how they get recruited' (Ekat 9).

In terms of radicalisation and recruitment, two interviewees (4%) said that the more radical form of social media content is delivered in stages and further up the recruitment process (Sama 7 and Astr 7). At first individuals receive innocuous messages on messaging apps such as WhatsApp or Telegram. Videos are shared too. Then content of a more religious nature is shared with them, which subsequently progresses to more serious material about jihad. A female factory worker in Samara explained:

On WhatsApp once came some stories about our Oisha-mother. I used to hear it from my grandmother. So I read what came to me on the phone. It was interesting. So I added the sender to my 'friends' list. Then other stories began to come, about our Prophet, about other saints. Then some more stories about jihad and other such ... My friend showed it to me, I immediately said that it was necessary to lock these messages down, expel from friends and erase. (Sama 7)

Some respondents described how recruiters would initially send their targets innocent videos about reading the Qu'ran before progressing to more violent content. This was explained by a construction worker in Astrakhan:

*Here, on the internet, wherever you want you can freely climb. Right.
There everything is simple and [you] come across all sorts of videos,
as they told me, first simple stories, or there are lessons on the correct
reading of the Qu'ran and others like that. And then they also send
other things that attract young people and all that. That is, they lure
gradually. See for yourself on the internet. As soon as you climb into
such a place, you will be lured, sent something. This was told to us.
Therefore, I have a simple phone only for communication. And the
young, we banned other phones. Only under our control. (Astr 7)*

A More Permissive Environment for Exposure to Alternative Ideas and People

An important finding from the data is that Russia potentially
presents a more conducive environment for the exposure to
alternative forms of religion and lifestyle than Central Asian
countries. This is due to a combination of complex and interrelated
factors.

First, governments in Central Asian countries are perceived to
have a less tolerant record of accommodating religion than Russia
in recent history. Two of the interviewees said that there is more
religious freedom in Russia than at home, as expressed by this
respondent in Samara: 'They enjoy freedom of religion, sometimes
more than at home' (Sama 22). This idea was echoed by an Uzbek
diaspora leader in Khabarovsk: 'In Russia, Muslims normally
feel themselves religiously, they are not forbidden to read namaz
[prayer] the mosque is officially registered' (Khab 25). Some
respondents suggested that some Islamists from Central Asian
countries who have been proscribed and exiled from their home
countries exploit the more permissive spaces found in Russia.

Second, there is an increased possibility for some migrant workers
to come into greater contact with either more puritanical readings
of Islam or more radical versions of Islam (the two are not the same,
nor are they necessarily linked), as well as a more diverse group of
people in Russia than back in their home countries. For a third
of interviewees, this greater exposure to more 'extreme' or radical
interpretations of Islam was blamed on either the 'Wahhabis',

recruiters from the Caucasus, and/or the internet. The frequency with which the term 'Wahhabi' was used among interviewees was particularly salient. The term was used pejoratively and was associated with 'extremism', often being blamed as the root cause behind a number of problems.

The term was associated with many things, including: the conflict in Syria; the growing Islamisation of Central Asians; Chechen recruiters; and the threat to the moderation embodied in the traditional school of jurisprudence (hanafi) that most Central Asians follow. For example, one interviewee blamed the US and Wahhabis for the conflict in Syria, stating that they were 'guilty of everything. Together they are destroying Muslims', while Russia was applauded for 'helping good Muslims fight against Wahhabism' (Novo 14). When another interviewee, a foreman in Astrakhan, was asked to define 'Wahhabi', he defined it as 'those who go into politics and forget about real faith ... they call for taking up arms' (Astr 11). He also went on to blame 'Wahhabis' for the civil war in Tajikistan.

Third, the cultural displacement that can be associated with migrating to Russia means a greater appeal to migrants of a global Islamic identity that transcends ethnic and national origins. For some individuals, the adoption of religion in a new and strange environment can be strategic; though it can also be emotional, intellectual and psychological, among other reasons. It can help the migrant to cooperate and establish a connection with other migrants, as well as to solicit support from a wider network of people. This group bonding often occurs through common rituals, something a professed attachment to a religious identity can facilitate. Outward expressions of religion can also be used to preserve identity and to prove to families back home that they have not entirely assimilated and forgotten their origins. The sociological process of this experience was highlighted by the Russian *professor in St Petersburg*:

When migrants come here, they try to build their relations. For example, in a hostel. What is the closest way to them? Of course, this is through Islamic ethics. At least outwardly, as observance of some elementary norms, including ritual ones. Therefore, for them, religiosity becomes more important for them than at home, since social ties must be built on some kind of ethics. It is the closest and most understandable. Therefore, Islam becomes an instrument for building internal relations; it is understandable, comfortable, and so on ... But sometimes you need to prove to your parents and relatives that you are not spoiled and that you have not become an alcoholic and that's why they keep their external Islamic ethics in their behaviour. (StPb 4)

However, while some individuals adopt 'external Islamic ethics', according to three respondents most Uzbek migrant workers were non-observant and did not practise Islamic religious rituals. For example, the leader of a diaspora organisation in Astrakhan said this about religious observance:

Since most are not completely religious, that is, they all consider themselves, of course, Muslims, but they do not adhere to religious rituals so much; especially those that are from Kashkadarya, Surkhandarya, Khorezm. And about 65% of Uzbek migrants come from Khorezm, since here they are geographically close. (Astr 12)

Perceptions of Individual Incentives

Money/Economic Incentives

According to 23 interviewees (44%), money was perceived as an incentive for joining violent extremist organisations. The standard narrative in these interviews was that the desire for money drives people towards violent extremism because many labour migrants are in severe debt. Their grave financial position is compounded for illegal migrants, as they have fewer opportunities available and less recourse to mainstream channels of support. In this vulnerable financial, social and psychological state they become prey for criminal gangs and, in some cases, violent-extremist recruiters. For fifteen interviewees (29%), it is at this point that violent extremist groups enter the picture: they promise to alleviate the financial woes of migrants and provide them with support. Once trust is earned, recruiters begin to deploy religious discourse and narratives to proselytise and persuade such individuals to fight in the Middle East. Migrants are also promised the prospect of new jobs and a regular salary as part of a package of taking part in the building of a new state – an Islamic State. This prevailing narrative was expressed by both a construction worker and a director of a company in Novosibirsk:

I heard about one guy from my hometown that disappeared in Moscow. He was young and unexperienced in life. He had no money as his boss wouldn't pay him. And he was robbed on the metro of everything he had left. Someone helped him then and convinced him to leave for Turkey. All because he had contact with some Wahhabis. (Novo 14)

As I said, if a cell is set up then they will try first of all to recruit those guys who have problems. Primarily money problems. When they have neither food nor money. I've heard of cases where a guy is promised 5,000 dollars to send to his family and he agrees to the deal, seeing it as the answer to all his problems. He doesn't think about the consequences and about how he just sold his life for those 5,000 dollars. (Novo 16)

However, four interviewees (8%) offered a different view on the primacy of monetary incentives. An Uzbek diaspora leader in Astrakhan, for example, noted that 'hundreds and thousands of migrants fall into hopeless situations. But they don't all run to pick up a rifle or get on a plane to Syria' (Astr 8). A couple of the participants mentioned that in fact some of the recruits had jobs and money and were not financially vulnerable. An Uzbek male from Ekaterinburg said that some of the recruits had 'a business, a job and rich parents' (Ekat 7), while an Uzbek male interviewee who ran a business in Novosibirsk described how 'a couple of young guys from Namangan were recruited' (Novo 16), even though they had good jobs and legal status.

Religion

Twelve interviewees (23%) mentioned religion as an incentive for becoming engaged with violent extremism. The data reveals two main perceptions on the role of religion in violent extremism. The first presents a picture of a particular version of Islam ('Wahhabis') as corrupting mainstream orthodoxy (the madhabs3) among Central Asians which leads to violence. The 'Wahhabis' were also notably blamed, along with the US, for the war in Syria by many of the participants. According to this view, labour migrants are deceived by a misunderstanding of Islam. It is a view that downplays the agency of radicalised labour migrants and depicts them as being manipulated and duped by 'Wahhabis'. An example of this understanding was articulated by the Russian professor in Astrakhan:

The scheme is simple. They approach a guy from Central Asia [in the bazaar] and ask: 'Are you a Muslim? If so, why do not you pray', and so on. They lead them to the mosque, where the bulk of them are Caucasians. So [the Central Asian] finds himself in the very environment that suppresses him and prepares him for manipulation. Therefore, the 'Islamization' of Muslims from Uzbekistan, for example, is reinforced here, but not in Uzbekistan. (Astr 10)

In contrast, the second view presents religion as a source of identity and acts as a moral standard which individuals feel obliged to take seriously. Rather than cause the problem of violent extremism per se, this view of the role of religion provides radicalised individuals with a sense of purpose and mission, either to defend Muslims against oppression – by the Assad government in Syria – or to help Muslims to create an Islamic State. In this view of religion, labour migrants are more empowered. An Uzbek leader in Astrakhan linked radicalisation to grievance: 'When a person sees constant violations of fairness and norms, he becomes something of a revolutionary, even extremist' (Astr 8). This idea was echoed by a director of a company in Novosibirsk, who remarked that some young people think that 'the war over there [Syria] is a war for justice, Islam, and Allah' (Novo 16).

Adventure

The third and least-referenced individual factor mentioned was the idea of seeking 'adventure': the notion some young people either seek to become 'heroes', or are bored with their lives and thus seek a sense of adventure. It is essentially about the hope for a different life. An Uzbek diaspora leader in Novosibirsk said that there were many newly religious recruits, mostly 'those who don't work and don't play sport, they have more free time' (Novo 17). On the whole, this desire was framed as something negative and foolish – the result of impulsive and impetuous youngsters. A religious leader in Samara acknowledged that, for some young people, the war in Syria is a 'jihad' and they are drawn to the adventure associated with it: 'It is very easy for them to believe that the war in Syria is a jihad. That is, they are also looking for some kind of adventure or even to be glorified as heroes. That is, completely without realizing what is happening' (Sama 22).

Perceptions of Vulnerable and At-Risk Populations

Interviewees identified the following categories of people as 'vulnerable' to violent extremism, presented here in order of the frequency with which each term was used:

1. Youth.

2. Illegal migrants.

3. Uneducated migrants: particularly an inability to speak Russian.

4. Loners: individuals disconnected from family and kinship groups.

More than half the respondents cited youth as a factor in recruitment. A construction worker from Novosibirsk described recruits as 'young, stupid, and inexperienced' (Novo 15), arguing that older men would be held back by thoughts of their family. This was supported by the former Islamist in Moscow, who said an older man would not join because 'he has responsibility, children and a family' (Mosc 1). An Uzbek leader in Astrakhan reinforced this view, claiming that 'Some team leaders only take unmarried guys. A married man has responsibilities and looks at the world differently' (Astr 8).

The second type of person identified as vulnerable to recruitment and radicalisation was illegal migrants. The distinction between legal and illegal has profound consequences for migrant workers. Legal migrant workers earn more, enjoy greater security and are less vulnerable to exploitation. The perception was that it was illegal migrant workers, rather than legal ones, who were preyed on by both violent-extremist recruiters and criminal networks because of financial difficulty and the absence of legal protections. According to a male in Ekaterinburg, 'Money comes above all else ... An illegal immigrant is easy to recruit if he is left without money' (Ekat 6).

Third, uneducated migrants were cited as vulnerable to recruitment. A female interviewee in Samara explained:

Most of them [Uzbeks] do not know Russian well, many who [have recently] come from kishlaks [rural settlements of semi-nomadic people], without [a profession], come on their own, without being called here by acquaintances and relatives. Of course, for adaptation such people are the most problematic,and it is they who become victims of fraudsters from intermediaries or even get involved in sects who are eagerly looking for just such ... many are very poorly literate. I'm not talking about religious, but about secular reading and writing. They do not know and do not understand local laws, customs or culture. This is also important for adaptation. (Sama 8).

Moreover, seven respondents (13%) mentioned the lack of language skills as a major source of vulnerability for migrant workers. The inability of many migrants to speak Russian hampered their ability to compete in the job market and made adaptation to social and cultural life in Russia a challenge. With respect to recruitment, this would suggest that contact with Caucasian violent extremists would be minimal, and would thus mean that the main agents of radicalisation are other Uzbeks. However, the data is silent on the link between the inability of some migrants to speak Russian and how it plays into violent extremists' recruitment methods. A man working in the migration adaptation centre in Krasnodar said those migrants unable to adapt risked becoming slaves: 'Out of 100 maybe only 5 have knowledge of Russian. They are the only ones with a chance to adapt properly. 50% of those coming were born in villages. They come here on the bus without any money and then end up on the streets. These are "prepared slaves"' (Kdar 7).

The last group vulnerable to violent extremism was lonely individuals or those migrants disconnected from family and ties of kinship. The absence of family in a foreign country and a lack of connection with other members of their own ethnic groups were cited as a form of vulnerability. One of the men from Ekaterinburg said those who came 'without relatives, neighbours or friends who know the situation and can find them work were vulnerable' (Ekat 7). The idea is that the lack of usual social or ethical standards provided by a group makes individuals more conducive and vulnerable to new ideas, practices and lifestyles. The effect of this isolation was described by a Russian professor as a form of 'psychological trauma':

Most have learned to adapt, create alternative networks. But some fall out of these networks. And for some of them it becomes some kind of psychological trauma. Therefore, it is necessary to look at specific cases separately. And such a suspended state, as you said, is the cause of the psychological weak spot that recruiters use. (StPb 4)

Perceptions of Resilience

Employment

Employment was seen by 21 respondents (40%) and all three in the focus group as the pre-eminent source of resilience. Labour migrants are in Russia to work and make money; many have responsibilities back in their home countries, with many participants in the study having families to support. Also, for six of the interviewees (12%), there were few or no employment opportunities in Uzbekistan. These factors provided strong incentives for labour migrants to focus their efforts on work. In fact, based on the response to a question regarding leisure and social life, for the majority of labour migrants in the study work consumed their life.

This was explained by a Russian academic in St Petersburg: 'the working migrant is working intensely here, getting tired, he already by and large has no time for abstract activities and therefore nothing of this kind is going on with him' (StPb 4). An Uzbek businessman in Astrakhan reiterated this point: 'No one will run off to a jamaat, they are busy only with their work and with providing for their family' (Astr 8). A male interviewee from Krasnodar described how providing for one's family could provide greater motivation than religion: 'I have other goals [aside from religion] – I have children and they need to stand on their own feet, so they can study somewhere good and then find their own life' (Kras 6).

Community Hierarchy and Leadership

Over half of respondents stressed the role of leadership and forms of communal hierarchy as a reliable source of resilience. Whether it is the figure of the foreman, the wise religious elder, or the community representative, the common idea that unites each is the notion of leadership and hierarchy. Interviewees conveyed a clear sense that among Uzbeks there is an established culture built around hierarchy, and that those in leadership positions are older and more experienced than younger labour migrants.

Another critical source of resilience is the role of the foreman in the workplace. The foreman is responsible for the direction and supervision of a group of workers, but also seems to have an active role in providing pastoral care to his 'brigade', such as by mentoring. This relationship between foreman and his team of workers, particularly in relation to violent extremism, is highlighted by one foreman in the construction industry who lives in Astrakhan: 'They [recruiters] are cunning, but we already understand everything. Now we don't have naifs and fools. We began to understand everything. All foremen speak with their people. And here at the construction sites and bazaars' (Astr 11).

An Uzbek leader of the diaspora in Astrakhan explained the role of the foreman in detail:

Of course the community is very hierarchical. The most senior of his group is the Senior Foreman. He is responsible for everything, even of the behaviour of his subordinates. At the second level [are the] foreman's assistants. In the community of countrymen, there are also the main foremen, but there are also authorities which know religious ethics, that is who can correctly direct religious ritual.

[On youth and where they chat:] mainly at work ... sometimes they sit in a café, but most often in our Uzbek chaikhanas [tea houses] – there are already many in Astrakhan. Young people particularly prefer these places ... but everything only with the permission of the foreman.

In several cases, if the foreman does not respond to certain requirements, people will leave his group and join another brigade. Therefore, foremen are forced to adhere to elementary rules ... we, that is our office and service – we are also for them an authority. (Astr 12)

The idea of a role model is a permanent feature of labour migrant lives. Respect for elders or the pious and wise older person is evident from the data. As one of the interviewees in Ekaterinburg put it, 'There are the elders and among us there are good experts in Islam. They also constantly warn us and especially our young people' (Ekat 6). A diaspora leader of Novosibirsk described how youngsters rely on the older men and 'ask them for advice when necessary' (Novo 17). Similarly, a labourer in Astrakhan said 'Us older guys in the team keep a close eye on the young ones', and also 'Here we are like soldiers. We must respect our commanders ... They are good people ... who will keep us from wrong' (Astr 11). It is important to stress that this relationship between older and younger generation and social arrangements configured along hierarchical lines can act as a strong source of resilience.

Positive Role of the Authorities

Another form of resilience is the positive role of the Russian authorities and their relationship to diaspora communities. Several interviewees stressed that diaspora communities have links to the Russian security services and they cooperate to remove recruiters. As one man from Ekaterinburg said, 'If we find them out, we will get them deported' (Ekat 8). Similarly, the diaspora leader in Krasnoyarsk claimed 'Our diaspora is in frequent contact with the security services' (Krsk 10), while a business owner in Ekaterinburg said 'We diaspora heads co-operate much with each other and the local security services' (Ekat 9). This relationship between the local authorities and the diaspora was explained by a representative of an Uzbek diaspora organisation in Khabarovsk:

We have not had such cases in Khabarovsk, everything is in sight in our community and if conversations about recruitment happen somewhere, it becomes immediately known. In addition, local authorities constantly warn us and we are working with the population to work – explaining to them that if they meet such people, then do not give in to their agitation. (Khab 25)

Community Support

Community support has been identified as a source of resilience to violent extremism. The data indicates that Uzbek labour migrants have established community networks in Russia, albeit rudimentarily in some cities. Parts of these new structures are connected to the closeknit configurations of families and friends that constitute local diaspora populations. An Uzbek construction worker in Novosibirsk explained the importance of having friends when arriving in Russia: 'When people from back home come here they don't understand that they need reliable friends. You can't live here without a reliable job and reliable friends' (Novo 14). Labour migrants are likely to travel to areas and cities where a family or friend is already living there. A leader of the Uzbek diaspora in Irkutsk explained:

Uzbeks are organised into groups by place/city of origin, or even smaller, and each has a senior person, starshiy [senior supervisor4] who is respected and serves as the focal point for local administration, the diaspora organisations, to reach the migrants, and who are the most trusted leaders for the migrants, who know all about every person in their circle. (Irku 16)

It is important not only to know about the availability of work in a particular industry (which can partly explain why certain industries and sectors of work become dominated by a particular ethnic group), but also to know about accommodation and general support. According to the data, the major figureheads of these community networks are diaspora leaders, mosque leaders, foremen, the consulate, and cultural centres. Each of these roles and spheres represent different practical and symbolic functions.

For example, the diaspora leader does not have an official obligation to help those who come to him requesting help, but they do so out of goodwill and social commitment. The data shows that some of the support that leaders provide ranges from helping migrants to fill in documents and forms, to providing them with national newspapers, helping with funeral arrangements, and general information and advice. This was explained by a male construction worker in Novosibirsk: '[Migrants have] no networks or communication outside their own group. But with some issues, they turn to diaspora leader —, he is very helpful and respected. Helps with getting patents, etc. Rarely, they also turn to the Consul' (Novo 19). The mosque plays a more pastoral role, emphasising a more spiritual, educational and moral source of support to migrant workers. According to two of the interviewees working in mosques (Sama 9 and 22), the mosque also acts as a place of refuge for vulnerable labour migrants.

Education

The importance of being 'educated' as a source of resilience to violent extremism was referred to by seventeen interviewees (33%), albeit it meant different things to different people. Depending on the context, education could refer to secular, moral, religious, or cultural education. For example, an Uzbek market trader in Samara highlighted a particular form of education that helped him when migrating to Russia and which acted as a form of protection against radicalisation

Because I'm a normal person, because, I got proper education at home. I was accompanied by the whole mahalla [community] when I left for the first time. The old men said different things, but warned – 'do not go along the crooked road.' All parents, whose children leave the house, whether for work or study, let them also gather the elderly and let their child listen to the aksakals [elders]. This is important. I will say so – children will be like their parents. (Sama 6)

From his comments, education is seen in terms of moral and social upbringing. Education, then, is perceived to act as a form of resilience in several ways. First, education provides labour migrants with the ability to challenge extremist interpretations of religion with greater confidence. Second, it equips labour migrants for life in Russia. Several interviewees spoke about the importance of speaking Russian. Third, education provides them with the skills to compete in the marketplace. Fourth, a good education increases the options and opportunities available to labour migrants seeking to integrate into Russian life, thereby mitigating the risk of being drawn into vulnerable situations.

Religion

For a third of respondents, a better understanding of Islam was seen as a form of resilience. Even a basic understanding of Islam allows labour migrants to challenge and evaluate violent-extremist ideology. An Uzbek teacher in Ekaterinburg explained that: 'A person will refuse a recruiter because he understands what Islam is and has listened to the imam' (Ekat 7). This knowledge does not have to be deep or extensive. Even a basic understanding of Islam can empower an individual to assertively challenge violent-extremist ideology, as illustrated in the following story from an Uzbek male construction foreman in Astrakhan recounting an incident in which one of his colleagues was told by a stranger in a mosque that he should go and fight in Syria:

One of my guys is not bad on religion. But he answered beautifully – 'go – fight there yourself, if you are so worried about these Wahhabis.' He stood up to fight – there the other guys stopped ... And I always tell guys that if they try to entice you somewhere, answer the same – let them go [to Syria]. [The extremists] themselves will not go, but they will count the dollars for each deceived, and put them in their pocket. (Astr 11)

However, 20 respondents (38%) identified with their mainstream religious traditions and cited jamaats and Salafist and Wahhabist deviations from recognised, established religious authorities as a form of vulnerability. The former Islamist, for example, stressed the necessity of staying 'with the Hanafi school of Islam, our trusted and correct path' (Mosc 1). Whilst remaining impartial on the issue of distinctions between the various internal dynamics of Islam, the perception of most of the Uzbek respondents are judged to be accurate: that the prevalence of a mainstream and recognised tradition of Islam can and does act as a form of resilience.

Perceptions of Violence and Politics

Four of the respondents expressed a lack of interest in politics. Their apolitical position was due to their very busy lifestyles as migrant workers. In other words, most migrant workers do not have time for leisure, let alone engaging with politics. This does not mean political views were not conveyed. Where political views were articulated, they seemed to mirror mainstream Russian narratives, particularly in relation to the conflict in Syria.

However, nine respondents (17%) condemned the use of violence to achieve political ends. This is articulated by a female factory worker in Samara:

To use violence, especially on behalf of Islam or another religion – this is not politics anymore, it's a psychological problem of these guys. They think – well, you stabbed a man and put this video on the Internet, and you're a hero. He's just an idiot and sick. But the worst thing is that after watching this information people in the world start to think that all Muslims and Muslim women are like that.

In particular, many felt that the conflict in Syria, particularly the existence and behaviour of Daesh, or what was often and misleadingly referred to as 'Wahhabi', had tarnished the image of Islam. Some participants suggested that one factor of resilience among migrant workers is that; on the whole, they are disengaged from politics compared to the wider population.

Labour Migrants from Kyrgyzstan

Sarah Lain

THIS SECTION IS divided into five sub-sections that follow the analytical framework used to analyse the data. This includes perceptions of structural motivation; perceptions of enabling factors; perceptions of individual incentives; perceptions of vulnerable and at-risk populations; and perceptions of resilience. This framework aims to analyse the drivers of radicalisation that takes into consideration the importance of context, as well as encompass the widest possible range of interconnected factors.

Perceptions of Structural Motivation

General Discrimination

Although discrimination was not necessarily explicitly linked to radicalisation by interviewees, it was mentioned as a common challenge and could be considered a structural motivation. Eleven individuals (13%) mentioned discrimination to varying degrees. Three (4%) referenced the use of the derogatory term churka (literally, 'block of wood') for Central Asians (Mosv 31, Ekat 14, and Khab 3). An Uzbek male from Osh, living in Moscow and working on a construction site, felt that Russians regard Central Asians as 'second-class citizens' (Mosc 23). Another male respondent living in Moscow working as a doctor felt that racism affected the progression of professionals in his field.

He said that in his clinic, 'people with less experience are getting promoted to leadership positions. That's because the latter are Slavic by ethnicity' (Mosc 27). However, discrimination was by no means a universal feeling or experience. At least three people (Othe 5, Krsk 15, and Sama 18) specifically said they had never had issues with discrimination or that where there were initial suspicions, they faded away with time. For example, an Uzbek male interviewee from Osh who lives in Moscow working as a manager at a microcredit organisation (Othe 5) did not feel there was any discrimination, and did not feel that his nationality or ethnicity had ever held him back.

Six people (7%) did make specific references to how assumptions, not just discrimination, can be linked to perceptions of Islam and terrorism (Sama 12, Othe 3, Mosc 24, Mosc 26, Mosc 28, and Kdar 15). One nineteen-year-old ethnic Uzbek student living in Samara said, 'I know people, Muslims, who have grown beards, and these are normal people. But here they think that if someone has a beard – he's an ISIL supporter' (Sama 12). Another ethnic Uzbek man who previously worked as a construction worker in Russia but now resides in Kyrgyzstan echoed this, saying that in Russia, 'peaceful Muslims are being kept in contempt. They are being blamed for terrorist acts. We are peaceful people. Discrimination of people is also leading to radicalization' (Othe 3).

Four individuals (Mosc 28, Mosc 24, Kdar 15, and Mosc 25) mentioned how they felt that some suspicions are directed at Central Asians in part due to Russian societal perceptions of their association with terrorism. Three mentioned the St Petersburg Metro bombing, carried out by a young ethnic Uzbek male from Kyrgyzstan in April 2017 (relatively recently to when the interviews took place). One ethnic Uzbek male interviewee working in construction in Moscow said that:

the events of recent times, such as the explosions in the metro, all that is presented in such a way that migrants are potential terrorists. Locals don't like when migrants gather in large numbers [for example, for prayers] and cause traffic jams, they don't like how migrants behave, and even how they dress. All that irritates the local population of Moscow. (Mosc 24)

Two other individuals – one ethnic Kyrgyz female living in Moscow (Mosc 28) and a Kyrgyz male living in Krasnodar (Kdar 15) – noted how monitoring and checks from Russian authorities had increased following the attack.

Discrimination by Authorities

Fifteen respondents (18%) mentioned that they had experienced discrimination by Russian authorities in some form. Most of the complaints related to abuse of position, with some respondents mentioning the practical need to pay bribes as well as a more general sense of injustice in the system. For example, one ethnic Uzbek male residing in Krasnodar, who runs a private company assisting migrants with documentation, said:

[T]here are many cases when the police stop the migrants without any reason, make arrests, and extort money … The pretext–the lack of proper documents. There were cases when police slipped counterfeit bills to the migrants and accused them of wrongdoing and extorted money. How can migrants protect themselves in such cases? (Kdar 2)

On the other hand, two respondents – an ethnic Uzbek male working in construction in St Petersburg (StPb 11) and an ethnic Kyrgyz male who works among the diaspora in St Petersburg (StPb 9) – said they had not had issues with authorities and suggested that, if migrants kept their documents in order, there should be no problem. In their view, therefore, issues with the authorities are usually the fault of the migrant workers themselves. In particular, the ethnic Kyrgyz male said '[other migrants] complain that they are stopped and arrested by militia [police in Russia]. I explain that I have not been stopped or detained for 30 years … if you behave yourself, nobody will touch you' (StPb 9).

One respondent believed that discrimination from the authorities could be a driver of radicalisation. This respondent was an ethnic Azerbaijani from Osh. He resides in Moscow, but had previously served time in prison in Kyrgyzstan for being part of the banned organisation, Hizb-ut-Tahrir.[1] He said, 'they join [ISIS], because they were persecuted, and they wish revenge … I know so many people who dream of revenge against [law enforcement agencies]' (Mosc 25). However, because of his past, his views might not necessarily be mainstream, and it is also important to note that his views are likely to have been negatively affected by his experience in prison.

Yet some support for this view also came from an ethnic Uzbek male living in St Petersburg, who provided insight as to why his brother left for Syria by reflecting on the negative role of law enforcement in Kyrgyzstan as a factor in his radicalisation process:

My brother went to Syria [from southern Kyrgyzstan]. Before he went there, he was given a very difficult time [by the law-enforcement agencies], was summoned to interrogations, put in jail, extorted money from, and finally he was pushed to go to Syria where he died [while fighting]. If I had the possibility and was given an automatic rifle, I would have killed every one of the offenders [from the authorities] of my brother, I would shoot each of them. (StPb 10)

Challenges Relating to Employment

Despite many Kyrgyz respondents repeatedly highlighting that since their country joined the Eurasian Economic Union in 2015, the process to start working in Russia has become easier, they still faced some challenges. Four interviewees (5%) mentioned issues around employers. Two (Kdar 3 and Irku22) said some migrant workers struggle because they fail to secure formal contracts with employers. A female Kyrgyz diaspora leader blamed this on employers, saying 'Russian employers do not want to pay taxes and therefore our people are hired without paperwork' (Kdar 03). An ethnic Kyrgyz male who represents the diaspora in Irkutsk instead blamed the migrant workers themselves, saying 'newly arrived migrants do not try to secure written agreement ... it happens due to lack of education. They don't know laws' (Irku 22).

Two others (Ekat 14 and Sama 13) complained of employers not paying wages on time, or at all. A male Kyrgyz seasonal migrant worker living in Ekaterinburg referred to his experience: '[the employer] fired us for no reason, but we worked without a contract – she did not give us a salary. We call, but she does not pick up. We can only blame ourselves, since we worked without an employment contract' (Ekat 14). Four people (Khab 4, Irku 13, Irku 14, and Kdar 9) mentioned the issue of intermediaries scamming migrant workers. For example, a Kyrgyz male who works for local government said, 'there are a lot of intermediaries. They find job offers/vacancies here and then invite their own people [to Russia]. They take their passports, allegedly for registration purposes, and then in such a way the exploitation begins' (Irku 13). A Kyrgyz male working as a doctor noted, 'yes, there are a lot of scammers among our fellow countrymen' (Irku 14).

Restrictions at Home

Four respondents (Irku 14, Othe 5, Mosc 25 and Mosc 24) felt that issues with radicalisation have their origins at home, particularly due to the control exercised by governments there, though most were quick to differentiate Kyrgyzstan as more open than Uzbekistan and Tajikistan. One Kyrgyz male who works as a doctor in Irkutsk specifically mentioned religious persecution in Tajikistan and Uzbekistan:

In the other republics other than Kyrgyzstan, Muslims are subjected to persecution, for example, in Tajikistan, Uzbekistan, repressions against those who wear scarves or beards. There is freedom in Russia; they can do what they are prohibited from doing in these countries ... When something is banned or people are limited, it leads to more interest and craving for all these forbidden things. (Irku 14)

Another ethnic Uzbek from Kyrgyzstan echoed this, saying, 'I, for example, am acquainted with the imam from Uzbekistan. According to him, the fact that the Uzbek authorities strongly control mosques and religious education promotes the growth of radical ideologies' (Othe 5).

Grievances at home were also specifically perceived as a driver of why people go to Syria. One ethnic Uzbek male interviewee who lives in Moscow said: 'we must understand that the preconditions for radicalizations happen in Central Asian countries. Some believers get pressured and pushed around by official religious bodies, they get abused by repressive activities of law enforcement agencies, too' (Mosc 24).

This rationale was also supported by another ethnic Uzbek who had previously worked in Novosibirsk and Khabarovsk, who said:

[M]oney and unemployment are not involved. Most of them had everything. Probably, some people were motivated by the repressive policies of the government, and the fact that they could not pray freely [in Kyrgyzstan] ... Initially, not understanding the situation, I, too, was supporting the war in Syria. But later, with God's help, I understood things better and saw everything in a different light. (Othe 3)

On the other hand, some Kyrgyz participants associated the relative freedom of Russia with a permissive environment in which radicalisation could take place. This somewhat paradoxical set of conclusions about the role of societal openness in the process of radicalisation – with, on the one hand, some believing that the relatively closed nature of Tajikistan and Uzbekistan drives radicalisation, while on the other, others believing that the relative openness of Russia and Kyrgyzstan can both drive radicalisation (in Russia) and act as a protective factor against radicalisation (in Kyrgyzstan) – highlights the degree to which it is not clear that freedom of expression is necessarily linked to the process of radicalisation. Whilst this is possibly a valid conclusion, the discussion could also more simply reflect ethnic bias, in that the Kyrgyz interview subjects are highlighting how their country is better than the other Central Asian countries.

Perceptions of the Enabling Factors

Mosques and Religious Leaders

Five respondents (6%) felt that mosques and imams could be involved in radicalisation. One male Kyrgyz business-owner from Jalalabad residing in Astrakhan described how recruitment took place at the 'Red Mosque' in Astrakhan. He noted that:

there, Kavkazi [people from the Caucasus] or Tajiks, or Uzbeks, approach young and inexperienced guys and offer them not-bad money for alleged work. But of course this is deception. At first, they give for a 'warm-up' USD 2–3,000 and then say that 'there' you will get more and persuade them to go. Few take the offer, but there were cases, when young guys fall for such tricks. (Astr 9)

One specifically mentioned a religious leader that was suspected of being radical (interestingly, he used 'Wahhabi' in this context synonymously with 'radical'): 'there was a Kyrgyz guy here. He was deputy imam. He was also a radical. Then he disappeared god knows where. The authorities put out a wanted notice for him ... It seems that he was pushing Wahhabi ideas' (Irku 11).

However, eight respondents (10%) were adamant that radicalisation did not take place in mosques. There was clearly respect for the mosque and religious leaders among these respondents, with two believing in particular that the role of imams was to 'keep order'

212

(Othe 5) and that radicalisation could not take place as 'there is control there by imams' (Sama 24). Mosques and the role of religious leaders were identified by these respondents as a source of resilience.

Recruitment

No interviewees had direct experience of recruiters. Nine offered their own perceptions of who the recruiters were likely to be – mostly Central Asians or people from the Caucasus, such as Dagestanis or Chechens. Four (Ekat 12, Kdar 14, Irku 11, and Astr 14) explicitly referred to Caucasians. For example, an individual from Ekaterinburg noted, 'I do not know about recruiters, but they talked about it on television. I heard that they are Caucasians who are offended by Russia and are now fighting in Syria. I heard that they seem to get more money for each recruit' (Ekat 12). Another deduced that 'maybe [recruiters] are Caucasus people. Because many Dagestanis have been arrested' (Kdar 14). Three individuals (Ekat 10, Mosc 32, and

Khab 3) specifically mentioned their opinion that Uzbeks are working to recruit people in Russia.

Locations of Radicalisation and Recruitment

Ninety per cent of the 83 interviewees and the focus groups mentioned people leaving for Syria. The detail and proximity of the respondents to the subject of the stories varied. For example, a Kyrgyz male living in Moscow offered little detail beyond saying that 'there was one moldo in Kara-Suu who was jailed for disseminating propaganda about the Syria war' (Mosc 32).2 But one ethnic Uzbek male living in St Petersburg (StPb 10) offered the most detail in a story regarding his brother who had left for Syria. Seven people (8%) commented on their own perceptions as to radicalisation taking place in Kyrgyzstan rather than by giving examples that they had specifically heard about. For example, a Kyrgyz male living in Irkutsk said 'from Russia mostly people from the Caucasus go to Syria. Central Asians ... mostly from Central Asia directly; not those who are in Russia' (Irku 21).

Eleven individuals (13%) and one focus group mentioned specific examples of and references to radicalisation in Russia. The majority of these stories pertained to people going to Syria. Some of the more concrete stories were echoed by two respondents in the same city. A Kyrgyz male residing in Irkutsk said, 'yes, a married woman from Osh, an Uzbek left [for Syria] with her children. The husband stayed. He didn't know that she had gone ... this was the first instance when a native from Kyrgyzstan went there' (Irku 11). Another man from Irkutsk who works at a migrant-aid organisation also highlighted seemingly the same story: 'the wife of a guy from Osh [an Uzbek] went there ... with two kids ... she went back to Osh to the wedding of her brother with kids, and then took the kids, left a note for her husband, and left' (Irku 23). This individual believed that the woman had been radicalised in Osh, but this was speculation. He noted, 'They say the woman's relatives had gone there [to Syria] before ... I think they invited her' (Irku 23).

However, radicalisation also took place at home: two respondents from Samara both had knowledge of a case in their city. A female Kyrgyz with Russian citizenship said that there were three young Uzbeks from Osh who left for Syria from Samara:

[The young Uzbeks] all died. I don't know how, but their parents found out and each at a different time held a memorial for their son ... Everyone asked each other how it happened, but no one knew exactly how ... [The parents] did not talk about it, but they did not grieve and did not curse the war in Syria. Now they trade at the bazaar, like always. (Sama 15)

The respondent was not aware of how these individuals were recruited or how they went to Syria, particularly as they were 'quiet guys, who helped their parents' (Sama 15). A Kyrgyz male also working in the bazaar in Samara referred to this story, saying that:

[I] personally saw these people in our bazaar, Osh Uzbeks, 18, 19, 20 years old who went to fight in Syria. We only found out about it when their parents started to organise memorial services for them. They are ordinary guys, didn't seem different from others at all ...

214

And they disappeared somehow, quietly, unnoticed, about half a year apart ... all thought that they left for family business. (Sama 17)

Two individuals referred to stories where suspected militants had either been detained or had attacked people. For example, a Kyrgyz female working as a diplomat in Ekaterinburg said that seven individuals suspected of being part of Daesh had been detained by the Federal Security Service (FSB) in Ekaterinburg in February 2016. She noted that they were 'Kyrgyz citizens of Uzbek ethnicity from the Osh region' (Ekat 10). A Kyrgyz male working as a trader in Astrakhan commented on perceptions of radical activity by non-Kyrgyz nationals after the St Petersburg Metro bombing. He said that 'immediately after the Uzbek from Osh blew himself up in the metro in St Petersburg, here in Astrakhan there was excitement. Four militants killed two RPS [Road Patrol Service] workers and wanted to arrange a terrorist attack ... they were Kazakhs and Caucasians, all Wahhabis' (Astr 14). Again, a specific definition of Wahhabi was not given. Six other respondents (7%) mentioned knowledge of people who had gone to Syria or who had encouraged others to go, but it was unclear from the transcripts from where they knew these examples – either at home in Kyrgyzstan or Russia.

Social Networks

Though recruiters were not specifically identified, social networks were said to be important. One Kyrgyz male living in Samara spoke of three classmates that he knew from Malovodnoye in Kyrgyzstan who had gone to fight in Syria. He said this 'took place under the influence of a classmate from Karachay' (Sama 20). Another Kyrgyz male spoke of an entire family he had heard about who had gone to Syria from Issyk-Kul (a widely reported case): 'twenty people! They took all their relatives and small children there. There, when they cross the border with Turkey, they take away all their documents and their families are taken hostage and men are told to go to fight; everything ends there' (Irku 14). One individual from the focus group in St Petersburg (StPb FG3) commented on how it was mainly Uzbeks from Kyrgyzstan going to fight.

Tools of Radicalisation: The Internet

Most respondents believed the internet was a key enabling factor in radicalisation. Eight people (10%) and one focus group mentioned this. For example, one Kyrgyz female living in Ekaterinburg said that she 'heard they communicate on the internet. [Recruiters] gather, maybe hypnotise them' (Ekat 12). Three individuals spoke of concrete cases. One ethnic Uzbek male studying in Samara said that 'in my city [Moscow] there was a case, I even saw it on the news. The girl somehow on the internet got acquainted with an ISIS supporter, and tried to leave for Syria, but she was detained at the airport' (Sama 12).

An ethnic Uzbek male from St Petersburg whose brother had gone to Syria said 'my brother was receiving information via the Internet through his acquaintances [in Turkey and Syria] and went there with their help' (StPb 10). A third individual, an imam living in Irkutsk, described how the Kyrgyz wife of one migrant went to Turkey without telling anyone, although he has some doubts as to her real whereabouts. He said that 'on social media, Instagram, she later sent a message saying "I'm in Turkey". But where she really is, in Turkey or elsewhere – remains unknown'. He said 'she was not [as far as he knows] meeting anyone, or joining any group. She learned how to pray and other things about religion via Internet' (Irku 22).

Perceptions of Individual Incentives

Money

Twenty individuals (24%) and three focus groups suggested that money is a motivation for migrant workers to go to Syria and fight with extremist organisations. It is important to note that this seemed based more on the personal opinion of interviewees rather than their own experience or first-hand knowledge. Of these, two respondents (Irku 14 and Sama 18) saw it almost as a business venture for those going to Syria. The latter noted that 'mostly, it is considered as business and if it pays well there then they go to fight for money. If they are not paid, they do not go', with the latter seeing it as a way to 'make big money quickly' (Sama 18).

Four other respondents (StPb 9, Mosc 31, Sama 13, and Khab 3) and two focus groups (StPb FG2 and Krsk FG1) believed people were deceived into leaving due to the deceptive lure or promise of money. For example, one respondent noted the perception that:

they are lured with money, saying that you will receive 10 thousand dollars a month, and the promise of three to four wives ... then he goes there, crosses the border and he disappears. They receive nothing. (StPb 9)

A Kyrgyz female interviewee working in a bazaar in Samara singled out Uzbeks, speculating that a key motivation was 'maybe money, big money. It is no secret that our Uzbeks love money more than anything else. Even more for bazaar Uzbeks, who never have enough money for turning over goods' (Sama 15). This comment might reveal common prejudices (that is, Uzbek stereotypes) by some of those within Kyrgyz society.

Eleven respondents (13%) were more specific and viewed the problem through the prism of a person falling on hard times or being affected by broader socioeconomic hardship. For example, an individual from St Petersburg noted that, 'Having arrived here without finding a job, they begin to suffer. And they begin to look for an easy way to earn money' (StPb 9). In a more vivid view, a respondent from Irkutsk stated:

because he has a desperate situation: problems with documents, problems with work, and problems with housing. At first, he takes the money to get out of this situation. Then they say to him: there is a way to work off this money. Then they begin: look, you have persecution here, they don't allow beards or headscarves. It is as if they need to take revenge or there is a way for you to get out of debt and return true Islam to your homeland. And they say, you have to go and work somehow. The person has already been caught now and goes, but naturally they do not say that he is going there to fight. (Irku 14)

Five of these respondents commented on the broader socioeconomic issues back home, citing the economy of Kyrgyzstan 'and the consequent lack of money' (Kdar 15), with another saying 'at the state level, the government must reduce the number of migrants, increasing the workplaces in our own country. Economic problems play a big role in radicalisation' (Sama 21).

However, not all interviewees agreed. Three respondents (4%) said that money was unlikely to be the driver. One (Mosc 5) gave no further detail as to their reasoning. Another offered an argument: 'I don't know about money. If he is to die there, why would he want money. If he cannot use that money, it does not make sense. I don't think it's about money' (Irku 23). One ethnic Uzbek male referred to someone they knew who had gone to Syria from his village, saying 'what's interesting is that people do not leave because of money. I have one more friend. Before leaving for Syria, he was a successful businessman in the village' (Othe 5).

Religious Belief

When asked why Central Asian migrant workers might leave Russia to go to Syria, the largest number of interviewees – 20, or about a quarter of the total – and respondents from two focus groups believed an influencing factor was the misinterpretation or misunderstanding of religion, with some citing poor religious teaching or a poor understanding of Islam as leaving people open to misinterpretations advanced by those participating in the conflict in Syria and Iraq. An alternative interpretation was given by five individuals (6%) and one focus group, who believed that some people went due to genuine religious conviction and faith. Speaking bluntly, a Kyrgyz male working at the bazaar in Samara made a direct link between religion and radicalisation, saying 'Uzbeks and Tajiks are more strictly Muslims, compared to the Kyrgyz, and more inclined to radicalisation, maybe according to their religion' (Sama 16).

Two respondents referred to misinterpretation of the Qu'ran. For example, one participant in Ekaterinburg said 'probably they misinterpret Islam. The Qur'an says that you cannot kill people or cause violence' (Ekat 12). Another in Irkutsk said 'many people are misled by partial, selective quotes from Quran that suggest violence, and rewards for it' (Irku 12). Two respondents

218

(StPb 2 and Sama 15) specifically cited a misinterpretation of jihad among those who have gone to Syria. Five respondents (Mosc 25, Kdar 9, Othe 5, Mosc 26, and Irku 14) cited people's own religious illiteracy due to limited knowledge of Islam or poor religious education. Three respondents (Irku 23, Mosc 27 and Irku 21) believed it is the fault of the religious leaders, particularly at home in Kyrgyzstan. Three respondents (Novo 11, StPb 9 and Irku 14) blamed the recruiters' deception and manipulation of religion.

Six respondents felt that there was an element of brainwashing during radicalisation and that certain conditions left people vulnerable to charismatic individuals. Two interviewees

(Mosc 30 and Othe 5) felt that those who had economic problems were most vulnerable to this. One respondent (Mosc 26) felt that migrants were particularly vulnerable to fanatical ideas when they feel isolated or alone, which they felt could easily happen when migrants were away from home. One ethnic Kyrgyz male working for the local authorities in Krasnodar made an interesting observation about the submissiveness of migrants and their willingness to obey orders, based on his own experience managing migrant workers from Central Asia:

For example, I have 700 migrants every day answerable to me. Wherever I lead, they follow. Wherever I tell them to stand, they'll stand, whatever I say, they'll do. They won't argue. Now imagine there was a psychologist or a good orator in their midst, that person would get into their souls, they would go [to Syria, and so on] under hypnosis. (Kdar 14)

Two respondents (StPb 13 and Astr 14) determined that the problem is 'Wahhabism' – without actually defining what they meant by this. Explicit mention of 'fanaticism' was also made by two interviewees (Irku 23 and Krsk 16) and one focus group (Krsk FG1): they saw people that go to Syria as those who had let religion go 'too far'.

Sense of Belonging and Solidarity

Four interviewees (5%) believed that individuals going to Syria had a sense of purpose and belonging, with two interviewees (Sama 14 and Mosc 29) citing the possibility that individuals with difficult childhoods or family situations might be more inclined to go. Two others suggested that people might also go to Syria in solidarity for what is happening there. For example, an interviewee from Moscow said, 'Well they have the strong conviction – that in Syria there is a mass murder of Muslims, and that it is necessary to stop this bloodshed and to rescue brothers of Muslims' (Mosc 5). Another in Moscow noted that:

> when I first heard that the faithful Muslims are subjected to oppression and deprivation, I thought of abandoning everything and going there to help my brothers and my sisters of faith ... [but his nephew] told me that in Syria a fratricidal war is taking place – where one Muslim fights with another Muslim, and it is not a righteous war. (Mosc 12)

Perceptions of Vulnerable and At-Risk Populations

Uzbeks from Kyrgyzstan

A large population of ethnic Uzbeks in Kyrgyzstan, particularly in the south, creates an important dynamic that was observable in the transcripts (and is in fact observable in the broader public discourse around radicalisation of Central Asians). In particular, Kyrgyz interviewees commented how this caused divisions within migrant communities within Russia. Some respondents believed that Uzbeks (either from Uzbekistan or Kyrgyzstan) behaved differently to ethnic Kyrgyz, and it was implied that these differences manifested in vulnerabilities to radicalisation and recruitment. When they mentioned 'Uzbeks', it was not always clear whether respondents were referring to ethnic Uzbeks from Uzbekistan or ethnic Uzbeks from Kyrgyzstan when it was not specifically stated.

Four Kyrgyz interviewees (Khab 3, Ekat 10, Novo 6, and Kdar 2) specifically expressed a view that ethnic Uzbeks from Osh were more isolated and restricted than Kyrgyz. For example, an interviewee from Khabarovsk said '[Osh Uzbeks] would like to be with us but they can't. And the Uzbeks from Uzbekistan don't accept them. They are on their own' (Khab 3). Another respondent, a Kyrgyz male working with the diaspora in St Petersburg, said that he had given an interview to the Bishkek radio station 'Azatyk' after the St Petersburg bombing. 'I said that we did not know [the terrorist] because he is Uzbek, and Uzbeks are not included in our diaspora. It's always been this way' (StPb 9).

When discussing radicalisation, six interviewees gave the opinion that Uzbeks were more likely to go to fight in Syria than the Kyrgyz. For example, an unemployed Kyrgyz male said he had 'heard that Uzbeks and Tajiks are recruiting and recruited. I did not hear about the Kyrgyz' (Ekat 11). Seven individuals said Uzbeks from Kyrgyzstan, including specifically from Osh, were likely to go to fight. Sometimes this highlighted conflicts between the Kyrgyz and Uzbek community. Four respondents (5%) mentioned the inter-ethnic clashes in Kyrgyzstan of 2010 and how they had caused friction between the migrant communities in Russia. One Kyrgyz male who works seasonally in Ekaterinburg offered his own conclusions about how such tensions might relate to radicalisation: 'Uzbeks of Kyrgyzstan probably get recruited because of 2010 conflict, because they feel angry, want to [get revenge] even here, doing bad things while carrying Kyrgyz passports' (Ekat 15). There were also concerns that there was a risk of blowback for all Kyrgyz when an ethnic Uzbek from Kyrgyzstan is involved in trouble. For example, a Kyrgyz female said:

> there were no cases among the Kyrgyz. I heard a conversation at a meal, one of my acquaintances said that we were disgraced by Osh Uzbeks, who are the ones persuaded to go to war or blow themselves up in Russia, and their passports are Kyrgyz, so they started not liking us Kyrgyz people in Russia. (Ekat 12)

There was clearly the perception among some interviewees that Kyrgyz were almost immune to such issues, embodying a sense of superiority towards other Central Asians. Some respondents (Sama 17, Mosc 32, Ekat 11, and Sama 16) expressed the perception that the Kyrgyz were more independent and self-reliant, and therefore were less easily deceived. For example, one Kyrgyz male who works in Samara bazaar said that 'the majority of Kyrgyz have immunity to "fairytales" no matter who tells them' (Sama 17). Again, showing the perceived contrast between Kyrgyz and Uzbek, a Kyrgyz male living in Moscow said 'only Uzbeks go to Syria or Iraq. Kyrgyz have no business being there ... Kyrgyz don't respect them [those who go to fight], but among young Uzbeks they are some kind of hero' (Mosc 32). Again, this is perhaps more a reflection of ethnic bias as opposed to anything else.

Seven respondents (8%) saw the Kyrgyz as far less religious than Tajiks or Uzbeks. Again, it is not clear here whether the respondents were considering ethnic Uzbek citizens of Kyrgyzstan as 'Uzbek' or 'Kyrgyz'. There was certainly the perception that religion played a role in a person's vulnerability to radicalisation. This was highlighted by a Kyrgyz male residing in St Petersburg, who, when asked why more migrant workers are not going to Syria, said 'the Kyrgyz are not religious fanatics, if they were, they would all leave' (StPb 13).

Lack of Education and the Russian Language

Ten individuals (12%) mentioned that poor education and/ or a poor understanding of the Russian language increased the challenges for migrant workers. For example, one nineteenyear-old ethnic Uzbek Kyrgyz male who is studying in Samara said that, 'when people come [to Russia], they find it difficult to get a job; if a person does not know the language, then it is twice as hard' (Sama 13). Another ethnic Uzbek Kyrgyz residing in Samara who translates documents for a living said:

> ....honestly, for those that don't have connections and money coming here is difficult. It is especially hard for those who don't know Russian. They become victims of police checks, their intermediaries often double cross them. They are the most defenceless and disenfranchised. (Sama 24)

Although it was not necessarily a universal assumption among all interviewees, there was clearly a logical link made among some between a lack of education and vulnerability. One Kyrgyz female diaspora leader in Krasnodar said that 'Uneducated people quickly succumb to deception. When you are in darkness and see light, you head towards it' (Kdar 3). A male Kyrgyz working in Novosibirsk echoed this by saying 'it seems to me that educated people will not go there [to Syria], there are so many opportunities to work, to self-actualise themselves. There is simply no time and no interest' (Novo 11).

Youth

A less prevalent theory on why people go to fight in Syria relates to youth and inexperience. Five people (6%) and one focus group commented on this. Interestingly, it was not only older interviewees that commented: the respondents were a 21-year-old Kyrgyz female (Novo 7), a 21-year-old Uzbek female (Sama 21), a 35-year-old Kyrgyz male (Khab 4), a 46-year-old Kyrgyz male (StPb 13), a 47-year-old Uzbek male (Sama 14), and a focus group of 19–30-year-old Kyrgyz males (StPb FG3). These respondents mainly identified young people as more vulnerable, citing issues such as manipulation over social media, financial persuasion, or simply not having their own skills to know who and what to trust. One respondent spoke of a 'new tendency among youth to grow a beard and turn to Islam', giving his own perception that 'everyone with a beard belongs in a sect, Wahhabi Muslims' (StPb 13). As before, the definition of 'Wahhabi' was not given.

Perceptions of Resilience

Community Relations

Many migrant workers felt that aspects of their community helped build resilience against radicalisation or people sowing discord in their community. Within this group, three respondents (Novo 11, Astr 17 and Sama 24) mentioned places or collective organisations where diaspora can gather to discuss issues. For example, a respondent in Novosibirsk (Novo 11) mentioned the House of Friendship in Novosibirsk; another interviewee in Astrakhan (Astr 17) mentioned the Congress of Uzbeks in Astrakhan, Russia.

An ethnic Uzbek female in Samara (Sama 24) mentioned that her husband was planning to open an affiliate office of the All-Russian Union of Uzbeks and Uzbekistanis in Samara.

Two respondents (Ekat 10 and Khab 27) mentioned diaspora leaders as respected figures who could help build cohesion and a sense of belonging within communities. The latter gave an example of her community: 'the head of the diaspora is a smart young man. We can be proud of him, he can build a relationship with locals, he works for the people and himself. He is not conceited, he is always approachable' (Khab 27). Three respondents (Mosc 29, Sama 20, and Ekat 11) mentioned how respected foremen or bosses were at work. One of the respondents said that:

> *at work we respect the foreman. He treats everyone equally and justly, and organises the work according to our strengths. He constantly teaches new things and how to do things better … If conflict situations come up, in the majority of working moments, then the foreman immediately solves everything. (Sama 20)*

Four respondents (Khab 03, Kdar 15, Othe 5, and Sama 25) and one focus group (StPb FG2) noted how the diaspora community often comes together to provide a support group, even if it is simply for social activity. For example, focus group participants noted that 'every two months we Kyrgyz gather to play football and make pilaf' (StPb FG2). The respondent from Khabarovsk noted how the community can monitor and discipline as a group; he said that there are no cases of recruitment because 'we keep tight control of the situation …. In 2010, we told everyone that if there were any problems, then we would kick out the troublemaker in three days … we would have invited the FSB in' (Khab 3). In contrast, three respondents (Kyrgyz female Astr 14; Kyrgyz male Astr 15 and Kyrgyz male Sama 20) seemed to highlight the independence of Kyrgyz migrant workers, stating that most people fended for themselves. However, they did also admit that the diaspora community can come together as a support group if necessary.

Religion

Eleven respondents (13%) and two focus groups mentioned the role that Islam could play in building up resilience against radicalisation. Seven of these mentioned either the fact that they had heard in mosques that imams are speaking out against radicalisation, or that they think it is a good idea for mosques to help combat radicalisation. For example, an interviewee in St Petersburg noted that:

> a lot depends on the imams, an imam should be very well educated ... I went to the mosque [in Irkutsk, built by the Kyrgyz] – the imam there is a young man, without a beard. But very educated ... He gives correct advice and guidance, in my view. (StPb 13)

A respondent from Irkutsk was more direct about making the link and the role mosques should play, saying that 'awareness-raising work needs to be done in the mosque' (Irku 22). In the focus group, one participant gave the opinion that '[recruiters] look for ones who are dead-beats, or the ones that do not go to the mosque. They go to such people. And they cannot come to those who pray, read and constantly go to the mosque' (StPb FG2).

Three respondents (Ekat 10, Irku 14 and Novo 9) noted specific visits from high-profile religious leaders and religious scholars. For example, a respondent from Irkutsk (Irku 14) reported that a former mufti (and Islamic legal expert) and rector of an Islamic university came to give seminars on the specifics of Kyrgyz and broader Central Asian Islam. One respondent (Ekat 11) and two focus groups (StPb FG2 and StPb FG3) commented on the importance of religious literature in keeping people on the right track. For example, a respondent from St Petersburg noted:

> You need to read proper books, which are published strictly by the mufti. Several receive this knowledge, pass it on to those they meet, they read, and then think that Islam is such ... and thoughts turn to the other side. (Respondent in StPb FG3)

Authorities

Eleven respondents (13%) cited the Russian authorities as a reason more Central Asian migrants did not turn to radical Islam. The authorities were not always seen in a positive light, but nevertheless were still seen as a deterrent factor. For example, four respondents (Astr 13, Astr 15, Astr 14, and Ekat 13) all mentioned FSB surveillance. A participant in Astrakhan explained 'we do not watch [videos about the conflict]. The FSB works here clearly, but we do not need to watch such videos' (Astr 14). The remaining seven interviewees of the eleven noted their interaction with local police and the control that they can exert over migrants to deter them from radical activity. One respondent, a Kyrgyz doctor, had a rather positive attitude towards engagement with the authorities, saying:

> we are invited to all the meetings concerning migrants that take place with law-enforcement bodies, and the local administration. There, they immediately voice all the problems that exist. Sometimes we are asked to control or influence in some way, and we tell them the problems our migrants are facing; what assistance is needed from the local administration. (Irku 14)

One other respondent did not mind when Russian law enforcement – in his view – overstepped their legal remit: an ethnic Uzbek male working in construction remarked that: '[Russian law enforcement] act tough and resolutely, often without any due process. Their goal – to cut the phenomenon at its roots ... I guess to some extent I even agree with such an approach' (Mosc 24). An ethnic Uzbek female document translator noted an interplay of various state actors, saying that 'most migrants in Samara are very far from radical ideas ... there is also adequate control over migrants here – FSB, prosecutor's office, FMS ... in order to prevent negative developments' (Sama 24). Generally, therefore, the work of the authorities was seen as a way of keeping in check those who might be tempted by radical behaviour.

Economic Factors

Eight respondents (10%) were explicit that positive economic factors – finding work and earning money – worked against radicalisation. (However, given the number that cited 'money' as a driving force for those going to Syria, it is likely that more respondents may have supported this view on the impact of positive economic factors had they been asked directly.) This answer was mainly given in response to the question of why more Central Asian migrants did not go to fight in Syria. For example, a respondent from Astrakhan said, 'decent people have nothing to do there. They can find money, but you can earn money here. We work hard and earn. We bought a house and a car. Our children are kept. You can work' (Astr 15).

Family

Despite the fact that some Central Asians who have gone to fight in Syria travelled as families, the family was seen as a major point of resilience for migrants. Four respondents (Ekat 15, Ekat 13, Sama 17, and Mosc 26) saw having a family as a deterrent: this was a reason to stay and earn money in Russia. For example, an interviewee from Ekaterinburg explained: 'why should I go there? I have a wife, children – everything is fine. You can earn money here and not risk your life' (Ekat 13) – the quote interestingly also highlights once again the perceived importance of money for those who go to Syria and Iraq. One young ethnic Uzbek female gave a specific example of someone who they knew was sympathetic to the extremist cause in Syria, but had benefited from family guidance:

> *[her friend] always talked about the conflict in Syria, and justified those that went to make war there ... we often had arguments ... Now she is different. She tells me that she was mistaken in her view of war in Syria ... she changed her mind due to circumstances in her family. She had an uncle who told her and her sister those [women] who go to Syria – they become suicide bombers. (Sama 21)*

227

Seven respondents (8%) and one focus group (Krsk FG1) mentioned the value of elders, at times referring to aksakaly – people the community or individuals respect. Most indicated also that the elders are those that either provide support or are obeyed. A 45-year-old ethnic Uzbek from Osh raised this in particular:

> *yes, there are older people who prevent young children. I myself, for example, also work in this direction. When I hear the opinion that it is necessary to go to Syria to support the Muslims, I'm going to besiege such people, convincing them that no one will benefit from this war, and that there will be a fratricidal war. (Mosc 12)*

III. Labour Migrants from Tajikistan

Nadine L Salman

THIS SECTION IS divided into five sub-sections that follow the analytical framework used to analyse the data. This includes: perceptions of structural motivation; perceptions of enabling factors; perceptions of individual incentives; perceptions of vulnerable and at-risk populations; and perceptions of resilience. This framework aims to analyse the drivers of radicalisation that takes into consideration the importance of context, as well as encompass the widest possible range of interconnected factors.

Perceptions of Structural Motivation

Migration Experience and Legal Issues

When discussing factors that can make some migrants more vulnerable to radicalisation, many Tajik interviewees highlighted difficulties with the migration process and economic hardship. These factors may contribute to vulnerability and feelings of desperation among migrants. Specifically, twelve interviewees (18%) mentioned difficulties registering documents and the cost of the work patent as important issues affecting Central Asian migrants in Russia. Of these, four specifically connected such difficulties to vulnerability, desperation and targeting by extremist recruiters. For example, a businessman and diaspora leader living in Novosibirsk, speaking from his experience of two cases within his community, said that 'Mostly, recruiters target those who upon arrival in Russia experience difficulties finding work, getting registered, and having material and moral difficulties' (Novo 12).

As further noted by five interviewees (8%), migrants also face persecution from the authorities over their legal status and documentation, which, despite not being explicitly linked to radicalisation, may contribute to the grievances and context in which radicalisation can occur. For example, an undocumented male Kyrgyz builder from Tajikistan, currently living in Krasnodar, warned:

> *If you don't have documents, the police will catch you and they will collect money. If you don't speak Russian, then they may even take your documents away ... if all the documents are in order, then here it is good. And if you don't have documents then you will be constantly running from the police. (Kdar 12)*

Indeed, eleven interviewees (17%) mentioned discrimination, both from the authorities and the wider community. A Tajik female working in a Russian-language assessment centre in Krasnodar highlighted that: 'In Russia, if you are a Muslim, then you are seen as a potential threat' (Kdar 10). Again, while not explicitly linked to radicalisation, these structural issues may further alienate and increase the vulnerability of migrants.

Economic Factors

As well as the difficulties with the registration process, the high costs of the process can leave migrants in considerable debt. Eight interviewees (12%) posited a link between desperation due to mounting debt, poverty and economic difficulties, and joining extremist groups. As theorised by a male administrative assistant living in Samara, 'Imagine a young migrant who came to work and couldn't find a job, he does not have any money, but has to pay for a patent, accommodation, food, etc. They offer him a lot of money to go to Syria or Iraq. He is forced out of desperation to agree to these conditions' (Sama 1).

229

Echoing this, a male undocumented porter living in Samara speculated that the cost of registration may be an important factor: 'I think some of our people can't cope with [the price] and are forced to agree to the proposals of [recruiters] who give them money and money for the journey' (Sama 2).

However, the cost of documents may only account for part of the economic struggles of migrants. According to five interviewees (8%), worsening economic conditions and sanctions have, according to a male head of a construction company in Astrakhan, 'severely affected the position of migrants' (Astr 3). As a result, a Tajik male shopkeeper in Astrakhan commented, 'In recent years in Astrakhan, for obvious reasons [referring to sanctions], there have been fewer work opportunities and more and more migrant workers coming' (Astr 1). This lack of jobs may further increase the desperation of migrants, which could exacerbate the presumed relationship between financial difficulties and extremist recruitment.

Perceptions of the Enabling Factors

The Internet

A third of the interviewees claimed that the internet is a key enabler of recruitment, and a common space for radicalisation to take place. The widespread use of internet-enabled devices and the ease of access may make it an easy tool for recruiters to use and for extremist messages to spread. In the words of a male working for the Representative Office of the Ministry of Migration in Irkutsk, 'The internet is everywhere. It is the source of whatever information you want' (Irku 1). The role of the internet in recruitment is starkly shown through one interviewee's description of his brother's experience in Box 7.

Box 7: Knowledge of Recruitment. A male bus driver living in Moscow described how his brother became radicalised online:

The internet is full of radical Islamic sermons and calls for jihad. I personally do not understand what interested my brother in this. He left for Syria in 2015 (at age of 23).

He sat at home on the internet all day, that's how he was sent to Syria. I think he was recruited over social networks ... He spent a lot of time on the internet on his phone. It turns out that he had joined an extremist group on the internet. I don't know what they said to him.

Now every week at work I look at my workers' phones and forbid them from going into town without a good reason. I invite people who give lectures on preventing radicalisation and the migrants' parents also welcome this initiative. (Mosc 7)

In addition, two interviewees also mentioned the perceived need to protect youth from watching online videos of violence uploaded by Daesh. A female translator living in Ekaterinburg said, 'I and my friends watch videos about these conflicts to understand what is happening there. But we prevent our children from watching them' (Ekat 1).

Community

However, many interviewees acknowledged that recruitment does not solely take place online. Thirteen interviewees (20%) suggested that radicalisation and recruitment take place within their communities – including in markets, workplaces and the homes of migrants. This is highlighted in two cases reported by one of the interviewees in Box 8.

Box 8: Knowledge of Recruitment

A male businessman and informal leader of the Isfara community in Novosibirsk describes two cases of recruitment within his community:

> *Three years ago, our co-villager who worked here secretly went to Syria with his family. But seeing the terrible truth there, by some great fortune managed to escape to Afghanistan. From Afghanistan, returned home ... Our co-villager must have been recruited at the bazaar where he worked. But he doesn't like to speak about it ... [He] said from Russia he went to Turkey, and from there to Syria.*

A month ago, a man came back from Moscow to Novosibirsk, where he worked before going to Moscow ... The person who lived with him there attempted to recruit him to go to Syria. Seeing what was going on, he lied to the recruiter and fled back to Novosibirsk and reported to our consul here, asking for protection from the recruiter. He [the consul] immediately advised to change his SIM-card and not respond to phone calls. (Novo 12)

Mosques

To a lesser extent, seven interviewees (11%) speculated that radicalisation could take place at mosques. However, they asserted that such mosques are in a minority, and that they did not identify with them. For example, an Uzbek male from Tajikistan working as a leader of a migration centre in Astrakhan said, 'Some mosques are apparently run by such people, and can become a base for recruitment. But generally, not' (Astr 4).Indeed, other interviewees were adamant that mosques are not places of recruitment, instead claiming that radicalisation takes place in external, informal prayer houses. This was highlighted by a Tajik male who works as a surgeon and is a community leader of Badakhshan migrants in Khabarovsk, who has some experience with radicalisation in his community: 'Official religious leaders and mosques have nothing to do with radicalism, but in informal prayer houses and markets, one can meet people who call for radicalism and intolerance' (Khab 5).

Salafis/Wahhabis

Ten interviewees (15%) specifically blamed 'Salafis' or 'Wahhabis' for extremist recruitment. A male human rights defender in Novosibirsk knew of a case of recruitment in his community: 'In principle, it [religion] shouldn't be [a factor]. But in reality, as we know, there are groups of Salafists and Hizb-ut-Tahriris.[1] It is their mosques and centres that spread extremist ideas' (Novo 5). However, despite these accusations, the interviewees did not seem to express an understanding of the relationship between Salafism, Wahhabism, groups such as Hizb-ut-Tahrir (a non-violent organisation and movement), and violent extremism, often using the terms interchangeably. Indeed, contrary to the suggestions of the interviewees, and public perceptions in general, there is no simple relationship between Salafism and violent extremism.[2]

Other Tajiks

Five interviewees who previously suggested that recruitment happens within their communities also specifically referred to the involvement of other Tajiks. One example of such a view was given by a male working for the Representative Office of the Ministry of Migration in Irkutsk: 'Salafi sermons incite groups against one another, and even Tajiks preach Salafism among the community' (Irku 1).However, a male Tajik employed in the administration of a district of Astrakhan argued that this is mainly an issue among Uzbek and Kyrgyz communities: 'We [Tajiks] haven't had any incidents. But the Kyrgyz and Uzbek migrants have. That was two or three years ago ... [and anyway migrants] are not radicalised in Russia ... Uzbeks of Kyrgyzstan (especially Osh) and Tajiks from the Shartuz, Kabadiyan and Isfara regions of Tajikistan [are radicalised back home in Central Asia]' (Astr 2). Again, however, this may be more reflective of an ethnic bias rather than the reality among migrants in Russia.

Caucasians

Four interviewees referred specifically to Caucasian recruiters, particularly Chechens and Dagestanis as being a particular source of concern. For example, a male head of a construction company in Astrakhan mentioned cases within his community: 'There were two to three cases. Young people without money and without a job or the means to live fall under the influence of Dagestanis, Chechens or Salafis and go to Syria and Iraq ... They say that these recruiters are from the North Caucasus' (Astr 3). However, the interviewees as a whole provided little detail on these recruiters; rather, the perceptions of the role of these recruiters appear to come from hearsay. This is something that is reflective of broader narratives around radicalisation within the Russian-speaking world in particular.

Perceptions of Individual Incentives

Money

Although the lack of work opportunities, mounting debt and poverty may lead some migrants to join extremist groups out of desperation, others who are in a better situation may also be drawn in by the promise of monetary reward. Indeed, the majority of those interviewed (over two-thirds), eight of whom had some direct knowledge of recruitment, believed that money is an important incentive for those joining extremist groups. Indeed, as an undocumented porter from Samara said, 'They are attracted above all, by money. More than they have ever seen. All the other reasons stated are myths' (Sama 2).Moreover, seven interviewees (11%) suggested that people join extremist groups because they do not want to work, or want 'easy' money. A male trader living in Samara explained: 'Everyone comes here to earn money. But some people want money, but don't want to work hard. Those must be the ones agreeing to go after easy money' (Sama 4). A third of those who highlighted money as an incentive speculated that money is particularly tempting to young and uneducated migrants.

Religion

Similarly, a third of interviewees, six of whom had some direct knowledge of recruitment, believed that religious fanaticism and a genuine belief in the 'caliphate' are important incentives for those who join extremist groups. This is highlighted by the statement of a prisoner convicted for terrorism offences in Box 9. However, it is worth noting that while this interviewee may have been attempting to give a religious justification after the fact for joining Daesh, he may have been motivated at the time by other reasons.

Box 9: Knowledge of Recruitment

A male prisoner in Moscow convicted for terrorism, disseminating extremist propaganda and supporting ISIS:

> I was accused of spreading extremist ideas over the internet. In Tajikistan, I received information and sermons and sometimes

spread them over the internet. But these were the true words of the great Islamic scholars Ibn Taymiyyah1 and Sheikh Al-Albani.2 Here I also spread such material among Tajik migrants over the internet.

Many people say that migrants join ISIS for money. That's not correct. People travel there [to Syria] for their faith. Money is just a means used to achieve our goals.In Iraq and Syria, there is a war for the creation of an Islamic Caliphate, as the prophet predicted. This is spiritual devotion to Islam. And the jihad will last to the day of judgement ... Those who are fighting in Syria today against the infidel state have already fulfilled their mission to God. They are already shahids [martyrs] and will go to paradise. They don't yet understand that you have to fight for religion. If they don't want to, Allah will abandon them. Many haven't yet decided what they need in the future. But with the help of sermons we will bring the true religion to them.

Mosques and religious leaders are not resolute and they defend the interests of infidels. (Mosc 6)

1 A medieval Sunni theologian (1263–1328) and a member of the Hanbali school of jurisprudence, Ibn Taymiyyah is a controversial scholar whose interpretations of the Qur'an and the Sunnah and his rejection of some aspects of classical Islamic tradition are believed to have had considerable influence on contemporary Wahhabism, Salafism and Jihadism.

2 A leading Islamic Salafi scholar (1914–99), Albani was an Albanian who taught in Saudi Arabia but built his reputation in Syria and spent his later years in Jordan. Albani had controversial views on jurisprudence and Islamic issues.

Among those who emphasised the role of religious fanaticism, four (6% of the interview sample) said that those who join violent extremist groups believe they are 'saving Islam'. This view was exemplified by a male working in Khabarovsk as a market vendor: 'I think that guys fall into these circles for the promise of big money. But you can find guys who are fanatics and think that by their participation they save Islam' (Khab 1).

This perspective was echoed to a degree by several interviewees. When asked for their perspective on the conflict in Syria and Iraq, twelve (18%) argued that those countries, and Muslims in those countries, are 'victims', particularly of foreign intervention. A respondent from St Petersburg noted: 'On this we all agree, that it is a war against the Muslims. The US has its own interests, Saudis – their own, Iran – its own, Russia – its own, but the most difficult is the Syrians' own lot' (StPb 6). This sense of grievance can be exploited by recruiters and used as an incentive by those who go on to join extremist groups.

Thirteen interviewees (20%) argued, based on their own perceptions, that rather than being religious fanatics, violent extremists use religion as a cover; and that recruiters, as well as politicians, abuse it to justify violence. For example, a male market seller in Khabarovsk claimed that 'ISIS covers up their inhumane actions with Islamic sermons, but what they do in Syria and Iraq is absolutely foreign to Islam' (Khab 7).

In addition, a quarter of interviewees believed religion is not related to violent extremism at all, while two claimed that migrants from other Central Asian countries are more susceptible due to their poor understanding of religion. In the words of a male Kyrgyz builder from Tajikistan, currently living in Krasnodar:

> *The Uzbeks are not that religious. People that know religion and observe it, they would not go to fight ever, because they know that this is a sin before God. Those that fight are those that don't understand and think that the whole world will convert to Islam. (Kdar 12)*

Yet, another interviewee, a male Tajik entrepreneur living in Irkutsk, said that 'It seems to me that this [recruitment on religious grounds] is truer for our compatriots from Kyrgyzstan, since in Uzbekistan and Tajikistan people are more literate in matters of religion' (Irku 18).

These conflicting statements from interviewees of different ethnicities highlight the subjectivity and biases in migrant beliefs about violent extremism in their communities, as well as their prejudice against those from different groups.

A Sense of Meaning

The interviewee in Box 10 had direct knowledge of recruitment. He recounts the story of his son joining Daesh. Unlike the dominant explanation of money and religious beliefs highlighted above, this respondent argues that his son was in a good position financially and that he was also not interested in religious ideas. He explains his son's motivation in terms of seeking 'spiritual peace'. It is not clear what is meant by this term or how it differs to what other religious adherents seek. However, the implicit suggestion here is that his son was looking for a sense of meaning through religious experience.

Box 10: Knowledge of Recruitment

A male private driver living in Moscow explains how his son joined ISIS after moving to Russia:

> *when he came here, he had no difficulties. He had a rented flat, had a job, went to the gym. There, he trained with Dagestanis and Chechens. From Central Asia, there were Uzbeks, Kyrgyz, Kazakhs. I never noticed any change in him, it was all as usual, he never raised his voice. All relatives and community members respected him. Who and how recruited him I don't know. How he got there, I don't know. After five days, I learned that he left. I asked his friends, those who knew him, trained with him, but all of them said they knew nothing. When I went to the gym the second time, there was no one. Nobody wanted to tell anything.*

About my son, if I said money was a factor that would be untrue … As for religious ideas, such things never really interested him. Those who are affected easiest by recruiters are those who are looking for some spiritual peace. (Mosc 8)

237

Perception of Vulnerable and At-Risk

Populations Education

A common factor increasing vulnerability given by interviewees was a lack of education – religious or otherwise. Almost a third of interviewees specifically highlighted religious ignorance or the general lack of education as an issue. A female street cleaner living in Khabarovsk exemplified this view: 'How can anyone believe someone you don't know? Because most are educated and understand these issues. Those who are uneducated fall prey to recruiters' (Khab 11). One male who works as a construction worker in Moscow argued that improving education could prevent violent extremism: 'We need to increase the knowledge of citizens, including migrant workers. An educated person will never … join an extremist group' (Mosc 14) .

Youth

A third of the interviewees speculated that young people are the most likely group to become involved in extremism. However, not all interviewees agreed on the reasons behind this. Fifteen interviewees (23%) said that young people are more likely to be drawn in by monetary rewards – either because they suffer from financial difficulties, or because they are tempted by 'easy' money. Nine interviewees blamed specific characteristics associated with youth – namely, a lack of experience, naivete, and a disobedience to authority. According to a 47-year-old female NGO director living in Irkutsk, who had no direct experience of recruitment:

> *Young people are not experienced and are quick to believe when talking about religion. Under the pretext of religion, they become interested and are then persuaded by the promise of large amounts of money. The money is received by other people, but uneducated young guys die. (Irku 2)*

Similarly, a 55-year-old male employed in the administration of a district of Astrakhan insisted that some young people join 'because they are trapped and have no way out and because of their

238

ignorance and stupidity' (Astr 2). These characteristics are further highlighted by a case in Box 11.

Box 11: Knowledge of Recruitment

A male janitor foreman living in St Petersburg describes how a young employee became radicalised:

So this guy from Khatlon is our only instance. He was lazy. He did not work with conscience, called at girls in the yard, bullied them. Then he got in touch with someone from his fellow countrymen from Kurgantep. He missed days of work. Then suddenly changed and became silent. He started teaching us things, saying that even [a local religious leader] is praying wrong, that he is talking wrongly about Islam and history. Everything was wrong for him. These are the young fools who started the war. So he disappeared, did not even show up for his last pay check.

He was a decent guy; he accepted everything and did not argue. He then became like a mad or sick man … We talked, but what's the use. Then, I had just become a foreman. He basically looked at us like he was looking at a wall. Then he collected his things in silence and left. But no one drove him out. We just warned him. And so he disappeared. Then, all these people came asking questions. I do not remember, [he was] 20-21. He was young, but he grew out his beard, like a Wahhabi. Well, what will become of him in the war? They killed him, probably. They show them on the TV – they are dying in batches. It can be seen. It is said that it is easiest to entice young people and also those who are left without money and without relatives or friends. (StPb 5).

Social Isolation

Three interviewees with some experience of recruitment stated that people who are isolated are more vulnerable to recruitment (see Box 11). According to one, a male private driver living in Moscow whose son was recruited, 'When a person is recruited, he doesn't tell anyone about that. It is known that recruiters isolate [their recruits] from society. Precisely that barrier/ isolation prevents the victims from seeking help with families and friends' (Mosc 8). A similar account is given in Box 12.

Box 12: Knowledge of Recruitment

A male head of a shopping centre department in Moscow describes how his brother-in-law left for Syria:

In 2012 I invited my wife's brother to work here, he was 22 then. Got him a job so he could support family. He left wife and a kid back home. In 2014, without saying a word to anyone, he went to Syria. There's war there, and they are victims of that war ... now I watch all news about Syria and Iraq ... Among those fighters, killing women and children, is the brother of my wife ... I never imagined a member of my family would go to the Syrian war. I probably didn't notice or missed something in the behaviour of the person ... We work from 6am till 11pm, where did he find time for that!

I suppose recruiters' job is not only to recruit a person, but if successful, also to organise their travel to Syria via Turkey. He wrote from Turkey to his cousin who worked with him that he was going to Syria, and asked not to search for him. When we informed police, they showed that a ticket was issued for him to Turkey.

The last time we heard from him was in August 2015. After that, twice, there were messages from others that he was doing alright ... The problem is that the recruits won't tell anyone about it. Maybe there is an agreement with recruiters that they must not tell anyone, or maybe they are threatened somehow if they tell. After getting recruited, they don't trust anyone except the recruiters.

I don't know when and how he got recruited ... [He] had no financial problems, had a normal job, enough for living. Young, just married ... I think he was recruited for religious reasons.

The mosque and traditional religious leaders are the only real power against radicalism ... But their power is also limited, some people join Salafists and other radical currents. Radicalism's parapet is the internet, and their space is very strong.

I think if a person got into the web of recruiters, he cannot freely walk out of it … Recruiters isolate the person from others, and create a virtual world – which is very convenient for further recruitment … The people who fall prey to recruiters must be those who couldn't find comfort in society, and were looking for a different world. (Mosc 11)

Perceptions of Resilience

Community Support

Alongside risk factors, most interviewees also mentioned ways in which members of their communities are resilient. Twelve interviewees (18%) discussed the role of diaspora leaders not just in terms of preventing radicalisation, but generally helping and solving problems within the community in which they are well respected. This was highlighted by a community leader living in Irkutsk: 'I help everyone who approaches me as they chose me as the leader of the community. I do not allow anyone to sow discord … Community leaders, along with educated people, are fighting against radicalisation' (Irku 3).

As shown here, one of the ways in which diaspora leaders help to prevent radicalisation is by resolving disputes in the community. Other interviewees also mentioned the role of community leaders in holding seminars, educating the community and cooperating with the authorities.

Nearly a third of interviewees talked about how ordinary members of the community help each other overcome various problems, including radicalisation. Again, this often involves resolving disputes, educating other members of the community, and monitoring each other. For example, the surgeon and community leader in Khabarovsk believed that 'organised diasporas and communities can protect their own from such ailments … educated young people among the migrants are actively working for the prevention of radicalism and extremism among the youth' (Khab 5).

A third of interviewees also mentioned the role of religious leaders (including mullahs and muftis – well educated and respected in religious matters) and mosques in actively preventing radicalisation, particularly through providing religious and moral guidance and education. For example, a male martial arts trainer living in Novosibirsk mentioned a case in which a mufti disrupted the recruitment of a community member: 'Our Mufti told us of a case when in 2016 one of the mosque attenders, an Uzbek, told him that his two sons wanted to go to Syria. And that he met those young men and in several conversations explained what was going on there. So the departure was aborted' (Novo 13).

Religion

In addition to the role of religious leaders and mosques in preventing radicalisation, a quarter of interviewees discussed how following religious teachings could be a protective factor by discouraging violence. For example, a female Russian examiner from Krasnodar stated, 'True faith and genuine belief in God – that's what helps me to reject violence' (Kdar 10). However, as previously noted, some interviewees speculated that a lack of understanding of religion could make some more susceptible to radicalisation, while still others speculate about the significance of religion at all.

Family

A quarter of interviewees also claimed that a sense of responsibility towards family is the primary reason why most migrants do not join violent extremist groups. This was characterised in either terms of financial responsibility, moral responsibility, or simply as a priority that took up most of their time. In the view of a female translator living in Ekaterinburg, migrants do not join violent extremist groups 'because they came to Russia to provide for their family. And for the sake of this, they are willing to endure the many difficulties which confront them at every step' (Ekat 1).

Economic Prospects

Thirteen interviewees also mentioned the positive aspects of migration to Russia – namely, more job opportunities, higher wages, and a better quality of life compared with Tajikistan. Not all of this, of course, was mentioned in the context of preventing radicalisation. Migrants who had this positive experience and stability may be less susceptible to recruitment, as suggested by the male assistant administrator at a bazaar in Samara: 'They want to find a good job and earn well. They have no use for going to Syria or Iraq' (Sama 3). Conversely, however, a lack of economic prospects, particularly due to difficulties with legalising their status, can make migrants more vulnerable. Similarly, an inability to provide economically for family members back home may also leave individuals vulnerable to extremist messaging.

The Positive Role of Authorities

Eleven interviewees mentioned the positive role that Tajik authorities can have, including in preventing radicalisation – although exactly how was not specified. Four specifically mentioned the role of the Tajik consulate, noted by a businessman in Novosibirsk: 'Diaspora leaders, authoritative individuals in the community and employees of the Tajik consulate in Novosibirsk [fight radicalisation]' (Novo 4). Furthermore, eight interviewees believed that the community should cooperate more with the authorities to fight violent extremism. A diaspora leader in Novosibirsk explained: 'Only through the joint efforts of diasporas, the government and state structures of the Russian Federation, can we resist violence and extremism' (Novo 3).

Education and Awareness

A quarter of interviewees pointed out that education and an awareness of the situation in Syria and Iraq makes migrants less likely to travel to these countries to fight for Daesh. For example, according to a male market seller in Irkutsk, the number of migrants going to fight in Syria or Iraq has been kept lower because of awareness of atrocities: 'At first, there was little information and people did not understand what was happening in Syria. As soon as videos or images of atrocities and mass executions of innocents began to appear on social networks or media, most people began to realise that this is the wrong way' (Irku 5).

Similarly, some of these interviewees pointed to the role of education and awareness initiatives. A community leader from Khabarovsk noted that 'Tajikistan and Russia have been carrying out extensive work to bring real information about ISIS and other extremist organisations to everyone' (Khab 5). Moreover, ten interviewees (15%) recommended that further improving education – particularly education on the realities of the actions of Daesh, as well as religious education – can help prevent extremism. For example, a male bus driver whose brother was recruited stated, 'The government needs to increase educational outreach and dialogue with young people in schools and universities' (Mosc 7).

IV. Analysis

Mohammed S Elshimi

IN TERMS OF structural motivations for engaging in violent extremism, this study shows that several 'push' factors were present that may have contributed to feelings of marginalisation, exclusion and alienation. First, the administrative and legal challenges of the migration process are such that some migrants end up with illegal status, and are therefore exposed to other vulnerabilities, including extremist recruiters. Second, the study identifies economic exploitation by various actors combined with financial hardship and poverty, which compels some down a path of criminality and, in a smaller number of cases, engagement with violentextremist recruiters who offer monetary incentives. Third, the discrimination, stigmatisation and securitisation of labour migrants can lead to social marginalisation and foster grievances that can be exploited by violent-extremist entities.

A key finding in the data is the perceived relationship between economic exclusion and violent extremism. In fact, the dominant explanation offered by respondents of why migrants might have turned to violent extremism was financial. This perception is striking because the poverty argument is contradicted by the evidence of other studies. Many rich and educated people take part in violent extremism, and in fact tend to form the leadership cadre of terrorist organisations.[1] This explanation dominates among the respondents who did not have a direct experience of radicalised individuals. This is contrasted with respondents who actually knew someone who had been recruited and radicalised to violent extremism, who stressed that money was not the motivation.

Recently, there has been a re-think among analysts on the role of poverty and economic factors, and the debate has moved beyond absolute poverty and instead onto relative poverty in relation to others in society[2] In the context of Central Asian labour migrants in Russia, it may be that absolute and not relative poverty plays a greater role in processes of marginalisation and exclusion that could push individuals towards violent extremism. This hypothesis will need to be tested. However, another key finding is the experience of social marginalisation that some labour migrants have to endure. This is due in large part to the growing securitisation of labour migration in Russia, a trend which according to interview subjects accelerated following the

St Petersburg Metro attack of April 2017

According to the data generated for this report, since the attacks, migrants have been framed as potential terrorists in the press and law enforcement agencies have taken a firmer approach with migrants. The symbolic and operational message is that migrants have become a security concern. However, securitisation adversely impacts the perception migrants have of their host society. It reinforces insider–outsider dynamics, leading many migrants to feel not only as outsiders in Russia, but also that their migrant identity is strengthened and reinforced. It also exacerbates grievances that feed into common narratives exploited by recruiters. At the same time, however, a great number of interview subjects expressed a view that there was positive cooperation with state structures and security authorities. They viewed these relationships as a factor of resilience rather than radicalisation. The point being that while it was clear that there was a sense of them being targeted and victimised more in the wake of the St Petersburg attack, there was also a realisation that this targeting was not universal.

The data indicates the existence of violent-extremist groups and networks operating on the ground in Russia. The names and details of those organisations were not disclosed, but a number of respondents highlighted the role of individuals from the Caucasus and others from Central Asia in recruitment processes. Assertions made by the bulk of interviewees about recruitment to violent extremism are based on perceptions and not verified facts. However, for cases where the interviewee had direct knowledge of someone who had been recruited or was in an otherwise informed position, the accounts are taken seriously. The perception of the sample group that some Caucasians are involved in violent extremism is compatible with what is known about the longer historical experience of violent extremism in the Caucasus.[3] It also makes sense from an operational point of view: Caucasians understand the culture and terrain of Russia well and have greater operational, logistical and technical capacity than Central Asians in Russia – not to mention international connections with other Salafi-Jihadi movements in the Middle East and South Asia.

A number of respondents pointed out that the first level of recruitment is normally managed by someone of the same ethnic background, who is in turn connected to wider Caucasian networks. This fits with the conclusions of other research that indicates that effective recruitment takes place over a long period of time, in small circles, with a lot of attention and care invested in individuals.[4] Recruitment is expedited in conditions of trust, companionship, and through shared acts and rituals, which strengthen the bonds between the recruiter and the recruited, between the individual and the group. This process is then more likely to take place between people who share a language and background–even if one of the most distinctive characteristics of the Salafi-Jihadi movement is its emphasis on globalised nodes of identification that are supposed to supersede conventional ethnic and national forms of identity. In this study, the data on recruitment focuses on the multiple tactics used to lure vulnerable people in – including money, religion and the internet.

Another important finding from the data is that Russia presents a more conducive environment for the promulgation and adoption of violent-extremist ideas than the Central Asian countries, due to a combination of complex factors. The authoritarian governments of Central Asia are less accommodating of religion in the public sphere than Russia. Migrant workers have a greater chance to come into contact with more radical versions of Islam in Russia than back in their home countries, including because of the greater access to the internet. Being away from home in a foreign land can push some to adopt a more categorical form of identity, such as a global Islamic identity. Finally, labour migrants, particularly illegal migrants, experience a heightened sense of vulnerability given the nature and precariousness of migrant life in Russia.

Respondents highlighted the role of online radicalisation and recruitment in violent extremism. It allowed young people to watch violent-extremist videos, as well as receive communications over apps such as WhatsApp and Telegram. Exposure to violent-extremist content was more prevalent in Russia because of better access to and affordability of smartphones and the internet in Russia. This was corroborated by two interviewees who knew someone who had been recruited. It is not clear from the data, however, what the role of social media is in pathways towards radicalisation. Nevertheless, it is important to note that the wider literature shows that the internet and social media do not themselves cause radicalisation to violent extremism: they encourage and ignite violent extremism once individuals have made up their mind.[5]

What, then, are the factors contributing to radicalisation and violent extremism among Central Asian migrants in Russia? There is a lack of consensus about what motivates an individual to leave his or her country to join a terrorist organisation elsewhere. The most common motivations cited in popular discourse and by policymakers and violent extremist themselves since 2002 are ideology and religion. The wider literature cites other incentives including belonging, status, revenge, coercion, identity, money and a sense of adventure.[6]

The most striking finding in the research for this report is that the majority of respondents believed monetary incentives were the primary motive for individuals joining violent-extremist groups. The emphasis of 'greed' (money) over 'creed' (ideology) as and explanation is different to the dominant discourse in the West, which stresses the role of creed in violent extremism. In this study, interviewees showed a notable lack of knowledge about ideology, both in terms of its doctrinal features and the role it plays in violent extremism. However, the authors of this report are cautious against putting too much trust into the respondents' views that economic hardship/poverty/material incentives drive radicalisation.

Data derived from the interviews with individuals who knew somebody closely who was radicalised is more reliable than others in the sample. If looked at in this way, it is noticeable that money and material incentives were not offered as an explanation, and it was more ideational, ideological and spiritual factors that featured in their responses. The economic incentive is a widespread view in the data, but is not backed by evidence – such as concrete examples, life stories or profiles of the arrested.

There is an explanation of why people would think so. First, since interview subjects are for the most part economic labour migrants, monetary incentives are the primary driving motive for their existence. Hence, they would lock onto that idea as a priority. Second, historically, these were at root Marxist societies, where an influence of economic determinism dominated. Many participants found it hard to believe in the driving power of ideas, which given their status as migrants from former Marxist societies, appeared alien to them. This might explain why some look for explanations which fit into their mental frames. At the same time, it is also important to consider that anecdotal evidence beyond the report shows that money does seem to be one of the many factors contributing to violent extremism, supporting this perception among interview subjects.

The role of religion was articulated in different and often contradictory ways. One view common to many respondents was that some individuals drawn into violent extremism were duped into embracing an extremist interpretation of Islam. Many particularly lay the blame on what they referred to as 'Wahhabis'.

In this view, Wahhabis are blamed for convincing gullible young migrants that it is their obligation to fight with Daesh. The wider literature confirms the idea that many who travelled to join Daesh were religious novices.[7] Yet, another view is that some individuals become motivated by the desire to help Muslims to fight against perceived oppressive regimes, for example in Syria. According to this view, violent extremist actors do not seem themselves as 'vulnerable', nor do they lack agency, but rather they are perceived as empowered altruistic individuals who have taken the responsibility to protect Muslims under siege in Assad's Syria.

Importantly, the data shows that there is no typical profile of a violent extremist or an inherent 'vulnerability' to radicalisation of labour migrants. The low volume of incidents and the relatively small number of individuals implicated mean that a typical profile of a would-be terrorist cannot be inferred. However, among labour migrants in Russia from Uzbekistan, Tajikistan and Kyrgyzstan, there are a minority of individuals who are vulnerable and at-risk of violent extremism.

The data shows that four types of person are perceived to be more vulnerable and at-risk to violent extremism: youth; illegal migrants; uneducated migrants; and lonely individuals. The perception that illegal migrants are at greater risk of being drawn into violent extremism needs to be investigated further. It is true that illegal migrants are exposed to a greater range of vulnerabilities than legal migrants, but the question is whether there is a greater relationship between illegal migrants and greater risk of being recruited. Here, caution must be exercised: the St Petersburg Metro suicide bomber, AkbarzhonJalilov, had Russian citizenship.[8]

Moreover, the perception that a lack of education increased vulnerability to violent extremism is a salient finding. This is because educated and integrated people too can be radicalised. In fact, the wider literature holds that some of those who became violent extremists in Russia among Central Asian communities are better educated than typical migrants to Russia.[9] Some scholars, such as Diego Gambetta and Steffen Hertog,[10] state the controversial thesis that individuals with higher levels of education, particularly in technical subjects, are more vulnerable to Islamist radicalisation. But in the context of labour migrants from Uzbekistan, Tajikistan, and Kyrgyzstan who are away from home, the question of whether low levels of education increase vulnerability to violent extremism needs to be investigated further.

A key element at the heart of this research which this report was unable to unpack was the impact of the detailed diversity among Uzbek, Tajik and Kyrgyz communities and the effect this might (or might not) have on violent extremism emanating from these communities. The many cultural, social, economic and historical differences between these countries and peoples are the topic of a much larger research project. But there were some noticeable issues that emerged from the research and in particular around people's perceptions of one another. For example, according to interview subjects, migrants from Kyrgyzstan hardly mix with other Central Asians, and see themselves as more individualistic and educated than other Central Asian migrants. Many interviewees also revealed a considerable degree of prejudice against ethnic Uzbeks, in particular ones from southern Kyrgyzstan who were seen as problematic.

Of the three migrant communities in this study, the Uzbeks had more to say about the challenges of Russia's migration system, in part due to the fact that, unlike migrants from Kyrgyzstan, they do not benefit from being in the Eurasian Economic Union (EEU). Migrants from Tajikistan were perceived to be the most religiously observant community of the three, as well as the most cohesive communally. Tajik interviewees were less concerned about their country not being a member of the EEU. Logically, membership of the EEU should make it easier for people to integrate and get jobs, which in turn should reduce the problems associated with radicalisation to violent extremism–the fact that this did not appear to be the case might be a significant finding, but one that is hard to support conclusively on the basis of available data.

It is also important to note that the volumes of labour migrants from the three countries at a national level are vastly different, with migrants from Uzbekistan constituting the overwhelming majority of Central Asian labour migrants in Russia. Given the bias and generalisation evident in participants' responses about their own and other ethnicnational communities, the authors of this report chose to avoid making sweeping comparisons about the difference between the three communities and how it shaped the emergence of violent extremism among a minority of individuals.

Based on the information gleaned from interviews, radicalisation and recruitment to violent extremism is a marginal issue for labour migrants from the three Central Asian countries covered in this research. Why is this? Several potential perceived sources of resilience were identified by participants: the Russian authorities; community leaders; employment; family, including the guidance of family elders or the foreman in the workplace; religion; and education. In fact, except for minor differences, these factors were consistently mentioned across the context of all three Central Asian countries.

However, there are two particular perceptions on sources of resilience worth highlighting here: (1) the positive role of the Russian authorities and (2) the positive role of community leaders. With regard to the first point, it is important to stress that the data can be contradictory. While negative experiences with the authorities – such as the clamp down on migrants by Russia's law enforcement agencies in the aftermath of the St Petersburg Metro bombing – were highlighted as a potential structural push factor, several interviewees nevertheless highlighted the government's security capacity as a protective factor. It is important to reiterate here that the literature suggests that a heavily securitised state approach can generate grievances.[11] However, the perception among several interviewees is that the net effect appears to be positive in terms of protecting against violent extremism and terrorism.

The second point about the perception of effective community leaders offers a valuable insight into factors of resilience. Many interviewees highlighted the positive role that community leaders have in supporting migrants, helping them adjust to life in Russia and, in some cases (such as mosque leaders), providing alternative narratives to those promulgated by violent extremists. Community leadership includes diaspora leaders, leaders of civil-society organisations, consular and diplomatic officials, entrepreneurs, foremen and union leaders in the workplace, and religious leaders. The dominant perception among respondents was that community leaders, in their various forms, had built a good relationship with the authorities, looked after the welfare and interests of their communities, and were positive role models for migrants. It is important to provide support for these spaces and leaders: they provide resilience.

V. Conclusion

Mohammed S Elshimi and RaffaelloPantucci

Violent extremism has substantial political, social, psychological and economic costs, as well as significant regional and international impact. This report sought to bridge the knowledge gap of why a minority of individual labour migrants in Russia from Uzbekistan, Tajikistan and Kyrgyzstan have turned to violent extremism. Through its milieu approach, this research project has generated data that both provides important new insights on radicalisation and recruitment into violent extremism among labour migrants from Uzbekistan, Tajikistan and Kyrgyzstan in Russia, and also reaffirms the results of other studies – raising questions for further research.

Looking more specifically at radicalisation to violent extremism, it is important to identify what natural sources of resilience already exist and bolster them. While relations between the state and labour migrant communities are not always perfect, research showed how in some contexts good networks of communication had been established and these played an important role in keeping people away from extremist ideas. These need to be encouraged. Furthermore, the problem of radicalisation is one that touches on all communities – so greater cooperation and discussion between Russia and the three Central Asian states is going to be important to manage this problem. Given that people are now leaving the battlefields in Syria and Iraq and in some cases heading home, the moment for closer cooperation and discussion is at hand.

Finally, the number of labour migrants who turn to violent extremism is very limited. This is important to remember as there is a danger otherwise that increased stigmatisation of the entire community will generate greater alienation and conflict, and ultimately exacerbate the problem of radicalisation. Given the growing number of Central Asians who have appeared in prominent roles in high-profile terrorist attacks around the world, there has already been a steady shift in the public discourse around Central Asians being involved in violent extremist activity. This trend should not be exacerbated further and it is important to keep the issue in appropriate proportion.

This Project is the product of a great deal of work from many people both within RUSI but also outside. First, a particular note of thanks is due to KeneshbekSainazarov for being the motor that kept the whole project going, as well as to his colleagues Samuel Fife, Kunduz Kydyrova and Michael Shipler. The completion of this research project would not be possible without their hard work and dedication. This report is principally produced by RUSI. The overall project was delivered in cooperation with Search for Common Ground; RAS; and teams of researchers from Uzbekistan, Tajikistan and Kyrgyzstan led by EmilbekDzhuraev from the American University of Central Asia; and RUSI. The team from Uzbekistan comprised Bakhtiyar Babadjanov (PhD, independent researcher) and Saida Arifkhanova (Center for Studying Regional Threats). The team from Tajikistan comprised AbdunabiSattorzoda (PhD, Tajik Academy of Science Named after Rudaki) and Mahram Anvarzod (independent researcher). The team from Kyrgyzstan comprised KayratbekDzhamangulov (PhD, Center for Social Studies, and Kyrgyz Academy of Science), NurbekOmuraliev (PhD, Center for Social Studies, and Kyrgyz Academy of Science) and Alisher Khamidov (independent researcher). Dr Mohammed S Elshimi is a Research Fellow in the National Security and Resilience Team (NSR) at the Royal United Services Institute (RUSI). RaffaelloPantucci is the Director of International Security Studies at the Royal United Services Institute (RUSI). Sarah Lain is an Associate Fellow at the

Royal United Services Institute (RUSI). Nadine L Salman is a PhD candidate at University College London (UCL). Understanding the Factors Contributing to Radicalisation among Central Asian Labour Migrants in Russia. Mohammed S Elshimi with RaffaelloPantucci, Sarah Lain and Nadine L Salman. Royal United Services Institute for Defence and Security Studies. 187 years of independent thinking on defence and security. The Royal United Services Institute (RUSI) is the worlds oldest and the UK's leading defence and security think tank. Its mission is to inform, influence and enhance public debate on a safer and more stable world. RUSI is a research-led institute, producing independent, practical and innovative analysis to address today's complex challenges. Since its foundation in 1831, RUSI has relied on its members to support its activities. Together with revenue from research, publications and conferences, RUSI has sustained its political independence for 187 years. Royal United Services Institute for Defence and Security Studies Whitehall London SW1A 2ET United Kingdom +44 (0)20 7747 2600 www.rusi.org. RUSI is a registered charity (No. 210639). Published in 2018 by the Royal United Services Institute for Defence and Security Studies. This work is licensed under a Creative Commons Attribution.

Chapter 9

Anti-Extremism and Anti-Terrorism in Legislation of Tajikistan: Problems of Application

Valijon Abdukhamitov and Rano Abdullayeva

Abstract

The paper considers the issues of implementing the standards of the international legislation on religious and extremist crimes in the national legislation of the Republic of Tajikistan. With regard to its ideology the category of extremism is reflected in the criminal law through the concept of extremist crime: crime for political, ideological, racial, national or religious hatred or hostility reasons or crimes resulting from hatred or hostility towards any social group. According to the understanding of hatred and hostility, which is deeply rooted within the criminal law, the latter one represents external practical (conflict, destructive) actions whereas the first one illustrates hostility without specific actions. The criminal law warrants five kinds of hatred or hostility motives: political, ideological, racial, national, religious hatred or hostility, as well as hatred or hostility towards any social group. These kinds partially overlap in their content, which requires their correct definition. In order to improve the criminal legislation the authors analyzed the disadvantages of the legislation of the Republic of Tajikistan and made certain suggestions.

1 Introduction

Counter-religion and counter-extremism efforts are urgent issues demanding law enforcement agencies to take stringent measures and coordinated actions aimed to prevent and suppress religious extremism. Today terrorism and extremism became the most dangerous global phenomenon preventing smooth development of international relations, destabilizing safety of many regions and entire countries. According to many experts, terrorism and extremism represent an asymmetrical response to global challenges, a reaction of the emerging postmodern 'network' world organization to pressure from traditional 'hierarchical' structures managing global processes. According to projections, in 2015 the income per capita across 56 countries of the world will be less than 5 thousand dollars.

Nearly 3 billion people (41% of the entire population) will live in these countries. Hunger, blatant poverty, especially against the background of welfare growth among advanced countries, will form a strong negative aspect of the world economy at the beginning of the 21st century. Among key parameters of global development the developed and rich countries will face an urgent need to create conditions for sustainable development of the poorest countries mainly led by the humanitarian viewpoint. The fear of uncontrolled immigration, growth of drug trafficking and terrorism in these countries will most likely force rich countries to develop and implement the economic development programs in poor countries.

The legal literature indicates that there are no clear distinctions between terrorism and extremism. Perhaps, due to such uncertainty the state often ignores the relation between these phenomena. Currently, the efforts of law enforcement agencies on counterterrorism do not serve as a warning but as a reaction to already committed illegal acts. The fight against extremism in some CIS countries is generally confined to suppression of terrorist activity while terrorism prevention shall become the main focus of such efforts since the political power purely relying on its authority to counteract terror and not fully utilizing diverse political and legal mechanisms of its prevention and suppression, has no future.

2 Problem Statements

The problem of counter extremism in a society, especially among young people of Tajikistan is among the major tasks since the government bears responsibility for compliance and protection of rights and freedoms of humans and citizens (Article 5, Constitution of the Republic of Tajikistan). The concept of 'radicalism' typical for social sciences means both conscious and unconscious extremity in views and actions (i.e. the assessment of extremity depends only on sociocultural level of individual development and its social conditions). Similar to any other extreme phenomenon, radicalism may be prosocial and anti-social. It should be considered that in severe crisis conditions (one of the largest is being developed in all countries now) the radical social elements holding extreme views possess the maximum destructive potential able to change the development trajectory of a society.

This quality of radicals, the majority of which is traditionally composed of young people, for many centuries has been provoking the idea to use them for power struggle by groups claiming for such power. The attribution of political concept to words and actions of radical groups regardless their personal interests and needs turns diverse youth groups into the tool of power struggle, i.e. into extremist groups and associations within the context of current legislation. Natural escalation of radicalism (the boundary of 'extreme' is shifted from words to actions and such 'actions' eventually result in violence) during political struggle inevitably forms the ideology and practice of legitimacy of any violent actions in fight for the 'bright future'. If the influence of destructive forces with regard to both internal and external impact on Tajikistan during the recent years is defined in theses, then they can be described approximately within the following time frames:

The first period–1990, February events leading to the first human losses in Dushanbe; The second period – 1991, rallies organized by new social, political and parochial organizations, groups; The third period – beginning of civil opposition and mass fratricidal war –1992-1994; The fourth period – beginning of negotiation process and signing of the Treaty of Peace and National Consent-1994-1997, attempts to interrupt the negotiation process by supporters of internal and external forces; The fifth period – a series of terrorist attacks by gangs of groups and paramilitary forces, which refused to sign and accept the Treaty of Peace and National Consent, and liquidation of remained illegal armed groups – 2001-2002 years; The sixth period – spate of new radical organizations and terrorist attacks in Dushanbe, in Sughd region – 2002-2009; The seventh period – recruitment of young people in various new radical terrorist organizations and participation of certain citizens of the Republic of Tajikistan in the Syrian Civil War as part of ISIL, escalation of illegal armed groups on the Tajik-Afghan border (on the Afghan side) – 2013-2015.

3 Purpose of the Study

The purpose of the study is to identify problems of applying the anti-extremism and anti-terrorism legislation of Tajikistan. This purpose implies not only the analysis of the existing legislation, but also the conditions aimed to update the forms of counterextremism and counter-terrorism in the conditions of the Republic of Tajikistan.

4 Research Methods

The methodology of the study is based on complex and system approaches. It also includes the methods of analysis, synthesis, and generalization, logical and legal (dogmatic), comparative and legal, historical and legal approaches. The study is built upon works of Kurbonzod B.Sh.[2], Laqueur W.[3] Petryanina A.V[4]], etc. The study of extremism also overlaps with the issues of discrimination, including linguistic discrimination, which was analyzed by Iskandarova et al [1].

5 Results and Discussion Findings

In recent years four external threats began to exert direct influence on national and regional security of the Central Asian states:

1. Drug trafficking, drug expansion or drug menace;

2. Illegal armed forces, radical and terrorist organizations generally recruiting young people, ideological opposition and ideological sabotage;

3. Increase in illegal small arms (in the Middle East), illegal arms trade, control over small arms and ammunition and risk of their transportation to the Central Asian countries;

4. Cyberwar, information and psychological propaganda of youth in the Republic of Tajikistan and the Central Asian states. Having gained its international significance, terrorism and extremism cannot but affect the Republic of Tajikistan (RT).

Since 2006, such organizations as Al-Qaeda, East Turkestan Islamic Movement, Turkestan Islamic Movement (TIM), Taliban, Muslim Brotherhood, Lashkar-e-Taiba, Islamic society of Pakistan, DzhamoatiTablig, SozmoniTabligot, TochikistoniOzod, HizbutTahrir are under ban of the Supreme Court of Tajikistan. Further efforts to reduce the level of radicalization were adopted after the official statement saying that since 2011 more than one thousand Tajiks have joined the militants in Syria and Iraq. Thus, according to statistics of the RT Main Information Analysis Center of the Ministry of Internal Affairs, during 2004-2016 over 271 extremist crimes were recorded in the republic, including 3 in 2010, [1] in 2011, 2 in 2012, 13 in 2013, 43 in 2014, 112 in 2015 and 97 in 2016 {1, P.4}. To counteract extremism and terrorism, Tajikistan adopted the Law "On Combatting Terrorism" [2] on 16 November 1999 and the Law "On Combatting Extremism" [3] on 8 December 2003. Besides, on 12 November 2016 the republic approved the National Strategy of the Republic of Tajikistan on counterextremism and counter-terrorism for 2016-2020[4] stipulating the main priority directions on counterextremism and counter-terrorism.

Nevertheless, anti-terrorism and anti-extremism legal acts of Tajikistan include some problems concerning their application. Let us consider some of them. First, despite the importance of counter-terrorism the anti-terrorist legislation of Tajikistan does not consider the uniform understanding of terrorism. The analysis of available legal (and not only) literature allows "identifying from 100 to 200 concepts of terrorism and extremism, however neither of them was recognized as a classical concept". In this respect the authors cannot but agree with American scientist W. Laqueur defining terrorism as "the term overloaded with concepts, which results in failure to develop a comprehensive and objective definition of terrorism. Such definition does not exist and will not be found in the near future".[5, 13] Second, the definition of extremism established in the anti-extremism legislation of Tajikistan represents almost a complete textual reproduction of the concept of extremist activity, which is contained in the initial edition of the anti-extremism legislation of the Russian Federation dated 2002.

Moreover, the Law of RT "On Combatting Extremism" (Article 3) describes extremism as "manifestation by legal entities and individuals of extreme forms of actions appealing to destabilization, change of constitutional system in the country, seizure of power and its authorization, racial, national, social and religious agitation". This norm conflicts Article 22 of the Criminal Code of RT, according to which only sane natural person[6] but not the legal entity is subject to criminal liability. Third, at present the legislation of Tajikistan ambiguously treats the concepts of 'extremist crime' and 'crime of extremist activity'. Moreover, the laws and regulations define the above notions similarly to such terms as 'crime of extremist character' and 'terrorist activity'. Thus, the Law of RT "On Combatting Organized Crime" [7] identifies the term 'extremism' as the concept of 'extremist activity' (Art. 5). In turn, the Laws of RT "On Political Parties" (Art. 4) [8] and "On National Security Structures of RT" (Art. 15) [9] apply the concept of 'extremist activity'.

The heading of Article 15 of the above law says: "Combatting Terrorist Activity and Organized Crime", however the text itself contains such statements as 'terrorist and extremist activity', and then 'organized crime'. The same situation may be observed in case of the Uniform Concept of the Republic of Tajikistan on

Combatting Terrorism and Extremism [10](Section 5 item 2; Section 10 item 2; Section 3 item 2, 3, 4), the Concept of Cooperation of the CIS Member States in Combatting Terrorism and other Violent Manifestations of Extremism[11] (Section 7 item 1; Section 4; Section 9; Section 15 item 2; Section 2; Section 3; Section 6; Section 8 item 3; Section 4 item 4), the Concept of Criminal and Legal Policy of RT [12] (Section 8 item 2) where in one case it states 'extremist activity' and in the other – 'activity of extremist character', i.e. the terms listed above are used several times as synonyms. Another problem, which is worth paying attention, is lack of systematization and unification of religious education in the Republic of Tajikistan.

Uncontrolled departure of Tajikistan citizens from the country in recent decades with their subsequent religious education abroad resulted in low level of education of local Muslim spiritual servants. Low education of confessors affects the quality of education in madrasah. Generally students study a short course of ceremonies, superficially get acquainted with the Islamic law, partially study the issues of worship, partially Islam history, gain some knowledge of Arabic. The situation becomes even worse due to the fact that the clergy is not able to resolutely and efficiently react to manifestations of religious extremism believing that over some time nonconventional religious trends in Tajikistan will recede into the past. However, the recent events demonstrated just the reverse. Several various directions of youth extremist organizations appeared recently.

Despite the apparent external discrepancy, they fit within the logic of any system, passing the stages of formation, maintenance, stabilization and further development in their urge to avoid chaos and disappearance. Unlike traditional extremist groups of various levels of organization and structure the majority of youth extremist organizations are rather sensitive and unstable. They function around norms not fixed in charters and guidelines and arise spontaneously in the course of communication therefore are perceived by all members and deeply rooted thus transforming into individual specific attitudes and value orientations. Nonconformists are characterized by various levels of organization. Quite often youth associations are unstable, do not have well defined structure and change their configuration. The age range of active members of extremist organizations of such type is generally from 14 to 35 years with organizational and administrative unit composed of certain senior actors. Teenagers and persons that have not reached their mature age yet but have clear separatist views are considered the most active representatives.

Thus, unlike traditional complex associations there is a clear tendency among young extremists towards association by the network principle implying high independence of network cells (youth extremist groups). With new forms of activity of extremist groups, their organizations and communities may change the role of their participants, in particular the organizer and the leader. The organizer does not always acts as the leader, which position for various reasons may be taken by another person. Religious extremism is similarly dangerous since it often implies illegal armed groups, organized criminal organizations specializing in terrorist crimes. However, religious extremism is not constraint by actions of certain terrorist and extremist organizations. As a rule, participants of extremist groups and organizations record their illegal acts using videos and photos, and then place them on corresponding websites in the Internet. Such websites are actively used by extremist groups, organizations and associations to promote their activity, to justify their actions, to disseminate data on their methods, for reconnaissance purposes, to recruit new members and collect donations.

Quite often the extremist and terrorist groups affiliated to them create 'short-lived websites' thus changing their formats and addresses, which complicates official recording of their illegal activity in electronic space. Rapid development of information technology leads to the fact that many social phenomena find immediate reflection in the so-called virtual worlds, i.e. in information environment with mass media, global computer telecommunication networks and systems. The increasing criminal control over these spheres poses extremely high danger to society. The development of the Internet, which does not use earlier applied mechanisms and principles of information environment control, opened up opportunities for extremists to carry out anonymous and unpunished promotion of criminal activity.

The extremist organizations consistently master cyberspace. Recruiters are active within networks through a wide use of information and manipulative mechanisms. Their main task is to make their image the most attractive to the young part of the Internet users and whenever possible to recruit the maximum number of them. In both cases there is no direct contact between people;therefore all manipulative tools are utilized without restrictions resulting in unconscious actions of the majority of website users, which do not understand that they take part in extremist activity. The search for candidates is accordingly carried out at corresponding forums, blogs and in cybercommunities presenting interest to extremist organizations, which identifies the most active participants able to competently and intelligibly express their thoughts and able to convince and argue their point. When attracting such persons to cooperation the recruiters apply 'an intelligent hook' and the candidates shall solve a challenging but rather interesting intelligent task.

By solving it they do not only help the extremist organization but also undergo testing for suitability. Alternatively, their entire activity in the organization can be focused on the solution of similar intelligent tasks or they can be involved in pure unwitting propaganda. New information technologies substantially promoted the formation of such organizations, made them manageable and lifted limits on the number and geography of access to information. This new quality allowed applying technologies, which were simply impossible before: flashmob, contactless manipulation, individual and mass programming of certain actions.

Without any doubt the domestic youth extremist organizations are fully ready to use all 'achievements' of destructive technologies, which requires law enforcement officers to bear thorough knowledge of these innovations and to be ready to counteract. First of all this refers to 'virtual' environment. The study of domestic and foreign experience showed that there are all chances to supplement traditional forms of counteraction with major investigative measures in virtual environment, which could make it possible to increase the efficiency of combatting extremist organizations.[6]

Conclusion

In conclusion it should be noted that human losses of Tajikistan as a result of the civil war, which mainly arose among the youth, cannot be measured in money and digital equivalents. The Republic of Tajikistan suffered the economic damage of over 7 billion dollars (in equivalent of 1990s), the country lagged behind 20-30 years, and all critical social and economic objects were destructed. Tajikistan did not even suffer such destructions during the World War II. The most severe consequence of the civil fratricidal war was the death of over 150 thousand people with 50 thousand orphan children and more than 30 thousand widows remaining in the republic. The civil war affected every single family in Tajikistan and marked a deep imprint of grief and suffering, pain and separation. It resulted in over 1 million internal displacements and external refugees.

After 25 years of national independence and 18 years from signing the Treaty of Peace and National Consent there are still some forces from abroad and within the country willing to play upon heartstrings of people and revive the feelings of religious, ethnic and parochial intolerance, promote ethnoegoistic, ethnocentric and ethnochauvinistic feelings and prejudices among young and naïve people. Thus, summing up the results it is possible to note that theoretical and practical aspects of the above problems will contribute to further positive improvement of anti-terrorism and anti-extremism situation in Tajikistan. *The Authors, published by EDP Sciences. This is an open access article distributed under the terms of the Creative Commons Attribution License 4.0 (http:// creativecommons.org/licenses/by/4.0/). SHS Web of Conferences 50, 01224 (2018) https://doi.org/10.1051/*

Chapter 10

Sunni-Shia Issue in Azerbaijan

Ilia Brondz1, Tahmina Aslanova

Abstract

Being constitutionally recognized as a secular country, due to its
Muslim majority Azerbaijan is known as a Muslim country in the
world. Most of the Muslim population belongs to Shia sect, which
is a minor part of Muslims all over the world and this peculiarity
differentiates Azerbaijan from other Islam dominated countries.
The issue of division of Islam shows itself, not that distinctly, but
somehow in Azerbaijan too. Considering the geographic position
of Azerbaijan that is one of the crucial factors being lucrative for
the foreign actors to some extent led to an imbalance between the
Sunni-Shia sects.

Since the analysis of Sunni-Shia controversies, the history and
spread of Islam in Azerbaijan are being studied by a number of
researches, this article will not be focused on the same issues. The
reason why Azerbaijan does not witness Sunni-Shia controversies
comparing with other Islamic countries has always been a topic of
discussion and this article aims to shed a light on some aspects of
this question. However, the fact that the recent developments in
rivalry between sects due to internal and foreign influences makes
us concern about its nature to cause hazardous situation in all
spheres of life.

Keywords:

Islam, Sunnism, Shiism, Azerbaijan, Foreign Actors, Secularism, İslamic Revival

1. Introduction

(Dissemination of Islam in Azerbaijan: First Signs of Sectarian Tensions)

Back in VII century Arabs started to storm the northern borders of Middle East as well as Azerbaijan, thus, started the spread of Islam in the territory of Modern Azerbaijan. Formation of the religion in this territory evolved through numerous steps over the centuries and has been a long complex process. The religious policy of states and nations who took control of these territories before and after Arabs had a huge impact not only on the ethnic identity, but on the distinction of Azerbaijani population's religious identity. It is noteworthy to mention the fact that the existence of Christianity, Zoroastrianism and Shamanism before Islam for centuries had influence on the spread of new religion in Azerbaijan. Azerbaijan as being the bridge between West and East, considering the motherland of people with Turkic origin—speaking Turkic language could not remain beyond the religious and ethnic conflicts of the medieval ages.

The aggravating of the conflict was not only due to the fact that the territory was surrounded by Muslim and Christian states. At the same time, becoming the field of struggle between Sunni Turkey and Shia Iran (Iran is used as a geographic location) added the religious patter into the political controversy as well. That to a certain extent led to the ideological disorientation of Azerbaijani people. When a state founded its authority over these territories, the religion he backed also dominated the area, while other sects and their adherents by taking opposition side continued the struggle for power. In XV-XVI centuries, internal Safavids—AqQoyunlu[1] and external Safavids—Ottomans religious clashes contributed to the sectarian hostility and became an inseparable part of the history of Azerbaijan until the beginning of XIX century.

266

1.1. Expansion of Sunni-Shia Division Process

The term Jafarism refers to Jafar al-Sadiq, who was principally responsible for defining Twelver Shia doctrine. It is in fact synonymous with Twelver Shia Islam.

One of the interesting sides of Islam is the adaptation to the local conditions of different areas. It had spread and got various regional forms without damaging the common principles. The regional form of Islam spread in Central Asia and Caucasus, especially Azerbaijan was Islamic mysticism—Sufizm[2]. Some Sufi brotherhoods whose influence grew in XIII-XV centuries headed the main social movements in Azerbaijan, Iran and Ottoman Empire. One of them was Safaviyya brotherhood [3]which was the first to raise Irfan or Shi'ite Sufism to the rank of a state ideology in XVI century, distinguishing Iranian Turks from others. Because of this policy Azerbaijan became a battlefield for endless wars between Safavids and Ottomans in XVI-XVIII centuries. During the reign of Tahmasib I Shiism was an absolute and even radical form of this sect dominating Azerbaijan and Iran. Only his son, Ismail II showed interest to Sunnis, and tried to remove radical form of Shiism and extreme hostile attitude towards Sunnis, but he couldn't. Because of his attempts he was killed in the second year of his reign [456]

1.2. Further Attempts for Reconciliation of Sunni-Shia Sects

In XVIII century, there was a new attempt to reconcile Sunni and Shia sects of Islam by Nader Shah—the ruler of the Afshar dynasty. In 1736, Nader, the military commander from the Turkoman Afshar tribe, overthrew the rule of the Safavid dynasty by declaring himself Shah. He introduced the term "Jafari"1 to describe mainstream Shias by repeating Sunni methodology. He launched a series of religious reforms aimed at easing differences between Shias and Sunnis. But he failed to achieve his goal, there were few changes as Shias were allowed to join Sunnis during the Hajj pilgrimage to Mecca[7].

Nader Shah was interested in gaining rights for his people to go to the Hajj in part because of revenues from the pilgrimage trade.

Among his reforms was the introduction of what came to be known as the kolah-e Naderi. This was a hat with four peaks which symbolized the first four caliphs. Since the times of Nader Shah, no further civil wars between Shia and Sunnis have been recorded. After his death, during the Khanates period in Azerbaijan, khanates such as Quba and Derbent, located in the north of Azerbaijan, close to Dagestan, were officially Sunni, while the southern ones were Shia, but nonetheless it didn't play a major political role[8].

2. Islam in Azerbaijan under the Russian Empire Conquest: From the Religious to the National Identity

Early in XIX century, Araxes River became a border between Russia and Iran after the Treaty of Turkmenchay, according to the terms, north of the Araxes was incorporated into Russian Empire and cut off from the major Shia cities of Qom, Mashhad and Tabriz. Turks remaining in the northern border of river in Russian—held Azerbaijan thoroughly differed from their compatriots remaining in the south of the river; while in the north, regions bordering with Dagestan and Chechens, also to the west part majority were Sunnis, but in the south part of Azerbaijan granted to Iran, Shi'as outnumbered Sunnis, which consequently resulted with involving North Azerbaijan in the secularization process by which to the political difference between North and South part of country was added religious factor[9.] The approach of Tsarist regime to Islam was not even, accompanied with the demonstration of tolerance to avoid forthcoming rebellions or when the weakness of the new government was apparent.

However generally as a "rival and fanatic religion" Islam was under pressure

The state and political officials could not come to an agreement regarding the religion, although the plan on centralizing the religious governance was prepared, the Tsarist government was concerned about unifying Caucasian Muslims even under official control. In this case, the tension in North Caucasus was more apparent and long-lasted. Creating a centralized clerical board remained unsettled, while in South Caucasus "The Resolution on Board of Shiite and Sunni Muslims of Transcaucasia" was adopted by Russian Tsar in 1872. Two Muslim administrative organ—Sunni and Shi'a's Spiritual Boards respectively headed by Mufti and Sheikhul-Islam was formed. They were under the control of Ministry of Internal Affairs and directly attached to the Viceroyalty[10.] The religious issues of South Caucasian Muslims were arranged by these two boards until Azerbaijan declared its Independence (1918-1920). In the beginning periods of tsar's conquest, the Russian authorities considered Sunnis more hostile and this sentiment was reinforced by the Sunni-dominated North Caucasus.

The long-lasted struggle of Imam Shamil against Russian Tsar' army inspired the Azerbaijani Sunnis whom by getting both spiritual and material support from mountainous nation started their rebellions against the regime in the 30s of XIX century. There are a number of facts prove that Russian government used even Shi'as for its purpose of neutralizing the followers of Muridism and Sunnis whose persecution changed the percentage of people in favour of Shi'as. It can be said that since this time Shi'as were composed the main part of all South Caucasus Muslims.[11,12] Overall, the Russian Tsarist government was interested in existence of resentment among different sects (tarikas) of Islam and gave its support to some of them.

This way had been estimated as an opportunity to deepen the conflicts among the sects by which Islam could internally be weakened. South Azerbaijan, ruled by Gajar dynasty was the territory where Babism and its reformist wing Bahaism widely spread and passed to the regions of North Azerbaijan, including Nakhchivan, Ordubad and namely to Baku. The Russian Tsarist regime allowed them to move from south of Araz river and be settled in the north regions of Azerbaijan by creating a favourable condition for them to spread their ideas. An orthodox Shia clericals and Islam adherents were concerned about the activity of Babis, Bahais, and the sect of Sheykhis, while the local people were seriously suffered from the internal conflicts too. The sects and split among them were openly depicted in the fictions referring to the mid-XIX century[13].

All these factors sometimes hindered Muslims to unite and solve their common problems that had been attempted to rise several times before government by February Revolution of 1917. Among these events can be listed Congresses of Russian Muslims held in 1905-1906, the activity of Muslim fraction in the Russian State Duma and etc., where regardless of inter-rivalry of Muslim nations somehow, they could make their voice to be heard[14]. During Armenian-Azerbaijanis (by then, Azerbaijanis were called Transcaucasian Muslims or Tatars) ethnic conflict during the Russian Revolution of 1905-1907 which was fomented by Tsarist government in order to distract the attention of subordinated nations from the social-political issues also eliminated the Sunni-Shia split, and consequently pushed Azerbaijani Muslims to merge their forces against Armenian threat regardless being bounded to Sunni-Shia sects and become the participants of the National Movement aimed to get rid of the oppression of the Russian Empire.

Secularization Line: Secular Intellectuals and Their Reforms

One of the main responsibilities of front-rank Azerbaijani intellectuals, who were the leaders of enlightenment and national-liberation movement from the second quarter of XIX century, was to suspend the Sunni-Shi'a split. By taking the pro-secularization position these open-minded people's target was not Islam itself, but hostility between the sects considering it as the main obstacle for the formation of national identity, educational development and cultural level of the nation? Even during the first Congress of All-Caucasian Muslims, which was held in Baku on 15 - 20 April, 1917, the question regarding to establishing single board for both Sunnis and Shias was put into discussion and with this, they called for the unity of all political trends by ending the sectarian rivalry. For them, the time was ripe for replacing the religious identity with the national one. In the works of these intellectuals, such as Seyyid Azim Shirvani, Sultan Majid Ganizade, Mahammad TaghiSidqi, MirzeAlekber Sabir, Mirza Fatali Akhundov, Mirza Kazem Bek, Mahammad agha Shahtakhtinski, Jalil Mammadguluzade, Hasan bey Zardabi, Abbasgulu Agha Bakikhanov-special attention was given to the propaganda of national-political revival of the nation and extent of secularization[15].

Bayram Balci, a professor studying religious issue in Azerbaijan lists the factors caused the weakening of Sharia system—Shiism in this period: if the secularization process and increasing the influence of intellectual trends comes first, he underlined the role of Pan-Turkism and Pan-Islamism ideologies also as the essential factors. The Pan-Turkists thought that the Shiism was a main obstacle for building great Turkic world, and on the other hand, pan-Islamism wanted to unite Sunni and Shia division and proclaimed the unity of Islam[16]. This tendency, as mentioned above, continued during Azerbaijan Democratic Republic (ADR) existence, the first democratic Republic in the East in 1918-1920, which resulted with the weakening influence of foreign religious forces on Islam in country. Unlike North Caucasus and Central Asia, sharia courts were replaced by secular courts in Azerbaijan as it became unacceptable to form such reliable courts on sharia rules[17].

3. Soviets and Islam

Despite the fact that all religions were persecuted during Soviet period, the Muslims' situation was much desperate, and they were trusted less. The reason was Soviet's belief that Islam is the main obstacle for Muslims' resistance against communism. However, their anti-religious, anti-Islam position was less effective, this can be proved by numerous facts such as covert practice of Islamic rites. Moreover, some Muslim communists from different peripheries of the Soviet Russia who held a leading position in their countries, such as Nariman Narimanov, the first Muslim communist leader of Azerbaijan, Mir Sayyid Sultanqaliyev, Galimdjan İbrahimov in Tatarstan, Uzbeks FayzullaKhojayev, AbdurraufFitrat in Bukhara, Kazakhs TurarRiskulovand Ahmed Baytursuncherished hope to get support for the idea of Islamic Communism[18].

Narimanov thought that state esteem for religious beliefs may help the Soviets to get support in the outskirts. Despite his opposition views against Bolsheviks, soviets tried to avoid any conflicts with Muslim nations and reduced their anti-Islam measures, even did not refuse their membership in the Communist Party, for neutralizing their influence they promoted loyal Muslim communists to the state positions. Only from the end of 1920th they started to liquidate these local communist leaders[19]. They were labeled as a "national" communist deprecating the main part line and eliminated them from the political stage. Forming the League of the Godless, closing mosques, religious schools and courts, pursuing clergies clearly demonstrated new government's antireligious—anti-Islam position from the beginning of 1920th[20].

The hostile approach of both Tsarist and Soviet Russia toward Islam was disguised as a struggle with the superstition and backwardness of the Muslims. Despite the elimination of the religious education and the pressure on religion, the Soviets were not able to destroy the country's deeply-embedded Muslim identity, however acquired a common distinctive identity as Soviet Muslims, with this they became estranged from their ethnic brethren and co-religionists both along and across the USSR borders.

Overall, estimating the result of the religious policy of Soviets in Azerbaijan nearly for 70 years it seems the strengthening of the feeling to be bound to Islam noticed before the islamophobia of Russian government, but generally as a first stage of consolidation of national-ethnic identity, this religion showed itself in the peculiarities of social and individual behavior and self-consciousness rather than in confession and strict observing religious rites. As T. Swietochovski noted the practicing religious rites limited within the family not publicly, so Islam was much more privatized than previous years. Especially, the city-dwellers revealed their Muslim identity only during the main events—such as circumcision and burial ceremony[21].

In the area of religious sects, it can be said that the secularization policy of pre-Soviet Azerbaijani intellectuals, additionally the atheist position by Bolsheviks explained the limited knowledge on Sunni-Shia rivalry and to attach themselves to any of these sects, especially noticeable among the young generation, eventually led to the dispersion of above-mentioned Soviet Muslims identity or

272

Soviet identity of Caucasian Muslims by giving its place to the ethnic-national "Muslim" identity.

4. The Role of Foreign Actors in Activization of Radical Islam in Modern Azerbaijan

The dissolution of the Soviet Union is marked with the revival of Islamic values in Azerbaijan. What was the peculiarity of it and which religious powers were fighting for it? What kind of differences can be observed in the attitude towards Islam and its sects between the Muslim population of pre-Soviet and post 1991 Azerbaijan? As mentioned above, anti-Islam policies of the USSR abated the Islamic mainstay but could not relinquish it completely. Islam was politically so vague. Despite the fact, it kept an important part to determine cultural and national identity and classify the nation ethnically.

Early years of independence witnessed the spread of Turkic values and pro-Turkish political tendencies. On the other hand, since they could not provide the society with religious knowledge, Azerbaijani Shia religious leaders lost their influence and leading position in revival. Thus, contrasting local religious communities starts to be formed eventually. Notwithstanding, those communities could not gain public support due to the same reasons and starting from mid-1990s, foreign religious groups start to grow financed by overseas countries[22,23.]Interestingly enough, Iranian and Turkish led ideologies caused public outrage among secular Azerbaijani population due to their Sunni-Shia confronting contents.

Hence, they resorted different, more effective tools to manipulate the sects. However, one cannot say that sect confrontation or differences among them were embedding. There were several reasons for that, disturbed by the foreign powers' interference, local government prepared action plans, less effective amendments in the legislatives and made it mandatory for all religious communities to be subject to the Caucasian Muslims Spiritual Board despite their different sects. Although there was some interest to get education at a university of a prestigious Islamic countries in early 90th, later due to the amendments made in the Law on Freedom of Religious

Belief in 2009, the people who got religious education abroad could not act as a religious person and conduct any religious rituals, that led to the less interest to the religion among the young generation for not being lucrative area. Simultaneously, all exchange programs were terminated.

In spite of these, during the first decade of XXI century, active influence of Shia sect can be observed in political processes. By all means, Shaykh al-Islām's association with Shiism was the major circumstance. With another word, political activities of Shia leaders assisted the revival of this sect. As witnessed during the recent years, government supervision on religious revival gets tighter, due to restrictions imposed by the government on Sunni Nur and Salafi communities, religious revival progresses with interruptions and stagnation[24]. In contrast to other religious groups, Nur or Nurchular, which was formed as a Turkish religious sect, is less radical and aggressive than that of radical Shi'a and Salafi schools. It is a combination of moral and ethical obligations of Muslims, and its audience includes educated strata of the Azerbaijani society. However, one of the two branches of Nurcus was called the people of Gulen or Fatullahcis (the followers of FatullahGulen), who does not limit on religious propaganda, but tries to penetrate into all areas of public-political life.

To prevent their influence, 10 private schools-lyceums and 1 university attached to "ChagOyretim" company, whose administration and teaching staff were primarily from Turkey, were closed step by step since 2014 with the order of the Azerbaijani government, while the decision was faced with strong discrepancy among the population[25]. Despite their success in modern Azerbaijan, pre-mentioned Islamic movements are not decisive in Azerbaijan. Main reason for that is crushing secular preference over religion in Azerbaijan. On the other hand, ongoing conflict with Christian Armenia pacifies religious confrontation between sects and preserves the importance of secular national and political identity for unity. In addition, Pew Research Center's survey of 2011-2012, which was carried out in 5 countries comprising Sunni and Shia population, reveals the nation's attitude towards one another. Survey was accomplished among 5000 Muslims. Among them Shias comprise the majority in Iran, Iraq and Azerbaijan? According to the results, tension between Sunnis and Shia's was confirmed only by 1% of the respondents [26].

Less tension among both sects in Azerbaijan is observed with overt practice of both religious beliefs, which are similar to each other except some key tenets of their faith. Among those rituals, remembrance of Prophet Mohammad's grandchild Huseyn's death on the 10th Ashura day and visiting major Shia saints' graves is not contradicted excessively by any of the sects (between Shias and Sunnis +93 and +86 percentage points, respectively). Such cases prove that there is no possibility that Azerbaijan will be another potential country hosting sect clash. Both the state policy and also Azerbaijani population themselves are motivated to be tolerant and publicly express religiously tolerant position[27]. Recently Heydar Mosque was constructed in Azerbaijan, being the largest Mosquein the entire South Caucasus region, named after Heydar Aliyev, the third President (1993-2003) of Azerbaijan. During the inauguration, religious, government and community leaders joined together to participate in a "unity prayer" of Shia and Sunni Muslims. Since then the Heydar Mosque has been holding joint Shia-Sunni prayers every Friday https://jewishjournal.com/news / israel/185602/.

5. Conclusion

To conclude all the noted facts, it should be emphasized that strong political Islam does not exist in Azerbaijan. Most Azerbaijanis consider Islam as a part of their national identity and any mix of religion with the political sphere is rejected by the vast majority of people. Sparked by the USSR's collapse, Islamic revival remains rather superficial. Since the revival was boosted by foreign powers with alien ideologies to the Azerbaijani society, some differences can be seen in their attitude towards pre-Soviet Islam and its influence on society. Although, great majority associate themselves either with Sunni Islam or Shia Islam, most of them do not know the main difference between them or do not want to know at all. Yet most people even consider overtly voicing one's sect inappropriate and it does not comply with mental etiquette to them.

Government-led propaganda rejecting the superiority of one sect over another and instead promoting unified and secularized Islam, thus, making religion cultural identity influences the current process as well. However, things could change. Relatively affluent natural resources of Azerbaijan (especially oil and gas) among other South Caucasian Republics attracts regional and global power's attention in this country and they try to utilize all available tools to enhance their political-economic spheres including ethnic-language and religious options. On the other hand, growing concern by the authorities over the influence of external religious influence and carrying out fierce and indiscriminate policy against some movements, along discrepancy of local population on socio-political developments might lead to the improvement of radicalization. If to express shortly, there is a serious concern for political Islam to become an influential force in Azerbaijan. In this case, many things depend on when and how the internal and foreign problems are going to be solved.

Brondz, I. and Aslanova, T. (2019) Sunni-Shia Issue in Azerbaijan. Voice of the Publisher, 5, 1-11. https://doi.org/10.4236/vp.2019.51001. Scientific Research Publishing Inc. (SCIRP) has played a prominent role in the Open Access movement starting from as early as 2007. All original research papers published by SCIRP are made freely and permanently accessible online immediately upon publication. SCIRP aims to operate at the very forefront of this movement while abiding by its highest possible standards. Scientific Research Publishing (SCIRP) is one of the largest Open Access journal publishers. It is currently publishing more than 200 open accesses, online, peer-reviewed journals covering a wide range of academic disciplines. SCIRP serves the worldwide academic communities and contributes to the progress and application of science with its publication. https://www.scirp.org/journal/paperabs.aspx?paperid=91359

Chapter 11

Chechens in Afghanistan: A Battlefield Myth That Will Not Die

Christian Bleuer

In 2001, as the United States and other allied military forces attacked Taleban and al-Qaeda forces in Afghanistan, numerous soldiers, journalists and Afghans allied to the Americans relayed stories of a fearless and deadly opponent, incomparably worse than any other enemy: the Chechen. Such reports have never gone away, despite no Chechen having ever been captured or definitively identified in Afghanistan during this time. In the first dispatch in a special two-parter, Christian Bleuer discusses the history of Chechens in Afghanistan – both real and imagined – while also analysing the reasons for the many mistaken reports.

A second dispatch will look at how difficult it is to identify Chechens and how the word 'Chechen' may just be used to mean 'unidentifiable foreign Muslim'. It also looks at the appropriation of the name by other jihadi fighters because of the fearsome and brave connotation of this 'brand'. On the night of the 14-15 April 2016, American and Afghan military forces attacked what they described as the house of a suspected al-Qaeda operative named Abu Abdullah in Logar's Kharwar district. Citing an "Afghan interior ministry incident report," The Wall Street Journal noted subsequently that, in addition to taking two captives, coalition forces killed seven Chechens. The accompanying commentary uncritically repeated a narrative[1] that has been regularly promoted in the media:

Extremist members of Chechnya's rebel movement adhere to ideas tied to jihad and the creation of an Islamist state. Afghan and foreign officials say as many as 7,000 Chechens and other foreign fighters could be operating in the country, loosely allied with the Taliban and other militant groups. Local reporting by Pajhwok News, sourced to the Logar governor's spokesman, was slightly different, naming the targets as "Taliban Commanders Mullah Saber, Mullah Sabawon and Mullah Bashir," but also noting the presence of Chechens – in this case, three Chechen women who were allegedly killed. Khaama Press also reported the incident, noting that "[f]oreign insurgents fighting the Afghan forces is not new as scores of militants from Chechnya and other countries are routinely reported killed during the fight with the Afghan forces," with the caveat that "[t]he anti-government armed militant groups have not commented regarding the report so far."

Why not ask the Russians?

What was missing from the reporting by foreign and Afghan journalists was any sign of an attempt to ask the Russian Embassy in Kabul about a report that American and Afghan forces had just killed seven Russian citizens. In fact, it does not seem that any media outlet working in Afghanistan has ever done this, despite journalists publishing hundreds of reports on Russian citizens (ie Chechens) fighting and dying in Afghanistan. There is a way to remedy this, and journalists in Pakistan (see here) did exactly this in May 2011 after Frontier Corps soldiers shot dead five suspected suicide bombers at a checkpoint in Quetta. Pakistani media outlets immediately reported on the incident, citing police officials who claimed that all five (two women and three men) were Chechens. The Russian Foreign Ministry immediately sought answers, and then spoke to Pakistani journalists about the mysterious travellers from Chechnya. The end result was the conclusion that the five travellers were not Chechen and had also not been armed.

The Russian Foreign Ministry identified three of the victims as non-Chechens from Dagestan in southern Russia, and the seven-month pregnant woman who died as Olga Shroeder, a Siberian native who had recently converted to Islam, dropped out of university and married a Dagestani man twice her age. The fifth was a citizen of Tajikistan. This group was certainly suspicious (no Pakistani visas in their passports), and the Russian media quickly identified two of the Dagestanis as 'Wahhabis' with ties to militants in the North Caucasus. Olga Shroeder, for her part, was noted for her social media enthusiasm for Sayyed Buryatsky, a now dead half-Russian, half Buryat Buddhist who converted to Islam and made a name for himself as an anti-Russian militant in the North Caucasus.[2]

Speaking to the Russian Embassy, it had been easy enough to determine who they were, and who they were not. And it was quick: the travellers' 'Chechen' identity was revealed as nothing of the sort in less than two weeks. In Afghanistan, by contrast, there appears to be an enthusiastic media boosting of reports of Chechen insurgents and terrorists fighting and dying throughout Afghanistan. Reports of Chechens in Afghanistan go all the way back to 1994 and cover every period since then up until the present day.

The first Chechens in Afghanistan

The first Chechens to visit in Afghanistan in any significant numbers were those serving in the Soviet military in the 1980s occupation, of which 47 died in Afghanistan, with zero desertions to the mujahedin. Later, 170 of these Chechen veterans of the war in Afghanistan would die in the course of the two Russian-Chechen wars (1994-1996, 1999-2000).[3] The most prominent of them was Dzhokhar Dudayev, who had served as a Soviet air force Major General in Afghanistan, leading bombing campaigns against mujahedin in 1986-87 in western Afghanistan. He later became the president of the (unrecognised) Chechen Republic of Ichkeria until Russian forces killed him in 1996.

The next Chechens to visit Afghanistan were the group of men who accompanied the Chechen terrorist, Shamil Basayev, to Peshawar and then on to Khost province in the Afghanistan-Pakistan border region in 1994. The United States State Department claimed this number to be several hundred and that they had gone on to form a part of al-Qaeda's 055 Brigade.[4] But according to the Egyptian Abu Walid al-Masri (AKA Hamed Mustafa, an al-Qaeda linked figure who later headed al-Jazeera's media operations in Afghanistan), Basayev only sent six of his men for training to a camp in Afghanistan where al-Masri was based. Of these, five would die fighting Russia in the First Chechen War. Basayev himself stated that 12 of his men were eventually trained in Khost, but that he had attempted to fly in 50 additional Chechens – all of whom were stopped at the airport in Karachi and immediately deported at Russia's request. The start of the war in Chechnya in December 1994 ended the travels of Chechens to Afghanistan. The next notable Chechen visit to this region – but not Afghanistan – was in 1998, when Chechen Defence Minister Ruslan Gelayev attended the World Muslim Congress in Pakistan.[5]

Ahmed Rashid very briefly mentioned Chechen fighters in his book, "Taliban: Militant Islam, Oil and Fundamentalism in Central Asia", published before 9/11. He did not connect them to the Taleban, however, but rather to the Islamic Movement of Uzbekistan and to then al-Qaeda deputy chief Ayman al-Zawahiri in Kandahar where, according to Rashid, Chechens, black American Muslims and others clustered around al-Qaeda circles.[6] However, intense scrutiny since then (that is to say, after 9/11) has not identified any Chechens or black American Muslims in al-Qaeda at this time in Afghanistan.[7]

Various other claims of a Chechen presence in Afghanistan during the 1990s have been made retroactively (ie, after 9/11), and usually alongside outlandish claims and obviously incorrect analysis – for example an alleged al-Qaeda chemical and nuclear materials stockpile near Herat.[8] A faulty line of reasoning often employed is that tens of thousands of Chechens fled the First Chechen War and therefore Chechens must have contributed considerably to terrorist networks worldwide. This statement from the Middle

East Briefing of the Orient Advisory Group based in Washington and Dubai (see here) is a good example:

At the time of the First Chechen War (1994-1996), an estimated 15,000 to 25,000 young Chechen men fled the fighting and took refuge in Afghanistan, Pakistan, Yemen, Egypt and other ungoverned regions of Eurasia. Over the ensuing two decades, they became a backbone of Al Qaeda and other jihadist organizations.[9] This analysis assumes that the young men – or at least a significant proportion of them – who fled Chechnya were not refugees, but terrorists (or soon to be terrorists) who desired to fight in places such as Afghanistan. In fact, many of these men went through refugee screening and the asylum process in various countries (mostly Turkey and Europe), and still live there.

A prominent example is the 30,000 strong communities of Chechens in Austria (see here and here), who were not lured to foreign battlefields in any numbers until the Syrian conflict commenced. Other Chechens followed traditional, centuries old ties to Turkey and to the Arab world, especially Jordan, Syria and Iraq (where Arabised Chechen communities still live). Reasons for this included: seeking education (secular and Islamic), pilgrimage to Saudi Arabia, or the region being simply the easiest place for a Chechen refugee to go (Turkey is very close and there are many Russian-speakers there).[10] Afghanistan obviously held no appeal on any of these grounds.

The Chechen embassy in Afghanistan

It is a later event that most writers cite as proof of Chechens' large-scale presence in Afghanistan: the recognition of Chechnya's independence by the Taleban in January 2000 and opening of a Chechen embassy. Two scholars who research Chechnya's international militant and terrorist connections focused on the perceptions that this event generated: "The importance of this relationship lay with the fact that it heralded the beginning of the association of the Chechens with the extremist ideology of the Taliban within the international community."[11]

The recognition of Chechnya's independence did not pass without notice: the Russian government was outraged, and journalists and United Nations personnel in Kabul immediately set off to locate the 'embassy'. The Russian government had already been involved in Afghanistan for a few years supporting anti-Taleban forces diplomatically and militarily, with weapons and materiel. A few months after the Taleban's recognition of Chechnya's independence, the Russia government openly threatened to bomb the Taleban, accusing it of supporting and training Chechen terrorists – accusations that the Taleban denied.[12]

This episode seems clear enough: Taleban Foreign Minister Wakil Ahmad Mutawakel stated publically that "the Islamic Emirate of Afghanistan has decided to accord immediate recognition to the government of an independent Chechnya," and that a Chechen embassy had been opened in Kabul in January 2000.[13] However, recently revealed private correspondence between Chechnya's foreign minister and president from this time reveal[14] that the 'Chechen embassy' was unauthorised and without any support from the official separatist government in Chechnya (soon to be in exile).

The Chechen who opened the embassy was Zelimkhan Yandarbiyev, who served at the time as a roving Chechen envoy to the Muslim world. A previous Chechen foreign minister (Movladi Udugov) had sent 'emissaries' to Afghanistan to make contact with the Taliban in 1998, but nothing came of this visit. Yandarbiyev then visited in 1999 and lobbied Mullah Muhammad Omar for official recognition of Chechnya – which was eventually granted in January 2000. Chechen foreign minister Ilyas Akhmadov was only informed of this recognition when a Russian asked him about it during a public appearance at Johns Hopkins University in Washington, DC.

Akhmadov was unprepared for the question, only offering his opinion that it was merely diplomatic recognition, and nothing else. Akhmadov then made a phone call to Chechen president Aslan

Maskhadov, who only had three minutes to talk as he was fighting the Russians for control of Chechnya's capital city, in the Battle of Grozny. Akhmadov, at first angry as he thought the Chechen president has sent Yandarbiyev on a diplomatic trip to Afghanistan without informing him, quickly realised that Yandarbiyev was on a completely unauthorised mission. President Maskhadov stated that he was not even sure where Yandarbiyev was, and that he only had a vague memory of him visiting Afghanistan.

This is plausible as the Chechen president and foreign minister were trying to gain diplomatic recognition for their independence from the United States and European countries, not from the Taleban. That is why President Maskhadov had sent his foreign minister to the United States (where he was rebuffed by the State Department [15]. Both Maskhadov and Akhmadov had been the victims of an attempt by Yandarbiyev to push power in the Chechen separatist movement towards the Islamist radicals (the military defeat at the hands of the Russians in the winter of 1999-2000 was the beginning of the trend towards the dominant Chechen moderates being marginalised [16]. As noted by Mark Kramer:

> The Chechen president had deep misgivings about the timing of the announcement, which he saw as "playing into Russians' hands" and tarnishing the Chechens' standing in the international community. Moreover, he and Akhmadov correctly sensed that Yandarbiyev's persistent overtures to the Taliban had been designed to marginalize the more moderate elements around Maskhadov.[17] In the end, the unauthorised Chechen mission to Afghanistan accomplished little for either the moderate or the Islamist elements in the Chechen separatist movement. The Chechen presence was minimal and not entirely cordial. In one anecdote, as noted by Wahid Muzhda (a former Taleban foreign ministry employee), officials from the Taleban Ministry for the Promotion of Virtue and the Prevention of Vice rudely lectured the Chechen delegation on how the democratic elections in Chechnya violated Islamic law.[18]

The Russian campaign to connect Chechnya to Afghanistan

A Russian threat to bomb the alleged camps in Afghanistan in 2000, which was made publically and loudly by many Russian government officials, can be interpreted in two different ways. The first is the obvious: the Russian government was angry that a foreign government had granted diplomatic recognition to a separatist force within the Russian Federation, and was concerned that Chechen insurgents and terrorists were being trained in Afghanistan. The second is that the Russians were making so much noise because, as Maskhadov and Akhmadov believed, the Russian government saw this as an opportunity to portray the Chechen separatist government as extremists backed by the Taleban – a foreign Islamist force.

The relations between the Taleban and Russia were already bad, as Russia was supporting Ahmad Shah Massud's anti-Taleban forces, and nothing changed after the excitement over the Taleban's recognition of Chechen independence. Between this event and the start of the American-led war in Afghanistan, the only time Chechens in Afghanistan were mentioned prominently (outside Russia), was when ArifAyub, the Pakistani ambassador to Afghanistan, argued (privately) that supporting the Taleban was a threat to Pakistani interests, namely its good relations with Saudi Arabia and China, while citing hundreds of Chechens as being among a long list of foreign fighters serving with the Taleban.[19] By 2002, the Russian government's top envoy to Afghanistan was claiming that up to 300 Chechen families had been living in the Shahr-e Naw and Wazir Akbar Khan neighbourhoods of Kabul. Yet of this alleged number, there is only one Chechen (an ethnic Chechen from Georgia) who has openly claimed to have fought as a jihadist in Afghanistan at any time since the withdrawal of Soviet troops.

Russia's attempt to connect Chechen separatism to Afghanistan and al-Qaeda was a failure, as western and Muslim governments continued to condemn Russian abuses in the war in Chechnya, rejecting Russian claims that all of its opponents in Chechnya were terrorists connected to a global Islamist force[20] (note: this was before the Chechen terrorist attacks at a theatre in Moscow in late 2002 and on a school in Beslan in 2004). However, al-Qaeda's attacks on 11 September 2001 gave Russia an opportunity to reframe its enemies – and it was very successful in doing so. As argued by Zbigniew Brzezinski, "...after 9/11, the Bush administration officials adopted the Russian view that the Chechen resistance was really part of an international terrorist movement, alleging (falsely as it turned out) that Chechen fighters were battling alongside Al-Qaeda in Afghanistan and Iraq."[21] The United States secured Russia's acquiescence to military bases in Central Asia, as well as a broad range of support in its fight against al-Qaeda and the Taleban.[22] In return, the US gave Russia what it wanted: the US government began to make references to Chechens as part of al-Qaeda, while repeating the Russian claim that there were many Chechen fighters in Afghanistan.[23]

The Northern Alliance promotes the Chechen myth

Former Chechen foreign minister Akhmadov has completely rejected the notion that Chechens were with the Taleban fighting in Afghanistan, arguing that the Russian government used its then ally, the Northern Alliance, to make what were false claims: Putin was trying to make his war in Chechnya look similar to the U.S. war in Afghanistan. Since Moscow had supplied the Northern Alliance for years, it was not problematic [for Putin] to have them regularly "discover" Chechen fighters in Afghanistan. This was a small thing for the Northern Alliance to do to repay their patron but it had a huge impact. Suddenly we Chechens were viewed as America's enemies.[24]

Brian Glyn Williams, a professor at the University of Massachusetts Dartmouth,[25] and Russian journalists[26] also cite Northern Alliance (officially: United Front) leaders as promoters of the belief in large numbers of Chechens in Afghanistan. It also was not strictly a phenomenon that occurred after the start of the US-led war in late 2001. The earliest sources where Northern Alliance sources tell reporters and researchers that they are fighting Chechens occurred in late May 2000, a few months after Russia loudly claimed that

Afghanistan was sheltering Chechen terrorists. In this case, the anti-Taleban Islamic State of Afghanistan government's embassy in Tajikistan told (see here) Russian journalists they could confirm a "large group" of Chechen militants in Afghanistan. Later, in October 2000, Massud's forces claimed they were fighting "Uighurs, Uzbeks and Chechens" near Taloqan, saying they had been flown in from a base near Kabul.[27]

The post-9/11 American discovery of Chechens in Afghanistan

In the early months of Operation Enduring Freedom, US Special Operations Forces and CIA officers were relying heavily on their Northern Alliance hosts for intelligence. As for the belief of Afghan fighters in the identity of their enemies, a New York Times reporter in Afghanistan noted that "The phrase 'Arabs, Chechens and Pakistanis' was uttered so often that it seemed to have been drilled into the mind of every alliance soldier." The same reporter then asked to see the prisoners that the Northern Alliance guards were advertising as 'Arab, Chechen and Pakistani', but found that "in fact the group appeared to be almost entirely from Pakistan." One Canadian journalist who had previously reported from Chechnya was particularly interested in finding Chechens in Afghanistan. But he came to a dead end. American Taleb John Walker Lindh gave him a hurried interview and stated briefly that he had met Chechens in the past, but that "Here, in Afghanistan, I haven't seen any Chechens."

American soldiers and CIA officers, in contrast, were far more gullible, for several reasons. The main reason is that their leaders were telling them they were fighting Chechens in Afghanistan. In late November 2001, Defence Secretary Donald Rumsfeld briefed journalists on the battle for Kunduz, claiming he would not allow foreign militants and terrorists to be evacuated in any sort of negotiated deal: And if they're looking for any kind of conditions whereby the foreigners — there's Chinese in there, there's Chechens in there, there's Arabs in there, there's Al Qaeda in there — any idea that those people should be let loose on any basis at all to leave that country and to go bring terror to other countries and destabilize other countries is unacceptable.

Notably, Rumsfeld did not mention the many Pakistani fighters who were actually in Kunduz, as Vice President Dick Cheney was, at this time, busy acquiescing to President Musharraf's request to evacuate Pakistani advisors from there – a request that was granted at the top level of the US government. It was worried that a slaughter of Pakistani ISI officers in Kunduz would worsen Pakistani-America relations yet further and possibly even result in upheaval in Pakistan.[28]

In March 2002, US Major General Frank Hagenbeck commented authoritatively on the Chechen presence while emphasising the foreign nature of the foe in Afghanistan, as Agence France-Presse reported (see here): "We know the history of the Chechens. They are good fighters and they are very brutal," Hagenbeck said. The general said he has heard of reports out of the Pentagon that a unit of 100-150 Chechens had moved into southern Afghanistan. Hagenbeck said US intelligence was exchanging information with foreign counterparts to help fight the Al Qaeda in Afghanistan, but he would not say if there had been any specific exchanges with Moscow over the Chechens.

US General Tommy Franks, the overall commander of the war against the Taleban and al-Qaeda in Afghanistan also spoke on the matter in early March 2002, stating that his forces has killed between 100 and 200 foreign fighters, including "Arabs, Chechens and Uzbeks" in the Shahikot Valley in Paktia. Later, he said "The number of nationalities represented in the detainees we have is about 35 and, to be sure, the Chechen nationality is represented among those nations." Notable is that there were no Chechens represented after detainees were identified [29] (even after detainee numbers increased ten-fold), and that General Franks was in Moscow when he commented on the Chechens. One Russian military affairs analyst, asked about the reports of Chechens in Afghanistan, said there were probably a few there, but that, "sometimes I wonder if the Americans don't emphasize the presence of Chechens in Afghanistan just to please Moscow."[30]

Another analyst, the head of the Institute for Caucasian Studies in Moscow, offered a cynical explanation for the sudden American enthusiasm for seeing Chechens everywhere in Afghanistan: they were attempting to discredit any Afghan resistance by painting them as being controlled by foreigners. This may have been the case, but Americans on the ground certainly believed they were fighting Chechens. In CIA officer Gary Schroen's memoirs of leading CIA and SOF forces in northern Afghanistan in late 2001, a local Afghan told him they were fighting Chechens, something that Schroen did not question, just as he did not question the intelligence provided by Bariullah Khan, a Northern Alliance commander, that in one instance they were up against "a key al-Qa'ida position, manned by Arab, Chechen, and Uzbek IMU (Islamic Movement of Uzbekistan) terrorists." [31]

The low-ranking Northern Alliance soldiers themselves also believed they were fighting Chechens. In one small battle, three unidentified insurgents charged Schroen, an American soldier identified as 'Craig', and 60 Northern Alliance soldiers, all of whom held the high position on top of a hill. Schroen described what happened next:

Then, one of the Afghans watching the three men steadily cross the open ground shouted, "Chechnya, Chechnya!" The cry was picked up by the others. "Chechnya!" A wave of panic and fear, so intense that Craig could feel it physically, swept through the line of men on the hilltop.[32] The 60 Afghans and the two Americans then fled from these three fighters after failing to hit them with their gunfire. The three 'Chechens' took the hilltop and proceeded to mock the Afghans until the US Army team called in an airstrike on them. They were vaporised in a subsequent airstrike and no identification was made.

Scepticism is offered, but brushed aside

While the Russian government was adamant that Chechens were in Afghanistan, independent Russian analysts were very sceptical. In late 2001 The Moscow Times surveyed (see here) a range of experts and researchers who focus on Chechnya or Afghanistan.

When asked if they believed there were large numbers of Chechens in Afghanistan, only one agreed (and he argued that the Chechen embassy in Afghanistan and Putin's subsequent threat to bomb alleged Chechen camps in Afghanistan was the necessary proof).[33] Chechen separatist media were even more sceptical, rejecting any notion of their compatriots being in Afghanistan, noting the inability of the American or Afghan forces to "produce even one Chechen as proof of the 'participation of hundreds and thousands of Chechen fighters' in the war in Afghanistan." For its part, the Russian Federal Security Service (FSB) told the media that, leading up to late 2001, hundreds of Chechen fighters travelled to Afghanistan to join the Taleban and al-Qaeda.

The Russian media was mixed in its support of the (both Russian and American government) narrative of Chechens being in Afghanistan. Newspaper articles did appear, uncritically relaying reports of Chechens being captured or killed in Afghanistan (see for example here and here) but Russian reporters on the ground in Afghanistan were encountering a problem: they could not find any Chechens, dead or alive. For example, Russian journalist Alexander Khokhlov collected many stories, but no proof. Another journalist with long experience reporting on Chechnya, Andrei Babitsky, travelled to Afghanistan in winter 2001-2002 and could find no trace of any Chechens. He noted that "All the Russian journalists in Afghanistan received instructions to find Chechens, but we inspected all of the jails, asked all of the [Afghan] field commanders – in vain." Carlotta Gall, a journalist with extensive experience reporting on Chechnya, also failed to find any Chechens in early 2002 despite Afghans telling her that they were holding prisoners from Chechnya.

Another Russian journalist, Yuri Kovalenko, asked this question: How has it happened that among the several thousand foreign fighters taken into prison in Afghanistan, not a single Chechen has been discovered? There are likewise none among the 500 prisoners in the hands of the Americans; including those interned at the Cuban base at Guantanamo…Not one Chechen has been found among the 3,000 fighters imprisoned in the dungeon of Shibirgan… One US publication, the Terrorism Monitor of the

Jamestown Foundation, sought answers (see here) to the Chechen question from the US government for several months, but never received an answer.

Many American news reports from this time are, on average, far less sceptical; in most cases they just relay the claims from the US military, Northern Alliance soldiers or unidentified sources without any sort of confirmation or questioning. In one instance, a source inside Kunduz told CNN that 60 Chechens drowned themselves in the Amu Darya rather than surrender. A quick look at a map begs the question, why 60 Chechens, instead of fighting to the death at the Kunduz airport, would break out of the containment by Afghan and American forces, safely cross the Khanabad River without drowning and hike 40 km to the Amu Darya to commit suicide. The stories from this era all have an element of the absurd, with Chechens vanishing without a trace – as opposed to Uzbeks, Arabs, and Pakistanis.

No Chechens, but the myth lives on

Any notion of a significant number of Chechens being in Afghanistan, not only in 2001 but subsequently, has been comprehensively analysed by one American researcher who focuses on Chechnya, Brian Williams, who makes his case in his recent 2015 book. After regular field research in Afghanistan and over a decade of researching the topic (including visits to Uzbek and Tajik Northern Alliance fighters), he addresses all the claims and roundly rejects the notion of Chechens being in Afghanistan.[34]

By 2013, Williams wrote that: To date, no Chechen has ever been captured, interviewed, nor has there been any evidence of one being killed in this region. Significantly, no Chechens were ever captured and sent to Guantanamo Bay by Coalition troops. In addition, in all my years of tracking on line martyrdom epitaphs I have never seen one of a Chechen in Afghanistan or Pakistan.[35]Since then, this author has found one single 'martyrdom' mention of an identified Chechen linked to Afghanistan (see here), that of Saifullah Shishani, who died in Syria, but whose epitaph claimed he had, at some unspecified point in the past, fought in Afghanistan.

In addition, there is a single instance of Afghan security forces naming a killed Chechen – but in this case (in Baghlan province in May of this year) identified as Chechen only by nom de guerre ('Omar Chechen') and no subsequent information or confirmation provided.

As for revelations of foreign detainees in Afghanistan, in 2014 AAN pieced together (see here) the identities of the foreign detainees at Bagram – a long-held secret. Among the names was one single citizen of Russia. However, he was not a Chechen, but an ethnic Tatar, IkrakHamidullan (he was subsequently taken to the United States and put on trial in a military court (see here). The question then is no longer "Are there many Chechens in Afghanistan?", but "Why do so many people still believe there are in 2016?"

Military Battlefield Reports of Chechens

Working hand-in-hand with many foreign journalists in Afghanistan are representatives of the American and other coalition militaries. Many journalists quote and cite the US military, and on the issue of Chechens many of them just repeat what the military tells them (unlike other controversies where journalistic scepticism is the norm). In ISAF-NATO's own media departments, and particularly in ISAF press releases, the Chechens live in large numbers. A survey of ISAF press releases[36] in 2010 reveals the following (underlining added):

> ...combined Afghan and coalition security forces killed more than 20 armed insurgents, including Arab, Chechen and Pakistani fighters. ... Afghan and coalition security force killed more than 20 armed insurgents, including Arab, Chechen and Pakistani fighters, during the latest deliberate clearing operation against Haqqani Network foreign fighters camps... ... while pursuing a Taliban commander who is responsible for smuggling Pakistani, Chechen and Arab fighters and improvised explosive device materials... ... Afghan and coalition security force killed more than 20 armed insurgents, including Arab, Chechen and Pakistani fighters... Afghan and coalition forces killed 23 armed insurgents, including Arab,

Chechen and Pakistani fighters during the operation. Other military news sources, like the Office of the US Secretary of Defense for Public Affairs (see here; or here), or Afghan military and police reports (excerpts here), can be cited saying the same thing.

When non-military news outlets and wire services report on Afghanistan, they regularly cite or quote US military commanders, many of who claim to be fighting Chechens. But American commanders are not the only ones making Chechen claims. For example, in November 2015, The Washington Post relied on a German Brigadier General for information when they reported that Chechens had participated in the recent fighting in Kunduz. A search of news archive results in news stories with the same components: coalition military commanders say they are fighting foreigners, including Chechens.

However, US commanders are not always so certain about Chechens, and occasionally make cautious statements. Reporting (see here) to a US Senate committee in October 2015, the overall commander in Afghanistan, General John Campbell, was pressed by a senator to provide a number for foreign fighters in Afghanistan. He would not–or could not-provide a definitive answer, merely repeating "There are reports," "we have seen reports," and mentioning "reports" of Chechens in the mix, notably in the north. And in May 2013, one media outlet reported that "[c]lose to 1,000 insurgents, including Arab and Chechen fighters allied with al Qaeda, launched a series of counter strikes against U.S. and ANSF positions in Sangin and Helmand provinces beginning Monday," though they did note that the American Major General who briefed reporters refused to identify the nationality of any of the foreign fighters.

From academics to analysts: Chechens are everywhere

Analysts, researchers and academics often like to say that journalists' work lacks rigour. But many researchers with experience in the region have also uncritically reported the presence of Chechens in Afghanistan in various scholarly publications [37] and think tank reports [38] over the last decade. References to Chechens have even appeared in UN reports [39] and made it into documents intended for US lawmakers and government officials to read.[40]None of them make any more than an off-hand reference, and none offer any convincing analysis or evidence. Still, it remains journalists who are on the frontlines of relaying reports of Chechens. From Kunar to Kunduz, foreign reporters regularly report Chechens on the battlefield, with some stating it as fact without any doubts or reservations (see two good examples here and here).

Chechens are fearless fighters; therefore, fearless fighters must be Chechen

Numerous American soldiers claim to have fought Chechens in Afghanistan, painting the image of a super-soldier insurgent. One journalist reported on Chechen fighters in Afghanistan, quoting various Special Operations Forces soldiers speaking in dramatic terms:

Chechens are a different breed. They fight till they die. They have more passion, more discipline and less regard for lives. A few of them could have just given up but decided they needed to die. What I always appreciated was their lack of tether. They will transplant anywhere. I don't think they ate or were even clear as to why they fight, wherever it is, but they're fighting most of the time. It's just a fire in their bellies. It's what they do.The same journalist, however, cautioned that this reputation "may have led many in the U.S. military and intelligence to inflate the Chechens' true numbers on a battlefield." Indeed, other soldiers he quoted were not so sure. One admitted that misidentifications were common, while another remarked that "It was a pervasive rumour at the time. But I never saw a Chechen. In fact, I'm not sure anyone did."

Technical military skills-Chechen

One Special Operations Forces soldier argued that Chechens were notable on the battlefield for their discipline, skill and, strangely, their tendency to wear expensive North Face brand ski jackets. Often, soldiers are certain they are fighting Chechens based on the fact that the foes they met on the battlefield were skilled and fearless and therefore must have been 'Chechen', as if only Chechens fighters have these attributes. This trope is even picked up by counterinsurgency experts, who see battlefield combat skills by insurgents as a sure sign that Chechens must be there, fighting in person or at least in an advisory role.[41] As the private intelligence firm Stratfor wrote in a short 2005 analysis: "The Chechens in Afghanistan are the insurgency's elite fighters."

Others, like two AAN guest authors (see here), note, much more critically, the habit of soldiers to see Chechens as the source of technical military skills. One of them, Antonio Giustozzi, added elsewhere, "The tendency among US officers was to attribute sniping skills to foreign volunteers, particularly Chechens."[42] Similarly, a former Force Recon Marine who served in Iraq and Afghanistan somewhat sceptically noted the same, especially in Iraq:

The Chechen jihadist fighter has achieved near-legendary status in the last decade-plus. "Chechen" has become synonymous with "militarily competent jihadist." Any time coalition forces have met jihadists on the battlefield who maneuver and shoot well, they are presumed to be Chechens. In 2005, the effective insurgent snipers in Iraq were all presumed to be Chechens. This is not just an idea that is generated and sustained at the lower levels of the US military. It is believed at command levels as well. For example, one soldier argues this:

Having been there, I can say without any reservation that from at least 2007-2008, there was no evidence of Chechens in Nangarhar, Nuristan, Konar, or Laghman provinces despite over 100 reports of their presence often trumpeted by the CJTF [Combined Joint Task Force]. It's very easy and comforting for commanders to blame every moderately well coordinated and "successful" insurgent attack on mythical "Chechens" rather than local fighters.

Those other, less sceptical, American and coalition soldiers never explain why they believe that, after Afghanistan having been at war since 1979 and Afghans having undergone training by the Soviet, Russian, American, European, Pakistani and other militaries, there should not be an Afghan who can shoot straight. Furthermore, the various accounts by British officers in the First and Second Anglo-Afghan Wars made it very clear that there was a generous, indigenous supply of Afghan snipers. This is not a skill that Afghans are, by nature, incapable of.[43] But the idea that only Chechens can shoot straight is not just an American soldier story. This idea extends into the ranks of other ISAF militaries and to Afghan soldiers as well. According to CIA officer Gary Schroen, the Northern Alliance soldiers also believe this. Schroen wrote:

> In every battle they had fought with the Taliban, there had been rumours and reports that a group of Chechens was fighting with the Taliban. They were reported to be fanatical, fierce fighters, well trained and experts with their weapons. After one particular tough engagement a few days earlier, a number of dead among the Karzai forces had been found to have been killed by a single shot to the head. This was incredible to the Afghans, none of whom actually aimed their weapons but rather trusted Allah to guide their bullets. They thought that such accurate fire had to be the work of the Chechens.[44]

Of course, this was not the first time Afghans had misidentified their enemy, as the mujahedin of the 1980s relayed stories of fighting a plethora of nationalities from communist countries allied to the Soviets. The most absurd was their 1980 claim that 10,000 Cubans had been deployed to Afghanistan. Two years later, the mujahedin claimed to have had a particularly hard and unsuccessful fight near Paghman against Cubans – who, they claimed, were superior to Soviet soldiers. This led an exasperated western diplomat working on Afghanistan to argue that the mujahedin had likely just fought against elite Soviet airborne troops, and had thought Soviet soldiers who had darkened their faces for night-time operations must have been Cuban.[45]

Deliberate misidentification of Chechens

While high-ranking American officials and military commanders may have played along with a non-existent Chechen presence in Afghanistan to gain the cooperation of Russia, and while lower-ranking US soldiers may be just repeating what they have been told by their superiors or by Afghans, there may be a part of the ISAF/NATO military forces that was deliberately spreading disinformation about Chechens as part of an information warfare campaign. For example, in the summer of 2007 in Helmand, unknown people distributed a pamphlet (see here) to local 'tribal elders' that announced:

We criticize the decision of Mullah Mohammad Omar. We don't accept any other commander. If they continue on this path, we will leave the movement. We only want to carry out jihad against Americans and this is our wish. And we will fight until the end against foreign troops. But the decision of the leadership council in Quetta was a wrong decision. They want to appoint Uzbeks or Chechens instead of a Taliban commander. And Mullah Mohammad Omar, you should know that Pashtuns never want to be slaves. We will not accept a Chechen or Uzbek commander. It is still unclear whether Uzbeks and Chechens are good Muslims. Death is better than accepting their commands. If this happens, we will stop and leave everything to Mullah Omar.

One of the Taleban spokesmen rejected the veracity of information in the pamphlet, while a more neutral observer, Ahmed Rashid, said, "I think there's a huge disinformation campaign – probably being carried out by NATO and the Americans – in order to present Mullah Omar in a light in which he is seen as being just a tool of Al-Qaeda and foreigners." Distributing pamphlets and trying to control information, perceptions and behaviour in warzones are the responsibility of the US military and CIA Psychological Operations groups. The leaked US military PSYOPS manual describes a tool called 'Black Products' that would fit the style of the above pamphlet Products that purport to emanate from a source other than the true one are known as black products. Black products are best used to support strategic plans.... The presumption of emanating from within an opponent country lends credibility and helps to demoralize the opponent by suggesting that there are dissident and disloyal elements within their ranks.

Regarding the US Army, both the 2nd and the 7th Psychological Operations Groups were deployed to Afghanistan around this time, but they do not openly communicate what they are doing, nor does the CIA's equivalent. The Afghan government could also be responsible for this pamphlet. It is also possible that some Taleban fighters genuinely thought Chechens were being deployed as Taleban commanders, and decided to print their own objections in pamphlet form. Canada, however, is more open about its information warfare. One Canadian media outlet published an article (see here) on the Royal 22nd Regiment's operations in Kandahar in 2007, which included these passages:

> "The Chechens are hard core. They are the best we face," said the soldier, a Montrealer who works in a secretive cell devoted to what the Canadian battle group calls Information Operations and what other armies sometimes call Information Warfare. "We're dealing with all kinds of insurgents. With Chechens, Egyptians, Saudis, Pakistanis, guys from the Yemen. It isn't one group more than the next." "Most Afghans dislike the Taliban, so imagine what they think of foreign fighters," the sergeant said. "For the foreigners, unlike the Afghans, the war is not about nationalism. The foreigners have an ideology and that ideology is Islamic fundamentalism. They try to use that to control the Afghans. The American military manual on information warfare clearly includes how to manipulate the media for strategic uses; it is possible that the Canadians here were using a similar playbook.

Afghan government, military and media reports of Chechens

Afghan media outlets are far more active than foreign journalists when it comes to reporting on Chechens. A search of Afghan media outlets, Tolo News for example, in both English and Persian returns numerous reports of Chechens in Afghanistan in the last few years, usually as part of a list of foreign fighters (search returns in English; in Persian). Pajhwok also published regular stories about Chechens in similar fashion. A survey of these articles shows that the sources of reports of Chechens are usually coalition military sources, Afghan security forces and local Afghan officials. The articles cite these officials uncritically, relaying the long list of foreign nationalities – including Chechens – fighting and dying in Badakhshan, Nangarhar, Logar, Faryab, etc. [46] In a two month period in early 2016, the Afghan Ministry of Defence spokesmen were particularly active in informing reporters that Chechens and other foreign fighters were active in Afghanistan. [47]

The narrative is clear: Afghan security forces are fighting a war against a foreign invasion – and Chechens are part of that force.

Surprisingly, it is also possible to find quotes like this from Taleban commanders. In 2011, Afghan officials put Mullah Habib, a Taleban commander in Kunduz on television sometime after he surrendered, identifying him as an al-Qaeda loyalist. Mullah Habib admitted that his network employed Chechen, Pakistani and Arab fighters, and he repeated the government line (see here): "I have realised that foreigners are working to destroy our country and the war has no benefit. I joined the peace process in the interest our people." However, the report did not offer the caveat that this Taleb was in government custody and may just have been so compliant due to having been freshly interrogated –or worse –similar to how captured American soldiers in Iraq have condemned American policies and renounced the war in video messages.

This narrative of foreign blame is also emphasised at the highest levels of the Afghan government. In 2006, SebghatullahMojaddedi, then the speaker of the Upper House of the Afghan Parliament and the chair of the National Peace and Reconciliation Commission, blamed the continued war on three factors: the actions of ISAF/ NATO troops, incompetent provincial officials and outside interference that manifests in foreigners among the insurgents– including Chechens. Three years later, then Defence Minister Rahim Wardak informed parliament (see here) that "4,000 Chechens, Chinese Muslims and Pakistani fighters had stolen into Afghanistan to carry out terrorist activities." More recently, both President Ashraf Ghani and Vice President Abdul Rashid Dostum have spoken on national TV and to newspapers about the Chechens and other foreign fighters who threaten Afghanistan on the battlefield. In a speech in March 2016, Ghani stressed that the war was being imposed on Afghanistan by outsiders, including Chechens:

The main element in this war is Al-Qa'idah, which is neither an Afghan element nor is Afghanistan the reason of Al-Qa'idah's war. Another element of the war is Da'ish. It is a matter of pride for us today that Afghanistan is the only country, where Da'ish is on the run. They are escaping from Nangarhar today and Afghanistan will be their grave. We can regard extremist groups from Uzbekistan, Tajikistan, Chechnya, Xinjiang and other places as the third factor of war in Afghanistan. They also have no attachment to our country.[48] Dostum and his commanders fighting in the northwest also make similar claims about foreign fighters, blaming Chechens, Uzbeks and Pakistanis.[49] Dostum is rare in Afghanistan – he is an Afghan who has actually been to Chechnya (in late 2015), where he met Chechen President and Putin vassal Ramzan Kadyrov, emphasising that both men were in a struggle against "international terrorism." It is notable that in late 2001, by contrast, Dostum rejected claims that Chechens were among the many foreign fighters he had captured. [50]

Case studies of the Afghan conflict that aspire to some sort of objectivity and neutrality do indeed reveal an important foreign component to the continuing war in Afghanistan – that being, of course, the various groups and individuals in Pakistan and within its security structures (as well as comparatively small numbers of foreign, non-Pakistani fighters). However, these case studies also reveal important local motivations for why Afghans would become insurgents: anger at the presence of a foreign and non-Muslim, American-led army, predatory Afghan government officials, civilian casualties, local political factional struggles, a desire to boost one's social standing, monetary incentives, a basic desire to fight, criminal activities, religious and ideological motivations, etc.[51] However, if one wants to blame outsiders (beyond looking at Pakistani state support) for the continuing insurgency in Afghanistan, Chechen and other foreigners become a convenient tool.

The Afghan People

Beyond the Afghan government, military and journalists, there are many Afghans who also believe that Chechens are, or were, in Afghanistan. Speaking to many Afghans about the destruction from the recent years of war, SlavomírHorák, a Czech researcher with a focus on Russia and Central Asia who went to Afghanistan for field research in 2002, found the question of Chechens did arise. Horák was sceptical, and he found that some locals gave a similar narrative: that the Taleban had committed atrocities, but that no Afghan would do such a thing, therefore foreigners accompanying the Taleban were to blame. In one interview, an Afghan said that they could recognise a Pakistani, but that the other foreign fighters who spoke a language they could not understand must be Chechen.[52]

Horák cites a social anthropologist who studies post-conflict societies, and argues that the attempt by local people to blame outside foreigners for atrocities is a form of a truce: they often know exactly who the perpetrators were, but they need to blame an absent outsider for the crimes committed in order to preserve the peace – in combination with the disinclination to blame someone from one's own group (eg, someone of the same ethnicity). In this line of reasoning, the Chechens serve as a 'scapegoat.'[53] More generally, Afghan denial that fellow Afghans could be responsible for killing Afghans was a feature of the rhetoric surrounding the beginning of the suicide bombing trend in Afghanistan. This was especially true at an early point, when foreigners would be blamed in place of the Afghans who were actually responsible.[54] As one Afghan-American journalist (see here) argued, "I don't think the Taliban are a primarily Afghan movement. [...] ...many of the suicide bombers, for example, have not been Afghan. They've been Chechens. They've been Arabs. They've been Pakistanis." These same viewpoints can be found repeatedly, including on the part of both the Afghan leadership and the Afghan people.

This dispatch analysed the phenomenon of Chechens being misidentified and misreported in Afghanistan, including the motivations for doing so (deliberately or accidentally). In the next dispatch, the author will look at the difficulties involved in actually attempting to identify Chechens. After all, they look like other north Caucasians and Muslims from elsewhere in the former Soviet Union and also can speak Russian. Moreover, 'Chechen' is a useful brand; identity theft by those keen to expropriate their terrifying battlefield image is also a factor in this tale. Researchers focusing on Chechen issues point to clear evidence that many Chechens are fighting in Syria, but roundly reject the notion of a Chechen presence in Afghanistan. In the first part of his special two-parter, Christian Bleuer looked at how Chechens became a battlefield myth for western soldiers and a tool for Afghan and US governments frame their fight as a struggle against foreign militants. In this second dispatch, he looks at the difficulties of identifying a Chechen and at how 'Chechen' has become a loose term that can mean different things to different people.

(Mis)identifying Chechens in Afghanistan: a few examples

Chechens (dead and alive) are reported frequently in Afghanistan, but that identification usually falls apart under scrutiny. For example, a United States officer reported the alleged capture by Afghan police of a Chechen in Paktia in summer 2007. But when the identity of the 'Chechen' was eventually revealed, although he did turn out to be a citizen of Russia, he was an ethnic Russian from Siberia called Andrei who had converted to Islam (see also this 2007 blog). Or, in another example from 2009, a reporter looking into the role of foreign fighters in the Afghan insurgency quoted a United States Army Major in Paktika stating confidently that Arab, Uzbek, Turkmen and Chechen fighters were entering his area of operation. A suspicious analyst personally contacted the major to confirm the report. The major said he had told the reporter that he and his team were fighting against local Afghans. "I never said the quote that he used," he said. "I stated that there have been reports that Chechens have been in the area, but that we have no way of verifying this information."

Documents allegedly identifying Chechens are also occasionally reported, such as a 2005 USA Today article citing a government spokesman in Zabul who stated that recently killed insurgents were positively identified as Pakistani and Chechen, as "documents found on the bodies of the three identified their nationalities." This may be the case for the dead Pakistanis, but very unlikely for the 'Chechens.' If they were carrying a passport, it would be a passport of the Russian Federation; in 1997 the Russian government removed the line in the passport where the Russian citizen identified their ethnicity. Of course, a birthplace is still listed, but in the Cyrillic Russian alphabet and by city only, not by republic or province (so the word 'Chechnya' would not be included). As for the unknown number of Chechen Republic of Ichkeria passports issued in 1997, none have turned up in warzones, but rather in asylum applications in Europe.[55]

In January 2011, the Deutsche Presse-Agentur (DPA) wire service circulated a fantastic story: fifteen Chechen women in Dasht-e Archi district of Kunduz had married Talebs and were assisting them as experts in the use of suicide vests and roadside IEDs (improvised explosive devices), and as nurses.[56]The source of this information was the interrogation by Kunduz police Chief Abdul Rahman Sayedkheli[57] of Taleban Mullah Jamaluddin – leaving open the possibility that these are the words of the police, put into the mouth of a Taleb prisoner. Furthermore, to believe this story, one must assume that fifteen Chechen women – who are also Islamist extremists, trained in suicide vest and IED construction– left Chechnya on their own and travelled all the way to Kunduz to marry Afghan Talebs. This story could be a play on the Russian 'Black Widow' female suicide bombers from the North Caucasus region, itself an exaggerated phenomenon. These women – also referred to as shahidka in Russian are overwhelmingly vulnerable widows manipulated into putting on suicide vests inside Russia, rather than globe-trotting insurgent and terrorist tactic experts.

In some incidents where foreign militants certainly were to blame, the Afghan government is still quick to name Chechens as the perpetrators. A good example is the February 2015 kidnapping of dozens of Hazaras on the Kabul-Kandahar highway. The governor of Zabul province immediately blamed the Pakistani terrorist group Lashkar-e Jangvi and Chechens. But unlike many other reports around the country that named Chechens as the guilty party, this incident generated a relatively large amount of media and public interest. The scrutiny dismantled the government's initial claims, and it was revealed quite decisively that Uzbeks of the Islamic Movement of Uzbekistan were responsible.[58] But for other reports of Chechens, there is usually no such fact-checking or scrutiny.

Positive identification of Chechens: 'racial' stereotyping

If some Afghan mujahedin had been misidentifying dead Soviet soldiers as Cubans in the 1980s (possibly because Soviet soldiers had darkened their faces for night-time fighting; see the author's previous dispatch), could contemporary American and Afghan soldiers be doing something similar?

Many, including Russians, think they can identify Chechens and fail badly, as noted in a widely circulated Russian article written by a Chechen titled "How to spot a Chechen." Basically, 'racial stereotypes' (anthropologists prefer the word 'phenotypes') such as hair type, facial features, skin colour, etc are not particularly useful as the Chechen population is a diverse group of people who speak a common language. A stereotypical Chechen 'look' will fail as a tool of identification. If ethnic Russians have problems identifying Chechens despite sharing a country with them, what chance do Afghans have? Even so, some American soldiers trust Afghans to identify dead bodies as Chechen. One soldier who served in Khost made this claim:

> ...there are Chechens fighting (and dying) in Khost, Paktika and Paktya and there have been for years. [...] How do i know? Because the Afghans know a Chechen dead guy from an Arab dead guy from an Afghan from a Pakistani when they see one, that's how.

In reality, identification of insurgent bodies in Afghanistan is undertaken in the crudest fashion. The Paktia provincial police chief in May 2007 for example, needed only the disembodied head of a suicide bomber to be able to declare that "the face complexion revealed he was a Chechen." An ISAF officer with years of experience in northern Afghanistan wrote this in 2011: "We see it here (Mazar-e Sharif) in the provincial hospital, where dead bodies of insurgent KIAs are brought to. When the bodies are not claimed by family members, they are automatically labeled Foreign Fighters and depending on their faces: Asiatic = Uzbeks; dark-skinned = Pakistani; and Caucasian = Chechens. This is done by doctors as well as police and everybody takes it at face value".[59]

Two other researchers whose works includes studies of both the North Caucasus and Afghanistan agree: corpses on the Afghan battlefield that "appeared Caucasian [ie 'white European'] was presumed to be Chechens." In another similar anecdote, an Afghan-American working for US forces near Khost as a cultural advisor said that local Afghans were referring to lighter-skinned foreign fighters generically as 'Chechens', partially because that is what they thought the Americans wanted to hear. Add to this the existence of light-haired and light-skinned Afghans, and it is clear as to why making an identification of a dead or live fighter based on crude racial stereotypes is unreliable.

Russian language in Afghanistan: Chechens, Central Asians and others

Analysis in Jane's Defence published in November 2001 identified Chechen units, bases and 'civilian communities' in Afghanistan as part of the Islamic Movement of Uzbekistan. This provides a possible example of how 'Chechen sightings' may be the result of linguistic and cultural confusion. As far as language identification goes the notion that the US military has deployed army linguists and signals intelligence operators proficient in Nokhchiynmott (the language of Chechens) was completely rejected by a researcher who spent time with the US military in Afghanistan. Outside the US military, in 2013, the terrorism researcher, Murad Batal Al Shishani (an Arab of Chechen descent – Arabic, lacking a 'ch' sound, replaces it with 'sh' instead), rejected the notion of a Chechen presence in Afghanistan based on the total lack of evidence of the Chechen language being used by any fighters in that country. But like other sceptics, he is convinced of Chechens being in Syria – based on the type of linguistic (and other) evidence found there, that is lacking in Afghanistan.

The use of the Russian language on the battlefield as proof of the presence of Chechens is even less useful. Chechens only comprise 1.5 million people out of Russia's over 16 million Muslims, and Russian is the dominant lingua franca between and among Central Asians and those from the North Caucasus region of Russia. Hearing Russian spoken or finding Russian language documents in Afghanistan thus does not mean that there are Chechens. However, Afghans have probably been led to assume that Central Asians speaking Russian were in fact Chechens.[60] Documents written in Russian have also been cited as a sign of Chechens in Afghanistan, but researchers familiar with Central Asian militants have instead assigned the papers to the Islamic Movement of Uzbekistan (for example, Russian documents found in the Kabul houses of foreign militants in December 2001).

A survey of publications by researchers with an expertise on the North Caucasus and/or Central Asia (as well as personal communication with them) returns an overwhelming consensus: Afghans and foreign military forces in Afghanistan, as well as some journalists and other researchers, are regularly mistaking Russian-speaking, foreign Muslims for Chechens. In particular, numerous people are mistaking Central Asian fighters of the Islamic Movement of Uzbekistan for Chechens, while others point also to non-Chechens from the North Caucasus as the source of the misidentification.[61] However, it goes beyond just the use of the Russian language. As two researchers of the Chechen conflict argue, "the ethnonym 'Chechen' has in fact been employed to describe almost all foreigners whose identity Afghans were unable to discover or whose language was incomprehensible (ie almost anyone but Pakistanis and Arabs)."[62] Even foreign Uzbeks who can speak local languages have been misidentified as Chechens, as the kidnapping incidents of Hazara bus passengers in Zabul demonstrated.

If 'Chechen' has become, for some Afghans, a generic term for unidentifiable foreign Muslims, it has followed numerous, similar,

305

historical linguistic practices (in ethnolinguistics, the 'incorrect' names of ethnic groups used by outsiders are called exonyms or xenonyms). For example, the Persian word farangi is derived narrowly from 'Frank', the western Germanic tribes in the Rhine region (eventually, the name 'France' was also derived from 'Frank'). Yet farangi and similar names were used throughout the Muslim world and as far as China and Southeast Asia to refer to anybody from western or Central Europe, or even just to European Christians in general. So, for example, a Persian in the 1800s could refer to a Swede, Portuguese, Czech or Irishman as a farangi, and be corrected by a European who would then identify them not as farangi (Frank), but by their actual nationality. However, both are correct in their own linguistic context.

Similarly, arguing with every Afghan police officer or soldier about whether someone is Chechen or not misses the point in a similar way: for Afghans, 'Chechen' could just mean 'foreign Muslim of unknown ethnicity', and this use would be correct for them even if the person they are identifying is not Chechen.[63] However, the listener may think they are hearing a reference to 'Chechen', meaning native of Chechnya. Similar examples of this are the numerous reports of Afghans in isolated areas referring to American and other coalition soldiers as 'Russian' or 'Soviet' (shurawi).[64] It is obviously wrong to say that American soldiers are Russians or indeed Soviets, but if in one's own linguistic and cultural context, shurawi refers to foreign, non-Muslim soldiers, then it is not incorrect – it is just a linguistic and cultural difference in terminology.

Real Chechens in Afghanistan

The first known (sort-of) Chechen to visit Afghanistan as a foreign volunteer was Fathi Muhammad Habib, also known as Shaykh Ali Fathi al-Shishani, in 1982. An elderly electrical engineer, he took on non-combat duties with Abdul Rab Rasul Sayyaf's Ittehad party. However, despite being 'al-Shishani' ('the Chechen' in Arabic), he was not actually from Chechnya. Rather he was a Jordanian Arab descended from Chechens who had emigrated during the Ottoman period.[65]More recently, another member of the Chechen diaspora fought in Afghanistan. The online 'martyr' tribute to Sayfullah Shishani, an ethnic Chechen from Georgia who died in Syria, mentions that he fought for a year in Afghanistan at some point in the past. Another researcher mentioned that he had seen a tribute to another 'Shishani' who died in Afghanistan.[66] On the opposite side to the Islamists, there was a Chechen who fought for Dostum against the Taleban and the Islamic Movement of Uzbekistan and who apparently was in Afghanistan out of a motivation to kill 'Wahhabis'. When asked in 2003, he said he had never seen another Chechen in Afghanistan, "despite his best efforts to locate his countrymen amongst the Talib prisoners."[67]

These few examples of Chechen foreign fighters are rare exceptions. Comprehensive studies of foreign fighters, their biographies and their 'martyr' tributes turn up almost nothing. A study of 'martyr biographies' killed in Afghanistan and Pakistan from 2002 to 2006 includes only five citizens of Russia, and based on their noms de guerre they were ethnic Tatars or from Dagestan, not Chechens.[68] Furthermore, a study focusing on foreign fighters in Afghanistan from 1980-2010 completely rejects the Chechen narrative.[69] When Russian citizens do show up in lists of 'martyrs', they are in tiny numbers and from other Russian regions – usually from Dagestan and Tatarstan – not Chechnya.[71] As for those captured alive, just as when the eight Russian citizens imprisoned in Guantanamo Bay turned out to be non-Chechens, a list compiled by AAN of detainees at Bagram turned up only a single Russian citizen: an ethnic Tatar.

The expropriation of Chechen identity on the battlefield

Najibullah Qurishi's documentary footage with Hezb-e Islami insurgents in northern Afghanistan from 2010 included a scene where a single insurgent was pointed out by a fellow fighter who declared, "This brother's from Chechnya." There are very few instances of Taleban fighters saying they worked together with one or more Chechens. The most prominent is in a 2009 Newsweek article by Sami Yousafzai. Yet there is reason to believe that even someone who self-identifies as a Chechen may not actually be Chechen. The first reason is that it is often difficult for a Russian

Muslim to explain their ethnic identity to Muslims and others from outside Russia. In the Russian North Caucasus region alone, there are Muslims whose ethnicity is Avar, Dargwa, Kumyk, Lezgin, Tabasaran, Karachay, Cherkess, Abazin, Kabardian, Ingush, et cetera. It is easier to just identify out of convenience with the better-known names of 'Chechen' or 'Dagestani' (which is not an ethnic identify, but rather someone of varied ethnicity from the Dagestan province of Russia).

But convenience aside, there are also insurgents and terrorists who do expropriate the Chechen identity 'brand' in order to better promote themselves and project an image of a fearsome and brave fighter. Chechen fighters in Syria have spoken publically of this identity theft. Joanna Paraszczuk, a researcher who focuses on Chechen fighters, reported on this phenomenon:

Meanwhile, Chechens in Syria have also complained that the West — and even other Islamist militant groups in Syria — are trying to claim the Chechen name, "Shishani" in Arabic, because they think this is associated with bravery on the battlefield.

"The name "Shishani" has become a brand," one Chechen militant in Latakia said via Facebook. "Lots of people want to be a Shishani, when they are not."

A reporter asked an American Special Operation Forces officer with an academic and research background on the North Caucasus and Chechnya about the practise of people 'stealing' the Chechen identity. He compared these people to Americans who lie and claim to be Special Forces: "So just as it's 'cool' here to be Special Forces, or to be a Navy SEAL, it is cool in that part of the world to be a Chechen." The main reasons he gives for the Chechen identity having this sort of value is that Chechens legitimately are good fighters, and that in the early to mid-1990s, videos from Chechnya circulating in the worldwide militant community of Chechens killing Russian soldiers boosted their reputation (as Islamic fighters). He even cites Islamic Movement of Uzbekistan fighters in Afghanistan lying and claiming to be Chechen in order to instil fear in their enemies.

What do Chechens have to say?

Aside from noting that other fighters are falsely claiming to be Chechen, Chechens – both pro-Russian and in the opposition – widely mock the notion that large numbers of their countrymen are in Afghanistan. One 2005 article published in the (anti-Russian) Chechen Press titled "Chechens as a Nightmare" (see here) mocked the "schizophrenic... hallucinations" that turned up Chechens on various battlefields around the world, comparing them to UFO sightings. Citing generals, police and the media, it found examples over several years of people 'seeing' Chechens fighting or planning terrorist attacks in Afghanistan, Israel, Azerbaijan, Pakistan, Iraq, India, China, Mexico and even Arizona (eventually, the Boston Marathon Bombers would provide the first real Chechen terrorists in the US).

In most cases, the Chechen sightings were accompanied by bizarre details and ludicrous claims.A year earlier in 2004, AkhmedZakayev, the deputy prime minister of the Chechen government in exile also denied claims that Chechens were in Afghanistan and Iraq. Other denials are far angrier, such as one in the anti-Russian website Kavkaz Center which ridicules and condemns the American soldiers and journalists who claim to be identifying Chechens in Afghanistan, stating that "the American Islam-haters speak only lies about Chechen Mujahideen."

Finally, the (pro-Russian) Chechen president himself, Ramzan Kadyrov, when vigorously denying that Chechens were fighting in Syria, cited the previous false rumours of Chechens in Afghanistan. By 2014, he begrudgingly admitted that there were a few Chechens in Syria, but that they were Chechens who had been born or raised in the West. Of course, Chechens now – in mid-2016 – have no choice but to acknowledge a Chechen presence in Syria, as there are numerous forms of proof, including video. Similarly, there is proof of Chechens fighting on both side of the war in Ukraine. Analysts and researchers who have argued that there were no significant numbers of Chechens in Afghanistan have demonstrated that they are perfectly able to acknowledge Chechens on foreign battlefields when presented with evidence (as in Syria).[72]

If there were actually large numbers of Chechens fighting in Afghanistan...

A common sentiment expressed by researchers, analysts, and contractors who work for the US government directly and indirectly is that, if there were truly large numbers of Chechens in Afghanistan, and if the US government and military truly believed this at the levels where the final intelligence products are produced and where funding is allocated, there would be unmistakable signs of this in US government structures and programmes. For example, Chechen would be a prominent and popular language at the Defense Language Institute and other government language schools, the study of Chechen and Chechnya would be given generous funding in various government-supported programs (academic language programmes, for example), contractors would be regularly advertising for Chechen (Nokhchinmott) linguists, and the experts and researchers with long experience studying Chechnya and Central Asia who work full or part-time for the US government and military would not be so dismissive of the idea that Chechens are in Afghanistan. Furthermore, names or at least noms de guerre would emerge from American targeted killings of Chechen terrorists and insurgents in Afghanistan and Pakistan (just as they do for Uzbeks, for example). As for US-Russian cooperation, there would be more signs of intelligence sharing, just as there are clear indications of that in Syria, at the moment, and in Afghanistan immediately after 9/11.

Conclusions: 'Generic' Chechens

Despite the very small-scale and rare visits of Chechens to Afghanistan in the 1990s, many people eventually came to believe that Chechen fighters were a common presence during that era. The Russian government, being regularly criticised by the US, European and Arab governments for its conduct in its fight against Chechen separatists, saw an opportunity to portray the entire spectrum of the Chechen independence movement to the world as extremists after the Taleban recognised Chechnya as an independent country. The 'Northern Alliance,' by the year 2000 heavily dependent on Russian military support, eagerly adopted the Russian view that there were significant numbers of transnational Chechen terrorists in Afghanistan – while Western governments rejected the Russian government view. But then the al-Qaeda attacks on 9/11 convinced the US government to adopt the Russian line on Chechnya in exchange for Russian cooperation in Operation Enduring Freedom (for more details see part one of this special two-parter).

From here the myth of Chechens in Afghanistan might have died, as no Chechens were captured or confirmed killed in Afghanistan. However, a renewed insurgency in Afghanistan made regular gains against the Afghan government and ISAF-NATO troops. The Afghan government and its US military backers, in an attempt to portray the insurgency as illegitimate, decided to frame the insurgency as a foreign phenomenon. Afghan and western forces fairly blamed elements of the state and society in Pakistan, but the Chechens were, without merit, added to the mix along with a long list of foreign fighters. Journalists, and even many analysts, did not question the regular statements about Chechen fighters by the Afghan government and by representatives of ISAF-NATO forces, allowing their articles and publications to uncritically disseminate what was at best a mistaken view, or at worst 'information warfare' intended to explain the motivations for the insurgency in a manner that absolved the Afghan government and its western backers of blame.

The Chechen myth was also enabled by smaller technical details, primarily the reputation of Chechens in the militant community owing to their successful campaign against Russia (roughly, 1994 to 2000), and the ambiguity of the use of the name 'Chechen' as a generic name in Afghanistan. Non-Chechen fighters expropriated the 'Chechen' name while Afghan and NATO-ISAF forces often assumed that competent and brave opponents must be Chechen. As for the name 'Chechen', it is clearly being used to describe a range of Muslim ethnic groups from the former Soviet Union – including ethnic Russian converts to Islam.

In the context of Afghanistan's full range of problems, the accidental and intentional misidentification of Chechens is not a major issue.

However, it can serve as a symbol of larger, systemic problems: poor intelligence collection and analysis by the US government and military forces and of those of other western allies, the blurring of lines between analysis and psychological operations, lazy journalism, blame-shifting and deflection by the Afghan and US governments, the manipulation of facts to serve Great Power politics (eg, between Russia and the United States) and the lack of critical inquiry by academics, analysts and the general public in the west and in Afghanistan. All of this, taken together, can distract from questions concerning the true nature of the conflict: who are the insurgents and terrorists? Why are they joining the insurgency? What needs to be done to address these problems? The phenomenon of Chechen misidentification in Afghanistan is just one of many problems encountered when trying to understand the conflict in Afghanistan. Now, as the Afghan government and its western backers attempt to absolve themselves of blame, the alleged large number of 'foreign fighters' may well continue to be a tool used in an attempt to manipulate public perceptions. Stories of Chechens in Afghanistan, therefore, will likely persist. Courtesy: AAN. *Christian Bleuer is an independent researcher based in Central Asia. From September-December 2015 he worked in Kabul for AAN. He can be reached at Christian.Bleuer@gmail. com.*

Chapter 12

When we are the violent: the Chechen Islamist Guerrillas Discourse on their own Armed Actions

AdrianTarin Sanz

Abstract

Over the last decades, the strategic profile of the discourse with which wars are narrated has been reinforced. This discourse has also varied in the light of a recent – and alleged – peace culture permeating Western societies. Whereas the war discourse in Russia during the Second Russian-Chechen War has been widely studied, this has not been the case of the rhetoric of the Chechen Islamist guerrillas. The aim of this paper is to contribute to bridging this gap in the academic literature on the North Caucasus, employing to this end a critical discourse analysis (CDA) of a selection of texts posted by the Kavkaz Center (KC) news agency. On the basis of this analysis, it can be concluded that one of the main discursive strategies revolved around the construction of an "us" embodying the Chechen victims of the initial aggression in a conflict provoked by the Russian "other".

Keywords: discourse, war, Chechnya, jihadism, Russia

1. Introduction

Over the last few decades, an alleged peace culture has apparently been established, which, in part, has modified the way of waging and legitimizing war (Nikken, 2011), making this the last political resort. "Material interest, conflict over scarce resources, or simple intergroup hatred has not been sufficient to legitimate political violence in our times" (Hollander, 2013: 518). Generally speaking, that legitimacy has to be sought in other parts, which in itself challenges the moral ideal that violence is not admissible under any circumstances (Tarín Sanz, 2015). One of those "other parts" revolves around legitimate defense or self-defense,[1] extenuating circumstances that, nowadays, appear as two of the foremost narratives for justifying political violence to global public opinion.

This last notion – that of presenting the event to others – is essential in just war theory (O'Boyle, 2002), which analyzes precisely the shift of the ideal of previous justice – the need for territorial expansion, amassing greater wealth, empire-building, etc.–toward another contemporary one in which it is crucial to bear in mind public opinion. Beyond the normative processes that regulate the internal and international relations of countries, even way beyond whatever those intervening directly in a conflict actually do, the moral issue of war is established by the opinions of humanity as a whole (Walzer, 2015). The reasons behind, or acts of, war are not as important as what is imagined by the body of citizens. That is why propaganda, the discourse employed to offer an account of war, is one of the key elements of military success (Miller, 2004).

In this respect, there is plenty of literature that has sought to unravel the discourses revolving around political violence.[2] But one of the most resorted to has to do with the collective yearning for a superior or horizontal order, objectively better than that which is being contested. This social, and personal, benefit is central to contemporary just war doctrine and has been used by organizations such as IRA, for which the redefinition of frontiers would improve the lot of the Irish people (Macfarlane, 1990); the North American far right, who regard themselves as a genuinely native vanguard that will transport the nation back in time to an idealized past of racial purity (Barkun, 2000); and the North American government itself during the Kosovo War, whose military success was narrated as a victory of all in pursuit of human rights, thanks to which the world would be a safer place (Stables, 2003).

According to O'Boyle (2002, 25), this war frame is based on consequentialist theory, "the doctrine that says that the right act in any given situation is the one that will produce the best overall outcome in terms of the identified end." Namely, there is an ultimate purpose that is just (or more equitable than the current design) and which makes political violence against those who stand in the way of a better world admissible. Using the aforementioned cases, it is just to kill the English to attain a country where we can live happily; it is just to kill coloured people to restore our nation to the peaceful racial harmony enjoyed by our ancestors; it is just to kill Serbs to protect the world.

But, in addition to resorting to violence to reach a loftier goal, it must also be adequately employed. The actors of an armed conflict must contend that this was the last resort, after having exhausted all other alternatives for a peaceful settlement and, moreover, that its use was responsible. This is the reason why the manuals of the Animal Liberation Front scrupulously establish that the only morally acceptable acts of violence are those carried out against the property of whoever is directly involved in animal exploitation, taking special care not to harm any animal – human or otherwise (Cordeiro-Rodrigues, 2016). Or, from a different perspective, it is the same reason why jihadist groups go to great lengths to justify martyrdom – the procedure and not the outcome – on the basis of the sacred texts (Slavicek, 2008). In the first case, the source of legitimacy lies in resorting to proportional violence and only against blatant aggressors. In the second case, it resides in a divine and, therefore, absolute code.

With respect to the main context of this paper, some studies have addressed the war discourse during the Russian-Chechen Wars, particularly the second war. As a rule, they coincide in underscoring that one of the central arguments employed by the Kremlin to justify its intervention was to place the conflict in the context of the North American War on Terror (Foxall, 2010, Lapidus, 2002, Russell, 2005, Vázquez Liñán, 2005, Vázquez Liñán, 2009). According to these analyses, after the 9/11 terrorist attacks the administration of Vladimir Putin experienced one of the periods of greatest rapprochement with its US counterpart, thanks, among other aspects, to its support for the war in Afghanistan and by presenting the Chechen conflict as yet another front of that battle. Thus, the narrative of the global threat to the West – or to the Christian world – with the twin towers collapsing in the background, was a frame central to Russia's war discourse:

The event that occurred in the US today goes beyond national borders. It is a brazen challenge to the whole humanity, at least to civilized humanity. And what happened today is added proof of the relevance of the Russian proposal to pool the efforts of the international community in the struggle against terrorism, that plague of the 21st century. Russia knows at first hand what terrorism is. So, we understand as well as anyone the feelings of the American people. Addressing the people of the United States on behalf of Russia I would like to say that we are with you, we entirely and fully share and experience your pain. We support you (Putin, 2001).

Nonetheless, there are remarkable shortcomings in the study of the Chechen discourse of justification, with the exception of Radnitz (2006), who analyzes the progressive "Islamization" of Russian and Chechen institutional language between the first and second war, and how religion gradually played a more important role in war rhetoric. This progressive "Islamization" had a special presence in the period studied (2001–2005): the previous moment of the institutional transition from pseudo-secular Chechen nationalism (the Maskhadov government) to pan-Caucasian jihadism (the Caucasus Emirate). It is thus a period in which the majority of the Chechen population were hesitant about the application of sharia (Akaev, 2014), and in which the propagandists – like MovladiUdugov – who during the first war spoke Russian and considered Western reporters as potential allies, during the second war began to employ a hostile jihadist discourse (Swirszcz, 2009).

This paper intends to contribute to partially filling that lacuna. The general objective is to analyze the arguments employed by the incipient Chechen jihadist guerrillas to present their own political violence in an acceptable light, during the government of Aslan Maskhadov. To this end, the English language version of the website of the Kavkaz Center (KC), recognized as the chief mouthpiece of these armed groups, was chosen as the object of study. The selected sample comprises news items dealing with the four violent events with greater coverage in the KC between 2001 and 2005: the storming of the DubrovkaTheater in 2002, with the subsequent death of dozens of hostages; the campaign of terrorist attacks sparked by the passing of the "pro-Russian" Chechen constitution in 2003; the assassination of the "pro-Russian" Akhmad Kadyrov and the tragic siege at Beslan School in 2004. A specific design of critical discourse analysis (CDA), called "ideological square", which will be described below, was used for data collection and analysis.

2. The outbreak of the conflict in 1999

After the First Russian-Chechen War (1994–1996) – the military reaction of the Kremlin to the unilaterally declared independence of what was then known as the Chechen Republic of Ichkeria (CRI)–the region was plunged into a deep depression caused by the ravages of the conflict, the consequent increase in crime, internal political disputes, and the pressure brought to bear by Moscow in order to hinder the peace process, among other aspects (Dannreuther, 2010, Galeotti, 2002, Galeotti, 2014, Gammer, 2005, Sagramoso, 2007, Souleimanov, 2005, Wilhelmsen, 2005). This state of affairs affected the nationalist government of Aslan Maskhadov, who, in spite of occupying the presidency until his death, provided ample proof of his inability to retain the monopoly of violence (Rivas Otero & Tarín Sanz, 2016). The vacuum generated by the "weak authority" of Maskhadov was exploited by the warlords and the incipient Islamist insurgency to occupy a greater number of positions of power (Le Huérou et al, 2014, Moore, Tumelty, 2009), a frame in which the uncontrolled incursion of Chechen Islamist guerrillas into Dagestan in 1999 must be understood.

317

After the collapse of the USSR, a thriving Salafi community consolidated its position in Dagestan[3] (Ibragimov&Matsuzato, 2014), edified in part on the deception caused by Soviet modernity and its chaotic transition toward capitalism (Ware, Kisriev, Patzelt, & Roericht, 2003). Its main stamping ground was located in the area of Kadar, an irregular strip of land between the capital Makhachkala and the small town of Gimry. This enclave has produced religious leaders such as Rustam Asilderov, the incumbent emir of the Islamic State's subsidiary in Russia (Vilayat Kavkaz), and, among others, three of the most outstanding personalities of the 1990s, the clerics Akhmad-KadiAkhtaev, BagautdinMagomedov, and Abbas Kebedov, these last two being half-brothers.[4]Akhtaev is retrospectively considered a moderate (Roshchin, 2003), at least bearing in mind his Salafism; albeit for the traditional Sufi Community, with historical roots in the Muslim Caucasus, he preached extremist religious interpretations typical of foreigners (Makarov, 2008).

In fact, this accusation – that Salafism is an imported vision far removed from local tradition – has been a constant bone of contention between both communities (Bobrovnikov, 2006). Moreover, Bagautdin and Abbas had ties with the most radical traditions advocating for political violence, and even went so far as to enter into strategic alliances with the Chechen warlords (Khanbabaev, 2010). Notwithstanding their different vision of Salafism, this did not prevent the Dagestanis Akhtaev, Bagautdin, and Abbas, in collaboration with the Chechen Islamist Khalimov,[5] from establishing contacts with Middle Eastern Islamist groups (Moore &Tumelty, 2008). These contacts were crucial for allowing Salafism to "reach" Dagestan, and, from there, vulnerable Chechnya (McGregor, 2012, Roshchin, 2012), caught up in the turmoil of war at the time.

In keeping with this new Islamist spirit, around 500 men – including Salafis, Dagestanis, foreign Mujahideen, and former Chechen nationalists – crossed the border between Chechnya and Dagestan between August and September of 1999, with the intention of creating an Islamic state that united the Caucasus (Giuliano, 2005). Even though the Dagestani administration had little control over the territories of Kadar, which appeared to be a de facto autonomous enclave, the attempt ended in failure, due mostly to the fact that the local population did not endorse the Salafi project (idem), but also because many refused to risk their lives in a Chechen enterprise led by guerillas with a recent and perfunctory knowledge of Islam (Matsuzato&Ibragimov, 2005)."In Dagestani public opinion, local Wahhabis were 'traitors' and Chechens were 'invaders' or an 'occupying force'" (Kisriev& Ware, 2000, 487). Parallel to this operation, bombs were detonated in four apartment blocks located in different parts of Russia, acts that Moscow attributed to the Chechen separatists. The invasion of Dagestan and the bombings, depicted by Russia as a consequence of the weak government of Maskhadov (Koltsova, 2000), served as a casus belli for launching the second war (Coppieters, 2003).

Although Boris Yeltsin, the then President of the Russian Federation, justified the second intervention with the same arguments and language that had been employed during the first conflict – the guerrillas were merely bandits devoid of any political or religious motivation, assassins who were plunging the region into chaos (Radnitz, 2006) – as has already been noted in the introduction, the 9/11 terrorist attacks presented his successor Vladimir Putin with the opportunity to "internationalize" the conflict, in line with the West's struggle in the War on Terror. The war was not only justified as a direct consequence of a prior aggression for which the Chechen authorities were responsible – the invasion of Dagestan and the apartment block bombings – but also because it contributed to improving global security by combating a politically antagonistic global enemy: international jihadist terrorism.

On the whole, the Chechen case was more complex due to the absence of a homogeneous public discourse – a result of the country's infighting. The political divide between the government of Maskhadov, who had inherited the secular nationalist vision of his predecessor Dzhokhar Dudayev, and the incipient Islamist guerillas, whose frame of interpretation of the conflict was in line with the rationale of religious war, had become manifest since the interwar period. These discrepancies, or parallel agendas, were not only expressed as part of a calm internal ideological debate, but also lead to armed confrontation, above all during the months running up to the outbreak of the second war, thus contributing to the aforementioned instability.

An example of this is an incident that occurred in the town of Gudermes (Chechnya) in 1998, in which the Chechen security forces repressed a group of militant Salafis who were acting as self-appointed "guardians of public morals", which left over 50 dead (Tarín Sanz, 2017). In this respect, Chechen institutional language "included [a] discourse amenable to the west, emphasizing Chechen victimization and Russian brutality, casting their role in the conflict as motivated by self-defense, and occasionally accusing Russia of trying to annihilate Muslims" (Radnitz, 2006, 251), though this discourse might not have coincided exactly with the Islamist insurgency's version of events. To approach this issue, and at the same time to provide empirical data for analysis, a CDA of Chechen jihadist propaganda was conducted.

3. Critical discourse analysis (CDA) and the ideological square

The study of war discourse implies establishing the antagonism between the ally who reacts to an aggression and the enemy responsible for the violence occasioning the conflict. This "us/ other" dichotomy6, whose construction is disputed in the field of discourse and which embodies the nature of politics as a discipline (Mouffe, 1995, Schmitt, 2007), entails a power relation. Assuming this premise to be the case, it was considered appropriate to use a version of discourse analysis with a notable track record in the study of the linguistic particles with which the actors in question are constructed: CDA.[7] CDA "primarily studies the way social power abuse, dominance, and inequality are enacted, reproduced, and resisted by text and talk in the social and political context," and thus "take explicit position" (Van Dijk, 2003a, 352) and are honored to do so (Van Dijk, 2003b).

For CDA, nonetheless, discourse is much more than a sequence of linguistic signs; it is, moreover, a three-dimensional entity: text, discursive practice, and sociocultural practice (Fairclough, 1995). It is text insofar as it is understood as a product of language. Its analysis – text analysis – is descriptive, focusing on the structure and formal aspects of discourse, such as vocabulary, grammar, deixis, and its organization. It is also discursive practice, linked to text production and interpretation, inasmuch as it is associated with an established genre or type of discourse connected to a particular social activity. And, lastly, it is sociocultural practice, seeing that it explains the relationship between the discursive process and social processes, since discourse constructs or reproduces a reality, transmits or transforms ideologies, perpetrates or subverts power relations and domination through its linguistic structures (Fairclough, 1992, Foucault, 1992, Wodak, Meyer, 2009).

These three dimensions are not expressed independently, but holistically. It is a material, delimited, and delimitable product – it is text – elaborated on the basis of specific patterns, practices, and hierarchies – it is discursive practice – and permeated by potentially transmittable beliefs, myths, imaginaries, and ideologies – it is social practice. In this regard, in the analysis conducted as part of this study attention was paid to the linguistic devices of Chechen Islamist propaganda, its structures of creation, and its possible sociocultural insertion, insofar as it tried to explain and justify its own violence against the Russian enemy.

To apply CDA a concrete research design, defined by Van Dijk (1998a, 33) as an "ideological square", involving a "strategy of polarization – positive ingroup description, and negative outgroup description," which "appears in most social conflict" and that "may be expressed in the choice of lexical items that imply positive or negative evaluations, as well as in the structure of whole propositions and their categories," was used. This design can be summarized in four vertexes that serve as a guide for the analysis: (1) "Emphasize our good properties/actions", (2) "Emphasize their bad properties/actions", (3) "Mitigate our bad properties/actions", and (4) "Mitigate their good properties/actions".

The ideological square has been successfully used in other media discourse analyses with similar characteristics. In some cases, its use is limited to that of a theoretical benchmark, as occurs in Karda (2012), whose paper describes the "us/other" strategies used by the Turkish media to combat the clandestine Ergenekon network; in Els (2013), a work revealing the xenophobic discourses appearing in the newspaper The Daily Sun; in Hearns-Branaman (2015), who compares the coverage of the diplomatic disputes between the US and Iran by different news agencies; or in the analysis of the discourse of the Russian website InoSMI with respect to the Crimea crisis, conducted by Spiessens and Van Poucke (2016).

Yet it has also been employed as a methodological tool with the same results, as shown in Turner (2008) on the construction of the lesbian community in the magazine Diva; in Arrunátegui (2010), who analyzes how the Peruvian press characterizes the indigenous subject; or in Mayer, Ajanovic, and Sauer (2014), dealing with the gender roles promoted by the Austrian extreme right. To approach the discourse employed by the Chechen Islamist guerrillas to justify political violence, this second path was taken, not only to detect the use of the specific linguistic structures proposed by Fairclough (1992) and Van Dijk (1998a), but also to deal with other more complex dimensions of this discourse – such as discursive and social practice – which the ideological square model is also capable of addressing (Philo, 2007).

A. Delimiting the object of study

In order to analyze the discourse employed by the Islamist guerrillas to justify their own violence, the KC website was chosen. After the First Russian-Chechen War, these armed groups saw in the Internet – and more specifically in the aforementioned news agency – an opportunity to disseminate their message with less restrictions and financial constraints (Campana &Ducol, 2015). But also because "Chechen websites were intended primarily for international, rather than domestic, audiences (since, presumably, Internet access would not be widespread in Chechnya during wartime), and can therefore be considered a source of public discourse" (Radnitz, 2006, 249).

As regards the period of study, content corresponding to events particularly relevant to the proposed analysis was selected – moments when the guerillas had to justify their own violence8 because of their relationship with the situational context in which the discourses were produced – since this allowed us to fine-tune the analysis of their ideological content (Van Dijk, 1998b). These events are framed between the birth of the English version of KC (2001) and the death of Aslan Maskhadov (2005), because this period holds a special importance: this is where "a war of identity" during the transition from nationalism to jihadism was fought, in which the discourse played a key role (Janeczko, 2014, 446).

So, content related to four events was taken into account: the hostage-taking at the DubrovkaTheater (2002); the campaign of terrorist attacks that accompanied the passing of the pro-Russian Chechen constitution (2003); the assassination of Akhmad Kadyrov (2004); and the massacre at Beslan School (2004).[9] Likewise, those forms of journalistic expression that could not be considered informative were discarded (Velásquez Ossa, 2011), since ideological discourse becomes a topic of special interest when the receivers are not forewarned (Van Dijk, 1998b). Thus, only 44 texts, corresponding to news items, communiqués, or interviews related to the above-mentioned events, were included. "Conducting a CDA analysis often involves the analysis of only a small number of texts" (Machin & Mayr, 2012, 207).

B. Method application

Emphasize our good properties/actions

Agency, responsibility, and merits

Agency can be understood as the real or potential position of an actor in a conflict, as well as the subject's own acts and capacity to act (Ema López, 2004). So, it possess an ideological-guiding role by placing a specific subject in a certain situation and, therefore, constructing an "us" with "our" good actions. This possibility of establishing agency allows us, among other things, to attribute certain responsibilities and merits of the acts integrated into the discourse. The latest suicide bombing by Chechen independence rebels, apparently an attempt to assassinate the region's most senior pro-Moscow figure, followed a truck bomb at government offices in the north of the territory on Monday which killed 59. [...] Pro-Russian [sic] officials said she had intended to kill Akhmad Kadyrov, the pro-Moscow head of the Chechen administration and a strong advocate of Putin's peace plan, who addressed the crowd of about 15,000 [...]. Local officials identified the bomber as 46-year old ShakhidaBaimuratova, a rebel fighter whose husband was killed in 1999 during the conflict.[10]

This extract refers to a suicide attack carried out in May 2003, whose clear intention was to murder Akhmad Kadyrov, who was at the time the person with every chance of becoming President of the Republic of Chechnya, the rival administration of the nationalist CRI. A month before, a new constitution replacing the separatist one of 1992 had been passed in a referendum vote, thus questioning the legitimacy of the government of Aslan Maskhadov. Despite the fact that their forces had been incapable of impeding the referendum, the Islamist guerrillas were indeed capable of launching a series of attacks that hindered the process and cast doubt on the official Russian account that argued that the passing of the new constitution and formation of a new government signaled the end of the war.

In this context, a "logical" explication was offered for the insurgency's own violence, since, first, it not only responded to a collective aggression against Chechen sovereignty – represented by Kadyrov – but also to an individual one against a citizen of "our" country; so, accordingly, Baimuratov's widow had adopted a combatant role. One of the essential characteristics of the construction of "us" resides in the fact that our history and acts are loaded with comprehensible reasons, whereas the "others" act without a cause worthy of the name (Alba Rico, 2015).

The small mountainous republic of Chechnya has been ravaged by conflict since 1994, with just three years of relative peace after the first Russian invasion of the region ended in August 1996 and the second began in October 1999.[11] Another logical explication for Chechen Islamist violence, which helps to place the actors involved in the action, is that it was the only alternative for reestablishing the prior status quo. According to the KC, the only brief moment of calm in the region was when Russian domination did not exist – the tumultuous inter-war period – interrupted by a foreign "invasion", a term that in and of itself possesses a high load of agency: invasions are in themselves aggressions.[12]

The strategy of intertextuality

What is understood by intertextuality is the relating of a discourse to another extraneous one (Kristeva, 2001, Todorov, 1998) which, together, form a new discourse; fragments that a reader glimpses in a text which belong to, or recall, other previous ones. In other words, intertextuality is "the presence of elements of some texts inside another one" (Fairclough, 2003, 39). The selection of these elements, called subtexts, necessarily involves an ideological attitude, inasmuch as "intertextuality is inevitably selective with respect to what is included and what is excluded from the events and texts represented" (Fairclough, 2003, 52). Seen from a wider viewpoint, all creative production can be regarded as intertextual, insofar as nothing emerges from the sterile vacuum of imagination. However, and while recognizing such limitations, a restricted vision of intertextuality grounded in linguistics was employed here, focusing solely on devices such as citation, mention, and allusion (Zavala, 1999). According to MovsarBarayev, Chechen fighters have the situation under their total control.[13]. Maskhadov has distanced himself from the attack, offering his condolences to the victims' families.[14]

In this case, both quotes correspond to texts covering the DubrovkaTheater hostage crisis in October 2002. During a play, a group of Chechen insurgents stormed the theater and took the audience hostage for several days. In the course of the questionable rescue operation carried out by the Russian security forces, using a gas whose composition was kept under wraps and which was partly blamed for the tragedy, more than 150 people died, including Russian civilians and Chechen militants. The first extract is an example of how the coverage of the attack was constructed: using the insurgency's own sources. Thus, it was a constant that the relevant actors, like MovsarBarayev, the leader of the operation, and Aslan Maskhadov, President of the CRI, made their own statements that then went on to form part of the official Chechen account.

But with a revealing appreciation: at the time, institutionalism was still represented by secular nationalism, and the official proclamation of the Caucasus Emirate, the Islamist organization that would virtually replace the RCI, was still five years away. Thus, the KC offered two different versions of the violence: the Islamist guerrillas' rendition for their followers who wanted to know that "the situation was under control" versus the contradictory information supplied by the Russian media; and the nationalist and institutional account, concerned that the international community might associate the hostage-taking with terrorist operations like that of 9/11. This discursive ambivalence echoed the circumstantial debate within the opposition to Russia and which prevailed for several years more.[15]

But, furthermore, it was customary that when the Chechen's own violence had to be presented with greater finesse, this coincided with the posting of communiqués or interviews with the foremost members of the government of the CRI or of the insurgency, such as the then minister AkhmedZakayev, President Aslan Maskhadov, and the Mujahideen leader Shamil Basayev. This led to these controversial events being narrated in the first person by the allied camp, while the arguments of the enemy were systematically omitted.

Emphasize their bad properties/actions

Unification of perspective or point of view

This device is the result of the "strategy of intertextuality", but instead of presenting a situation in which one or several quotes or allusions ideologically guide the discourse, what is being referred to here is a general tendency in the text, where the great majority or all of the sources or allusions point to a sole point of view, disregarding other possible discourses that could flesh out or corroborate the reasons behind the violence. "Inherent in the notions of ideology, attitudes and the specific opinions based on them is the notion of 'position'. Events are described and evaluated from the position, point of view or perspective of the speaker" (Van Dijk, 1998a, 43). That war in [sic] ended in 1996, after which Chechnya had de facto independence from Russian control. But Russian forces went storming back in to the region in October 1999.[16]

The outbreak of war in 1999 is an event on which there currently exist different views – a strategy to promote the image of Vladimir Putin; the national-popular necessity to construct the limits of a new Russia; a consequence of the widespread instability in Chechnya due to the CRI's loss of authority; a counter-terrorist operation in the face of the challenge posed by Al-Qaeda; etc.– and its outcome was influenced by multiple variables. However, the Chechen Islamist guerrillas ignored all those explications that might have implied a certain degree of responsibility of their own, placing their discourse in the frame of invasion. The insistence on this account during the DubrovkaTheater hostage crisis contributed to fostering the idea that the operation was justified (from the point of view of the Islamist insurgency), or, at best, attenuated (from the viewpoint of the secular nationalists). Opposition politicians said the attack underscored Moscow's weak control over the predominantly Muslim province.[17]

In this quote, the campaign of attacks suffered by Russia as a result of the passing of the constitution of 2003 is presented from the perspective of political opposition. The Russian viewpoint was only admissible when it served to underpin the opposition's vision of the war. As a matter of fact, in that same text Vladimir Putin's statements only appear in a paraphrased form, preceded by the word "defiant", with clearly pejorative undertones. Lastly, other information that contextualized Chechen Islamist violence was described from just one perspective – that favoring the Chechens' own theses – including the violation of human rights by the Russians, war reports, or the alleged link between the guerrillas and Al-Qaeda.

Agency, responsibility, and blame for the acts. In the same manner as agency is useful for attributing merits, it can also be used to apportion blame, employing identical mechanisms: by localizing and characterizing the actors in the discourse. Nonetheless, this can be achieved not only by narrating and describing their acts, but also through the ordination of words, predication, and lexical selection. The incident comes as Russia is launching a crackdown in the republic following the seizing of hundreds of hostages last week in Moscow by a group of heavily armed Chechens.[18] Capture of civilians in Moscow, the capital of the aggressor country, is the consequence of the mass and purposeful extermination of civilian population not only in the capital, but also in all other cities and villages of the victimized country. Whatever outcome the incident will have, the whole responsibility will fully lie on those who unleashed the criminal war against the Chechen people.[19]

The representative of the President of CRI, A. Maskhadov in RF, S. Maigov stated in his brief interview with Grani.ru news agency about the explosion in Iliskhan-Yourt–'We are the witnesses of the escalation of violence in Chechnya. Obviously, this is the consequence of the fact that Kremlin did not succeed in implementing the declared promises in the case of the success of referendum. [...] This is response to that terror against Chechen people.'[20] Shaheeds do not resort to personal revenge. They were taking revenge for our desecrated religion, for our entire nation, for our land, and for the entire Islamic Ummah.[21] But it would have been dishonest to the victims and irresponsible to the survivors if, having condemned the killers, we had failed to name the political causes of the tragedy and had failed to try – even without much hope for success – to once again urge the world to condemn the policy that makes tragedies like this not only possible, but inevitable.[22]

In the Chechen Islamist discourse, it was commonplace to encounter linguistic constructions that suggested a "cause–effect" relationship between Russian violence and its own. Thus, typical expressions included "come as", "the consequence", "[the attack] is a response", "taking revenge for", or the explicit "the responsibility will lie" in order to emphasize that Russia was to blame for the guerrillas seizing theatres and schools, and bombing apartment blocks. In this respect, it is noteworthy that the storming of School No. 1 at Beslan, when a commando retained hundreds of pupils and teachers for several days, and whose outcome was similar to that of the DubrovkaTheater episode, with dozens of deaths after a failed rescue operation, was regarded as "inevitable". In this case, Chechen violence was neither less brutal nor the consequence of another greater violence, foreign and primeval, but, furthermore, the assassination of Russian children ceased to be a (inevitable) voluntary act, given that the country's government had left the insurgents no alternative.

Liberal members of parliament are demanding an inquiry into the way the crisis was handled – in reference to the cold-blooded way in which Russian authorities opted to end the hostage-taking crisis.[23]Insha Allah, sooner or later, whether they want it or not, both the people and the government of Russia will be forced to stop this bloody slaughter.[24] [...] killed eight Russian invaders from among the so-called subdivision of combat reconnaissance of invaders. The detachment of aggressors was ambushed.[25] [...] carry out a special operation on the elimination of the formations of invaders and collaborators.[26] But in addition to justifying its own violence on the basis of its nature – since it was a response to another prior violence – the Chechen Islamist discourse also addressed another of the aforesaid sources of legitimacy: the procedure with which the said violence was used. Thus, the armed actions of the Russians were unlawful because they were "aggressions", the product of an "invasion" launched "in cold blood" and with "bloody" consequences. They were not, therefore, as proportional and restrained as the Chechens' own actions.

Local coherence

As noted by Van Dijk (1998a, 36), local coherence is "one of the crucial semantic conditions of textuality" and "the property of sequential sentences (or propositions) in text and talk that defines why they 'hang together' or forro [sic] a 'unity', and do not constitute an arbitrary set of sentences." So, some clauses only reveal their ideological meaning in relation to others and by means of a basic and repeatable structure (Van Dijk, 1998b). These schemes "may involve causal or conditional relations between the facts as represented by a model" (Van Dijk, 1998a, 36–37); viz., the reproduction of structural skeletons of texts that on their own guides the interpretation of a specific meaning, as with cause-effect relationships or contrasts (Van Dijk, 1998b).

MovsarBarayev's assistant told during his interview to Kavkaz Center over the phone at about 10:00 AM Moscow Time that they are getting ready to release 30 foreigners and are warning the Russian command not to shoot at the hostages. MovsarBarayev reported to Kavkaz Center that General Aslakhanov left him a phone number of the Russian headquarters, where Mr. Barayev is going to call. He already called this number once, but did not get through.[27] At least 117 hostages and around 50 Chechen hostage-takers were killed, most of them gassed to death by Russian forces in an assault on the theatre where more than 800 people were taken by the militants on Wednesday. Zakayev was in Denmark as an envoy of rebel Chechen president Aslan Maskhadov, who on Monday again said he was prepared for negotiations with Moscow to put an end to the bloodshed in the tiny breakaway republic.[28]

After the theatre siege, France and other Western states urged Moscow to talk with the rebels. But Yastrzhembsky echoed President Vladimir Putin's longstanding rejection of any talks with "terrorists".[29] Some of the texts included in the sample achieve discursive coherence by contrasting two consecutive clauses that express "our" good deeds, before underscoring the wrongdoings of the "other". The order of the sentences stresses the coherence of the second clause –that which places the blame on the Russians or extols the Chechens. In the first of the aforementioned cases, this contrast was achieved when the KC informed that the hostage-takers who had stormed the DubrovkaTheater claimed that they were willing to free a number of hostages, but for this to happen they needed a direct line to the Kremlin, which never replied. Both clauses attempt to express the will of the Chechen guerrillas to find a negotiated solution to the conflict, whereas the Russians continued stubbornly to refuse to reach a compromise. This is also illustrated, more clearly if possible, in the following two quotes, in which it was explained that Moscow did not negotiate with Maskhadov on the principle of "do not negotiate with terrorists".

Mitigate our bad properties/actions

Modalization (verbal)

Modalization is a grammatical device that, on specific occasions, is used to explain the degree of confidence with which the speaker transmits a "truth". Thus, when the particle that expresses that degree of confidence is a verb – generally, modal verbs that act as auxiliaries to others – the phenomenon is usually described as "verbal modalization", the verbs "to be able to" or "to have to" being normally used, or others in their conditional form (Fairclough, 1992). In the discourse employed by the Chechens to justify their own violence, modalization was used to mitigate the offences of the insurgency, since the degree of confidence of their own wrongdoings was narrated with a level of certainty that was lower than the usual force with which they broached "Russian crimes".

If the fact that the theater has really been seized by Chechens confirms [sic], then it must be considered as the gesture of extreme despair.[30] In this proposition, two elements expressing uncertainty (if/must + be) as regards how the DubrovkaTheater hostage crisis should be interpreted are introduced. The clause begins with a conditional form, expressing doubts about whether the action was really the work of Chechen insurgents, and then claims that, if so, it could only be interpreted as a gesture of extreme despair, presupposing that this was the product of Russian criminality. A personal act of violence, expressed with uncertainty, is thus eclipsed by that of the enemy which was indeed presented as self-evident.

On other occasions, modal markers were used in the discourse under study (paraphrasing). Attributions of third-party statements not only catered to the "strategy of intertextuality" or the "unification of perspective", but, when these were made erroneously, the discourse could be restructured for ideological purposes (Fairclough, 1992), manipulating statements to its own benefit or discrediting the sources of the enemy: Tass said in a separate report, without giving a source, that some teachers may have been killed.[31]

The Russian news agency TASS stated that some teachers were killed during the Beslan School No. 1 hostage crisis, but in order to undermine the credibility of the press release the Chechen Islamists stressed that the piece was not backed by any source. This being a reasonable demand that, on the other hand, they never made with regard to the original news items appearing on the KC website.

Mitigate their good properties/actions

Semantic shift

What is meant by semantic shift is the resignification and redirection of specific propositions. Albeit commonly used in linguistics to refer to a form of lexical evolution, this phenomenon is also employed as a discursive tool to "shift" a proposition with a positive ideological strategy toward a negative one. In some instances, it is presented using paralipsis (Van Dijk, 1998a), but in the texts analyzed here it is found more frequently in contrasts similar to those of "local coherence". In the case in point, however, the sequential propositions both refer to the enemy and are connected by nexuses like the preposition "but", which takes on specific ideological connotations here by blaming Russia for a violence that outweighed any good deed of which it might have been capable.

He also reported that General Aslakhanov contacted him over the phone and offered Ruslan Khasbulatov as the negotiator. But the Mujahideen rejected that proposal, stating that Khasbulatov is stained with the blood of the Chechen people.[32] For instance, this material mentions that Putin keeps repeating over and over again that Al-Qaeda is involved in these acts on the Russian soil. But international intelligence agencies are casting doubts on the proofs that he brings to back his point of view with.[33]

In the first quote, after several hours during which the guerrillas who seized the DubrovkaTheater denounced Russia's refusal to negotiate, the commando's spokesman reported that the Kremlin had already got in contact with them for that purpose. This proposition, which shows the conciliatory spirit of the enemy, is followed by another discrediting it. It is thus possible to observe the discursive shift that starts with the conjunction "but" and ends with the explicit expression "stained with the blood of the Chechen people". In the second quote, a similar structure (a positive proposition mitigated by another negative one) is applied, this time to debunk the basic arguments with which the Kremlin justified the second war.

Russian sources reported that Putin's "amnesty" will apply to the individuals who committed "acts dangerous for the public within the borders of the former Chechen-Ingushetian Autonomous Soviet Socialist Republic over the period starting August 1, 1993, to the day when the State Duma resolution takes effect". At the same time it was especially stressed that those who "stopped armed resistance or who voluntarily turned in their weapons and military equipment before 12:00 AM August 1, 2003" will fall under amnesty. [...] "The so-called 'amnesty' that Putin is talking about has legally nothing to do with the Chechen citizens or the Chechen State. From the Shariah viewpoint, as well as from the viewpoint of the so-called 'international community', this is a totally illegitimate act that the Kremlin is doing, it has [a] purely propagandistic and totally speculative nature aimed to plant Moscow's allegations in the minds of the people that Chechnya is allegedly a part of Russia".[34]

Lastly, another form of semantic shift that is observed in the Chechen Islamist discourse occurred on a structural level, rather than by means of conjunctive lexical markers. Thus, at the beginning of the extract Vladimir Putin's intention to offer an amnesty to political prisoners and insurgents who laid down their arms is described in detail. Two paragraphs further on, in contrast, Commander Sahad, a member of the State Defence Council (Majlis al-Shura), is cited, contending that from the point of view of both Islamic Law and the international community the amnesty was illegitimate, propagandistic, and speculative. In this manner, an authoritative argument discrediting a positive action of the enemy is introduced to ideologically "shift" the discourse in order to complete the last vertex of the ideological square.

4. Conclusions

On the whole, the Chechen Islamist guerrillas justified their own violence by constructing an "us" free from any responsibility for the tragedies that they provoked, and a criminal "other" to blame for the aggression giving rise to the conflict; something that is very common in war propaganda: "The construction of the Enemy is accompanied by the construction of the identity of the Self as clearly antagonistic to the Enemy's identity. In this process, not only is the radical otherness of the Enemy emphasized, but also the Enemy is presented as a threat to 'our own' identity. Ironically (...) the evilness of the Enemy is a necessary condition for the articulation of the goodness of the Self (Carpentier, 2007, 03).

Chechen armed actions were always in legitimate self-defense against the Russian "invasion" of their territory, even when the victims were civilians, who were considered the Government's accomplices.[35] To this end, all direct references to the Russian discourse were omitted, and when it did indeed appear it was disparaged. By the same token, Russian actions that audiences might have interpreted as positive were always presented as an illusion or driven by covert, malicious intentions. Conversely, the Chechen separatists – nationalists and Islamists – were habitually depicted as noble victims pushed by the circumstances to storm theaters and schools and bomb buildings. This unity of action is noteworthy to the extent that, for years, both factions had been immersed in a struggle to monopolize the separatist movement. However, this propaganda strategy ultimately backfired in 2007, when Doku Umarov proclaimed the establishment of the Caucasus Emirate and the KC published a series of articles accusing AkhmedZakayev, the CRI's representative in exile, of treason and complicity with Russia (Tarín Sanz, 2017).

Although this narrative is commonplace in war propaganda (HuiciMódenes, 2010), the Chechen Islamist discourse at the time (between 2001 and 2005) displayed some characteristics that distanced it from conventional jihadist narratives. First, the Chechens' own violence was seemingly devoid of any exhibitionism, as was not the case in the contemporary Iraq of Abu Musab al-Zarqawi or currently in the Islamic State. On the contrary, the violence was occasionally presented as a lesser evil, as the inevitable consequence of Russian military aggression. This exceptionality could have been due to multiple factors, one of which being that, at that moment, the legitimate authority of the Chechen separatist movement was still wielded by the secular nationalist Aslan Maskhadov. Controversial though his mandate was, and in spite of the fact that for some authors he was in cahoots with the Islamists, the truth is that Maskhadov was an actor more inclined to negotiate and implement peace policies than his Islamist successors (Rivas Otero &Tarín Sanz, 2016).

Therefore, Islamist rhetoric had to coexist with a more cautious Westernized discourse, attentive to the international community, something that contributed to tempering the presentation of its own violence.36 As matter of fact, in that period the narratives framed in the deontology theory were few and far between, which, according to O'Boyle (2002), is typical of jihadist groups and assumes the existence of a set of superior (divine) moral principles that should never be violated, even if the consequences are beneficial. Instead, the central arguments have more to do with human motives –a widow of the conflict who blows herself up, a nation defending itself against an aggression – than divine ones –a mandate of Allah to punish the violence of the infidels. This does not mean to say that religious rhetoric was conspicuous by its absence – in fact, it is one of the differences between the first and second war (Radnitz, 2006) – but that, in comparison with other conflicts involving jihadist elements, it had to be played down since it coexisted with the nationalist narratives still controlled by the executive power.

In short, the Chechen war discourse could serve as a compass for taking our bearings in the process of progressive Islamization that affected the region after the first war,[37] since it reflects some of the main changes and contradictions that gradually transformed the separatist movement, as well as contributing to unraveling the power relations, political disputes, and social imaginaries (in the process of being) shared by the Chechen opposition to Russia.

Volume: 8 issue: 2, page(s): 185-195, Article first published online: July 1, 2017; Issue published: July 1, 2017. Adrián TarínSanzartarin@ uce.edu.ec, Faculty of Social Communication, Central University of Ecuador, Bolivia y Eusorgio Salgado Oe7-132, Quito, Ecuador.

Chapter 13

The Future of Chechens in ISIS

Anna Borschevskaya

Executive Summary

Russia is now third among top countries from which ISIS receives its recruits. The majority come from the North Caucasus, but also increasingly from Central Asia. The most prominent North Caucasians among the ISIS ranks have been the Chechens. While the Chechens have a reputation of being fierce warriors who fought the Russian state for twenty years, the majority have come from the Chechen diaspora and did not participate in war prior to joining ISIS. Nonetheless, a number of North Caucasian fighters in the ISIS ranks, including Chechens, have stood out. This report includes profiles of several of these individuals. While the Russian government routinely says it faces the same terrorist struggle as the West, the radicalization among Russia's Muslims is rooted in Russia's mistreatment of these people, which has a history that spans roughly 200 years. Until very recently, Russia's Muslims who radicalized did not see themselves as part of the global terrorist struggle. Rather, they saw the Russian government as their main enemy.

Their cause was different and more limited. Many who traveled to Syria wanted to fight the Russian government, but Russia's policies, especially in the run-up to the 2014 Sochi Olympics, also encouraged many North Caucasians to leave Russia for Syria, thus contributing to global terrorism, rather than fighting it. ISIS continues to decline, but the ideology will remain, and the Russian government has not addressed the root causes that led to radicalization in Russia in the first place. Most North Caucasians fighting for ISIS are unlikely to return to Russia. Instead, they are more likely to come to Europe. But it doesn't take many individuals to create acts of terrorism. Until the Russian government changes its approach, Russia will continue to be a source of instability, and an inadvertent contributor to terrorism, rather than a fighter of it.

Introduction

In recent years, Russia has emerged as third among the top five countries from which ISIS receives its recruits.[1]Most fighters come from Russia's restless North Caucasus, and increasingly also from Central Asia. This trend has been long in the making. On 23 June 2015, official ISIS spokesman Abu Muhammad al-Adnani declared the formation of a new wilayat, or governorate, in Russia's North Caucasus.[2] The announcement marked a turning point. Never before had ISIS made a territorial claim inside Russia, as press reports noted at the time. Al-Adnani's announcement came just days after reports that thousands of Islamic militants in Dagestan, Chechnya, Ingushetia, and Kabardino-Balkaria–four declared provinces of the Caucasus Emirate, Russia's main jihadist group–had formally pledged allegiance to ISIS (Islamic State of Iraq and Syria).

In doing so, these fighters echoed a December 2014 declaration of allegiance to ISIS by several of the Emirate's senior militants.[3] Al-Adnani's June 2015 announcement raised questions about the extent of ISIS influence in Russia. It also hinted at the possibility of an end to the Caucasus Emirate (also known as Imarat Kavkaz, or IK), or at least signaled IK's decline. While the Emirate's decline had been visible before, Al Adnani's announcement highlighted the decline more definitively. As these trends continue, what is next for the North Caucasian fighters in ISIS, and for Russia?

Rise and Decline of the Emirate

The Caucasus Emirate originates in the sectarian conflict that has raged in Russia's North Caucasus for a little more than two decades as a result of the collapse of the Soviet Union and the Kremlin's subsequent efforts to control its increasingly unruly hinterlands. The present conflict is actually the latest chapter of a struggle spanning more than two centuries between Moscow and the fiercely independent tribes and clans of the North Caucasus. The peoples of this region are traditionally moderate Sufi and predominantly Chechen, Dagestani, and Circassian. They always resisted tsarist rule and periodically rebelled even after the Kremlin incorporated them into the Russian empire in the late 1800s. Rebellions tended to arise at times when the Kremlin was weak domestically, and Moscow always responded with harsh repression. Moscow also historically questioned the loyalty of the North Caucasians and feared rebellion from the region and controlled it through expulsions and forcible relocations.

In February 1944, Soviet premier Josef Stalin summarily rounded up and deported approximately 1.4 million people from this region to the Siberian gulags under a false pretext of Nazi collaboration. Out of approximately a dozen nationalities that comprised this group, the largest was the Chechens. The deportations were horrific and at least a third of those involved died along the way. Survivors were not allowed to return until 1956, after Stalin's death, only to find their homes taken by strangers. The importance of this event cannot be overstated. The experience of deportation altered group identities: Chechens began to think of themselves as belonging to a distinct Chechen nationality, rather than a teip, or clan, as they had previously.[4] When the Soviet Union fell apart in 1991; many former Soviet holdings declared and received independence. In 1991, speaking at in the predominantly Muslim Tatarstan, Russian President Boris Yeltsin told regional leaders to "take as much sovereignty as you can swallow."[5]

A year later Tatarstan held a referendum on independence (despite Moscow's attempts to prevent it) and granted Tatarstan autonomy within the Russian Federation. In this context, local

339

leader Dzhokhar Dudayev proclaimed an independent Chechen Republic of Ichkeria in November 1991. But in this case Moscow met the declaration with armed opposition. At the time, Yeltsin's advisors were convinced that denying Chechnya its independence was essential to preserving the integrity of the fledgling Russian state, and that the resulting military victory, which they were sure would be quick and easy, would boost Yeltsin's failing presidency.[6] Thus, Moscow went to war with Chechnya in December 1994. That year Chechens had been commemorating the 50th anniversary of Stalin's deportations with many signs throughout Grozny, Chechnya's capital.

The Russian army didn't wait for the commemorations to end, and the signs were among its first targets.[7] This is an important element of the war that speaks volumes of Russia's relationship with this region. The fighting ended in August 1996, but Yeltsin's advisors had been very wrong; the war had proved both costly and difficult for Moscow. On the Chechen side, it also transformed a "nationalist cause into an Islamist one, with a jihadi component," according to the International Crisis Group.[8] Writing about this transformation, Israeli author Ya'ovKarny highlighted Moscow's historic efforts to erase the very memory of Chechens as a people as part of its struggle with the region. "The Chechen independence struggle, begun in increments in 1990, was born in the shadow of this partial amnesia, which is why it proved easy prey to foreign Islamic militants whose espousal of the Chechen cause is a mere subterfuge for the imposition of their own intolerant and aggressive theological dogma."[9]

In October 2007, Dokku Umarov, then the president of the declared Republic of Ichkeria, formally announced the establishment of the IK as an umbrella organization to unite militant jamaats (fighting units) in the North Caucasus. The agenda, however, was both local and global. "Our enemy is not Rusnya [Russia] only, but everyone who wages war against Islam and Muslims," Umarov declared at the time. Umarov's comment was a clear indicator of the increasingly transnational nature of Islamist ideology that had come to animate the Chechen resistance.[10]The Kremlin for its part declared a second war with Chechnya in 1999 following a series of apartment bombings in Moscow. Although questions remain to this day about who was ultimately responsible for the blasts, the Russian government was quick to blame the Chechens.

The resulting war spilled into neighboring Dagestan, and while it formally concluded in 2000 with the Russian army razing Grozny to the ground,[11]Russian military occupation and Islamist opposition continued until 2009. During this period, Vladimir Putin installed the Kadyrov family, former anti-Kremlin insurgents who switched sides, to be in charge of Chechnya. Violence in the region continued to grow, and in April 2009 IK openly declared its allegiance to global jihad, pledging an oath to the premier international terrorist actor of the day, al-Qaeda.[12] Less than a year later, in June 2010, the US State Department recognized this shift by designating Umarov a Specially Designated Global Terrorist under US Executive Order 13224.[13] But while the IK had global partners, it preferred to act locally. Indeed, scholar Elena Pokalova of the US National Defense University wrote that "much of the independent evidence suggests that links between Al Qaeda and North Caucasus insurgents have been tactical and operational at best.

No clear evidence suggests a merger between the two at the strategic level. Further, no evidence suggests that the groups pursued the same goals."[14] Umarov himself prioritized domestic targets over international ones, even though the latter would have been more consistent with al-Qaeda's approach. Moreover, the group funded itself primarily through local criminal activity and overwhelmingly targeted Russian government forces – although it also took credit for a number of high-profile attacks in Russia, such as a November 2009 bombing of a Nevsky Express train, a March 2010 suicide attack on the Moscow Metro, February 2011 attacks on Moscow's Domodedovo airport, and two suicide bombings in Volgograd in December 2013.

Thereafter, however, the IK's presence in Russia, and its pace of activity, was deeply affected by developments in the Middle East. After the Syrian uprising started in March 2011 – a peaceful protest that quickly radicalized in no small part because of Syrian President Bashar al-Assad, who injected radicals into the protest movement – Russian and Western press reports began periodically to note that there were Chechens fighting in Syria. Indeed, the complexion of Chechen Islamism was altered profoundly by the conflict underway in Syria – and by the lure of Islamist groups like al-Qaeda and the Islamic State, which were active in that arena.

By late 2011 and early 2012, hundreds of foreign fighters – including from Russia and other parts of Eurasia – migrated to the Syrian battlefield. There, Chechen fighters quickly rose to the forefront of the Islamist opposition against Bashar al-Assad's regime. Chechens had a reputation as fierce fighters, which helped them rise through the ranks. By 2013, at least three Syria-based jihadist groups were reportedly led by Chechen emirs from the North Caucasus.[15]These factions, like other Islamist elements in Syria and beyond, would subsequently be caught up in the escalating struggle for control over the Syrian opposition then playing out between al-Qaeda and its one-time affiliate. IK's loyalties lay with al-Qaeda, at least initially.

The IK and ISIS differed significantly in their ideologies, their approaches to recruitment and violence, and their very structures. The IK's new leader, Magomed Suleymanov, reportedly was angry at the excesses of IS, seeing public beheadings and other acts of wanton violence perpetrated by the group as "unnecessary." Operationally, too, the groups were dissimilar, with the IK operating as what regional expert OrkhanDzemal has called a "night-time government" with a purely military structure, while IS adopted a "day-time" approach and called on entire families to join it. Such distinctions, however, wouldn't remain. In July 2014, IS leader Abu Bakr al-Baghdadi named Russia and the US the two leading enemies of the Muslim world, insisting that both were "mobilized by the Jews."[16]

This appeared to be the first time that ISIS had given such importance to Russia, and it coincided with a decline of the Emirate. In March 2014, Russian security forces killed Umarov. He was succeeded by Ali Abu Muhammad al-Dagestani, who became the IK's first non-Chechen leader and appeared to be al-Qaeda supporter.[17] Russian forces killed him only a year later. His death, coupled with stepped-up counterterrorism measures on the part of the Russian government, reverberated through the IK. According to Russian expert Artur Ataev, the IK, post-Dagestani, "no longer had charismatic leaders and completely lost financing." The reversal of fortune was profound. The group was unable to recruit new members and suffered from low morale.[18]

Russian-Language Speakers in ISIS

This situation added to the appeal of the ISIS narrative in Russia. The Islamic State's military victories in the context of IK decline did not go unnoticed by Muslims in the North Caucasus. Since 2013, Russian officials say, ISIS has carried out an extraordinarily effective propaganda campaign in Russia and neighboring countries, targeting Muslim youth with little education and feelings of disenfranchisement. In doing so, the group has played on underlying societal issues such as religious and ethnic profiling, discrimination, and continuous, often violent, harassment by the Russian security forces directed at ethnic minorities in Russia – all of which exacerbate feelings of resentment towards the Russian state. According to a harrowing in-depth report by Svoboda, a Russian human rights watchdog, hundreds and possibly thousands of Chechens are held Russian prisons on trumped-up charges, where Russian security services routinely subject them to torture.[19]

Simultaneously, the rise of far-right nationalism and xenophobia in Russian society has contributed to feelings of rejection among Muslims in Russia. The effects have been profound. Russian has emerged as the third most popular language for ISIS propaganda after Arabic and English. Indeed, ISIS began publishing a magazine in Russian, called Istok (The Source).[20] According to Igor Malashenko of the Carnegie Moscow Center, IS spreads its message through "tens of thousands of internet accounts and sites," including those in the Russian language such as the popular social media website Odnoklassniki, a Russia version of Facebook. According to Malashenko, these recruitment networks have become a de facto part of the "structure of all-Russian Islamism."[21] They have also served as a tool of mobilization, with Russian

Muslims indoctrinated by IS propaganda being propelled to leave the country and join the jihad in the Middle East.

Estimates of the number of North Caucasian fighters in Syria and Iraq vary dramatically – from several hundred to several thousand. Shortly before Russia's Syria intervention, the Russian government claimed that between 2,000 and 5,000 militants had joined ISIS; weeks after the entry of Russia into the conflict, however, that figure jumped to 7,000 out of a total of approximately 30,000 foreign fighters active within the ranks of the Islamic State. Independent experts tend to agree that it is difficult to ascertain the veracity of these claims, and that the Russian government inflates the numbers.[22] Ultimately, no one truly knows how many Russian-language speakers and Russian citizens are fighting for ISIS–not even ISIS. Many Chechens fighting in Syria and Iraq came from the diaspora in Europe, and not all of them necessarily to fight for the Islamic State. Another factor is that many who leave Russia to join ISIS leave with their families, since ISIS presents itself as a state enterprise, so not everyone who leaves participates in fighting.

Indeed, according to recent press reports ISIS prevents widows and children of deceased fighters from returning home, claiming they are the property of the Islamic State.[23] While Chechens continue to enjoy an international reputation of fierce warriors who fought the Russian government for over twenty years, the majority who came to Syria did not fight in the first or second Chechen wars. Furthermore, many in the Middle East tend to assume that a Russian speaker in the ISIS ranks is a Chechen, but that need not be so. While accurate figures may be elusive, the anecdotal evidence is unmistakable: ISIS is exerting a growing influence on Russia's Muslims and on their counterparts in Central Asia.

Many North Caucasians, including Russian citizens, have indeed joined the Islamic State. Russia's Syria intervention, meanwhile, has only served to increase anti-Russian sentiment among the country's Muslims, many of whom already felt disenfranchised as a result of Moscow's policies.[24] To be more precise, North Caucasian fighters have come to the Islamic State in two waves. Between 2011-2013, they were primarily from the European diaspora. Many were related to Chechens who fought in the first or second Chechen war. They came to Syria because they couldn't fight in the North Caucasus, according to Jean-François Ratelle, assistant professor at Ottawa University and a North Caucasus expert.

During these years, he writes IK militants and Salafists in the North Caucasus saw Russia as the real enemy. The second wave began in late 2013, when many North Caucasians from Russia began travelling to Syria and Iraq. These people were ideologically driven and preferred "the utopian views of the Islamic State" rather than the fight in the North Caucasus.[25] Some experts, as reported by The Telegraph, believes ISIS "fields at least three exclusively Russian-speaking 'Caucasian' battalions of about 150 men each. Often led by Chechens, the rank and file of these battalions is believed to have been drawn from across the north Caucasus and other parts of the former Soviet Union."[26] A number of these individuals, according to the report, live in Mosul, where they enjoy a degree of autonomy. Until recently, they also retained access to hard-to-obtain consumer goods. Chechen nationalism within ISIS remains strong. Thus, reportedly, when Chechen ISIS fighters capture another Chechen, they torture him less cruelly than someone of another ethnicity, so he has a higher change of survival.[27]

Russia's Policies: Encouraging Fighters to Leave As a number of credible press reports have indicated, Russia's various intelligence services have actually aided Islamic militants in joining the jihad in Syria, typically via Turkey.[28] Turkey is the ideal transit point because it already has a large North Caucasian diaspora, a porous border with Syria, visa-free entry, and a large flow of tourists that allows these people to blend in easily.[29] By 2013-2014, before the Sochi Olympics but during the war in Ukraine, "law enforcement began to virtually physically expel Salafis to Syria, telling them, 'Go there and die there.'"[30]

Many people in the region truly wanted to fight, and saw an opportunity "to realize themselves in this struggle," while others didn't go to fight but rather settled in certain neighborhoods and suburbs of Istanbul, where many Russian-speaking migrants lived.[31] To the Kremlin, the practice of driving militants out of Russia both echoes Russia's historic methods of dealing with problems (and thereby exacerbating them), and remains preferable to addressing the true causes of radicalization in the Russian context – the societal and economic inequality that has contributed to Muslim alienation.[32]The practice of encouraging people to leave for Syria was especially widespread in the run-up to the Sochi Olympic Games, which Putin wanted to go without a terrorist incident.

The games were symbolic for several reasons. Putin held games in Sochi on the 150th anniversary of the tsarist war, massacre and deportations of Circassians that occurred at the same site – though the Kremlin denies any connection. It was another case of Russia's erasing of memory. The games both spurred peaceful protest and encouraged radicals to take up the Circassian cause in the name of their own ideology, independent of much real concern for the plight of Circassians. Furthermore, the government for the first time banned the commemoration of Stalin's deportations of the Chechens. The commemoration was to fall on the last day of the Sochi Olympics, 23 February. Earlier, the Chechen government, headed by Ramzan Kadyrov, had ordered a demolition of a memorial to the deportations.[33]

Profiles of Several Fighters

Experts note that many Russian citizens in the ISIS's ranks have come to realize that their future is bleak. "[T]hey will be forced to defend themselves until the end," wrote MaazBilalov for RFE/RL's Caucasus site, Kavkaz.Realii, in November 2016.[34] "They are going to die ... they know that, that's why they're fighting to the end," said Vera Mironova in a telephone interview with the author in March of this year. Mironova is a pre-doctoral research fellow in the BelferCenter's International Security Program and a Ph.D. candidate in political science at the University of Maryland. Her research explores individual-level behaviour in conflict environments and she has conducted fieldwork in many conflicts, from Bosnia to Yemen.

Mirnova told me these individuals are also disillusioned. "Everything they came for is not happening, [there's] no Islam," she

346

said, referring to a vast gap between the Islamic state they imagined and one they have experienced.[35] It's difficult to find accurate details about Chechens or other North Caucasians fighting for various Islamist groups in the Middle East. Those who have been killed, or who hold senior positions, tend to be the exceptions.[36] Below are several profiles of such individuals. Together, they demonstrate a complex picture of different motivations and loyalties towards Islamist groups.

Omar al-Shishani ("Omar the Chechen," or "Abu Meat")

TarkhanTayumurazovichBatirashvili, known by his nom de guerre Omar AlShishani (the Chechen), was the most famous North Caucasian fighter in ISIS, and held the position of war minister. Tarkhan was born to an ethnic Georgian and Orthodox Christian father and a Muslim Kist (ethnic Chechen of the Melkhi clan) mother. The Kist people are a subgroup of Georgia's Pankisi Gorge, Tarkhan converted to Islam and was radicalized after fighting in the 2008 Russo-Georgian war. He was wounded in Shaddadi, Syria, as a result of US air strikes and died of his wounds on 4 March 2016.[37] Al-Shishani had come to Syria in about 2012 and served in command positions in different militant Islamist groups. In an interview with the BBC in July 2014, Omar's father said his son actually left home because his family was poor, though his stated reason was his new-found religion. But his father thought money was not the reason his son remained in Syria.[38]

He doesn't say what the real reason was, though the context of the interview suggests it was likely that radical ideology had taken over. Al-Shishani joined ISIS in 2013 and quickly rose through its ranks. He commanded Katibat al-Aqsa – the most famous Chechen brigade within ISIS.[39] On 24 September 2014 The US Treasury Department added al-Shishani to its Specially Designated Global Terrorists list and several months later announced a reward up to USD 5 million for information leading to his capture. Even within ISIS al-Shishani was somewhat of a mystery, according to press reports. He had a reputation as a fierce warrior yet gained the nickname "Abu Meat" for sending young men to die from behind a desk. He also excelled at recruitment. His death thus reportedly meant a reduction in ISIS's recruitment capabilities.

AkhmadChataev (AkhmadShishani, "Akhmad the One Armed")

AkhmadChataev, nom de guerre AkhmadShishani, or Akhmad the One Armed, was born in Vedeno in Chechnya's Vedesnky District and reportedly participated in the insurgency against the Russian government that began in the 1990s. The Russian authorities captured and tortured him. Chataev is missing an arm and a foot, which explains the epithet "One Armed" and variations of it. Chataev reportedly claimed that Russian authorities had chopped off his arm in prison as part of torture that also included electric shocks, though the veracity of his claim is impossible to ascertain.[40] He has subsequently been wanted by the Russian government for perpetrating terrorist acts. According to press reports Chataev left Russia either in 2001 or 2004 for Western Europe, where he was arrested several times and in the fall 2012 Georgian authorities arrested him as a member of an armed group that had clashed earlier that year with Georgian troops at Lopota Gorge, close to the Russian border, though he was soon acquitted.

In 2015 he appeared in ISIS territory and in October 2015 the US and UN designated him as a terrorist.[41] According to one reported YouTube Video, Chataev pledged allegiance to ISIS in February 2015 and began working on training and recruitment as commander of the Yarmouk Battalion, the second most well-known Chechen battalions within ISIS.[42] Georgia Journal wrote in January 2015 that "[a]ccording to a trustworthy source from Istanbul, it is precisely Chataev who oversees the transit of young recruits from Pankisi [Georgia] to Syria. It is also said that he gets paid $1,000 for every recruit he manages to hook in."[43] Recent press reports indicated Chataev commanded at least 130 men within the Islamic State.[44] Reportedly Chataev was the mastermind behind a major Istanbul airport bombing in June 2016 that resulted in at least 40 deaths and 240 injuries.

Salahuddin al-Shishani

PayzullaMargoshvili, nom de guerre Salahuddin al-Shishani, is far less known than his fellow Kist Chechen, Omar al-Shishani. In 2012, Doku Umarov sent Salahuddin al-Shishani to Syria as his representative to gain military experience and gain valuable contacts. He first joined Jaishal-MuhajreenwaalAnsar (JMA)–a group that Omar al-Shishani created and once headed and that analysts have described as Caucasus Emirate's branch in Syria.[45] When Omar al-Shishani joined ISIS in spring 2013, Salahuddin al-Shishani took the reins in running the group, but was ousted from the group in June 2015.[46] JMA briefly aligned with ISIS, but quickly took an increasingly anti-ISIS stance and formally pledged allegiance to al-Qaeda in September 2015. Most Russian citizens moved to other groups. Salahuddin meanwhile was ousted from his position in a internal leadership struggle and proclaimed himself a leader of a subgroup of JMA, Imarat Kavkaz v Shame (ImaratKavkas in Sham), but the group fell apart in June 2015.

Russia's Novaya Gazeta reports that his new group, Jaish al-Usra, fought together with Kurds in Sheikh Masoud in February 2016.[47] Though the US State Department has designed JMA as a terrorist organization, Joanna Parasczhuk wrote that there is no record of this group kidnaping foreigners or killing civilians, and the group instead focused on fighting Syrian President Bashar al-Assad's regime in Aleppo, primarily north-western Aleppo. While it would have been accurate to designate the group as a terrorist organization when it fought with ISIS under Omar al-Shishani's leadership, the group weakened significantly after he left and the description of terrorist no longer applies.[48]

Abdul KhakimShishani

Rustam Azhiev, nom de guerre Abdul KhakimShishani, is the leader of Khalifa Jamaat in Latakia. According to Joanna Paraszczuk, a long-time observer and chronicler of information about Chechens in Syria, he is interesting because unlike most Chechens in Syria Abdul KhakimShishani is a veteran of the Russo-Chechen war, and couldn't return to Chechnya because of an injury. Nohchicho, an independent Chechen website,[49] published an interview with him in February 2017 in which he stated that his group has never had any connection to ISIS. Earlier, he published a letter on the same site on the anniversary of Stalin's deportations of Chechens. "The occupying powers and their dogs are using all their strength to erase that crime [Stalin's deportations], that date, from our memory," he wrote. "Today, what Stalin did to an entire people, they continue to do to the families of mujahideen. They will not cease in this, because this is a war against all Muslims. May Allah save us from this and strengthen us in Islam."[50]

Abu Jihad

Islam Seit-UmarovichAtabiyev, nom de guerre Abu Jihad, is an ethnic Karachay from Karachay-Cherkessia in the North Caucasus, and reportedly was a close friend of Omar al-Shishani.[51] "While Abu Jihad does not appear to have taken part in any military action on behalf of IS, in 2013 and 2014 he was frequently seen alongside Umar Shishani and has since become a prominent ideologue within IS's North Caucasian contingent. More recently, he has begun reaching out to jihadis in Syria and the Russian Federation via regular Russian-language audio lectures on the Zello platform," wrote Paraszczuk on 21 April 2015.

Abu Jihad has rejected Imarat Kavkaz and instead placed himself firmly in the proISIS camp. In April 2015, Abu Jihad made what Paraszczuk described as a "bold attempt at control and domination of the Islamist insurgency in the North Caucasus as well as of Russian-speaking jihadis in Syria." He made a video address calling on jihadists in the North Caucasus to join groups that pledged allegiances to ISIS, rather than the Caucasus Emirate.This move "should be viewed as the latest development in the ongoing and increasingly fierce power struggle between Umar Shishani's North Caucasians in IS and those in the CE and its affiliate in Syria," according to Paraszczuk.[52] As of August 2016, Abu Jihad denied that he ever even pledged allegiance to Imarak Kavkaz. [53]

Adam Magomadov

Adam Magomadov, a young man of Chechen origin living in Norway, travelled to Syria in August 2014 with an older man, Hasan Ahmed, a Norwegian of Pakistani origin. Both men returned to Norway and were reportedly planning to return to Syria in 2015, when the Norwegian authorities arrested them.54 In August 2016 an Oslo court found that the two men while in Syria had pledged allegiance to ISIS and participated in training, though Magomadov stayed in Syria longer and, according to the court's findings, also participated in combat. The court therefore sentenced him to seven and a half years in prison rather than the six years given to Hasan Ahmed.[55]

Russia's Failed Policies and Future Prospects

In the summer of 2015 a story about 19-year-old Moscow State University student Varvara Karaulova made headlines. According to Russian press reports, she had met online with several people, including one man who made her fall in love with him, convinced her to convert to Islam and to leave for Syria to marry him.[56]Karaulova's father pushed for intensive search efforts soon after her disappearance. Officials found her on the Turkish-Syrian border before she could enter Syria and brought her home. But Russian security services arrested her on charges of communicating with ISIS recruiters, even though by many accounts she appeared to be a victim of ISIS brainwashing rather than a criminal.[57]Karaulova never harmed or sought to harm anyone, and would no doubt have benefited from psychological counselling, but the Russian court sentenced her to four and a half years in person in December 2016.[58] Her case most poignantly highlights the Russian government's failure to craft adequate policies to address radicalization issues.

More broadly, while Russian authorities tend to focus on the mosques in Chechnya and Dagestan, most recruiting takes place outside of them.[59] In fact, those who receive Islamic education are less likely to succumb to radical ideas. When it comes to charging an individual with the crime of recruitment into ISIS, the charges can be arbitrary. Anyone who simply reposts radical information on social media could face an accusation of recruitment if someone testifies that the individual who posted the information was a recruiter. Russian security services do not shy away from torture, and are eager to demonstrate success.

In addition, most recruiters are outside of Russia to begin with.[60] After Karaulova's story became public Yelena Sutormina, a member of Russia's Civic Chamber, issued brochure advising teachers and parents how to deal with attempted recruitment by ISIS. The Civic Chamber also created the "Resistance to the Islamic State Recruiters" project, which Sutormina heads.[61] No information is available about the success of these efforts. But Russia's struggle to integrate returnees from ISIS is known. By Russian law, individuals involved in terrorist activities typically face between five and 10 years in prison; in reality it is often solitary confinement.

The definition of involvement, moreover, is vague, meaning that Karaulova could face the same sentence as someone involved in actual violence. Anecdotal accounts describe Russia's imprisonment system as more conducive to radicalization rather than reform, particularly among individuals who are put in solitary confinement.[62] "The youth have despaired, [and] terrorists use this, lie to them about religious oppression, and lure them into the underground," said one Russian expert. "Let's start with the fact that none of them knows the Sharia at a high level. Even in Dagestan there are no such specialists and Sharia textbooks also do not exist."[63] In addition, Russian officials according to one report are so ignorant of Islam that they inadvertently end up helping radical imams spread their message in Russia.[64] Eduard Urazayev, a former official in Dagestan who is now a political analyst, says, "If the high level of corruption and unfavorable socio-economic situation remain, it may further fuel protest sentiments and increase sympathy for the IS."[65]

Russia's Muslim community and even some people outside it are now a receptive audience for radical Islamic ideas, regardless of source. ISIS may soon fall, but the ideology will remain. The Kremlin says it got involved in Syria in part to kill radicals there so they don't return to Russia. While some no doubt will be able to return to Russia and participate in terrorist activities, many will likely try to travel elsewhere, such as Europe, because they know they will probably face harsh interrogation in Russia upon entry, and even if released will continue to be watched. "Foreign fighters usually prefer to export their jihadist cause abroad rather than engaging in riskier insurgent and terrorist activities at home," according to Jean-François Ratelle, assistant professor at Ottawa University and a North Caucasus expert.[66] Of course, it only takes a few fighters to conduct insurgent or terrorist activities. Some could slip back into Russia through Georgia or Azerbaijan.[67] Still, the Russian government's policies tend to exacerbate radicalization and instability primarily within Russia and it is from within Russia that the effects emanate far and wide. Until the Kremlin changes its approach, the reverberations are likely to be felt.

The Future of Chechens in ISIS. Anna Borschevskaya, October 9, 2017.

https://www.hate-speech.org/new-report-the-future-of-chechens-in-isis/andhttps://www.google.com/search?ei=f8MDXvSLMJeT8gLGw JyAAQ&q=hate+speech+international&oq=hate+speech+interna tional&gs_l=psy-ab.1.1.0l2j0i22i30l3j0i333.186016.194253..1981 93...0.0..0.115.1738.23j2......1....1..gws-wiz.......0i273i70i251j0i273 j0i67j0i131j0i67i70i249.kklxGaqZHDk Hate Speech International is an independent network of journalists employing cooperative models of cross-border research into extremism, hate speech and hate crime. Investigative reporting is indispensable to democracy. Freedom of speech and freedom of information are primary weapons against those who cynically misuse their own democratic freedoms in an attempt to violate basic human rights. Its goal is to create an international network of reporters and academics that investigate, analyse and report on hate speech and hate crime. HSI was founded by Norwegian journalists KjetilStormark and ØyvindStrømmen in the spring of 2013. Initial funding for a two–year pilot project has been provided by the Freedom of Expression Foundation (Fritt Ord) of Oslo as well as the Norwegian Ministry of Foreign Affairs. HSI operates independently. Its material and stories may not be edited, except for minor adjustments to time and location references or to suit different editorial style guidelines with regard to such matters as spelling and punctuation. If one publish its story online, HS expects to link to the original story (on our web pages). HS expects to be credited, preferably in the byline, in the following style: "Author Name, Hate Speech International". Its vision is to elevate the public understanding of extremism as a phenomenon and to increase the overall ability, knowledge and will of media organizations to report on such matters. The primary task in HSI's first phase is to contribute to the development of research and reporting that elevates the total volume of reporting on hate speech, hate crime and extremism in Europe. Seeks to make freedom of speech and the right to information primary weapons against those who violate, or seeks to violate, basic human rights through their exploitation of those same freedoms. HS Editor-in-Chief & Executive Director is KjetilStormark, and Managing Editor, is ØyvindStrømmen. This work by Hate Speech International is licensed under a Creative Commons Attribution-NoDerivs 3.0 Unported License.

Chapter 14

Counter-Terrorism Cooperation between China and Central Asian States in the Shanghai Cooperation Organization

Wang Jin and Kong Dehang

Abstract

As Islamic extremist threats have grown to be a common issue of focus and a major cooperation area between China and Central Asian states since the 1990s, the Shanghai Cooperation Organization (SCO) provides China with an important regional and even international counter-terrorism platform. Highlighting sustainable security cooperation and countering terrorism in a peaceful way under the "Shanghai Spirit," the SCO helps stabilize China's internal security environment while enhancing the country's economic and cultural cooperation with its Central Asian neighbours.

This article reviews the Islamic extremist and terrorist challenges to China and the counter-terrorism cooperation between China and Central Asian states under the framework of the SCO, with a focus on how to tackle the weaknesses of such cooperation. It is concluded that SCO member states must be prudent in taking further steps in counter-terrorism cooperation, especially with regard to whether the organization should be transformed into a quasi-military and political alliance.

Keywords: Shanghai Cooperation Organization (SCO); counter-terrorism; "Shanghai Spirit"; Central Asia.

In 1996, five regional countries China, Russia, Tajikistan, Kyrgyzstan, and Kazakhstan announced the founding of a new organization in Shanghai, the "Shanghai Five," to resolve border disputes among themselves.[1] With the inclusion of Uzbekistan in 2001, it became the Shanghai Cooperation Organization (SCO), an important regional cooperation mechanism to combat terrorism and facilitate the development of its member states in inland Asia. Though substantially larger than the North Atlantic Treaty Organization (NATO) and the European Union in terms of total population, landsize, and natural resources,[2] the SCO is far less strong and integrated than the NATO.

The major concern of the SCO is to curb the expansion of terrorism, extremism and separatism in Central Asia and China's Xinjiang Uygur Autonomous Region How well have China and other SCO members cooperated on counterterrorism over the past two decades? And what challenges does the SCO face in the future? This article aims to address these two questions with a focus on the counter-terrorism cooperation between China and Central Asian states. It first reviews the Islamic extremist and terrorist threats in China and Central Asia; it then examines the major achievements of the SCO in countering terrorism as well as the limitations and challenges faced by the organization. The concluding section discusses the future trends of the SCO with regard to the changing geopolitical circumstances in Asia and different foreign policies of SCO member states.

Security Concerns of SCO Members

Central Asian Islamic terrorism is not a new phenomenon. It can be traced back to the 1970s when the Soviet ideology was losing its charm in Central Asia. Many Islamic clergies and groups' financed by both Arab states and some Western states established branches in the region from the 1970s to the 1980s to disseminate Islamic extremism through underground activities. With the collapse of the Soviet Union and the ensuing nation-state building process of Central Asian states including Uzbekistan, Kyrgyzstan, Kazakhstan, Turkmenistan, and Tajikistan, many Islamic groups, some of which were extremism groups, expanded their influence in Central Asia. As a Turkish American scholar observes, "[b]y the end of the Soviet era the number of local clergy had shrunk, while the demand (of Islamic knowledge) for them across Russia and Eurasia was mushrooming."[3] Meanwhile, the defeat of the Soviet Union by Islamic Mujahidin in Afghanistan left a legacy of trans-Islamic networks in Central Asia.[4] Against this backdrop, many Islamic extremist groups, such as the Islamic Movement of Uzbekistan and Hizbut-Tahrir (Party of Liberation), started to penetrate into Central Asia and provoked Islamic revolution in Central Asian states.

Afghanistan under the Taliban served as an important base for Islamic extremism in Central Asia; many Islamic extremists and terrorists were trained in the country. A number of Islamic extremists and terrorists in China's Xinjiang Uygur Autonomous Region also received training and supplies from Al-Qaeda and the Taliban in Afghanistan. Incomplete statistics indicate that over the past three decades, "separatist, terrorist and extremist forces launched thousands of terrorist attacks in Xinjiang, killing large numbers of innocent people and hundreds of police officers, and causing immeasurable damage to property."[5] To be more exact, from 1990 to 2001, Uygur extremists and terrorists implemented more than 200 terrorist attacks, killing 162 people and injuring over 400 in Xinjiang.[6] The Al Qaeda, led by Osama bin Laden,established training camps in Afghanistan for the Chinese Islamic extremists, and the Taliban-dominated Afghanistan became a major external threat to social stability and security in China's Xinjiang.[7] Some of the Uygur extremists and terrorists also penetrated into Central Asian states and Russia to join the local terrorist groups.

After the American invasion of Afghanistan, many Central Asian Islamic extremists fought side by side with the Taliban against the Washington-led coalition forces in 2001. Some Islamic extremists from Central Asia fled to Pakistan and entered into the complex system of local Pashtun tribal allegiances.[8] After the Arab Spring especially the Syrian civil war brokeout in 2011, thousands of

Islamic extremists, including some from Central Asia and China, went to Syria and Iraq to join the "Islamic State (IS)" and other Islamic extremist groups.[9] Meanwhile, some Islamic extremists and terrorists pledged allegiance to the IS leader Abu Bakr al-Baghdadi and set up their own branches in Afghanistan and Pakistan.[10] A network connecting the Islamic extremists from Central Asia and Southeast Asia was also constructed. Reports of IS recruiters in Hong Kong approaching Indonesians and using Malaysia as a hub for gathering potential fighters further put Beijing on alert as more Uygurs joined the IS ranks. In July 2013, Chinese leading media Global Times accused Uygur Islamic terrorists of receiving training and support from rebel groups in Syria and Turkey.[11]

The threat of Uygur extremists became obvious in August 2015 when several Uygur Islamic terrorists killed almost two dozen people at the Hindu Erawan Shrine in Bangkok, Thailand. As warned by Vice Minister of Chinese Public Security Meng Hongwei, the biggest concern for China is a possible mass return of Uygur Islamic militants.[12] Although a mass return of trained militants to Central Asian states is less likely, for they may be relocated to new terrorist attacks elsewhere, yet in the long term, the influx of such militants will still pose serious threats to Central Asia.One reasonis that Islamic extremism is misused by many extremists to provoke dissatisfaction and hatred among the general public; another reason is that Islamic extremists try to brainwash people with the narrowly defined notion of "Jihad," abetting them to participate in violent and terrorist activities against innocent civilians. Since "[a]ll this indicates their denial of modern civilization, rejection of human progress, and gross violation of the human rights of their fellow citizens,"[13] religion-based terrorism has become a common threat to both China and Central Asian states that entails their close cooperation and, when necessary, joint efforts with the international society.

Achievements of the SCO in Counter-Terrorism Cooperation

The SCO can be traced back to a set of bilateral and multilateral boundary-monitoring and trust-building mechanisms between

China and its Central Asian neighbours in the early 1990s. As mentioned previously, the "Shanghai Five" was established in 1996 with the signature of the Treaty on Deepening Military Trust in Border Regions in Shanghai. At the 2001 summit in Shanghai, leaders of the "Shanghai Five" agreed to accept Uzbekistan into the group and upgrade it into the Shanghai Cooperation Organization. The "Shanghai Spirit," which features mutual trust, mutual benefit, equality, consultation, respect for cultural diversity and pursuit of common development, thus became the founding values of the SCO and continued promoting the development of the organization not only for the benefit of its members, but also for regional peace and stability.[14]

To confront the challenges posed by the expansion of the "three evil forces (terrorism, secessionism and extremism) in Central Asia and Xinjiang, it became necessary for China as a leading member of the SCO to enhance counter-terrorism cooperation in the organization. Since 2001, a number of key documents on counter-terrorism cooperation have been signed by SCO members. With the signing of various important documents and agreements, counter-terrorism cooperation has been strongly enhanced, highlighting mutual trust and the openness of the SCO.[15] Most importantly,China and other SCO members have agreed on the definition of such key concepts as "terrorism", "terrorist groups,""secessionism" and "extremism."

Table 1. SCO Documents on Counter-Terrorism Cooperation.

Issue Date	Place	Name of Document
June 2001	Shanghai, China.	Shanghai Convention of Counter-Terrorism Counter-Extremism and Counter-Secessionism
June 2002.	St. Petersburg, Russia	Chapter of Shanghai Cooperation Organization; Agreement over-Counter-Terrorism
June 2004	Tashkent, Uz-bekistan.	Agreement over Counter- Terror-ism Database

Issue Date	Place	Name of Document
June 2006	Shanghai, China	Cooperation Guideline of Counter-Terrorism, Counter-Extremism,and Counter-Secessionism, 2007–2009
June 2007	Bishkek, Kyrgyzstan	Agreement over Military Exercise
August 2008	Dushanbe, Tajikistan	Agreement over, Counter-terrorism Exercise; Agreement over Cracking Down, Smuggling Weapons, Explosives and Ammunition
March 2009	Tashkent, Uzbekistan	Agreement Between Afghanistan and SCO member states over Cracking Down Drugs Smuggling, Terrorism and Organized Crimes; Agreement over Counter-Terrorism Training; Agreement over the Procedures of Counter-Terrorism Exercise; Cooperation Guideline of Counter-Terrorism, Counter-Extremism and Counter-Secessionism, 2010–2012; Convention of the Shanghai Cooperation Organization against Terrorism
August 2010	Tashkent, Uzbekistan	Declaration of Tashkent
June 2011	Astana, Kazakhstan	Declaration of Astana
June 2012	Beijing, China	Cooperation Guideline of Counter-Terrorism, Counter-Extremism and Counter-Secessionism, 2013–2015
June 2017	Astana, Kazakhstan	Statement by the Heads of the SCO on Joint Counteraction to International Terrorism

Source: SCO website (http://scochina.mfa.gov.cn/chn/).

According to the Shanghai Convention of Counter-Terrorism, Counter-Extremism and Counter-Secessionism signed in 2001 and the Convention of the Shanghai Cooperation Organization against Terrorism signed in 2009, all the SCO member states were "[a]ware that terrorism, separatism and extremism constitute a threat to international peace and security, promotion of friendly relations among States as well as enjoyment of fundamental human rights and freedoms."[16] Meanwhile, SCO counter-terrorism cooperation has expanded to other areas to restrain the financial resources of the terrorist networks in the region.

For example, because the smuggling of drugs is a major source of funds for Islamic extremists and terrorists in Central Asia, SCO members signed the Agreement on Cooperation in Combating Illicit Traffic of Narcotic Drugs, Psychotropic Substances, and Precursors in 2004, calling for all countries to "promote bilateral and multilateral international cooperation in combating illicit trafficking of narcotics and their precursors, and in prevention and control of drug use."[17] With time, various cooperation mechanisms among SCO member states have been constructed, with the Council of Heads of State (CHS) serving as its top decision-making body and Council of Heads of Government (CHG) working as the second-highest body inside the SCO.

Both the CHS and the CHG hold summits annually to discuss major directions and events of the SCOin one of the member states' capital cities. Apart from the CHS and the CHG, the Council of Foreign Ministers and the Council of National Coordinators also hold regular meetings, where the former is focused on discussion of the international situation and the SCO's interaction with other international organizations and the latter coordinates multilateral cooperation of member states within the framework of the SCO. The Secretariat of the SCO, located in Beijing, is the primary executive body of the organization. It serves to implement organizational decisions and decrees, draft proposed documents (such as declarations and agendas), arrange specific activities within the SCO framework, and promote information sharing about the SCO. In 2004, a special office for counter-terrorism was set up in Toshkent to facilitate information sharing and intelligence cooperation among SCO states.

Table 2. Major SCO Counter-Terrorism Exercises.

Time	Exercise Code	Location	Participants
October 2002	"Exercise-01"	China-Kyrgyzstan border	China and Kyrgyzstan
August 2003	"Union-2003"	China and Uzbekistan	China, Russia, Uzbekistan, Kyrgyzstan, Tajikistan and Kazakhstan
August 2005	"Peace-Mission 2005"	China and Russia	China and Russia
August 2006	"Tianshan Mountain No. 1"	China and Kazakhstan	China and Kazakhstan
September 2006.	"Coordination 2006"	Tajikistan	China and Tajikistan
September 2007	"Peace Mission 2007"	China and Russia	China, Russia, Uzbekistan, Kyrgyzstan, Tajikistan and Kazakhstan
July 2009	"PeaceMission2009"	Russia and China	China and Russia
September 2010	"PeaceMission2010"	Kazakhstan	China, Russia, Uzbekistan, Kyrgyzstan, Tajikistan and Kazakhstan
May 2011	"Tianshan Mountain No. 2"	China	China, Tajikistan and Kyrgyzstan

Time	Exercise Code	Location	Participants
June 2012	"PeaceMis-sion2012"	Tajikistan	China, Russia, Uzbekistan, Kyrgyzstan, Tajikistan and Kazakhstan
August 2014	"Peace Mission 2014"	China	China, Russia, Uzbekistan, Kyrgyzstan, Tajikistan and Kazakhstan

Source: Selected from the Regional Anti-Terrorism Structure of Shanghai Cooperation Organization, http://ecrats.org/cn/.

These mechanisms cover various fields ranging from defense and diplomacy to law enforcement, culture communication and economic relations. All levels of meetings and panels have been held regularly, including the SCO Summits, Prime Ministers' Meetings, Parliament Speakers' Meetings, Defense and Foreign Ministers' Meetings, Chief Procurators' Meeting, and Interior Ministers/Public Security Ministers' Meetings, among others. Over the past two decades, different SCO member states have cooperated on various multilateral counter-terrorism exercises and China has participated in all the exercises. Infact, the SCO military exercises have become an important platform for both Chinese military forces and armed police, for it was in those SCO exercises that the Chinese military and police personnel had the first regular encounter with their foreign counterparts. The "Exercise-01" in 2002 was the first military drill by Chinese military forces with foreign states, while the "Union-2003" was the first joint exercise conducted on the soil of a foreign country.[18]

With the ever closer cooperation among SCO members, the drug-trafficking network between Afghanistan and other Central Asian states has been significantly restricted.[19] At the same time, the SCO has attempted to tap the collective economic potentials of its member states by encouraging trade and economic exchange among themselves, emphasizing the necessity of "expanding trade and investment, facilitating joint ventures and trade activities, and creating suitable conditions for gradual free movement of goods, capital, services and technologies."[20] As a result, the SCO has become an important regional mechanism to facilitate communication, mutual understanding and cooperation among its member states, in order to curb the expansion of Islamic extremism in Central Asia and to counter the threats from Islamic extremists and terrorists in the region.[21]

Challenges for the SCO on Counter-Terrorism

In June 2010, the SCO approved the procedure of admitting new members and several states participated as observers. In June 2017, India and Pakistan became full members of the SCO, while Turkey, Iran[22] and some other states have expressed strong willingness to become full members in the future.[23] With the enlargement of the SCO, several challenges also emerge in counter-terrorism cooperation among its member states. Above all, mistrust and conflicts of all sorts among SCO member states may seriously undermine their willingness for counter-terrorism cooperation. For example, since India and Pakistan became member states; the SCO has witnessed more disagreement and disputes on its action agenda due to the enmity between the two states, which might lead to possible division between China and Russia as well.

For although China fully supports Pakistan's participation in the SCO, Russia tends to have some reservations because Islamabad supported mujahidin during the Soviet Union's invasion of Afghanistan in the 1980s. Meanwhile, India is widely regarded as a strategic partner of Russia, yet to many observers, China and India are regional competitors apart from their unresolved territorial disputes. Similarly, Uzbekistan and Tajikistan have been bogged down in enduring territorial disputes the former even suspended gas supply to the latter in 2013 for that reason. Uzbekistan also strongly opposes Kyrgyzstan's plan to construct dams over the Naryn River; and military skirmishes between the two countries are not unusual. As many empirical studies have demonstrated that territorial disputes are central to the breakout of interstate wars and conflicts,[24] they seriously hinder the cooperation among SCO members on their common cause of counterterrorism.

Second, the definitions of "terrorists" and "terrorist groups" have become more blurry and sensitive with the SCO enlargement, for different SCO members have varied definitions and standards concerning counter-terrorism, despite the many documents signed in the past in this regard. For example, although China, India and Russia agreed to treat the Jaish-e-Mohammed, an Islamic extremist group based in Pakistan, as a "terrorist group" in 2017,[25] Pakistan opposes the definition and is reluctant to take actions against the group. Likewise, China's counter-terrorism measures taken by local security agencies in Xinjiang are often criticized by Central Asian states as "persecution against Muslims."[26]

Indeed, the disagreement among SCO members on the status of some Muslim groups in Central Asia will continue to be a major challenge for China to further enhance counter-terrorism cooperation with its Central Asian neighbours. Third, there remains much debate and doubt about whether the SCO should develop into a quasi-military and political alliance in the long run, which may affect the counter-terrorism cooperation among SCO members and, in particular, with non-member states.[27] As a matter of fact, the SCO was designed as an endeavour to strengthen regional cooperation mechanisms rather than compete with the United States or the West as a whole. As an issue-oriented regional organization, both the establishment and expansion of the SCO are based on shared concerns of its member states over terrorist threats.

Although the population and area of SCO member states are much larger than that of Europe and the United States, and cooperation in various fields have been ever closer over the past few years, the SCO should not be perceived as an anti-U.S. or anti-West bloc, since that would harm the interests of all member states that are in need of working with the West in trade, investment, education, science and technology, as well as in other areas. Take China, for example. With China's active participation and leading role in the SCO, the organization has managed to reach many important agreements on expanding cooperation in various fields (Table 3).

Table 3. SCO Documents on Economic and Social Development (2013-18).

Year	Document	Cooperation Area
2013	Agreement on Scientific and Technical Cooperation	Science and Technology,
2014	Agreement on Creating Favorable Conditions for International Road Transportation	Infrastructure
2015	Development Strategy of the SCO until 2025	Overall Cooperation
2015	Agreement on Cooperation and Interaction on Border Issues	Border Management
2015	Statement by the Heads of Member States of the SCO on Drug	Threat Drugs Prohibition
2016	Program for Expanded Tourism Cooperation	Tourism
2018	Statement by the Heads of the SCO Member States on Joint Efforts against the Threat of Epidemics	Health and Diseases Control

Source: SCO Website: http://scochina.mfa.gov.cn/chn/.

Yet China has no intention to expand its sphere of influence or foster a coalition against a third party. On the contrary, China has taken strenuous efforts to enhance its economic and strategic relations with the United States and Europe while remaining prudent at every step of SCO institutionalization, lest its efforts be misinterpreted as certain strategic ambition. In a similar vein, its "Belt and Road Initiative (BRI)" is aimed at further promoting economic globalization, thus facilitating its peaceful development, instead of challenging the established interests of the United States, Europe or any other party.[28]

In addition, as two powers with overwhelming political, economic and military strengths, China and Russia maintain a sensitive relationship within the SCO. Russia has been worried that the expanding cooperation of the organization especially between China and Central Asian members may increase China's political influence in Central Asia and put Russia in a risky position.[29] Therefore, it is necessary for China to manage the balance between ever closer cooperation within the SCO and potential concerns of other member states.

Conclusion

During the past decades, Islamic extremist and terrorist groups have gradually connected with each other across the world and a country' local terrorist and extremist threats might be provoked or planned from a distant region. It is thus important for international society to tackle and constrain these threats through closer cooperation in regional or global arena as, where the SCO serves as a good example. For decades, it has not only helped its member states effectively manage the threats of the "three evil forces," but its cooperation in other fields like finance, education, culture and counter-crime has also contributed to the economic well-being and social stability of the whole region. With the enlargement of the SCO, an important question to ask is: in what direction will the organization develop in the future? Will the SCO become a quasi-political and military alliance against the West? Or will it evolve into a supranational organization like the European Union?

Some states may perceive the organization as a bargaining chip or a strategic counterbalance against the United States or the European Union. For instance, with the Turkey-U.S. relationship deteriorating after the failed military coup against the Justice and Development (AKP) government in mid-2016, Turkish leaders have many a time reiterated the necessity for Turkey to join the SCO form or political support from international society, in particular Russia and China. In another instance, after President Trump decided to withdraw from the Joint Comprehensive Plan of Action (JCPOA) signed in 2015, the Iranian government expressed a strong willingness to further enhance its relations hip with Russia and China by joining the SCO, in order to safeguard Iran's security and development.[30] For China, however, the SCO should be kept as an international platform that aims to tackle those non-traditional security threats and uphold its "new security concept" featuring "mutual trust, mutual benefit, equality and cooperation,"rather than as a vehicle to bring all countries in to a new Cold War.[31]

Thus, it is of great importance that China and other SCO members are prudent in accepting new members while accommodating the security needs of each other. In the meantime, the enlargement of the SCO reflects the growing need of its members and other regional countries for closer cooperation on the most salient security and development issues, as well as for enhanced communication between the SCO and the regional or international organizations and groups. For sure, effectiveness and efficiency of the SCO largely depend on the common needs and joint efforts of its member states; and the many collective initiatives such as the "Greater Eurasian Partnership" proposed by Russia and the BRI proposed by China make it possible for SCO members to be more deeply engaged in cooperation in areas beyond security and counterterrorism. Nevertheless, SCO cooperation on economy, trade, education, culture as well as science and technology remains limited regardless of the many agreements signed among its members, such as the Inter-governmental Agreement on Facilitation of International Road Transport signed in 2014 and the Agreement on Customs Cooperation and Mutual Assistance signed in 2017.

The SCO member states still lack a clear common vision for economic cooperation under the SCO. For example, although many SCO members call for closer trade and economic exchange within the organization and the idea of establishing an "SCO Free Trade Zone" has been under discussion for quite a few years, trade promotion was largely left out from the Development Strategy of the Shanghai Cooperation Organization until 2025, an important guideline for SCO members approved in 2015.32 On the other hand, due to many reasons, bilateral rather than multilateral cooperation seems to remain a major trend among SCO members, which in turn hinders the institutionalization of the SCO and expansion of cooperation areas among SCO member states. Therefore, in the foreseeable future,constraining the expansion of terrorism and Islamic extremism will remain a priority task for the SCO.

China Q of Int' l Strategic Stud 2019.05:65-79. Downloaded from www.worldscientific.com by 82.39.249.120 on 12/03/19. This article is funded by the National Social Sciences Fund of China under Grant number 16ZDA096.° c 2019 World Century Publishing Corporation and Shanghai Institutes for International Studies China Quarterly of International Strategic Studies, Vol. 5, No. 1, 65–79 DOI: 10.1142/ S2377400195002765. *Wang Jin is Research Fellow at the Syria Research Center of Northwest University in China. His mailing address is: 39th building, Dianjian Community, Jiaozuo City, Henan 454000, China.He can also be reachedat warmjohn@live.com. Kong Dehang is Directorof Central China Economic Region Research Institute. His mailing address is: Room 1308, Qianxi Square, Zhengdong District, Zhengzhou City, Henan 450000, and China. He can also be reached at ccerri@ccerri. org.*

Chapter 15

Geopolitics at the World's Pivote: Exploring Central Asia's Security Challenges

Jacqueline Lopour

Executive Summary

Central Asia's five countries — the Republic of Kazakhstan, the Kyrgyz Republic, the Republic of Tajikistan, Turkmenistan, and the Republic of Uzbekistan — hold considerable geopolitical significance for global security. The Central Asian countries share borders with Russia, China, Iran and Afghanistan, and are rich in natural resources, including oil, gas, uranium, and coal, gold, copper, aluminium and hydroelectric power. Central Asia's unique geopolitical placement, valuable resources and the legacy left by the former Soviet Union have resulted in a host of complicated security challenges, including water security and transboundary water management; energy security; terrorism; narcotrafficking; migration and human trafficking; nuclear security; and border management. The issues transcend national boundaries and lend themselves to multilateral approaches. To date, regional cooperation has been piecemeal and stymied by the fact that many issues are inherently tangled with the others.

Central Asia's security challenges closely align with Canada's national security and foreign policy priorities, as well as with

Canada's trade and investment interests, and thus suggest natural pathways for Canada to expand engagement in the region. The Centre for International Governance Innovation (CIGI) has launched a project to work closely with the Central Asian states to explore new security and governance models that address their security priorities, with the aim of facilitating multilateral cooperation and helping the Central Asian states drive innovative, tangible and practical security solutions.

Introduction

Central Asia is a complex geopolitical region that has significant implications for global security. With a population of 66 million, it lies at the crossroads of Europe, the Middle East and Asia, and has vast natural resources, many of which are only beginning to be explored. Historically, these advantages have placed it at the heart of tensions between some of the world's most powerful states and contributed to an array of thorny transboundary security issues. The governments of the Central Asian states have identified several main themes as key security priorities: water security and transboundary water management; energy security; terrorism; narco-trafficking; migration and human trafficking; nuclear security; and border management.

Although these issues primarily affect the region itself, they have important implications for Canada's national interests. Central Asia's security challenges are closely aligned with Canada's foreign policy and national security priorities, which include a focus on Asia, supporting effective governance, increasing Canadian investment abroad—including in developing countries—addressing counterterrorism and non-proliferation, and reducing global drug and human trafficking. Furthermore, Canada's interests and investments in Central Asia are diverse and include sectors such as mining, agricultural machinery, agri-food, knowledge industries, aerospace and infrastructure, as well as education and training programs. Canada's continued success and participation in these areas relies on the region maintaining stability, security and good governance. Canada can play an important role in leading a multilateral dialogue with the Central Asian states to

371

identify how best practices developed in Canada can be adapted to fit the unique local circumstances of the governance and security challenges in Central Asia.

This paper introduces Central Asia's geopolitical significance and explores several inter-related security challenges. For each security issue, this paper provides a brief overview of the issue explains why or how it developed and looks at the issue's significance within the broader security environment. The paper then turns to Canada's role in Central Asia and addresses opportunities to expand engagement in the security realm.

The Pivot of the World

It is easy to attribute Central Asia's importance to its neighbourhood. The five countries of Central Asia — Kazakhstan, the Kyrgyz Republic, Tajikistan, Turkmenistan, and Uzbekistan — sit amid Russia to the north, China to the east, Afghanistan to the south, and Iran to the southwest. Equally important, the region is rich in key natural resources—including oil, gas, hydroelectric power, uranium, coal, gold, copper and aluminium—and only a fraction of these resources have been developed. Kazakhstan is the largest uranium producer in the world, producing 38 percent of the global supply in 2013 (World Nuclear Association 2015a). Turkmenistan has the world's fourth-largest natural gas reserves (British Petroleum 2014), and Tajikistan alone has four percent of the world's hydro power potential—the second-largest percentage in the world (United Nations Development Programme [UNDP] 2013). The Kyrgyz Republic also has immense hydro power potential (Renner 2010), and Uzbekistan has over 1,800 known mineral deposits, contains extensive uranium reserves, and is a leading producer of gold, nitrogen, oil, gas, iodine and sulphur (Safirova 2011). The region also is heavily agrarian, with agriculture—primarily cotton and wheat — serving as one of the region's primary sectors and accounting for over 15 percent of the states' GDP on average (Central Intelligence Agency 2015).

Central Asia's geopolitical significance is not a new development. Starting in the second century BC, Central Asia formed a pivotal segment of the Silk Road trade network, which connected the East to the West and shaped global civilization as we know it today. In modern times, nineteenth-century Britain and Russia battled for influence over Central Asia in a struggle famously known as "The Great Game." Decades later, the founding father of geopolitics, Sir Halford Mackinder, argued that Central Asia's geography made it the world's most important place, describing it as the "pivot region of the world's politics" and the "Heartland." He went on to assert that command of this "Heartland" inevitably leads to command of the entire world: *Who rules the Heartland commands the WorldIsland; Who rules the World-Island commands the world. (Mackinder 1919, 194)*

Unfortunately, global powers for years have, arguably, treated Central Asia as collateral to what they considered more important policy objectives (see Blank 2012; Cornell and Swanström 2006; McCoy 2015; Nourzhanov 2009; Peyrouse, Boonstra and Laruelle 2012). For example, the US Department of State launched its "New Silk Road" Central Asia policy in 2011 to great fanfare, but a senior official testified before Congress the same year that its Central Asia policy revolved around the situation in Afghanistan (Blank 2012). In the East, China's approach to Central Asia serves as both a domestic and a foreign policy. China wants to lock up natural resources to support domestic economic growth, seeks to prevent terrorism from spilling across its borders and tries to hedge against US influence in its own backyard (McCoy 2015; Peyrouse, Boonstra and Laruelle 2012). Even the European Union's robust programs in Central Asia play second fiddle to its primary focus on European energy security and relations with its neighbouring countries, China and India (Blank 2012; Peyrouse, Boonstra and Laruelle 2012).

Nonetheless, the Central Asian regimes—25 years after achieving independence—are emerging as self determining and forceful players determined to plot their own trajectories. The regimes are growing adept at playing countries against each other and at driving their own terms for bilateral and multilateral engagement (Nourzhanov 2009; Peyrouse, Boonstra and Laruelle 2012; Saipov 2012). According to Central Asia expert Daniel Burghart, "for too long, Central Asia has been defined in terms of what others sought to gain there…what is different is that since 1991, the region has begun to define itself" (cited in Blank 2012).

Central Asian governments and scholars are taking the lead in determining their own security priorities, which span a range of transnational issues such as water resource management, energy security, terrorism, drug and human trafficking, nuclear security and border management. In 2013, Erlan Idrissov, Kazakhstan's minister of foreign affairs, told the OSCE Ministerial Council that it should give more attention to transnational issues in Central Asia, including the six topics mentioned above. He called for ongoing regional cooperation to "resolve long-standing conflicts [and to] prevent the build-up of tensions" (Idrissov 2013).

In its official "Concept of the Foreign Policy of the Republic of Tajikistan" (2015), Tajikistan's foreign affairs ministry lists regional cooperation and the same six topics as fundamental priorities of its government. The website for Uzbekistan's Ministry of Foreign Affairs (2015) includes regional cooperation, transboundary water management, and border delimitation and demarcation as policy priorities; the President of Uzbekistan also frequently discusses Islamic extremism in public statements. Likewise, the Kyrgyz Ministry of Foreign Affairs lists regional cooperation, terrorism, narco-trafficking, and border delimitation as foundational elements of Kyrgyz foreign policy (Embassy of the Kyrgyz Republic to the Kingdom of Saudi Arabia 2015).

Central Asia's security picture is complicated, because addressing one issue almost certainly impacts others and can spark controversy. Virpi Stucki et al. (2012) compare water security in Central Asia to a Rubik's cube, with six faces, nine stickers on each side and six different colours: "Moving one face can easily bring disorder to all the other faces; just when you thought you were getting one face in order, you discover another face in disorder. In the case of water and security in Central Asia, there are many 'faces', including not only the Central Asian states but also the neighbouring countries, the US, China, and the EU; 'stickers' such as policies, practices, causes and impacts; and 'colours' such as the different stakeholders."

Stucki's analogy applies far beyond water, aptly describing the difficulty of addressing most of Central Asia's security challenges. Potential policies on managing water resources, stemming narco-trafficking and preventing the spread of Islamic extremism inevitably lead to debates on border management. Addressing transboundary water resource management has implications for energy security, agriculture and the environment. Curtailing drug trafficking and creating stricter migration regulations could stymie terrorist funding but also might negatively impact the economy of those Central Asian countries that rely heavily on remittances and other grey economy sources.

Key Security Priorities

Central Asia's unique geopolitical situation, valuable resources and legacy from the former Soviet Union have resulted in a complex array of security problems common to all five countries. The following section provides an overview of each key security issue identified by the Central Asian governments explains why or how each issue developed and explores the topic's significance within the broader security environment.

Water Security

Water resources in Central Asia are a story of "have" and "have not," a dichotomy that has aggravated tensions among the individual republics since their independence. The region's major rivers are shared and transit multiple countries. Upstream countries—Tajikistan and the Kyrgyz Republic—are water controllers, with access to 90 percent of Central Asia's water resources (Renner 2010). Tajikistan and the Kyrgyz Republic use water resources to fuel their hydroelectric dams, which produce electricity for export and domestic use. Downstream countries—primarily Uzbekistan and Turkmenistan—are water consumers and depend on upstream countries to supply water for irrigation, as agriculture is a linchpin of their respective economies. Turkmenistan, for example, is 80 percent desert and depends almost entirely on irrigation for agriculture, which employs nearly 50 percent of its workforce (FAO 2012).

The Central Asian countries also have different priorities and perspectives regarding the role of water resources. One primary disagreement involves whether to prioritize downstream irrigation or upstream hydro power. Another difference involves timing. Downstream states need water most during the spring and summer growing seasons. Upstream states prefer to conserve water and build up their reservoirs in the summer, so that they have enough supply to generate hydro power in the winter, when domestic energy needs are at their peak. Adding to tensions, downstream countries are vulnerable to flooding during the winter months after upstream hydroelectric dams release water for energy production. The situation is further exacerbated by the fact that water-rich countries view water as a commodity that can be sold — similar to oil and gas — while downstream countries, such as Uzbekistan, view it as a free public good and basic right (Kraak 2012; Pannier 2008).

Friction over access to water has its origins in a resourcesharing system devised by the former Soviet Union. Moscow created a centrally administered integrated water and energy exchange system for all of Central Asia. The Soviets prioritized cotton production, and they built one of the world's most complex irrigation systems of dams, canals, reservoirs and pumps. Their goal was to transform Central Asia into the Soviet Union's agricultural heartland, where upstream states provided irrigation water to downstream states in return for coal, gas and oil for energy. Water resource management is directly tied to domestic and regional security.

According to the Food and Agriculture Organization (FAO) of the United Nations, water is Central Asia's "most precious resource and its use is the most conflict-prone" (Frenken 2013). Some scholars assess that the ouster of Kyrgyz President KurmanbekSaliyevich Bakiyev in 2010 was a "hydroelectric revolution" stemming from public discontent over mismanaged water resources, water shortages and two years of rolling blackouts (Wooden 2014). The five Central Asian states have signed several water-sharing agreements since their independence, but these have failed to fully resolve tensions (Abdolvand et al. 2014; Granit et al. 2010). In a thinly veiled threat directed to Tajikistan and Kyrgyzstan, Uzbek President

Regional Cooperation-A Brief Overview

The Central Asian states belong to a number of regional organizations, including, but not limited to:The Commonwealth of Independent States (formed in 1991): promotes economic and security cooperation among the former Soviet republics. Member states include Armenia, Azerbaijan, Belarus, Kazakhstan, the Kyrgyz Republic, Moldova, Russia, Tajikistan and Uzbekistan. Turkmenistan—in line with its UNrecognized international neutrality—is an associate member, as is Ukraine. The Collective Security Treaty Organization (formed in 1992): an intergovernmental military alliance—similar to the North Atlantic Treaty Organization (NATO)—that includes Armenia, Belarus, Kazakhstan, the Kyrgyz Republic, Russia and Tajikistan.

The International Fund for Saving the Aral Sea (formed in 1993): facilitates regional cooperation on water resources and helps finance projects aimed at rehabilitating the Aral Sea and its surrounding areas. Members include Kazakhstan, the Kyrgyz Republic, Tajikistan, Turkmenistan and Uzbekistan. Shanghai Cooperation Organisation (formed in 1996): aims to strengthen regional cooperation, confidence, stability and economic growth. Members include China, Kazakhstan, the Kyrgyz Republic, Russia, Tajikistan and Uzbekistan, with India and Pakistan expected to join in 2016. Central Asia Regional Economic Cooperation (formed in 1997): an initiative, supported by the Asian Development Bank that focuses on increasing development and reducing poverty. Members include Afghanistan, Azerbaijan, China, Kazakhstan, the Kyrgyz Republic, Mongolia, Pakistan, Tajikistan, Turkmenistan and Uzbekistan. Eurasian Development Bank (formed in 2006): promotes economic growth and cooperation between member states, which include Armenia, Belarus, Kazakhstan, the Kyrgyz Republic, Russia and Tajikistan. Eurasian Economic Union (established in 2015): a regional trading bloc; its members include Armenia, Belarus, Kazakhstan, the Kyrgyz Republic and Russia.

The Central Asian states also participate in or cooperate with a number of other international organizations and financial institutes, including the Asian Development Bank, the Economic Cooperation Organisation, the European Bank for Reconstruction and Development, the International Monetary Fund, the Islamic Development Bank, the NATO Partnership for Peace, the Organization for Security and Co-operation in Europe (OSCE), the Organization of Islamic Cooperation, the United Nations Office on Drugs and Crime (UNODC), the World Bank Group and the World Trade Organization (WTO).

Islam Karimov in 2012 warned that water conflict could lead to serious confrontation and that "even wars could be the result" (Nurshayeva 2012). Uzbekistan continues to feud with the Kyrgyz Republic and Tajikistan regarding the Kambarata-1 and Rogun dams (Frenken 2013). In the coming years, management of water resources will become even more pivotal to regional security and stability. The Soviet-era canal systems that facilitate irrigation in downstream countries have reached the end of their lifespan and will only deteriorate further. The FAO reports that leaking and inefficient canals in some Central Asian countries already result in the loss of 65 percent of irrigation water before it even reaches the fields (ibid.). A review by the US Embassy Bishkek assessed that up to 30 percent of energy produced by hydro power is lost before it can get to market (Zozulinsky 2010). In addition, more and more water sources are being polluted or salinized through over-irrigation, excessive fertilization and improper handling of industrial, nuclear and human waste (Frenken 2013). As demand for clean, usable water rises, so will interstate tensions.

Energy Security and Pipeline Politics

Central Asia is rich in natural gas and oil reserves, but the individual states, as they do with water, exist in a dichotomous state of "have" and "have not." The downstream countries of Kazakhstan, Turkmenistan and Uzbekistan are rich in hydrocarbon resources.

Turkmenistan has the fourth-largest natural gas reserves in the world, while Kazakhstan has the twelfth-largest oil reserves, including the world's single largest oil field outside of the Middle East (British Petroleum 2014; Energy Information Administration 2013). Both Tajikistan and the Kyrgyz Republic, however, are dependent on oil and gas imports from the other Central Asian states to fill energy gaps, as their hydro power infrastructure is able to handle only a small fraction of their hydro power potential.

Soviet-era infrastructure complicates the energy picture. During the Soviet regime, all oil and gas pipelines in Central Asia ran north to Russia. After independence, these aging pipelines significantly limited Central Asia's export potential and provided Russia with a de facto monopoly over the sector (Chow and Hendrix 2010). Energy inefficiency plays a key role in energy security, illuminating why energy supply often fails to meet domestic consumption needs. Decaying equipment, obsolete technology and gas flaring contribute to why the World Bank considers emerging Europe and Central Asia to be among the most energy-inefficient regions in the world, with over 60 percent of the region's potential electricity lost in processing or delivery (World Bank 2013a; World Bank 2013c).

Since the fall of the Soviet Union, the Central Asian states have explored new oil and gas pipeline routes to diversify into new markets and increase exports. The primary obstacle for regional exporters is geographic: Central Asia is landlocked and there is no direct route to transport oil and gas to sea and shipping lanes. Going west is costly, as it requires circuiting the Caspian Sea or building an expensive underwater pipeline. Pipelines would have to stretch across all of China to reach the Pacific Ocean and access to the Arabian Sea requires transiting through volatile Afghanistan or controversial Iran (Fishelson 2007).

International and regional politics further complicate pipeline options. Pipelines provide significant economic and political benefits for the countries they transit: construction creates jobs and investment opportunities; countries can demand significant transit fees; countries can obtain oil and gas for domestic needs;

379

and transit countries could even disrupt pipeline flow for political or economic leverage (Bahgat 2006; Fishelson 2007). The crux of the issue is that "whoever controls the pipelines controls the energy they contain" (ibid.), and as a result, proposed pipeline routes have played key roles in the Central Asian states' foreign policies (Coburn 2010).

The Central Asian governments have faced immense pressure from external actors — Russia, China, the United States and the European Union — regarding the location and control of new pipelines. In pressing for their own preferred routes, Russia wants to preserve its monopoly on oil and gas in the region; China desires energy security to support sustained domestic economic growth; the European Union seeks new sources of gas; and the United States looks to hedge against Russia, China and Iran (ibid.). Despite these pressures, several new pipelines have been built since the Soviet Union dissolved, including the Kazakhstan–China oil pipeline (first stage completed in 2003); the Central Asia–China natural gas pipeline (2009), which connects Turkmenistan, Uzbekistan and Kazakhstan to Chinese markets; and the Korpeje–Kordkuy (1997) and Dauletabad–Sarakhs–Khangiran (2010) natural gas pipelines, which connect Turkmenistan to Iran. Nonetheless, these new pipelines largely continue the practice of extremely high dependence on a single country or energy market — for example, several of the new pipelines substitute dependence on Russia for reliance on China.

Terrorism

The Islamic Movement of Uzbekistan (IMU) — and its offshoot, the Islamic Jihad Union (IJU) — are perhaps the most infamous terrorist groups operating in Central Asia, although there are several other active groups. The IMU, founded in 1998, aims to overthrow the Uzbek government and establish an Islamic state governed by sharia. Despite its small size, the IMU is "tough and battle-hardened, having been engaged in military operations almost fulltime since their creation" (Quinn-Judge 2010).

IMU fighters spent many of the post-2001 years in North and South Waziristan, Pakistan, gaining battlefield experience and developing close ties with al-Qaeda and the Taliban. As a result of this networking, the organization has diversified and now includes fighters from across Central Asia, the Caucasus and Russia, to include ethnic Kazakh, Kyrgyz, Tatar, Dagestani and Chechen fighters. Reinfiltration of IMU forces has reached into almost all of the Central Asian states, including Tajikistan, Uzbekistan, Turkmenistan and Kyrgyzstan (ibid.). The IMU and IJU have been responsible for a number of high-profile attacks in Central Asia, including*suicide attacks and embassy bombings, as well as for attempted assassinations of political leaders in Pakistan and plots to attack the West (Balci and Chaudet 2014).

Since 2001, the threat of radicalization and terrorism in Central Asia has grown. Paul Quinn-Judge (2010) of the International Crisis Group notes that Islamism in Central Asia "has a rich environment in which to develop further," citing corruption by those in power, poverty, rising unemployment, and a large youth population as reasons why the traditionally moderate Muslims in Central Asia are starting to consider the appeal of conservative Islamic based governments. Terrorist recruiters in Central Asia also are taking advantage of the economic situation. Groups such as the Islamic State of Iraq and al-Sham (ISIS) have seized the opportunity to lure unemployed workers with promises of large salaries, even if prospective fighters are not necessarily ideologically sympathetic to the cause. As one unemployed Tajik worker told The Washington Post, "Many people in this situation are very desperate. They need money so badly that they could follow some groups that would offer them money" (Demirjian 2015).

Central Asia's proximity to terrorist groups in Afghanistan and Pakistan also plays a significant role in explaining the threat of terrorism in Central Asia (Nourzhanov 2009; Swanström 2010). One Kyrgyz diplomat blamed Afghanistan for the rise in the terrorist threat, deeming it one of the main "challenges of a new era" (cited in Nourzhanov 2009). Tajik officials also have warned of the threat from thousands of Islamic militants located just across the border in Afghanistan (Romin 2015). The conflict in Syria and ascendance of ISIS has complicated the terrorist threat. The most visible symptom was the high-profile defection of the Tajik Special Forces commander Colonel GulmurodKhalimov, who joined ISIS in June 2015 and filmed a video calling on thousands of Tajik workers to follow him (Demirjian 2015). IMU also has jumped on the ISIS bandwagon; IMU leader Usman Gazi in 2014 swore allegiance to ISIS and its leader Abu Bakr alBaghdadi (Agence France Press 2014). An estimated 500 to 1,000 Central Asian fighters operate in Syria, and ISIS has used Kazakh child fighters in propaganda videos (Snow 2015; Wyke and Boyle 2014). The primary fear is that those who leave to fight in Syria might eventually return home to possibly conduct attacks or spread extremism within their communities.

Narco-Trafficking

Central Asia is one of the world's primary narco-trafficking hubs. Neighbouring Afghanistan produces 90 percent of the global supply of opium and one-quarter of the heroin it produces transits through Central Asia (UNODC 2015; 2012). All five of the Central Asian countries are impacted: heroin enters Tajikistan from Afghanistan, after which it is trafficked into Uzbekistan, Kyrgyzstan and then Kazakhstan (UNODC 2012). Porous borders, high levels of corruption and endemic poverty reinforce the industry.

Narco-trafficking plays a significant role in the economies of some Central Asian countries. The UNODC reports that drug traffickers in 2010 made a net profit of US$1.4 billion from opiates that transited Central Asia — the equivalent of almost one-third of the Kyrgyz Republic's or Tajikistan's GDP (ibid.). Narco-trafficking is linked to widespread corruption or tacit approval by officials; alleged drug kingpins have been elected to the Kyrgyz Parliament (in 2000) and have served as senior law enforcement officials in Kyrgyzstan and Tajikistan (Cornell and Swanström 2005; Trofimov 2012). Efforts to boost legitimate trade—such as the US-funded bridge across the Panj River connecting Tajikistan and Afghanistan—have had the unintended consequence of facilitating drug trafficking. As one Tajik official told The Wall Street Journal, "Why take it on a donkey if you can drive it by the truckload?" (ibid.).

Drug trafficking severely undermines the political, economic and social stability of Central Asia. It enfeebles state institutions, allows corruption to flourish, stagnates the economy and facilitates the spread of disease, as well as terrorism and other forms of crime (Swanström 2010; UNODC 2015). Narco-trafficking literally can overturn governments — the instigators of the Kyrgyz revolution in 2005 likely were financed by drug money (Swanström 2010). Officials of all levels, from high-level government to low-paid bureaucrats and law enforcement officers, are lured by high profit margins (Cornell and Swanström 2006).

Also, an increasing number of terrorist and insurgent groups rely on drug trafficking as a source of funding (Balci and Chaudet 2014, Cornell and Swanström 2006). Although the majority of drugs are destined for foreign markets, the number of Central Asian addicts is soaring, and human immunodeficiency virus/acquired immune deficiency syndrome (HIV/AIDS) and hepatitis C epidemics directly correspond to narco-trafficking transit routes (Swanström 2010). Drug trafficking also impacts other security areas, because traffickers take advantage of established drug routes to transfer other contraband, including weapons, natural resources, nuclear waste and trafficked humans (UNODC 2015).

Migration and Human Trafficking

A significant percentage of Central Asia's population work as migrant labourers abroad, and their remittances play a major role in the states' economies. According to the International Organization for Migration (IOM), an estimated 10 million people in Central Asia are on the move.[1] In Tajikistan alone, the World Bank estimates that half of its working-age males are employed abroad, as well as a significant percentage of Kyrgyz and Uzbek labourers (World Bank 2013b). Russia traditionally has been one of the primary destinations for Central Asian migrant workers, who in 2014 made up 40 percent of all foreign residents there (IOM 2015b). Many migrant labourers also stay within Central Asia and seek employment in Kazakhstan, where high economic growth has created demand for seasonal and skilled workers alike (ibid.). Remittances from migrant labourers are hugely important to the economy; in 2013, remittances comprised approximately 50 percent of Tajikistan's GDP and 30 percent of the Kyrgyz Republic's GDP, according to World Bank estimates.

The extent of migration has significant implications for the region's economic stability and security. Migration increases the threat of ideological radicalization, because migrant workers are isolated from their communities and often face hostile conditions abroad. This situation makes them vulnerable to hardline religious organizations, which are able to step into the void and provide community and spiritual support. Radicalized migrant workers have then returned home and attempted to spread extremist ideology (Mohapatra 2013). Terrorist groups also capitalize on migration trends.

Russia's strict new migration laws and economic downturn have left thousands of migrant workers in the lurch. Badly needed remittances have declined, and terrorist recruiters have stepped in to lure newly unemployed workers with promises of large salaries (Demirjian 2015). There are also close links between migration and the spread of HIV/AIDS, particularly when migrant labourers become infected abroad, return home and infect their wives and families (Mohapatra 2013). Other male labourers stay abroad for extended periods of time, sometimes fully abandoning their wives and families. These women have few economic opportunities, making them vulnerable to exploitation and reinforcing the poverty cycle (ibid.).

Irregular migration is closely linked to human trafficking for labour (IOM 2015b). Over one million people in Central Asia are at risk for trafficking, and over 69 percent of trafficking victims are men (IOM 2015a). Many of the same factors that drive migration also contribute to human trafficking, including high unemployment, poverty, a growing youth population and corruption (IOM 2015b). The trafficking problem in Central Asia is threefold: the region is simultaneously the origin, the transit and the destination state for human trafficking. The US Department of State "Trafficking in Persons Report" (2015) indicates that adult male labour migrants working abroad are at greatest risk for trafficking, primarily in the agricultural, forestry, construction, domestic service and textile industries. The wives and families that migrant workers leave behind also are vulnerable to sexual trafficking; some women from Tajikistan have been forced into marriages or debt bondage in Afghanistan. Trafficked children are forced to beg, sell drugs or participate in other criminal behaviour. They are also forced to pick cotton or tobacco and sexually trafficked. Despite decreasing levels of forced child labour in Uzbekistan's cotton fields, compulsory adult labour is on the rise in both Uzbekistan and Turkmenistan. Those who refuse to help with the cotton harvest face harassment or lose their jobs (ibid.).

Nuclear Security

Central Asia has vast uranium resources and is a top supplier of uranium for nuclear energy. Kazakhstan is the world's leading uranium producer and as of 2013 provided 38 percent of the global supply (World Nuclear Association 2015a). Uzbekistan is the seventh-largest supplier and is increasing production (World Nuclear Association 2015c). Kyrgyzstan has signed agreements with foreign companies to explore uranium reserves and Tajik officials claim the country has huge uranium reserves, the size of which are classified as a state secret (Kassenova 2010; Nuclear Threat Initiative 2014; World Nuclear Association 2015b).

Kazakhstan recently has moved beyond exporting raw material and built a plant to process raw material into nuclear fuel pellets, an endeavour that promises even greater economic return (Kassenova 2010; World Nuclear Association 2015a). Additionally, the government of Kazakhstan and the International Atomic Energy Agency agreed in April 2015 to establish a low-enriched uranium (LEU) fuel bank in Kazakhstan, which would ensure that nuclear power plants have a steady supply of LEU if the commercial market were somehow disrupted (World Nuclear Association 2015a).

Historically, Central Asia played a pivotal role in the Soviet Union's nuclear ambitions, but the region has since become one of the greatest success stories in nuclear disarmament and non-proliferation. The Soviets mined and milled significant amounts of uranium ore across Kazakhstan, the Kyrgyz Republic, Tajikistan and Uzbekistan. After the collapse of the Soviet Union, Kazakhstan inherited 1,410 nuclear warheads and repatriated all of them to Russia by 1995. Kazakhstan also worked closely with the US government in the mid-1990s to remove half a ton of highly enriched uranium from a poorly secured facility in a classified mission dubbed "Project Sapphire" (Hoffman 2009).

There is little to no risk that the Central Asian governments will attempt to proliferate or militarize their nuclear programs, given the states' strong commitment to non-proliferation. All five Central Asian countries signed the Treaty on the Non-Proliferation of Nuclear Weapons and the Comprehensive Nuclear-Test-Ban Treaty. In a rare show of regional unity, in 2006 the five countries also signed the Central Asian Nuclear-Weapon-FreeZone (CANWFZ) treaty, which prohibits developing, acquiring, testing or possessing nuclear weapons. The CANWFZ treaty was ground-breaking in that it created a denuclearized area in the middle of several powerful nuclear countries: Russia, China, Pakistan and India. The CANWFZ treaty could serve as a model for future efforts to increase regional cooperation, because the five Central Asian states successfully navigated and resolved significant disagreements during the treaty negotiations (Kassenova 2010).

Many of Central Asia's nuclear waste sites lack sufficient security measures, however, raising the prospect of terrorists drawing from the region's vast nuclear waste to obtain material for a "dirty bomb." International security agencies and experts repeatedly have warned of ISIS and al-Qaeda's interest in dirty bombs and efforts to use nuclear material in improvised explosive devices (Blake and Hope 2011; Withnall 2015). The late al-Qaeda leader Osama bin Ladin even advised the late Taliban leader Mullah Omar to look toward Central Asia for "nonconventional military industries" — a reference to nuclear expertise and resources (bin Ladin 2002). In Central Asia, there are significant amounts of uranium tailings or other nuclear waste stored in poorly secured sites or abandoned mining facilities (see Figure 2).

The United Nations in 2012 warned that there was nearly 55 million tons of radioactive waste in Tajikistan that was stored in sites with inadequate security measures (Agence France Press 2012). Similarly, the Nuclear Threat Initiative in 2009 expressed concern that many sites in the Kyrgyz Republic "have no security measures, allowing the general population to scavenge for radioactive metals and other waste" (Humphrey and Sevcik 2009). Additionally, the proximity of nuclear waste sites to densely populated areas and the threat of natural disaster (such as earthquakes, floods and landslides) pose significant environmental and health risks (ibid.). The five Central Asian states are aware of these threats and take them seriously, but most still lack the necessary resources needed to mitigate all risks and ensure comprehensive nuclear safety and security programs (Kassenova 2010).

Border Management and Security

Twenty years after independence, none of the five Central Asian states have fully demarcated all of their borders. The borders are porous and difficult to monitor and span a wide variety of difficult terrain, from the Eurasian steppes to isolated mountain passes. The dissolution of the Soviet Union in 1991 forced the Central Asian states to patch together border authorities from the remnants of Soviet bureaucracy, a task complicated by the fact that several borders of the individual republics were unclear (Gavrilis 2012). Contested areas remain, and delimitation proceedings have devolved into heated political battles in which Central Asian leaders have accused "one another of deliberately mismanaging their borders" (ibid.).

Border security in Central Asia is complicated by Soviet historical legacy. Moscow deliberately created borders that were administrative in nature —rather than following natural geographic features or ethnic lines — to forestall potential separatist sentiments. Soviet planners also created multiple "enclaves"—small territorial islands belonging to one state that are completely encircled by another —as well as a complex system of land leases in which one republic leased a parcel of land or natural resource from another. As the International Crisis Group

(2002) explains, these factors "combined to create a complex stew of territorial claims and counterclaims once the Central Asian republics became independent states." There is little chance that border disputes will erupt into full-blown war, but local clashes are frequent. One of the most fiercely disputed regions is the Ferghana Valley, the "agricultural heartland" of Central Asia and a historically important staging point on the Silk Road(Figure 3).

The valley is shared by Uzbekistan, Tajikistan and the Kyrgyz Republic, and all three have long-standing historic, economic and ethnic claims to the area. The European Union calls the Ferghana Valley "one of the most curious border patterns in the world" because of its dense population, mix of ethnic groups, and history of "disastrous gerrymandering by Soviet planners" (EU 2009). Various ethnic groups compete among each other for pastures, water rights, territory and economic opportunities, and chafe against the closed borders that inhibit their access to these. In the Ferghana Valley, as well as other areas, border crossings have been indiscriminately closed, bribery and corruption are rampant, and the situation has devolved into occasional small firefights with counterparts on the other side (Gavrilis 2012).

Most border authorities in Central Asia require capacity building. Although multiple international assistance programs are addressing these issues, many border officials in Central Asia are poorly paid, insufficiently trained and under-equipped; work in substandard facilities; and suffer from low morale and high corruption levels, according to the European Union Border Management Programme (EU 2009). In some of the more remote border post locations, guards must resort to harsh subsistence living, including growing their own crops and hunting their own food. The mental strain is intense, and some guards are unable to cope and turn to suicide or homicide (Gavrilis 2012).

Border management and security is intrinsically linked to almost all other security areas. The International Crisis Group (2002) labels border security as the "fundamental stumbling block to wider regional cooperation in economics, security and ethnic relations." Murky border lines complicate efforts to improve cooperation on water resource management and energy security. Poorly monitored borders allow for illegal migration and trafficking in drugs, people, contraband and nuclear waste. Terrorist groups take advantage of weak border security to conduct cross-border activity, recruit new fighters or set up safe havens. Despite all of these risks, there must be a balance between secure borders and those open enough for trade and economic development. According to the European Union Border Management Programme, "increased levels of cross-border trade are...vital to the economic development of the landlocked countries of Central Asia" (EU 2009).

Canada's Role in Central Asia

Central Asia's security challenges closely align with Canada's national security and foreign policy priorities, providing natural pathways for Canada to expand engagement in the region. Canada's Department of Foreign Affairs, Trade and Development (DFATD)2 lists expanding economic and political engagement in Asia, supporting effective governance globally and improving Canadian investment opportunities in developing countries as some of its 2015–2016 foreign policy priorities. Central Asia's advantageous geopolitical position makes it a natural partner in this endeavour. Central Asia's security challenges also correspond to other DFATD and Public Safety Canada priorities,3 including tackling the threat of terrorism, preventing nuclear proliferation, promoting the peaceful use of nuclear energy, addressing human smuggling and stemming transnational crime, including the global drug trade.

Canada can deepen collaboration with Central Asia in the security realm because it has extensive experience navigating many of the same security issues as Central Asia, including managing extensive uranium and hydrocarbon resources; nuclear security, waste management and inspections by the International Atomic Energy Agency; managing transboundary and trans-provincial waterways;

working multilaterally to address contested international borders; and managing its own lengthy terrestrial border, as just a few examples. The entangled nature of these security issues suggests that a cooperative regional arrangement would benefit all attempting to address them. Canada's capacity and expertise in this realm makes for a natural partnership, one in which Canada could play an important role in leading a multilateral dialogue with the Central Asian states.

Jacqueline Lopour is a research associate in CIGI's Global Security & Politics Program. At CIGI, her research interests include exploring major security challenges in Central Asia. She also works on CIGI's Fixing Climate Governance project, which is designed to generate fresh ideas on how to more effectively approach climate change negotiations. Prior to joining CIGI, Jacqueline spent 10 years as a political and leadership analyst at the Central Intelligence Agency in Washington, DC. She provided numerous written and verbal briefings to top United States government officials and participated in meetings with various international leaders and government representatives. Her main areas of focus were political developments in South Asia and the Middle East, and she has lived in and travelled extensively throughout the region. Jacqueline holds a B.A. with Honors in English Literature and History from the University of California, Los Angeles. CIGI Papers No. 80-November 2015, Geopolitics at the World's Pivot Exploring Central Asia's Security Challenges. Jacqueline Lopour. This work is licensed under a Creative Commons Attribution—Non-commercial — No Derivatives License. To view this licence, visit (www.creativecommons.org/ licenses/by-nc-nd/3.0/). For re-use or distribution, please include this copyright notice. The Centre for International Governance Innovation is an independent, non-partisan think tank on international governance. Led by experienced practitioners and distinguished academics, CIGI supports research, forms networks, advances policy debate and generates ideas for multilateral governance improvements. Conducting an active agenda of research, events and publications, CIGI's interdisciplinary work includes collaboration with policy, business and academic communities around the world. CIGI's current research programs focus on three themes: the global economy; global security & politics; and international law. CIGI was founded in 2001 by Jim Balsillie, then co-CEO of Research In Motion (BlackBerry), and collaborates with and gratefully acknowledges support from a number of strategic partners, in particular the Government of Canada and the Government of Ontario.

Chapter 16

Theory-Testing Uyghur Terrorism in China

Andrew Mumford

Abstract

Analysis of terrorism perpetrated by Uyghurs inside China and
the presence of Uyghur fighters in the warzones from Afghanistan
to Syria has been divided as to whether such violence constitutes
the alignment of Uyghur groups like the East Turkestan Islamic
Movement (ETIM) and the Turkestan Islamist Party (TIP) with
the broader constellation of global jihadi organisations pushing an
extremist religious cause, or if it is representative of a more inward-
looking push for the secession of Xinjiang province. Testing the
causes, conduct and organisational structure of Uyghur terrorism
against prevalent theories in the field, this article argues that
Uyghur terrorism actually constitutes a hybrid model of modern
terrorist group in which religious discourse is used to underline the
push for a separatist agenda. Keywords: China, Uyghur, Xinjiang,
Terrorism

Introduction

Uyghur terrorism is not easy to categorise given the predominant
paradigms in contemporary terrorism studies. The religious
rhetoric used by groups such as the East Turkestan Islamic
Movement (ETIM), its successor group the Turkestan Islamist
Party (TIP), and the presence of some Uyghurs in contemporary

warzones from Afghanistan to Syria has encouraged a portion of analysis to suggest that this constitutes a Chinese contribution to the global jihadist threat. Yet the limited size of the Uyghur presence in jihadist groups outside of China, and indeed the targets of attacks within the country, have prompted counter-arguments that point not to an outward-looking international jihadist agenda but to an inward-looking separatist one that is bent on self determination for the Uyghur people.

This mixed picture has bifurcated the academic literature on terrorism in China (or Chinese terrorism more generally). Having to determine whether Uyghur violence is either separatist or jihadist begs the question of how it can be best theorised in order to help explain the phenomenon. It is the aim of this paper to better understand terrorism in modern China by theory-testing Uyghur political violence inside and outside the country against prominent theories of modern terrorism, including the instrumental v. psychological debate, David Rapoport's four waves theory, as well as against attempts to contemporise his work by sign-posting to a possible 'fifth wave'.

This article is therefore not just about the state of terrorism in China but an assessment of what the Chinese case tells us about the state of modern terrorism. This subject arguably combines two of the most influential factors shaping twenty-first century international politics: the rise of China as a global superpower and the proliferation of non-state violence.[1] Surprisingly little of the growing literature on terrorism in China engages with the phenomenon from a theoretical perspective[2] Much of the literature is concerned with either analysing the repressive nature of Chinese counter-terrorism policies[3] or understanding the nature of Uyghur nationalism.[4]

Ultimately this paper argues that a hybrid assessment of Uyghur terrorism is most appropriate because it is too nationalist to be considered part of a 'fourth wave' of terrorism, not millenarian or web-savvy enough to be 'fifth wave', not organised enough to be instrumentalist, and not accessible enough to withstand credible psychological interpretations. This is the multivariate platform on which theoretical explanations of modern Uyghur violence arguably stand. It is not the purpose of this theory-testing exercise to dismiss the intellectual foundations of the theories themselves – each has its own merits and strong scholarly credentials that have advanced the field in important ways.

Instead, this article aims to highlight that the empirical base of our knowledge about terrorism from ethnic Uyghur groups indicates a complex picture that negates singular explanatory frameworks. This article will firstly offer some background detail on the state of current terrorism inside China, and then engage in turn with leading theories in the field in order to stand the Uyghur case up to their main tenets. It ends by reasserting the case for a hybrid theoretical assessment of terrorism in China given the absence of a strong fit with any one theoretical model.

Terrorism in Xinjiang: A Brief History Located in the far west of the country, Xinjiang (which is officially called the Xinjiang Uyghur Autonomous Region or XUAR for short) is China's biggest province, whose terrain is mainly either desert or mountain range. To trace the historical antecedents of contemporary Uyghur violence would mire the reader in centuries of conflict, repression and reprisal.[5] Its modern manifestation is the by-product of a combustible mix of nationalism, separatism and religion. Only fully integrated into Beijing's political sphere after the founding of the People's Republic of China in 1949, Xinjiang's Sunni Muslim, Turkic-speaking Uyghur population constitute 44% of the province's population today.[6]

After the end of the Cold War Beijing simultaneously loosened the ideological grip of communism and moved to strengthen the legitimacy of the Chinese Communist Party (CCP). In political terms this set loose a new wave of ethnic nationalism among the Han majority, resulting in a backlash of non-Han resentment across the provinces dominated by minorities.[7] The Uyghurs of Xinjiang were foremost among those minority groups to respond through acts of resistance, resenting what they perceived was an attack on their religion, language and ethnicity[8] The East Turkistan Islamic Movement (ETIM) was founded in 1989 by Ziyauddin Yusuf with the aim of separating Xinjiang from China which could then be governed by Islamist precepts.

Yusuf believed that the Turkic-speaking people of Central Asia should be free from either Soviet or Chinese control. This panTurkic ideology, infused with Islamist theology, was spurred by the defeat of the Soviet Union's invasion of Afghanistan by the mujahedeen and foreign jihadist fighters. Yet after the collapse of the USSR most Central Asian satellite states such as Kazakhstan, Tajikistan, Kyrgyzstan, and Uzbekistan achieved their independence. ETIM attempted to wrestle Xinjiang from China by the use of extremist violence to achieve its political aim of an independent state – East Turkestan. But to the ruling cadre in Beijing the issues of Uyghur separatism and Islamic extremism were, and still are, two sides of the same coin.[9] This interpretation is a deliberate ploy by the CCP to elicit international sympathy for their fight against what they perceive to be networked pan-national Islamist violence.

Such a depiction of ETIM activity seemingly justified their domestic crackdown on religious and political activity and simultaneously delegitimised calls for greater Uyghur autonomy[10] Citing fears of Islamist violence (concerns easily related to by the West) was a Trojan Horse for enhanced repression of Uyghur separatism. As such, in the years after the 9/11 attacks on the United States, the Chinese government forwarded three main justifications for its actions against Uyghurs: first, detained Uyghurs were being supported by Islamist groups, notably al-Qaeda; second, Uyghur groups were peddling a violent Islamist ideology that was undermining the Chinese state; and third, that this had international ramifications and that action was in line with the broader aims of the 'Global War on Terror'.[11]

This counter-terrorism rhetoric was amplified in the years running up to the 2008 Beijing Olympic Games when YouTube videos started to emerge in 2006 indicating that ETIM had undergone a transformation and was now branding itself as the Turkestan Islamic Party (TIP). These videos by TIP members promised a renewed wave of domestic terrorism, although very little direct evidence exists as to their operational capabilities rendering their claims of responsibility for some acts of violence dubious.[12]

Given the mutual fears of mass catastrophic terrorism at a major sporting event and the shared narrative of global jihadist threats, the authorities in Beijing were given a metaphorical free pass by the West to instigate an internal crackdown on terrorist suspects in Xinjiang. It is only in recent months, nearly two decades after the 9/11 attacks, that Western political and media scrutiny have returned to Chinese counter-terrorism policy and practice.

In May 2014, the government of Xi Jinping launched a renewed 'Strike Hard Campaign against Violent Terrorism' in Xinjiang (previous 'Strike Hard' campaigns had been instigated in the 1990s), scaling up its military presence in the region and introducing stringent restrictions on freedom of movement and assembly[13] Since then, the number of people placed under arrest increased three-fold compared to the previous five-year period, with Human Rights Watch accusing the Chinese government in September 2018 of overseeing a system of "mass arbitrary detention, torture, and mistreatment of Turkic Muslims"[14] Media reports focussed on evidence heard by the UN Committee on the Elimination of Racial Discrimination in August 2018 of the detention of up to one million Uyghurs in 'political education camps' under the auspices of countering terrorism.[15]

This article does not aim to explain this draconian Chinese counter-terrorism response in Xinjiang – this has been done excellently elsewhere[16] Instead it argues that we must make further headway in trying to understand the phenomenon of Uyghur terrorist violence in the first place. This requires a more vigorous theoretical assessment of what it represents in terms of cause, conduct and consequence. Thus, a systematic exercise in theory-testing is appropriate in order to shed much-needed light on a conflict that is still making headlines globally because of China's illiberal approach to countering terrorist activity[17]

Uyghur Terrorism: Instrumental vs. Psychological Explanations

The emergence of the field of terrorism studies brought with it two broad schools of thought: the instrumentalist approach and the psychological approach. From an instrumentalist point of view, Martha Crenshaw argued that the recourse to terrorism is a logical strategic choice willingly chosen by groups to further their political agenda. Terrorism thus has, Crenshaw posits, a 'collective rationality'[18] Such a strategic choice approach requires the de facto presence of an identifiable organisation and leadership structure capable of fostering rational intragroup discussion. No such coherent structures exist in the Uyghur case given the flimsy coherence of ETIM and the absence of key figures around which the cause revolves when the group evolved into TIP.

It is difficult to see how terrorism in Xinjiang can be the product of rational strategic choice when there is no organisational structure to foster the fomentation of such a strategy. Furthermore, there is also a noticeable strategic diversity, possibly even confusion, in the Uyghur case. There is no central, unifying strategic objective. Acts of terror are depicted by the Chinese authorities as an admixture of separatism, jihadism, and Uyghur nationalism[19] Compounding this is the absence of any effective communications strategy from TIP, beyond sporadic YouTube videos that attempt to claim credit for the perpetration of attacks.[20]

Conceptually, strategic choice theory is of limited use explaining Uyghur violence due to the absence of a discernible group structure to hold rational strategic debates and the fragmented nature of strategic objectives inside the community of violent Uyghurs. Conversely, psychological explanations of terrorism posit, as Jerrold Post has done, that individuals "are driven to commit acts of violence as a consequence of psychological forces and that their special psycho-logic is constructed to rationalize acts they are psychologically compelled to commit"[21] Innately using bifurcated rhetoric dividing 'us and them', terrorists are, according to Post, united by common personality traits, including a damaged sense of self, often the result of childhood psychological trauma. Such individuals become drawn to terrorist activity precisely to commit acts of violence because it offers a sense of self-significance that bounds the individual's entire identity and self-worth. Yet there are still similar restrictions in making the case for a psychological approach to explain Uyghur violence as there are for an instrumentalist one.

JIHAD IN CENTRAL ASIA

The main one is methodological. It is very difficult for terrorist researchers to access detained Uyghurs for interview as a means of asserting their psychological motives, given restrictions placed on the region by the authorities. This does not mean, however, that Beijing may not be guilty of fomenting terrorism in Xinjiang through its own repressive counter-terrorism policies. Terrorists may not be born, but they can be made. The policy consequences of state counter-terrorism will have a psychological effect on individual Uyghurs, but we are not yet at a stage of methodological confidence to make those assertions accurately.

Terrorism inside China:

Which 'Wave'? David Rapoport's 'four waves theory' of modern terrorism has been a terrorism studies industry standard explanation of the evolution of modern political violence in the years since its publication.[22] Rapoport described the modern history of terrorism as having four distinct but over-lapping 'waves', each with their own defining set of common tactics and motives: the Anarchist wave (1880-1920); the Anti-Colonial wave (1920-1960); the New Left wave (1960s-1979); and the Religious wave (1979-onwards). Rapoport's theory has heavily influenced post-9/11 studies of terrorism as a global phenomenon and still retains utility as a conceptual benchmark against which to interpret the characteristics of terrorist groups.

So how does Uyghur terrorism fit into this theory? The separatist agenda of groups like ETIM and then TIP, as well as the subsequent crackdown by the central authorities, has ensured that there are overtones of anti-colonialism to the Uyghur struggle. This brings with it echoes of Rapoport's 'second wave'. Beijing acknowledged that between 1990 and 2001 there were over 200 incidents of Uyghur violence that killed more than 160 people, injuring 440.[23] Since then the pattern of terrorism inside China has, according to Philip Potter, indicated two broad trends:1) terrorist attacks are a response to "broader geopolitical circumstances and strategic opportunities (e.g. 9/11 and the Olympics)";2) "tensions and grievances can remain dormant for significant periods of time only to flare dramatically"[24]

398

The 9/11 attacks in America marked a watershed moment in Beijing's approach to Uyghur violence inside China. Two months after the Twin Towers attack the Foreign Ministry explicitly stated that ETIM was under the control of Osama bin Laden and that Uyghur fighters had received training in Afghanistan.[25] The launching of a global 'War on Terror' by President Bush furnished Beijing with an opportunity to change its approach to Uyghur violence by framing such incidents as their own domestic struggle against terrorism. A crackdown on the activities of ETIM ensued, resulting in a dip in violence. Yet one of the 'dramatic flares' observed by Potter occurred in 2014. A series of three knife attacks at train stations in Kunming, Urumqi and Guangzho in the spring of that year left 32 people dead, whilst a bomb in Urumqi in May 2014 killed a further 39 persons.

This denoted a distinct tactical shift by militants away from hitting government and military targets and towards softer civilian targets, notably at transport hubs that are the mainstay of Beijing's economic and infrastructural plans for Xinjiang.[26] After these attacks President Xi Jinping vowed that government counter-terrorism policy would be "long-term, complicated and acute."[27] But it would be churlish to theorise the Uyghur struggle as 'anti-colonial'. Not only does it fall decades after Rapoport contended that the 'anti-colonial' wave had crested, but it would also be reductionist to equate domestic acts of terrorism with a fight against a perceived imperial power. Uyghur terrorist targeting has shifted away from symbols of Beijing's political and military presence, and there is a notable lack of anti-imperialist language in Uyghur terrorist discourse.[28] Separatism is not de facto anti-colonialism by another name.

Terrorism outside China:Uyghurs as 'Fourth Wave' Jihadists?

Assumptions as to the predominant religious motivation of Uyghur violence have held sway within the authorities in Beijing, begging the question of whether Rapoport's religiously-inspired 'fourth wave' of terrorism is a more apt model to apply. Most Uyghurs practice Hanafi Islam, the jurisprudence of which allows for non-Arabic languages to be used in prayer and is also suffused with other pan-Asian religious influences including Sufism and Buddhism.[29] Yet it is misleading to interpret Uyghur's Muslim faith as an indication of their belonging to the 'fourth wave' of religiously-motivated terrorism.

They are not millenarian in their faith (a key tenet of Rapoport's typology). Their grievances are not motivated by faith outright but by a combination of local governmental restrictions on their worship as well as their wider ethnic and national identity. Indeed, there does not appear to be much homogeneity in the political demands of Uyghurs, with calls ranging from equality with the Han population to demands for complete independence of Xinjiang province.[30] Assessments as to the quantity and motive of Uyghurs fighting with Islamist groups outside of China vary wildly. Alarmist reports emanated from the Jerusalem Center for Public Affairs in June 2014 suggesting that there were up to 1,000 Chinese jihadists receiving training at a paramilitary base in Pakistan, with an additional (but undetermined) number fighting alongside other jihadi groups inside Syria.[31]

Clarke and Kan put the number of Uyghur fighters inside Syria and Iraq at somewhere between 100-300 arguing that organisations like TIP have become "a noticeable part of the constellation of globally active jihadist terror groups."[32] Yet despite the acknowledged presence of Uyghurs joining ISIS and Jabhat Fateh al-Sham (formerly the al-Qaeda affiliated al-Nusra Front) in Syria this is more likely to be a sign of Middle Eastern jihadist groups fostering recruitment channels from southeast Asia to perpetuate the fight in Syria and Afghanistan rather than a sign of an imminent extension of activity from Uyghur foreign fighters into China itself. TIP has no known independent operational capabilities outside Afghanistan where its small number of members is based.[33]

Further evidence pointing to a lack of desire by Uyghur militants to return to China to commit attacks is firstly their willingness to appear in propaganda videos, thus revealing their identity to the Chinese authorities (two Uyghurs appeared in an online ISIS video in March 2017), and secondly the way such foreign fighters have often sold their homes and possessions in Xinjiang in order to finance their travel to Syria and Afghanistan. Many bring their whole families with them.[34] The presence of a small number of Uyghurs in conflict zones outside China will always stoke concerns as to the regional network being fostered by groups like TIP. For example, in September 2014 four Uyghurs were arrested in Indonesia, with another four arrested five months later, all on suspicion of liaison with the ISISaffiliated Mujahidi Indonesia Timur in Central Sulawesi.[35]

However, a small, yet dispersed, Uyghur presence across the Muslim world falls short of a global network of militant Uyghur jihadists. The sum parts in this case do not add up to a whole. Not only are the actual numbers of foreign fighters unverified, the actual pattern of activity by Uyghurs once encamped in third countries reveals an ethos discernibly more anti-China than pro-jihad. These two motives are distinct and should not be seen as two sides of the same coin. For this reason, Uyghur militancy is not strictly representative of Rapoport's 'fourth wave' of modern terrorism.

Uyghurs and the 'Fifth Wave' of Modern Terrorism Scholarly attempts to build upon Rapoport's four waves have become a cottage industry in recent years. As the 'War on Terror' attempted to eliminate the threat of jihadist groups globally, academics have sought to make sense of the evolution of terrorism. In between the fall of al-Qaeda as a centrally-controlled organisation based in Afghanistan and the rise of the Islamic State's self-proclaimed caliphate across Syria and Iraq three broad contending themes have emerged that purport to show how the religious wave identified by Rapoport has ended. Firstly, Jeffrey Kaplan has argued that a fifth wave of modern terrorism has crested and it is "particularistic, localistic, and centered on the purification of the nation through perfection of a race or tribal group."[36]

Labelling this wave 'new tribalism', Kaplan aimed to highlight the local, as opposed to global, dynamics that led to terrorism with a particular emphasis on 'racial or tribal mysticism' as a motive.[37] Yet Kaplan's 'new tribalism' fifth wave theory is not fully substantiated in the Chinese case. Kaplan outlines 17 ideal-type characteristics of this new form of terrorism, of which the Uyghur example barely complies with half (for example, Uighur groups do not use rape as a weapon, do not claim to establish some form of new calendar, do not belief in human perfectibility, do not place faith in the logic of genocide, and have not embarked on a campaign of apocalyptic violence). Secondly, Jerrold Post et al have intimated that a fifth wave (a possible 'tsunami' even) will be social mediainspired acts of lone actor terrorism.[38]

The internet has facilitated what has been labelled a 'virtual community of hatred', allowing for online radicalisation to inspire the next generation of political violence. This fifth wave hypothesis is also not really applicable in the China case mainly because of strong central government control over internet access inside the country. The online 'community of hatred' that Post holds as key to facilitating this wave is largely off-limits to Uyghurs because of nationwide web censorship. Thirdly, Honig and Yahel argue that Rapoport's fourth religious wave has been superseded by a fifth wave constitutive of what they label 'terrorist semi-states'. These entities "control portions of a weak state's territory... but still launch terrorist attacks against third party victim states."[39]

They point to groups like ISIS, Al-Shabaab, Boko Haram, Hezbollah and Hamas as examples of these territorially established groups that embrace a mix of conventional and unconventional tactics. Yet this too is not fully applicable for the Uyghurs as their cause is nominally secessionist within the context of exceptionally strong central political control over the territory and governance structures of Xinjiang province. There is little chance of a 'state within a state' emerging. Honig and Yahel's model only really applies to instances where there is initial weak governmental control over the contested space. China has over the decades ensured a strong political, economic and military presence in Xinjiang, fostered by a programme of government-sponsored migration of ethnic Han into the province.[40]

Conclusion

The Case for a Hybrid Theory The Chinese government has asserted that Uyghur groups are guilty of promulgating what it labels the 'three evils': terrorism, separatism and religious extremism.[41] This veritable shopping list of perceived crimes against the state reveals that even Beijing has a hybrid interpretation of what Uyghur violence represents – at turns jihadist, anti-communist, and nationalist. Terrorism perpetrated by Uyghurs is thus not easily categoriseable, rendering any theoretical explanation somewhat of a hydra. It is too diffuse organisationally to be fully explainable from an instrumentalist perspective. Crenshaw's emphasis on strategic rationale is dampened in the Uyghur case by the scant evidence offered by either TIP members themselves or the Chinese security forces to back up claims of responsibility for attacks. TIPs claims via internet videos to be behind attacks, including an explosion at a factory in Guangzhou and bus bombs in Shanghai and Kunming in 2008 were largely uncorroborated, even by the security forces.[42]

Research on Uyghur terrorism is too unsubstantiated methodologically to belong fully to the realm of a psychological explanation as advocated by the likes of Post. Restrictions imposed by the Chinese authorities on academic freedom of movement make access to interviewees very difficult, and ensures that much face-to-face interaction with Uyghurs (including those suspected of terrorism) is done predominantly with exiles that have fled China.[43]

Furthermore, Uyghur terrorism lacks a comfortable fit within any of the identified 'waves' of modern terrorism identified by Rapoport and others due to its fusion of ethno-nationalist ideology and Islamic theology, not to mention the absence of genocidal violence and the online orchestration of terror acts. Uyghur groups are of course not the only terrorist movement in recent history to combine a number of ideological motives. Hybrid is not a synonym for unique. What some might term 'old' terrorist groups exuded a mix of political catalysts. Euskadi Ta Askatasuna (ETA), for example, was simultaneously socialist, separatist and Basque nationalist in its outlook.

The Liberation Tigers of Tamil Eelam (LTTE or the Tamil Tigers) imbued a similar concoction of revolutionary socialism and ethnic nationalism in the name of separatism. Even what some would label 'new' terrorist groups, including the recent iteration of the self-proclaimed caliphate of Islamic State, are hybrid entities in as much as they combine a profound religious agenda with a rejection of the Westphalian state system of sovereign borders. Yet what makes the Uyghur case stand out is, firstly, how the religious beliefs of the perpetrators have been seized on by the counter-terrorist state to manipulate global opinion to create a permissive environment for repressive responses, and secondly, how the political, media and academic assessment of political violence by Uyghurs oscillates between religious and secular motives.

If the 'old' groups like ETA and LTTE were firmly secular groups, and 'new' groups like al-Qaeda and ISIS are undeniably religious in their motive, then Uyghur groups like ETIM/TIP fall between two stools analytically. Understanding the violence occurring inside China, and Beijing's response to it, are of increasing international importance given President Xi Jinping's recent declaration that China had entered a 'new era' when it would "take centre stage in the world."[44]

The abrogation of leadership on global issues and in international institutions by the United States under the Trump administration stands in stark contrast to China's willingness to shoulder more international responsibilities abandoned by the US. China's global strength is being pushed through the construction of the Belt and Road Initiative, the enhancement of the Shanghai Cooperation Organization and contributions to United Nations peacekeeping missions. Consequently, it is essential to investigate how terrorism is framed in China as the experiences the Chinese government has gained are likely to be transplanted into its global security agenda. There is a growing literature on terrorism in China. However, theoretical perspectives are still largely missing from this pool. Explaining the nature of acts of terrorism perpetrated by Uyghurs is an

PERSPECTIVES ON TERRORISM Volume 12, Issue 5-- Volume XII, Issue 5 October 2018. Perspectives on Terrorism (PoT) is a joint publication of the Terrorism Research Initiative (TRI), headquartered in Vienna, Austria, and the Institute of Security and Global Affairs (ISGA) of Leiden University, Campus The Hague. PoT is published six times per year as a free, independent, scholarly peer-reviewed online journal available in both HTML and PDF versions at http://www. terrorismanalysts.com and in PDF version (only) at https://www. universiteitleiden.nl/perspectives-on-terrorism. PERSPECTIVES ON TERRORISM Volume 12, Issue 5 important endeavour. This article is just a first step towards initiating a bigger conversation in the field. The Terrorism Research Initiative (TRI) seeks to support the international community of terrorism researchers and analysts by facilitating coordination and engaging in cooperative projects. The globally-circulated online journal Perspectives on Terrorism has 8,000 regular subscribers and is viewed by many more occasional website visitors annually. The Terrorism Research Initiative is the parent organisation of Perspectives on Terrorism (PoT). Perspectives on Terrorism is a peer-reviewed online journal published by Prof. em. Alex P. Schmid and Prof. James J.F.

Chapter 17

Why States Won't Give Nuclear Weapons to Terrorists

Keir A. Lieber and Daryl G. Press

For the last two decades, U.S. leaders have focused on the possibility of nuclear terrorism as a serious threat to the United States. In the wake of the terrorist attacks of September 11, 2001, those fears grewe even more acute. In his State of the Union Address four months after the attacks, President George W. Bush warned a worried nation that rogue states "could provide [weapons of mass destruction] to terrorists, giving them the means to match their hatred."[1] Both Vice President Dick Cheney and National Security Adviser Condoleezza Rice amplified the president's warning in order to justify the war against Iraq. According to Rice, "Terrorists might acquire such weapons from [Saddam Hussein's] regime, to mount a future attack far beyond the scale of 9/11. This terrible prospect could not be ignored or wished away."[2] Such fears continue to shape policy debates today: in particular, advocates of bombing Iran's nuclear facilities often justify a strike based on the idea that Iran might give nu- clear weapons to terrorist groups.[3]

Even President Barack Obama, who as a senator opposed the war against Iraq, declared, "The American people face no greater or more urgent danger than a terrorist attack with a nuclear weapon."[4] For U.S.leaders, the sum of all fears is that an enemy might give nuclear weapons to terrorists. But are those fears well founded? The concern that a nuclear-armed state might transfer weapons to terrorists is part of the foundation of U.S. non-proliferation policy. Non-proliferation is pursued for a variety of reasons, including the fear that new nuclear states will use their weapons directly against adversaries, even in the face of a clear risk of retaliation; lose control of their nuclear weapons or materials through regime incompetence, corruption, or instability; trigger regional proliferation cascades among nervous neighbours; or be emboldened to use nuclear weapons as a "shield" for undertaking aggressive diplomatic and military actions, confident that other states could thus be deterred from responding forcefully.[5]

The concern that a state might transfer nuclear weapons to terrorists, however, is among the greatest of these worries, and to many analysts it is the most compelling justification for costly actions—including the use of military force—aimed at preventing proliferation. Despite the issue's importance, the danger of deliberate nuclear weapons transfer to terrorist's remains understudied.[6] Scholars have scrutinized many other proliferation concerns more extensively. Analysts have investigated the deductive and empirical bases for claims that new nuclear states would be deterrable;[7] the likelihood that Iran, in particular, would behave rationally and avoid using nuclear weapons recklessly;[8] and the risks of proliferation cascades,[9] "loose nukes,"[10] and nuclear-armed states using their weapons as a shield for aggression or blackmail.[11] To the extent that analysts have debated the possibility of covert state sponsorship of nuclear terrorism, however, the arguments have consisted mostly of competing deductive logics—with little empirical analysis. This article assesses the risk that states would give nuclear weapons to terrorists.

We examine the logical and empirical basis of the core proposition: that a state could surreptitiously transfer a nuclear weapon to a like-minded terror group, thus providing the means for a devastating attack on a common enemy while remaining anonymous and avoiding retaliation. The strategy of nuclear attack by proxy hinge so none key question: What is the likelihood that a country could sponsor a nuclear terror attack and remain anonymous? We examine this question in two ways. First, having no data on the aftermath of nuclear terrorist incidents, we use the ample data on conventional terrorism to discover attribution rates. We examine the fraction of terrorist incidents attributed to the perpetrating terrorist organization and the patterns in the rates of attribution. Second, we explore the challenge of tracing culpability for a nuclear terror event from the guilty terrorist group back to its state sponsor. We ask: How many suspects would there be in the wake of a nuclear detonation? How many foreign terrorist organizations have state sponsors? Of those that do, how many state sponsors do they typically have? And how many state sponsors of terrorism have nuclear weapons or sufficient stockpiles of nuclear materials on which to base such a concern?

We conclude that neither a terror group nor a state sponsor would remain anonymous after a nuclear terror attack. We draw this conclusion on the basis of four main findings. First, data on a decade of terrorist incidents reveal a strong positive relationship between the number of fatalities caused in a terror attack and the likelihood of attribution. Roughly three-quarters of the attacks that kill 100 people or more are traced back to the perpetrators. Second, attribution rates are far higher for attacks on the U.S. homeland or the territory of a major U.S. ally—97 percent (thirty-six of thirty-seven) for incidents that killed ten or more people. Third, tracing culpability from a guilty terrorist group back to its state sponsor is not likely to be difficult: few countries sponsor terrorism; few terrorist groups have state sponsors; each sponsored terror group has few sponsors (typically one); and only one country that sponsors terrorism, Pakistan, has nuclear weapons or enough fissile material to manufacture a weapon.

In sum, attribution of nuclear terror incidents would be easier than is typically suggested, and passing weapons to terrorists would not offer countries an escape from the constraints of deterrence.[12] This analysis has two important implications for U.S. foreign policy. First, the fear of terrorist transfer seems greatly exaggerated and does not—in itself—seem to justify costly measures to prevent proliferation. Nuclear proliferation poses risks, so working to prevent it should remain a U.S. foreign policy goal, but the dangers of a state giving nuclear weapons to terrorists have been overstated, and thus arguments for taking costly steps to prevent proliferation on those grounds—as used to justify the invasion of Iraq and fuel the debate over attacking Iran—rest on a shaky foundation. Second, analysts and policymakers should stop understating the ability of the United States to attribute terrorist attacks to their sponsoring states. Such rhetoric not only is untrue, but it also undermines deterrence. States sometimes exaggerate their capabilities to deter an enemy's attacks;[13] but U.S. analysts and leaders, by understating U.S. attribution capabilities, inadvertently increase the odds of catastrophic terrorist attacks on the United States and its allies.

The remainder of this article is divided into five main sections. The first section examines the logic that might tempt foreign leaders to give nuclear materials to terrorists. The second section uses data from thousands of terrorist incidents to determine historical rates of attribution and critical patterns in these data. The third section explores the challenge of linking terrorist groups with their state sponsors. The fourth section rebuts several counterarguments, and the conclusion discusses the implications of this analysis for U.S. foreign policy.

The Logic of Nuclear Transfer to Terrorists: Assessing the Challenges

If a state were undeterrable—that is, if its leaders did not fear retaliation— it would presumably conduct a nuclear strike itself rather than subcontract the job to a terrorist group, ensuring that the weapons were used against the desired target at the desired time (not against a target ultimately chosen by terrorists). The calculated, "back-door" approach of transferring weapons to terrorists makes sense only if a state fears retaliation. The core of the nuclear attack-by-proxy argument is that a state otherwise deterred by the threat of retaliation might conduct an attack if it could do so surreptitiously by passing nuclear weapons to terrorists. Giving nuclear capability to a terrorist group with which the state enjoys close relations and substantial trust could allow the state to conduct the attack while avoiding devastating punishment.

Some analysts are skeptical about such sponsored nuclear terrorism, arguing that a state may not be willing to deplete its small nuclear arsenal or stock of precious nuclear materials. More important, a state sponsor would fear that a terrorist organization might use the weapons or materials in ways the state never intended, provoking retaliation that would destroy the regime.[14] Nuclear weapons are the most powerful weapons a state can acquire, and handing that power to an actor over which the state has less than complete control would be an enormous, epochal decision—one unlikely to be taken by regimes that are typically obsessed with power and their own survival. Perhaps the most important reason to doubt the nuclear-attack-by-proxy scenario is the likelihood that the ultimate source of the weapon might be discovered.[15]

One means of identifying the state source of a nuclear terrorist attack is through "nuclear forensics"—the use of a bomb's isotopic fingerprints to trace the fissile material device back to the reactors, enrichment facilities, or uranium mines from which it was derived. In theory, the material that remains after an explosion can yield crucial information about its source: the ratio of uranium isotopes varies according to where the raw uranium was mined and how it was processed, and the composition of weapons-grade plutonium reveals clues about the particular reactor used to produce it and how long the material spent in the reactor.[16] The possibility that the covert plot could be dis covered before being carried out also acts as a deterrent. For these and other reasons, some analysts argue that nuclear terrorism is unlikely. Other policy analysts are more pessimistic.

Many find the attribution problem particularly significant, largely because of the technical and political challenges involved in trying to pinpoint the source of nuclear material after a detonation. They argue that the United States has not developed a reliable and credible attribution capability, and they highlight the difficulty of building and maintaining strong nuclear forensic capabilities. A 2010 report by the National Research Council, Nuclear Forensics: A Capability at Risk, found the U.S. ability to identify the source of nuclear explosive debris to be "fragile, under-resourced and, in some respects, deteriorating."[17] The technical challenge of post-explosion forensics has been described as "among the most difficult problems in physics."[18]In practice, significant challenges arise from the many bomb designs that could be used, as well as from the challenge of building a comprehensive "library" with samples from all the world's uranium mines, centrifuges, reactors, and related sites. These challenges make it daunting to determine with a high degree of confidence the origin of nuclear material through physical forensics.[19] As a result, some analysts conclude that nuclear attribution currently provides little deterrent value for countries that might consider diverting nuclear weapons or materials to terrorists.[20]

Other pessimistic analyses highlight an important conundrum limiting the ability of nuclear forensics to deter attack: deterrence would be bolstered if the United States made more of its nuclear forensic capabilities public, but greater transparency would give terrorists and their potential sponsors' greater knowledge of weaknesses. In sum, pessimism about post-explosion attribution abounds. If one cannot pinpoint those states responsible for the materials used in a terrorist nuclear attack, the ability to deter those states by threatening nuclear retaliation is greatly weakened. The future sounds dire—but are these threats overblown?

Empirical Evidence from Terrorist Attacks

There have been no nuclear terror attacks, so it is impossible to directly test the proposition that terrorists could conduct such attacks and remain anonymous. In the past few decades, however, there have been thousands of conventional terrorist incidents. It is thus possible to explore rates of attribution after those incidents and seek patterns in the data that might shed light on the prospects for attributing nuclear terrorism.[21] To explore the history of terrorist attribution, we use the Global Terrorism Database (GTD), a widely referenced dataset compiled by the National Consortium for the Study of Terrorism and Responses to Terrorism, which includes incidents dating back to 1970.[22] The version employed here ends in 2008 and includes more than 87,000 terrorist events. We use a subset of the GTD data that includes 18,328 terrorist incidents that occurred from 1998 to 2008.[23]

411

Figure 1. Terrorist Incidents and Rate of Attribution by Number of Fatalities

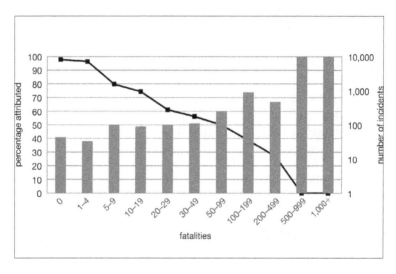

We rely on this portion of the data because GTD first started recording whether terror groups claimed responsibility for an attack in 1998, an important consideration in assessing the data on attribution rates.[24] Figure shows the number of terror incidents that occurred from 1998 to 2008, and the rate of attribution, organized by the number of fatalities. The solid line, corresponding to the logarithmic scale along the right y-axis, indicates the number of terrorist incidents for each level of fatalities.[25] The columns, corresponding to the lefty-axis, reveal the rate of attribution per fatality. The data in figure-1 yield two key findings. First, of the 18,328 attacks conducted from 1998 to 2008, GTD researchers identified the attacker 42 percent of the time. That estimate of the "attribution rate," however, implies greater precision than is warranted, because the researchers who coded the data did not have all the information then or currently available to intelligence and law enforcement agencies.

Therefore, some cases that the researchers coded as "unattributed" may, in fact, have been attributed; and on the other hand, some of the perpetrators identified in the GTD data set may have been incorrectly accused. Despite the possibility of errors in both

412

directions, the data suggest that the perpetrators of terror attacks are identified slightly less than half the time. The implication of a 40–45 percent attribution rate is subject to competing interpretations. On the one hand, states that seek to retaliate after terrorist attacks may desire a much higher rate of attribution. On the other hand, from the perspective of a potential perpetrator, knowing that a covert nuclear terror attack has only about a 60 percent chance of remaining anonymous should be sobering.

The second principal finding reflected in figure-1 is that the rate of attribution is strongly tied to the number of fatalities caused by the attack. Mostterror attacks kill relatively few people? In fact, most of the incidents in the sample caused 0 to 4 deaths; and only 40 percent of those were attributed by GTD to the perpetrator. But as fatalities increase, so does the rate of attribution. Of the 49 attacks that killed more than 100 people, the guilty party was identified 73 percent of the time. Based on these data, a terror group contemplating a mass casualty attack should not expect to remain anonymous. While figure 1 reveals a link between the level of fatalities and the likelihood of attribution, most of the underlying data are derived from events unlike the kind of incident that drives U.S. fears about proliferation and terrorism: an anonymous nuclear terror strike on the United States or a U.S. ally.

The 18,000-plus cases in the dataset are mostly failed attacks, in foreign lands, against target countries with less-capable intelligence agencies than those of the United States and many key U.S. allies. To shed more light on the prospect of attributing nuclear terror strikes on the United States or a key U.S. ally, we focused on a narrower subset of the GTD data composed of attacks against the United States or its principal allies.[26] We also restricted the analysis to attacks on those states' home territory—thereby excluding incidents such as roadside bombings against military convoys in distant lands. By focusing on attacks on the home soil of these countries, we created a sample of 2,089 cases that provides greater leverage for evaluating whether the United States or a close ally could be struck anonymously.

Figure 2 compares the attribution rates for attacks against the United States and U.S. allies to attacks on the rest of the world. Two major observations emerge from the data. First, across all fatality levels, the United States and its allies substantially outperform the "average" country in attributing terrorist incidents. Second, the rate of attribution for the United States and its allies increases as a function of fatalities—as do the aggregate data in figure 1, but more steeply and reaching higher levels. Specifically, the United States and its allies suffered thirty-seven homeland attacks that killed ten or more people and identified the perpetrators in thirty-six of those cases (97 percent). One should not infer from this that the United States and U.S. allies are the best at attributing attacks—some other countries (e.g., Russia) also have high attribution rates.

Figure 2. Attribution Rates by Number of Fatalities: "U.S. and Allies" and All Others

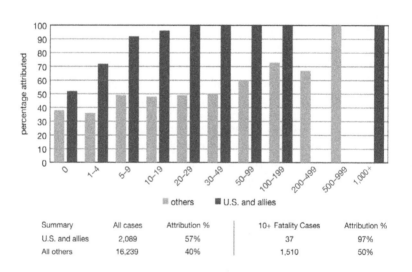

Summary	All cases	Attribution %	10+ Fatality Cases	Attribution %
U.S. and allies	2,089	57%	37	97%
All others	16,239	40%	1,510	50%

The claim is merely that when terrorists kill even a moderate number of Americans or citizens of U.S. allies on their home soil, the perpetrators are almost always identified. The data presented in figures 1 and 2 include cases in which terror groups claim responsibility for their attacks and those in which they do not. Even the cases in which the guilty terror group takes responsibility should be considered "successful attribution," because successful attacks often induce multiple groups to take credit—requiring the victim to evaluate the competing claims and also look for possible culprits among those who have not taken credit. Furthermore, in some cases the attacks were attributed before the claims of responsibility were issued (for example, the September 11 attacks were attributed to al-Qaida before the group claimed responsibility). For both of those reasons, removing the "claimed" cases from the dataset may exclude many cases of successful attribution.

Nevertheless, figure 3 displays data on the subset of cases in which the guilty party never claimed credit for the attack. As the figure reveals, the unclaimed cases look similar to the claimed ones: the likelihood of attribution increases with the number of fatalities, especially for attacks on the "U.S. and allies." Furthermore, even when incidents produced only moderate fatalities (5-plus people killed), the United States and its allies identified the perpetrators 83 percent of the time—a rate that should chasten those who might pass nuclear weapons to terrorists. Taken together, the data on conventional terrorism suggest that nuclear attacks—especially those that target countries with sophisticated intelligence agencies—would not remain anonymous for long. In fact, both because of its shocking nature and because of fears of an additional follow-up nuclear terror attack, any instance of nuclear terror would trigger an unprecedented global investigation. The data in this section, therefore,likely understate the probability of attribution. For a state leader contemplating giving a nuclear weapon to terrorists, the implication is clear: your proxy will very likely be identified.

Linking Terrorists to Their Sponsors

The data presented above reveal that devastating attacks are usually attributed to the responsible terrorist organization. But to deter states from passing nuclear weapons or materials to terrorists, one must also be able to connect the terrorists to their state sponsor. How difficult would it be to do this? Passing nuclear weapons or material to a terrorist group under any circumstances would be a

415

remarkably risky act. A leader who sponsored nuclear terrorism would be wagering his life, the lives of family members, his regime, and his country's fate on the hope that the operation would remain anonymous. If the terror group used the weapon against a different enemy, or revealed the source of the weapon, or if the terror group's operatives or senior leadership were penetrated by foreign intelligence, the consequences could be catastrophic for the sponsor.

Figure 3. Attribution after Unclaimed Attacks

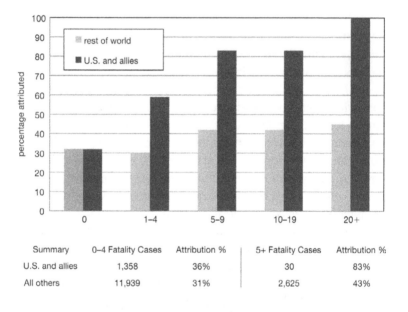

Summary	0–4 Fatality Cases	Attribution %	5+ Fatality Cases	Attribution %
U.S. and allies	1,358	36%	30	83%
All others	11,939	31%	2,625	43%

Given the enormous risks involved, it is difficult to imagine a state's leaders placing so much faith in a terrorist organization unless they already had a long-running, close, and trusting relationship with that group, and unless that group had repeatedly demonstrated its reliability, competence, and ability to maintain secrecy. Furthermore, leaders considering giving nuclear weapons to terror groups would need to find a group with the demonstrated capability to conduct complex operations across international borders.[27] Many violent nonstate groups can plant roadside bombs or conduct small-scale ambushes against unsuspecting targets, but those relatively simple attacks do not imply an ability to conduct complex international operations involving training, travel, visas, finances, and secure communications.[28]

In short, both the complexities of the mission and the need for unwavering trust mean that a state seeking to orchestrate a nuclear attack by proxy would be limited to collaborations with well-established terrorist organizations with which it has existing relationships, simplifying the task of connecting terrorist perpetrators to their state sponsors. To assess the difficulty of connecting terrorists to their sponsors, we compiled a list of terror organizations—focusing on those with close relationships to one or more countries. We began with the U.S. State Department's list of foreign terrorist organizations (FTOs), which we then adjusted, as described below, to account for potential omissions.[29] The adjustments generally involved adding state-sponsored terror groups to the State Department's list, which, by itself, would make it harder to establish our claim that victims could trace attacks from guilty terrorists to their sponsors. According to the State Department, there are fifty-one FTOs, only nine of which have state sponsors.[30] Furthermore, according to the State Department, only four countries actively sponsor terror groups: Cuba, Iran, Libya, and Syria.[31]

Table 1: State-Sponsored Foreign Terrorist Organizations (FTOs)

	Syria	Iran	Libya	Paki-stan	Ven-ezuela	Cuba
Popular Front for the Liberation of Palestine	✔					
AbuNidal Organization	✔	✔	✔			
Hamas	✔	✔				
Hezbollah	✔	✔				
Palestinian Islamic Jihad	✔	✔				

	Syria	Iran	Libya	Paki-stan	Ven-ezuela	Cuba
Popular Front for the Liberation of Palestine— General Command	✔	✔				
Al-Aqsa Martyrs Brigade		✔				
Kata'ib Hezbollah		✔				
Al-Qaida		✔				
Haqqani Network				✔		
Indian Mujahideen				✔		
Jaish-e-Mohammed				✔		
Lashkar-e-Tayiban				✔		
National Liberation Army					✔	
Revolutionary Armed Forces of Colombia					✔	✔

NOTE: *Shading indicates the only FTOs that have multiple sponsors. Pakistan is the only sponsor of terrorism that has bomb quantities of fissile material. No FTO has multiple nuclearcapable sponsors, which would remain true even if Iran acquires nuclear weapons.*

We made three significant adjustments to this list. Some experts argue that the State Department understates Pakistan's and Venezuela's roles in supporting various FTOs, so we added four FTOs that are alleged to have close ties to Pakistan and two that are often linked to Venezuela.[32] Furthermore, several terror experts note that al-Qaida has meaningful ties with Iran, even if their relationship is plagued by substantial distrust.[33] (For example, Iran has held key al-Qaida members and their families hostage, perhaps in order to deter al-Qaida from attacking Iran or to gain release of Iranian hostages held by the organization.[34] But because ties between the state and the group exist, we include al-Qaida on our list.) We are thus left with fifteen terror groups and six states that sponsor terrorism.[35]

Table 1 appears to present a daunting list of FTOs and states, but the data show that tracing an attack from a terror group to its sponsor would be relatively simple. First, nearly all of the terror groups listed have only one or two sponsors: nine FTOs have a single sponsor; five have two sponsors; and only one—the Abu Nidal Organization—has three (and it might soon have only a single sponsor).36 Furthermore, only one of the sponsors has nuclear weapons or bomb quantities of fissile material (Pakistan). If Pakistan were to consider giving a weapon to terrorists, it would not turn to Hezbollah or Hamas, with which it has weak connections. Nor, for the same reason, would Iran give nuclear weapons or material to Jaish-e-Mohammed.

The implication is clear: if a terrorist group is identified in a nuclear attack, the list of possible sponsors will be short. In almost every conceivable case, a single nuclear-armed suspect will stand out. Finally, table 1 does not capture the momentous changes under way in the Middle East. It is unclear whether post-Qaddafi Libya will continue to sponsor terrorism or whether Syria (currently enmeshed in civil war) will remain a sponsor for long. If those two states were to cease supporting FTOs, then no FTO would have more than a single sponsor—making it simple to trace an attack from an identified group to the country that supplied it. This discussion highlights the fundamental conundrum for a country seeking to sponsor nuclear terror: given the incredible risks, it must collaborate with a group that it trusts completely. At the same time, it must choose a terror partner with whom it has weak (and hence untraceable) ties. These two goals are fundamentally contradictory. Only a terrorist group with a long association and deep ties (and a record of effective operations) could be trusted with a nuclear weapon; such a group, however, would be unlikely to stay below the radar of Western intelligence agencies and hide those close ties.

Counterarguments

Critics of our analysis might offer several counterarguments. First, the problem of "loose nukes" might give state sponsors of nuclear terrorism an opportunity for avoiding responsibility for their actions. Second, one might discount empirical evidence about the attribution rate of conventional terror attacks because attributing a nuclear attack would be different—and harder—than attributing an act of conventional terrorism. Third, one might argue that some states will still be tempted to resort to nuclear attack by proxy because the threat of retaliation by the victim would lack credibility given the inherent uncertainty that would persist even in a case of so-called successful attribution.

Counterargument #1: Capitalizing on "loose nukes"

In the wake of a nuclear detonation, investigators would need to consider the possibility that the nuclear device or fissile materials were obtained without the consent of any state. The attack might not have resulted from a state's attack-by-proxy strategy, but rather from the problem of "loose nukes"— poorly secured nuclear weapons or materials falling into the wrong hands through illicit means. Knowing that a victim would need to at least consider the possibility of nuclear theft, a state sponsor might hope to succeed with its nuclear handoff under one of two logics. First, a state might give nuclear weapons or materials to a terrorist organization with full awareness that it would be identified as the source, but then try to avoid responsibility by claiming that the weapons or materials had been stolen from its stockpiles. Second, a state might give nuclear weapons or materials to a terrorist organization and try to avoid responsibility by claiming that the weapons or materials were stolen from a different foreign stockpile.

The first strategy—giving nuclear weapons to terrorists and then pleading guilty to the lesser charge of maintaining inadequate stockpile security—is highly dubious. Any state rational enough, to seek to avoid retaliation for a nuclear attack would recognize the incredible risk that this strategy entails. In the wake of an act of nuclear terrorism, facing an enraged and vindictive victim, would the state sponsor step forward to admit that its weapons or materials were used to attack a staunch enemy, with the hope that the victim would believe a story about theft and grant clemency on those grounds? If that logic does not appear implausible enough, recall that no state would be likely to give its nuclear weapons or materials to a terrorist organization with which it did not have a long record of cooperation and trust. Thus, a state sponsor acknowledging that it was the source of materials used in a nuclear attack would be doing so in light of its enemies' knowledge that the terrorists who allegedly stole the materials happened to have been its close collaborators in prior acts of terrorism. This strategy would be nearly as suicidal as launching a direct nuclear attack.[37]

The second strategy—giving nuclear weapons to terrorists, and then hiding behind the possibility that they were stolen from some unspecified insecure foreign source—deserves greater scrutiny. The list of potential global sources of fissile material seems long. Nine countries possess nuclear weapons, and eleven more have enough fissile material to fashion a crude fission device.[38] In 2011 the world's stockpile of highly enriched uranium (HEU), the fissile material most likely to be sought by terrorists,[39] was about 1.3 million kilograms, meaning that the material needed for a single crude weapon could be found within the rounding error of the rounding error of global stocks. Perhaps, therefore, nearly all twenty countries with sufficient stocks of fissile material would need to join the lineup of suspects after a terrorist nuclear attack, not as possible sponsors but as potential victims of theft. And if enough fissile material to make a nuclear weapon could be purloined from any of these countries, then perhaps the victim would be unable to rule out all possible sources and thus be unable to punish the real culprit.

This gloomy picture overstates the difficulty of determining the source of stolen material after a nuclear terrorist attack. In the wake of a detonation, the possibility of stolen fissile material complicates the task of attribution—but only marginally. At the end of the Cold War, several countries—particularly in the former Soviet Union—confronted major nuclear security problems, but great progress has been made since then.[40] Although no country has perfect nuclear security, today the greatest concerns surround just five countries: Belarus, Japan, Pakistan, Russia, and South Africa.[41]

In addition, not all of those states are equally worrisome as potential sources of nuclear theft. Substantial concerns exist about the security of fissile materials in Pakistan and Russia (the latter if simply because of the large size of its stockpile), but Belarus, Japan, and South Africa would likely be quickly and easily ruled out as the source of stolen fissile material. Belarus has a relatively small stockpile of fissile material—approximately 100 kilograms of HEU[42]—so in the wake of a nuclear terrorist attack, it would be easy for Belarus to show that its stockpile remained intact.[43] Similarly, Japan (one of the United States' closest allies) and South Africa would be keen to allow the United States to verify the integrity of their full stocks of materials. (In the wake of a nuclear terror attack, a lack of full cooperation in showing all materials accounted for would be highly revealing.) Iran is not believed to have any weapons-usable nuclear material to steal,[44] although that could change. In short, a nuclear handoff strategy disguised as a loose nukes problem would be very precarious.[45]

Counterargument #2: conventional versus nuclear attribution

The evidence presented above shows that the perpetrators of terror attacks against the United States or its allies in which ten or more people are killed on home territory are almost always identified. But these data are based solely on conventional terror attacks. Might acts of nuclear terror be harder to attribute than their conventional cousins? With no actual cases of nuclear terrorism to examine, it is impossible to know for sure how the challenges of attribution after a nuclear attack would compare to the difficult police and intelligence work that led to attribution in the thousands of cases of conventional terrorism. Logic suggests at least one reason why it might be harder to identify the perpetrators of nuclear terrorism, but many other factors suggest that nuclear attribution would be easier than solving conventional incidents of terrorism. Taken together, these arguments suggest that the data presented above may well understate the actual likelihood of nuclear attribution.

Identifying the perpetrators of a nuclear terror attack, as opposed to a conventional terror incident, would be harder because a nuclear detonation would destroy much of the evidence near the site of the attack. In the aftermath of a conventional bombing, investigators check near by security cameras for images of the attackers, sift through the debris to recover physical evidence, and interview witnesses. This sort of evidence has proved useful in several terror investigations. For instance, investigators found the vehicle identification number (VIN) from the trucks used to bomb the World Trade Centre in 1993 and to destroy the Alfred P. Murrah Federal Building in Oklahoma City in 1995.[46] Anu clear detonation, however, would leave little (if any) of such evidence.

Although investigators always prefer to have physical evidence from the scene of a bombing, in high-profile investigations such evidence is used in conjunction with vast quantities of other data: for example, information about the activities of terror groups already under surveillance before the attack; intercepted cellphone and internet communications; reports from agents embedded with known terror groups; and similar types of information shared by friendly governments. In fact, while the VIN number was useful in solving the 1993 World Trade Centre attack, it was far less important in the Oklahoma City bombing investigation, because the key suspect was in custody before the on-site evidence was gathered. Nevertheless, the loss of evidence from the attack site would complicate the attribution of a nuclear terror attack relative to a conventional terror incident.

There are at least five reasons; however, to expect that attributing a nuclear terrorist attack would be easier than attributing a conventional terrorist attack. First, no terrorism investigation in history has had the resources that would be deployed to investigating the source of a nuclear terror attack—particularly one against the United States or a U.S. ally. Rapidly attributing the attack would be critical, not merely as a first step toward satisfying the rage of the victims but, more importantly, to determine whether additional nuclear attacks were imminent. The victim would use every resource at its disposal— money, threats, and forces—to rapidly identify the source of the attack.[47] If necessary, any investigation would go on for a long time; it would never "blow over" from the victim's standpoint. The second reason why attributing a nuclear terror attack would be easier than attributing a conventional terrorist attack is the level of international assistance the victim would likely receive from allies, neutrals, and even adversaries.

An attack on the United States, for example, would likely trigger unprecedented intelligence cooperation from its allies, if for no other reason than the fear that subsequent attacks might target them. Perhaps more important, even adversaries of the United States—particularly those with access to fissile materials—would have enormous incentives to quickly demonstrate their innocence. To avoid being accused of sponsoring or supporting the attack, and thus to avoid the wrath of the United States, these countries would likely go to great lengths to demonstrate that their weapons were accounted for, that their fissile materials had different isotopic properties than the type used in the attack, and that they were sharing any information they had on the attack. The cooperation that the United States received from Iran and Pakistan in the wake of the September 11 attacks illustrates how potential adversaries may be motivated to help in the aftermath of an attack and stay off the target list for retaliation.[48] The pressure to cooperate after an anonymous nuclear detonation on U.S. soil would be many times greater.[49]

Third, the strong positive relationship between the number of fatalities stemming from an attack and the rate of attribution (as depicted in figures 1 to 3 above) suggests that the probability of attribution after a nuclear attack—with its enormous casualties—should be even higher. The 97 percent attribution rate for attacks that killed ten or more people on U.S. soil or that of its allies is based on a set of attacks that were pinpricks compared to nuclear terrorism. The data in those figures suggest that our conclusions understate the actual likelihood of nuclear attribution. Fourth, the challenge of attribution after a terrorist nuclear attack should be easier than after a conventional terrorist attack, because the investigation would begin with a highly restricted suspect list. In the case of a conventional terror attack against the United States or an ally, one might begin the investigation at the broadest level with the U.S. Department of State's list of fifty-one foreign terrorist organizations. In the case of a nuclear terror attack, only fifteen of these FTOs have state sponsors—and only one sponsors

(Pakistan) have either nuclear weapons or fissile materials. (If Iran acquires nuclear weapons, that number will grow to two, but there is no overlap between the terror groups that Pakistan supports and those that Iran assists.)

Finally, any operation to detonate a nuclear weapon would involve complex planning and coordination—securing the weapon, learning to use it, planning the time and location of detonation, moving the weapon to the target, and conducting the attack. Even if only a small cadre of operatives knew the nuclear nature of the attack, the planning of a spectacular operation would be hard to keep secrets.[50] For example, six months prior to the September 11 attacks, Western intelligence detected numerous indications that al-Qaeda was planning a major attack. The intelligence was not specific enough—or the agencies were not nimble enough—to prevent the operation, but the indicators were "blinking red" for months, directing U.S. attention to al-Qaida as soon as the attacks began.[51]

Counterargument #3: uncertainty and failed deterrence

Skeptics of our confidence in the feasibility of post-nuclear attack attribution might emphasize the role of uncertainty in constraining the response of the victim. Attribution, after all, is not a binary outcome but a matter of probabilities. Each of the cases of "successful attribution" in the data we used rejects a consensus among GTD researchers that a particular group carried out an attack—but there are few cases in which the list of the guilty parties is certain. Without such certainty, a victim of nuclear terrorism would arguably be constrained in its response against a suspected sponsor. Believing this, a state comparing the option of a direct nuclear attack to sponsorship of a terrorist strike might prefer the latter, counting on residual attribution uncertainty to dampen the response. There are two problems with this counterargument.

First, while attribution uncertainty might restrain a state from responding to an act of nuclear terror with a major nuclear retaliatory strike, that option is not the only devastating response available to a country such as the United States or one of its allies.

Indeed, regardless of the level of attribution certainty, a nuclear strike might not be the preferred response. For example, in the wake of a nuclear terror attack against the United States thought to be sponsored by Pakistan, Iran, or North Korea, U.S. leaders might not feel compelled to determine those countries' guilt "beyond a reasonable doubt" or to narrow down the suspect list further; Washington might simply decide that the era in which "rogue states" possessed nuclear weapons must end, and threaten to conquer any country that refused to disarm or that was less than forthcoming about the terror attack.[52]

Second, this counterargument would be unlikely to carry much weight with a leader contemplating nuclear attack by proxy. A leader tempted to attack because of the prospect of residual attribution uncertainty and the hope that such uncertainty would restrain his victim from lashing out in retaliation would need enormous confidence in the humaneness of his enemy, even at a time when that enemy would be boiling over with rage. For example, could one really imagine an Iranian aide convincing the supreme leader that if Iran gave a nuclear bomb to Hezbollah, knowing that Israel would strongly suspect Iran as the source, Israel's leaders would be too restrained by their deep humanity and lingering doubts about sponsorship to retaliate harshly against Tehran?

In fact, the U.S. response to the September 11 attacks, including the invasions of Afghanistan and Iraq, indicates a willingness to retaliate strongly against those directly culpable (al-Qaida), their associates (the Taliban), and others simply deemed to be troublemakers in the neighborhood (Iraq). There was debate in the United States over the strategic wisdom of invading Iraq, but none of Saddam Hussein's crimes—either known, suspected, or fabricated— were held to an evidentiary standard even close to certainty.[53] States that consider giving nuclear weapons to terrorists cannot be certain how the victim will react, but basing one's hope for survival on a victim's reluctance to act on partial evidence of culpability would be a tremendous gamble.

A nuclear terror strike would have momentous consequences. In the case of an attack on the United States, such a strike would draw the full investigative, diplomatic, and military might of the world's only superpower. In that environment, the incentives for allies, neutrals, and adversaries to cooperate would be immense. Therefore, the data offered in figures 1 to 3 (which show attribution rates after attacks that are, by comparison to a nuclear event, mere pinpricks) probably greatly underestimate the odds of attribution. Uncertainties about the full list of possible accomplices might endure, but the notion that a victim of a nuclear terrorist attack would be paralyzed by those uncertainties is far-fetched.

Conclusion

President Obama has identified nuclear terrorism as "the single biggest threat to U.S. security," describing it as "something that could change the security landscape of this country and around the world for years to come."[54] The prospect of an adversary state covertly giving a nuclear weapon or nuclear materials to a terrorist organization has been the animating force in U.S. grand strategy for more than a decade. The scenario was used to justify the invasion of Iraq and toppling of the Iraqi regime in 2003; and in 2012 and 2013, proponents of a preventive military strike on Iran's nuclear facilities frequently argued that such attacks are necessary to eliminate the possibility of Iran trying a nuclear attack by proxy against Israel or the United States. We demonstrate here that such fears are overblown. The rationale for state sponsorship of nuclear terrorism lacks sound deductive logic and is empirically unsupported by the most relevant available evidence.

The United States and its allies should be able to deter nuclear-armed states from passing their weapons to terrorists, because a terrorist nuclear strike would not remain anonymous for long and would soon be traced back to the originating state. This conclusion is based on two empirical findings. First, among the relevant past cases of conventional terrorist attacks—those targeting the homelands of powerful states and causing significant casualties—almost all were successfully attributed to the perpetrating terrorist organization. Second, linking the attributed terrorist organization to a state sponsor would not be difficult. Few foreign terrorist organizations have state sponsors; those that do typically have only one; and only one suspected state sponsor of terrorism (Pakistan) has nuclear weapons or sufficient stockpiles of nuclear materials.

Furthermore, potential sponsors of nuclear terror face a wicked dilemma: to maintain distance by passing the weapon to a terrorist group they do not know well or trust, or to maintain control by giving it to a group they have cooperated with repeatedly. The former strategy is mind-bogglingly dangerous; the latter option makes attribution from terror group to sponsor simple. Our findings have two important policy implications. First, the fear of nuclear attack by proxy by itself does not justify costly military steps to prevent nuclear proliferation. Nuclear proliferation may pose a variety of other risks, and the appropriate level of U.S. efforts to stop proliferation should depend on the cumulative effect of these risks, but the dangers of a nuclear handoff to terrorists have been overstated. For example, Iranian leaders would have to be crazy or suicidal to think that they could give a nuclear weapon to one of their terrorist collaborators and face no repercussions.

If leaders were that irrational, the bigger problem would be direct nuclear attack without concern for the retaliatory consequences, not the alleged problem of a nuclear handoff. A second implication is that instead of publicly stressing the dangers of nuclear attack by proxy and lamenting the limits of U.S. nuclear forensic capabilities (and thus potentially misleading enemies to overestimate the feasibility of an anonymous attack against America), the United States should be advertising its impressive record of attributing highly lethal terrorist attacks. Understating one's own capabilities is a reasonable strategy for luring an enemy into making an unwise attack, but it is a disastrous policy if the goal is deterrence. The most effective way to deter countries from passing weapons to terrorists is to demonstrate the ease of nuclear attribution and the devastating consequences of such attribution to the sponsoring state.

Keir A. Lieberis Associate Professor in the EdmundA. Walsh School of Foreign Service and the Department of Government at Georgetown University. Daryl G. Press is Associate Professor of Government at Dartmouth College. The authors thank Daniel Byman, Gregory

Koblentz, Jennifer Lind, James Wirtz, and participants in the Institute on Global Conflict and Cooperation Nuclear Security D.C. Policy Series for helpful comments on earlier drafts of this article. They are also grateful to Benjamin Chuchla, Kunal Malkani, and Lauren Weiss for their valuable research assistance. The MIT Press journals division has a long-standing commitment to open access content and makes hundreds of articles freely accessible on its websitemitpressjournals.org. Articles included in MIT Press OA journals are rigorously reviewed and allow immediate access upon publication.MITPJ open access articles are normally published-under-a-Creative-Commons-Attribution-4.0International Licensehttps://creativecommons.org/licenses/by/4.0/ (CC BY 4.0) although some are published under a Creative Commons Attribution 3.0 International License (CC BY 3.0). Articles posted under either a CC BY 3.0 or 4.0 license allow users to share, copy, and redistribute the material in any medium of format, and adapt, remix, transform, and build upon the material for any purpose, even commercially. Reusing under a CC BY license requires that appropriate attribution to the source of the material must be included along with a link to the CC BY license, with any changes made to the original material indicated.Why States Won't Give Nuclear Weapons to Terrorists. Keir A. Lieber and Daryl G. Press. International Security, Vol. 38, No. 1 (Summer 2013), pp. 80–104, doi:10.1162/ISEC_a_00127 © 2013 by the President and Fellows of Harvard College and the Massachusetts Institute of Technology.

Chapter 18

Islamic State and Technology–A Literature Review

Truls Hallberg Tønnessen

Abstract

This article offers an overview of the literature on how the Islamic State has used different technologies, primarily within the fields of drone technology, CBRN and communication technology. The author argues that the primary strength of the Islamic State and terrorist groups in general, is not in the acquisition and use of advanced technology, but the innovative and improvised use of less advanced, but easily accessible, technology. A gap identified in the existing research is the question of priority – why and under what circumstances would a terrorist group allocate some of its (usually) limited resources in order to develop or acquire new technological capabilities?

Keywords: Technology, Terrorism, Islamic State, CBRN, Drones, Internet.

Introduction

The aim of this article is to offer a brief overview of the literature on Islamic State (IS) and technology. The intention is to identify knowledge gaps within the literature and to make some preliminary observations on the Islamic State's use of specific technology. Since it is somewhat difficult to separate the literature on technology and Islamic State from the more general literature on terrorism and technology, this article will, indirectly, also be a presentation of the larger literature on terrorism and technology. However, given the unprecedented scale of the Islamic State's territorial control, financial resources and the number of recruits, the Islamic State has, at least until its recent demise, been at the forefront of technological development among contemporary terrorist groups. In this overview, three fields of technology that have received most attention in the literature-drone technology, communication technology and CBRN – have been singled out. These fields are also some of the fields where the Islamic State has been most innovative. All of these technologies can be used as part of offensive operations.

One main argument made here is that while the general literature on terrorism and technology tends to focus on the most advanced and most lethal scenarios, the primary strength of terrorist groups is their innovative use of less advanced and easily accessible technology. The present study finds that, like most terrorist groups, the Islamic State has used some of this technology mainly for defensive purposes and when the group has used technology offensively, it has done so in a crude, improvised and "low-tech" manner. It is also argued that, although the Islamic State has been innovative in the use of technology and made technological improvements, this is mainly an effect of IS' ability and willingness to exploit new opportunities given by the rapid technological development and by the sheer size of the group. The primary gap in the literature identified in this review is the issue of priority – why and under what circumstances would a terrorist group allocate some of its (usually) limited resources in order to develop or acquire new technological capabilities?

General Observations on the Literature

The literature on terrorism and technology can generally be divided into two categories. On the one hand is what we may refer to as "what if" writings and scenario-oriented literature, looking mainly at which capabilities a non-state actor would require to engage in, for instance, a CBRN attack or in an act of cyber-terrorism, and the probability that a non-state actor would be able to acquire the resources and competence needed.[1] Given the (fortunate) rarity of incidents of CBRN attacks and acts of cyber-terrorism, this literature is often highly technical and theoretical.[2] This literature has at times been criticized for exaggerating the threat and the probability of highly advanced and potentially very lethal attacks[3]

There has also been a tendency in some of this literature to conflate non-state actors with their limited resources with states that have developed highly advanced technology[4] For advanced technological fields, like CBRN and cyber, it is undoubtedly states, and not non-state actors that represent the greatest threat, if they choose to use it offensively. However, it cannot be ruled out that non-state actors could directly or indirectly be given access to advanced technologies and resources by states that, for instance, want to avoid attribution.[5] Thus, a major caveat of this literature review is that it has not looked at the literature on technology and state-sponsored terrorism.

Another type of literature looks at terrorist organisations' motivation to use certain technologies. For instance, some of this literature discusses a non-state actor's motivation and various incentives and disincentives for the use of CBRN.[6] This literature is often more empirical –either based on actual incidents or focusing on statements of intent from terrorist groups or key individuals.[7] However, as this article will illustrate, it is often not enough to look at terrorist groups' stated intent. Intent does not equal capability, certainly not in technologically more advanced fields.

Islamic State and CBRN

There has been no shortage of politicians and security analysts warning that Islamic State (or other terrorist organisations) may use various forms of CBRN weapons, even nuclear weapons, for an attack.[8] And there is no doubt that the motivation to use CBRN weapons indeed is present – in 2014 it was estimated that there have been 50 registered incidents where al-Qaida or its affiliates have attempted to acquire, produce or deploy CBRN weapons during the last two decades.[9] There have also been a handful of incidents in Europe where CBRN materials have been considered in the planning phase of a terrorist attack.[10] However, the low number of actual incidents including CBRN indicates that ambition fortunately has so far exceeded capabilities. Jihadists' lack of competence and lack of development within the field of CBRN has been confirmed by a 2015 study based on the discussions of CBRN weapons and various CBRN "recipes" posted on online jihadist forums.[11]

Symptomatically, terrorist groups have so far primarily used the least advanced form of CBRN – chemical weapons. The University of Maryland's Global Terrorism Database (GTD) has registered 303 incidents of terrorist attacks including chemical weapons worldwide. In comparison, GTD has registered 32 incidents of biological terrorism worldwide, resulting in 9 fatalities, no incidents of nuclear terrorism, and 13 incidents of (attempted) radiological terrorism, resulting in no fatalities.[12] Of the al-Qaida affiliates, it is the Islamic State and its predecessors that have been regarded as the most successful in the development and use of chemical weapons.[13]. Al-Qaida's history of experimenting with, and using, chemical weapons goes back to the 1990s when Abu Musab al-Zarqawi, the Jordanian founder of al-Qaida in Iraq, established a camp for foreign fighters in Herat, Afghanistan.[14] In 2007 the Islamic State of Iraq, as the group was known at the time, was responsible for a series of attacks that combined truck bombs with canisters of chlorine. Many died as a result of the attacks, but apparently not due to the chlorine, but due to the conventional explosion itself.[15]

Following the establishment of the Islamic State in 2014, there was a rapid increase in the group's use of chemical weapons. According to an estimate by IHS Conflict Monitoring, the Islamic State is believed to have been responsible for 71 incidents of chemical attacks between July 2014 and June 2017.[16]

There are also indications that there has been an improvement in the Islamic State's chemical capabilities since 2014. This development was the result of what may be referred to as a chemical weapons program, including some veterans from Saddam Hussein's chemical weapons program.[17] For instance, the Islamic State has been able to manufacture shells filled with chemical agents and successfully delivered them over a greater distance, using mortar grenades. Chlorine was still the most frequently used chemical, but IS has also succeeded in both manufacturing and weaponising mustard gas.[18] This is a worrisome development that should raise some concerns. However, so far few incidents attributed to IS having been reported where the chemicals alone have caused causalities. The impact of the Islamic State's use of chemical weapons has thus far primarily been psychological, not physical.

Taking into account the group's access to substantial financial resources, its vast pool of recruits, its territorial control and the group's long history of experimenting with chemical weapons, it is rather surprising that the group's capabilities did not evolve more than they did. As pointed out by Geoffrey Chapman elsewhere in this Special Issue, what characterizes the Islamic State's use of chemical weapons is the scale of its use, not its technological sophistication.[19] So far, concerns that IS should acquire more weapons-grade and more advanced chemical weapons, such as sarin, from the stock-piles of the Syrian regime appear to have been unfounded. IS has primarily used crude and improvised chemical weapons and most reports point to the Syrian regime as the culprit behind sarin attacks in Syria.[20]

There have also been concerns that IS could succeed in weaponising other forms of CBRN materials than chemicals, such as radiological substances building a radiological dispersal device (RDD) or "dirty bomb". The Islamic State had access to various sources of radioactive material in Iraq, particularly in Mosul's hospitals and university institutes. This has led to concerns that the group could be able to develop an RDD.[21] However, experts have concluded that the radiological material IS had access to had limited utility for constructing a dirty bomb.[22] There have also been concerns voiced that the Islamic State could be able to buy some sort of nuclear device or materials on the black market.[23]

An article published in Islamic State's magazine Dabiq alluded to the fact that IS might be able to use its unprecedented access to financial resources to obtain a nuclear device from Pakistan and smuggle it to the United States and detonate it there. The author of the article admits that this might be a far-fetched scenario, but that the scenario nevertheless would be the "sum of all fears of Western intelligence agencies".[24] In addition, the possibility that a state in possession of nuclear weapons, like, for instance, Pakistan, should willingly sell a nuclear device to a non-state actor has been discredited.[25]

However, an incident in Belgium illustrates the typical "low-tech" and asymmetrical threat that IS, and other terrorist organizations, may represent. Members of the IS-linked attack cell that was responsible for the attacks in Paris November 2015 and in Brussels in March 2016 had been spotted on several hours of video surveillance footage targeting a Belgian nuclear scientist working at a nuclear research centre. One police theory is that the cell planned to abduct him and force him to provide them access to radiological materials.[26] The same cell reportedly also planned mixing certain animal excrements with explosives to construct a primitive "biological weapon."[27] Additionally, a Belgian recruit of Moroccan origin, who used to work at a nuclear power plant before travelling to Syria, illustrates the potential of insider threats.[28]

Islamic State and Drone Technology

The Islamic State has made their most technological progress in the field of drone technology.[29] One of the most comprehensive reports on terrorist groups' use of drones, published in 2016, identifies four groups with discernable "drone programs"–Hizballah, Hamas, Islamic State and Jabhat Fatah al-Sham (formerly known as Jabhat al-Nusra). Tellingly, all four had territorial control to varying degrees and three of them have been involved in the ongoing conflict in Syria.[30] Hizballah and Hamas were pioneers when it came to exploiting the possibilities offered by drone technology, but the rapid development of the drone program of the Islamic State is striking. According to the report, it took approximately seven years from Hizballah demonstrating some interest in drone technology until the successful use of a drone as part of an operation, while the same trajectory took only about one year for the Islamic State.[31] This rapid development is even more striking, knowing that Hizballah received some support from Iran, while the Islamic State did not enjoy such state support.[32] A partial explanation is that the rise of the Islamic State coincided with a rapid development of the availability and commercialisation of drone technology.

The Islamic State primarily used commercially available drones that were modified for military use but also experimented with constructing simple surveillance drones 'in-house'. Conflict Armament Research has identified several IS-drone workshops, for instance in Ramadi and in Mosul, where IS modified and weaponized drones and also manufactured some from scratch.[33]

The Islamic State initially used drones for surveillance and for propaganda purposes, but there has been a rapid increase of weaponised drones. In September and October 2016 it was reported that the Islamic State had managed to weaponise drones by attaching explosives that could be released when the drone hovered over an intended target.[34] In October 2016 two Kurdish Peshmerga soldiers were killed and two French Special Forces badly injured in what has been described as the first confirmed incident causing casualties following a terrorist organization's use of a weaponised drone. This incident also illustrates the unconventional and innovative offensive use of drones by the Islamic State. The drone in question was brought down to a landing without any casualties, but it had been rigged with explosives that blew up when the Kurdish Peshmerga soldiers were inspecting the drone[35.]

There was a rapid increase in reports on the Islamic State's use of weaponised drones after the group announced the establishment of a separate drone unit in January 2017. According to a publication by the IS-affiliated al-Yaqin foundation, the Islamic State's drones succeeded in killing 39 persons and destroying 43 vehicles in February 2017 alone.[36] These numbers are probably exaggerations, but there has been a steady uptick of deadly drone attacks. In September 2017, media reported that a dozen Iraqi soldiers had been killed by Islamic State drones.[37]

This rapid development seems to have been the result of a concentrated effort by IS to develop a drone program. The existence of such a drone program was confirmed by the discovery of the so-called "drone papers" in Mosul in 2016. Most of the documents found were produced in 2015; – these papers indicated that IS had, at least to some extent, developed a streamlined and bureaucratised program for development and weaponisation of drones. Several of the documents pertaining to acquisition of drone parts were signed by the Aviation section (qism al-tayaran) of the group's Committee of Military Manufacturing and Development (Hai'a al-tatwir w al-tasni` al-`askari). The existence of a specific committee for military manufacturing and development illustrates that this was something the group prioritised[38] A 2017 report, based on information obtained from several local sources based in Syria, illustrates the extent of the group's drone program. The report identified separate centers for training, weaponisation, modification and maintenance, as well as the existence of a center for storage and distribution. Each of these centers had its own director, and all were based in Raqqa. The overall leader (or emir) of the Islamic State's drone program was identified to be a Muhammad Islam, a European citizen of Malaysian descent who holds a degree in information technology from a British university.[39]

Although the Islamic State has made rapid improvements in the use and weaponisation of drones, it can be argued that drone technology in itself has worked against the Islamic State since many of its top leaders have been killed by the technologically much more advanced U.S drones. For instance, by March 2016 it was estimated that 90 senior and mid-level IS leaders had been killed by drone strikes.[40] This supports the general observation that technology, especially more advanced technology, often works to the disadvantage rather than the advantage for non-state actors.

In addition, there are a number of anti-drone measures that might reduce the threat from non-state actors' use of drones. For instance, through use of geo-fencing, DJI, the producer of the most popular commercial drones, has prevented its models from flying in parts of IS-controlled areas in northern Syria and Iraq.[41]

The U.S-led Coalition Forces in Iraq have also used several anti-drone tools against the drones of the Islamic State, such as the anti-drone rifle Battelle DroneDefener and one called Dronebuster.[42] This illustrates that although non-state actors start using more advanced technology, their opponents still stay ahead of the curve because states are more capable of rapid technological development than non-state actors are. However, the rapid commercialisation of drone technology has contributed to reducing this gap - a development likely to continue.[43]

Islamic State and the Internet

The literature on Islamic State and the Internet falls mainly in two categories. The first category is literature focusing on how the group has taken advantage of the opportunities provided by the Internet and especially by social media, for instance in the fields of recruitment and dissemination of propaganda.[44] A large part of this literature focuses on the actual content of the propaganda and not on the Islamic State's use of internet technology per se.[45] The second category is of a more technical nature and focuses on the online infrastructure of the Islamic State - such as which platforms they use, how they disseminate their propaganda and how they maintain an online presence despite counter-measures against it.[46]

These two categories also correspond with two different categories in the literature on counter-terrorism online. One type of literature focuses on how to respond and counter the propaganda from the Islamic State, through, for instance, counter-narratives.[47] Another category focuses more on the technical and judicial aspects of preventing the Islamic State and similar groups from using the Internet for propaganda and recruitment purposes.[48]

This is not a new development – the Internet has been central for the propaganda and recruitment strategy of most terrorist groups for a number of years. However, as with the their use of drones, the rise of the Islamic State coincided with a rapid technological advance in the form of the development and popularisation of a vast array of apps and platforms the Islamic State could exploit.[49] Especially important was the popularisation of apps that provided end-to-end encryption, such as Telegram and WhatsApp.[50] The proliferation of encrypted apps has made it easier and safer for members and sympathisers of the Islamic State to communicate with each other and to meet potential recruits online. Especially worrying is the new phenomenon of so-called remote-controlled plots and virtual entrepreneurs grooming and micro-managing potential attackers through various encrypted social media platforms.[51] Encrypted apps have been reportedly used immediately before or during attacks in Europe where handlers abroad communicate with a remotely-controlled operative.[52]

The online community of sympathisers has also contributed to the technological advances of the Islamic State (and similar groups) through posting instruction manuals and how-to-tips online, for instance, on how to increase the range of drones or how to communicate securely.[53] In February 2016 a Telegram channel for "Islamic State Scientists & Engineers" was launched. The channel was only open to those who had pledged allegiance to the Caliph and who had a technical degree such as engineering, aeronautics, physics and biology. The stated intent behind the channel was to gather a group of qualified people who could do research in order to support "the military industry in the Islamic State."[54]

The Islamic State was of course far from the only terrorist group capable to take advantage of the opportunities provided by new communications technology. Yet, as with the Islamic State's attacks with chemical weapons, the group distinguishes itself mainly through the scale and volume of its use of Internet and social media. The extent of IS' territorial control and the sheer number of attacks committed by the group, provided it with a large reservoir of battle footage and pictures that could be turned into slick productions that gained worldwide distribution. Like its predecessor al-Qaida in Iraq, the Islamic State has exploited the new technology to receive worldwide attention by broadcasting brutal executions. Abu Musab al-Zarqawi, regarded by the Islamic State as its historical founder, gained worldwide notoriety in 2004 when he was seen beheading the U.S hostage Nicholas Berg in the first video issued by his group on the Internet. This was years before the rise of social media; the video was released on the jihadi web forum that was the main platform for disseminating jihadi material at the time. The movie did, however, gain attention far beyond the jihadi forums - the search string "Nick Berg" was the second most popular Google search for May 2004, second only to "American Idol".[55]

Islamic State has not only used the Internet to distribute propaganda, but also for more offensive purposes, mainly through its so-called "Cyber Caliphate Army" (jaysh al-khilafa al-iliktruni).[56] However, this "Army" has primarily been engaged in what has been referred to as cyber vandalism and hacktivism. So far the general assessment is that the Islamic State capabilities in the realm of cyber are low and unsophisticated.[57] It has also been claimed that some of the activities of the Cyber Caliphate originated from Russia.[58] Moreover, there have been reports that Islamic State members and/or supporters have used virtual currencies such as Bitcoin, but so far the evidence is mainly anecdotal.[59] The Islamic State has also been accused of using the Internet for raising money, for instance, through fake eBay transactions.[60]

To sum up, the most innovative use of the Internet by the Islamic State is that they have been using encryption not only in order to spread propaganda but also for offensive purposes by remotely directing and coaching operatives immediately before and during ongoing terrorist operations.

Innovation in Zones of Ongoing Armed Conflict

Although both capabilities and intention are crucial factors for estimating the potential technological threat from a non-state actor, the perhaps most important factor is the question of priority. For instance, if the Islamic State and its predecessor have been experimenting to develop and use chemical weapons since 1999, with few enemy casualties, it can hardly be said to have been a "success" from the viewpoint of the terrorists - the more so when compared to the staggering number of casualties these groups have been responsible for through other and less technological advanced modi operandi.

Thus, given that there exists technologically less advanced and less resource-intensive modi operandi that have proven to be more effective in terms of creating deaths and destruction, the question raises: why and under what circumstances would a non-state actor decide to allocate a large amount of its (usually limited) resources to develop more advanced technology? This question is not properly addressed in the literature, but a promising avenue of research that might help to answer such a question is by studying the internal decision-making processes and the internal organisation of terrorist groups. For instance, how do terrorist groups manage their resources?

How does a group that frequently loses resourceful professionals and key leaders secure organisational learning and transfer knowledge within the organisation? How are terrorist groups set up for processes such as innovation, adaption and training?[61] It has been pointed out that due to the lack of sources that there has been a paucity of studies on the internal decision-making of terrorist groups or the background of its recruits.[62] However, due to the increasing availability of internal documents and lists of members from the Islamic State, it is now possible to gain a better insight into the internal processes of IS.[63]

It is beyond the scope of this article to provide in-depth analysis of these questions. This review has, however, illustrated that one favourable condition for non-state actors acquiring and using more advanced technology is territorial control. For instance, all of the insurgent groups with discernable drone programs had territorial control and three out of four were involved in the conflict in Syria. Previous studies of terrorist innovation have also found that territorial control and operating in an armed conflict zone offering frequent possibilities to test innovations often are drivers for technological progress.[64]

In Iraq and Syria, the Islamic State's territorial control has also enabled the group to experiment with less advanced technology in a DIY-way. According to internal documents, the Islamic State had a separate Research and Development Division (Qism al-buhuth w al-tatwir). This division experimented, for instance,

441

with producing remote-control car bombs, a robot operated by a solar-panel that was intended to function as a decoy, an automatic steering system for artillery weapons, etc.[65] Sky News was provided with several hours of unedited videos by a Syrian rebel group, showing documentation of what is referred to as an Islamic State "jihad university" in Raqqa. The video shows how the Islamic State is experimenting with developing a driverless car bomb.[66] The Islamic State has also constructed a fleet of armored cars, with a high DIY improvised "Mad Max" factor.[67] Insurgent groups operating in Syria have also been experimenting with various forms of remotely-controlled and tele-operated weapons.[68]

Conclusion: "Low-Tech Terrorism"?

This review of the Islamic State's use of technology has found that what distinguishes the group's use of technology from other non-state actors is primarily its ability to exploit the opportunities offered by commercial technology development as well as the extent of its use of technology. This is primarily an effect of the unprecedented size of the Islamic State. Another explanation is that the rise of the Islamic State partly coincided with a rapid technological development within the fields of drone and communication technology. In that sense, the Islamic State was uniquely poised to exploit this, given its size and the degree of its territorial control.

Another observation is that terrorist groups, including the Islamic State, mainly use technology for defensive and not offensive operations. As an illustration, a large share of the technological innovation and concern from Islamic State and al-Qaida has been within the field of operational security and how to defend and protect the organisation from the technology used against them. For instance, until recently most of the publications from al-Qaida were concerned with how to protect themselves from U.S. drones rather than focusing on how to use drones themselves.[69] The Islamic State and its supporters online have also spent considerable resources and energy on how to maintain their presence on Twitter and other social media platforms and how to communicate securely, sharing information on digital security and encryption.[70]

This review has illustrated that even in cases when the Islamic State used more advanced technology, such as drones, or attempted to use CBRN weapons, the group has done so in an improvised, crude and DIY manner. Even a terrorist group like the Islamic State, with its unprecedented access to resources, is incomparable in strength to a real state. The group's primary asset is its innovative use of already existing technologies and modi operandi, like booby-trapped drones. This is also supported by previous research that has found that the primary originality and innovation of terrorists has historically been to creatively modify or combine pre-existing and relatively "simple" modi operandi.[71]

This underlines the difficulties for a non-state actor to acquire and use more advanced technology. However, it may also indicate that to acquire advanced technology is not a priority for most terrorist groups. The primary knowledge gap identified by this literature review is precisely the question of prioritisation – why and under what circumstances would a terrorist group decide to use some of its limited resources in order to acquire new technological capabilities? In order to answer this question, it is necessary to gain a more in-depth insight into internal factors such as various groups' internal decision-making and what role technology and innovation plays in the strategic thinking of the groups' leaders.

Finally, what are the implications for use of technology in terrorist attacks in areas outside the conflict theater, e.g. in Europe? While there has been some technological innovation in conflict areas like Iraq and Syria, recent studies of the modus operandi of jihadi terrorism in Europe indicate that terrorists have become less technologically advanced–using relatively "low-tech" means such as knives, firearms and rented vehicles as weapons.[72] This is also something that has been recommended both by the Islamic State and by al-Qaida in their respective online publications.[73] Al-Qaida in the Arabian Peninsula (AQAP) hailed the perpetrator who on 22 March 2017 drove a car into pedestrians on London's Westminster Bridge for employing "the art of the possible" and urged other lone wolves to do the same.[74]

This has led some observers to refer to a trend of "low-tech terrorism" where terrorists "routinely transform everyday tools into low-tech weapons or attack vehicles—whether cars, trucks, scooters, or kitchen knives".[75] This is probably an adaption to the growth of security measures in Europe, but it also illustrates and supports previous studies concluding that terrorists tend to be pragmatic and conservative in terms of their uses of technology and their modus operandi.[76]

In terms of technological innovation, this implies that terrorist groups in the West will primarily use relatively simple, but easily accessible, commercially available technology that could potentially be transformed into a weapon. For instance, one potential scenario is to steer a swarm of drones towards a crowd, using the drone blades themselves to inflict damage on the crowd or to use drones as part of a coordinated attack.[77] In 2017 it was reported that the Islamic State had achieved a swarm-level capacity of drone use.[78] We have also seen that various encrypted apps have enabled handlers based in a conflict area to remotely assist and guide attackers in Europe – something that is likely to continue.

In the immediate future, there are also other technological developments that can be exploited by the Islamic State or other terrorist organizations, like 3D printing. This allows terrorists to produce parts to a drone for instance, or even 3D printed firearms.[79] There have so far not been any incidents of 3D printed firearms among terrorists registered, but there have been instances of 3D printing used by criminals and drug-cartels.[80] In the longer term, the rapid technological development and increasing commercialisation of new technologies may lead to terrorism taking unexpected turns.

About the Author: Truls Hallberg Tønnessen is a Research Fellow at the Norwegian Defence Research Establishment (FFI), specialising in Salafi-jihadi insurgent groups in Iraq and Syria. In 2016, he was a visiting scholar at the Center for Security Studies, Georgetown University. He obtained his PhD in history from the University of Oslo in 2015, with a dissertation on the rise of al-Qaida in Iraq in 2003-2006. This work is licensed under a Creative Commons

Notes to Chapters

Chapter 1

1. The term 'Second Great Game' refers to the first 'Great Game' of the nineteenth century, in which Russia and the UK struggled for strategic dominance in Central Asia.

2. We include trade figures of Kazakhstan, Kyrgyzstan, Uzbekistan and Tajikistan. Turkmenistan is not included due to the lack of reliable trade data. Noteworthy, official trade figures likely underestimate intraregional trade since they do not include the informal 'bazaar trade', which accounts for 20–30% of the total trade volume in Central Asia. The biggest international bazaars are the Dordoi market (Bishkek), Barakholka (Almaty), Kara-Suu (Osh) and Korvon (Dushanbe) (Wang 2014, p. 228).

3. Notably, at a recent peak of oil prices in 2013, Kazakhstan's GDP reached 236 bln, but fell sharply in the coming three years, rising again only in 2017.

4. GDP numbers are taken from the World Bank (data.worldbank.org/data-catalog/GDP-ranking-table) .

5. In autumn 2017, after the construction of the Kazakhstan-China gas pipeline, a 1-year 5 3 bln m3deal with China was put in place. In late 2018, it was extended by 5 years and 10 bln m3(Erubaeva 2018).

6. While the Central Asian states are secular, domestically Islam holds an important place (Spechler 2002). Due to poverty and political marginalisation, the region has become a growing source of foreign fighters, with up to 4000 people joining ISIS (International Crisis Group 2015).

7. Originally, Uzbekistan was a member of the CSTO as well, but it withdrew its membership in 2012.

8. The fifth Central Asian country, Turkmenistan, has followed a very isolationist policy since independence, and it has not joined any regional organisation at all. It is not even a full, but only an associate member of CIS.

9. While in the early 1990s the Russian and Chinese economies were about the same size, the speed of the Chinese economic growth and

the resulting power imbalance raised concerns for Moscow (Kembayev 2018).

10. As of 2017, remittances constituted about one-third of the Kyrgyz and Tajik GDP (data.worldbank.org/indicator/BX.TRF.PWKR. CD.DT).

Springer Nature remains neutral with regard to jurisdictional claims in published maps and institutional affiliations.

References - Chapter 1

1. Acharya A (2005) Do norms and identity matter? Community and power in Southeast Asia's regional order. Pac Rev 18, 95–118CrossRefGoogle Scholar

2. Allison R (2004) Regionalism, regional structures and security management in Central Asia. Int Aff 80, 463–483Google Scholar

3. Allison R (2008) Virtual regionalism, regional structures and regime security in Central Asia. Cent Asian Surv 27, 185–202CrossRefGoogle Scholar

4. Bobokulov I (2006) Central Asia: is there an alternative to regional integration? Cent Asian Surv 25, 75–91CrossRefGoogle Scholar

5. Bohr A (2004) Regionalism in Central Asia: new geopolitics, old regional order. Int Aff 80, 485–502CrossRefGoogle Scholar

6. British Petroleum (BP) (2018) BP statistical review of world energy (www.bp.com/content/dam/bp/en/corporate/pdf/energy-economics/statistical-review/bp-stats-review-2018-full-report.pdf)

7. Collins K (2009) Economic and security regionalism among patrimonial authoritarian regimes: the case of Central Asia. Eur Asia Stud 61, 249–281CrossRefGoogle Scholar

8. Collins N, Bekenova K (2017) Fuelling the new great game: Kazakhstan, energy policy and the EU. Asia Europe Journal 15, 1–20CrossRefGoogle Scholar

9. Cooley A (2012) Great games, local rules: the new great power contest in Central Asia. University Press, OxfordCrossRefGoogle Scholar

10. Dave B, Kobayashi Y (2018) China's silk road Economic Belt initiative in Central Asia: economic and security implications. Asia Europe Journal 16, 267–281CrossRefGoogle Scholar

11. Doing Business (2019) Economy profile Kazakhstan. World Bank (www.doingbusiness.org/content/dam/doingBusiness/country/k/kazakhstan/KAZ.pdf). 21 Jan 2019

12. Erubaeva G (2018) Kazakhstan expands gas exports to China. Caspian News 30 November 2018 (caspiannews.com/news-detail/kazakhstan-expands-gas-exports-to-china-2018-11-29-42). 21 Jan 2019

13. Eurasian Economic Commission (2017) China and the EAEU declared the conclusion of negotiations on the agreement on trade and economic cooperation (www.eurasiancommission.org/en/nae/news/Pages/2-10-2017-5.aspx). 21 Jan 2019

14. Eurasian Review (2012) Kazakhstan energy profile: second largest oil reserves among former Soviet Republics (www.eurasiareview.com/06052017-kazakhstan-energy-profile-second-largest-oil-reserves-among-former-soviet-republics-analysis-2). 21 Jan 2019

15. Frankopan P (2016) The silk roads: a new history of the world. Knopf, New YorkGoogle Scholar

16. Gabuev A (2017) Bigger, not better: Russia makes the SCO a useless Club. Carnegie Moscow Center, MoscowGoogle Scholar

17. Gleason G (2001) Inter-state cooperation in Central Asia from the CIS to the Shanghai forum. Eur Asia Stud 53, 1077–1095CrossRefGoogle Scholar

18. Guangcheng X (2015) The strategic interests of China and Russia in Central Asia. In: Denoon D (ed) China, the United States and the future of Central Asia. New York University Press, New York-Google Scholar

19. Guliev I, Mekhdiev E (2017) The role of fuel and energy sector in the Eurasian economic community integration process. Int J Energy Econ Policy 7, 72–75Google Scholar

20. Haas EB (1961) International integration: the European and the universal process. Int Organ 15, 266–292CrossRefGoogle Scholar

21. Haftel YZ (2007) Designing for peace: regional integration arrangements, institutional variation, and militarized interstate disputes. Int Organ 61, 217–237CrossRefGoogle Scholar

22. Holzinger K (2003) Common goods, matrix games and institutional response. Eur J Int Relat 9, 173–212CrossRefGoogle Scholar

23. Hurley J, Morris S, Portelance G (2018) Examining the debt implications of the belt and road initiative from the policy perspective. Center for Global Development Policy Paper 121 (www.cgdev.org/sites/default/files/examining-debt-implications-belt-and-road-initiative-policy-perspective.pdf). 21 Jan 2019

24. IMF (International Monetary Fund) (2016) Regional Economic Outlook: Caucasus and Central Asia (www.imf.org/~/media/Files/Publications/REO/MCD-CCA/2016/October/cca1016.ashx). 21 Jan 2019

25. International Crisis Group (2015) Syria calling: radicalisation in Central Asia. Europe and Central Asia Briefing 72 (www.crisisgroup.org/europe-central-asia/central-asia/syria-calling-radicalisation-central-asia). 21 Jan 2019

26. International Crisis Group (2017) Central Asia's silk road rivalries. Europe and Central Asia Report 245 (www.crisisgroup.org/europe-central-asia/central-asia/245-central-asias-silk-road-rivalries). 21 Jan 2019

27. Jenish N (2015) Walls and windmills: economic development in Central Asia. In: Denoon D (ed) China, the United States and the future of Central Asia. New York University Press, New York, 20–74Google Scholar

28. Jonson L (2001) Russia and Central Asia. In: Allison R (ed) Central Asian security. Brookings Institution, Washington, 95–126Google Scholar

29. Kassenova N (2012) Kazakhstan and Eurasian economic integration: quick start, mixed results and uncertain future. RussieNei Reports 14. InstitutFrancais des Relations Internationales (IFRI), ParisGoogle Scholar

30. Kembayev Z (2018) Implementing the silk road Economic Belt: from the Shanghai cooperation organisation to the silk road union? Asia Europe Journal 16, 37–50CrossRefGoogle Scholar

31. Konopelko A (2018) Eurasian economic union: a challenge for EU policy towards Kazakhstan. Asia Europe Journal 16, 1–17CrossRefGoogle Scholar

32. Krapohl S (2015) Financial crises as catalysts for regional cooperation? Chances and obstacles for financial integration in ASEAN+3, MERCOSUR and the Eurozone. Contemp Polit 21, 161–178CrossRefGoogle Scholar

33. Krapohl S (2017a) Two logics of regional integration and the games regional actors play. In: Krapohl S (ed) Regional integration in the global south: the external influence on economic cooperation in ASEAN, MERCOSUR and SADC. Palgrave, Basingstoke, 33–62CrossRefGoogle Scholar

34. Krapohl S (2017b) ASEAN: extra-regional cooperation triggers regional integration. In: Krapohl S (ed) Regional integration in the global south: the external influence on economic cooperation in ASEAN, MERCOSUR and SADC. Palgrave, Basingstoke, 115–146CrossRefGoogle Scholar

35. Krapohl S, Fink S (2013) Different paths of regional integration: trade networks and regional institution-building in Europe, Southeast Asia and Southern Africa. J Common Mark Stud 51, 472–488Google Scholar

36. Krapohl S, Meissner KL, Muntschick J (2014) Regional powers as leaders or rambos of regional integration? Unilateral actions of Brazil and South Africa and their negative effects on MERCOSUR and SADC. J Common Mark Stud 52, 879–895Google Scholar

37. Krickovic A, Bratersky M (2016) Benevolent hegemon, neighborhood bully, or regional security provider? Russia's efforts to promote regional integration after the 2013–2014 Ukraine crisis. Eurasian Geogr Econ 57, 180–202CrossRefGoogle Scholar

38. Kubicek Paul (1997): 'Regionalism, nationalism and Realpolitik in Central Asia', in: Europe-Asia Studies, 49:4, 637–655Google Scholar

39. Kuzmina.N.(2010) EkonomicheskiyeinteresyRossii v ZentralnoyAziiZentralnayaAziya: AktualnyeAkzentyMezhdunarodnogo-Sotrudnichestva. MGIMO University, Moscow, 23–39Google Scholar

40. Lake DA (2009) Regional hierarchy: authority and local international order. Rev Int Stud 35, 35–58CrossRefGoogle Scholar

41. Mansfield ED, Milner HV (1999) The new wave of regionalism. Int Organ 53, 589–627CrossRefGoogle Scholar

42. Mattli W (1999) The logic of regional integration: Europe and beyond. Cambridge University Press, CambridgeGoogle Scholar

43. Mazorenko D (2014) Skolko Kazakhstan zarabatyvaetnatransitegazainefti? Vlast 10 September 2014 (vlast.kz/jekonomika/

skolko_kazahstan_zarabatyvaet   na_tranzite_gaza_i_nefti-7306. html)

44. Melnykovska I, Plamper H, Schweickert R (2012) Do Russia and China promote autocracy in Central Asia? Asia Europe Journal 10, 75–89CrossRefGoogle Scholar

45. Mesheryakov K (2012) IntegracionniyeProzessynaPostsovetskom-ProstranstveiUchastiye v NikhRossii. Skiphia Print, St Petersburg-Google Scholar

46. Ministry of Foreign Affairs of the Russian Federation (2005) On the Summit of CACO, Saint Petersburg, 6 October 2005 (www.mid.ru/central-noaziatskoe-soobsestvo-cas-/-/asset_publisher/0vP3hQoCPRg5/content/id/ 425166)

47. Moravcsik A (1998) The choice for Europe: social purpose and state power from Messina to Maastricht. Cornell University Press, Itha-caGoogle Scholar

48. Muntschick J (2017) SADC: extra-regional trade relations constrain deeper market integration. In: Krapohl S (ed) Regional Integration in the Global South: External Influence on Economic Cooperation in ASEAN, MERCOSUR and SADC. Palgrave, Basingstoke, 179–208CrossRefGoogle Scholar

49. Myant M, Drahokoupil J (2008) International integration and the structure of exports in central Asian republics. Eurasian Geogr Econ 49, 604–622CrossRefGoogle Scholar

50. Naarajärvi T (2012) China, Russia and the Shanghai cooperation organisation: blessing or curse for new regionalism in Central Asia? Asia Europe Journal 10, 113–126CrossRefGoogle Scholar

51. Peyrose S, Raballand G (2015) Central Asia: the new silk road Initiative's questionable economic rationality. Eurasian Geogr Econ 56, 405–420CrossRefGoogle Scholar

52. Pollack MA (2003) The engines of European integration: delegation, agency, and agenda-setting in the EU. Oxford University Press, OxfordCrossRefGoogle Scholar

53. Pomfret R (2009) Regional integration in Central Asia. Econ Chang Restruct 42, 47–68CrossRefGoogle Scholar

54. Raballand G, Andresy A (2007) Why should trade between Central Asia and China continue to expand? Asia Europe Journal 5, 235–252CrossRefGoogle Scholar

451

55. Roberts SP, Moshes A (2016) The Eurasian economic union: a case of reproductive integration? Post-SovAff 32, 542–565CrossRef-Google Scholar

56. Rolland N (2017) China's 'Belt and road initiative': underwhelming or game-changer? Wash Q 40, 127–142CrossRefGoogle Scholar

57. Russel M (2019) Connectivity in Central Asia: reconnecting the silk road. European parliamentary research service briefing (www.europarl.europa.eu/RegData/etudes/BRIE/2019/637891/EPRS_BRI(2019)637891_EN.pdf)

58. Samokhvalov V (2016) The new Eurasia: post-soviet space between Russia, Europe and China. Eur Polit Soc 17, 82–96CrossRefGoogle Scholar

59. Schirm SA (2002) Globalization and the new regionalism: global markets, domestic politics and regional cooperation. Wiley, CambridgeGoogle Scholar

60. Sheives K (2006) China turns west: Beijing's contemporary strategy towards Central Asia. Pac Aff 79, 205–224CrossRefGoogle Scholar

61. Söderbaum F, Sbragia A (2011) EU studies and the 'new regionalism': what can be gained from dialogue? J Eur Integr 32, 563–582CrossRefGoogle Scholar

62. Spechler M (2002) Regional cooperation in Central Asia. Probl of Post-Communism 49, 42–47CrossRefGoogle Scholar

63. Stein AA (1982) Coordination and collaboration: regimes in an anarchic world. Int Organ 36, 299–324CrossRefGoogle Scholar

64. Stronski P, Ng N (2018) Cooperation and competition: Russia and China in Central Asia, the Russian Far East, and the Arctic. Carnegie Endowment for International Peace (carnegieendowment.org/2018/02/28/cooperation-and-competition-russia-and-china-in-central-asia-russian-far-east-and-arctic-pub-75673). 21 Jan 2019

65. Stubbs R (2014) ASEAN's leadership in east Asian region-building: strength in weakness. Pac Rev 27, 523–541Google Scholar

66. Sultanov B (2014) Kazakhstan and Eurasian integration. In: Dutkiewicz P, Sakwa R (eds) Eurasian Integration—The View Within. Palgrave, Basingstoke, 97–110Google Scholar

67. The Diplomat (2017) Belt and road attendees list (thediplomat.com/2017/05/belt-and-road-attendees-list/). 21 Jan 2019

68. Trenin D (2017) Russia's evolving grand Eurasia strategy: will it work? Carnegie Moscow Center, MoscowGoogle Scholar

69. Vinokurov E (2018) Introduction to the Eurasian economic union. Palgrave, BasingstokeCrossRefGoogle Scholar

70. Von Hauff L (2018) Towards a new quality of cooperation? The EU, China, and Central Asian security in a multipolar age. Asia Europe Journal (online first)Google Scholar

71. Wang W (2014) The effect of regional integration in Central Asia. Emerg Mark Financ Trade 50, 219–232CrossRefGoogle Scholar

72. Warleigh-Lack A, Rosamond B (2010) Across the EU-studies-new regionalism frontier: invitation to a dialogue. J Common Mark Stud 48, 993–1013CrossRefGoogle Scholar

73. Xin L, Daleng X (2015) Chinese and Russian economic interests in Central Asia: comparative analysis. In: Denoon D (ed) China, The United States and The Future of Central Asia. New York University Press, New York, 130–153Google Scholar

74. Yapıcı U (2018) From positive neutrality to silk road activism? The continuities and changes in Turkmenistan's foreign policy. J Balkan Near East Stud 20, 293–310CrossRefGoogle Scholar

75. Yuan J-D (2010) China's role in establishing and building the Shanghai cooperation organization (SCO). J Contemp China 19, 855–869CrossRefGoogle Scholar

76. Zürn M (1993) Problematic social situations and international institutions: on the use of game theory in international politics. In: Pfetsch F (ed) International Relations and Pan-Europe: Theoretical Approaches and Empirical Findings. Lit Verlag, Münster, 63–84Google Scholar

Chapter 2: Jihadists from Ex-Soviet Central Asia: Where Are They? Why Did They Radicalize? What Next? Edward Lemon Vera Mironova William Tobey

1. Saradzhyan, Simon and Monica Duffy Toft, "Islamic State and the Bolsheviks: Plenty in Common and Lessons to Heed," Russia Matters, Dec. 16, 2016, https://www. russiamatters.org/analysis/islamic-state-and-bolsheviks-plenty-common-and-lessons-heed.

2. Kramer, Andrew E. and Rukmini Callimachi, "ISIS Says It Killed 4 Cyclists in Tajikistan," The New York Times, July 30, 2018, https://

www.nytimes. com/2018/07/30/world/asia/tajikistan-attack-cylists.
html.

3. Nechepurenko, Ivan, "Suicide Bomber Attacks Chinese Embassy in
Kyrgyzstan," The New York Times, Aug. 30, 2016, https://www.ny-
times.com/2016/08/31/ world/asia/bishkek-china-embassy-kyrgyz-
stan.html.

4. Global Terrorism Database, https://www.start.umd.edu/gtd/.

5 The European Commission's Radicalization Awareness Network estimated in a July 2017 report that more than 42,000 "foreign terrorist
fighters" from over 120 countries had joined terrorist organizations
in 2011-2016. See: https://ec.europa.eu/ home-affairs/sites/homeaf-
fairs/files/ran_br_a4_m10_en.pdf.

6 According to the World Bank, the combined total population of Kazakhstan, Kyrgyzstan, Tajikistan, Turkmenistan and Uzbekistan for
2017 was just over 71.3 million out of a global population of more
than 7.5 billion. See: http://databank.worldbank.org/ data/reports.
aspx?source=2&series=SP.POP.TOTL&country=.

7 "DataBank | World Development Indicators," The World Bank,
2018, http://databank.worldbank.org/data/reports.aspx? source=
2&series=SP.POP.TOTL&country=.

8 Spada, Andrea, "About 500-600 people originating from Kazakhstan
fighting alongside ISIS," Islam Media Analysis, Apr. 11, 2017, http://
www.islamedianalysis.info/   about-500-600-people-originating-
from-kazakhstan-fighting-alongside-isis/.

9 KNB: 150 Kazakhstantsevvoyuyut v SiriiiIrake [NSC: 150 Kazakhstanis Fighting in Syria and Iraq]," Tengri News, June 29, 2015,
https://tengrinews.kz/tv/novosti/obschestvo/4278/. This number
comes from Kazakhstan's Committee of National Security, which estimated at the time that the fighters were accompanied by more than
200 wives, widows and children.

10 Matveeva, Anna, "Radicalisation and Violent Extremism in Kyrgyzstan: On the Way to the Caliphate?" The RUSI Journal, 163, (1), 2018,
https://www.tandfonline.com/ eprint/gXEVaGDNChmtBTJGUXJe/
full. The paper's author cites official figures of 863 Kyrgyz citizens
who had "left ... for foreign fighting zones," including 185 women
and 83 minors.

11 "Kyrgyzstan Apprehends ISIL Terrorist in Bishkek," FARS
News Agency, July 23, 2016, http://en.farsnews.com/newstext.

aspx?nn=13950502000746. Figure based on statements by Kyrgyz officials, with 205 women and children subtracted from the total of "over 500."

12 An estimated 200 women have been subtracted from the figures given in the cited articles: http://www2.unwomen.org/-/media/field office eca/attachments/publications/2017/iii_unw_eca_tajikistan chapter_final-02 final.pdf?la=en&vs=1241

13 Murodov, Abdumajid, "Peshgiriijalbijavononbatashkilotiterroristī vazifaijomeaishahrvandīniz hast [Civil Society Also Has a Role in Preventing Young People From Participating in Terrorist Groups]," Sadoimardum, Nov. 15, 2018, http://sadoimardum.tj/ma-lisi-ol/peshgirii-albi-avonon-ba-tashkiloti-terrorist-vazifai-omeai-sharvand-niz-ast/.

14 "VlastiTadzhikistanaozabochenyvozvrascheniem "dzhikhadistov" izSirii [Authorities in Tajikistan Concerned by the Return of "Jihadists" From Syria]," Ozodlik, July 11, 2016, https://rus.ozodlik.org/a/28610097.html.

15 "Policy Briefing," International Crisis Group, Jan. 20, 2015, https://d2071andvip0wj.cloudfront.net/b72-syria-calling-radicalisation-in-central-asia.pdf.

16 Dyner, Anna, Arkadiusz Legieć and KacperRękawek, "Ready to Go? ISIS and Its Presumed Expansion into Central Asia," PolskiInstytut SprawMiędzynarodowych (PISM), June 2015, https://www.pism.pl/files/?id_plik=20020.

17 Barrett, Richard, "Beyond the Caliphate: Foreign Fighters and the Threat of Returnees," The SoufanCenter, October 2017, http://thesoufancenter.org/wp-content/ uploads/2017/11/Beyond-the-Caliphate-Foreign-Fighters-and-the-Threat-of-Returnees-TSC-Report-October-2017-v3.pdf.

18 "V ryadakh IGIL voyuyutokolo 200 grazhdanUzbekistana [Around 200 Citizens of Uzbekistan Fighting for ISIS]," Regnum, Mar. 26, 2015, https://regnum.ru/%20 news/1908975.html.

19 Data from the EU Terrorism Situation and Trend reports (https://www.europol.europa.eu/activities-services/main-reports/eu-terrorism-situation-and-trend-report#fndtn-tabs-0-bottom-2) for 2014, 2015, 2016 and 2017.

20 By way of comparison, we were unable to find any reliable reports of Russian nationals' involvement in terrorist acts in the EU in the same

time period. However, one IS-related terror attack (https://www. telegraph.co.uk/news/2018/05/12/knifeman-shot-dead-french-po-lice-stabbing-several-people-paris/) in Paris in May 2018 involved a naturalized French citizen born in Russia's republic of Chechnya. (After the deadly knife attack, Chechen President Ramzan Kadyrov claimed (https://apostrophe. ua/news/world/ex-ussr/2018-05-13/ krovavaya-reznya-v-parije-kadyirov-nashel-vinovatogo/129932) the 20-year-old assailant had not renewed his Russian passport, as he was supposed to and hence wasn't a Russian national.)

21 Seehttps://www.europol.europa.eu/activities-services/main-re-ports/eu-terrorism-situation-and-trend-report#fndtn-tabs-0-bot-tom-2.

22 Global Terrorism Database, https://www.start.umd.edu/gtd/.

23 Priimark, Artur and Pavel Skrilnikov, "Bumerang radicalism voz-vrashchyayetcyzizSredneiAzii," Nezavisimaya Gazeta, April 19, 2017, http://www.ng.ru/ facts/2017-04-19/9_419_bumerang.html.

24 Tsvetkova, Maria and Andrew Osborn, "Nanny who beheaded Russian girl cites revenge for Putin's Syria strikes," Reuters, March 3, 2016, https://www.reuters. com/article/us-russia-murder-child/ nanny-who-beheaded-russian-girl-cites-revengefor-putins-syria-strikes-idUSKCN0W50OH.

25 "471: The Convert," This American Life, https://www.thisamerican-life.org/471/ transcript.

26 Shallwani, Pervaiz, Rebecca Davis O'Brien and Andrew Grossman, "Three Brooklyn Men Arrested and Accused of Plot to Join Islamic State," The Wall Street Journal, Feb. 25, 2015, https://www.wsj.com/ articles/three-brooklyn-men-accused-ofplot-to-join-islamic-state-1424888001?mod=article_inline.

27 "Country Reports on Terrorism 2016 - Foreign Terrorist Organi-zations: Islamic Movement of Uzbekistan (IMU)," United States Department of State, July 19, 2017, https://www.refworld.org/ docid/5981e3d7a.html.

28 Mitchell, Kirk, "Denver federal jury finds Uzbekistan refugee guilty of aiding terror group," The Denver Post, June 21, 2018, https:// www.denverpost. com/2018/06/21/denver-jury-jamshid-muhtorov-guilty/.

29 At least one news report (https://www.theguardian.com/world/2014/ jun/11/ uzbek-militant-group-imu-karachi-airport-assault-paki-

stani-taliban-drone) put the number at 36; the BBC (https://www.
bbc.com/news/world-asia-27790892) and later the U.S. State Department (https://www.state.gov/documents/organization/272488.
pdf) put it at 39.

30   Guistozzi, Antonio and Anna Matveeva, "The Central Asian Militants: Cannon Fodder of Global Jihadism or Revolutionary Vanguard?" Small Wars and Insurgencies, 29, (2), 2018, https://www.
tandfonline.com/doi/abs/10.1080/09592318.2018.1433472

31   Donati, Jessica and Paul Sonne, "New York Attack Underlines Central Asia as Growing Source of Terrorism," The Wall Street Journal,
Oct. 31, 2017, https://www.wsj. com/articles/new-york-attack-un-
derlines-central-asia-as-growing-source-of-terrorism-1509508624.

32   Kranz, Michal, "Here's how the region the New York attacker immi-
grated from became fertile ground for terrorism," Business Insider,
Nov. 1, 2017, https://www.businessinsider.com/central-asia-fertile-
ground-for-terrorism-sayfullo-saipov-2017-11.

33   Matveeva, Anna, "Radicalisation and Violent Extremism in Kyrgyzstan: On the Way to the Caliphate?" The RUSI Journal, 163, (1), 2018,
https://www.tandfonline.com/ eprint/gXEVaGDNChmtBTJGUXJe/
full.

34   Tucker, Noah, "What Happens When Your Town Becomes an ISIS
Recruiting Ground? Lessons from Central Asia about Vulnerability, Resistance and the Danger of Ignoring Injustice," Central Asia
Program, July 2018. http://centralasiaprogram.org/ wp-content/up-
loads/2018/06/Tucker-CAP-Paper-July-2018.pdf.

35   "Uzbek militant group IMU claims involvement in Karachi airport
assault," The Guardian, June 11, 2014, https://www.theguardian.
com/world/2014/jun/11/uzbek-militant-group-imu-karachi-air-
port-assault-pakistani-taliban-drone.

36   Weiss, Caleb, "State adds Uzbek jihadist group to terror list," Long
War Journal, Mar. 22, 2018, https://www.longwarjournal.org/tags/
imam-bukhari-jamaat. Weiss, Caleb, "Jihadists celebrate in key
Idlib city after defeating Syrian regime," Long War Journal, Apr. 27,
2015, https://www.longwarjournal.org/archives/2015/04/jihadists-
celebrate-in-key-idlib-city-after-defeating-syrian-regime.php. Paraszczuk, Joanna and BarnoAnvar, "The Last Moments Of A Suicide
Bomber In Syria," Radio Free Europe, Sep. 21, 2015, https://www.
rferl.org/a/uzbek-suicide-bomber-syria/27260806.html.

37   Many observers have been skeptical about the IRPT's involvement. See Edward Lemon, "Violence in Tajikistan Emerges from within the State," CACI-Analyst, Sept. 23, 2015, https://cacianalyst.org/publications/analytical-articles/item/13279-violence-in-tajikistan-emerges-from-within-the-state.html.

38   Galdini, Franco and ZukhraIakupbaeva, "The Strange Case of Jaysh al-Mahdi and Mr. ISIS: How Kyrgyzstan's Elites Manipulate the Threat of Terrorism," CERIA Briefs, 2016, http://centralasiaprogram.org/archives/10075.

39   Baizakova, Zhulduz and Roger N. McDermott, "Reassessing the Barriers to Islamic Radicalization in Kazakhstan," U.S. Army War College, July 29, 2015, https:// apps.dtic.mil/dtic/tr/fulltext/u2/a621437.pdf.

40   On manipulation of the threat, see John Heathershaw and David Montgomery. "Islam, Secularism and Danger: A Reconsideration of the Link Between Religiosity, Radicalism and Rebellion in Central Asia." Religion, State and Society, 2016, 44, (3): 192–218; Rustam Burnashev. 2014. "Why Islamists are not the most important regional security challenge for Central Asian states." In: Johan Norberg and Erika Holmquist, (ed.). ISAF's Withdrawal from Afghanistan - Central Asian Perspectives on Regional Security. Stockholm: Ministry of Defense.

41   "Tajikistan seizes momentum to tar opposition as terrorists," Eurasianet, Aug. 2, 2018, https://eurasianet.org/tajikistan-seizes-momentum-to-tar-opposition-as-terrorists.

42   "Tajikistan: A mystery Islamic State conversion for a hopeless young man," Eurasianet, July 31, 2018, https://eurasianet.org/tajikistan-a-mystery-islamic-stateconversion-for-a-hopeless-young-man.

43   Orazgaliyeva, Malika, "Kazakh President Declares June 9 as National Day of Mourning," The Astana Times, June 9, 2016, https://astanatimes.com/2016/06/kazakh-president-declares-june-9-as-national-day-of-mourning/.

44   "Country Reports on Terrorism 2016," United States Department of State, July 2017, https://www.state.gov/documents/organization/272488.pdf.

45   Weiser, Benjamin, "Bike Path Terrorism Suspect Seeks Plea Deal to Avoid Death Penalty," The New York Times, Jan. 17, 2018, https:// www.nytimes. com/2018/01/17/nyregion/saipov-bike-path-terrorist-death-penalty.html.

46   For a discussion of the limits of our knowledge in the context of Central Asia, see John Heathershaw and David Montgomery. "Who Says Syria's Calling? Why It Is Sometimes Better to Admit That We Just Do Not Know," CEDAR Network, 17 February 2015, http://www.cedarnetwork.org/2015/02/17/who-says-syrias-calling-why-it-issometimes-better-to-admit-that-we-just-do-not-know-by-john-heathershaw-and-david-w-montgomery/

47   Matveeva, Anna and Antonio Giustozzi, "The Central Asian Militants: Cannon Fodder of Global Jihadism or Revolutionary Vanguard?" Small Wars & Insurgencies, 29, (2), 2018, https://www.tandfonline.com/doi/abs/10.1080/09592318.2018.1433472.

48   Roy, Olivier, "France's Oedipal Islamist Complex," Foreign Policy, Jan. 7, 2016, https://foreignpolicy.com/2016/01/07/frances-oedipal-islamist-complex-charlie-hebdo-islamic-state-isis/.

49   Roy, Olivier, "Who Are the New Jihadis?" The Guardian, April 13, 2017, https:// www.theguardian.com/news/2017/apr/13/who-are-the-new-jihadis.

50   Nasritdinov, Emil, Zarina Urmanbetoeva, KanatbekMurzakhililov and MamatbekMyrzabaev, "Vulnerability and Resilience of Young People in Kyrgyzstan to Radicalization, Violence and Extremism: Analysis Across Six Domains," Research Institute for Islamic Studies, 2018; Elshimi , Mohammed S. et al. "Understanding the Factors Contributing to Radicalisation Among Central Asian Labour Migrants in Russia," RUSI, Apr. 26, 2018, https://rusi.org/publication/occasional-papers/understanding-factors-contributing-radicalisation-among-central-asian

51   "Kyrgyzstan: Probe Forces' Role in June Violence," Human Rights Watch, Aug. 16, 2010, https://www.hrw.org/news/2010/08/16/kyrgyzstan-probe-forces-role-june-violence.

52   "Kyrgyzstan: Widening Ethnic Divisions in the South," International Crisis Group, Mar. 29, 2012, https://www.crisisgroup.org/europe-central-asia/central-asia/ kyrgyzstan/kyrgyzstan-widening-ethnic-divisions-south.

53   "Corruption Perceptions Index 2017," Transparency International, Feb. 21, 2018, https://www.transparency.org/news/feature/corruption_perceptions_index_2017 .

54   "Worldwide Governance Indicators," The World Bank, 2018, http://info.worldbank.org/governance/wgi/index.aspx#reports.

55 Event transcript: "Sergey Abashin – Central Asian Migrants in Russia: Will There Be a Religious Radicalization?" Central Asia Program, George Washington University, Apr. 24, 2017, http://centralasiaprogram.org/archives/10989.

56 Lemon, Edward, "Pathways to Violent Extremism: Evidence from Tajik Recruits to Islamic State," The Harriman Magazine, May 2018, http://www.columbia.edu/cu/   creative/epub/harriman/2018/summer/Pathways_to_Violent_Extremism.pdf; Nasritdinov, Emil, Zarina Urmanbetoeva, KanatbekMurzakhililov and MamatbekMyrzabaev, "Vulnerability and Resilience of Young People in Kyrgyzstan to Radicalization, Violence and Extremism: Analysis Across Six Domains," Research Institute for Islamic Studies, 2018.

57 Beissembayev, Serik, "Religious Extremism in Kazakhstan: From Criminal Networks to Jihad," The Central Asia Fellowship Papers, 15, 2013, http://centralasiaprogram.org/wp-content/uploads/2016/02/CAF-Paper-15-Serik-Beissembayev.pdf.

58 "'Congratulations, Your Brother's Become a Martyr': How Moscow's Migrant Workers Became Islamic State Fighters," Meduza, Apr. 27, 2015, https://meduza.io/en/ feature/2015/04/27/congratulations-your-brother-s-become-a-martyr.

59 For two scholarly discussions of the linkages between sports and criminal violence in the former Soviet Union see "Criminal Networks in Georgia and Kyrgyzstan and Young Male Sportsmen" (2008) by Alexander Kupatadze (https://books.google. com/books?hl=en& lr=&id=xCW6nVReyAcC&oi=fnd&pg=PA170&dq=georgia+kyr gyzstan+sports+violence&ots=RBi_pwek0M&sig=HMiFJBZAU-g1xScIVm9DBWab3vk#v=onepage&q=georgia%20kyrgyzstan%20 sports%20violence&f=false) and "Violent Entrepreneurs: The Use of Force in the Making of Russian Capitalism" (2002) by Vadim Volkov.

60 "Why Did a Tajik Student & Mixed Martial-Arts Champ Die for IS in Iraq?" Radio Free Europe, Feb. 23, 2015, https://www.rferl.org/a/tajik-isis-fighter/26864323. html.

61 Naumkin, Vitaly, "Radical Islam in Central Asia: Between Pen and Rifle," Lanham, MD: Rowman & Littlefield, 2005.

62 Tucker, Noah, "What Happens When Your Town Becomes an ISIS Recruiting Ground? Lessons from Central Asia about Vulnerability, Resistance and the Danger of Ignoring Injustice," Central Asia Program, July 2018, http://centralasiaprogram.org/ wp-content/uploads/2018/06/Tucker-CAP-Paper-July-2018.pdf; Lemon, Edward,

"Daesh and Tajikistan: The Regime's (In)Security Policy," The RUSI Journal, 160:5, 68-76, https://rusi.org/publication/rusi-journal/daesh-and-tajikistan-regimes-insecurity-policy.

63   Mironova, Vera, Ekaterina Sergatskova and Karam Alhamad, "The Lives of Foreign Fighters Who Left ISIS: Why They Escaped and Where They Are Now," Foreign Affairs, Oct. 27, 2017, https://www.foreignaffairs.com/articles/2017-10-27/lives-foreignfighters-who-left-isis.

64   "Syria Calling: Radicalisation in Central Asia," International Crisis Group Europe and Central Asia Briefing, N°72, 2015, https://www.crisisgroup.org/europe-central-asia/central-asia/syria-calling-radicalisation-central-asia

65   "Tajikistan pardons over 100 ex-militants in Syria, Iraq wars," PressTV, Feb. 8, 2018, http://www.presstv.com/Detail/2018/02/08/551716/Tajikistan-pardon-returnees-Iraq-Syria; Matveeva, Anna, "Radicalisation and Violent Extremism in Kyrgyzstan: On the Way to the Caliphate?" The RUSI Journal, 2018, 163, (1), https://www.tandfonline.com/eprint/gXEVaGDNChmtBTJGUXJe/full; https://eurasianet.org/s/kazakhstan-to-spend-840m-on-countering-religious-extremism.

66   Lang, Josef, "Exporting Jihad – Islamic terrorism from Central Asia." OSW Commentary, No. 236, April 12, 2017, https://www.osw.waw.pl/en/publikacje/osw-commentary/2017-04-12/exporting-jihad-islamic-terrorism-central-asia.

67   "Amaq Reports IS Fighter Behind Attack That Sparked Prison Riot in Tajikistan," SITE Intelligence Group, Nov. 8, 2018, https://ent.siteintelgroup.com/State   ments/amaq-reports-is-fighter-behind-attack-that-sparked-prison-riot-in-tajikistan. html.

68   "Tajikistan admits to prison massacre," Eurasianet, Nov. 23, 2018, https://eurasianet.org/tajikistan-admits-to-prison-massacre.

69   Ibid.

70   Ratelle, Jean-Francois, "Terror Threat from Russian-Speaking Jihadists Won't End with World Cup, and the West Should Care," Russia Matters, June 13, 2018, https:// www.russiamatters.org/analysis/terror-threat-russian-speaking-jihadists-wont-endworld-cup-and-west-should-care. The author focuses on Russian-speaking fighters, primarily from the North Caucasus, but many of his assessments may apply to Central Asians as well.

71 "Emomali Rakhmon: tadzhikskieboyevikikperemestilis' s Blizhne-goVostoka v Afganistan [Emomali Rahmon: Tajik Militants Have Moved from the Middle East to Afghanistan]," Radio Ozodi, May 12, 2018, https://rus.ozodi.org/a/29222903.html; "Official: 150 Kyrgyz Citizens Killed In Syria Fighting Alongside IS," RFE/RL, June, 28,2018, https://www.rferl.org/a/official-150-kyrgyz-citizens-killed-in-syria-fighting-alongsideis/29325374.html; "Cvishe 220 GrazhdanKazakhstanaPogiblo v BoyevihDeistviyahnaBlizhnyemVostoke" [Over 220 Citizens of Kazakhstan Died in Fighting in the Middle East], BNews.Kz, Dec. 12, 2017, https://bnews.kz/ru/news/svishe_220_grazhdan_kazakhstana_pogiblo_v_boevih_deistviyah_na_blizhnem_vostoke

72 "'They deserve no mercy': Iraq deals briskly with accused 'women of Isis,'" The Guardian, May 22, 2018, https://www.theguardian.com/world/2018/may/22/ they-deserve-no-mercy-iraq-deals-briskly-with-accused-women-of-isis.

73 "Russian-Speaking Foreign Fights in Iraq and Syria," CSIS Report, December 2017, https://csis-prod.s3.amazonaws.com/s3fs-public/publication/180726_Russian_   Speaking_Foreign_Fight.pdf?VyUdcO2D6TJdW_Zm4JkmIpRkJxoXEZU6

74 Lynch III, Thomas, Michael Bouffard, Kelsey King and Graham Vickowski, "The Return of Foreign Fighters to Central Asia: Implications for U.S. Counterterrorism Policy," Strategic Perspectives, 2016. 21.

75 Lemon, Edward, "To Afghanistan Not Syria? Islamic State Diverts Tajik Fighters South," Eurasia Daily Monitor, March 15, 2017, https://jamestown.org/program/   afghanistan-not-syria-islamic-state-diverts-tajik-fighters-south/.

76 Ali, Obaid, "New Confusion About ISKP: A case study from Sare Pul," Afghanistan Analysts Network, Sep. 7, 2018, https://www.afghanistan-analysts.org/new-confusion-about-iskp-a-case-study-from-sar-e-pul/.

77 For an overview of ISKP's expansion and incorporation of Central Asian groups see Giustozzi, Antonio, The Islamic State in Khurasan, London: Hurst and Company, 2018, pp. 139-159.

78 Osman, Borhan, "ISKP's Battle for Minds: What are its Main Messages and Who Do They Attract?" Afghanistan Analysts Network, Dec. 12, 2016, https://www. afghanistan-analysts.org/iskps-battle-

for-minds-what-are-their-main-messages-andwho-do-they-attract/.

79   Obaid Ali, "Still Under the IS's Black Flag: QariHekmat's ISKP Island in Jawzjan after His Death by Drone," Afghanistan Analysts Network, 15 May 2018, https:// www.afghanistan-analysts.org/stillunder-the-iss-black-flag-qari-hekmats-iskp-islandin-jawzjan-afterhis-death-by-drone/.

80   Borhan Osman, "ISKP's Battle for Minds: What are its Main Messages and Who Do They Attract?" Afghanistan Analysts Network, Dec. 12, 2016, https://www. afghanistan-analysts.org/iskps-battle-forminds-what-are-their-main-messages-andwho-do-they-attract/.

81   Stepanova, Ekaterina, "The ISIS Factor in Afghanistan: How Much of a Challenge For Russia?" Bishkek Project, March 30, 2017, https:// bishkekproject.com/memos/21.

82   "Russian General Says About 10,000 Militants Deployed in Afghanistan," Asia Plus, April 17, 2018, https://www.news.tj/en/news/ world/20180417/russian-generalsays-about-10000-militants-deployed-in-afghanistan.

83   Lamothe, Dan, "Senior ISIS leader killed in northern Afghanistan, highlighting shifting militant allegiances," The Washington Post, April 9, 2018, https://www.washingtonpost.com/news/checkpoint/wp/2018/04/09/senior-isis-leader-killed-in-northern-afghanistan-highlighting-shifting-militant-allegiances/?utm_term=.da3aa49e1f98.

84   "Statement of General Joseph L. Votel on the Posture of U.S. Central Command," House Armed Services Committee Hearing, Feb. 27, 2018.

85   "Twenty-second report of the Analytical Support and Sanctions Monitoring Team submitted pursuant to resolution 2368 (2017) concerning ISIL (Da'esh), Al-Qaida and associated individuals and entities," United Nations Security Council, July 16, 2018, http://www.un.org/en/ga/search/view_doc.asp?symbol=S/2018/705&referer=/english/&Lang=E.

86   Seldin, Jeff, "Afghan Officials: Islamic State Fighters Finding Sanctuary in Afghanistan," VOA News, Nov. 18, 2017, https://www.voanews.com/a/afghan-officials-islamic-state-finds-sanctuary-in-afghanistan/4122270.html.

87 Shalizi, Hamid, "Embassy, mosque attacks fuel fears ISIS bringing Iraq war to Afghanistan," Reuters, Aug. 2, 2017, https://www.reuters.com/article/us-afghanistan-islamic-state/embassy-mosque-attacks-fuel-fears-isis-bringing-iraq-war-to-afghanistan-idUSKBN1AI0V1.

88 "Country Reports on Terrorism 2015: Special Briefing," United States Department of State, June 2, 2016, https://web.archive.org/web/20160603121929/https:/   www.state.gov/r/pa/prs/ps/2016/06/258013.htm.

89 Ali, Obaid, "QariHekmat's Island: A Daesh enclave in Jawzjan?" Afghanistan Analysts Network, Nov. 11, 2017, https://www.afghanistan-analysts.org/qari-hekmatsisland-a-daesh-enclave-in-jawzjan/.

90 Saeed Khan, August 2016; Sheikh Abdul Hasib, May 2017; Abu Saeed, July 2017.

91 Dickinson, Amanda, "How the Islamic State Got a Foothold in Afghanistan," The Washington Post, March 21, 2018, https://www.washingtonpost.com/news/worldviews/wp/2018/03/21/how-the-islamic-state-got-a-foothold-in-afghanistan/?noredirect=on&utm_term=.7967b4b66aa5.

92 Zahid, Farhan, "Islamic State Emboldened in Afghanistan," Terrorism Monitor, 16(12), https://jamestown.org/program/islamic-state-emboldened-in-afghanistan/.

93 Giustozzi, Anotonio, "Taliban and Islamic State: Enemies or Brothers in Jihad?" Center for Research and Policy Analysis, Dec. 14, 2017, https://www.crpaweb. org/single-post/2017/12/15/Enemies-or-Jihad-Brothers-Relations-Between-Taliban-and-Islamic-State.

94 Ibid.

95 Sharifi, Shoaib and Louise Adamou, "Taliban threaten 70% of Afghanistan, BBC finds," BBC, Jan. 31, 2018, https://www.bbc.com/news/world-asia-42863116.

96 Chughtai, Alia, "Afghanistan: Who controls what," Aljazeera, Oct. 19, 2018, https://www.aljazeera.com/indepth/interactive/2016/08/afghanistan-controls-160823083528213.html.

97 Almukhtar, Sarah, "How Much of Afghanistan Is Under Taliban Control After 16 Years of War With the U.S.?" The New York Times, Aug. 23, 2017, https://www.nytimes. com/interactive/2017/08/23/world/asia/afghanistan-us-taliban-isis-control.html.

98 "Quarterly Report on the Protection of Civilians in Armed Conflict: 1 January to 30 September 2018," United Nations Assistance Mission in Afghanistan, Oct. 10, 2018, https://unama.unmissions. org/sites/default/files/unama_protection_of_civilians_in_armed_ conflict_3rd_quarter_report_2018_10_oct.pdf.

99 Giustozzi, Anotonio, "Taliban and Islamic State: Enemies or Brothers in Jihad?" Center for Research and Policy Analysis, Dec. 14, 2017, https://www.crpaweb. org/single-post/2017/12/15/Enemies-or-Jihad-Brothers-Relations-Between-Taliban-and-Islamic-State.

100 Special thanks to Thomas Ruttig for confirming with Afghan sources that Moawiya was an ethnic Uzbek from Afghanistan, and not from Uzbekistan as suggested by earlier reporting in The Washington Post. (See https://www.washingtonpost. com/news/checkpoint/ wp/2018/04/09/senior-isis-leader-killed-in-northern-afghanistan-highlighting-shifting-militant-allegiances/.)

101 Rahim, Najim and Rod Nordland, "Taliban Surge Routs ISIS in Northern Afghanistan," The New York Times, Aug. 1, 2018, https:// www.nytimes.com/2018/08/01/ world/asia/afghanistan-taliban-isis. html.

102 "Quarterly Report on the Protection of Civilians in Armed Conflict: 1 January to 30 September 2018," United Nations Assistance Mission in Afghanistan, Oct. 10, 2018, https://unama.unmissions. org/sites/default/files/unama_protection_of_civilians_in_armed_ conflict_3rd_quarter_report_2018_10_oct.pdf.

103 "At Least 200 IS Fighters 'Surrender' In Afghanistan," Radio Free Europe, Aug. 2, 2018, https://www.rferl.org/a/at-least-200-is-fighters-surrender-in-northern-afghanistan/29402416.html.

104 Musavi, Sayed Aref, "Jawzjan Governor Says Province 'Is Clear Of Daesh,'" Tolo News, Aug. 2, 2018, https://www.tolonews.com/afghanistan/jawzjan-governor-saysprovince-'-clear-daesh'.

105 Weiss, Caleb, "Foreign Islamic State fighters captured by Taliban in Jawzjan," Long War Journal, Aug. 4, 2018, https://www.longwarjournal.org/archives/2018/08/ foreign-islamic-state-fighters-captured-by-taliban-in-jawzjan.php.

106 "Emomali Rakhmon: tadzhikskieboyevikikperemestilis' s Blizhne-goVostoka v Afganistan [Emomali Rahmon: Tajik Militants Have Moved from the Middle East to Afghanistan]," Radio Ozodi, May 12, 2018, https://rus.ozodi.org/a/29222903.html.

107 "Kabul extradirovalgrazhdankuTadzhikistanas dvumyamalolet nimi det'mi [Kabul Has Extradited a Tajik Woman with Two Small Children]," Radio Ozodi, May 6, 2018, https://rus.ozodi.org/a/29210981.html.

108 Rakhmatzoda, Makhmuddzhon, "'Vernitesynadomoy'. Kak 18-letniy migrant okazalsya v afganskomNangarkhare ['Return my son home'. How an 18-year old migrant ended up in Nangarhar, Afghanistan]," Radio Ozodi, Jan. 26, 2018, https://rus. ozodi.org/a/28999437.html.

109 "How Former 'Islamic State' Militants Wind Up in Ukraine," Hromadske, Aug. 8, 2017, https://en.hromadske.ua/posts/how-former-islamic-state-militants-wind-up-inukraine.

110 Barrett, Richard, "Beyond the Caliphate: Foreign Fighters and the Threat of Returnees," The SoufanCenter, October 2017, http://thesoufancenter.org/research/ beyond-caliphate/; Hegghammer, Thomas and PetterNesser, "Assessing the Islamic State's Commitment to Attacking the West," Perspectives on Terrorism, 4(9), 2015, http://www.terrorismanalysts.com/pt/index.php/pot/article/view/440/html.

111 Sonmez, Gotkug, "Violent Extremism among Central Asians: The Istanbul, St. Petersburg, Stockholm, and New York City Attacks." CTC Sentinel, 10 (11), 2017; "Istanbul Nightclub Massacre Suspect Goes On Trial," Radio Free Europe, Dec. 11, 2017, https://www.rferl.org/a/uzbek-istanbul-nightclub-attack-islamic-state-trial-begins/28908886.html.

112 "Stockholm Attack Suspect Deported from Turkey in 2015 While on Way to Join ISIL in Syria," Hurriyet, 12 April 2017, http://www.hurriyetdailynews.com/stockholm-attack-suspect-deported-from-turkey-in-2015-while-on-way-to-join-isil-in-syria-111959.

113 "Tadzhiksky sled v terakte v Stokgolme" [Tajik Link in the Act of Terrorism in Stockholm], Radio Ozodi, 9 February 2018, https://rus.ozodi.org/a/29029512.html.

114 "Podozrevaemyy v terakte v PeterburgebyldeportirovanizTurtsii [Suspect in Petersburg terrorist attack had been deported from Turkey]," Radio Free Europe, Apr. 11, 2017, https://www.svoboda.org/a/28422548.html.

115 "PravookhraniteliproveryayutdannyeobobucheniiterroristaDzhalilova v ryadakh IG v Sirii [Law enforcement checking information about the training of the terrorist Jalilov in the ranks of ISIS in Syria]," TASS, Apr. 5, 2017, https://tass.ru/proisshestviya/4157978.

116 "St Petersburg bombing: Group says al-Qaeda chief ordered attack," BBC, Apr. 25, 2017, https://www.bbc.com/news/world-europe-39713324.

117 Solopov, Maksim, Amalia Zatari and German Petelin, "Terakt v Peterburgeprivyol k Abu Salakhu [Terrorist Act in St. Petersburg led to Abu Salah]," Gazeta.ru, Apr. 21, 2017, https://www.gazeta.ru/army/2017/04/21/10638311.shtml.

118 "St. Pete Metro Blast Suspect Received Money From Terrorist Group in Turkey," Sputnik News, Apr. 20, 2017, https://sputniknews.com/russia/201704201052820547-st-petersburg-metro-blast-suspect-money-turkey/.

119 Ratelle, Jean-Francois, "Terror Threat from Russian-Speaking Jihadists Won't End with World Cup, and the West Should Care," Russia Matters, June 13, 2018, https:// www.russiamatters.org/analysis/terror-threat-russian-speaking-jihadists-wont-endworld-cup-and-west-should-care.

120 Najibullah, Farangis, "Life After Islamic State: Pardoned Tajik Militants Navigate Road to Reintegration," RFE/RL, Aug. 6, 2017, https://www.rferl.org/a/tajikistan-islamic-state-pardoned-militants-reintegration/28661770.html.

121 "More than 30 pardoned Tajiks have rejoined IS terror group, said Sughd chief police officer," Asia-Plus, Feb. 5, 2018, http://news.tj/en/news/tajikistan/security/20180205/more-than-30-pardoned-tajiks-have-rejoined-is-terror-group-saidsughd-chief-police-officer.

122 Kharzhaubayeva, Ainur, "Frontier Migration Between Kazakhstan and Russia: The Case of the West Kazakhstan," unpublished PhD dissertation, Charles University, Prague, 2013, p. 62, https://is.cuni.cz/webapps/zzp/download/140027754.

123 "2017 Report on Compliance with and Adherence to Arms Control, Nonproliferation, and Disarmament Agreements and Commitments," U.S. Department of State, https://www.state.gov/t/avc/rls/rpt/2017/270330.htm#CHEMICAL%20WEAPONS%20CONVENTION%20(CWC).

124 "Poisoned Legacy," The Economist, July 9, 2015, https://www.economist.com/ asia/2015/07/09/poisoned-legacy.

125 Tobey, William, "What Lies Beneath," Foreign Policy, April 30, 2012, https:// foreignpolicy.com/2012/04/30/what-lies-beneath/.

126 Ibid.

127 "Project Sapphire After Action Report," November 1994, declassified U.S. government document, https://nsarchive2.gwu.edu/NSAEBB/ NSAEBB491/docs/01%20 -%20After%20Action%20report%20 DTRA.pdf.

128 "GTRI Plans for FY2011," International Panel on Fissile Materials Blog, Feb. 5, 2010, http://fissilematerials.org/blog/2010/02/gtri_ plans_for_fy2011.html.

129 Miller, Judith, "Poison Island: A Special Report, at a Bleak Asian Site, Killer Germs Survive," The New York Times, June 2, 1999, p. A01, https://www.nytimes. com/1999/06/02/world/poison-island-a-special-report-at-bleak-asian-site-killergerms-survive.html.

130 Miller, Judith, William Broad, and Stephen Engelberg, Germs: Biological Weapons and America's Secret War, (New York: Simon and Schuster, 2001) pp. 165-67.

131 Budjeryn, Mariana, "Sen. Sam Nunn: 'We Have a Choice Between Cooperation or Catastrophe,'" Russia Matters, June 20, 2017, https:// russiamatters.org/analysis/ sen-sam-nunn-we-have-choice-between-cooperation-or-catastrophe.

132 Tobey, William, "What Lies Beneath," Foreign Policy, April 30, 2012, https:// foreignpolicy.com/2012/04/30/what-lies-beneath/.

133 Butler, Kenley, "Weapons of Mass Destruction in Central Asia," Nuclear Threat Initiative, Oct. 1, 2002, https://www.nti.org/analysis/ articles/weapons-mass-destruction-central-asia/.

134 Ibid.

135 Zhantikan, Timur, "Strengthening Security of Radioactive Sources in Central Asia," slide presentation, May 24, 2017, https://inis.iaea. org/collection/NCLCollectionStore/_Public/48/078/48078661. pdf?r=1&r=1.

136 "Pathways to Cooperation," (Washington, DC: Nuclear Threat Initiative, November 2017), p. 18, https://www.nti.org/media/documents/Pathways_to_Cooperation_FINAL.pdf.

137 Binder, Marcus K., Jillian M. Quigley, Herbert F. Tinsley, "Islamic State Chemical Weapons: A Case Contained by Its Context," CTC Sentinel, March 2018, Vol. 11, Issue 3, p. 27, https://ctc.usma.edu/ islamic-state-chemical-weapons-case-contained-context/

138 Ibid., p. 30.

139 Quoted in David Albright and Sarah Burkhard, "Daesh Hype About Stealing Nuclear Weapons," Institute for Science and International Security, Oct. 2, 2015, pp. 1-2, https://isis-online.org/uploads/isis-reports/documents/Daesh_Hype_about_Nuclear_Weapons_Oct_2_2015-final1.pdf

140 Ibid.

141 Warrick, Joby and Loveday Morris, "How ISIS Nearly Stumbled on Ingredients for a 'Dirty Bomb,'" The Washington Post, July 22, 2017, https://www.washingtonpost. com/world/national-security/how-isis-nearly-stumbled-on-the-ingredients-for-a-dirtybomb/2017/07/22/6a966746-6e31-11e7-b9e2-2056e768a7e5_story.html.

142 Bunn, Matthew, et al., "Advancing Nuclear Security: Evaluating Progress and Setting New Goals," BelferCenter for Science and International Affairs, March 2014, p. 39, pp. 39-40, https://www.belfercenter.org/sites/default/files/legacy/files/advancingnuclearsecurity.pdf

143 Malashenko, Alexey and Alexey Staroshin, "The Rise of Nontraditional Islam in the Urals," Carnegie Moscow Center, Sept. 15, 2015, http://carnegie.ru/2015/09/30/ rise-of-nontraditional-islam-in-urals-pub-61461

144 Ter, Marta and RyskelkiSatke, "Conditions for Central Asians in Russia Boost Radicalism," European Council on Foreign Relations, March 17, 2016, https://www. ecfr.eu/article/commentary_conditions_for_central_asians_in_russia_boost_radicalism_6034

145 Donnelly, D., Kovchegin, D., Mladineo, S., Ratz, L. and Roth, N., "Corrupting Nuclear Security: Potential Gaps and New Approaches to Insider Risk Mitigation," Institute for Nuclear Materials Management Paper, 2015, p. 3, https://www.belfercenter. org/sites/default/files/files/publication/a525_1%20%281%29.pdf

146 Karim, Iskander, "Identifying Instability Pockets," School of Advanced Military Studies, U.S. Army Command and General Staff College, 2014, p. 11, http://www.dtic. mil/dtic/tr/fulltext/u2/a614169.pdf

147 "Four Russians Sentences for Smuggling Radioactive Sources Across the Russian Kazakh Border," ITAR-Tass, Jan. 23, 2008, https://www. nti.org/analysis/ articles/four-russians-sentenced-smuggling-radioactive-sources-across-russian-kazakh-border/

148 "Russian-Speaking Foreign Fighters in Iraq and Syria: Assessing the Threat from (and to) Russia and Central Asia," Center for Strategic and International Studies, December 2017, https://csis-prod.s3.amazonaws.com/s3fs-public/publication/180726_Russian_Speaking_Foreign_Fight.pdf?VyUdcO2D6TJdW_Zm4Jk-mIpRkJxoXEZU6

Chapter 3: The Return of Foreign Fighters to Central Asia: Implications for U.S. Counterterrorism Policy. Thomas F. Lynch III, Michael Bouffard, Kelsey King, and Graham Vickowski

1   The Islamic State of Iraq and the Levant (ISIL), al-Qaeda, the al-Nusra front, and numerous other Salafi jihadist organizations fit under the much broader U.S. category of violent extremist organizations. See Fact Sheet: The White House Summit on Countering Violent Extremism (Washington, D.C.: The White House, February 18, 2015), available at <www.whitehouse.gov/the-press-office/2015/02/18/fact-sheet-white-house-summit-countering-violent-extremism>; Paul Davis, Influencing Violent Extremist Organizations and Their Supporters without Adverse Side Effects, Working Paper WR-909-OSD (Washington, DC: RAND, March 2012), 3–8, available at <www.rand.org/content/dam/rand/pubs/   working_papers/2012/RAND_WR909.pdf>.

2   In early 2016, U.S. Ambassador-at-Large and Coordinator for Counterterrorism Tina Kaidanow observed that, "the international terrorist threat picture has been transformed by ISIL's territorial expansion, the promulgation of its so-called caliphate, and its campaign aimed at the West. Weak or failed governance has allowed ISIL to take territory in Syria and Iraq and continues to provide an enabling environment for ISIL and its affiliates, notably in the Sinai, Libya, and Yemen. ISIL's seizure of territory in Iraq and Syria; its continued access to significant numbers of foreign terrorist fighters; its increased number of global branches; its unprecedented use of social media to spread its message, radicalize and recruit individuals to violence; and its external plotting through directed and inspired attacks has elevated it to our most pressing counterterrorism priority at this moment." See Tina S. Kaidanow, "Countering the Spread of ISIL and Other Threats," remarks at the Center for Strategic and International Studies Washington, DC, February 3, 2016, available at <www.state.gov/j/ct/rls/rm/252082.htm>.

3   Eugene Rumer, Richard Solilsy, and Paul Stronski, U.S. Policy Toward Central Asia 3.0 (Washington, DC: Carnegie Endowment for International Peace, January 25, 2016), available at <http://carnegieendowment.org/2016/01/25/u.s.-policy-toward-central-asia-3.0/itlr>.

4   Data demonstrating U.S. assistance trajectory is presented later in the paper.

5   Described in more detail later in the paper. See Syria Calling: Radicalisation in Central Asia, Europe and Central Asia Briefing No. 72 (Brussels: International Crisis Group, January 20, 2015), 1–3, available at <www.crisisgroup.org/~/media/Files/asia/central-asia/b072-syria-calling-radicalisation-incentral-asia.pdf>.

6   Peter R. Neumann, "Foreign Fighter Total in Syria/Iraq Now Exceeds 20,000; Surpasses Afghanistan Conflict in the 1980s," International Center for the Study of Radicalization, January 26, 2015, available at <http://icsr.info/2015/01/foreign-fighter-total-syriairaq-now-exceeds-20000-surpasses-afghanistan-conflict-1980s>.

7   Of note, there is a grand debate among experts about the factors that contribute to individual radicalization and the propensity to become a terrorist group member, including a Salafi jihadist group member. Some experts find an absence of economic opportunity to be a factor, if not a major one. Other scholars dispute the role of economic deprivation in the process of radicalization, pointing to the number of rich and privileged joining terrorist organizations. Many scholars view repressive political climates as a key factor in the alternative expression of needs, wants, and grievances as violence. Others minimize the factor of political repression in the individual choice for radicalism and terrorism. Some scholars argue that national programs for identification and reintegration of one-time terrorists and jihadists are a critical factor in reducing the risks from radicalization and instability. Others have found that these programs produce uncertain results and may not be of much value. For a review of these and other academic debates regarding radicalization and the choice to violent action, see Matthew Francis, "What Causes Radicalisation? Main Lines of Consensus in Recent Research," RadicalisationResearch.org, January 24, 2012, available at <www.radicalisationresearch.org/guides/francis-2012-causes-2/>; Randy Borum, "Radicalization into Violent Extremism II: A Revie of Conceptual Models and Empirical Research," Journal of Strategic Security 4, no. 11 (Winter 2011), 37–62, available at <http://scholarcommons.usf.edu/cgi/viewcontent.cgi?article=1140&context=jss>; SalihaMetin-

soy, "What Are the Common Factors That Drive Radicalization," Newsweek.com, June 17, 2016, available at <www.newsweek. com/ what-drives-radicalization-471661>. With these debates noted, this paper develops the important role that poor economic conditions, political repression, and an absence of credible means for generating social connections within the Central Asian republic states play in the preconditions for radicalization and the choice to jihad. Each of these factors contributes to what the majority of radicalization literature agrees is a common trait in those ripe for radicalization: the feeling of social alienation and the desire for positive social relations and solidarity that the cells of a terrorist organization provide. For a general review of this consensus on radicalization, see Max Abrahms, "What Terrorists Really Want: Terrorist Motives and Counterterrorism Strategy," International Security 32, no. 4 (Spring 2008), 78– 105; Martha Crenshaw, "The Logic of Terrorism: Terrorist Behavior as a Product of Strategic Choice," in Origins of Terrorism: Psychologies, Ideologies, Theologies, States of Mind, ed. Walter Reich (Cambridge: Cambridge University Press, 1990), 7–24.

8   For ISIL's advances in terrorist organization marketing and social media use, see J.M. Berger, "How ISIS Games Twitter," Atlantic.com, June 16, 2014, available at <www.theatlantic.com/international/ archive/2014/06/isis-iraq-twitter-social-media-strategy/372856/>; Javier Lesaca, "On Social Media, ISIS Uses Modern Cultural Images to Spread Anti-modern Values," Brookings Institution, September 24, 2015, available at <www.brookings.edu/blogs/techtank/ posts/2015/09/24-isis-socialmedia-engagement>.

9   Estimates of non-Syrian fighters joining jihad there and in Iraq between 2011 and late 2015 range from a low of 27,000 to a high of 31,000. All points in this range indicate the great importance of foreign fighters to the jihad in Syria and the Levant. See Charles R. Lister, The Syrian Jihad: Al Qaeda, The Islamic State and the Evolution of an Insurgency (Oxford: Oxford University Press, 2015), 1; Foreign Fighters: An Updated Assessment of the Flow of Foreign Fighters into Syria and Iraq (New York: The Soufan Group, December 2015), 4–9, available at <http://soufangroup.com/wp-content/ uploads/2015/12/ TSG_ForeignFightersUpdate3.pdf>.

10 National Strategy for Counterterrorism (Washington, DC: The White House, 2011), 6, available at <www.whitehouse.gov/sites/default/files/counterterrorism_strategy.pdf>.

11 In part, this is now done through the Department of Defense Counterterrorism Partnership Funds (CTPF) established in 2014. Here Central Asia is among the regions for CTPF partnership-fund focus. The fund targeted $20 million in CT money toward Central Asia in fiscal year 2016 and proposes an increase to $30 million for fiscal year 2017. The fiscal year 2017 plan proposes assistance to Tajikistan as a feature state and with focus on security programs for countering regional terrorist groups, while assisting security forces to improve border security intelligence, construction, and mobility as a priority—but not exclusive—security effort. See Counterterrorism Partnerships Fund: Department of Defense Budget for Fiscal Year (FY) 2017 (Washington, DC: Office of the Under Secretary of Defense [Comptroller)], February 2016), 1, 10–11.

12 See Joshua Kucera, "Pentagon Proposes $50 Million Program to Help Tajikistan Fight Terrorists," Eurasianet.org, February 16, 2016, available at <www.eurasianet.org/node/77366.

13 Maciej Falkowski and Józef Lang, Homo Jihadicus: Islam in the former USSR and the Phenomenon of the Post-Soviet Militants in Syria and Iraq (Warsaw: Center for Eastern Studies, September 2015), 40, available at <www.osw.waw.pl/sites/default/files/homojihadicus.pdf>. Also see Foreign Fighters, 10, 14–15.

14 Here, ummah denotes the Sunni Islam population worldwide. See Falkowski and Lang, 40.

15 Syria Calling, 1–3; Neumann.

16 See Thomas Grove, "Vladimir Putin Sympathizes with Turkey after Airport Killings," Wall Street Journal, June 29, 2016, available at <www.wsj.com/articles/vladimir-putin-sympathizes-withturkey-after-airport-killings-1467196514>.

17 Ibid., 43.

18 Syria Calling, 13–14.

19 Edward Lemon, "Assessing the Threat of Returning Foreign Fighters from Central Asia," Geopolitical Monitor.com, September 18, 2014, available at <www.geopoliticalmonitor.com/assessing-threatreturning-foreign-fighters-central-asia/>.

20 For examples, see, Bayram Balci and Didier Chaudet, "Jihadism in Central Asia: A Credible Threat After the Western Withdrawal from Afghanistan?" Carnegie Endowment.org, August 13, 2014, available at <http://carnegieendowment.org/2014/08/13/jihadism-in-central-

asia-credible-threatafter-western-withdrawal-from-afghanistan-pub-56381>; Reid Standish, "Shadow Boxing with the Islamic State in Central Asia," ForeignPolicy.com, February 6, 2015, available at <http://foreignpolicy. com/2015/02/06/shadow-boxing-with-the-islamic-state-in-central-asia-isis-terrorism/>; RyskeldiSatke, Casey Michel, and SertaçCanalp Korkmaz, "The Islamic State Threat in Central Asia: Reality or Spin?" Terrorism Monitor 13, no. 6 (March 2015), available at <www.jamestown.org/programs/tm/single/?tx_ttnews%5Btt_news%5D=43680&cHash=0675ecbfd7e509e815ff002b4143e228#.V40YBPnR_mE>.

21 Frank J. Cilluffo, "Wanted: Foreign Fighters—The Escalating Threat of ISIL in Central Asia," testimony before the Commission on Security and Cooperation in Europe (Helsinki Commission), June 10, 2015, available at <https://cchs.gwu.edu/sites/cchs.gwu.edu/files/downloads/CentralAsianForeignFighters.pdf>; Mark Kramer, The Return of Islamic State Fighters: The Impact on the Caucasus and Central Asia, PONARS Eurasia Memo 381 (Washington, DC: Elliott School of International Affairs, August 2015), available at <www.ponarseurasia.org/memo/return-islamic-state-fighters-impact-caucasus-andcentral-asia>. For an earlier, similarly worrisome conclusion, see John C.K. Daly, "Islamic Movement of Uzbekistan Flirts with ISIS," SilkRoadReporters.com, October 13, 2014, available at <www.silkroadreporters.com/2014/10/13/islamic-movement-uzbekistan-flirts-isis/>.

22 "ISIL Child Training Camp Discovered in Istanbul: Report," Hurriyet Daily News (Turkey), October 19, 2015, available at <www.hurriyetdailynews.com/isil-child-training-camp-discovered-in-istanbulreport-.aspx?pageID=238&nID=90052&NewsCatID=341>; "The Child Soldiers of Islamic State," RFERL. org, October 30, 2014, available at <www.rferl.org/content/islamic-state-child-fighters/26666558.html>.

23 UranBotobekov, "ISIS and Central Asia: A Shifting Recruiting Strategy," The Diplomat, May 17, 2016, available at <http://thediplomat.com/2016/05/isis-and-central-asia-a-shifting-recruiting-strategy/>.

24 Antony J. Blinken, "An Enduring Vision for Central Asia," remarks at the Brookings Institute, Washington, DC, March 31, 2015, available at <www.state.gov/s/d/2015/240013.htm>. This U.S. policy approach toward Central Asia remained unaltered in 2016.

25 In addition to these two main policy aims, the United States asserts sustained "connectivity" to the region as an official policy objec-

tive. See Blinken; Reid Standish, "Watchdogs Say U.S. Turned Blind Eye to Uzbek Abuse," ForeignPolicy.com, April 15, 2015, available at <http://foreignpolicy. com/2015/04/15/amnesty-international-uzbekistan-central-asia-war-on-terror-torture/>.

26 In 2010, the U.S. security assistance was 56 percent of its overall $385 million in total aid to the Central Asia region. But in 2014, direct security assistance it was 41 percent of its ≈ $194 million in overall regional aid. Much if not all of this general security assistance decline is scheduled to be offset by CTPF funds for targeted security support in 2016 and 2017. See details in text associated with table 1 of this paper. Also see the Center for International Policy's Security Assistance Monitor, available at <http://securityassistance.org>.

27 Catherine Putz, "Tajikistan Battered with Criticism, but U.S. Waives Sanctions," The Diplomat, April 2016, available at <http://thediplomat.com/2016/04/tajikistan-battered-with-criticism-butus-waives-sanctions/>.

28 For an in-depth exploration of Russian and other external support for Central Asian militaries, see Dmitry Gorenburg, External Support for Central Asian Military and Security Forces (Stockholm: SIPRI, January 2014), available at <www.sipri.org/research/security/afghanistan/central-asia-security/ publications/SIPRI-OSFno1WP.pdf>.

29 Approximately $6 million worth of International Military Education and Training annually, which as of 2014 translated to 109 trainees, per SecurityAssistance.org.

30 In 2015, there were approximately 3,000 officers from Uzbekistan alone studying at Russian military schools. See Dmitry Gorenburg, "Ever Wondered about the Military Balance in Central Asia?" RussiaInsider.com, July 3, 2015, available at <http://russia-insider.com/en/politics/ever-wonderedabout-military-balance-central-asia/ri8488>.

31 See Security Assistance Monitor. Data for total 2015 U.S. aid and security assistance was not fully available at the time of this writing. However, incomplete 2015 information did reveal a substantial cut to the category of U.S. military and police aid for all regional countries, with much of the past funding in this category evolving to management under the new, targeted CTPF in 2016 and 2017. After a 25 percent decline from 2014 to 2015, U.S. humanitarian and de-

velopment aid for 2016 and 2017 forecasts a return to a level slightly above 2014 numbers.

32 This rise and decline in U.S. assistance to the states of Central Asia largely paralleled the increase in U.S. military and security forces pushed into Afghanistan during the U.S. and North Atlantic Treaty Organization troop surge there from 2009 to 2013. Washington's attention toward Central Asia spiked during the Afghanistan surge as Central Asia and Russia provided critical rail and air access—through what became known as the Northern Distribution Network—for the additional troops and support personnel moving during the surge. See Deirdre Tynan, "Afghanistan: The Pressure Is Now on Central Asian Supply Route," Eurasianet.org, December 7, 2011, available at <www.eurasianet.org/node/64650>; John C.K. Daly, "Russia Shutters Northern Distribution Network," Eurasia Daily Monitor 12, no. 111 (June 15, 2015), available at <www.jamestown.org/single/?tx_ttnews%5Btt_ news%5D=44034&no_cache=1#.V4famoTR9aQ>.

33 Security Assistance Monitor.

34 Ibid.

35 Countering violent extremism (CVE) refers to proactive actions to counter efforts by violent extremists to radicalize, recruit, and mobilize followers to violence and to address specific factors that facilitate violent extremist recruitment and radicalization to violence. See Department of State & USAID Joint Strategy on Countering Violent Extremism (Washington, DC: Department of State, May 2016), 4, available at <www.state.gov/documents/organization/257913. pdf>. Also see Peter Romaniuk, Does CVE Work? Lessons Learned from the Global Effort to Counter Violent Extremism (Goshen, IN: Global Center on Cooperative Security, September 2015), available at <www.globalcenter.org/wp-content/ uploads/2015/09/Does-CVE-Work_2015.pdf>; Owen Frazer and Christian Nunlist, The Concept of Countering Violent Extremism, No. 183 (Zurich: Center for Security Studies, December 2015), 1, available at <www.css.ethz. ch/content/dam/ethz/special-interest/gess/cis/center-for-securities-studies/pdfs/ CSSAnalyse183-EN.pdf>.

36 Here the authors include the Islamic Movement of Uzbekistan's breakaway offshoot, the Islamic Jihad Union, as part of this main group with extraregional consequence. See "Islamic Jihad Union," Terrorism Research Analysis Consortium, available at <www.track-ingterrorism.org/group/ islamic-jihad-union-iju>; Daly, "Islamic Movement"; Bill Roggio and Caleb Weiss, "Islamic Jihad Union

Details Its involvement in Taliban's Azm Offensive," The Long War Journal, July 25, 2015, available at <www.longwarjournal.org/archives/2015/07/islamic-jihad-union-details-its-involvement-in-talibansazm-offensive.php>.

37 Falkowski and Lang, 69.

38 Ibid., 40.

39 Anna Dyner, Arkadiusz Legieć, and KacperRękawek, Ready to Go? ISIS and Its Presumed Expansion into Central Asia, PISM Policy Paper No. 19 (121) (Warsaw: Polish Institute of International Affairs, June 2015), available at <www.pism.pl/files/?id_plik=20020>.

40 Syria Calling, 6.

41 Paul Goble, "80 Percent of Tajiks Fighting for ISIS Recruited While in Russia, Dushanbe Says," Window on Eurasia, January 19, 2016, available at <http://windowoneurasia2.blogspot. com/2016/01/80-percent-of-tajiks-fighting-for-isis.html>; Catherine Putz, "Central Asia's Migrants Face Suspicion in Russia," The Diplomat, April 1, 2016, available at <http://thediplomat.com/2016/04/centralasias-migrants-face-suspicion-in-russia/>.

42 "From Tajikistan to Russia: Vulnerability and Abuse of Migrant Workers and Their Families," International Federation for Human Rights, October 2014, available at <www.fidh.org/IMG/pdf/russie641uk2014hd.pdf>.

43 Ibid., 11.

44 Noah Tucker, Public and State Responses to ISIS Messaging: Kazakhstan, CERIA Brief No. 13 (Washington, DC: Institute for European, Russian, and Eurasian Studies, February 2016), available at <https://app.box.com/s/q2deq68fvhjkgn8ijp2ywy7xshpuqzt9>; Goble.

45 Umida Hashimova, What 2015 Is Promising for Labor Migrants from Central Asia, CERIA Brief No. 23 (Washington, DC: Institute for European, Russian, and Eurasian Studies, March 2015), available at <https://app.box.com/s/bwoq8p80wfbn7brg2wyczzusx2p8ljhn>.

46 United Nations (UN), Department of Economic and Social Affairs, Population Division, "Trends in International Migrant Stock: Migrants by Destination and Origin," POP/DB/MIG/Stock/ Rev.2015. UN data are calculated mid-year every 5 years and as such does not cover the last year of further cutbacks in migrant flows.

47   Dugald McConnell and Brian Todd, "ISIS Fighter Was Trained by State Department," CNN, May 30, 2015, available at <http://edition. cnn.com/2015/05/29/politics/isis-man-trained-in-us/>.

48   Marnie O'Neill, "U.S.-Trained Police Sniper Colonel Gulmurod-Khalimov Made 'ISIS Minster of War,' News.com, September 8, 2016, available at <www.news.com.au/world/middle-east/ ustrained-police-sniper-colonel-gulmurod-khalimov-made-isis-minister-of-war/news-story/5469ea355 13f9c8a4eba5cf553d5171c>.

49   John C.K. Daly, "Tajikistan Worried by Islamic State's Threat to Central Asia," SilkRoadReporters.com, December 04, 2014, available at <www.silkroadreporters.com/2014/12/04/tajikistan-worried-islamic-states-threat-central-asia/>.

50   Falkowski and Lang, 2.

51   Ned Levin and Ayla Albayrak, "Istanbul Airport Bombers Were from the Former Soviet Union, Turkey Says," Wall Street Journal, June 30, 2016, available at <www.wsj.com/articles/turkey-detains-13-in-raids-linked-to-istanbul-airport-terror-attack-1467282081>; Thomas Grove, "Former Soviet Republics Are Fertile Ground for ISIS Recruiting," Wall Street Journal, June 30, 2016, available at <www. wsj.com/articles/former-soviet-republics-are-fertile-ground-for-isis-recruiting-1467311228>.

52   Neumann.

53   Tucker.

54   "Senior U.S. Delegation in Astana for the Central and South Asia Regional Conference on Countering Violent Extremism," Media Note, Department of State, Washington, DC, June 26, 2015, available at <www.state.gov/r/pa/prs/ps/2015/06/244422.htm>; ibid.

55   Joanna Paraszczuk, "Kyrgyz Official Blames Minority Uzbeks For Syria Presence," RFERL. org, March 17, 2015, available at <www. rferl.org/content/isis-kyrgyzstan-kyrgyz-uzbeks-syria-fightersis-lamic-state/26905648.html>; Tucker.

56   "Twenty-Two Kyrgyz Nationals Killed in Syria," RFERL.org, February 2, 2015, available at <www.rferl.mobi/a/kyrgyzstan-22-killed-syria/26825435.html>.

57   Ibid., 3.

58   Neumann.

59 An August 30, 2016, suicide car bombing against the Chinese embassy in Bishkek, Kyrgyzstan, corroborated analysis that the limited linkages that do exist between Salafi jihadist groups in Syria and militant operatives in Kyrgyzstan mainly come from the al-Nusra Front, the al Qaeda affiliate in Syria. Kyrgyzstan's State National Security Committee reported that the suicide bomber had been identified as a Kyrgyzstan citizen (born in Osh), who had joined the anti-China East Turkestan Islamic Movement (ETIM) and then trained in Syria in explosive attacks before returning to Kyrgyzstan on a Tajik passport under ETIM orders in June 2016. ETIM groups in Syria operate under the al-Nusra front umbrella organization. See "Jabhat al-Nusra Behind Attack on Chinese Embassy to Kyrgyzstan—Kyrgyz Security Agency," Interfax.com, September 6, 2016, available at <www.interfax.com/news.asp?y=2016&m=9&d=6&pg=3>.

60 Umar Farooq, "Kyrgyzstan and the Islamists," The Diplomat, November 16, 2015, available at <http://thediplomat.com/2015/11/kyrgyzstan-and-the-islamists/>.

61 "Tajikistan," in The CIA World Factbook, available at <www.cia.gov/library/publications/theworld-factbook/geos/ti.html>.

62 "Рахмон: «Более 1000 таджиковвоюютвСириииИраке» [Rahmon: "More than 1,000 Tajiks Fighting in Syria and Iraq"], Radio Azattyk, January 25, 2016, available at <http://rus.azattyk.org/ content/tajikistan-more-than-thousand-fighters-syria-iraq/27508035.html>; Neumann.

63 Noah Tucker, Public and State Responses to ISIS Messaging: Tajikistan, CERIA Brief No. 11 (Washington, DC: Institute for European, Russian, and Eurasian Studies, February 2016), 3, available at <https://app.box.com/s/o4q4porur5wg0xu1ngvseukxgwgkjiew>.

64 Ibid.

65 Catherine Putz, "Tajikistan Uses Laws to Crush Islamist Opposition," The Diplomat, July, 10 2015, available at <http://thediplomat.com/2015/07/tajikistan-uses-laws-to-crush-islamist-opposition/>.

66 Tucker, Public and State Responses to ISIS Messaging: Tajikistan, 3.

67 Ibid.

68 Ibid.

69 Bruce Pannier, "All Unquiet on the Tajik-Afghan Frontier," RFERL.org, March 12, 2016, available at <www.rferl.org/content/qishloq-ovozi-unquiet-tajik-afghan-border/27606705.html>.

70 Noah Tucker, Public and State Responses to ISIS Messaging: Turkmenistan, CERIA Brief No. 15 (Washington, DC: Institute for European, Russian, and Eurasian Studies, February 2016), 3, available at <https://app.box.com/s/k6qqvl3b2gsr08tyqu45flg211hz7icg>.

71 Neumann.

72 Tucker, Public and State Responses to ISIS Messaging: Turkmenistan, 33.

73 Ibid.

74 Noah Tucker, Public and State Responses to ISIS Messaging: Uzbekistan, CERIA Brief No. 12 (Washington, DC: Institute for European, Russian, and Eurasian Studies, February 2016, available at <http://centralasiaprogram.org/blog/2016/02/16/public-and-state-responses-to-isis-messaginguzbekistan/>.

75 Tucker, Public and State Responses to ISIS Messaging: Turkmenistan, 2.

76 Thomas F. Lynch III, Islamic State as Icarus: A Critical Assessment of an Untenable Threat (Washington, DC: The Woodrow and Wilson Center for International Scholars, October 2015), 15–16, 26, available at <www.wilsoncenter.org/sites/default/files/theislamicstateasicarus.pdf>; Jacob Zenn, "Al Qaeda–Aligned Central Asia Militants in Syria Separate from Islamic State-Aligned IMU in Afghanistan," Terrorism Monitor 13, no. 11 (May 29, 2015), available at <www.jamestown.org/programs/tm/single/?tx_ ttnews%5Btt_news%5D=43968&cHash=618bae17a86c2d23c30b7e219c3c731c#.V1hqhI-TR9aQ>.

77 See John Heathershaw and David W. Montgomery, The Myth of Post-Soviet Muslim Radicalization in the Central Asian Republics (London: Chatham House, November 2014), 6, 10–12, available at <www.chathamhouse.org/sites/files/chathamhouse/field/field_document/20141111PostSovietRadicaliz ationHeathershawMontgomery.pdf>; Standish, "Shadow Boxing."

78 Noah Tucker, "Uzbek Extremism in Context, Part 2: The Internet, Social Media and Religious Speech", Registan.net, October 14, 2013, available at <http://registan.net/2013/10/14/uzbek-extremismin-context-part-2-the-internet-social-media-and-religious-speech/>. After quarter century as Uzbekistan's only president, Islam Karimov died of a stroke on September 2, 2016. See "President Islam Karimov of Uzbekistan Dies at Age 78," New York Times, September 2, 2016, available at <www.nytimes. com/aponline/2016/09/02/

world/asia/ap-as-uzbekistan-president-profile.html?_r=0>; Andrew Roth, "Islam Karimov, Uzbekistan Strongman Who Exploited Anti-Terror Fight, Dies at 78," Washington Post, September 2, 2016, available at <www.washingtonpost.com/world/islam-karimov-uzbekistan-strongman-who-exploited-anti-terror-fight-dies-at-78/2016/09/02/3e08f846-7059-11e6-8365-b19e428a975e_story.html>.

79 Ibid.

80 In addition to earlier citations focused on these fears, see Dylan Morris, "ISIS in Central Asia: Threat or Illusion," ForeignBrief.com, March 21, 2016, available at <www.foreignbrief.com/isiscentral-asia-threat-illusion/>.

81 Daniil Turovsky, "'Congratulations, Your Brother's Become a Martyr': How Moscow's Migrant Workers Became Islamic State Fighters," Meduza Project, April 2015, https://meduza.io/en/feature/2015/04/27/congratulations-your-brother-s-become-a-martyr.

82 NazaraliPirnazarov, "Barely Guarded Afghan Border Puts Ex-Soviet Tajikistan in Peril," Reuters, April 21, 2016, available at <http://www.reuters.com/article/us-tajikistan-afghanistan-borderidUSKC-N0XI107>; Ovozi.

83 Tucker, "Public and State Responses to ISIS Messaging: Tajikistan," 3.

84 Joshua Kucera, "Turkmenistan Asks U.S. for Military Aid to Address Afghan Border Instability," Eurasianet.org, March 2015, available at <www.eurasianet.org/node/72761>.

85 OlzhasAuyezov, "Exclusive: Suspect in Kazakh Shooting Posted Islamic State-Linked Video," Reuters, June 8, 2016, available at <www.reuters.com/article/us-kazakhstan-shooting-exclusiveidUSKC-N0YU1TM>.

86 Mansur Mirovalev, "Kazakhstan: 17 Killed in Series of 'Extremist' Attacks," Al-Jazeera.com, June 6, 2016, available at <www.aljazeera.com/news/2016/06/kazakhstan-17-killed-series-extremistattacks-160606105755961.html>.

87 Bank of Russia, "External Sector Statistics," available at <www.cbr.ru/eng/ statistics/?PrtId=svs>.

88 Authors' interview with former U.S. Defense Attaché to Moscow, Washington, DC, February 15, 2016; National Endowment for Democracy, "Eurasia," available at <www.ned.org/region/eurasia/>.

89 "ISIS training Militants from Russia in Afghanistan, 'U.S. and UK Citizens among Instructors,'" RT.com, October 8, 2015, available at <www.rt.com/news/317989-afghanistan-isis-train-russians/>.

90 See Counterterrorism Partnerships Fund, 1, 10–11.

91 John Heathershaw and Sophie Roche, Islam and Political Violence in Tajikistan, Ethnopolitics Papers No. 8 (Exeter, United Kingdom: Exeter Centre for Ethno-Political Studies, March 2011).

92 AnoraSarokova, "Tajikistan's Battle Against Beards to 'Fight Radicalisation,'" BBC.com, January 2016, available at <www.bbc.com/news/world-asia-35372754>.

93 Ibid.

94 Pirnazarov; Counterterrorism Partnerships Fund, 10–11.

95 See Counterterrorism Partnerships Fund, 10–11.

96 Embassy of the United States, Dushanbe, Tajikistan, "U.S. Embassy Conducts Countering Violent Extremism Seminar," February 1, 2016, available at <http://dushanbe.usembassy.gov/pr020116.html>.

97 Tucker, Public and State Responses to ISIS Messaging: Turkmenistan, 3.

98 Kucera, "Turkmenistan Asks."

99 Mirovalev.

100 See Department of State, "Central and South Asia Regional Conference on Countering Violent Extremism (CVE) (Summary Report)," available at <www.state.gov/documents/organization/245601.pdf>.

101 Farooq.

102 "Kyrgyzstan Detains Imam for 'Encouraging Followers to Fight for ISIS,'" The Guardian, February 18, 2015, available at <www.theguardian.com/world/2015/feb/18/kyrgyzstan-imam-encouraging-followers-fight-for-isis>; ibid.

103 Standish, "Watchdogs Say."

Chapter 4: Islamic Movement of Uzbekistan a Strategy of Survival in Afghanistan-Pakistan Region Re-shift of Focus to Central Asia. Sayed Mujtaba Hashimy

A): Central Asian Jihadists under Al Qaeda's & Taliban's Strategic Ties. UranBotobekov

Chapter 5: Central Asian Jihadists in the Front Line. Ely Karmon

1   "St. Petersburg subway blast was suicide attack, officials say," The Associated Press, April 4, 2017, URL: http://www.cbc.ca/news/world/st-petersburg-russia-explosion-investigation-1.4054197

2   Filipov, David and Roth, Andrew, "Russia arrests possible accomplices of presumed St. Petersburg bomber," The Washington Post, April 6, 2017.

3   "St Petersburg attack: Russian police question new suspect," Reuters, April 17, 2017. URL: https://www.theguardian.com/world/2017/apr/17/st-petersburg-attack-russian-police-question-new-suspect

4   "Russia Arrests 12 Central Asians On Extremism Charges in Kaliningrad," Radio Free Europe/Radio Liberty, April 27, 2017. URL: http://www.rferl.org/a/russia-arrests-12-central-asians-extremism-charges-kaliningrad-sakhalin-islamic-state-/28454312.html

5   "Police arrest SIX more suspects over the Stockholm truck attack as three are bundled out of a car linked to the atrocity and special forces raid a property 20 km from the scene where four were killed," MailOnline, April 8, 2017. URL: http://www.dailymail.co.uk/news/article-4392736/Homemade-BOMB-hijacked-beer-truck-Stockholm.html

6   "Akilov linked to network around jihadist leader," Swedish Radio News, May 12, 2017. URL: http://sverigesradio.se/sida/artikel.aspx?programid=83&artikel=6694525

7   "Uzbeks Arrested For Allegedly Trying To Join Al-Qaeda Group In Syria," Radio Free Europe/Radio Liberty, November 6, 2015. URL: https://www.rferl.org/a/uzbekistan-al-qaeda-group-syria-jannat-oshliqari/27349840.html

8   "Terrorists who attacked in Stockholm and St. Petersburg deported by Turkey," Stockholm Center for Freedom, April 13, 2017. URL: http://stockholmcf.org/terrorists-who-attacked-in-stockholm-and-st-petersburg-deported-by-turkey.

9   Dominique Soguel and Suzan Fraser, "Attention in Istanbul bombing focused on Chechen extremist," The Associated Press, July 1, 2016. URL: https://apnews.com/fad6ca6eda9142bead29b11b7b259981/turkish-official-mastermind-feb-terror-attack-killed .

10 "Turkey remembers Istanbul airport attack blamed on ISIL," Agence France-Presse, June 28, 2017. URL: http://www.hurriyetdailynews.

com/turkey-remembers-istanbul-airport-attack-blamed-on-isil-.as px?pageID=238&nID=114880&NewsCatID=341.

11   Ahmet S. Yayla, "The Reina Nightclub Attack and The Islamic State Threat to Turkey," CTC Sentinel, Combating Terrorism Center, Vol. 10, Issue 3, March 10, 2017.

12   Ibid.

13   Ibid.

14   "Istanbul Reina attack suspect says nightclub was chosen at random," BBC News, January 19, 2017. URL: http://www.bbc.co.uk/news/world-europe-38673154

15   Göktuğ Sönmez, "Reina Attack, Masharipov and Radicalization in Central Asia," Orsam Review of Regional Affairs, No.56, January 2017. URL: http://www.orsam.org.tr/files/Degerlendirmeler/56/56eng.pdf

16   Ahmet S. Yayla, op. cit.

17   Neal Baker and Mark Hodge, "Inside the Killer's Lair." The Sun, January 17, 2017.

18   "Two Daesh suspects planning Reina-style attack nabbed in Istanbul," Daily Sabah, March 16, 2017.

19   Tamer Badawi, "Daesh in Eurasia," Al-Jazeera Centre for Studies, December 4, 2014. URL: http://studies.aljazeera.net/en/dossiers/decipheringdaeshoriginsimpactandfuture/2014/12/201412311921865343.html .

20   Martin Berger, "Radical Islamic Terrorism Spreading Across Central Asia Like Fire," New Eastern Outlook, July 9,.2016. URL: http://journal-neo.org/2016/07/19/radical-terrorism-is-spreading-across-central-asia-as-fire/ .

21   "Germany Probing Possible Extremism Among Chechen Migrants," Radio Free Europe/Radio Liberty, October 25, 2016. URL: http://www.rferl.org/a/germany-extremism-chechen-migrants/28074011.html .

22   Tamer Badawi, op. cit.

23   "Chinese Jihadis' Rise in Syria Raises Concerns at Home," Dawn, April 23, 2017. URL: https://www.dawn.com/news/1328675 .

24   Christina Lin, "The Changing Nature of Terrorism in China," The Cipher Brief, September 27, 2016. URL: https://www.thecipherbrief.com/article/asia/changing-nature-terrorism-china-1089 .

25 Ely Karmon, "The Demise of the Caliphate: Quo Vadis ISIS?" International Institute for Counter-Terrorism (ICT) website, December 19, 2016. URL: https://www.ict.org.il/Article/1878/the-demise-of-the-caliphate-quo-vadis-isis .

26 Nathaniel Barr, "Wilayat Khorasan Stumbles in Afghanistan," Terrorism Monitor, The Jamestown Foundation, Vol.15, Issue: 5, March 3, 2016. URL: https://jamestown.org/program/wilayat-khorasan-stumbles-in-afghanistan/ .

27 Michael Safi, "Isis militants disguised as doctors kill 38 in Kabul hospital attack." The Guardian, March 8, 2017.

28 "10,000 ISIS fighters in Afghanistan 'trained to expand to Central Asia, Russia,'" RT NEWS, April 19, 2016. URL: https://www.rt.com/news/340200-isis-afghanistan-threaten-russia/ .

29 "Isis letter reveals tribal rifts in Afghanistan faction amid war with Taliban and US," Associated Press, June 7, 2017. URL: http://www.ibtimes.co.uk/isis-letter-reveals-tribal-rifts-afghanistan-faction-amid-war-taliban-us-1625127 .

30 Scott Shane and Eric Schmitt, "Norway Announces Three Arrests in Terrorist Plot," New York Times, July 8, 2010.

31 MuhTaufiqurrohman and Ardi Putra Prasetya, Today, December 15, 2016; URL: http://m.todayonline.com/commentary/radical-terrorist-man-behind-five-terror-plots-indonesia .

32 Jonathan Head, "The surreal investigations into Thailand's unresolved bombings," BBC News, August 17, 2016. URL: http://www.bbc.com/news/world-asia-37091825 .

33 Philip Wen, "Xinjiang attack: vehicle rams into government compound killing several," The Sydney Morning Herald, December 29, 2016.

34 "Eight dead after knife attack in China's western Xinjiang region," Associated Press, February 15, 2017. URL: http://www.telegraph.co.uk/news/2017/02/15/eight-dead-knife-attack-chinas-western-xinjiang-region/ .

35 Bloody Islamic State video puts China in cross hairs, South China Morning Post, March 1, 2017.

36 Nectar Gan, "Details emerge of 'terrorism suspect' arrest during armed raid in China," South China Morning Post, April 17, 2017.

Chapter 6: Talebs in Tajikistan: The 'Terrorist Spill-Over' Hype. Thomas Ruttig

1   They cite an interesting example: 'In the 1980s, during the Soviet oc-
    cupation of Afghanistan, the CIA in fact tried to facilitate the spread
    of insurgency from the mujahedeen it was supporting to infect the
    Washington's ideological rival to the north. Yet they found the ma-
    jority of Soviet Central Asians unsympathetic to the Afghan cause.'

2   It is sometimes written that the IMU has renamed itself, or joined
    with other groups, to form IPT. This is incorrect. See the comment at
    the end of this article.

3   Analysts in Dushanbe say OzodTojikiston (Free Tajikistan) is led by
    former Tajik army colonel Mahmud Khudoiberdiev, an ethnic Uzbek
    and former ally of the Rahmon government, who broke ranks, left
    the country, led an unsuccessful military incursion into the country
    in 1998, was wrongly reported dead and now is reportedly based in
    Uzbekistan, close to both the Tajik and Afghan borders (see here;
    more background about him here; only the author had to revise his
    opinion later about the colonel's death). Claims by Tajik authorities
    in 2009 that fighters of this group have joined al-Qaeda do not sound
    very convincing.

4   Ansarullah is reportedly led by a Tajik, Mulla Amruddin, and op-
    erates 'in Pakistan and Afghanistan'. The Kabul-based Ariana News
    website quoted Afghan intelligence sources in June last year saying
    that 'some Tajik terrorists are being trained in Pakistan and said
    that a movement called Ansarollah has been attracting young Ta-
    jiks to train them and dispatch back to Tajikistan'. The Jamestown
    Foundation, another terrorism watch institute, writes that 'Jamaat
    Ansarullah is believed to have close ties with both the IMU and the
    Taliban.... While the group has not successfully attacked Tajikistan
    since 2010, they have been actively recruiting members via their
    webpage and through Twitter.' It adds that some Tajik opposition
    activists question the group's existence.

5   The origin of the SCO is the 2001 Shanghai Convention on Com-
    bating Terrorism, Separatism and Extremism concluded between
    China, Russia, Tajikistan, Kazakhstan and Uzbekistan (which later
    left the organisation) (see here; see also here).

6   The AEI's Critical Threats Project distinguishes between affiliated
    groups, like al-Qaeda in the Islamic Maghreb or the Islamic Emir-
    ate of the Caucasus, and associated groups, like Boko Haram (in

Nigeria), the TTP, LeT and SSP (all in Pakistan) and the Haqqani network; it does not include the Afghan Taleban as such, though. It writes: "Identifying formal inclusion in the network is straightforward: the al Qaeda emir recognizes certain groups that have pledged their allegiance, bayat, to him. All of these recognized groups share al Qaeda's ideology, and their leaders justify the groups' operations with that ideology. The formally recognized groups also share resources.... They also have a common signature: similar structures, training procedures, and patterns and methods of operations." In contrast, "many" of al-Qaeda's associates, the organisation says, "focus their efforts almost exclusively on local agendas" (see also here).

7   The LWJ report has more such information: ISAF previously identified the Burkah district as 'a Taliban and [IMU] safe haven'; also that ISAF said it has targeted there "a Taliban commander who is linked to the Islamic Movement of Uzbekistan and leads approximately 80 foreign fighters of Uzbek, Chechen and Tajik descent". ISAF also had "begun to identify the location of safe havens and training camps in the north for the Taliban and the allied Islamic Movement of Uzbekistan. Both terror groups maintain a strong presence in the northern Afghan provinces of Badakhshan, Baghlan, Balkh, Faryab, Jawzjan, Kunduz, Samangan, Sar-i-Pul, and Takhar, and have established suicide training camps in the north over the past several years. As the two groups expand their presence in the north, top leaders of the Islamic Movement of Uzbekistan have integrated into the Taliban's shadow government in the northern provinces." LWJ also repeats the quote of "a Taliban commander from Baghlan named Mustafa" in the Asia Times, saying that "jihadis from Central Asia, including 'Chechnya, Uzbekistan, Tajikistan, and Russia,' make up a significant portion of the fighters in the Afghan north and that they are setting their sights on the neighboring country of Uzbekistan".

8   One of them was MirzoZiyoev, the civil war-time commander-in-chief of the opposition guerrilla force who, so far, has lived peacefully in the Rasht valley, the scene of most of the 2008–10 fighting. Ziyoev was accused of having joined the IMU, an assertion that was quickly denied by the late IMU leader Yuldashev. This led to speculations that MulloAbdullo's move was a provocation set up by the Dushanbe government to get rid of Ziyoev who had been one of the highest-ranking former opposition government members after the peace deal. He was dismissed by President Rahmon in 2006.

9   Roche and Heathershaw wrote immediately after the events that "the
     government has set up an information blackout. It has issued threat-
     ening statements against Tajikistan's beleaguered independent press
     and threatened criminal charges against journalists who report more
     than the official line". They also detail the social problems in the area
     where the fighting took place, speak about young men disappearing
     into the mountains because they fear reprisals by the government
     forces (which makes them 'rebels' in the official accounts) and about
     the 'phantom of foreign Islamism' evoked by the government in Du-
     shanbe.

10   The March 2012 attack happened while President Karzai was in
     Dushanbe for joint Nawruz celebrations with other Central Asian
     heads of state. But none of the author's interlocutors in Tajikistan
     mentioned the Karzai visit when talking about the episode (he only
     discovered the coincidence later), so he assumes they did not see a
     connection.

11   Background on the original main moderate opposition groups Erk
     and Birlik, which were suppressed starting in 1992 here and about
     the current state of the non-violent Uzbek opposition here and here.

12   Meanwhile, in 2011 and 2012, the IMU lost its main military com-
     mander and Yuldashev's successor in drone strikes in Pakistan (here
     and here).

13   In September 2010, the Christian Science Monitor, referring to "US
     estimates", suddenly has 3,000 Uzbeks in Waziristan, "not to men-
     tion a number of militants belonging to other Central Asian states".

14   The report, picked up by LWJ, contains ISAF claims about an "Ira-
     nian-based Uzbek Islamic Movement of Uzbekistan facilitators" and
     that "a senior US intelligence official" told the website that a captured
     IMU facilitator operated "in Iran with the support of Qods Force,
     the special operations branch of Iran's Islamic Revolutionary Guards
     Corps". The US official added, "Qods Force helps the IMU and al Qa-
     eda move fighters into Afghanistan, and backs local Taliban groups".

Chapter 7: Kazakhstan, Kyrgyzstan, Tajikistan, Turkmenistan, Uzbekistan. NodirbekSoliev

1 Some of these figures were put forth by lawenforcement officials from
  the respective Central Asian countries during the regional counter-
  terrorism experts meeting held in Tbilisi, Georgia in September

2018, where the author attended as a speaker. However, they prefer their identity and affiliation to remain anonymous.

2 "IG iNovieUgrozyBezopasnostiPostsovetskikhGosudarst (IS and New Security Threats to the PostSoviet Countries)," Sputniknews.uz, March 9, 2016, https://ru.sputniknewsuz.com/analytics/20160309/1965841.html.

3 Mumin Ahmadi, "Boeviki 'IslamskogoGosudarstva' UgrojayutTadjikistanu 'Djihadom (Islamic State' Fighters Threaten Tajikistan with Jihad')," Radio Ozodi, January 4, 2015, http://rus.ozodi.org/content/article/26775997.html.

4 "Islamic State Claims Attack That Killed Four Foreign Cyclists In Tajikistan," RFE/RL's Tajik Service, July 30, 2018, https://www.rferl.org/a/tajikistan-terrorism-possibleattack-four-foreign-cyclists/29398154.html.

5 "Two Guards Killed in Khujand Prison Riot," Asia Plus, November 12, 2018, https://news.tj/en/news/tajikistan/incidents/20181112 /two-guards-killed-in-khujand-prison-riot.

6 Rohan Gunaratna, "East Asia Part of IS's Grand Strategy for Expansion," BenarNews, September 25, 2017, https://www.benarnews.org/english/commentaries/as ia-pacific-threat-update/singapore-link09252017123147.html.

7 A low-tech attack is a form of terrorist operations involving the use of simple tactics and primitive weapons that can be easily obtained and used by anyone at any time. This mode of attack does not require extensive planning and professional experience from the perpetrator. In the light of heightened propaganda calls, vehicular assault, stabbing and arson have become the most fashionable tactics for attacks carried out by IS inspired individuals in many parts of the world, including Central Asia. For more details see: Kumar Ramakrishna, "ISIS "Weaponisation of Everyday Life"," RSIS Commentaries, March 27, 2017, https://www.rsis.edu.sg/rsispublication/nssp/co17054-london-march-2017-isisweaponisation-of-everyday-life/#.XBifr_kzaM8

8 Oved Lobel, 'Is Al-Qaeda's Syrian Affiliate Adopting Islamic State Tactics in Russia?' Al-ArabyAlJadeed, July 4, 2018, https://www.alaraby.co.uk/english/comment/2017/7/5 /is-al-qaedas-syrian-affiliate-adopting-is-tactics-inrussia.

9   This is a derogatory term used by Islamist terrorist groups to describe Shia and Alawite forces whom they regard as heretics and apostates.

10 Thomas Joscelyn, "Analysis: Jihadists in Syria react to Sochi agreement," FDD's Long War Journal, October 16, 2018, https://www.longwarjournal.org/archives/2018/10/an alysis-jihadists-in-syria-react-to-sochiagreement.php.

11 Ninth report of the Analytical Support and Sanctions Monitoring Team submitted pursuant to resolution 2368 (2017) concerning ISIL (Da'esh), AlQaida and associated individuals and entities, UN Security Council, May 30, 2018, https://www.ecoi.net/en/file/local/1435051/1226_152 8897591_n1813039.pdf.

12 "Russian, Kyrgyz Troops To Hold Counterterror Drills In Eastern Kyrgyzstan," RFE/RL's Kyrgyz Service, September 25, 2018, https://www.rferl.org/a/russia-kyrgyz-troops-to-holdantiterror-drills-in-eastern-kyrgyzstan/29508580.html.

13 "Media Note of the United States Department of State on "State Department Terrorist Designation of Katibat al-Imam al-Bukhari," March 22, 2018, https://www.state.gov/r/pa/prs/ps/2018/03/279454.ht m.

14 Rafael Fakhrutdinov, "V rezultatespetsoperatsiizaderjano 60 inostrannykhgrajdan (As a result of special operation, 60 foreign citizens were detained)," Gazeta.ru, March 13, 2018, https://www.gazeta.ru/social/2018/03/13/11681395.s html.

15 Kathrin Hille, "Russia And Radicalisation: Homegrown Problem," The Financial Times, December 8, 2015, https://www.ft.com/content/77156ed2-9ab0-11e5be4f-0abd1978acaa.

16 "Origins and Destinations of the World's Migrants, 1990-2017," Pew Research Center, February 28, 2018, http://www.pewglobal.org/2018/02/28/globalmigrant-stocks/?country=RU&date=2017.

17 Jamshed Marupov, "Why Do Isfara Residents Become Jihadists?" CABAR, November 1, 2018, https://cabar.asia/en/why-do-isfara-residentsbecome-jihadists-multimedia/; "150 Kyrgyz CitizensKilled In Syria Fighting Alongside IS,"RFE/RL's Kyrgyz Service, June 28, 2018, https://www.rferl.org/a/official-150-kyrgyz-citizenskilled-in-syria-fighting-alongside-is/29325374.html.

18 The propaganda speech of KTJ's leader Abu Saloh that appeared on a YouTube channel run by an anonymous supporter of the group:

"Shomahliningsobitqadamligi (The Devotion of the Syrian People),"
YouTube (YangiDarslar) August 16, 2018, https://www.youtube.
com/watch?v=D505mFX8BrA.

19 KanymgulElkeeva, "Ekstremizmpytajetsaproleztcherezlyubuyushel
(Extremism Is Seeking to Penetrate Through Any Gap)," RFE/RL's
Kyrgyz Service, January 10, 2018, https://rus.azattyk.org/a/kyrgyz-
stan_extremism_sites _internet/28967239.html.

Counter Terrorist Trends and Analyses. Volume 11, Issue 1 January
2019

**Chapter 8: Understanding the Factors Contributing to Radicalisation
among Central Asian Labour Migrants in Russia. Mohammed S
Elshimi with RaffaelloPantucci, Sarah Lain and Nadine L Salman**

1. For example, see Ahmed Rashid, Jihad: The Rise of Militant Islam in
Central Asia (Penguin, 2003). The concerns were much exacerbated
in the wake of the 9/11 attacks on the US, but were already present
in the background from the fall of the Soviet Union.

2. Radio Free Europe, 'Kyrgyzstan Sentences Three Over Chinese Embassy Attack', 28 June 2017.

3. Estimates of numbers, however, vary substantially. A report by the
Soufan Group in December 2015 identified just over a thousand
or so from Central Asia, while a report by the International Crisis
Group in January 2015 identified between 2,000 and 4,000. See Sou-
fan Group, 'Foreign Fighters: An Updated Assessment of the Flow of
Foreign Fighters into Syria and Iraq', December 2015; International
Crisis Group, 'Syria Calling: Radicalisation in Central Asia', Europe
and Central Asia Briefing No. 72, January 2015.

4. For a history of the degree to which Central Asian fighters have been
involved in Afghanistan, see Christian Bleuer and Said Reza Kazemi,
'Between Co-operation and Insulation: Afghanistan's Relations with
the Central Asian Republics', report, Afghan Analysts Network, June
2014. For a more recent example in Pakistan, see the Islamic Movement of Uzbekistan attack on Karachi airport in June 2014, or recent
Afghan government statements about foreign fighters in Afghanistan.

5. Noah Tucker, 'Central Asian Involvement in the Conflict in Syria
and Iraq: Drivers and Responses', USAID, 4 May 2015.

6. Ibid.; Edward Lemon, 'Daesh and Tajikistan: The Regime's (In)Security Policy', RUSI Journal (Vol. 160, No. 5, October/November 2015).

7. UranBotobekov, 'ISIS Uses Central Asians for Suicide Missions', The Diplomat, 1 December 2016.

8. Tucker, 'Central Asian Involvement in the Conflict in Syria and Iraq'; Marlene Laruelle, 'The Paradox of Uzbek Terror: Peace at Home, Violence Abroad', Foreign Affairs, 1 November 2017.

9. Lemon, 'Daesh and Tajikistan'.

10. Tucker, 'Central Asian Involvement in the Conflict in Syria and Iraq'.

11. Lemon, 'Daesh and Tajikistan'.

12. International Crisis Group, 'Syria Calling'.

13. John Heathershaw and David Montgomery, 'The Myth of Post-Soviet Muslim Radicalization in the Central Asian Republics', research paper, Chatham House, November 2014.

14. Eric McGlinchey, 'Violent Extremism and Insurgency in Central Asia: A Risk Assessment', USAID, September 2013.

15. International Organization for Migration (IOM), 'Migrant Vulnerabilities and Integration Needs in Central Asia: Root Causes, Social and Economic Impact of Return Migration', regional field assessment, 2016, p. 9.

16. Ibid.

17. International Crisis Group, 'Syria Calling'; The Soufan Group, 'Foreign Fighters', p. 15.

18. Sergey Ryazantsev, 'Labour Migration from Central Asia to Russia in the Context of the Economic Crisis', Russia in Global Affairs, 31 August 2016.

19. Stefan Malthaner and Peter Waldmann, 'The Radical Milieu: Conceptualizing the Supportive Social Environment of Terrorist Groups', Studies in Conflict & Terrorism (Vol. 37, No. 12, 2014).

20. The first three elements of the framework – structural motivation, individual incentive and enabling factors – were developed by James Khalil and Martine Zeuthen, 'Countering Violent Extremism and Risk Reduction: A Guide to Programme Design and Evaluation', RUSI Whitehall Report, 2-16 (June 2016).

21. RUSI, 'Countering Violent Extremism, Regional Training Curriculum,' European Commission 2018.

22. IOM, 'Who is a Migrant?', <https://www.iom.int/who-is-a-migrant>, accessed 26 March 2018.

23. See Minerva Nasser-Eddine et al., 'Countering Violent Extremism (CVE) Literature Review', Counter Terrorism and Security Technology Centre, Defense Science and Technology Organisation, Australian Department of Defence, 2011, p. 9; James Khalil, 'Know Your Enemy: On the Futility of Distinguishing Between Terrorists and Insurgents', Studies in Conflict & Terrorism (Vol. 36, No. 5, 2013), pp. 419–30.

24. UN, 'Plan of Action to Prevent Violent Extremism', Report of the Secretary-General, 24 December 2015, p. 1.

25. Ibid., p. 1.

26. Definition adapted from European Commission, STRIVE for Development: Strengthening Resilience to Violence and Extremism, revised edition (Luxembourg: Publications Office of the European Union, 2016).

27. Psychologists such as Randy Borum and John Horgan have been particularly critical of what they see as the received wisdom that extreme violence is caused by radical views. See John Horgan, The Psychology of Terrorism, 2nd edition (Abingdon and New York, NY: Routledge, 2014); Randy Borum, 'Understanding Terrorist Psychology', Mental Health Law & Policy Faculty Publications, Paper 576, January 2010.

28. European Commission, STRIVE for Development, p. 55

29. Ibid.

30. This quote is followed by a code in brackets that identifies the city and interviewee number, so that 'Novo' is short for Novosibirsk, and the number 15 denotes the fact that this interviewee is the 15th participant to be interviewed. This convention is used throughout the report.

31. The Hanafi School is one of the four religious Sunni Islamic schools of jurisprudence (fiqh). It is named after the scholar Abu Hanifa An-Nu'man ibn Thabit (d. 767), It has the largest number of followers among Sunni Muslims and dominates in the countries that were once part of the Ottoman Empire.

32. The four main Islamic schools of jurisprudence in Sunni Islam.

33. A Russian word referring to seniority of age or rank. In this context, it means senior supervisor.

34. Hizbut-Tahrir (Party of Liberation) is an international pan-Islamist political organisation. It was founded in 1953 as a Sunni Muslim organisation in Jerusalem by Taqiuddin Al-Nabhani. Since then, Hizbut-Tahrir has spread to more than 50 countries. It aims to re-establish 'the Islamic Khilafah (Caliphate)' or Islamic State. The new caliphate would unify the Muslim community (Ummah) in a unitary superstate of unified Muslim-majority countries. The proposed state would enforce Islamic Sharia law. Although it is a non-violent organisation, Hizbut-Tahrir is banned in many countries.

35. Moldo in Kyrgyz translates as 'mullah'.

36. Hizbut-Tahrir (Party of Liberation) is an international pan-Islamist political organisation. It was founded in 1953 as a Sunni Muslim organisation in Jerusalem by Taqiuddin Al-Nabhani. Since then, Hizbut-Tahrir has spread to more than 50 countries. It aims to re-establish 'the Islamic Khilafah (Caliphate)' or Islamic State. The new caliphate would unify the Muslim community (Ummah) in a unitary superstate of unified Muslim-majority countries. The proposed state would enforce Islamic Sharia law. Although it is a non-violent organisation, Hizbut-Tahrir is banned in many countries.

37. QuintanWiktorowicz, 'Anatomy of the Safali Movement', Studies in Conflict & Terrorism (Vol. 29, No. 3, 2006), pp. 207–39.

38. Diego Gambetta and Steffen Hertog, Engineers of Jihad: The Curious Connection Between Violent Extremism and Education (Princeton, NJ: Princeton University Press, 2017).

39. Thomas Heghammer, 'The Future of Jihadism in Europe: A Pessimistic View', Perspectives on Terrorism (Vol. 10, No. 6, December 2016); European Institute of Peace, 'Molenbeek and Violent Radicalization: "A Social Mapping"', June 2017.

40. John Russell, 'The Geopolitics of Terrorism: Russia's Conflict with Islamic Extremism', Eurasian Geography and Economics (Vol. 50, No. 2, 2013), pp. 184–96; PreetiBhattacharji, 'Chechen Terrorism (Russia, Chechnya, Separatist)', Council on Foreign Relations, April 2010.

41. Scott Atran, 'The Devoted Actor: Unconditional Commitment and Intractable Conflict Across Cultures', Current Anthropology (Vol. 57, No. S13, June 2016).

42. Tim Stevens and Peter R Neumann, 'Countering Online Radicalisation: A Strategy for Action', policy report, International Centre for the Study of Radicalisation and Political Violence, 2009.

43. Khalil and Zeuthen, 'Countering Violent Extremism and Risk Reduction'.

44. United Nations Office of Counter-Terrorism, 'Enhancing the Understanding of the Foreign Terrorist Fighters' Phenomenon in Syria', report, July 2017.

45. BBC News, 'St Petersburg Metro Bomber "from Kyrgyzstan"', 4 April 2017.

46. Lemon, 'Daesh and Tajikistan'.

47. Gambetta and Hertog, Engineers of Jihad.

48. Marc Sageman, Misunderstanding Terrorism (Philadelphia, PA: University of Pennsylvania Press, 2017); Shadi Hamid, Islamic Exceptionalism: How the Struggle Over Islam Is Reshaping the World (New York, NY: St Martin's Press, 2016).

Chapter 10: Sunni-Shia Issue in Azerbaijan. Ilia Brondz1, TahminaAslanova

1. Wikipedia, the Free Encyclopedia, AqQoyunlu. https://en.wikipedia. org/wiki/Aq_Qoyunlu [Citation Time(s):1]

2. Aleskerova, N. (2007) Sufism in Azerbaijan. The Caucasus and Globalization, 1, 111-119. https://www.ca-c.org/c-g/2007/journal_eng/c-g-4/11.shtml [Citation Time(s):1]

3. Nazeer, A. (2001) History of Islam. An Encyclopedia of Islamic History. https://historyofislam.com/contents/the-land-empires-of-asia/the-emergence-of-the-safavids/ [Citation Time(s):1]

4. Bearman, P., Bianquis, Th., Bos-worth, C.E., van Donzel, E. and Heinrichs, W.P. (2001) Middle East and Islamic Studies. Encyclopaedia of Islam, Second Edition. https://referenceworks.brillonline. com/browse/encyclopaedia-of-islam-2/alpha/i [Citation Time(s):1]

5. Laina, F.-H. (2002) Charles Melville, ed. Safavid Persia: The History and Politics of an Islamic Society. Comparative Civilizations Review,

47, Article 13. https://scholarsarchive.byu.edu/ccr/vol47/iss47/13 [Citation Time(s):1]

6. Chehabi, H.E. and Mneimneh, H. (2006) Distant Relations: Iran and Lebanon in the Last 500 Years. Centre for Lebanese Studies and IB Tauris & Co. Ltd., Oxford and London. https://www.lebanesestudies. com/portfolio-item/distant-relations-iran-and-lebanon-in-the-last-500-years/ [Citation Time(s):1]

7. Goyushov, A. (2012) Islam in Azerbaijan (Historical Background). The Caucasus Analytical Digest, 44, 2-4. [Citation Time(s):1]

8. Cornell, S.E. (2006) The Politicization of Islam in Azerbaijan. Central Asia-Caucasus Institute & Silk Road Studies Program, Washington DC. https://www.silkroadstudies.org/resources/pdf/SilkRoad-Papers/2006_10_SRP_Cornell_Islam-Azerbaijan.pdf [Citation Time(s):1]

9. Balci, B. (2004) Between Sunnism and Shiism: Islam in Post-Soviet Azerbaijan. Central Asian Survey, 23, 205-217. https://doi.org/10.10 80/02634930410001310544 [Citation Time(s):1]

10. Сампиев, И. (2008) Историческиепараллелиисламскойполит икиРоссиинаСевернomКавказе. Кавказиглобализация, 2, 63-73. (In Russian) https://cyberleninka.ru/article/v/istoricheskie-paralleli-islamskoy-politiki-rossii-na-severnom-kavkaze [Citation Time(s):1]

11. Swietochowski, T. (2002) Azerbaijan: The Hidden Faces of Islam. World Policy Journal, 19, 69-76. https://doi.org/10.1215/07402775-2002-4009 [Citation Time(s):1]

12. Svanberg, I. and Westerlund, D. (1999) Islam outside the Arab World. Curzon, Richmond. https://www.amazon.com/Islam-Out-side-World-Ingvar-Svanberg/dp/0700711244 [Citation Time(s):1]

13. Ismayilova, S.A. (2016) Azərbaycantarixininöyrənilməsindəbədiiə dəbiyyatmənbəkimi (XIX əsrin II yarısıŞimaliAzərbaycanbədiiədə biyyatıüzrə), Bakalavrhazirliğiüçün, Dərsvəsaiti, AzərbaycanRespu blikasiTəhsilNazirliyi, BakiDövlətUniversiteti, Avrora, Baki. Translation of Title to English: History of Azerbaijan (on the Literature of Northern Azerbaijan in the Second Half of XIX Century (2016)). The Ministry of Education of Azerbaijan Republic, Baku State University, Avrora, Baku. (In Azerbaijan) [Citation Time(s):1]

14. Seyidzade, D. (2011) Azerbaijan in the Beginning of XX Century: Roads Leading to Independence. Second Edition, Baku, 38-100. http://www.anl.az/el_en/s/sd_abXX.pdf [Citation Time(s):1]

15. Goyushov, A., Caffee, N. and Denis, R. (2010) The Formation of Contemporary Azerbaijani Society: The Role of the Russian Conquest in the Rise of a New Elite. Azerbaijan in the World, 3, 16-17. http://biweekly.ada.edu.az/vol_3_no_16-17/The_formation_of_contemporary_Azerbaijani_society_The_role_of_the_Russian_conquest.htm [Citation Time(s):1]

16. Motika, R. (2001) Islam in Post-Soviet Azerbaijan. Archives de sciences sociales des religions, 115, 111-124. http://assr.revues.org/18423 https://doi.org/10.4000/assr.18423 [Citation Time(s):1]

17. Goyushov, A. (2008) Islamic Revival in Azerbaijan. Current Trends in Islamist Ideology, 7, 66-81. https://www.hudson.org/research/9815-islamic-revival-in-azerbaijan [Citation Time(s):1]

18. Баберовски, Й. (2010) Врагестьвезде: СталинизмнаКавказе, Российскаяполитическаяэнциклопедия (РОССПЭН). (In Russian) http://mirknig.su/knigi/history/59414-vrag-est-vezde-stalinizm-na-kavkaze.html [Citation Time(s):1]

19. Беннигсен, А. (1983) МусулманивСССР. YMCA Press, Paris. (In Russian) https://vtoraya-literatura.com/pdf/benigsen_musulmane_v_sssr_1983_text.pdf [Citation Time(s):2]

20. Fazlur, R. (1979) Evolution of Soviet Policy toward Muslims in Russia: 1917-1965. Institute of Muslim Minority Affairs, Journal, 1, 28-46. https://doi.org/10.1080/02666957908715792 [Citation Time(s):1]

21. Yemelianova, G. (2014) Islam, Nationalism and State in the Muslim Caucasus. Caucasus Survey, 1, 3-23. https://doi.org/10.1080/23761199.2014.11417291 [Citation Time(s):1]

22. Valiyev, A. (2005) Azerbaijan: Islam in a Post-Soviet Republic. Middle East Review of International Affairs, 9, 1-13. https://www.researchgate.net/publication/293054146_Azerbaijan_Islam_in_a_Post-Soviet_Republic [Citation Time(s):1]

23. Valiyev, A. (2005) The Rise of Salafi Islam in Azerbaijan. Terrorism Monitor, 3. https://jamestown.org/program/the-rise-of-salafi-islam-in-azerbaijan/ [Citation Time(s):1]

24. Göyüşov, A. and Rövşǝnoğlu, K. (2018) The Brief History of Salafism in Azerbaijan. Baku Research Institute. https://bakuresearchin-

stitute.org/az/a-brief-history-of-salafism-in-azerbaijan/#_edn36 [Citation Time(s):1]

25. Mammadli, N. (2018) Islam and Youth in Azerbaijan. Baku Research Institute. https://bakuresearchinstitute.org/az/islam-and-youth-in-azerbaijan/ [Citation Time(s):1]

26. (2013) Many Sunnis and Shias Worry about Religious Conflict. Pew Research Center, Religion & Public Life, 7. http://www.pewforum. org/2013/11/07/many-sunnis-and-shias-worry-about-religious-conflict/ [Citation Time(s):2]

27. Wistrand, S.J. (2012) Azerbaijan and "Tolerant Muslims". Caucasus Analytical Digest, 44, 5-8. http://www.css.ethz.ch/content/dam/ ethz/special-interest/gess/cis/center-for-securities-studies/pdfs/ CAD-44-5-8.pdf [Citation Time(s):1]

Chapter 11: Chechens in Afghanistan: A Battlefield Myth That Will Not Die. Christian Bleuer

1   For example, see the articles cited by Alex Strick van Linschoten and Felix Kuehn in the "Chechens in Afghanistan" website: see here. For more recent examples, see: Examples: Rob Taylor, 'Insurgents increasing in east Afghanistan, but army sees gains', Reuters, 8 July 2013, (see here); Shamil Shams, 'Who is fighting in northern Afghanistan?', Deutsche Welle, 07 October 2015; Omar Al Saleh, 'On the front line of Afghanistan's battle with ISIL', Al Jazeera, 25 January 2016. For an extreme example, see: Bill Roggio, 'Arab, Pakistani, Chechen, and Uzbek fighters' spotted in Logar', The Long War Journal, 30 May 2013.

2   'MID Rossii: troyeubitykh v Pakistaneinostrantsevokazalis' urozhentsamiDagestana', KavkazskiyUzel, 24 June 2011; 'V Pakistaneopoznayutrossiyan, ubitykhpolitseyskimi: tsel' ikhpoyezdkibylaso-vsem ne mirnoy', News.ru, 2 June 2011; YuriySyun and Igor Petrov, 'Said Buryatskiypozval v Pakistan: Opoznayutubitykhpolitsiyeyros-siyan', Kommersant, 2 June 2011,

3   'Chechenskiye «shuravi» 25 let spustya', Kavpolit, 22 February 2014; 'Spisokchechentsev, pogibshikh v 1980-kh v Afganistane', Vaynahi, 13 May 2015.

4   The 055 Brigade was al-Qaeda's contribution in the field to the Taleban army.

5   Cerwyn Moore and Paul Tumelty, 'Foreign Fighters and the Case of Chechnya: A Critical Assessment', Studies in Conflict & Terrorism 31 (2008), 424.

6   Ahmed Rashid, Taliban: Militant Islam, Oil and Fundamentalism in Central Asia, Yale University Press 2000, 136.

7   The list of Americans of any race or ethnicity in al-Qaeda is well known (as a starting point, see for example: 'Category: American al-Qaeda members' on Wikipedia). The only black American to be identified is Sharif Mobley, an-Qaeda suspect imprisoned in Yemen, and he is far too young to have been in Afghanistan at this time. On the very limited phenomenon of Americans in al Qaeda, see: J.M. Berger, 'Al Qaeda's American Dream Ends', Politico Magazine, 23 April 2015.

8   As an example, see the claim of an al-Zarqawi training camp for Chechens near Herat, accompanied by information about al-Qaeda chemical and nuclear material being stockpiled in the vicinity: Sean M. Maloney, 'Army of darkness: The jihadist training system in Pakistan and Afghanistan, 1996–2001', Small Wars & Insurgencies 26 (2015), 530-531.

9   'Chechens Re-Emerge as Leading Global Jihadis', Middle East Briefing, Orient Advisory Group, 13 January 2014.

10 Cerwyn Moore and Paul Tumelty, 'Foreign Fighters and the Case of Chechnya: A Critical Assessment', Studies in Conflict & Terrorism 31 (2008), 416, 425.

11 Cerwyn Moore and Paul Tumelty, 'Foreign Fighters and the Case of Chechnya: A Critical Assessment', Studies in Conflict & Terrorism 31 (2008), 424.

12 Ian Traynor, 'Russia threatens to bomb Afghan terror camps Russia', The Guardian, 25 May 2000; 'Russia threatens Afghan air strikes', BBC News, 24 May 2000; Brian Glyn Williams, 'Shattering the al-Qaeda-Chechen Myth (Part II): Exploring the Links Between the Chechen Resistance and Afghanistan', Chechnya Weekly 4 (2003), 1-2.

13 Thomas D. Grant, Current Development: Afghanistan Recognizes Chechnya, American University International Law Review 15 (2000), 869-870.

14 Ilyas Akhmadov and Nicholas Daniloff, Chechnya's Secret Wartime Diplomacy: Aslan Maskhadov and the Quest for a Peaceful Resolution, New York, Palgrave Macmillan 2013, np.

15 Thomas D. Grant, Current Development: Afghanistan Recognizes Chechnya, American University International Law Review 15 (2000), 881.

16 See, for example: Robert W. Schaefer, The Insurgency in Chechnya and the North Caucasus from Gazavat to Jihad, Santa Barbara, CA, Praeger Security International 2010.

17 Mark Kramer, 'Preface', in ibid.

18 Robert D. Crews, 'Moderate Taliban?', in The Taliban and the Crisis of Afghanistan, Robert D. Crews and Amin Tarzi, eds, Cambridge, MA, Harvard University Press 2008, citing Wahid Muzhda, Afghanistan wapanjsalsulta-ye Taleban, Tehran, Nashr-e ney 1382 [2003], 55.

19 He stated in January 2001 that in Afghanistan there were numerous foreign fighters, including 500 Arabs, 500 Chechens, 100 Uighurs, 100 Uzbeks, 100 Tajiks, 100 Bengalis, 100 Moros and 5,000 Pakistanis. See: Tim Judah, 'The Taliban Papers', Survival 44 (2002), 74.

20 See, as one of many examples: Emil Souleimanov&OndrejDitrych, 'The Internationalisation of the Russian-Chechen Conflict: Myths and Reality', Europe-Asia Studies 60 (2008), 1202.

21 Zbigniew K. Brzezinski, 'Foreword', in Ilyas Akhmadov and Miriam Lanskoy, The Chechen Struggle: Independence Won and Lost, New York, Palgrave Macmillan 2010, xiii.

22 Fiona Hill, '"Extremists and Bandits": How Russia Views the War against Terrorism', PONARS Policy Memo No. 246, Brookings Institution, April 2002, 1-3; Simon Shuster, 'How the War on Terrorism Did Russia a Favor', Time, 19 September 2011.

23 Brian Glyn Williams, 'Shattering the al-Qaeda-Chechen Myth (Part II): Exploring the Links Between the Chechen Resistance and Afghanistan', Chechnya Weekly 4 (2003), 1-2.

24 Ilyas Akhmadov and Miriam Lanskoy, The Chechen Struggle: Independence Won and Lost, New York, Palgrave Macmillan 2010, 200-201.

25 Brian Glyn Williams, 'From "Secessionist Rebels" to "Al-Qaeda Shock Brigades": Assessing Russia's Efforts to Extend the Post-Sep-

tember 11th War on Terror to Chechnya', Comparative Studies of South Asia, Africa and the Middle East 24 (2004), 26.

26 Alexander Khokhlov, 'Zachemamerikantsyskupili v Afganeplennykhchechentsev? Po $8-10 tysyach za golovu', Izvestiya, 23 July 2002.

27 V.V. Naumkin, Radical Islam in Central Asia: Between Pen and Rifle, Lanham, MD, Rowman & Littlefield 2005, 96, citing SultonKhamadov, 'Mezhdunarodnyikontekst-afganskiifaktor', in Religioznyiextremizm v TzentralnoiAzii: problem iperspectivy, Dushanbe, Organization for Security and Cooperation in Europe 2002, 147. For more on allegations that significant numbers of Chechens were based in Kabul, see: Alexander Khokhlov, 'Zachemamerikantsyskupili v Afganeplennykhchechentsev? Po $8-10 tysyach za golovu', Izvestiya, 23 July 2002, (see here).

28 Ahmed Rashid, Descent into Chaos: The United States and the Failure of Nation Building in Pakistan, Afghanistan, and Central Asia, New York, Viking Press 2008, 92; Michael Mora, 'The 'airlift of evil': Why did we let Pakistan pull 'volunteers' out of Kunduz?', MSNBC, November 2001.

29 For a full list of, and information on, detainees, see: Andrei Scheinkman et al., 'Detainees: Citizens of Russia', The New York Times, no date. Cross-referencing these names with the Russian media will reveal all nine as non-Chechens.

30 Fred Weir, 'Chechnya's warrior tradition: Guerrillas from Russia's longtime nemesis take their fighting skills to Afghanistan', The Christian Science Monitor, 26 March 2002. A variety on this Russian theme was offered by a military analyst at the Moscow Carnegie Center: 'The West is interested in dragging Russia into the war now as the ground operation is unfolding. The publications that link bin Laden to the Chechen rebels are to demonstrate to the world that Russia and the West are jointly opposing Islamic terrorism.' See: Nabi Abdullaev, 'Are Chechens in Afghanistan?', The Moscow Times, 14 December 2001.

31 Gary Schroen, First In: How Seven CIA Officers Opened the War on Terror in Afghanistan, New York, Random House 2005, 139, 331.

32 Ibid, 281.

33 See also: Fred Weir, 'Chechnya's warrior tradition: Guerrillas from Russia's longtime nemesis take their fighting skills to Afghanistan', The Christian Science Monitor, 26 March 2002.

34 Brian Glyn Williams, Inferno in Chechnya: the Russian-Chechen wars, the Al Qaeda myth, and the Boston Marathon bombings, Lebanon, NH, ForeEdge 2015, especially chapter 7 ('The Chechen Ghost Army of Afghanistan').

35 Brian Glyn Williams, 'On the Trail of the 'Lions of Islam': Foreign Fighters in Afghanistan and Pakistan, 1980-2010', Orbis 55 (2011), 236.

36 Examples cited: Office of the Secretary of Defense Public Affairs, 'Afghanistan Command Provides Details of Recent Operations', Defense Video & Imagery Distribution System, 16 August 2010; ISAF Joint Command, 'More than 20 insurgents killed in Haqqani clearing operation', Defense Video & Imagery Distribution System, 14 August 2010; ISAF Joint Command, 'IJC Operational Update, July 10', Defense Video & Imagery Distribution System, 10 July 2010; ISAF Joint Command, 'Afghan and coalition forces disrupt Haqqani operations in K-G Pass', Defense Video & Imagery Distribution System, 15 August 2010; ISAF Joint Command, 'Afghan, international forces disrupt Haqqani and Taliban networks', Defense Video & Imagery Distribution System, 23 June 2010; ISAF Joint Command, 'Afghan, coalition forces round up hundreds in August', Defense Video & Imagery Distribution System, 1 September 2010.

37 A few examples on many: Thomas Barfield, Afghanistan: A Cultural and Political History, Princeton University Press 2010, 260-266; KerstiLarsdotter, 'Regional Support for Afghan Insurgents: Challenges for Counterinsurgency Theory and Doctrine', Journal of Strategic Studies 37 (2014), 149; Sean M. Maloney, 'Army of darkness: The jihadist training system in Pakistan and Afghanistan, 1996–2001', Small Wars & Insurgencies 26 (2015), 525-531.

38 Seth Jones, Counterinsurgency in Afghanistan, Santa Monica, RAND 2008, 43; Deirdre Tynan, 'Tajikistan: An ever-more fragile state in a brittle region', International Crisis Group, 28 January 2016; 'Tajikistan: The Changing Insurgent Threats', Crisis Group Asia Report N°205, 24 May 2011.

39 Example: 'Report of the Analytical Support and Sanctions Monitoring Team pursuant to Security Council resolutions 1267 (1999), 1988 (2011) and 1989 (2011) concerning linkages between Al-Qaida and the Taliban as well as other individuals, groups, undertakings and entities associated with the Taliban in constituting a threat to the peace, stability and security of Afghanistan', UN Security Council, 21 December 2011, 12.

40 Examples: 'US CENTCOM's Unclassified Executive Summary: U.S. Central Command Investigation into Civilian Casualties in Farah Province, Afghanistan on 4 May 2009', United States Central Command, 18 June 2009, 4; John Rollins et al, 'Al Qaeda and Affiliates: Historical Perspective, Global Presence, and Implications for U.S. Policy', Congressional Research Service, 25 January 2011, 8.

41 David Kilcullen, The Accidental Guerrilla: Fighting Small Wars in the Midst of a Big One, Oxford University Press 2009, 55-6, 84.

42 Antonio Giustozzi, Koran, Kalashnikov, and laptop: the neo-Taliban insurgency in Afghanistan, New York, Columbia University Press 2008, 151.

43 A search for 'jezail' (the Afghan musket rifle) in any book about the Anglo-Afghan Wars (particularly the first one), will return numerous examples of Afghan sniping skill.

44 Gary Schroen, First In: How Seven CIA Officers Opened the War on Terror in Afghanistan, New York, Random House 2005, 281-2.

45 Associated Press, 'Cubans fighting in Afghanistan?', 20 October 1982. See also: Bruce J. Amstutz, Afghanistan: The first five years of Soviet Occupation, Washington, NDU Press 1986, 179.

46 Examples: Mahbob Shah Mahbob, 'Panjabi, Chechen fighters sneak into Batikot', Pajhwok, 23 August 2014; Gul Muhammad Tanha, 'Chechens, Uzbeks among 15 killed in Warduj', Pajhwok, 29 October 2014; Abdul Maqsood Azizi, 'Taliban pressure Daesh commander into fleeing Logar', Pajhwok, 28 July 2015; Qutbuddin Kohi, 'Dostum to Taliban: Surrender or face consequences', Pajhwok, 4 April 2015.

47 'Afghan government vows to eliminate Taliban', BBC Monitoring Afghanistan news, 19 April 2016, citing Ariana TV, 17 April 2016; 'Punjabis and Arabs among foreigners fighting in Afghanistan – defence ministry', BBC Monitoring Afghanistan news, 13 April 2016, citing Khaama Press, 13 April 2016; 'Afghan morning headlines: Fight against insurgents, security', BBC Monitoring Afghanistan news, 2 April 2016, citing Ariana TV, 1 April 2016.

48 'Warning to militants, Taleban reject peace talks', BBC Monitoring Afghanistan news, 8 March 2016, citing speech by Ashraf Ghani to graduates of an Afghan military academy, broadcast on all main Afghan TV channels on 7 March 2016.

49 'Afghan first vice-president may meet Taleban commanders for peace talks', BBC Monitoring Afghanistan news, 7 March 2016, cit-

ing Ariana TV report on 5 March 2016; Ahmad Shah Erfanyar, 'Gen. Dostum seeks military assistance from Russia', Pajhwok News, 2 September 2015.

50 Brian Glyn Williams, 'Shattering the al-Qaeda-Chechen Myth (Part II): Exploring the Links Between the Chechen Resistance and Afghanistan', Chechnya Weekly 4 (2003).

51 I base this on many dozens of studies of the Afghan insurgency. See, for example, the many books, articles and reports collected in previous and the forthcoming Afghanistan Analyst Bibliography: (see here).

52 SlavomírHorák, Afghánskýkonflikt, Prague, Public History 2005, 100-101, 136-137, 148. Note: one interviewee said that unidentified people told them that the foreigners were Chechen.

53 SlavomírHorák, Afghánskýkonflikt, Prague, Public History 2005, 137.

54 'Suicide Attacks in Afghanistan (2001-2007), UNAMA, 1 September 2007, 64-67

55 In 1997, during the period between the First and Second Chechen Wars, the de facto independent government of Chechnya did print an uncertain number of passports. See: 'Chechen leader unveils "unofficial" passports – Russian report', BBC News, 27 November 1997. These passports (adorned with a wolf on the front) were never accepted as official travel documents: 'Information Concerning the Non-Exhaustive List of Known Fantasy and Camouflage Passports, as Stipulated by Article 6 of the Decision No. 1105/2011/EU (to which a visa may not be affixed)', European Union, 18 August 2015, 5.

56 Cited in: 'Afghan police look for 15 female Chechen militants', Trend, 31 January 2011; Bill Roggio, 'Afghan police search for 15 Chechen women aiding the Taliban in Kunduz', Threat Matrix, 31 January 2011.

57 Two months later, the BBC posted an obituary for the police chief, noting that he had to contend with hundreds of foreign fighters: Pakistanis, Arabs and Chechens. See: Bilal Sarwary, 'Sayedkhili: Afghan police chief who took on the Taliban', BBC News, 14 March 2011.

58 'Afghanistan kidnap video: Hostage beheaded 'by Uzbek gunmen', BBC News, 7 April 2015; 'Afghanistan Hazara kidnapped passengers released', BBC News, 11 May 2015.

59 Personal correspondence with former ISAF officer with several years' experience in northern Afghanistan, October 2011. For another example of 'body inspections', see the somewhat less clear example here: Leigh Neville, Special Operations Forces in Afghanistan, New York, Osprey Publishing 2012, 25.

60 Brian Glyn Williams, 'Shattering the al-Qaeda-Chechen Myth (Part II): Exploring the Links Between the Chechen Resistance and Afghanistan', Chechnya Weekly 4 (2003).

61 Guido Steinberg, 'A Chechen al-Qaeda? Caucasian Groups Further Internationalise the Syrian Struggle', SWP Comments 31 (2014), 1; Laura Miller, 'Chechens: Legendary tough guys', Salon, 20 April 2013; James Gordon Meek, 'The Secret Battles Between US Forces and Chechen Terrorists', ABC News, 19 February 2014; Mark MacKinnon Twitter post, 23 September 2013, citing comments by Lawrence Sheets at the 2013 Global Security Seminar; Brian Glyn Williams, 'From "Secessionist Rebels" to "Al-Qaeda Shock Brigades": Assessing Russia's Efforts to Extend the Post-September 11th War on Terror to Chechnya', Comparative Studies of South Asia, Africa and the Middle East 24 (2004); Thomas de Waal, 'Chechens I Used to Know', Carnegie Endowment for International Peace, 19 April 2011.

61 Emil Souleimanov&OndrejDitrych, 'The Internationalisation of the Russian-Chechen Conflict: Myths and Reality', Europe-Asia Studies 60 (2008), 1215-1216.

62 I ran this line of argument by other researchers and they agree it is either plausible or likely, though as academics they say it is unproven without archival research and dedicated field trips to Afghanistan.

63 Some examples: Marty Compton et al, Home from War: How Love Conquered the Horrors of a Soldier's Afghan Nightmare, Edinburgh, Mainstream 2009, np; Ann Marlowe and Derrick Hernandez, 'Ain't Reporting Hell: Sebastian Junger's Afghanistan', World Affairs, November/December 2010; Jeff Courter, Afghan Journal: A Soldier's Year in Afghanistan, Flossmoor, IL, CreateSpace 2008, 150; P.J. Tobia, 'How I spent my fall vacation…in Afghanistan', Nashville Scene, 26 March 2009; Tom Bowman, 'For U.S. Troops, One More Big Push In Afghanistan', NPR, 30 May 2012. There are numerous other examples of this, mostly American soldiers posting comments on online forums.

64 Cerwyn Moore and Paul Tumelty, 'Foreign Fighters and the Case of Chechnya: A Critical Assessment', Studies in Conflict & Terrorism 31 (2008), 416.

65 Personal correspondence in 2011 with anonymous researcher who viewed martyrs' videos in Arabic.

66 'No evidence of Chechens in Afghanistan', Chechnya Weekly, Volume IV, Issue 33, 12 September 2003.

67 Anne Stenersen, 'Al Qaeda's Foot Soldiers: A Study of the Biographies of Foreign Fighters Killed in Afghanistan and Pakistan Between 2002 and 2006', Studies in Conflict & Terrorism 34 (2011), Appendix A., 187-193. The author notes that the study is Arab-centric, and the compiler of the bibliographies noted that he had not been able to collect all of the Uzbek and Uyghur biographies.

68 Brian Glyn Williams, 'On the Trail of the 'Lions of Islam': Foreign Fighters in Afghanistan and Pakistan, 1980-2010', Orbis 55 (2011), 216-239.

69 For example, see the Islamic Movement of Uzbekistan official list of martyrs for the Hijri year 1432 (ending in November 2011), which lists one citizen of Russia: an ethnic Tatar: 'O'zbekistonIslomiyHarakatining 1432 hijriyyil (melodiy 2011) shahidlar', Furqon.com (November 2011). Another IMU martyr tribute in video form paid tribute to a Dagestani Russian named Khattab who died in Kunduz in 2010 (source: video screenshot received via personal correspondence with anonymous researcher).

70 As one of several examples, see: Brian Glyn Williams, Inferno in Chechnya: the Russian-Chechen wars, the Al Qaeda myth, and the Boston Marathon bombings, Lebanon, NH, ForeEdge 2015, especially chapter 7 ('The Chechen Ghost Army of Afghanistan').

Chapter 12: When we are the violent: The Chechen Islamist Guerrillas' Discourse on their own Armed Actions. AdrianTarin Sanz

Akaev, 2014: V. AkaevThe history and specifics of contemporary Islamic Revival in the Chechen Republic

Anthropology &Archeology of Eurasia, 53 (2) (2014), pp. 79-102, 10.1080/10611959.2014.1022431

CrossRefView Record in ScopusGoogle Scholar

Alba Rico, 2015

S. Alba RicoIslamofobia

Icaria, Barcelona (2015)

Google Scholar

Arrunátegui, 2010

C. ArrunáteguiIdeología y prensaescritaen el Perú: el casoBagua

Lexis, 14 (2) (2010), pp. 353-368

View Record in ScopusGoogle Scholar

Barkun, 2000

M. BarkunViolence in the name of democracy: Justifications for separatism on the radical right

Terrorism and Political Violence, 12 (3–4) (2000), pp. 193-208,
10.1080/09546550008427576

CrossRefView Record in ScopusGoogle Scholar

Bobrovnikov, 2006

V. Bobrovnikov'Traditionalist' versus 'Islamist' identities in a Dagestani
collective farm

Central Asian Survey, 25 (3) (2006), pp. 287-302,
10.1080/02634930601022559

CrossRefView Record in ScopusGoogle Scholar

Campana, 2009

A. CampanaCollective memory and violence: The use of myths in the
Chechen separatist ideology, 1991–1994

Journal of Muslim Minority Affairs, 29 (1) (2009), pp. 43-56,
10.1080/13602000902726756

CrossRefView Record in ScopusGoogle Scholar

Campana, Ducol, 2015

A. Campana, B. DucolVoices of the 'Caucasus Emirate': Mapping and
analyzing north Caucasus insurgency websites

Terrorism and Political Violence, 27 (2015), pp. 679-700,
10.1080/09546553.2013.848797

CrossRefView Record in ScopusGoogle Scholar

Carpentier, 2007

N. CarpentierCulture, trauma and conflict: Cultural studies perspectives
on war

Cambridge Scholar Publishing, Newcastle (2007)

Google Scholar

Coppieters, 2003

B. CoppietersSecession and war: A moral analysis of the Russian–Chechen conflict

Central Asian Survey, 22 (4) (2003), pp. 377-404, 10.1080/0263493042000202607

View Record in ScopusGoogle Scholar

Cordeiro-Rodrigues, 2016

L. Cordeiro-RodriguesIs the Animal Liberation Front morally justified in engaging in violent and illegal activism towards animal farms?

Critical Studies on Terrorism (2016), 10.1080/17539153.2016.1142797

Google Scholar

Dannreuther, 2010

R. DannreutherIslamic radicalization in Russia: An assessment

International Affairs, 86 (1) (2010), pp. 109-126, 10.1111/j.1468-2346.2010.00871.x

CrossRefView Record in ScopusGoogle Scholar

Els, 2013

C. ElsConstructing xenophobic discourses: The case of the Daily Sun

Language Matters: Studies in the Languages of Africa, 44 (2) (2013), pp. 47-67, 10.1080/10228195.2013.803147

CrossRefView Record in ScopusGoogle Scholar

Ema López, 2004

J.E. EmaLópezDelsujeto a la agencia (a través de lo politico)

Athenea Digital: Revista de pensamiento e investigación social, 6 (2004), pp. 1-24

View Record in ScopusGoogle Scholar

Fairclough, 1992

N. FaircloughDiscourse and social change

Polity Press, Cambridge (1992)

Google Scholar

Fairclough, 1995

N. FaircloughCritical discourse analysis. The critical study of language

Longman, London (1995)

Google Scholar

Fairclough, 2003

N. FaircloughAnalyzing discourse. Textual analysis for social research

Routledge, New York (2003)

Google Scholar

Foucault, 1992

M. FoucaultElorden del discurso

Tusquets, Buenos Aires (1992)

Google Scholar

Foxall, 2010

A. FoxallDiscourses of demonisation: Chechens, Russians, and the Stavropol' Riots of 2007

Geopolitics, 15 (4) (2010), pp. 684-704, 10.1080/14650040903504355

CrossRefView Record in ScopusGoogle Scholar

Galeotti, 2002

M. Galeotti'Brotherhoods' and 'Associates': Chechen Networks of Crime and Resistance

Low Intensity Conflict and Law Enforcement, 11 (2–3) (2002), pp. 340-352, 10.1080/0966284042000279072

CrossRefView Record in ScopusGoogle Scholar

Galeotti, 2014

M. GaleottiRussia's wars in Chechnya 1994–2009

Osprey, Oxford (2014)

Google Scholar

Gammer, 2005

M. GammerBetween Mecca and Moscow: Islam, politics, and political Islam in Chechnya and Dagestan

Middle Eastern Studies, 41 (6) (2005), pp. 833-848, 10.1080/00263200500261829

CrossRefView Record in ScopusGoogle Scholar

Giuliano, 2005

E. GiulianoIslamic identity and political mobilization in Russia: Chechnya and Dagestan compared

Nationalism and Ethnic Politics, 11 (2) (2005), pp. 195-220, 10.1080/13537110591005711

CrossRefView Record in ScopusGoogle Scholar

Hearns-Branaman, 2015

J.O. Hearns-BranamanOfficial enemies in commercial and soft power media

Journalism Studies (2015), 10.1080/1461670X.2015.1074865

Google Scholar

Hollander, 2013

P. HollanderRighteous Political Violence and Contemporary Western Intellectuals

Terrorism and Political Violence, 25 (4) (2013), pp. 518-530

http://dx.doi.org/10.1080/09546553.2013.814491

CrossRefView Record in ScopusGoogle Scholar

HuiciMódenes, 2010

A. HuiciMódenesGuerra y propaganda en el siglo XXI. Nuevosmensajes, viejasguerras

Alfar, Sevilla (2010)

Google Scholar

Ibragimov, Matsuzato, 2014

M.R. Ibragimov, K. MatsuzatoContextualized violence: politics and terror in Dagestan

Nationalities Papers: The Journal of Nationalism and Ethnicity, 42 (2) (2014), pp. 286-306, 10.1080/00905992.2013.867932

CrossRefView Record in ScopusGoogle Scholar

Janeczko, 2014

M. Janeczko'Faced with death, even a mouse bites': Social and religious motivations behind terrorism in Chechnya

Small Wars & Insurgencies, 25 (2) (2014), pp. 428-456, 10.1080/09592318.2014.903975

CrossRefView Record in ScopusGoogle Scholar

Johnston, 2008

H. JohnstonRitual, strategy, and deep culture in the Chechen national movement

Critical Studies on Terrorism, 1 (3) (2008), pp. 321-342

CrossRefView Record in ScopusGoogle Scholar

Karda, 2012

T. KardaNo laughing matter: Visualizing Turkey's Ergenekon in political cartoons

Middle East Critique, 21 (2) (2012), pp. 203-223, 10.1080/19436149.2012.688587

Google Scholar

Khanbabaev, 2010

K. KhanbabaevIslam and Islamic Radicalism in Dagestan

G.M. Yemalianova (Ed.), Radical Islam in the former Soviet Union, Routledge, New York (2010), pp. 82-111

Google Scholar

Kisriev, Ware, 2000

E. Kisriev, R.B. WareConflict and catharsis: A report on developments in Dagestan following the incursions of August and September 1999

Nationalities Papers: The Journal of Nationalism and Ethnicity, 28 (3) (2000), pp. 479-522, 10.1080/713687475

CrossRefGoogle Scholar

Kisriev, Ware, 2002

E. Kisriev, R.B. WareIrony and Political Islam: Dagestan's Spiritual Directorate

Nationalities Papers, 30 (4) (2002), pp. 663-689, 10.1080/00905992.2002.10540512

CrossRefView Record in ScopusGoogle Scholar

Koltsova, 2000

E. KoltsovaChange in the coverage of the Chechen Wars: Reasons and consequences

Javnost – The Public, 7 (3) (2000), pp. 39-54, 10.1080/13183222.2000.11008749

CrossRefView Record in ScopusGoogle Scholar

Kristeva, 2001

J. KristevaSemiótica

Fundamentos, Madrid (2001)

Google Scholar

Laclau, 1996

E. LaclauEmancipación y diferencia

Ariel, Buenos Aires (1996)

Google Scholar

Lapidus, 2002

G.W. LapidusPutin's war on terrorism: Lessons from Chechnya

Post-Soviet Affairs, 18 (1) (2002), pp. 41-48, 10.1080/1060586X.2002.10641512

View Record in ScopusGoogle Scholar

Le Huérou et al, 2014

A. Le Huérou, A.R. Aude Merlin, E.S. KozlowskiChechnya at war and beyond

Routledge, New York (2014)

Google Scholar

Macfarlane, 1990

L. MacfarlaneThe right to self-determination in Ireland and the justification of IRA violence

Terrorism and Political Violence, 2 (1) (1990), pp. 35-53, 10.1080/09546559008427049

CrossRefView Record in ScopusGoogle Scholar

Machin, Mayr, 2012

D. Machin, A. MayrHow to do critical discourse analysis: A multimodal introduction

Sage, Los Angeles (2012)

Google Scholar

Makarov, 2008

D.V. MakarovNesostoyavsheesyavozrozhdenieumerennogoislamizma v Dagestane. Islam.ru

Retrieved from

www.islamrf.ru/news/library/islam-word/2585 (2008)

(Accessed June 2, 2015)

Google Scholar

Matsuzato, Ibragimov, 2005

K. Matsuzato, M.R. IbragimovIslamic politics at the sub-regional level in Dagestan: Tariqa brotherhoods, ethnicities, localism and the spiritual board

Europe-Asia Studies, 57 (5) (2005), pp. 753-779, 10.1080/09668130500126577

CrossRefView Record in ScopusGoogle Scholar

Mayer et al, 2014

S. Mayer, E. Ajanovic, B. SauerIntersections and inconsistencies. Framing gender in right-wing populist discourses in Austria

NORA-Nordic Journal of Feminist and Gender Research, 22 (4) (2014), pp. 250-266, 10.1080/08038740.2014.964309

CrossRefView Record in ScopusGoogle Scholar

McGregor, 2012

A. McGregorMilitary Jamaats in the North Caucasus: A continuing threat

G.E. Howard (Ed.), Volatile borderland: Russia and the North Caucasus, Jamestown Foundation, Washington (2012), pp. 237-264

Google Scholar

Miller, 2004

D. MillerInformation dominance: The philosophy of total propaganda control?

Y.R. Kamalipour, N. Snow (Eds.), War media and propaganda: A global perspective, Rowman & Littlefield, New York (2004), pp. 7-16

ArticleDownloadPDFView Record in ScopusGoogle Scholar

Moore, Tumelty, 2008

C. Moore, P. TumeltyForeign fighters and the case of Chechnya: A critical assessment

Studies in Conflict & Terrorism, 31 (2008), pp. 412-433, 10.1080/10576100801993347

CrossRefView Record in ScopusGoogle Scholar

Moore, Tumelty, 2009

C. Moore, P. TumeltyAssessing unholy alliances in Chechnya: From Communism and Nationalism to Islamism and Salafism

Journal of Communist Studies and Transition Politics, 25 (1) (2009), pp. 73-94, 10.1080/13523270802655621

CrossRefView Record in ScopusGoogle Scholar

Mouffe, 1995

C. MouffePost-Marxism: Democracy and identity

Environment and Planning. D, Society and Space, 13 (1995), pp. 259-265, 10.1068/d130259

CrossRefView Record in ScopusGoogle Scholar

Nikken, 2011

P. NikkenSobre el concepto de Derechos Humanos

RevistaPensamiento Penal, 133 (2011), pp. 23-52

View Record in ScopusGoogle Scholar

O'Boyle, 2002

G. O'BoyleTheories of justification and political violence: Examples from four groups

Terrorism and Political Violence, 14 (2) (2002), pp. 23-46, 10.1080/714005612

CrossRefView Record in ScopusGoogle Scholar

Philo, 2007

G. PhiloCan discourse analysis successfully explain the content of media and journalistic practice?

JournalismStudies,8(2)(2007),pp.175-196,10.1080/14616700601148804

CrossRefView Record in ScopusGoogle Scholar

Putin, 2001

V. PutinDiscourse on 9/11

Retrieved from

http://archive.kremlin.ru/eng/speeches/2001/09/11/0003_
type82912_138531.shtml (2001)

(Accessed June 15, 2015)

Google Scholar

Radnitz, 2006

S. RadnitzLook who's talking! Islamic discourse in the Chechen wars

Nationalities Papers: The Journal of Nationalism and Ethnicity, 34 (2)
(2006), pp. 237-256, 10.1080/00905990600720328

CrossRefView Record in ScopusGoogle Scholar

Rivas Otero, Tarín Sanz, 2016

J.M. Rivas Otero, A. TarínSanzLeadership style and war and peace policies in the context of armed conflict: The case of Maskhadov and
Umarov

Problems of Post-Communism (2016), 10.1080/10758216.2016.1138847

Google Scholar

Roshchin, 2003

M. RoshchinFundamentalism v DagestaneiChechne

Otechestvennyezaposki, 5 (14) (2003)

Google Scholar

Roshchin, 2012

M. RoshchinIslam in the North Caucasus: The case of Dagestan

G.E. Howard (Ed.), Volatile borderland: Russia and the North Caucasus,
Jamestown Foundation, Washington (2012), pp. 159-179

View Record in ScopusGoogle Scholar

Russell, 2005

J. RussellTerrorists, bandits, spooks and thieves: Russian demonization of
the Chechens before and since 9/11

Third World Quarterly, 26 (1) (2005), pp. 101-116,
10.1080/0143659042000322937

CrossRefView Record in ScopusGoogle Scholar

Sagramoso, 2007

D. SagramosoViolence and conflict in the Russian North Caucasus

International Affairs, 83 (4) (2007), pp. 681-705, 10.1111/j.1468-2346.2007.00647.x

CrossRefView Record in ScopusGoogle Scholar

Said, 1978

E. SaidOrientalism

Random House, New York (1978)

Google Scholar

Schmitt, 2007

C. SchmittThe concept of the political

Chicago University Press, Chicago (2007)

Google Scholar

Schwarzmantel, 2010

J. SchwarzmantelDemocracy and violence: a theoretical overview

Democratization, 17 (2) (2010), pp. 217-234, 10.1080/13510341003588641

CrossRefView Record in ScopusGoogle Scholar

Slavicek, 2008

D.J. SlavicekDeconstructing the shariatic justification of suicide bombings

Studies in Conflict & Terrorism, 31 (6) (2008), pp. 553-571, 10.1080/10576100802064833

CrossRefView Record in ScopusGoogle Scholar

Souleimanov, 2005

E. SouleimanovChechnya, Wahhabism and the invasion of Dagestan

Middle East Review of International Affairs, 9 (4) (2005), pp. 48-71

View Record in ScopusGoogle Scholar

Spiessens, Van Poucke, 2016

A. Spiessens, P. Van PouckeTranslating news discourse on the Crimean crisis: Patterns of reframing on the Russian website InoSMI

The Translator (2016), 10.1080/13556509.2016.1180570

Google Scholar

Stables, 2003

G. StablesJustifying Kosovo: Representations of gendered violence and U.S. military intervention

Critical Studies in Media Communication, 20 (1) (2003), pp. 92-115, 10.1080/0739318032000067047

CrossRefView Record in ScopusGoogle Scholar

Swirszcz, 2009

J. SwirszczThe role of Islam in Chechen national identity

Nationalities Papers: The Journal of Nationalism and Ethnicity, 37 (1) (2009), pp. 59-88, 10.1080/00905990802373637

CrossRefView Record in ScopusGoogle Scholar

Tarín Sanz, 2015

A. TarínSanzMiradaslibertarias

Catarata, Madrid (2015)

Google Scholar

Tarín Sanz, 2017

A. TarínSanzLayihadenRusia: De Emirado del Cáucaso al Estado Islámico

Icaria, Barcelona (2017)

Google Scholar

Todorov, 1998

T. TodorovMikhail Bakhtin. The dialogical principle

Minnesota University Press, Minneapolis (1998)

Google Scholar

Turner, 2008

G. TurnerThe road to the lesbian nation is not an easy one: 'Us' and 'them' in Diva magazine

Social Semiotics, 18 (3) (2008), pp. 377-388, 10.1080/10350330802217147

CrossRefView Record in ScopusGoogle Scholar

Vázquez Liñán, 2005

M. Vázquez LiñánDesinformación y propaganda en la guerra de Chechenia

Padilla, Sevilla (2005)

Google Scholar

Vázquez Liñán, 2009

M. Vázquez LiñánPutin's propaganda legacy

Post-Soviet Affairs, 25 (2) (2009), pp. 137-159, 10.2747/1060-586X.24.2.137

Google Scholar

Van den Broek, 2015

H.P. Van den BroekLabelling and legitimization: Justifying political violence in the Basque Country

Terrorism and Political Violence (2015), 10.1080/09546553.2014.995788

Google Scholar

Van Dijk, 1998a

T.A. Van DijkOpinions and ideologies in the press

A. Bell, P. Garrett (Eds.), Approaches to media discourse, Blackwell, Oxford (1998), pp. 21-63

Google Scholar

Van Dijk, 1998b

T.A. Van DijkIdeology. A multidisciplinary approach

SAGE, New York (1998)

Google Scholar

Van Dijk, 2003a

T.A. Van DijkCritical discourse analysis

D. Schiffrin, D. Tannen, H.E. Hamilton (Eds.), The handbook of discourse analysis, Wiley-Blackwell, New Jersey (2003), pp. 352-371

Google Scholar

Van Dijk, 2003b

T.A. Van DijkIdeología y discurso

Ariel, Barcelona (2003)

Google Scholar

Van Dijk, 2009

T.A. Van DijkSociety and discourse: How social contexts influence text and talk

Cambridge University Press, Cambridge (2009)

Google Scholar

Velásquez Ossa, 2011

C.M. VelásquezOssaUnaaproximación a los génerosperiodísticos

V.M. García, L.M. Gutiérrez (Eds.), Manual de génerosperiodísticos, Universidad de La Sabana, Bogotá (2011)

Google Scholar

Walzer, 2015

M. WalzerJust and unjust wars: A moral argument with historical illustrations

Basic Books, New York (2015)

Google Scholar

Ware et al, 2003

R.B. Ware, E. Kisriev, W.J. Patzelt, U. RoerichtPolitical Islam in Dagestan

Europe-Asia Studies, 55 (2) (2003), pp. 287-302, 10.1080/0966813032000055886

View Record in ScopusGoogle Scholar

Wilhelmsen, 2005

J. WilhelmsenBetween a rock and a hard place: The Islamisation of the Chechen Separatist Movement

Europe-Asia Studies, 57 (1) (2005), pp. 35-59, 10.1080/0966813052000314101

CrossRefView Record in ScopusGoogle Scholar

Wodak, Meyer, 2009

R. Wodak, M. MeyerMethods for critical discourse analysis

SAGE, New York (2009)

Google Scholar

Wright, 2008

F. WrightThe theory of justification and excuse and its application to self-defence

Journal of Commonwealth Law and Legal Education, 6 (1) (2008), pp. 55-73, 10.1080/14760400802547599

CrossRefView Record in ScopusGoogle Scholar

Zavala, 1999

L. Zavala"Elementos para el análisis de la intertextualidad"

Cuadernos de literatura, 5 (10) (1999), pp. 26-52

View Record in ScopusGoogle Scholar

1 For a more in-depth legal debate on legitimate defense, see Wright (2008).

2 In this work, political violence is understood "as the use or threatened use of physical coercion to achieve political ends. Such actual or threatened acts of coercion are, in the present definition, carried out by identifiable persons, whether they are acting as agents of the state or as members of non-state bodies opposing the state. Political violence is here understood as the use (actual or threatened) of physical coercion to achieve a change in the nature of the political order, or (when carried out by agents of the state) to defend that order in its existing form" (Schwarzmantel, 2010, 218). Therefore, criminal or structural violence is excluded, in spite of the fact that it also responds to profoundly political reasons.

3 To delve deeper into the origins of Islam in Dagestan, from the 8th century to post-Soviet Russia, see Kisriev and Ware (2002).

4 Bagautdin and Abbas do not share the same surname because they have different fathers.

5 During the Independence process of the CRI, Dzokhar Dudayev, its leader and first president, "was also fully aware that his own Islamic credentials were weak and he thus infused much of his rhetoric with Islamic reference points," for which reason he chose Islam Khalimov as his religious assessor (Moore &Tumelty, 2009, 83).

6 Here, the dichotomy is used in the same terms in which Said (1978, 3) defined the relationship between the West (Us) and the Orient (Other): the Other "is not a free subject of thought and action" and the US "gained in strength and identity by setting itself off against [the Other] as a sort of surrogate and even underground self".

7   A review of the work of the leading theorists of CDA, like Fairclough, Wodak, Martín Rojo, and Van Dijk, shows how it is largely used to study the conditions of inequality in which the "us/other" dialectic, such as sexism, racism, anti-Semitism, globalism, etc., is constructed. In this work, in contrast, the idea is to discover how both actors were characterized in order to make them legitimately murderable and legitimately murderers.

8   According to Van Dijk (2009), contexts are subjective moments, whose relevance is defined by those participating in the situation. Given that the events selected received ample, in-depth coverage on KC, suitable contexts relevant to the Chechen Islamist guerrillas were taken into account.

9   As is typical in CDA, texts "are selected according to the interests of the analysts, where perhaps they have observed ideology in operation" (Machin & Mayr, 2012, 207).

10   Second suicide attack, 15 May 2003. Accessed: 14 December 2014; available at: http://www.kavkazcenter.com/eng/content/2003/05/15/1304.shtml.

11   Gunmen take 400 people hostage at Russia [sic] school, 2 September 2004. Accessed: 14 December 2014; available at: http://www.kavkazcenter.com/eng/content/2004/09/02/3147.shtml.

12   Terminological controversies are essential in discourses justifying violence – or in any other political exercise (Laclau, 1996) – and have parallels in other armed conflicts (Van den Broek, 2015). Thus, the Chechen Islamists provided ample proof of their attempts to appropriate language, calling the Russian soldiers "terrorists" or regarding the intervention of Moscow as an "invasion"; both concepts were, in turn, used by the Kremlin to describe the Chechen combatants and the jihadist operation of 1999 in Dagestan.

13   Protest demonstration of Chechen refugees in Baku, 24 October 2002. Accessed: 16 December 2014; available at: http://www.kavkazcenter.com/eng/content/2002/10/24/548.shtml.

14   Major manhunt, 1 November 2002. Accessed: 16 December 2014; available at: http://www.kavkazcenter.com/eng/content/2002/11/01/566.shtml.

15   There is thus a paradox that made the discourses of the two different national sentiments relatively compatible: that of those who advocated for a Western-style secular nation-state for Chechnya; and that of those who defended a theocratic government of a regional

character for the Muslim Caucasus. To this effect, it must be borne in mind that MovladiUdugov, the then director of the KC, had formed part of the administration of the CRI, insofar as he had been Prime Minister from 1996 to 1997, but after the outbreak of the second war he provided ample proof of his rapport with the Islamist guerrillas. Neither this about-turn nor the bitter feuds between both factions, noted above, prevented Udugov – and his website – from treating the government of Maskhadov as an ally against the common enemy: Russia. Even so, this alliance came up against a hurdle that was difficult to overcome: while the discourse of the legally elected President attempted to build a rapprochement with the "international community" (Radnitz, 2006), the KC strongly criticized the West and, above all, the US, the main culprit of the contemporary occupations of Muslim Afghanistan and Iraq. Thus, while on the home front the agency tried to underscore the positive aspects of the government of Maskhadov and conceal its shortcomings, on the international stage it did not hesitate to "boycott" the "pro-Western" strategy implemented by the Chechen administration. Proof of this was the publication on 27 January 2004 of an article entitled, "The US is now in the hands of a group of extremists," in which the agency had no qualms about describing the Americans as "criminal agents" and "extremists" incapable of respecting international treaties.

16   Top Chechen official arrested in Copenhagen, 30 October 2002. Accessed: 17 December 2014; available at: http://kavkazcenter.com/eng/content/2002/10/30/560.shtml.

17   Troops in Chechnya missed truck explosives – paper, 14 May 2003. Accessed: 17 December 2014; available at: http://kavkazcenter.com/eng/content/2003/05/14/1296.shtml.

18   Russian helicopter 'downed' in Chechnya, 30 October 2002. Accessed: 14 December 2014; available at: http://www.kavkazcenter.com/eng/content/2002/10/30/554.shtml.

19   Zakayev made a statement, 24 October 2002. Accessed: 14 December 2014; available at: http://kavkazcenter.com/eng/content/2002/10/24/544.shtml.

20   Eight invaders killed [in] Eshelkhatoy village, 15 May 2003. Accessed: 14 December 2014; available at: http://www.kavkazcenter.com/eng/content/2003/05/15/1305.shtml.

21 Abdallah Shamil: There was no personal revenge..., 19 May 2003. Accessed: 14 December 2014; available at: http://www.kavkazcenter. com/eng/content/2003/05/19/1328.shtml.

22 Address by President of C.R.I.A. Maskhadov to the Chechen people, 6 September 2004. Accessed: 14 December 2014; available at: http:// www.kavkazcenter.com/eng/content/2004/09/06/3166.shtml.

23 Russia arrests 30 citizens for helpig [sic] Chechens [sic] fighters, 31 October 2002. Accessed: 14 December 2014; available at: http:// www.kavkazcenter.com/eng/content/2002/10/31/561.shtml.

24 Chechen Commander claimed responsibility [sic], 1 November 2002. Accessed: 14 December 2014; available at: http://kavkazcenter. com/eng/content/2002/11/01/605.shtml.

25 Eight invaders killed [in] Eshelkhatoy village, 15 May 2003. Accessed: 14 December 2014; available at: http://www.kavkazcenter. com/eng/content/2003/05/15/1305.shtml.

26 Special-operation in Vedeno, 20 May 2003. Accessed: 14 December 2014; available at: http://kavkazcenter.com/eng/content/2003/05/20/1330.shtml.

27 Protest demonstration of Chechen refugees in Baku, 24 October 2002. Accessed: 16 December 2014; available at: http://www.kavkazcenter.com/eng/content/2002/10/24/548.shtml.

28 Top Chechen official arrested in Copenhagen, 30 October 2002. Accessed: 16 December 2014; available at: http://kavkazcenter.com/eng/content/2002/10/30/560.shtml.

29 Major manhunt, 1 November 2002. Accessed: 16 December 2014; available at: http://www.kavkazcenter.com/eng/content/2002/11/01/566.shtml.

30 Zakayev made a statement, 24 October 2002. Accessed: 20 December 2014; available at: http://kavkazcenter.com/eng/content/2002/10/24/544.shtml.

31 Gunmen take 400 people hostage at Russia [sic] school, 2 September 2004. Accessed: 20 December 2014; available at: http://www.kavkazcenter.com/eng/content/2004/09/02/3147.shtml.

32 Protest demonstration of Chechen refugees in Baku, 24 October 2002. Accessed: 22 December 2014; available at: http://www.kavkazcenter.com/eng/content/2002/10/24/548.shtml.

33 Spiegel: No links between Chechens and Al-Qaeda, 6 September 2004. Accessed: 17 December 2014; available at: http://kavkazcenter. com/eng/content/2004/09/06/3167.shtml.

34 No chance for Putin to get amnestied, 17 May 2003. Accessed: 5 May 2014; available at: http://www.kavkazcenter.com/eng/content/2003/05/17/1318.shtml.

35 Discussions on nationality, 9 December 2002. Accessed: 10 March 2014; available at: https://2r2tz6wzqh7gaji7.tor2web.fi/eng/content/2002/12/19/722.shtml.

36 Something especially relevant to a culture that had built around itself – with "Orientalist" help from Russian intellectuals – a warrior myth (Johnston, 2008) which justified, on its own, the political violence (Campana, 2009).

37 For a deeper understanding of this process, see Akaev (2014). Copyright © 2017, Asia-Pacific Research Center, Hanyang University. Production and hosting by Elsevier Ltd. https://doi.org/10.1016/j. euras.2017.05.002Get rights and content Under a Creative Commons license open access

Chapter 13: The Future of Chechens in ISIS. Anna Borschevskaya

1. ЕкатеринаСокирянская, "АбуМясо. ТаквИГИЛпрозваличе ченскогокомандира, отправляющегосвоихбойцовнасмерт ь," Novaya Gazeta, 20 May 2016, https://www.novayagazeta.ru/ articles/2016/05/11/68546-abu-myaso-tak-v-igil-prozvali-ch-echenskogokomandira-otpravlyayuschego-svoih-boytsov-na-smert Ian Bremmer, "The Top 5 Countries Where ISIS Gets Its Foreign Recruits," Time, 13 April 2017, http://time.com/4739488/isis-iraq-syria-tunisia-saudi-arabia-russia/.

2. Harleen Gambhir, "ISIS Declares Governorate in Russia's North Caucasus," Institute for the Study of War, 23 June 2015, http:// understandingwar.org/backgrounder/isis-declares-governorate-russia%E2%80%99snorth-caucasus-region#sthash.r2anmNPy.dpuf

3 Meredith Hoffman, "Caucasus Emirate Militants Pledge Allegiance to the Islamic State in a Video," VICE, 20 December 2014. https://news. vice.com/article/caucasus-emirate-militants-pledge-allegiance-to-the-islamic-state-in-newvideo; "Russia's Caucasus Islamists 'pledge allegiance' to ISIS," Agence France-Presse, 24 July 2015, http://www. dailystar.com.lb/News/World/2015/Jun-24/303595-russias-cauca-sus-islamists-pledge-allegianceto-isis.ashx#sthash.9nZXucQd.dpuf "Six North Caucasus Insurgency Commanders Transfer Allegiance

To Islamic State," Radio Free Europe/Radio Liberty, 2 January 2015, http://www.rferl.org/content/islamic-state-north-caucasus-insurgencycommanders-allegiance/26773615.html.

4   See Svante E. Cornell, "The 'Afghanization' of the North Caucasus: Causes and Implications in a changing conflict," in Stephen J. Blank, ed., Russia's Homegrown Insurgency: Jihad in the North Caucasus (Carlisle Barracks, Pa.: US Army War College Strategic Studies Institute, 2OL2), p. 126.

5   Steven Erlanger, "Tatars Vote on a Referendum All Agree Is Confusing,", New York Times, 22 March 1992 http://www.nytimes.com/1992/03/22/world/tatars-vote-on-a-referendum-all-agree-is-confusing.html

6   Rajan Menon, "Russia's Quagmire: On ending the standoff in Chechnya," Boston Review, 1 June 2004 http://bostonreview.net/rajan-menon-chechnya-russia.

7   Yo'avKarny, "Chechen Nightmare, Russian Amnesia. Memories of a Day No One Should Forget," Washington Post, 20 February 2000

8   "The North Caucasus: The Challenges of Integration (I), Ethnicity and Conflict," International Crisis Group, Europe Report No. 220, 19 October 2012, http://www.crisisgroup.org/en/regions/europe/northcaucasus/220-the-north-caucasus-the-challenges-of-integration-i-ethnicity-and-conflict.aspx .

9   Yo'avKarny, "Chechen Nightmare, Russian Amnesia. Memories of a Day No One Should Forget," Washington Post, 20 February 2000, http://www.washingtonpost.com/wp-srv/WPcap/2000-02/20/001r022000-idx.html

10 "Imarat Kavkaz/Caucasus Emirate," IHS Jane's World Insurgency and Terrorism, 2014, https://www.ihs.com/pdf/IHS-Janes-World-Insurg-Terror_Imarat-Kavkaz_146073110913052132.pdf.

11 Ian Traynor, "Russia Set to Destroy Grozny," The Guardian, 12 November 1999, https://www.theguardian.com/world/1999/nov/13/chechnya.iantraynor https://www.theguardian.com/world/1 999/nov/13/chechnya.iantraynor James Rodgers, "Chechnya: Destruction defying description," BBC, 7 June 2000, http://news.bbc.co.uk/2/hi/europe/780073.stm

12 "Caucasus Emirate," Mapping Militant Organizations, Stanford University, 11 April 2014, http://web.stanford.edu/group/mappingmilitants/cgi-bin/groups/view/255.

13 US Department of State, Bureau of Public Affairs, "Designation of Caucasus Emirate," 26 May 2011, http://www.state.gov/r/pa/prs/ps/2011/05/164312.htm . "In the Matter of the Designation of Rustam Aselderov, aka Abu Mukhammad al-Kadar, aka Abu Muk-hammadKadarsky, aka Abu MukhammadKadarskiy, aka Abu Mohammad al-Qadari, aka Abu Muhammad al-Kadarskii, aka Rustam Asildarov, aka Rustam Aseldarov as a Specially Designated Global Terrorist Pursuant to Section 1(b) of Executive Order 13224, as Amended," Federal Register, 1 October 2015, https://www.federal-register.gov/articles/2015/10/01/2015-25043/in-the-matter-of-the-designation-of-rustamaselderov-aka-abu-mukhammad-al-kadar-aka-abu-mukhammad.

14 Elena Pokalova, "The Al Qaeda Brand: The strategic Use of the 'terrorist' label," Terrorism and Political Violence, DOI: 10.1080/09546553.2016.1169175 http://dx.doi.org/10.1080/0954655 3.2016.1169175

15 Subcommittee Hearing: "Assessing Terrorism in the Caucasus and the Threat to the Homeland Counterterrorism and Intelligence Subcommittee," 311 Cannon House Office Building, 13. April 2014 https://homeland.house.gov/hearing/subcommitte-hearing-assess-ing-terrorism-caucasus-and-threathomeland/ Alan Cullison, "Meet the Rebel Commander in Syria That Assad, Russia and the U.S. All Fear," Wall Street Journal, 19 November 2013, http://www.wsj.com/articles/SB10001424052702303309504579181962177007316.

16 Andrei Ostalskiy, "Халифатвсеближе," Radio Svoboda, 21 October 2015, http://www.svoboda.org/content/article/26644660.html.

17 "Caucasus Emirate," Mapping Militant Organizations. Bill Roggio and Thomas Joscelyn, "Russian troops kill leader of Islamic Caucasus Emirate," Long War Journal, 19 April 2015, http://www.longwarjournal.org/archives/2015/04/russian-troops-kill-leader-of-islamic-caucasus-emirate.php.

18 "ИГИЛугрожаетРоссии: чегождатьоттеррористов, которыев ернут сянаКавказ," MoskovskyKomsomolets (Moscow), 29 October 2015, http :// www.mk.ru /politics /2015/10/29/ igilugrozhae-trossiichegozhdatotterroristovkotoryevernutsyana kavkaz.html.

19 Amina Umarova, "Еслиназемлеестьад, тоя – вэтомаду," Radio Svoboda, 4 October 2010, http :// www . svoboda .org / content / article /27286075. html.

20 Istok is available from: http://jihadology.net/category/istok-maga-zine/

21 "Эксперт: ВербовочнаясетьИГИЛвРоссииужепревратиласьвусто йчивуюструктуру," RosBalt, 12 October 2015, http ://www .ros-balt .ru /main /2015/10/12/1450165. html.

22 Anecdotally, for example, some Chechens who lived through the Chechen wars remember that at the very height of the Chechen in-surgency against Moscow there were, in their estimation, no more than 2,000 fighters in all of Chechnya fighting Moscow. Based on author conversation with SufianZhemukhov, Senior Research Asso-ciate at PONARS, Eurasia, 23 March 2017, Washington, D.C

23 Joanna Paraszczuk, "'Your Kids Belong To IS,' Militants Tell Tajik Widow," RFE/RL, 13 May 2015. http://www.rferl.org/a/islamic-state-tajik-widow-syria-children/27013281.html

24 "ПротивникиавиаударовпоСирииизчислажителейКавказаопас аютсяжертвсредимирногонаселения," KavkazskiyUzel, 9 October 2015, http://www .kavkazuzelru articles /270315/ .

25 Jean-François Ratelle (2016), "North Caucasian foreign fight-ers in Syria and Iraq: assessing the threat of returnees to the Russian Federation," Caucasus Survey, 4:3, 218-238, DOI: 10.1080/23761199.2016.1234096

26 Roland Oliphant, "'Your son has become a Martyr': The Russian fighters from Dagestan rising up the ranks of Islamic State," The Telegraph, 30 July 2016.

27 ЕкатеринаСокирянская, "АбуМясо. ТаквИГИЛпрозваличе ченскогокомандира, отправляющегосвоихбойцовнасмерт ь," Novaya Gazeta, 20 May 2016 https://www.novayagazeta.ru/articles/2016/05/11/68546-abu-myaso-tak-v-igil-prozvali-ch-echenskogokomandira-otpravlyayuschego-svoih-boytsov-na-smert

28 Michael Weiss, "Russia is Sending Jihadis to Join ISIS," The Dai-ly Beast, 23 August 2015, http://www.thedailybeast.com/arti-cles/2015/08/23/russia-s-playing-a-double-game-with-islamic-ter-ror0.html.

29 Denis Sokolov, forthcoming report.

30 Denis Sokolov, forthcoming report.

31 Denis Sokolov, forthcoming report.

32 Broadly speaking, individuals certainly radicalize even when not alienated by the state, but in Russia, the authorities' treatment of Muslims has been the primary issue.

33 Valery Dzutsati, "Official Grozny Fails to Mark 70th Anniversary of the Chechen Deportations,"Eurasia Daily Monitor, Volume 11, Issue 42, 5 March 2014. http://www.jamestown.org/regions/the-caucasus/single/?tx_ttnews%5Bpointer%5D=4&tx_ttnews %5Btt_news%5D=42045&tx_ttnews%5BbackPid %5D=639&cHash=20fae 6f93ccf34d461a6379fc38d9c90#.Vx0N5zArJ3I.

34 MaazBilalov, "Последнийбастион," Kavkazr.com, 29 November 2016, http://www.kavkazr.com/a/posledniy-bastion/28146313.html

35 Author telephone interview with Vera Mironova, 17 March 2017.

36 MaazBilalov, "Последнийбастион," Kavkazr.com, 29 November 2016, http://www.kavkazr.com/a/posledniy-bastion/28146313.html

37 Eric Schmidt and Michael S. Schmidt, "Omar the Chechen, a Senior Leader in ISIS, Dies After U.S. Airstrike," New York Times, 15 March 2016, https://www.nytimes.com/2016/03/15/world/middleeast/omarchechen-isis-killed-us-airstrike-syria.html?ref=world&_r=0

38 NinaAkhmeteli, "The Georgian roots of Isis commander Omar al-Shishani," BBC, July 2014. http://www.bbc.com/news/world-europe-28217590

39 Joanna Paraszczuk, "Russian Citizen Linked To Lopota Gorge Incident Now Heads IS Battalion In Syria," RFE/RL, 25 February 2015, http://www.rferl.org/a/russia-lopota-gorge-incident-islamic-state-syria/26869379.html

40 William Watkinson, "One-armed Chechen warlord AkhmedChataev reportedly behind Ataturk massacre," International Business Times, 30 June 2016, http://www.ibtimes.co.uk/istanbul-airport-attack-one-armedakhmed-chataev-reportedly-behind-ataturk-massacre-1568359

41 AkhmadChataev profile, Counter Extremism Project, https://www.counterextremism.com/extremists/akhmed-chatayev.

42 Joanna Paraszczuk, "Russian Citizen Linked To Lopota Gorge Incident Now Heads IS Battalion In Syria," RFE/RL, 25 February 2015, http://www.rferl.org/a/russia-lopota-gorge-incident-islamic-state-syria/26869379.html

43 "'Ahmed One Arm' – The man who sends Jihadists From Pankisi to Syria," Georgian Journal, 31 January 2015. http://www.georgianjournal.ge/military/29509-ahmed-one-arm-the-man-who-sends-jihadists-frompankisi-to-syria.html

44 William Watkinson, "One-armed Chechen warlord AkhmedChataev reportedly behind Ataturk massacre," International Business Times, 30 June 2016, http://www.ibtimes.co.uk/istanbul-airport-attack-one-armedakhmed-chataev-reportedly-behind-ataturk-massacre-1568359 Fionn Hargreaves, "Freed to Kill. One-armed ISIS warlord behind Istanbul massacre 'was due to be sent to Russia on terror charges… but court ruled it breached his human rights,'" The Sun, 1 July 2016, https://www.thesun.co.uk/news/1375182/one-armed-isis-warlord-behind-istanbul-massacre-was-due-to-be-sent-to-russia-on-terror-charges-but-court-ruled-it-breached-his-human-rights/.

45 Bill Roggio, "Jaish al Muhajireenwal Ansar leader accuses Islamic State of creating 'fitna' between jihadist groups," The Long War Journal, 28 May 2015, http://www.longwarjournal.org/archives/2015/05/jaish-al-muhajireen-wal-ansar-leader-accuses-islamic-stateof-creating-fitna-between-jihadist-groups.php

46 Joanna Paraszczuk, "SaahuddinShishani in New Video Address: 'Our Position Will Remain as Before,'" ChechensinSyria.com, 26 September 2015, http://www.chechensinsyria.com/?p=24157#more-24157

47 ЕкатеринаСокирянская "АбуМясо. ТаквИГИЛпрозваличеченскогокомандира, отправляющегосвоихбойцовнасмерть," Novaya Gazeta, 20 May 2016 https://www.novayagazeta.ru/articles/2016/05/11/68546-abu-myaso-tak-v-igil-prozvali-chechenskogokomandira-otpravlyayuschego-svoih-boytsov-na-smert

48 Joanna Paraszczuk, "SaahuddinShishani in New Video Address: 'Our Position Will Remain as Before,'" ChechensinSyria.com, 26 September 2015, http://www.chechensinsyria.com/?p=24157#more-24157

49 See: http://nohchicho.com/tribune/abdulhakim-about-23-february/

50 Joanna Paraszczuk, "Interview and Letter from Ajnad al-Kavkas Amir Abdul Hakim Shishani," ChechensinSyria.com, 24 February 2017 http://www.chechensinsyria.com/?p=25309 See also: http://nohchicho.com/interview/abdul-hakim-interview/

51 Michael Weiss, "Russia's Double Game with Islamic Terror," The Daily Beast, 23 August 2015 http://www.thedailybeast.com/arti-

cles/2015/08/23/russia-s-playing-a-double-game-with-islamic-terror0.html

52 JoannaParaszczuk, "Umar Shishani's Right Hand Man Calls on North Caucasian Jihadis to Join IS in Dagestan and Chechnya," Jihadology, 21 April 2015, http://jihadology.net/2015/04/21/guest-post-umar-shishanis-right-hand-man-calls-on-north-caucasian-jihadisto-join-is-in-dagestan-chechnya/

53 Joanna Paraszczuk, "Umar Shishani's Biographer Distances from Imarat Kavkaz Bayah," ChechensinSyria.com, 1 August 2016, http://www.chechensinsyria.com/?p=25200#more-25200

54 "ВНорвегииосужденыдвоепособниковИГИЛ," RIA Novosti, 3 August 2016 https://regnum.ru/news/society/2162851.html

55 "Two jailed in Norway for joining ISIS in Syria," The Local, 4 August 2016, https://www.thelocal.no/20160804/two-jailed-in-norway-for-joining-isis-in-syria

56 VladimirVashchenko,   "Карауловарассказалаовербовке," Gazeta.ru, 27 October 2015 http://www.gazeta.ru/social/2015/10/27/7848623.shtml

57 "ПолучилапродолжениегромкаяисториявокругвербовкивИГИЛ студенткиМГУ," TV Channel 1, 28 October 2015, https://www.1tv.ru/news/2015/10/28/8474poluchila_prodolzhenie_gromkaya_istoriya_vokrug_verbovki_v_igil_studentki_mgu.

58 "Карауловаполучилачетыресполовинойгодаобщегореж има," Vesti.ru, 22 December 2016, http://www.vesti.ru/doc.html?id=2835970 Vladimir Vashchenko, "Основнаяидеябыла — выйтизамужзамусульманина," Gazeta.ru, 17 November 2016, https://www.gazeta.ru/social/2016/11/17/10341713.shtml Daria Litvinova, "IS Fighter or a Girl in Love?" The Moscow Times, 20 October 2016, https://themoscowtimes.com/articles/daddy-i-made-a-mistake-take-me-home-55796

59 "95% of foreign fighters who join ISIS are recruited by friends and family and radicalization 'rarely occurs in mosques', claims an Oxford University terrorism expert," Daily Mail, 25 November 2015. See also International Crisis Group, "The North Caucasus Insurgency and Syria: an Exported Jihad?" https://www.crisisgroup.org/europe-central-asia/caucasus/north-caucasus/north-caucasus-insurgency-andsyria-exported-jihad

60 "The North Caucasus Insurgency and Syria: an Exported Jihad?" p. 18.

61 "Russia Publishes Guidelines on Avoiding IS Recruitment," The Moscow Times, 7 December 2015, http://www.themoscowtimes. com/news/article/russia-publishes-guidelines-on-avoiding-isre-cruitment/552135.html.

62 Based on SufianZhemukhov's comments during presentation of International Crisis Group report, "The North Caucasus Insurgency and Syria."

63 "ИГИЛугрожаетРоссии: чегождатьоттеррористов, которыевер нутсянаКавказ," MoskovskiyKomsomolets, October 2015, http://www.mk.ru/politics/2015/10/29/igil-ugrozhaet-rossii-chego-zhdat-otterroristov-kotorye-vernutsya-na-kavkaz.html.

64 Evgeniy Balabas, "КакгосчиновникивРФфактическипотворст вуютисламистам," MoskovkiyKomsomolets, 10 November 2015, http://www.mk.ru/politics/2015/11/10/kak-goschinovniki-vrf-fak-ticheskipotvorstvuyut-islamistam.html

65 ArsenMollayev and Vladimir Isachenkov, "Russia is feeding hundreds of fighters to ISIS – and some are starting to return," Business Insider, 28 October 2015, http://www.businessinsider.com/ap-islamic-state-onrecruitment-spree-in-russia-2015-10.

66 Jean-François Ratelle (2016), "North Caucasian foreign fighters in Syria and Iraq: assessing the threat of returnees to the Russian Federation," Caucasus Survey, 4:3, 218-238, DOI: 10.1080/23761199.2016.1234096

67 Author telephone interview with Jean-François Ratelle, 24 April 2017.

Chapter 14: Counter-Terrorism Cooperation between China and Central Asian States in the Shanghai Cooperation Organization. Wang Jin and Kong Dehang

1 The "Shanghai Five" mechanism can be traced back to the late 1980s when China and the Soviet Union started negotiation over their border disputes. After the Soviet Union collapsed in 1991, the border negotiation mechanism was retained and transformed into the China-Russia-Central Asian states negotiation mechanism, which was later called the "Shanghai Five."

2   Today, the SCO consists of 8 formal members, including China, Russia, Kazakhstan, Kyrgyzstan, Tajikistan, Uzbekistan, India and Pakistan. Afghanistan, Belarus, Iran and Mongolia are accepted as "observer states," while Armenia, Azerbajian, Cambodia, Nepal, Sri Lanka and Turkey are treated as "dialogue states." In addition, Turkmenistan and three international organizations including the Commonwealth of Independent States (CIS), the Association of Southeast Asian Nations (ASEAN) and the United Nations (UN) are welcomed as "guest attendances" for the SCO.

3   Zeyno Baran, Hizbut-Tahrir: Islam's Political Insurgency (Washington D.C.: The Nixon Center, December 2004), p. 71.

4   Samuel Huntington, The Clash of Civilizations and the Remaking of World Order (New York: Touchstone, 1997), p. 247.

5   The State Council Information Office of the People's Republic of China, "The Fight Against Terrorism and Extremism and Human Rights Protection in Xinjiang," March 2019, http://www.scio.gov.cn/ zfbps/32832/Document/1649931/1649931.htm.

6   ['Eastern Turkistan Groups' Commit Crimes in Xinjiang After Training in Afghanistan]," Global Times, February 1, 2002, p. 2.

7   Brynjar Lia, Architect of Global Jihad: The Life of Al-Qaeda Strategist Abu Mus'ab al-Suri (London: Hurst Publisher, 2007), pp. 247–248.

8   David Witter, "Uzbek Militancy in Pakistan's Tribal Region," Institute for the Study of War, January 27, 2011, http://www.understandingwar.org/sites/default/files/BackgrounderIMU 28Jan.pdf.

9   Most Uygur Islamic extremists are concentrated in Idlib province of Syria. See "Turkey's De-escalation Efforts around Idlib Come with Risks," Al-Monitor, May 21, 2018, https://www.al-monitor.com/ pulse/originals/2018/05/turkey-syria-de-escalation-effortsaround-idlib-risky-1.html.

10   Caleb Weiss, "Uzbek Groups Part of New Offensive in Southern Aleppo," Long War Journal, June 7, 2016, http://www.longwarjournal.org/archives/2016/06/uz-bek-groups-partof-new-offensive-in-southern-aleppo.%20php.

11   "Syria Ambassador to China: At Least 30 ETIM Members Went to Syria," Global Times, July 2, 2018, http://world.huanqiu.com/exclusive/2013-07/4081528.html.

12 "Chinese Islamic Extremists Might Return to China," Zaobao News, May 8, 2011, http://www.zaobao.com/special/report/politic/cnpol/story20110508-140335.

The State Council Information Office of the People's Republic of China, "The Fight Against Terrorism and Extremism and Human Rights Protection in Xinjiang."

14 "'Shanghai Spirit," Secret of SCO's Success, Xinhua News, June 6, 2017, http://www. chinadaily.com.cn/world/2017xivisitskazakhstan/2017-06/06/content 29640474.htm.

15 Jean-Pierre Cabestan, "The Shanghai Cooperation Organization, Central Asia and Great Powers: An Introduction," Asian Survey, Vol. 53, No, 3 (2013), p. 424.

16 Shanghai Cooperation Organization, Shanghai Convention of Counter-Terrorism, Counter-Extremism and Counter-Secessionism, Article 1(2), http://chn.sectsco.org/documents/; and Shanghai Cooperation Organization, Convention of the Shanghai Cooperation Organization against Terrorism, Article 1(3), http://chn.sectsco.org/documents/.

17 Shanghai Cooperation Organization, Agreement on Cooperation in Combating Illicit TrafficofNarcoticDrugs,PsychotropicSubstances,andPrecursorsbetweentheMemberStatesofthe Shanghai Cooperation Organization, Article 1, http://chn.sectsco.org/documents/.

18 Unlikemostotherexercises,"PeaceMission2014"receivedmanyobserversincluding Iran, Pakistan, Afghanistan, Mongolia, India, Sri Lanka, Belarus, Turkey and more than 60 military attaches in China.

19 Ruslan Maksutov, "The Shanghai Cooperation Organization: A Central Asian Perspective," Stockholm International Peace Research Institute (August 2006), p. 11.

20 Gregory Logvinov, "The Shanghai Cooperation Organization: A New Qualitative Step Forward," Far Eastern Affairs, Vol. 30, No. 3 (2002), p. 22.

21 JosephYu-hekCheng,"TheAfghanistanSituationandChina'sNewApproachtothe SCO," Asian Survey, Vol. 55, No. 2 (2015), p. 246.

22 For more about Iran's consideration of joining the SCO, see Shahram Akbarzadeh, "Iran and the Shanghai Cooperation Organization: Ideology and Realpolitik in Iranian Foreign Policy," Australian Journal of International Affairs, Vol. 69, No. 1 (July 2014).

23 In 2012, Armenia, Azerbaijan, Bangladesh, Nepal and Sri Lanka applied for observer status within the SCO.

24 See, for example, John Vasquez, The War Puzzle (New York: Cambridge University Press, 1993), Chapter 4.

25 Jaish-e-Mohammed, the Haqqani network and Lashkar were all designated as terrorist groups in the Xiamen Declaration issued at the BRICS Summit held in China in September 2017.

26 "The Plot Behind China's Suppression of Uygurs in Xinjiang," Central Asia Program, January 8, 2018, http://centralasiaprogram.org/archives/12048.

27 See, for instance, Kathleen A. Collins and William C. Wohlforth, "Defying `Great Game' Expectation," inRichardJ.Ellingsetal.,eds.,St rategicAsia2003-04:FragilityandCrisis (Washington, D.C.: The National Bureau of Asian Research, 2003).

28 Ouyang Xiangying, " :[Russia and China: Misplacement and Connection over the Belt and Road Initiative]," International Economic Review, 2017(2), p. 50.

29 GeirFlikke, "Balancing Acts: Russian-Chinese Relations and Developments in the SCO and CSTO," Norwegian Institute of International Affairs (No. 1, 2009), p. 23.

30 "Advisor to Iran's Supreme Leader Outlines Steps to Boost Nuclear Program," AlMonitor, May 31, 2018, https://www.al-monitor.com/pulse/originals/2018/05/iran-nuclearprogram-jcpoa-deal-velayati-uf6-ir8-centrifuges.html.

Chapter 15: Geopolitics at the world's pivot: Expanding Central Asia's security challenges. Jacqueline Lopour

Abdolvand, Behrooz, Lutz Mez, Konstantin Winter, Shabnam Mirsaeedi-Gloßner, BrigittaSchütt, Karl Tilman Rost and Julia Bar. 2014. "The Dimension of Water in Central Asia: Security Concerns and the Long Road of Capacity Building." Environmental Earth Sciences 73 (2): 897–912. doi:10.1007/s12665-014-3579-9.

Agence France Press. 2012. "UN Sounds Alarm on Unsecured Uranium Waste in Tajikistan." Phys.org, December 14. http://phys.org/news/2012-12-alarmunsecured-uranium-tajikistan.html.

2014. "Uzbek Militants Declare Support for Islamic State." Dawn News, October 6. www.dawn.com/ news/1136578.

Bahgat, Gawdat. 2006. "Central Asia and Energy Security." Asian Affairs 37 (1): 1–16. doi:10.1080/03068370500456819.

Balci, Bayram and Didier Chaudet. 2014. "Jihadism in Central Asia: A Credible Threat after the Western Withdrawal from Afghanistan?" Carnegie Endowment of International Peace, August 13. http://carnegieendowment.org/2014/08/13/jihadism-incentral-asia-credible-threat-after-western-withdrawalfrom-afghanistan.

Bin Ladin, Osama. 2002. Letter to Mullah Omar, June 5. United States Military Academy Counterterrorism Center, document #AFGP-2002-600321. https://www. ctc.usma.edu/wp-content/uploads/2010/08/AFGP2002-600321-Trans.pdf.

Blake, Heidi and Christopher Hope. 2011. "WikiLeaks: al-Qaeda 'is planning a dirty bomb.'" The Telegraph, February 2. www.telegraph.co.uk/news/worldnews/ wikileaks/8296956/WikiLeaks-al-Qaeda-is-planninga-dirty-bomb.html.

Blank, Stephen. 2012. "Rethinking Central Asia and Its Security Issues." UNISCI Discussion Papers, No. 28. Research Unit on International Security and Cooperation (UNISCI). www.isn.ethz.ch/Digital-Library/ Publications/Detail/?lang=en&id=143766.

British Petroleum. 2014. BP Statistical Review of World Energy 2014. London, UK: BP. www.bp.com/content/dam/ bp/pdf/Energy-economics/statistical-review-2014/BPstatistical-review-of-world-energy-2014-full-report.pdf.

Central Intelligence Agency. 2015. The World Factbook. Washington, DC: CIA.

Chow, Edward C. and Leigh E. Hendrix. 2010. "Central Asia's Pipelines: Field of Dreams and Reality." National Bureau of Asian Research Special Report #23, September. http://csis.org/files/publication/1009_ EChow_LHendrix_CentralAsia.pdf.

Coburn, Leonard L. 2010. "Central Asia: Pipelines Are the New Silk Road." International Association for Energy Economics. https://www.iaee.org/en/publications/ newsletterdl.aspx?id=113.

Cornell, Svante and NiklasSwanström. 2005. "Kyrgyzstan's 'Revolution': Poppies or Tulips?" The Central AsiaCaucuses Analyst, May 18. www.cacianalyst.org/ publications/analytical-articles/item/9959-analyticalarticles-caci-analyst-2005-5-18-art-9959.html.2006. "The Eurasian Drug Trade: A Challenge to Regional Security." Problems of Post-Communism 53 (4): 10–28. doi:10.2753/PPC1075-8216530402.

Demirjian, Karoun. 2015. "How Russia's Labor Migration Policy Is Fueling the Islamic State." The Washington Post, July 11. https://www.washingtonpost.com/world/ asia_pacific/how-russias-labor-migration-policy-isfueling-the-islamic-state/2015/07/08/15b9300e-1 14111e5-a0fe-dccfea4653ee_story.html.

DFATD. 2015. "Priorities for 2015–2016." Government of Canada. Last updated April 8. www.international.gc.ca/ department-ministere/priorities-priorites.aspx?lang=eng.

Embassy of the Kyrgyz Republic to the Kingdom of Saudi Arabia. 2015. "Foundations of Foreign Policy." www. kyrgyzembarabia.kg.

Energy Information Administration. 2013. "Kazakhstan Consortium Achieves First Oil Production from Kashagan Field." United States Energy Information Administration, September 18. www.eia.gov/todayinenergy/detail.cfm?id=13011.

EU. 2009. The European Union's Border Management Programme in Central Asia (BOMCA) Phase 6. www. undp.org/content/dam/undp/documents/projects/ KGZ/00048932_BOMCA%206_DoA_prodoc.doc.

FAO. 2012. Turkmenistan Agricultural Sector Review: FAO Investment Centre Country Highlights. www.fao.org/ fileadmin/user_upload/tci/docs/Turkmenistan_ web_OK.pdf.

Fishelson, James. 2007. "From the Silk Road to Chevron: The Geopolitics of Oil Pipelines in Central Asia." Vestnik, The Journal of Russian and Asian Studies 7 (1), December 12. www.sras.org/geopolitics_of_oil_pipelines_ in_central_asia.

Frenken, Karen. 2013. Irrigation in Central Asia in figures. Aquastat Survey-2012. Food and Agriculture Organization of the United Nations. FAO Water Reports No. 39.

Gavrilis, George. 2012. "Central Asia's Border Woes and the Impact of International Assistance." Open Society Foundations Central Eurasia Project, Occasional Paper Series No. 6.

Granit, Jakob, Anders Jägerskog, Rebecca Löfgren, Andy Bullock, George de Gooijer, Stuart Pettigrew and Andreas Lindström. 2010. Regional Water Intelligence Report Central Asia. Baseline Report. Regional Water Intelligence Reports, Paper 15.

Hoffman, David E. 2009. "How U.S. Removed Half a Ton of Uranium from Kazakhstan." The Washington Post, September 21. www.washingtonpost.com/wpdyn/content/article/2009/09/20/AR2009092002881. html?sid=ST2009092002315.

Humphrey, Paula and Margarita Sevcik. 2009. "Uranium Tailings in Central Asia: The Case of the Kyrgyz Republic." Nuclear Threat Initiative, October 16. www. nti.org/analysis/articles/uranium-tailings-kyrgyzrepublic/.

Idrissov, Erlan. 2013. "Statement by His Excellency Mr. Erlan Idrissov, the Minister of Foreign Affairs of the Republic of Kazakhstan, at the 20th OSCE Ministerial Council." MC.DEL/35/13. OSCE, December 6. www. osce.org/mc/109291?download=true.

International Crisis Group. 2002. Central Asia: Border Disputes and Conflict Potential. International Crisis Group, Asia Report No. 33.

IOM. 2015a. "Human trafficking in Central Asia: Facts and Figures." International Organization for Migration. Received June 2015 in Astana, Kazakhstan.2015b. Mapping on Irregular Migration in Central Asia 2014. International Organization for Migration, Astana 2015.

Kassenova, Togzhan. 2010 "Uranium Production and Nuclear Energy in Central Asia: Assessment of Security Challenges and Risks." The China and Eurasia Forum Quarterly 8 (2): 221–41.

Kraak, Eelke. 2012. "Central Asia's Dam Debacle." China Dialogue, January 3. https://www.chinadialogue.net/ article/4790-Central-Asia-s-dam-debacle.

Mackinder, Halford. 1919. Democratic Ideals and Reality. London: Constable and Company.

McCoy, Alfred. 2015. "The Geopolitics of American Global Decline." TomDispatch.com (blog), June 7. www. tomdispatch.com/blog/176007/.

Ministry of Foreign Affairs of the Republic of Tajikistan. 2015. "Concept of the Foreign Policy of the Republic of Tajikistan." January 27. http://mfa.tj/en/law-basefp/concept-of-the-foreign-policy-of-the-republic-oftajikistan.html.

Ministry of Foreign Affairs of the Republic of Uzbekistan. 2015. "International Cooperation." www.mfa.uz/en/ cooperation/.

Mohapatra, Nalin Kumar. 2013. "Migration and Its Impact on Security of Central Asia." India Quarterly: A Journal of International Affairs 69 (2): 133–57. doi:10.1177/0974928413481883.

Nourzhanov, Kirill. 2009. "Changing Security Threat Perceptions in Central Asia." Australian Journal of International Affairs 63 (1): 85–104. doi:10.1080/10357710802666133.

Nuclear Threat Initiative. 2014. "Tajikistan: Overview." www.nti.org/country-profiles/tajikistan/.

Nurshayeva, Raushan. 2012. "Uzbek Leader Sounds Warning over Central Asia Water Disputes." Reuters, September 7. www.reuters.com/article/2012/09/07/ centralasia-water-idUSL6E8K793I20120907.

Pannier, Bruce. 2008. "Central Asia: Age-Old Water Problem Brings Tensions to a Boil." Radio Free Europe Radio Liberty, June 15. www.rferl.org/content/ article/1144627.html.

Peyrouse, Sebastien, Jos Boonstra and MarléneLaruelle. 2012. "Security and Development Approaches to Central Asia. The EU Compared to China and Russia." EUCAM Working Paper No. 11.

Public Safety Canada. 2015. "National Security." Last modified August 1. www.publicsafety.gc.ca/cnt/ntnlscrt/index-eng.aspx.

Quinn-Judge, Paul. 2010. "Conventional Security Risks to Central Asia: A Summary Overview." The China and Eurasia Forum Quarterly 8 (2): 53–63.

Renner, Michael. 2010. "Troubled Waters: Central and South Asia Exemplify Some of the Planet's Looming Water Shortages." World Watch, May 1. http:// isites.harvard.edu/fs/docs/icb.topic1239113.files/Troubled%20waters.%20Central%20and%20South%20 Asia.pdf.

Romin, Romish. 2015. "Tajiks Talk Up Afghan Spillover Risks." Institute for War & Peace Reporting, July 13. https://iwpr.net/global-voices/tajiks-talk-afghanspillover-risks.

Safirova, Elena. 2011. "The Mineral Industry of Uzbekistan." In 2011 Minerals Yearbook. Uzbekistan [Advance Release]. United States Geological Survey, United States Department of the Interior.

Saipov, Zabikhulla S. 2012. "New Foreign Policy Strategy Paper Codifies Uzbekistan's Reluctance Toward Restrictive Alliances." Eurasia Daily Monitor 9 (153).

Snow, Shawn. 2015. "ISIS Looks for Foothold in Central Asia." The Diplomat, January 18. http://thediplomat. com/2015/01/isis-looks-for-foothold-in-central-asia/.

Stucki, Virpi, Kai Wegerich, Muhammad MizanurRahaman, and Olli Varis. 2012. "Introduction: Water and Security in Central Asia — Solving a Rubik's Cube." International Journal of Water Resources Development 28 (3): 395–97. doi:10.1080/07900627.2012.684301.

Swanström, Niklas. 2010. "Traditional and Non-Traditional Security Threats in Central Asia: Connecting the New and the Old." The China and Eurasia Forum Quarterly 8 (2): 35–51.

Trofimov, Yaroslav. 2012. "Afghan Drug Trade Sends Tremors." The Wall Street Journal, August 3. www.wsj. com/articles/SB1000087239639 04435455045775634141 82938548.

UNDP. 2013. Tajikistan. Rapid Assessment and gap analysis. United Nations Development Programme, June 24. www.tj.undp.org/content/tajikistan/en/home/ library/environment_energy/sustainable-energy-forall.html.

UNODC. 2012. Opiate Flows through Northern Afghanistan and Central Asia: A Threat Assessment. Vienna, Austria: United Nations Office on Drugs and Crime. https:// www.unodc.org/documents/ data-and-analysis/ Studies/Afghanistan_northern_route_2012_web.pdf.

2015. Programme for Central Asia. A Partnership Framework for Impact Related Action in Central Asia 2015– 2019. Vienna, Austria: United Nations Office on Drugs and Crime. https://www.unodc. org/documents/ centralasia//MOU/programme_for_central_asia_20152019_en.pdf.

US Department of State. 2015. "Trafficking in Persons Report 2015." US Department of State. www.state. gov/j/tip/rls/tiprpt/2015/index.htm.

Withnall, Adam. 2015. "ISIS's Dirty Bomb: Jihadists Have Seized 'Enough Radioactive Material to Build Their First WMD.'" The Independent, June 10. www. independent.co.uk/news/world/middle-east/isiss-dirty-bomb-jihadists-have-seized-enough-radioactivematerial-to-build-their-first-wmd-10309220.html.

Wooden, Amanda. 2014. "Kyrgyzstan's Dark Ages: Framing and the 2010 Hydroelectric Revolution." Central Asian Survey 33 (4): 463–81. http://dx.doi.org/1 0.1080/02634937.2014.989755.

World Bank. 2013a. "Energy." Europe and Central Asia Brief, June 5. www.worldbank.org/en/region/eca/ brief/energy.

2013b. "Migration and Remittance Flows in Europe and Central Asia: Recent Trends and Outlook, 2013–2016." World Bank, October 2. www.worldbank. org/en/news/feature/2013/10/02/migration-an-dremittance-flows-in-europe-and-central-asia-recenttrends-and-outlook-2013-2016.

2013c. "Uzbekistan: The Economics of Efficiency." World Bank, April 30. www.worldbank.org/en/ results/2013/04/30/uzbekistan-the-economics-ofefficiency.

World Nuclear Association. 2015a. "Uranium and Nuclear Power in Kazakhstan." www.world-nuclear.org/info/ Country-Profiles/Countries-G-N/Kazakhstan/.

2015b. "Uranium in Kyrgyzstan." www.worldnuclear.org/info/Country-Profiles/Countries-G-N/ Kyrgyzstan/.

2015c. "Uzbekistan Uranium." www.worldnuclear.org/info/Country-Profiles/Countries-T-Z/ Uzbekistan/.

Wyke, Tom and Darren Boyle. 2014. "ISIS Release Shocking New Video of Child Soldiers from Kazakhstan Being Trained with AK47s." The Daily Mail Online, November 22. www.dailymail.co.uk/news/article-2845531/ISIS-releaseshocking-new-video-child-soldiers-Kazakhstan-trainedAK47s.html.

Zozulinsky, Artyom. 2010. "Kyrgyzstan: Power Generation & Transmission." US Embassy Bishkek, October. http:// photos.state.gov/libraries/kyrgyzrepulic/328656/ pdfs/Kyrgyz%20Power%20Industry%20Report%20 _2_.pdf.

Chapter 16: Theory-Testing Uyghur Terrorism in China, Andrew Mumford

1   Edward Schwarck, "Terrorism and China: Seeing the Threat Clearly," RUSI Analysis, 28 March 2014; URL: https://www.rusi. org/analysis/commentary/ref:C53394FCDD0B99/#.U3B42qhdXuk

2   There are a few notable exceptions. For a collective action theory explanation see Joshua Tschantret, "Repression, Opportunity, and Innovation: The Evolution of Terrorism in Xinjiang, China," Terrorism and Political Violence, Vol.30 No.4 (2018), pp.56988. For a securitization theory approach see Marie Trédaniel and Pak K. Lee, "Explaining the Chinese Framing of the 'Terrorist' Violence in Xin-

jiang: Insights from Securitization Theory," Nationalities Papers: The Journal of Nationalism and Ethnicity, Vol.46 No.1 (2018), pp.177-95.

3   For example see: Zachary Abuza, "The Uighurs and China's Regional Counter-Terrorism Efforts," Terrorism Monitor, 15 August 2017; URL: https://jamestown.org/program/the-uighurs-and-chinas-regional-counter-terrorism-efforts/ ; Jeffrey Reeves, "Ideas and Influence: Scholarship as a Harbinger of Counterterrorism Institutions, Policies, and Laws in the People's Republic of China," Terrorism and Political Violence, Vol.28 No.5 (2016), pp.827-47; Liselotte Odgaard and Thomas Galasz Nielsen, "China's Counterinsurgency Strategy in Tibet and Xinjiang," Journal of Contemporary China, Vol.23 Issue 87 (2014), pp.535-55; Elena Pokalova, "Authoritarian Regimes Against Terrorism: Lessons From China," Critical Studies on Terrorism, Vol.6 No.2 (2013), pp.279-98; and Martin Purbrick, "Maintaining a Unitary State: Counter-Terrorism, Separatism, and Extremism in Xinjiang and China," Asian Affairs, Vol.48 No.2 (2017), pp.236-56.

4   For example see: Abanti Bhattacharya, "Conceptualising Uyghur Separatism in Chinese Nationalism," Strategic Analysis, Vol.27 No.3 (2003), pp.357-81; and Elizabeth Van Wie Davis, "Uyghur Muslim Ethnic Separatism in Xinjiang, China," Asian Affairs, Vol.35 No.1 (2008), pp.15-30.

5   For a useful overview of the historical roots of the violence see Van Wie Davis, "Uyghur Muslim Ethnic Separatism."

6   Norwegian Peace Building Resource Centre report, "Islam and Political Instability in China's Xinjiang," March 2014; URL: https://www.files.ethz.ch/isn/179639/3ba335a7680451de2612c693a481eb96.pdf

7   Bhattacharya, "Conceptualising Uyghur Separatism in Chinese Nationalism," pp.357-81.

8   For a thorough assessment of the Uyghur resistance to Han nationalism see Gardner Bovingdon, "The Not-So-Silent Majority: Uyghur Resistance to Han Rule in Xinjiang," Modern China, Vol.28, No.1 (2002), pp.39-78.

9   Yitzhak Shichor, "Blow Up: Internal and External Challenges of Uyghur Separatism and Islamic Radicalisation to Chinese Rule in Xinjiang," Asian Affairs, Vol.32 No.2 (2005), pp.123.

10   Michael Clarke, "China, Xinjiang, and the Internationalisation of the Uyghur Issue," Global Change, Peace and Security, Vol.22 No.2 (2010), p.221.

11 Liza Steele and Raymond Kuo, 'Terrorism in Xinjiang?', Ethnopolitics, Vol.6 No.1 (2007), p.9.

12 Sean Roberts, "Imaginary Terrorism? The Global War on Terror and the Narrative of the Uyghur Terrorist Threat," PONARS Eurasia Working Paper (March 2012), pp.19-20; URL: http://www.ponarseurasia.org/sites/default/files/Roberts_WorkingPaper_ March2012.pdf

13 Wall Street Journal, "Xinjiang Arrests Nearly Doubled in '14, Year of 'Strike-Hard' Campaign," 23 January 2015; URL: https:// blogs.wsj.com/chinarealtime/2015/01/23/xinjiang-arrests-nearly-doubled-in-14-year-of-strike-hard-campaign/; The Guardian, "Xinjiang steps up fight against religious extremists in China," 17 January 2014; URL: https://www.theguardian.com/world/2014/ jan/17/xinjiang-religious-extremists-china-terrorism

14 Human Rights Watch, "'Eradicating Ideological Viruses": China's Campaign of Repression Against Xinjiang's Muslims', 9 September 2018; URL: https://www.hrw.org/report/2018/09/09/eradicating-ideological-viruses/chinas-campaign-repressionagainst-xinjiangs

15 For example, see BBC News, "China Uighurs: One million held in political camps, UN told," 10 August 2018; URL: https:// www.bbc.co.uk/news/world-asia-china-45147972; Al-Jazeera, "China holds one million Uighur Muslims in concentration camps," 13 September 2018; URL: https://www.aljazeera.com/indepth/opinion/china-holds-million-uighur-muslims-concentrationcamps-180912105738481.html; Reuters, "U.N. calls on China to free Uighurs from alleged re-education camps," 30 August 2018; URL: https://www.reuters.com/article/us-china-rights-un/u-n-calls-on-china-to-free-uighurs-from-alleged-re-education-campsidUSKCN1LF1D6

16 For example, see Tschantret, "Repression, Opportunity, and Innovation"; Trédaniel and Lee, "Explaining the Chinese Framing of the 'Terrorist' Violence in Xinjiang"; and Purbrick, "Maintaining a Unitary State.

17 The Washington Post, "China's repugnant campaign to destroy a minority people," 20 May 2018; URL: https://www. washingtonpost.com/opinions/chinas-repugnant-campaign-to-destroy-a-minority-people/2018/05/20/9fe061b4-5ac0-11e8-b656a5f8c2a9295d_story.html?noredirect=on&utm_term=.feefd1ed9849

18 Martha Crenshaw, "The Logic of Terrorism: Terrorist Behaviour as a Product of Strategic Choice," in Walter Reich (Ed.), Origins of Ter-

rorism: Psychologies, Ideologies, Theologies, States of Mind (Washington DC: Woodrow Wilson Center Press, 1990), p.8.

19 Nick Holdstock, China's Forgotten People: Xinjiang, Terror and the Chinese State (London: I.B Tauris, 2015), p.4.

20 See the appendix in Roberts, "Imaginary Terrorism?" for analysis of alleged TIP attacks.

21 Jerrold Post, "Terrorist Psycho-Logic: Terrorist Behavior as a Product of Psychological Forces," in Walter Reich (Ed.), Origins of Terrorism: Psychologies, Ideologies, Theologies, States of Mind (Washington DC: Woodrow Wilson Center Press, 1990), p.25.

22 David Rapoport, "The Four Waves of Modern Terrorism," in Audrey Kurth Cronin and James M. Ludes (Ed.), Attacking Terrorism: Elements of a Grand Strategy (Georgetown University Press, 2004).

23 Martin I. Wayne, China's War on Terrorism: Counter-Insurgency, Politics and International Security (Abingdon: Routledge, 2008), p.8.

24 Philip B.K. Potter, "'Terrorism in China: Growing Threats with Global Implications," Strategic Studies Quarterly, Vol.7 No.4 (2013), p.88.

25 Holdstock, China's Forgotten People, p.159.

26 Zachary Keck, "Why China's Terrorists are Targeting Train Stations," The Diplomat, 9 May 2014; URL: https://thediplomat. com/2014/05/why-chinas-terrorists-are-targeting-train-stations/

27 Quoted in Ben Blanchard, "China says three killed in attach at Xinjiang train station," Reuters, 30 April 2014; URL: https://www.reuters.com/article/us-china-xinjiang-blast/china-says-three-killed-in-attack-at-xinjiang-train-stationidUSBREA3T0HX20140430

28 Holdstock, China's Forgotten People, p.76.

29 Ibid., p.12

30 Ibid., p.76.

31 Herb Keinon, "JCPA analyst: 1,000 Chinese jihadists training in Pakistan," The Jerusalem Post, 25 June 2014; URL: https:// www.jpost.com/Middle-East/JCPA-analyst-1000-Chinese-jihadists-training-in-Pakistan-360469

32 Colin P. Clarke, and Paul Rexton Kan, "Uyghur Foreign Fighters: An Underexamined Jihadist Challenge," International Centre for Counter-Terrorism policy brief #5 (November 2017), pp.1 & 7; URL:

https://icct.nl/wp-content/uploads/2017/11/ClarkeKanUyghur-For-eign-Fighters-An-Underexamined-Jihadist-Challenge-Nov-2017-1. pdf

33   NodirbekSoliev, "Uyghur Militancy in and Beyond Southeast Asia: An Assessment," Counter Terrorist Trends and Analyses, Vol.9 No.2 (2017), p.14.

34   Clarke and Kan, "Uyghur Foreign Fighters," p.6.

35   Marc Julienne, Moritz Rudolf and Johannes Buckow, "Beyond Doubt: The Changing Face of Terrorism in China," The Diplomat, 28 May 2015; URL: https://thediplomat.com/2015/05/beyond-doubt-the-changing-face-of-terrorism-in-china/

36   Jeffrey Kaplan, Terrorist Groups and the New Tribalism: Terrorism's Fifth Wave (Abingdon: Routledge, 2007), p.1.

37   Ibid., p.72.

38   Jerrold Post, Cody McGinnis, and Kristen Moody, "The Changing Face of Terrorism in the 21st Century: The Communications Revolution and the Virtual Community of Hatred," Behavorial Sciences and the Law, 32 (2014), pp.314.

39   Or Honig and IdoYahel, "A Fifth Wave of Terrorism? The Emergence of Terrorist Semi-States," Terrorism and Political Violence, (2017), p.2; URL: https://doi.org/10.1080/09546553.2017.1330201

40   Human Rights, Watch, "Eradicating Ideological Viruses."

41   Holdstock, China's Forgotten People, p.4.

42   See Roberts, "Imaginary Terrorism?"

43   For example, the September 2018 Human Rights Watch report 'Eradicating Human Viruses' is based on 58 interviews with Uyghur exiles.

44   "China's leader Xi Jinping declares the start of a 'new era'", The Economist, 21 October 2017; URL: https://www.economist. com/china/2017/10/21/chinas-leader-xi-jinping-declares-the-start-of-a-new-era

Chapter 17: Why States Won't Give Nuclear Weapons to Terrorists. Keir A. Lieber and Daryl G. Press

1.   President GeorgeW.Bush warned,"Stateslike[Iraq],andtheirterroris tallies,constituteanaxis of evil, arming to threaten the peace of the world. By seeking weapons of mass destruction, these regimes pose

a grave and growing danger. They could provide these arms to terrorists, giving them the means to match their hatred." Bush, "State of the Union Address," January 29, 2002. See also White House, The National Security Strategy of the United States of America (Washington, D.C.: White House, September 2002), pp. 13–16.

2. Condoleezza Rice, speech given to the Chicago Council on Foreign Relations, Chicago, Illinois, October 8, 2003. Rice repeatedly connected Iraq's alleged pursuit of nuclear weapons with terrorism.She explained the case for war against Iraq by arguing, "The problem here is that there will always be some uncertainty about how quickly he [Saddam Hussein] can acquire nuclear weapons. But we don't want the smoking gun to be a mushroom cloud....There is certainly evidence that al-Qaida people have been in Iraq. There is certainly evidence that Saddam Hussein cavorts with terrorists. . . . Weknow that he is acquiring weapons of mass destruction, that he has extreme animus against the United States." Rice, interview by Wolf Blitzer, Late Edition with Wolf Blitzer, CNN, September 8, 2002. Similarly, in the lead-up to the invasion, Vice President Dick Cheney asked rhetorically, "Where might these terrorists acquire weapons of mass destruction, chemical weapons, biological weapons, nuclear weapons? And Saddam Hussein becomes a prime suspect in that regard because of his past track record. . . . Weknow he's trying once again to produce nuclear weapons and we know that he has a long-standing relationship with various terrorist groups, including the al-Qaida organization." Cheney, interview by Tim Russert, Meet the Press, NBC, March 16, 2003.

3. Emblematic of this concern is Norman Podhoretz's depiction of "the menacing shadow of an Iran armed with nuclear weapons, and only too ready to put them into the hands of the terrorist groups." He continues, "Even if [President Mahmoud] Ahmadinejad did not yet have missiles with a long enough range to hit the United States, he would certainly be able to unleash a wave of nuclear terror against us. If he did, he would in all likelihood acts through proxies, for whom he would with characteristic brazenness disclaim any responsibility even if the weapons used by theterroristsweretobeartelltalemarkingsidentifyingthemasofIranianorigin."Podhoretz,"The Case for Bombing Iran," Commentary, June 2007, pp. 17–23, at p. 19.

4. White House, The National Security Strategy of the United States (Washington, D.C.: White House, May 2010), p. 23. For the views of other U.S. leaders, see also the 2004 and 2008 presidential candi-

dates' statements by John Kerry, George W. Bush, John McCain, and Barack Obama in Francis J. Gavin, "Same As It Ever Was: Nuclear Alarmism, Proliferation, and the Cold War," International Security, Vol. 34, No. 3 (Winter 2009/10), pp. 7–37, at p. 7.

5. An additional potential consequence of proliferation is not emphasized in the literature or in policymakers' statements: that an adversary's nuclear weapons will be used to stalemate U.S. conventional military power, and hence complicate the United States' global national security strategy. See Keir A. Lieber and Daryl G. Press, "The Nukes We Need: Preserving the American Deterrent," Foreign Affairs, Vol. 88, No. 6 (November/December 2009), pp. 39–51.

6. For an analysis focusing on Iran and arguing that the risk of deliberate transfer of chemical, biological, or nuclear weapons to terrorists is low, see Daniel L. Byman, "Iran, Terrorism, and Weapons of Mass Destruction," Studies in Conflict and Terrorism, Vol. 31, No. 3 (Spring 2008), pp. 169–181. See also the discussion in Daniel L. Byman, "Do Counterproliferation and Counterterrorism Go Together?" Political Science Quarterly, Vol. 122, No. 1 (Spring 2007), pp. 25–46. For a more pessimistic assessment, see Richard A. Falkenrath, Robert D. Newman, and Bradley A. Thayer, eds., America's Achilles' Heel: Nuclear, Biological, and Chemical Terrorism and Covert Attack (Cambridge, Mass.: MIT Press, 1998), which concludes that the risk of states using terrorists to de liver weapons of mass destruction is a significant and growing threat to the United States. See also Michael A. Levi, Deterring State Sponsorship of Nuclear Terrorism (Washington, D.C.: Council on Foreign Relations, 2008).

7. Scott D. Sagan and Kenneth N. Waltz, The Spread of Nuclear Weapons: A Debate Renewed (New York:W.W.Norton,2002);KennethN. Waltz,"Nuclear Myth sand Political Realities,"AmericanPolitical Science Review, Vol. 84, No. 3 (September 1990), pp. 731–745; Kenneth N. Waltz, The Spread of Nuclear Weapons: More May Be Better, Adelphi Papers, No. 171 (London: International Institute for Strategic Studies, 1981); and Robert Jervis, The Meaning of the Nuclear Revolution: Statecraft and the Prospect of Nuclear Armageddon (Ithaca, N.Y.: Cornell University Press, 1989).

8. Kenneth N. Waltz, "Why Iran Should Get the Bomb: Nuclear Balancing Would Mean Stability," Foreign Affairs, Vol. 91, No. 4 (July/August 2012), pp. 2–5. Evidence suggests that the Iranian government's leadership is "rational" in the sense that its leaders are goal oriented and do not seek their own destruction in pursuit of reli-

gious or ideological goals. On how Iran's postrevolution leadership has modulated its behavior in response to costs and risks, see Brenda Shaffer, "The Islamic Republic of Iran: Is It Really?" in Shaffer, ed., The Limits of Culture: Islam and Foreign Policy (Cambridge, Mass.: MIT Press, 2006), pp. 219–239. See also Juan Cole, Engaging the Muslim World (New York: Palgrave Macmillan, 2009), chap. 6.

9. Empirically, evaluations find that nuclear acquisition by one country barely increases the odds that any of its neighbours or enemies will acquire nuclear weapons. See William C. Potter, with Gaukhar-Mukhatzhanova, eds., Forecasting Nuclear Proliferation in the 21st Century: The Role of Theory, Vol. 1 (Palo Alto, Calif.: Stanford University Press, 2010), especially Philipp C. Bleek, "Why Do States Proliferate? Quantitative Analysis of the Exploration, Pursuit, and Acquisition of Nuclear Weapons," in ibid., chap. 8. See also William C. Potter, with GaukharMukhatzhanova, eds., Forecasting Nuclear Proliferation in the 21st Century: A Comparative Perspective, Vol. 2 (Palo Alto, Calif.: Stanford University Press, 2010); Moeed Yusuf, "Predicting Proliferation: The History of the Future of Nuclear Weapons," Brookings Institution Foreign Policy Paper Series, No. 11 (Washington, D.C.: Brookings Institution, January 2009); William C. Potter and GaukharMukhatzhanova, "Divining Nuclear Intentions: A Review Essay," International Security, Vol. 33, No. 1 (Summer 2008), pp. 139–169; Jacques E.C. Hymans, Achieving Nuclear Ambitions: Scientists, Politicians, and Proliferation (New York: Cambridge University Press, 2012); and Johan Bergenas, "The Nuclear Domino Myth," Snapshot, Foreign Affairs, August 31, 2010, http://www.foreignaffairs.com/articles/66738/ johan-bergenas/the-nuclear-domino-myth. John Mueller takes "cascadological hysteria" to task in Mueller, Atomic Obsession: Nuclear Alarmism from Hiroshima to Al-Qaeda (New York: Oxford University Press, 2010), pp. 90–95.

10. This hypothesis has been intensely debated. See John Mueller, "Think Again: Nuclear Weapons," Foreign Policy, No. 177 (January/February 2010), pp. 38–44; Micah Zenko and Michael A. Cohen, "Clear and Present Safety," Foreign Affairs, Vol. 91, No. 2 (March/April 2012), pp. 79–93; Kenneth N. Luongo, "Loose Nukes in New Neighborhoods: The Next Generation of Proliferation Prevention," Arms Control Today, Vol. 35, No. 4 (May 2009), pp. 6–14; Graham T. Allison, Owen R. Coté Jr., Richard A. Falkenrath, and Steven E. Miller, Avoiding Nuclear Anarchy: Containing the Threat of Loose Russian Nuclear Weapons and Fissile Material (Cambridge, Mass.:

MIT Press, 1996); Matthew Bunn, Securing the Bomb 2010: Securing All Nuclear Materials in Four Years (Cambridge, Mass.: Project on Managing the Atom, BelferCenter for Science and International Affairs, Harvard Kennedy School, 2010); Mueller, Atomic Obsession, pp. 165–168, 208–210, 238; Gary Milhollin, "Can Terrorists Get the Bomb?" Commentary, February 2002, pp. 45–49; and Karl-Heinz Kamp, "An Overrated Nightmare," Bulletin of the Atomic Scientists, Vol. 52, No. 4 (July/August 1996), pp. 30–34.

11. See Todd S. Sechser and Matthew Fuhrmann, "Crisis Bargaining and Nuclear Blackmail," International Organization, Vol. 67, No. 1 (Winter 2013), pp. 173–195; and Kyle Beardsley and Victor Asal, "Nuclear Weapons as Shields," Conflict Management and Peace Science, Vol. 26, No. 3 (July 2009), pp. 235–255. For earlier analyses, see Barry R. Posen, "U.S. Security Policy in a NuclearArmed World (Or: What If Iraq Had Had Nuclear Weapons?)," Security Studies, Vol. 6, No. 3 (Spring 1997), pp. 1–31; Jervis, The Meaning of the Nuclear Revolution, chap. 1; and Richard K. Betts, Nuclear Blackmail and Nuclear Balance (Washington, D.C.: Brookings Institution Press, 1987), chaps. 1–3, 6.

12. The danger of nuclear attack by proxy has two requirements: (1) that states are willing to transfer such weapons or materials; and (2) that terrorist groups seek to carry out such destructive attacks. In this article, we puncture the first proposition. Other analysts debate the second, articulated in Brian Jenkins's classic statement that "terrorists want a lot of people watching and a lot of people listening and not a lot of people dead." See Jenkins, "International Terrorism: ANew Mode of Conflict," in David Carlton and Carlo Schaerf, eds., International Terrorism and World Security (London: Croom Helm, 1975), p. 15; Bruce Hoffman, Inside Terrorism (New York: Columbia, 2006); Mueller, Atomic Obsession, pp. 199–216; and Byman, "Iran, Terrorism, and Weapons of Mass Destruction," pp. 173, 179.

13. Two examples of leaders intentionally overstating their military capabilities are Nikita Khrushchev's exaggerated claims about the Soviet nuclear arsenal in the 1950s and, more recently, KimJong-un's fauxintercontinentalballisticmissiles(ICBMs)onparadeinPyongyangin2012.On the former, see John J. Mearsheimer, Why Leaders Lie: The Truth about Lying in International Politics (New York: Oxford University Press, 2011), pp. 31–32. On the latter, see Markus Schiller and Robert H. Schmucker, "A Dog and Pony Show: North Korea's New ICBM," Arms Control Wonk, blog, April 18, 2012, http://

lewis.armscontrolwonk.com/ᵃles/2012/04/KN-08_Analysis_Schiller _Schmucker.pdf ; Jeffrey Lewis, "DPRK ICBM Items," April 19, 2012, Arms Control Wonk, http:// lewis.armscontrolwonk.com/ archive/5150/dprk-icbm-items; and Jeffrey Lewis, "Real Fake Missiles?" Arms Control Wonk, blog, May 1, 2012, http://lewis.armscontrolwonk.com/archive/5198/ real-fake-missiles.

14. See, for example, Bunn, Securing the Bomb 2010, p. 20.

15. For examples of these arguments, see Mueller, Atomic Obsession, pp.163–164, and sources cited therein; and Falkenrath, Newman, and Thayer, America's Achilles Heel. Note that even analysts deeply concerned about the problem of nuclear terrorism arising from other sources (e.g., theft or black-market purchase of nuclear materials) can be more sanguine about the possibility of deliberate state transfer. See Bunn, Securing the Bomb 2010, p. 20; and Matthew Bunn, "A Mathematical Model of the Risk of Nuclear Terrorism," Annals of the American Academy of Political and Social Science, Vol. 607, No. 1 (September 2006), pp. 103–120, at pp. 115–116.

16. Nuclear weapons use uranium or plutonium as fissile material—that is, split to release the energy associated with a nuclear detonation. The uranium used in nuclear weapons is typically U-235, a rare isotope that is acquired by separating the desired isotope from the vastly more plentiful U-238. This separation (i.e., "enrichment") can be done using various methods; currently, feeding uranium hexafluoride gas through cascades of spinning centrifuges is the most common approach. Plutonium is an element that does not exist in meaningful quantities in nature; it is created in nuclear reactors as a by-product of fission.

17. National Research Council, Nuclear Forensics: A Capability at Risk, as cited in William J. Broad, "Nuclear Forensics Skill Is Declining in U.S., Report Says," New York Times, July 29, 2010.

18. Michael Miller, "Nuclear Attribution as Deterrence," Non-proliferation Review, Vol. 14, No. 1 (March 2007), p. 41.

19. Charles D. Ferguson, Preventing Catastrophic Nuclear Terrorism (New York: Council on Foreign Relations, 2006), p.6; and Miller,"Nuclear Attributionas Deterrence,"p.40.The political obstacles to establishing an effective nuclear attribution capability may be as challenging as the technical ones. As one analyst observes, "The main problem with relying on nuclear forensics to identify those responsible for a nuclear explosion . . . is theneed to secure the co-

operation of the same countries that could be targets of a nuclear attribution investigation." Richard Weitz, "Nuclear Forensics: False Hopes and Practical Realities," Political Science Quarterly, Vol. 126, No. 1 (Spring 2011), pp. 54–55. Specifically, the likelihood of securing widespread participation by countries in an international database of nuclear materials—which would entail contributing nuclear samples and divulging highly sensitive information—is remote, given that the ultimate purpose of the enterprise is to identify and punish them if they misbehave or allow material to be stolen. This fundamental problem is compounded by additional practical factors: states that have previously shared nuclear materials with other states have an incentive not to release samples that would implicate them in these proliferation activities; states could submit false information or misleading samples to hide past activity or frame a rival state; and states that legitimately sell or lease nuclear reactor fuel to other countries would fear wrongful accusation if that material were used in an attack. Ibid., pp. 55–66.

20. Broad, "Nuclear Forensics Skill Is Declining in U.S., Report Says." Although the National Re search Council report is generally sanguine about the potential contribution of nuclear forensics to the attribution mission, the report highlights several major areas of concern about U.S. capabilities, stemming from issues of organizational complexity, lack of direction, and lack of consensus; declining funding; skilled personnel spread too thin and working in out dated facilities; and outdated equipment and procedures. National Research Council, Nuclear Forensics: A Capability at Risk (Washington, D.C.: National Academies Press, 2010). On other technical and political obstacles to effective U.S. nuclear forensic capabilities, see Weitz, "Nuclear Forensics," pp. 53–75; Michael M. May, Reza Aberdin-Zadeh, Donald Barr, Albert Carnesale, Philip E. Coyle, Jay Davis, William Dorland, William Dunlop, Steve Fetter, Alexander Glaser, Ian D. Hutcheon, Francis Slakey, and Benn Tannenbaum, Nuclear Forensics: Role, State of the Art, and Program Needs (Washington, D.C.: American Association for the Advancement of Science Center for Science Technology and Security Policy, February 2008); National Academy of Sciences, Making the Nation Safer: The Role of Science and Technology in Countering Terrorism (Washington, D.C.: National Academies Press, 2002); and Debra Decker, "Comments Provided for the Subcommittee on Oversight of Government Management, the Federal Workforce, and the District of Columbia of the U.S. Senate Committee on Homeland Security and Government Af-

fairs Regarding the Status of U.S. Response Following a Nuclear or RDD Attack," November 15, 2007. Michael Miller, however, argues that the flaws in nuclear forensic capabilities are "such that nuclear attribution currently provides little deterrent value." Miller, "Nuclear Attribution as Deterrence," pp. 33–60, at p. 33. For a balanced analysis of the link between improved nuclear forensics capabilities and the problem of deterring nuclear terrorism, see Caitlin Talmadge, "Deterring a Nuclear 9/11," Washington Quarterly, Vol. 30, No. 2 (Spring 2007), pp. 21–34.

21. Important works on "conventional" terrorism include Bruce Hoffman, Inside Terrorism (New York: Columbia University Press, 2006); Daniel Byman, Deadly Connections: States That Sponsor Terrorism (New York: Cambridge University Press, 2005); Robert A. Pape, Dying to Win: The Strategic Logic of Suicide Terrorism (Ithaca, N.Y.: Cornell University Press, 2005); Michael E. Brown, Owen R. Coté Jr., Sean M. Lynn-Jones, and Steven E. Miller, eds., Contending with Terrorism: Roots, Strategies, and Responsibilities (Cambridge, Mass.: MIT Press, 2010); Audrey Kurth Cronin, How Terrorism Ends: Understanding the Decline and Demise of Terrorist Campaigns (Princeton, N.J.: Princeton University Press, 2011); and John Mueller and Mark G. Stewart, "The Terrorism Delusion: America's Overwrought Response to September 11," International Security, Vol. 37, No. 1 (Summer 2012), pp. 81–110.

22. National Consortium for the Study of Terrorism and Responses to Terrorism (START), Global Terrorism Database (GTD), 2011, http://www.start.umd.edu/gtd.

23. The GTD dataset includes 20,234 incidents from 1998 to 2008. For two reasons, however, our consolidation of the data left us with 18,328 data points. First, a large number of the attacks in the GTD-datasetarereportedmorethanonce.TheGTDisdesignedtocapturede-tailedinformationon the weapons and tactics of terrorist groups, so an attack in which,forexample,terrorists detonated a bomb outside a building and then armed men stormed the facility would be recorded as two incidents. For our purposes, it would introduce bias if we "double-counted" complex attacks, so we consolidated the data to generate a single data point from each single attack. Second, because a key variable we explore is how attribution varies with fatality level, we ignored the roughly 2.5 percent of incidents for which the number of fatalities is not reported in the dataset.

24. We replicated our analysis with the Worldwide Incidents Tracking System (WITS) database, another major source for data on terrorist acts, and all the major findings reported here are confirmed. We have replicated figures 1 and 2 in this article using WITS data; they are available from the authors upon request.

25. We use algorithmic scale to allow readers to see the number of attacks, and how they decline, as a function of fatalities. Because the data are skewed toward the low-fatality side of the distribution, a linear scale would obscure the number of incidents that killed thirty or more people and the variation among the high-fatality categories.

26. For this group, we counted the United States; other NATO members; and Australia, Israel, Japan, and South Korea. Some countries became members of NATO during the decade in question; we counted attacks on their territory starting the year in which they joined the alliance.

27. For a thorough discussion of the task, see Mueller, Atomic Obsession, pp. 161–198.

28. For example, a complex international terror operation, such as the September 11 terrorist attacks, requires loyal and competent operatives who can travel to the target state. This often involves gaining entrance visas, establishing secure communication procedures, training the operatives to conduct the mission, moving money across borders, and moving the weapon itself to the victim state. As the September 11 attacks illustrate, sophisticated terrorist groups such as al-Qaida can execute complex operations such as these, but the organizational requirements are far more advanced than the capabilities of local militias and most terrorist groups.

29. U.S. Department of State, "Foreign Terrorist Organizations," September 28, 2012, http:// www.state.gov/j/ct/rls/other/des/123085. htm. For a description of each foreign terrorist organization (FTO), see U.S. Department of State, "Country Report on Terrorism, 2011" (Washington, D.C.: U.S. Department of State, July 31, 2012), chap. 6, http://www.state.gov/j/ct/rls/crt/. The State Department deªnes an FTO as a group that either engages in terrorism or retains the capability and intent to do so and whose terrorist activities threaten the citizens or interests of the United States. The last criterion means that the list principally includes anti-American terrorists, but it is nevertheless useful for two reasons. First, even though the list excludes terror groups whose interests align with those of the United States, unless "anti-American" terrorist groups have, on average, signifi-

cantly fewer or significantly more state sponsors than pro-American terror groups, the State Department list offers good insight into the number of state sponsors per terrorist group. Second, although one purpose of this article is to explore the challenge of terrorist attribution generally, a related goal is to explore the challenge of attribution for the United States. The terrorist organizations excluded from this list would not be prime suspects in a nuclear terror strike against the United States.

30. The number of FTOs comes from U.S. Department of State, "Foreign Terrorist Organizations." The number of FTOs with state sponsors is culled from U.S. Department of State, "Country Report on Terrorism, 2011."

31. The State Department also lists Sudan on its list of state sponsors of terror, but only because of Sudan's inability to adequately police its territory (and hence to effectively combat terrorist groups on its own territory). The State Department does not claim that Sudan funds, arms, or gives safe haven to any FTO.

32. In 2008, Pakistan was described as "perhaps the world's most active sponsor of terrorist groups." Daniel L. Byman, "The Changing Nature of State Sponsorship of Terrorism," SabanCenter Analysis Paper Series (Washington, D.C.: Brookings Institution, May 2008), p. 7. On Pakistan's more recent support for terrorists, see Peter Tomsen, "Pakistan: With Friends Like These..."World Policy Journal, Vol. 28, No. 3 (September 2011), pp. 82–90. The Pakistan-linked groups are Lashkare-Taiba, Jaish-e-Mohammed, the Haqqani Network, and the Indian Mujahedeen. The groups linked to Venezuela are the Revolutionary Armed Forces of Colombia and the National Liberation Army. See Mark P. Sullivan, "Venezuela: Issues for Congress" (Washington, D.C.: Congressional Research Service, October 12, 2012).

33. Daniel L. Byman, "Unlikely Alliance: Iran's Secretive Relationship with Al-Qaeda," Iranian Sponsorship of Terrorism, IHS Defense, Risk, and Security Consulting, July 2012.

34. Mark Hosenball, "Documents Show Tense Al Qaeda Relationship," Reuters, May 3, 2012.

35. Other critics question North Korea's absence from the State Department's list of FTOs. On the decision to remove North Korea from the list, see Helene Cooper, "U.S. Declares North Korea off TerrorList," NewYorkTimes,October12,2008.AlthoughtheNorthKoreangovern-

menthascarried out numerous attacks against South Korea over the past ᵃve decades, the North Korean military conducted those attacks, not terrorist groups. For a discussion of these attacks, see Jennifer Lind, "Why North Korea Gets Away with It," Snapshot, Foreign Affairs, April 12, 2012, http://www.foreignaffairs.com/articles/137399/jennifer-lind/why-north-korea-gets-away-with-it.

36. Given regime change in Libya and the civil war in Syria, it is unclear whether the organization will continue to receive significant support from those states.

37. For example, if Israel suffered a nuclear attack, and Tehran admitted that the weapon used was Iranian but blamed Hezbollah for stealing it, it is unlikely that Israel would believe Iran's story. It might not temper its response even if it did, because it could be argued that Iran's long history of support for Hezbollah makes Tehran responsible for Hezbollah's actions.

38. The nine states with nuclear weapons are China, France, India, Israel, North Korea, Pakistan, Russia, the United Kingdom, and the United States. The eleven states with at least 15 kilograms of highly enriched uranium or about 5 kilograms of plutonium—the minimum threshold considered necessary to build a crude nuclear device—are Belarus, Belgium, Canada, the Czech Republic, Germany, Italy, Japan, Kazakhstan, the Netherlands, Poland, and South Africa. On fissile material thresholds, see International Panel on Fissile Materials, Global Fissile Material Report 2011 (Princeton, N.J.: Program on Science and Global Security, Princeton University, 2011), p. 27. On the countries meeting these minimum thresholds, see ibid.; James Martin Center for Nonproliferation Studies, "Civil Highly Enriched Uranium: Who Has What?" http://www.nti.org/media/pdfs/ HEU_who_has _what.pdf; and Office of the Press Secretary, "Fact Sheet: Ukraine Highly Enriched Uranium Removal," Washington, D.C., March 27, 2012, http://www.whitehouse.gov/the-pressofice/2012/03/27/fact-sheet-ukraine-highly-enriched-uranium-removal. Although we credit any state with 15 kilograms of HEU as having bomb quantities of fissile material, a uranium-based weapon constructed by terrorists would likely be a simple design (perhaps a "gun-type" weapon) that would require substantially more than 15 kilograms of HEU—possibly in the 50-kilogram range. See, for example, Union of Concerned Scientists (UCS), "Weapon Materials Basics" (Cambridge, Mass.: UCS,April2004),http://www.ucsusa.org/nuclear_weapons_and_global_security/ nuclear_terrorism/tech-

nical_issues/ᵃssile-materials-basics.html; and "Nuclear Terrorism 101" (Cambridge, Mass.: BelferCenter for Science and International Affairs, Harvard Kennedy School, n.d.), http://nuclearsummit .org/ nuclear_terrorism_101.html.

39. HEU is less radioactive than plutonium and is therefore easier to handle and harder for sensors to detect. HEU can also be used in a crude gun-type fission bomb, a relatively simple device to build. Plutonium, by contrast, is highly radioactive and therefore difficult to handle without inducing debilitating radiation poisoning; it is easier to detect; and it must be detonated through a sophisticated implosion device, which is technically demanding to build—probably beyond the capabilities of terrorist groups.

40. Bunn, Securing the Bomb 2010, p. 23–59, gives a detailed account of the progress in securing nuclear material and the remaining risks. Note that our focus in this article is on the security of fissile material, not weapons. All nine nuclear weapon states place great emphasis on security at their nuclear weapons storage sites. Even Pakistan, the country that rightfully inspires the greatest nuclear security concerns, keeps its weapons consolidated at a small number of highly defended facilities, and apparently stores its weapons disassembled with each nuclear core located separately from the rest of the device. On Pakistan storing its weapons disassembled, see Hans M. Kristensen and Robert S. Norris, "Pakistan's Nuclear Forces, 2011," Bulletin of the Atomic Scientists, Vol. 67, No. 4 (July/August 2011), pp. 91–99; and David Albright, "Securing Pakistan's Nuclear Infrastructure," in Lee Feinstein, James Clad, Lewis Dunn, and David Albright, A New Equation: U.S. Policy toward India and Pakistan after September 11 (Washington, D.C.: Carnegie Endowment for International Peace, 2002). Furthermore, most nuclear weapons have sophisticated, integrated locks to prevent unauthorized detonation.

41. According to the Fissile Materials Working Group, "The stocks of nuclear weapons or weapons-usable nuclear material that are most likely to fall into terrorist hands today exist in Russia, Pakistan, and countries with research reactors that use large quantities of highly enriched uranium (HEU)—like Belarus, South Africa, and Japan." Fissile Materials Working Group, "Nuclear Security's Top Priority," Bulletin of the Atomic Scientists, online edition, June 12, 2012, http://www .thebulletin.org/web-edition/columnists/fissile-materials-working-group/nuclear-securitys-toppriority. See also Bunn, Securing the Bomb 2010, pp. 27–43, on risks emanating from Russia

and Pakistan, and pp. 43–45 on risks at HEU research reactors. Bunn identifies Belarus, Kazakhstan, and South Africa as posing the greatest dangers, as summarized in Bunn, Securing the Bomb 2010, table 3.5. Bunn's list of top concerns includes Kazakhstan, but that country has subsequently eliminated almost all of its highly enriched uranium, and its remaining stock—mostly in the range of 22 to 36 percent enrichment—would be inordinately difficult for a terror group to process into material for a nuclear bomb. Bunn's discussion also includes Ukraine, but Ukraine has subsequently removed all HEU from its territory. On Ukraine, see Office of the Press Secretary, "Fact Sheet: Ukraine Highly Enriched Uranium Removal."

42. Fissile Materials Working Group, "Nuclear Security's Top Priority."

43. As discussed above, a crude, gun-type HEU bomb—the type that terrorists might be able to construct—requiresroughly50kilogram sofHEU,approximately half of Belarus'sentirestockpile. It would be simple for Belarus to demonstrate its innocence.

44. Bunn, Securing the Bomb 2010, p. 21. Iran has roughly 7 kilograms of irradiated research reactor fuel. 45. Similar to the first strategy, this strategy of trying to capitalize on the problem of loose nukes is confounded by the need for the state sponsor to work with terrorist groups with which they have had long-established relations. For example, if a terrorist nuclear attack were attributed to Lashkar-e-Taiba, it would seem impossible for Pakistan to pin the blame for stolen ªssile materials on Japan or South Africa.

46. Robert L. Jackson, "Bomb Case Built a Stub, a Shard, a Shell at a Time," Los Angeles Times, De cember 13, 1993; "Turning to Evidence; Axle and Fingerprints," Kingman Daily Miner, April 29, 1997; and Richard A. Serrano, "McVeigh Guilty in Bombing: Death Penalty Trial Next in Oklahoma Tragedy," Los Angeles Times, June 3, 1997, text of infobox.

47. It is possible that the strong positive relationship between attribution rate and fatalities, as shown in ªgures 1 to 3, is a reªection of the greater investigative resources devoted to higherfatality terror attacks.

48. James Dobbins, "Engaging Iran," in Robin B. Wright, ed., The Iran Primer: Power, Politics, and U.S. Policy (Washington, D.C.: United States Institute of Peace Press, 2010), chap. 47. After the September 11 attacks, Pakistan captured terrorist suspects, allowed the United

States to use Pakistani airports and bases for operations into Afghanistan, and provided other kinds of logistical support.

49. The United States invasion of Iraq in 2003 arguably created another incentive for states to cooperate in any investigation. The United States attacked Iraq, toppled its regime, and spent billions of dollars waging a war that devastated the country—even though the evidence connecting Saddam Hussein to September 11, al-Qaida, or the active pursuit of weapons of mass destruction was extraordinarily °imsy. Those actions, despite many other costs to the United States and its interests, likely bought the United States a heavy measure of future cooperation from countries seeking to prove their innocence in the wake of a nuclear terrorist attack. One might argue that some states would withhold cooperation with a future U.S. investigation so as not to be responsible for assisting in the initiation of a massive retaliatory war launched by the United States against the state sponsor. States are unlikely, however, to value these reputational consequences above their own security interests, which would be jeopardized by noncooperation with the United States after a nuclear terror attack.

50. Mueller, Atomic Obsession, chaps. 12, 13.

51. "The 9/11 Commission Report," chap. 8.

52. There is precedent for this approach. When Japan attacked Pearl Harbor, the United States framed the attack in a broader context—not solely about the evils of Japan,but the need to stop the Axis—setting the United States down a course to conquer Germany, Italy, and Japan—three far more powerful states in relative conventional terms than Iran, North Korea, and Pakistan today.

53. For example, according to Lawrence Wright's authoritative account, the Taliban was not complicit in the planning of the September 11 attacks. Wright, The Looming Tower: Al-Qaeda and the Road to 9/11 (New York: Vintage, 2006).

54. Barack Obama, speech given at the Nuclear Security Summit, Washington, D.C., April 10, 2010.

Chapter 18: Islamic State and Technology–A Literature Review. Truls Hallberg Tønnessen

1   Wolfgang Rudischhauser, "Could ISIL Go Nuclear?," NATO Review, 2015 and Nomi Bar-Yaacov, "What If Isis Launches a Chemical Attack in Europe?," The Guardian, 27 November 2015.

2   For a recent overview of the literature see Brecht Volders and Tom Sauer, eds., Nuclear Terrorism: Countering the Threat, (London: Routledge, 2016).

3   Nicole Alexandra Tishler, "C, B, R, or N: The Influence of Related Industry on Terrorists' Choice in Unconventional Weapons," Canadian Graduate Journal of Sociology and Criminology 2 (2), 2013: 52–72, Nada Eweiss, "Non-State Actors & WMD: Does ISIS Have a Pathway to a Nuclear Weapon?" British American Security Information Council, March 2016 and Dina Esfandiary and Matthew Cottee, "The Very Small Islamic State WMD Threat," Bulletin of the Atomic Scientists, 15 October 2014.

4   See for instance Peter D. Zimmerman, "Do We Really Need to Worry? Some Reflections on the Threat of Nuclear Terrorism," Defence Against Terrorism Review 2 (2), 2009: 1–14; Reshmi Kazi, "The Correlation between Non-State Actors and Weapons of Mass Destruction," Connections 10 (4) 2011: 1–11.

5   For a critical view see for instance Keir A. Lieber and Daryl G. Press, "Why States Won't Give Nuclear Weapons to Terrorists," International Security 38 (1) 2013: 80–104.

6   Stephanie E. Meulenbelt and Maarten S. Nieuwenhuizen, "Non-State Actors' Pursuit of CBRN Weapons: From Motivation to Potential Humanitarian Consequences," International Review of the Red Cross 97 (899) July 2016: 831–58, BeyzaUnal and Susan Aghlani, "Use of Chemical, Biological, Radiological and Nuclear Weapons by Non-State Actors: Emerging Trends and Risk Factors" Chatham House - the Royal Institute of International Affairs, 2016.

7   Rolf Mowatt-Larssen, Al Qaeda Weapons of Mass Destruction Threat: Hype or Reality? (Cambridge, MA.:BelferCenter for Science and International Affairs, January 2010), and Meulenbelt and Nieuwenhuizen, "Non-State Actors' Pursuit of CBRN Weapons," International Review of the Red Cross 97 (899) July 2016: 831–58.

8   In 2014 then British Home Secretary Theresa May warned that ISIL, if given support from states, could acquire "chemical, biological or even nuclear weapons to attack us". "Theresa May: Speech to Conservative Party Conference 2014," accessible from http://press. conservatives.com/post/98799073410/theresa-may-speech-to-conservative-party For more examples see Esfandiary and Cottee, "The Very Small Islamic State WMD Threat."

9   Gary A. Ackerman, "Jihadists and WMD: A Re-Evaluation of the Future Threat," CBRNe World, October 2014.

10   PetterNesser and Anne Stenersen, "The Modus Operandi of Jihadi Terrorists in Europe," Perspectives on Terrorism 8 (6) 2014: p. 7.

11   Anne Stenersen, "Toxic Taster: Jihadists' Chemical Weapons Use Remains Crude," Jane's Intelligence Review (April 2015), 44-49.

12   University of Maryland, «Global Terrorism Database»; URL: https://www.start.umd.edu/gtd/ .

13   Chris Quillen, "The Islamic State's Evolving Chemical Arsenal," Studies in Conflict & Terrorism 39 (11) April 2016: 1019–30 and Peter Bergen, "Al Qaeda's Track Record with Chemical Weapons," CNN, 7 May 2013.

14   For a detailed overview of the group's experimenting with chemical weapons see Quillen, "The Islamic State's Evolving Chemical Arsenal."

15   Bruce Hoffman, "Low-Tech Terrorism," National Interest, March - April 2014.

16   ColumbStrack, "Islamic State's chemical weapons capability degraded," IHS Markit, 29 June 2017.

17   Helene Cooper and Eric Schmitt, "ISIS Detainee's Information Led to 2 U.S. Airstrikes, Officials Say," The New York Times, 9 March 2016 and Andrea Taylor, "FACTBOX: Evolution of the Islamic State's Chemical Weapons Capacity," Atlantic Council, 23 November 2015.

18   Beatrix Immenkamp, "ISIL/Daesh and 'Non-Conventional' Weapons of Terror," European Parliamentary Research Service, December 2015, Quillen, "The Islamic State's Evolving Chemical Arsenal," and C.J Chivers, "ISIS Has Fired Chemical Mortar Shells, Evidence Indicates," The New York Times, 17 July 2015.

19   Geoffrey Chapman, "Islamic State and Al-Nusra: Exploring Determinants of Chemical Weapons Usage Patterns," Perspectives on Terrorism, Vol. XI, Issue 6, December 2017.

20   See for instance Higgins, "A History of Sarin Use in the Syrian Conflict," Bellingcat, 6 September 2017 and"Death by Chemicals: The Syrian Government's Widespread and Systematic Use of Chemical Weapons," Human Rights Watch, 1 May 2017.

21 Rudischhauser, "Could ISIL Go Nuclear?", JobyWarrick and Loveday Morris, "How ISIS Nearly Stumbled on the Ingredients for a 'dirty Bomb,'" Washington Post, 22 July 2017.

22 Rob Downes and Geoffrey Chapman, "Dirty Business - Challenges remain to Islamic State RDD usage," IHS Jane's Intelligence Review, April 2016.

23 Stephen Hummel, "The Islamic State and WMD: Assessing the Future Threat," CTC Sentinel 9 (13) 2016: 18–21.

24 "The Perfect Storm," Dabiq, Issue 9, May 2015, pp.74 - 77.

25 Lieber and Press, "Why States Won't Give Nuclear Weapons to Terrorists." See also Carole N. House, "The Chemical, Biological, Radiological, and Nuclear Terrorism Threat from the Islamic State," Military Review 96 (5) 2016: 68 and Esfandiary and Cottee, "The Very Small Islamic State WMD Threat."

26 Ian Johnston, "Brussels attacks: Belgium fears Isis seeking to make 'dirty' nuclear bomb," The Independent, 25 March 2016, Gregory S. Jones, "ISIS and Dirty Bombs," RAND, 3 June 2016 and Pamela S. Falk, "The Dirty Bomb Threat," Foreign Affairs, 4 April 2017.

27 Siobhan McFadyen, "ISIS Plotting Biological Warfare: Brussels Jihadi Found with Bag of Animal Testicles," The Express, 6 May 2016.

28 Patrick Malone and Jeffrey R. Smith, "The Islamic State's Plot to Build a Radioactive 'Dirty Bomb,'" Foreign Policy29 February 2016. For more on topic of insider threat see Matthew Bunn and Scott D.Sagan,Insider Threats(Cornell University Press, 2017).

29 The most detailed reports on Islamic State and drones are Don Rassler, "Remotely Piloted Innovation: Terrorism, Drones and Supportive Technology," Combating Terrorism Center, October 2016, Don Rassler, Muhammad al-Ubaydi, and Vera Mironova, "CTC Perspectives – The Islamic State's Drone Documents: Management, Acquisitions, and DIY Tradecraft" Combating Terrorism Center, 31 January 2017, Nick Waters, "Types of Islamic State Drone Bombs and Where to Find Them," Bellingcat, 24 May 2017 and Asaad Almohammad and Anne Speckhard, "ISIS Drones: Evolution, Leadership, Bases, Operations and Logistics" The International Center for the Study of Violent Extremism, 5 May 2017.

30 Don Rassler, "Remotely Piloted Innovation: Terrorism, Drones and Supportive Technology," Combating Terrorism Center, October 2016.

31 Ibid.

32 Asaad Almohammad and Anne Speckhard, "ISIS Drones: Evolution, Leadership, Bases, Operations and Logistics" The International Center for the Study of Violent Extremism, 5 May 2017.

33 "Islamic State's Weaponised Drones," Conflict Armament Research, 2016 and JobyWarrick, "Use of Weaponized Drones by ISIS Spurs Terrorism Fears," Washington Post, 21 February 2017.

34 Rassler, "Remotely Piloted Innovation: Terrorism, Drones and Supportive Technology."

35 Ibid.

36 Bayt al-Ma'ādir, "[Image] Islamic State – Al-Yaqīn Foundation: 'Drones of the Islamic State – Until: 1st March 2017 – One Month,'" Bayt Al-Ma'ādir, 1 March 2017.

37 Eric Schmitt, "Pentagon Tests Lasers and Nets to Combat a Vexing Foe: ISIS Drones," New York Times, 23 September 2017.

38 Don Rassler, Muhammad al-Ubaydi, and Vera Mironova, "CTC Perspectives – The Islamic State's Drone Documents: Management, Acquisitions, and DIY Tradecraft," Combating Terrorism Center, 31 January 2017.

39 Asaad Almohammad and Anne Speckhard, "ISIS Drones: Evolution, Leadership, Bases, Operations and Logistics" The International Center for the Study of Violent Extremism, 5 May 2017.

40 Linda Robinson, "Assessment of the Politico-Military Campaign to Counter ISIL and Options for Adaptation," RAND, 2016.

41 Catherine Shu, "DJI Adds Much of Iraq and Syria to Its List of No-Fly Zones for Its Drones," TechCrunch, 27 April 2017 and Gareth Corfield, "Drone Maker DJI Quietly Made Large Chunks of Iraq, Syria No-Fly Zones," The Register, 26 April 2017.

42 Thomas Gibbons-Neff, "The U.S. Is Apparently Using Anti-Drone Rifles against the Islamic State," Washington Post, 26 July 2016.

43 Brynjar Lia, Globalisation and the Future of Terrorism: Patterns and Predictions (London: Routledge, 2005), 170–71.

44 Adam Hoffman and Yoram Schweitzer, "Cyber Jihad in the Service of the Islamic State (ISIS)," Strategic Assessment 18 (1) 2015: 71–81, "Overview of Daesh's Online Recruitment Propaganda Magazine, Dabiq" The Carter Center, December 2015). P.W Singer and Emerson Brooking, "Terror On Twitter: How ISIS Is Taking War To Social

Media," Popular Science, 11 December 2015 and Walid Magdy, Kareem Darwish, and Ingmar Weber, "#FailedRevolutions: Using Twitter to Study the Antecedents of ISIS Support," First Monday 21 (2) 2016.

45 Charlie Winter, "The Virtual 'Caliphate': Understanding Islamic State's Propaganda Strategy," Quilliam Foundation, July 2015, Haroro J. Ingram, "An Analysis of Islamic State's Dabiq Magazine," Australian Journal of Political Science 51 (3) 2016: 458–77, Brandon Colas, "What Does Dabiq Do? ISIS Hermeneutics and Organizational Fractures within Dabiq Magazine," Studies in Conflict and Terrorism 40 (3) 2016: 173–90, Monica Maggioni and Paolo Magri, "Twitter and Jihad: The Communication Strategy of ISIS" Italian Institute for International Political Studies, 2015) and Harleen Gambhir, "The Virtual Caliphate: ISIS's Information Warfare" Institute for the Study of War, December 2016).

46 Ali Fisher, "Swarmcast: How Jihadist Networks Maintain a Persistent Online Presence," Perspectives on Terrorism 9 (3) 2015: 3–20. J.M Berger and Jonathon Morgan, "The ISIS Twitter Census: Defining and Describing the Population of ISIS Supporters on Twitter," Brookings Institution, March 2015). N. F. Johnson et al., "New Online Ecology of Adversarial Aggregates: ISIS and beyond," Science 352 (6292) 2016: 1459–63, Ali Fisher and Nico Prucha, "The Call-up: The Roots of a Resilient and Persistent Jihadist Presence on Twitter," Combating Terrorism Exchange 4 (3) 2014), J.M Berger and Heather Perez, "The Islamic State's Diminishing Returns on Twitter" The Program on Extremism, George Washington University, February 2016.

47 Alberto M Fernandez, "Here to Stay and Growing: Combating ISIS Propaganda Networks" Brookings Institution, 2015, Jared Cohen, "How To Fight The Islamic State Online," Foreign Affairs 94 (December 2015).

48 Elizabeth Bodine-Baron et al.,"Examining ISIS Support and Opposition Networks on Twitter" RAND 2016 and Berger and Perez, "The Islamic State's Diminishing Returns on Twitter."

49 For an overview of various platforms and apps see Laith Alkhouri and Alex Kassirer, "Tech for Jihad: Dissecting Jihadists' Digital Toolbox Archives," Flashpoint, July 2016.

50 Ahmad Shehabat, TeodorMitew, and Yahia Alzoubi, "Encrypted Jihad: Investigating the Role of Telegram App in Lone Wolf Attacks in

the West," Journal of Strategic Security 10 (3) 2017: 27–53 and Jamie Bartlett and Alex Krasodomski-Jones, "Online Anonymity - Islamic State and Surveillance," Demos, March 2015

51   See for instance Alexander Meleagrau-Hitchens and Seamus Hughes, "The Threat to the United States from the Islamic State's Virtual Entrepreneurs," CTC Sentinel 10 (3) 2017: 1–8. DaveedGartenstein-Ross and Madeleine Blackman, "ISIL's Virtual Planners: A Critical Terrorist Innovation," War on the Rocks, 4 January 2017.

52   See for instance Rukmini Callimachi, "Not 'Lone Wolves' After All: How ISIS Guides World's Terror Plots From Afar," The New York Times, 4 February 2017.

53   Nico Prucha, "IS and the Jihadist Information Highway – Projecting Influence and Religious Identity via Telegram," Perspectives on Terrorism 10 (6) 2016: 48–58 and Steven Stalinsky and R. Sosnow "A Decade Of Jihadi Organizations' Use Of Drones – From Early Experiments By Hizbullah, Hamas, And Al-Qaeda To Emerging National Security Crisis For The West As ISIS Launches First Attack Drones," MEMRI, 21 February 2017. See also Anne Stenersen, "'Bomb-Making for Beginners': Inside Al Al-Qaeda E-Learning Course," Perspectives on Terrorism 7 (1) 2013: 25–37

54   Stalinsky and Sosnow, "Jihadi Drones - ISIS Al-Qaeda Hamas Hizbullah& Others."

55   Gabriel, Weimann, Terror on the Internet. (Washington D.C: United States Institute of Peace Press, 2006), p. 110.

56   Hoffman and Schweitzer, "Cyber Jihad in the Service of the Islamic State (ISIS)," 73–74.

57   Laith Alkhouri, Alex Kassirer, and Allison Nixon, "Hacking For ISIS: The Emergent Cyber Threat Landscape," Flashpoint, April 2016), Jose Pagliery, "ISIS Is Attacking the U.S. Energy Grid (and Failing)," CNN, 16 October 2015, Jack Moore, "ISIS Cyber Jihadis Are 'garbage' at Hacking, Top Researcher Says," Newsweek, 26 September 2017.

58   "Islamischer Staat'-Cyberattacken Als Werk Russischer Hacker Enttarnt," Spiegel Online, 18 June 2016

59   Zachary K. Goldman et al., "Terrorist Use of Virtual Currencies" (Washington D.C: Center for a New American Security, May 3, 2017), Iwa Salami, "Terrorism Financing with Virtual Currencies

– Can Regulatory Technology Solutions Combat This?," Studies in Conflict and Terrorism, August 11, 2017.

60 McCallister, "ISIS Used eBay As Part of Terror Network, Unsealed FBI Affidavit Shows," NPR, 11 August 2017.

61 Truls Hallberg Tønnessen, "Training on a Battlefield: Iraq as a Training Ground for Global Jihadis,"Terrorism and Political Violence 20 (4) 2008: 543–62, Mia Bloom, "Constructing Expertise: Terrorist Recruitment and 'Talent Spotting' in the PIRA, Al Qaeda, and ISIS,"Studies in Conflict and Terrorism40 (7) 2017: 603–23 and Adam Dolnik,Understanding Terrorist Innovation: Technology, Tactics and Global Trends, (London: Routledge, 2007).

62 Rassler, "Remotely Piloted Innovation: Terrorism, Drones and Supportive Technology." Meulenbelt and Nieuwenhuizen, "Non-State Actors' Pursuit of CBRN Weapons." Rudischhauser, "Could ISIL Go Nuclear?"

63 Aymenn Jawad Al-Tamimi, "Archive of Islamic State Administrative Documents," accessible from http://www.aymennjawad. org/2016/01/archive-of-islamic-state-administrative-documents-1, 11 January 2016 and Johnston et al. Foundations of the Islamic State: Management, Money, and Terror in Iraq, 2005–2010. (Santa Monica: RAND Corporation, 2016)

64 Dolnik, Understanding Terrorist Innovation, p.152.

65 "New ISIS Document Reveals Group's Electronic Warfare Projects," Zaman al-wasl, 19 February 2017.

66 Stuart Ramsay "Exclusive: Inside IS Terror Weapons Lab," Sky News, 5 January 2016.

67 Jamie Seidel, "Islamic State Goes 'Mad Max' in Its Fight for Mosul with Homemade Armoured Vehicles," News Corp Australia Network, 31 October 2016.

68 "Captured Daesh Remote Controlled SVD," The Firearm Blog, 3 June 2015. For an overview of how various insurgent groups have employed remote controlled arms in Syria see Robert J. Bunker and Alma Keshavarz, "Terrorist and Insurgent Teleoperated Sniper Rifles and Machine Guns" (Foreign Military Studies Office, 2016).

69 Stalinsky and Sosnow, "Jihadi Drones - ISIS Al-Qaeda Hamas Hizbullah& Others," 43–46 and Don Rassler, "Drone, Counter Drone: Observations on the Contest Between the United States and Jihadis," CTC Sentinel 10 (1) 2017: 23–27.

70 Edward Blake, "Islamic State Supporters Share Edward Snowden Video to Explain Need for Encryption," Washington Times, 11 February 2016. For an overview see Berger and Perez, "The Islamic State's Diminishing Returns on Twitter."

71 Lia, Globalisation and the Future of Terrorism: Patterns and Predictions. Hoffman, "Low-Tech Terrorism."

72 See for instance PetterNesser and Anne Stenersen, 'The Modus Operandi of Jihadi Terrorists in Europe', Perspectives on Terrorism 8, no. 6 (18 December 2014) and PetterNesser, Anne Stenersen, and Emilie Oftedal, "Jihadi Terrorism in Europe: The IS-Effect," Perspectives on Terrorism 10, no. 6 (2016): 3

73 See for instance Alastair Reed and Haroro Ingram, "Exploring the Role of Instructional Material in AQAP's Inspire and ISIS' Rumiyah" (The Hague: ICCT, 2016).

74 "Inspire Guide, Issue 5: The British Parliament Operation in London," al-Malahim Media, 23 March 2017. URL:https://azelin.files. wordpress.com/2017/04/al-qacc84_idah-in-the-arabian-peninsula-e2809cinspire-guide-5-the-british-parliament-operation-in-london22.pdf .

75 CorriZoli, "Lone-Wolf or Low-Tech Terrorism? Emergent Patterns of Global Terrorism in Recent French and European Attacks," Lawfare, 17 August 2016 and Bruce Hoffman, "Low-Tech Terrorism," The National Interest, April 2014.

76 B. Lia, Globalisation and the Future of Terrorism: Patterns and Predictions. Hoffman, "Low-Tech Terrorism."

77 "Hostile Drones: The Hostile Use of Drones by Non-State Actors against British Targets," Oxford Research Group, January 2016 and Stalinsky and Sosnow, "Jihadi Drones - ISIS Al-Qaeda Hamas Hizbullah& Others."

78 Christopher Dickey,"As ISIS Prepares Its Terror Resurrection, Watch Out for Drone 'Swarms,'" The Daily Beast, 28 February 2017.

79 Larry Friese, "Special Report No. 2: Emerging Unmanned Threats – The Use of Commercially-Available UAVS by Armed Non-State Actors,"Armament Research Services, 8 February 2016.

80 Robert J. Bunker, "Home Made, Printed, and Remote Controlled Firearms," Trends Institution, 21 June 2015.

Index

CPSIA information can be obtained
at www.ICGtesting.com
Printed in the USA
LVHW030406220720
661196LV00002B/171